Series Editors:
Marc E. Fey, Ph.D.
Alan G. Kamhi, Ph.D.

# Late Talkers

Communication
and Language
Intervention
Series

# Late Talkers

*Language Development,
Interventions, and Outcomes*

edited by

**Leslie A. Rescorla, Ph.D.**
Bryn Mawr College
Pennsylvania

and

**Philip S. Dale, Ph.D.**
The University of New Mexico
Albuquerque

·P·A·U·L·H·
**BROOKES**
PUBLISHING C<sup>O</sup> ®

Baltimore • London • Sydney

**Paul H. Brookes Publishing Co.**
Post Office Box 10624
Baltimore, Maryland 21285-0624

www.brookespublishing.com

Copyright © 2013 by Paul H. Brookes Publishing Co., Inc.
All rights reserved.

"Paul H. Brookes Publishing Co." is a registered trademark
of Paul H. Brookes Publishing Co., Inc.

Typeset by Apex CoVantage, LLC, Herndon, Virginia.
Manufactured in the United States of America by
Sheridan Books, Inc., Chelsea, Michigan.

Cover photo © istockphhoto/AmmentorpDK.

The individuals described in this book are composites or real people whose situations are masked and
are based on the authors' experiences. In all instances, names and identifying details have been changed
to protect confidentiality.

**Library of Congress Cataloging-in-Publication Data**

Late talkers : language development, interventions, and outcomes / edited by Leslie A. Rescorla, Ph.D.,
Bryn Mawr College, Pennsylvania and Philip S. Dale, Ph.D., The University of New Mexico, Albuquerque.
        pages        cm. — (Communication and Language Intervention Series)
    Includes bibliographical references and index.
    ISBN-13: 978-1-59857-253-7 (pbk.)
    ISBN-10: 1-59857-253-9 (pbk.)
    1. Verbal ability in children.   2. Children—Language.   3. Language acquisition.   4. Language
awareness in children.   5. Language disorders in children.   I. Rescorla, Leslie, editor of compilation.
BF723.C57L38 2013
155.4'136—dc23                                                                              2013007330

British Library Cataloguing in Publication data are available from the British Library.

2017   2016   2015   2014   2013

10   9   8   7   6   5   4   3   2   1

# Contents

## IV  Interventions

## V  Conclusion

# Series Preface

The purpose of the *Communication and Language Intervention Series* is to provide meaningful foundations for the application of sound intervention designs to enhance the development of communication skills across the life span. We are endeavoring to achieve this purpose by providing readers with presentations of state-of-the-art theory, research, and practice.

In selecting topics, editors, and authors, we are not attempting to limit the contents of this series to viewpoints that we agree with or that we find most promising. We are assisted in our efforts to develop the series by an editorial advisory board consisting of prominent scholars representative of the range of issues and perspectives to be incorporated in the series.

Well-conceived theory and research on development and intervention are vitally important for researchers, educators, and clinicians committed to the development of optimal approaches to communication and language intervention. The content of each book in the series reflects our view of the symbiotic relationship between intervention and research: Demonstrations of what may work in intervention should lead to analysis of promising discoveries and to insights from developmental work that may, in turn, fuel further refinement by intervention researchers. We trust that the careful reader will find much that is of great value in this book.

An inherent goal of the series is to enhance the long-term development of the field by systematically furthering the dissemination of theoretically and empirically based scholarship and research. We promise the reader an opportunity to participate in the development of this field through debates and discussions that occur throughout the pages of the *Communication and Language Intervention Series.*

# Editorial Advisory Board

# About the Editors

**Leslie A. Rescorla, Ph.D.,** Professor of Psychology, Bryn Mawr College, 101 North Merion Avenue, Bryn Mawr, PA 19010

Leslie A. Rescorla is Professor of Psychology and Director of the Child Study Institute and the Thorne Early Childhood Programs at Bryn Mawr College. Educated at Radcliffe College in Massachusetts, the London School of Economics, and Yale University in New Haven, Connecticut, she obtained clinical training at the Yale Child Study Center, the Philadelphia Child Guidance Center, and the Children's Hospital of Philadelphia. Dr. Rescorla's research interests include language delays in young children, longitudinal patterns of school achievement, and empirically based assessment of emotional and behavioral problems.

**Philip S. Dale, Ph.D.,** Professor, Department of Speech and Hearing Sciences, The University of New Mexico, 1700 Lomas Blvd NE, Suite 1300, Albuquerque, NM 87131

Philip S. Dale received his doctorate in communication sciences from the University of Michigan. He is a Fellow of the American Speech-Language-Hearing Association and the Association for Psychological Science, and he has served as President of the International Association for the Study of Child Language. Dr. Dale's research has focused on the causes and consequences of individual differences in language development, the relationship between oral language and early literacy development, and evaluations of treatment effectiveness.

# About the Contributors

**Edith L. Bavin, Ph.D.,** Honorary Professor, School of Psychological Science, Faculty of Science, Technology and Engineering, La Trobe University, Melbourne, Victoria 3086, Australia

Edith L. Bavin obtained her Ph.D. at the University of Buffalo. Her early research was on the acquisition of Warlpiri, an indigenous language spoken in central Australia. More recent research has been on specific language impairment, focusing on memory. She is a chief investigator on the Early Language in Victoria Study, a longitudinal study on the natural history of language impairment and literacy development. Other current research is the language processing of children with autism using eye tracking and the language and the cognitive development of young children with cochlear implants. She served as editor of the *Journal of Child Language* 2006–2012 and edited the *Cambridge Handbook of Child Language*, published by Cambridge University Press in 2009.

**Nan Bernstein Ratner, Ed.D.,** Professor and Chair, Department of Hearing and Speech Sciences, The University of Maryland, College Park, 0100 Lefrak Hall, College Park, MD 20742

Nan Bernstein Ratner is Professor and Chair, Department of Hearing and Speech Sciences, The University of Maryland, College Park. She has published widely in the areas of typical and atypical language development, fluency and stuttering, and parent–child interaction. She is the coauthor of the texts *Psycholinguistics* (Harcourt Brace College Publishers, 1998) and *The Development of Language, Eighth Edition* (Pearson, 2012), both with Jean Berko Gleason, and *A Handbook on Stuttering, Sixth Edition* (Delmar Cengage Learning, 2008), with the late Oliver Bloodstein. She is a Fellow of the American Speech-Language-Hearing Association.

**Dorthe Bleses, Ph.D.,** Professor, Center Director, Center for Child Language, Institute for Language and Communication, University of Southern Denmark, Campusvej 55, DK-5230 Odense M, Denmark

Dorthe Bleses is a linguist and applied researcher in early childhood language and literacy development, educational interventions, and development of assessment tools. She directs the Center for Child Language at the University of Southern Denmark.

**Lesley Bretherton, Ph.D.,** Associate Professor, University of Melbourne, Head of Clinical Psychology, Psychology Service, The Royal Children's Hospital, Flemington Road, Parkville, Victoria 3052, Australia

Lesley Bretherton is a child and adolescent clinical psychologist. She is currently Head of Clinical Psychology at The Royal Children's Hospital, Clinical Associate Professor in Psychological Sciences at the University of Melbourne, and Honorary Fellow at Murdoch Childrens Research Institute. Her research interests include child language and cognitive development and child psychopathology. She undertook study leave with Professor Dorothy Bishop at the University of Oxford and is a reviewer of research project grants and manuscripts for a variety of journals and for the National Health and Medical Research Council. She has been a member of the Early Language in Victoria Study since 2000.

**Stephen Camarata, Ph.D.,** Professor, Hearing and Speech Sciences, Vanderbilt University School of Medicine, 1215 21st Avenue South, Suite 8310, Nashville, TN 37232

Stephen Camarata is a nationally and internationally renowned clinician-scientist who studies late-talking children. His research focuses on the assessment and treatment of speech and language disorders in children with disabilities such as autism, Down syndrome, and specific language impairment. He also studies children whose late onset of talking appears to be a natural developmental stage rather than a symptom of a broader developmental disability.

**Christine Dollaghan, Ph.D,** Professor, Callier Center for Communication Disorders, University of Texas at Dallas, 1966 Inwood Road, A.128, Dallas, TX 75235

Christine Dollaghan is a professor at the University of Texas at Dallas. Her research interests include child language development and disorders, the validity of diagnostic measures, and the latent structure of diagnostic categories. Her publications include *The Handbook of Evidence-Based Practice in Communication Disorders* (Paul H. Brookes Publishing Co., 2007). She was awarded the Honors of the American Speech-Language-Hearing Association in 2012.

**Cindy Earle, M.A.,** Speech-Language Pathologist, The Hanen Centre, 1075 Bay Street, Suite 515, Toronto, ON M5S 2B1, Canada

Cindy Earle has worked as a speech-language pathologist with The Hanen Centre for more than 30 years. She is the program director for Target Word—The Hanen Program for Parents of Children who are Late Talkers and the author of the *Target Word—Making Hanen Happen Leaders Guide* (The Hanen Centre, 2011) and the *Target Word Parent Handbook, Third Edition* (The Hanen Centre, 2011).

**Susan Ellis Weismer, Ph.D.,** Professor, Department of Communication Sciences and Disorders, Associate Dean, College of Letters and Science, University of Wisconsin–Madison, Waisman Center, 1500 Highland Avenue, Madison, WI 53705

Susan Ellis Weismer is a professor in the Department of Communication Sciences and Disorders, a Waisman Center principal investigator, and an associate dean in the College of Letters and Science at the University of Wisconsin–Madison. She also holds affiliate faculty positions in the Departments of Psychology and Educational Psychology. Her research focuses on understanding the developmental course and mechanisms underlying language disorders in late talkers, children with specific language impairment, and children on the autism spectrum. She is a Fellow of the American Speech-Language-Hearing Association, past editor of the *Journal of Speech, Language, and Hearing Research*, and former member of the National Institutes of Health Language and Communication Study Section grant review panel.

**Anne Fernald, Ph.D.,** Associate Professor, Josephine Knotts Knowles Professor of Human Biology, Department of Psychology, Stanford University, 450 Serra Mall, Stanford, CA 94305

Anne Fernald has done pioneering research on the early development of skill in language processing, developing high-resolution measures of the time course of infants' understanding as they learn to interpret language from moment to moment. In longitudinal studies with English- and Spanish-learning children from advantaged and disadvantaged families, this research reveals the vital role of early language experience in strengthening speech processing efficiency, which in turn facilitates language learning. A central goal of this research program is to help parents understand that they play a crucial role in providing their infant with early linguistic nutrition and language exercise.

**Marc E. Fey, Ph.D.,** Professor, Speech and Hearing Department, School of Allied Health, University of Kansas Medical Center, 3901 Rainbow Boulevard, Kansas City, KS 66160

Marc E. Fey has published numerous articles, chapters, and software programs on children's speech and language development and disorders and has written or edited three books on child language intervention. He was Editor of the *American Journal of Speech-Language Pathology* 1996–1998 and served as Chair of the American Speech-Language-Hearing Association (ASHA) Publications Board 2003–2005. He is a Fellow of the American Speech-Language-Hearing Association and also holds ASHA Honors.

**Lizbeth H. Finestack, Ph.D.,** Assistant Professor, Department of Speech-Language-Hearing Sciences, University of Minnesota, Room 54 Shevlin Hall, 164 Pillsbury Drive SE, Minneapolis, MN 55455

Lizbeth H. Finestack is an assistant professor in the Department of Speech-Language-Hearing Sciences at the University of Minnesota. Her research focuses on identifying effective language interventions for children and adolescents with significant language impairment. She is currently examining the efficacy of using an explicit teaching approach to target grammatical forms when working with children with primary language impairment.

**Luigi Girolametto, Ph.D.,** Professor, Department of Speech-Language Pathology, University of Toronto, 160-500 University Avenue, Toronto, ON M5G 1V7, Canada

Luigi Girolametto is a speech-language pathologist and researcher at the University of Toronto. He teaches coursework on child language disorders and language intervention. He has conducted research on parent-focused intervention for late-talking children. His currently funded research focuses on 1) the facilitation of emergent literacy skills and 2) language acquisition in preschoolers who speak more than one language.

**Marianna E. Hayiou-Thomas, D.Phil. (Oxon),** Department of Psychology, University of York, Heslington, York, YO10 5DD, United Kingdom

Following completion of her doctoral work at the University of Oxford on cognitive processing in children with specific language impairment, Marianna E. Hayiou-Thomas joined the Twins Early Development Study for her postdoctoral training in behavioral genetics. Since then, she has combined her work in behavioral genetics with experimental approaches in order to examine the etiology of language impairment over the course of development, as well as its relationship to literacy.

**James Law, Ph.D.,** Professor of Speech and Language Science, Institute of Health and Society, School of Education, Communication and Language Sciences, Newcastle University, Victoria Road, Newcastle-upon-Tyne, NEI 7RU, United Kingdom

James Law graduated with a degree in linguistics before qualifying as a speech and language therapist. His principal research interests are child language and language learning difficulties, evidence-based practice and intervention, and mapping longitudinal outcomes for children with language difficulties. He has had a wide range of research funding, most recently as a principal investigator on the £1.5m Better Communication Research Programme in the United Kingdom and the Centre for Research Excellence in Child Language in Victoria, Australia.

**Laurence B. Leonard, Ph.D.,** Rachel E. Stark Distinguished Professor, Speech, Language, and Hearing Sciences, Purdue University, 500 Oval Drive, Heavilon Hall, West Lafayette, IN 47907

Laurence B. Leonard studies childhood language disorders, with special reference to children with specific language impairment. Much of his work in recent years has dealt with the grammatical deficits of these children. Together with collaborators, Dr. Leonard has studied children with specific language impairment from diverse language groups, including Cantonese, Finnish, Hebrew, Hungarian, Italian, and Spanish, as well as English.

**Michelle MacRoy-Higgins, Ph.D.,** Assistant Professor, Hunter College, The City University of New York, Brookdale Campus, 425 East 25th Street, Mailbox #727, New York, NY 10010

Michelle MacRoy-Higgins is Speech-Language Pathologist and Assistant Professor at Hunter College, The City University of New York. Her research and clinical interests include language and phonological development and disorders in children and children with autism spectrum disorders.

**Virginia A. Marchman, Ph.D.,** Research Associate, Department of Psychology, Jordan Hall, Building 420, 450 Serra Mall, Stanford, CA 94305

As a developmental psychologist, Virginia A. Marchman's main areas of research are language development, language disorders, and early childhood development. Her specific interests include individual differences in typically developing and late-talking children and lexical and grammatical development in monolingual and bilingual learners. She has worked extensively with the MacArthur-Bates Communicative Development Inventories (CDIs), Second Edition (Paul H. Brookes Publishing Co., 2007), developing the CDI Scoring Program, and serving on the CDI Advisory Board. Dr. Marchman's current studies explore links between children's speech processing skill, early learning environments, and individual differences in English and Spanish learners from diverse backgrounds.

**Rhea Paul, Ph.D.,** Professor, Founding Director, Department of Speech-Language Pathology, Sacred Heart University, 5151 Park Avenue, Fairfield, CT 06825

Rhea Paul is Professor and Founding Director of the Department of Speech-Language Pathology at Sacred Heart University. She is the author of more than 90 refereed journal articles, 40 book chapters, and 8 books and is Editor for Language at the *Journal of Speech, Language, and Hearing Research*. Recipient of the Editor's Award from the *American Journal of Speech-Language Pathology* in 1996, and the Ritvo/Slifka Award for Innovative Clinical Research from the International Society for Autism Research I, 2010, she is a Fellow of the American Speech-Language-Hearing Association.

**Barbara Zurer Pearson, Ph.D.,** Research Associate, Department of Linguistics, University of Massachusetts Amherst, 226 South College, 150 Hicks Way, Amherst MA 01003

Barbara Zurer Pearson received her Ph.D. from the University of Miami, where she was the coordinator of the Bilingualism Study Group for 10 years and a major contributor to *Language and Literacy in Bilingual Children* (Oller & Eilers; Multilingual Matters, 2002). She is currently a research associate and codirector of the Language Acquisition Research Center at the University of Massachusetts Amherst. Her book for a popular audience, *Raising a Bilingual Child* (Random House, 2008), has been published in Spanish and Polish and is being translated into Chinese.

**Mabel L. Rice, Ph.D.,** Distinguished Professor, 3031 Dole Human Development Center, University of Kansas, 1000 Sunnyside Avenue, Lawrence, KS 66045

Mabel L. Rice is the Fred and Virginia Merrill Distinguished Professor of Advanced Studies at the University of Kansas. She is an internationally recognized researcher with a productive line of inquiry that focuses on language acquisition and language impairments; morphosyntax (grammar markers of language impairment); genetics of language, reading, and speech impairments; language acquisition and impairments in twins; language impairments in children affected by HIV; and language impairments in children with autism. Her investigations are funded by competitive awards from the National Institutes of Health, involving international, cross-disciplinary collaborations with other investigators.

**Richard G. Schwartz, Ph.D.,** Presidential Professor, Ph.D. Program in Speech-Language-Hearing Sciences, The Graduate Center, The City University of New York, 365 Fifth Avenue, New York, NY 10016

Richard G. Schwartz is a speech-language pathologist who has conducted research on typical and atypical language acquisition in toddlers and school-age children. His research interests have included early phonology and lexical acquisition in children with specific language impairment (SLI), lexical and sentence processing in children with SLI, children with auditory processing disorders, and the neurological bases of childhood language impairments. He has published extensively in these areas.

**Catherine L. Taylor, Ph.D., PGradDipHlthSc, BAppSc,** Professor, The University of Western Australia, Telethon Institute for Child Health Research, 100 Roberts Road, Subiaco, Western Australia 6008, Australia

Catherine L. Taylor's primary research is in language development and disorders in childhood and related developmental outcomes, such as school readiness, school achievement, and social and emotional well-being. Her research investigates individual differences in language and literacy development, what factors account for these differences, and what these differences mean for children's progress at school and through life. The overarching aim of this research is to contribute to the evidence base that delivers equitable developmental opportunities for children, particularly in the early years.

**Donna J. Thal, Ph.D.,** Distinguished Professor Emerita, School of Speech and Hearing Sciences, San Diego State University, 5500 Campanile Drive, San Diego, CA 92182; Research Psychologist, Center for Research in Language, University of California, San Diego, 9500 Gilman Drive, La Jolla, CA, 92093

Donna J. Thal is a developmental psycholinguist and a certified and licensed speech-language pathologist. She has carried out research on typical and atypical development of language and cognition, language development in children with focal brain injury, and children with delayed onset of language. She has also studied language development in Spanish-speaking infants and toddlers and children with hearing impairments who use cochlear implants. Her major research program, funded by the National Institutes of Health National Institute of Deafness and Other Communicative Disorders, has focused on early identification of risk for clinically significant language impairment.

**J. Bruce Tomblin, Ph.D.,** D.C. Spriestersbach Distinguished Professor, Department of Communication Sciences and Disorders, University of Iowa, Iowa City, IA 52242

J. Bruce Tomblin is a Fellow and Honors recipient of the American Speech-Language-Hearing-Association. He also received the Callier Prize in Communication Disorders. He is a speech-language pathologist holding the Certificate of Clinical Competence in Speech-Language Pathology. His research has been concerned with the causes, course, and consequences of developmental language impairments. This research has focused on children with specific language impairment and children with hearing loss.

**Werner Vach, Ph.D.,** Professor, Clinical Epidemiology, University Medical Center Freiburg, Germany, Stefan-Meier-Str. 26, D-79104 Freiburg, Germany

Werner Vach is statistician with a diploma and a Ph.D. from the Department of Statistics, University of Dortmund, Germany. He has been a professor of statistics at the Faculty of Medicine and at the Faculty of Humanities, University of Southern Denmark. Currently he is a professor of clinical epidemiology at the University of Freiburg. He has worked together with researchers from medicine, linguistics, archeology, and anthropology on both applied projects and methodological issues.

**Elaine Weitzman, M.Ed.,** Adjunct Professor, Department of Speech-Language Pathology, University of Toronto; Executive Director, The Hanen Centre, 1075 Bay Street, Suite 515, Toronto, ON M5S 2B1, Canada

Elaine Weitzman is Executive Director of The Hanen Centre, Toronto, Canada, and Adjunct Professor in the Department of Speech-Language Pathology at the University of Toronto. Ms. Weitzman is coauthor of three resources for caregivers on how to facilitate children's language and literacy development: *It Takes Two to Talk: A Practical Guide for Parents of Children with Language Delays* (The Hanen Centre, 2004); *Learning Language and Loving It: A Guide to Promoting Children's Social, Language, and Literacy Development in Early Childhood Settings* (The Hanen Centre, 2002); and *ABC and Beyond: Building Emergent Literacy in Early Childhood Settings* (The Hanen Centre, 2010). Her research has focused on the efficacy of caregiver-implemented early language intervention.

**Stephen R. Zubrick, Ph.D.,** Winthrop Professor, Centre for Child Health Research, The University of Western Australia, Telethon Institute for Child Health Research, 100 Roberts Road, Subiaco, Western Australia 6008, Australia

Stephen R. Zubrick is Winthrop Professor of Research at The University of Western Australia. Trained at the University of Michigan in audiology, speech pathology, and psychology, he is one of the founding investigators of the Longitudinal Study of Australian Children and is a leading expert in population studies of child development. For the past decade, he has been the Head of the Division of Population Science at the Telethon Institute for Child Health Research.

# Preface

Like every other aspect of human behavioral development, the emergence of language is characterized by variation. Because language is so significant for social life, and because it is uniquely salient as a complex cognitive behavior, parents and others have expectations of young children. Not surprisingly, then, a delay in beginning to speak is one of the most common reasons for parents to seek professional consultation. Until fairly recently, however, the phenomenon of late talking had received little in the way of rigorous scientific research. Instead, a certain amount of folklore had grown up, not always internally consistent: late talkers were overwhelmingly boys, they were late in talking because their parents provided poor or insufficient input, they generally grew out of it, it was an early positive sign of nonverbal development foretelling a future in engineering, it was an early sign of autism and other developmental disorders, and more. These very understandable parental and clinical concerns formed one motivation for the research programs which emerged in the 1980s and 1990s.

This book provides a comprehensive summary of what the research since the early 1980s has revealed about late talkers. We define *late talkers* as children identified with delayed expressive language before about 3–3½ years of age. We differentiate late talkers from children with other conditions for whom expressive language delay is a secondary symptom (e.g., autism spectrum disorder, intellectual disability). However, we include in the group of late talkers children who have a receptive language delay in conjunction with an expressive language delay, as well as children who have typical receptive language. The book has four major sections: Identification and Classification of Late Talkers, Characteristics and Causes, Longitudinal Course/Outcomes, and Interventions. Each section contains several chapters written by major contributors to the field. Throughout the book, implications of research findings for clinical practice are emphasized. The book also contains two concluding chapters. We hope that the book proves useful for researchers, practicing speech-language pathologists, and graduate students in communication disorders.

## SECTION I: IDENTIFICATION AND CLASSIFICATION OF LATE TALKERS

Chapters in this section of the book review the literature on epidemiological research focused on late takers. Among the questions addressed in these chapters are what instruments and criteria can be validly used to identify late talkers, what percentage of children ages 2–3 years can be considered late talkers; what are the differential diagnostic issues in identifying late talkers; what are the issues involved in identifying late talkers among children growing up in non–English-speaking or bilingual home environments; and what demographic, health, and family history factors are associated with being a late talker? Because two of these chapters (Chapters 1 and 2) summarize longitudinal studies, this section also provides some information on outcomes of late talking identified at young ages.

## SECTION II: CHARACTERISTICS AND CAUSES

Chapters in this section of the book describe major findings about the characteristics of late talkers, with a focus on factors that may help to explain etiology. Thus, this section focuses on what research findings suggest may be important causes of early expressive language delay. This section also addresses the main theoretical approaches that have been used to explain late talkers. Among the questions addressed in these chapters are what is the evidence for categorical versus dimensional accounts of early expressive language delay and what basic mechanisms (e.g., information processing deficits, phonological deficits) have been found to be associated with late talking that may reflect the underlying causes of early language delay?

## SECTION III: LONGITUDINAL COURSE/OUTCOMES

This section of the book reviews major research findings on the outcomes of late talkers. Important questions addressed include what percentage of late talkers "recover" at different ages, are there residual effects of early language deficits/weakness on specific aspects of later language and/or literacy, what are the best early predictors of outcome for late talkers, and when should parents and practitioners seek intervention for young late talkers?

## SECTION IV: INTERVENTIONS

This section of the book focuses on promising interventions for late talkers, both those delivered in clinic-based settings and those delivered from a public health model. Important questions addressed include at what age should intervention be begun and for which late talkers, what does research indicate are the most efficacious interventions for late talkers, what are the relative benefits of different models of service delivery (i.e., whether intervention is delivered by parents, clinicians, or child care/preschool staff), and does intervention produce short-term or long-term benefits over and above spontaneous remission?

## SECTION V: CONCLUSION

This concluding section of the book contains two chapters. The first chapter provides a broad, contextualized theoretical overview about late talkers in light of the data presented in the previous chapters. The concluding chapter, written by the editors, summarizes the main messages for practitioners provided by the research to date, plus important questions that remain to be addressed in future research.

# Acknowledgments

We thank Alan Kamhi and Marc Fey as series editors for inviting us on behalf of Paul H. Brookes Publishing Co. to organize this book project. We have been gratified by the willingness of so many distinguished researchers to join us and by their promptness and responsiveness to editorial feedback and suggestions. It has been not just a stimulating project but a very enjoyable one. We believe this spirit of cooperation reflects a consensus that the time has been right to bring together the knowledge accumulated about late talkers, both to help clinicians and to set a research agenda for the future.

# Identification and
# Classification of Late Talkers

# The Early Language in Victoria Study

## *Late Talkers, Predictors, and Outcomes*

Edith L. Bavin and Lesley Bretherton

There is a great deal of variation in the overall rate of language development among children. One of the known contributing factors is gender—girls produce more words than boys in the early stages of development (Fenson et al., 1994, 2007; Klee et al., 1998; Rescorla, 1989)—but there is also variation in developmental trajectories. Some children start with delayed language onset but catch up, others seem to have a typical start but then slow down, and others show more varied pathways (Ukoumunne et al., 2012). Low expressive vocabulary has often been used as an indicator of delayed language onset. Because vocabulary level predicts early grammatical development (Bates & Goodman, 1997), late talkers (LTs)—children who produce fewer words than expected for their chronological age—are of concern. Prevalence estimates for LTs generally fall within the range of 10%–20% (e.g., Desmarais, Sylvestre, Meyer, Bairati, & Rouleau, 2008; Klee et al., 1998; Rescorla, 1989). Expressive language can emerge late for a number of reasons, including sensory, cognitive, or neurological problems, but these have not been identified as causal factors for many LTs.

Identifying LTs for whom there is no clear explanation for the delay (e.g., deafness, autism, Down syndrome, intellectual impairment) is important because they are generally considered to be at risk for later language impairment (Bishop &

We would like to acknowledge the members of the Early Language in Victoria Study team, Australia's National Health and Medical Research Council for research funding, and the support from the Victorian Government's Operational Infrastructure Support Program. The working memory study was conducted by Nadia Petruccelli as the research component of her doctoral degree in clinical psychology awarded by La Trobe University in Melbourne, Victoria, Australia, and supervised by the two authors of this chapter. Dr. Petrucelli was funded by a La Trobe University scholarship.

Edmundson, 1987). Much of the follow-up research on LTs has focused on how many of the children will resolve and how many will continue to have delayed or impaired language. For example, Paul, Spangle-Looney, and Dahm (1991) found that at age 3, nearly half of a group of 21 LTs remained delayed in expressive language, with a third also delayed in receptive language. Of particular interest is whether identifying LTs will help screen for specific language impairment (SLI)—that is, impaired language but development in other areas appearing to be in the normal range. Children with SLI are at risk for poor social, behavioral, and academic outcomes (e.g., Beitchman et al., 1996, 2001; Botting & Conti-Ramsden, 2000). SLI is estimated to affect 7% of children (Leonard, 1989).

Although not all LTs go on to be language impaired, research findings suggest that 20%–70% of a sample of LTs might be identified as having SLI by school age (e.g., Leonard, 1998; Paul, 1993). However, the number of LTs and how many go on to be impaired in language depends to a large extent on the composition of the sample and measures used. Much of the published research on LTs reports on clinical samples—that is, children who have been referred because of some concern—rather than community-based samples. Thus research findings may not be representative. A study by Tomblin et al. (1997), for example, found that only 29% of the children who met the criteria for SLI on a test battery had previously been identified as language impaired. Whether samples are clinical or not, there is a problem in generalizing across research findings if they vary in composition.

Identifying children as LTs implies that there are clear expectations about typical language development at specific ages. LTs are typically identified at age 2, or just prior to that age, when it is assumed that children will be producing words and starting to combine them. Two parent report checklists with normative data are frequently used to estimate children's expressive vocabulary and whether or not they have moved to a stage of combining words: the Language Development Survey (LDS; Rescorla, 1989) and the MacArthur-Bates Communicative Development Inventories (CDIs; Fenson et al., 2007). The LDS, developed with the purpose of screening for language delay, lists 310 words commonly found in children's early vocabularies, representing 14 semantic categories. Parents are asked to check which words their child uses and to indicate if their child combines words—and, if so, how frequently. Fewer than 50 words or not combining words are the usual criteria for identifying LTs. However, others have been adopted. Rescorla and Achenbach (2002) identified 18- to 23-month-olds as LTs if they fell below the 15th percentile on the LDS, whereas Paul et al. (1991) identified children with delayed expressive language at 18–23 months if their expressive vocabulary was fewer than 10 words on the LDS and at 24–34 months if their expressive vocabulary consisted of 50 words or less or they did not use two-word combinations.

The CDIs were developed as a way of tapping into parents' knowledge about their child's language. There are three age-appropriate inventories, and short versions of two of them—the CDI: Words and Gestures and the CDI: Words and Sentences. The full CDI: Words and Sentences was designed to be used with children of ages 16–30 months, which covers the age range for identifying LTs. It includes a vocabulary checklist of 680 words representing 22 semantic categories, and parents are asked to indicate which words their child says. The published percentile scores are based on gender and age in months (Fenson et al., 2007). Most studies using the Words and Sentences checklist adopt the 10th percentile as the cutoff for identifying children as LTs (e.g., Dale, Price, Bishop, & Plomin, 2003; Ellis Weismer & Evans, 2002), but other criteria have been used, including the more stringent 5th percentile (Girolametto, Pearce, & Weitzman, 1996).

In a prospective study of 1,766 singleton children at 24 months, Zubrick, Taylor, Rice, and Slegers (2007) used a different checklist to estimate early communicative development. They classified children with late language emergence on the basis of parent responses to the six questions comprising the communication scale of the Ages & Stages Questionnaires® (ASQ; Bricker & Squires, 1999; Squires & Bricker, 1993; Squires, Bricker & Potter, 1997; Squires, Potter, & Bricker, 1999). The questions tap into receptive as well as expressive language. Using the cutoff of –1.0 standard deviation (*SD*), Zubrick et al. found late language emergence in 13.4% of the sample.

Some LTs resolve or appear to resolve ("resolved late talkers" [RLTs] or "late bloomers"; Paul, 1991; Rescorla, Roberts, & Dahlsgaard, 1997). Although their scores may be in the normal range on most language assessments, there may still be a delay in specific areas of language. Furthermore, RLTs often score lower on language tasks than children with typical language development through to adolescence (Rescorla, 2009). Rescorla, Dahlsgaard, and Roberts (2000) measured expressive language at ages 3 and 4 of a group of 34 children identified as LTs between 24 and 31 months. Scores on the Index of Productive Syntax (IPSyn; Scarborough, 1990) showed that only 34% were above the 10th percentile at age 3 and 29% at age 4. The mean length of utterance (MLU) for 41% of the group was above the 10th percentile at age 3, and this increased to 71% by age 4. Because there is great improvement in scores on the IPSyn for children with typical development, the results indicate that LTs lag behind more in IPSyn than in MLU.

In reporting on a sample of LTs identified between the ages of 18 and 34 months, Paul and Alforde (1993) examined the use of grammatical morphemes in spontaneous speech samples collected from the LTs at age 4 compared with a group of non-LTs matched on nonverbal cognitive skills, socioeconomic status, birth order, race, and sex ratio. The results showed that although the 15 RLTs had acquired more grammatical morphemes than those who continued to show language delay, they had acquired fewer than the typically developing group. Such findings illustrate that "catching up" depends on which aspects of language are assessed and at which age.

Rescorla and colleagues followed a group of LTs to age 17 years (e.g., Manhardt & Rescorla, 2002; Rescorla, 2002, 2005, 2009) and found language-related problems emerging in the later school years when more advanced language-related skills, including narrative and reading skills, are developing. When compared with children with typical expressive language development matched on age, socioeconomic status (SES), and nonverbal ability, RLTs may achieve lower scores in some language areas during their school years (Ellis Weismer, 2007; Roos & Ellis Weismer, 2008).

Rescorla (2002) proposed that late language emergence indicates vulnerability for slow language acquisition; those children who catch up can be considered less impaired than those children who are later identified as having SLI. Despite the requirement that children with SLI are in the normal range for nonverbal cognitive ability, problems in verbal working memory, particularly phonological working memory, have been well documented for children with SLI (Archibald & Gathercole, 2006; Ellis Weismer, Evans, & Hesketh, 1999; Gathercole & Baddeley, 1990).

Along with word list and digit list recall, nonword repetition tasks have been used to assess phonological memory. Because there is no mental representation for novel words, the child must rely on short-term memory in order to repeat them. Scores for children with SLI are lower than children with typical development on nonword repetition tasks, particularly for longer words (Bishop, North, & Donlan, 1996; Gathercole & Baddeley, 1990)—indicating a storage deficit, a capacity limitation that affects linking of acoustic information and articulatory patterns (Evans, Alibali, & McNeil, 2001). RLTs have also been found to have low scores on nonword repetition tasks (Bishop, 2006; Bishop et al., 1996; Conti-Ramsden, Botting, & Faragher, 2001; Ellis Weismer et al., 2000), supporting the view that there may be a common underlying problem for RLTs and nonresolved LTs.

As discussed by Bishop (2008), there is likely to be a collection of risk factors that conspire to disrupt language development. Possible predictors/risk factors for both delayed language at age 2 and SLI in the preschool years have been investigated (e.g., Dale et al., 2003; Ellis Weismer et al., 2000; Ellis Weismer, Murray-Branch, & Miller, 1994; Paul et al., 1991; Thal & Tobias, 1994; Thal, Tobias, & Morrison, 1991; Zubrick et al., 2007). Selection criteria for samples vary, however, and only a few factors may be considered in any specific study. Family history of language problems has been documented as a risk factor, but other variables interact because not all children with a family history will be identified as language impaired. As discussed in Reilly et al. (2006), prospective, longitudinal, population-based studies are needed to document the influence of biological and environmental factors on the growth of linguistic skills in order to better understand why some children who are initially delayed in language development go on to be language impaired and others catch up. If it is possible to predict which LTs will go on to be language impaired, professionals may be in a better position to develop appropriate intervention programs to promote better language outcomes.

In the next sections, we provide an overview of the Early Language in Victoria Study (ELVS), including details of the sample and the measures used to determine the number of LTs at age 2 and language outcomes at age 4 (focusing on SLI), and predictors of LT status at age 2 and language scores at age 4. We also discuss a follow-up study on memory with a subsample of ELVS participants at age 5, including LTs who were identified as SLI, RLTs, and children with typical language development.

## THE EARLY LANGUAGE IN VICTORIA STUDY

ELVS is a prospective study concerned with the evolution of language and literacy problems over the first 7 years of life. The sample was drawn from across the socioeconomic spectrum in the greater Melbourne area in the state of Victoria, Australia, between September 2003 and April 2004. Melbourne had a population of 3.6 million at that time (Australian Bureau of Statistics, 2006).

The children were recruited with the help of maternal and child health nurses in six noncontiguous areas of the total 31 local government areas (LGAs) when children attended their regular 8-month checkup at state government–funded Maternal and Child Health clinics. Approximately 82% of eligible families attend this checkup. We selected six LGAs based on the Socio-Economic Indexes for Areas (SEIFA), derived from the 2001 Australian census data. SEIFA scores are determined from a number of factors that contribute to disadvantage (including income, education level, and unemployment) and are standardized for the Australian population to a mean of 1,000 and an *SD* of 100, with higher scores indicating greater advantage. Disadvantage scores are calculated for each postcode of residence. We stratified the 31 LGAs into three tiers. Two LGAs were selected from each tier (low, mid, and high) to represent the geographic spread of greater Melbourne.

The maternal and child health nurses were asked to distribute information about the study to all eligible families who attended the clinics in the time frame of interest. Families with children aged 7.5–10 months were targeted; exceptions were families in which the parents did not understand English or the children were known to have developmental delay (e.g., cerebral palsy, Down syndrome, serious physical or intellectual disability). Infants were also recruited at hearing screening sessions in the LGAs. A total of 2,335 eligible participants were approached, and 1,910 families returned the baseline questionnaire, accounting for approximately 35% of all eligible participants in the six LGAs. Of the 1,910 children, 50.5% were male. The sample included 54 twins (2.8%) and 50 children born prematurely—that is, at less than 36 weeks' gestation (3.15%). A total of 127 families reported a language background other than English (6%). Retention rate was excellent, with 1,759 questionnaires returned in the second wave of data collection (12 months); 1,741 in the third wave (24 months); and 1,623 (85%) in the fifth wave (4 years).

As described in our previous publications (Reilly et al., 2006, 2007, 2009, 2010), data were collected through a combination of parent questionnaires and direct assessment. Parents were sent a questionnaire package soon after the family was recruited and informed consent received. A questionnaire package was then sent annually starting with the second package sent soon after the child's first birthday. In addition to measuring early communication, language, and pre- and early literacy development, the questionnaires covered family history, general development and health, sociodemographic information, mental health and family stress factors, parent–child interactions, and child behavior and temperament. We focus on those measures that are relevant to the topic of this chapter. First, we briefly summarize the results at 12 months.

## Results at 12 Months

In reporting the communication skills of the ELVS sample at age 12 months, Reilly et al. (2006) conducted a regression analysis for which they selected predictor variables from possible risk factors listed in a Systematic Evidence Review for the U.S. Preventive Services Task Force on screening for speech and language delay in preschool (Nelson, Nygren, Walker, & Panoscha, 2006). The factors selected from the list were those for which 8- and 12-month data were available. Some factors related to child characteristics (gender; birth order; perinatal factors: twin birth, prematurity, and birth weight), others related to maternal characteristics (education level, age at child's birth), and others related to family characteristics (family history of language difficulties, SES, and minority status). SES was identified from the SEIFA Index of Disadvantage (Australian Bureau of Statistics, 2001). Minority status was based on whether English was the main language spoken in the home to the child, an indicator of families who have migrated recently to Australia from any of 100 countries. Two additional variables were included as likely predictor variables:

maternal vocabulary, because children's early language development is influenced by language input (Hart & Risley, 1995; Hoff-Ginsburg, 1998), and maternal mental health status, which has an impact on children's language development (Noel, Peterson, & Jesso, 2008; Stein et al., 2008). Maternal vocabulary was collected using the written multiple-choice modified version of the Mill Hill Vocabulary Scale (Raven, 1997). The total correct score, with a possible maximum of 44, was used. Mothers' mental health was measured with The Non-specific Psychological Distress Scale (Kessler-6; Kessler & Mroczek, 1994). A score of 4 or more of a possible 24 is considered an indication of the presence of a mental health problem.

The output measure for the regression was the score on the Communication and Symbolic Behavior Scales Developmental Profile™ (CSBS DP™) Infant-Toddler Checklist (Wetherby & Prizant, 2002), which was included in the 8- and 12-month questionnaire packages. The Infant-Toddler Checklist is a 24-item parent-report checklist, which provides a standard total score based on three domains: Social, Speech, and Symbolic. Questions cover Emotion and Eye Gaze, Communication, Gestures, Sounds, Words, Understanding, and Object Use. We examined the relationship between the possible risk factors and change in communication levels using a linear regression, adjusting for the 8-month CSBS DP Infant-Toddler Checklist scores. Because it allows for the correlation between the responses of twins, the random effects model was used to fit the linear regressions. The analysis showed that communication skills at 8 months were strongly associated with communication skills at 12 months. The CSBS DP Infant-Toddler Checklist scores at 8 months accounted for 37% of the variance. Female gender, twin birth, and family history of language and speech difficulties were associated with the output measure, but family and maternal factors explained very little variance, less than 6%. These results indicate that biological factors had more influence on communicative development in the first 12 months than environmental (family) factors.

## Age 2 and Age 4 Data

In the age 2 questionnaire package (24-month data collection), we included the MacArthur-Bates Communicative Development Inventory (CDI): Words and Sentences (Fenson et al., 2007), modified with permission of the authors and publishers to accommodate Australian usage (24 vocabulary items were changed, e.g., *crocodile* for *alligator, footpath* for *sidewalk*). At age 4, trained assistants conducted face-to-face assessments of the children in the sample. The Clinical Evaluation of Language Fundamentals–Preschool, Second Edition–Australian (CELF-P2; Wiig, Secord, & Semel, 2006) was used to assess receptive and expressive language. Expressive language was measured with three subtests: Word Structure, Expressive Vocabulary, and Recalling Sentences. Receptive language was also measured with three subtests: Sentence Structure, Concepts and Following Directions, and Basic Concepts. The Matrices subtest of the Kaufman Brief Intelligence Test, Second Edition (K-BIT2, Kaufman & Kaufman, 2004) was used to assess nonverbal cognitive abilities. Assessment sessions for most children were held in the local community child health center unless parents preferred to have their children assessed in their home.

## Outcomes at Age 2

From the age 2 data, we restricted the analysis of the CDI vocabulary production and LT status to parent reports that had been completed between 23.5 and 25.5

months. On the basis of gender-specific normative values (Fenson et al., 2007) and following common practice, we identified as LTs those children whose vocabulary scores on the CDI: Words and Sentences were at or below the U.S. 10th percentile. Regression analyses were used to determine the extent to which the 12 potential risk factors examined in our 12-month data were associated with the CDI vocabulary scores at age 2 and also LT status.

The mean number of words produced was 260 ($SD$ = 162) with a median of 247 and a range of 0 to 679 (Reilly et al., 2007). For girls the mean was 287.7 ($SD$ = 159.7, range: 0–679), and for boys the mean was 234.7 ($SD$ = 160.6, range: 0–679). A total of 333 children (19.7% of the sample of 1,691) were classified as LTs based on the U.S. 10th percentile. Of this group of LTs, 184 were reported not to be combining words. Of note was the large difference between the mean vocabulary score for the boys (mean = 39) and girls (mean = 65) who were LTs. The percentage of LTs identified is

**Table 1.1.** Late talker status using number of words produced on the CDI: Words and Sentences component of the MacArthur-Bates Communicative Development Inventories (CDIs; Fenson et al., 2007) ($n$ = 1,570)

| Variable | Odds ratio | 95% Confidence interval | $p$ |
|---|---|---|---|
| Female % | 0.86 | 0.66, 1.12 | |
| Twin birth % | 0.66 | 0.19, 2.26 | |
| Preterm birth (< 36 weeks) % | 1.16 | 0.44, 3.00 | |
| Birth weight (kg) | 0.92 | 0.70, 1.21 | |
| Birth order (first child reference) | | | .06 |
|   Second child | 1.16 | 0.85, 1.58 | |
|   Third child | 1.81 | 1.21, 2.71 | |
|   Fourth child | 1.69 | 0.17, 4.04 | |
|   Fifth child or more | 0.66 | 0.06, 6.97 | |
| Non–English-speaking background | 2.48 | 1.33, 4.61 | .004 |
| Disadvantage score (SEIFA first quintile reference) | | | .24 |
|   Second quintile | 1.17 | 0.52, 2.19 | |
|   Third quintile | 0.74 | 0.44, 1.26 | |
|   Fourth quintile | 1.01 | 0.60, 1.68 | |
|   Fifth quintile (least disadvantaged) | 0.77 | 0.44, 1.37 | |
| Family history of language difficulties | 1.58 | 1.18, 2.11 | .002 |
| Maternal vocabulary scores | 0.98 | 0.95, 1.01 | .18 |
| Mental health problem (mother) | 1.01 | 0.76, 1.34 | .96 |
| Maternal education level (≤ 12 years reference) | | | .04 |
|   13 years | 0.62 | 0.44, 0.87 | |
|   Degree | 0.67 | 0.45, 0.99 | |
|   Higher degree | 0.67 | 0.42, 1.05 | |
| Maternal age at birth of child | 1.02 | 0.99, 1.05 | .27 |

Reproduced by permission from Reilly, S., Wake, M., Bavin, E.L., Prior, M., Williams, J., Bretherton, L., Eadie, P., Barrett, Y., & Ukoumunne, O. (2007). Predicting language at 2 years of age: A prospective community study. *Pediatrics, 120e*, e1441–e1449. Copyright © 2007 by the AAP.

*Key:* SEIFA, Socio-Economic Indexes for Areas.

high but falls within the estimated range cited previously. The high percentage may be accounted for, in part, by the lower mean scores obtained for the sample than those published for the U.S. normative sample. As discussed in Bavin et al. (2008), lower scores have also been reported in studies using versions of the CDIs in the United Kingdom and New Zealand, suggesting that children in English-speaking nations vary in the number of words produced at age 2, or that there is variation in how confident their parents are in reporting the words their child knows.

We fitted a logistic regression model to LT status using the 12 risk factors as predictors. As shown in Table 1.1, those factors associated with late talking status were a non–English-speaking background, family history of speech and language difficulties, and low maternal education (≤ 12 years). However, the variation explained by the model was only 4% (Reilly et al., 2007). We ran another regression analysis in which we included the 12-month CSBS DP Infant-Toddler Checklist total score (restricted to children whose assessment was between 11.5 and 13.5 months). This early communication measure was a better predictor of LT status (odds ratio [$OR$] = 0.95; 95% CI [0.94, 0.96]; partial $R^2$ = 5.3%) than the 12 potential risk factors (child, family, and maternal characteristics).

## Outcomes at Age 4

Characteristics of the ELVS sample retained at age 4 were similar to those at recruitment at 8 months. Table 1.2 provides a comparison of the children who participated and those lost to the sample at age 4.

We investigated how many of the sample at age 4 could be identified as SLI in expressive language, receptive language, or both, and how many of these had been LTs. To identify the children in the sample as SLI, we used a cut-off score on the CELF-P2 of –1.25 $SDs$ below the mean for the normative population, in line with standard research practice (e.g., Tomblin, Records, & Zhang, 1996). This criterion equates to a standard score of 81 or less on expressive or receptive language or both. In addition, the children identified as SLI were required to have nonverbal scores on the K-BIT2 matrices task in the average range, to be of English-speaking background, and to have no developmental problems identified other than language. The cutoff for average nonverbal ability was a standard score of 86 on the K-BIT2; this was used rather than the published norm of 85 based on our distribution and the fact that the 4-year-old U.S. normative sample for the K-BIT2 was small ($N$ = 100).

From the eligible sample of 1,299 children, 215 had been LTs at age 2. Of these, 81 children (37.7%) were identified as SLI at age 4: 27 (12.6%) with expressive SLI, 20 (9.3%) with receptive SLI, and 34 (15.8 %) with mixed expressive–receptive SLI. A higher percentage of LT girls than LT boys were identified with expressive SLI (13.3% of the girls vs. 11.8% of the boys), but there was a higher percentage of LT boys than girls identified with receptive and mixed expressive–receptive SLI (receptive: 7.6% of the girls vs. 10.9% of the boys; mixed: 11.4% of the girls vs. 20.9% of the boys). Of the children from this sample who had resolved ($n$ = 134), 67.6% of the girls resolved, and 57.3% of the boys resolved. Of particular interest, however, was that 96 children (8.9%) of the non-LTs were classified as SLI at age 4. Of these, 52 were receptive SLI, 15 expressive SLI, and 29 mixed. There was a higher percentage of boys (11% of the non-LT boys and 6.7% of the non-LT girls).

**Table 1.2.** Characteristics of children participating and not participating at age 4

| Characteristic | Participating[a] $n = 1,596$ | Not participating[b] $n = 314$ |
|---|---|---|
| Female % | 48.6 | 53.8 |
| Twin birth % | 2.8 | 2.8 |
| Preterm birth (< 36 weeks) % | 3.2 | 2.5 |
| Birth weight (kg; mean) | 3.4 | 3.4 |
| Birth order % | | |
| First child | 50.1 | 50.3 |
| Second child | 35.3 | 35.7 |
| Third child | 12.2 | 10.4 |
| Fourth child | 2.5 | 3.6 |
| Non–English-speaking background % | 5.5 | 12.4 |
| Maternal education level % | | |
| ≤ 12 years | 21.0 | 31.7 |
| 13 years | 40.8 | 36.6 |
| Degree | 38.1 | 31.7 |
| Disadvantage score (SEIFA) | 1039 | 1023 |
| Family history of speech-language problems % | 25.1 | 23.6 |
| Mental health problem (mother) % | 31.7 | 31.5 |
| Vocabulary score (mother) | 27.7 | 27.7 |
| Maternal age at birth of child (years) | 31.3 | 30.3 |

From Reilly, S., Wake, M., Ukoumunne, O.C., Bavin, E.L., Prior, M., Cini, E., Conway, L., Eadie, P., & Bretherton, L. (2010). Predicting language outcomes at 4 years of age: Findings from the Early Language in Victoria Study. *Pediatrics, 126e,* e1530–e1537. Copyright © 2010 by the AAP.

[a]Sample size ranged from 1,519 to 1,596.
[b]Sample size ranged from 232 to 314.
*Key:* SEIFA, Socio-Economic Indexes for Areas.

Most were identified as SLI on the basis of their receptive scores: 33 boys and 19 girls, with 20 boys and 9 girls low on both expressive and receptive language. That is, more than half of the children we identified as SLI at age 4 had not been LTs based on parent report of number of words produced at age 2 (i.e., 96 non-LTs vs. 81 LTs).

The mean for CELF-P2 receptive standard scores at age 4 was 96.7 (*SD* = 14.9), and the mean for expressive standard scores was 99.6 (*SD* = 15.1. The extent to which the 12 potential risk factors contributed to receptive and expressive language scores at age 4 was examined in regression analyses. Because LT status is generally considered to be a risk factor for language outcome, we then repeated the analyses including age 2 LT status as a predictor variable.

As shown in Table 1.3, the predictor variables contributed 20.9% of the variance for expressive language scores (*n* = 1,442) and 18.9% for receptive language scores (*n* = 1,473). The predictors associated with receptive and expressive language for the sample at age 4 were male gender, birth weight, non–English-speaking background, maternal education, maternal vocabulary, SEIFA disadvantage score, family history of speech-language difficulties, and maternal age. For

**Table 1.3.** Multivariable linear regression of the Clinical Evaluation of Language Fundamentals–Preschool, Second Edition–Australian (Wiig, Secord, & Semel, 2006) standardized scores on potential baseline predictors

| Predictor | Expressive ($n = 1,442$) | | | Receptive ($n = 1,473$) | | |
|---|---|---|---|---|---|---|
| | Odds ratio | 95% Confidence interval | p | Odds ratio | 95% Confidence interval | p |
| **Child** | | | | | | |
| Male gender | −2.9 | 1.5, 4.3 | <.001 | 4.6 | 3.2, 6.0 | <.001 |
| Twin birth | −0.9 | −5.4, 3.6 | .69 | 0.1 | −4.4, 4.6 | .96 |
| Preterm birth (< 36 weeks) | 1.6 | −2.9, 6.0 | .49 | 2.9 | −1.6, 7.4 | .20 |
| Birth weight (kg) | 1.7 | 0.3, 3.2 | .02 | 2.0 | 0.5, 3.5 | .01 |
| Birth order (first child reference) | | | <.001 | | | .003 |
| Second child | −1.6 | −3.2, −0.02 | | −0.6 | −2.2, 1.0 | |
| Third child | −6.5 | −8.8, −4.2 | | −2.9 | −5.2, −0.7 | |
| Fourth child | −8.8 | −13.4, −4.2 | | −7.3 | −11.9, −2.6 | |
| **Family** | | | | | | |
| Non-English-speaking background | −12.6 | −16.1, −9.2 | <.001 | −11.9 | −15.4, −8.5 | <.001 |
| SEIFA disadvantage, per 100 unit increase | 2.5 | 1.3, 3.8 | <.001 | 2.7 | 1.5, 4.0 | <.001 |
| Family history of speech-language difficulties | −3.8 | −5.4, −2.2 | <.001 | −3.3 | −4.9, −1.6 | <.001 |
| **Mother** | | | | | | |
| Education level (≤ 12 years reference) | | | <.001 | | | <.001 |
| 13 years | 1.4 | −0.5, 3.3 | | 1.1 | −0.8, 3.0 | |
| Degree | 4.1 | 2.2, 6.1 | | 4.8 | 2.8, 6.8 | |
| Mental health problem | −0.37 | −1.9, 1.1 | .63 | −0.36 | −1.8, 1.1 | .64 |
| Vocabulary score | 0.62 | 0.46, 0.78 | <.001 | 0.48 | 0.32, 0.65 | <.001 |
| Age at birth of child (years) | 0.22 | 0.04, 0.40 | .02 | 0.21 | 0.03, 0.39 | .02 |
| | | $R^2 = 20.9\%$[a] | | | $R^2 = 18.9\%$[b] | |

Reproduced by permission from Reilly, S., Wake, M., Ukoumunne, O.C., Bavin, E.L., Prior, M., Cini, E., Conway, L., Eadie, P., & Bretherton, L. (2010). Predicting language outcomes at 4 years of age: Findings from the Early Language in Victoria Study. *Pediatrics, 126e*, e1530–e1537. Copyright © 2010 by the AAP.

[a]With late-talking status added to the expressive language regression, $R^2$ increased to 30.4% (coefficient = −12.9; 95% CI [−14.6, −11.1]; $p <$ .001).

[b]With late-talking status added to the receptive language regression, $R^2$ increased to 27.9% (coefficient = −11.4; 95% CI [−13.1, −9.7]; $p <$ .001).

*Key:* SEIFA, Socio-Economic Indexes for Areas.

boys, the mean scores on the CELF-P2 were lower than for girls. Children whose mothers had a higher level of education (a degree) had higher scores compared with children whose mothers had not completed high school, and children from families with higher SEIFA scores had higher language scores. A stronger association was found for non–English-speaking background (minority status) with low expressive language than with receptive language. Twin birth, preterm birth, and maternal mental health problems were not associated with the CELF-P2 scores, and when regression models excluded these three variables, nearly identical values were obtained as when all 12 variables were included (Reilly et al., 2010).

As noted at the bottom of Table 1.3, LT status significantly increased the percentages of variance explained: to 23.6% for receptive language (coefficient = –11.4; 95% CI [–13.1, –9.7]; $p < .001$) and to 30.4% for expressive language (coefficient = –12.9; 95% CI [–14.6, –11.1], $p < .001$). That is, LT status played a greater role in predicting expressive language than in predicting receptive language.

Of note is that more variance for CELP-P2 scores at age 4 was explained by the 12 potential predictors than for the age 2-year sample. Gender, birth order, English-speaking background, and family history of speech-language difficulties were significant predictors of vocabulary scores at age 2, but they explained only 7.0% of the variance (Reilly et al., 2007). At age 4, environmental factors had a greater impact on language outcome; in addition to these four factors, social disadvantage, maternal vocabulary, and maternal education also made significant contributions.

## Follow-Up Study: Working Memory in Resolved Late Talkers and Children with Specific Language Impairment

In our analyses of the ELVS sample, we did not initially consider children's memory in relation to LT status. Given the established association between word learning and verbal memory (Gathercole & Baddeley, 1990), we would expect that delayed memory development might be a factor influencing their low vocabulary scores. Previous research has reported that RLTs as well as those LTs who are identified as having SLI score low on the repetition of nonwords. Thus, we would predict low scores on a nonword repetition task for the RLTs in the ELVS sample. This section gives an overview of a follow-up study conducted with a subsample from ELVS at age 5. The study was designed to investigate whether the children whose late talking had resolved by age 4 showed similar performance on memory tasks as those children whose late talking had not resolved and were therefore identified as having SLI at age 4.

A criterion for identifying SLI is dissociation between language and nonverbal cognitive performance. However, children with SLI are known to have problems processing information. In particular, as previously discussed, SLI is associated with poor working memory. Research on memory limitations in SLI has focused on verbal memory, particularly phonological memory, but there are several different memory components. In Baddeley's model of working memory, the most frequently cited in research in the area of language disorders, there are four components (Baddeley, 1986, 1992, 2000). Verbal information is stored temporarily in the phonological loop. The fact that RLTs as well as children with SLI have been reported to have low scores on phonological memory tasks, particularly nonword repetition (Bishop & Adams, 1990; Bishop et al., 1996; Gathercole & Baddeley, 1990), indicates a limited storage capacity for both groups. A delay or impairment in visuospatial memory has also been shown for children with SLI (Bavin, Wilson, Maruff, & Slee-man, 2005; Hoffman & Gillam, 2004; Marton, 2008), but the extent to which RLTs are delayed in this aspect of memory is not known. Another task in which both SLI and RLTs show poor accuracy is recalling sentences (Bishop & Adams, 1990; Ellis Weismer, 2007), which has been suggested as a clinical marker for SLI (Archibald & Joanisse, 2009; Conti-Ramsden et al., 2001). Recalling sentence tasks assess the episodic buffer component of Baddeley's working memory model (Alloway, Gather-cole, Willis, & Adams, 2004); this is involved in the integration of information from different components of memory and can justify why more words in a sentence context can be recalled than from a word list. Children with SLI a few years older than in the current study (e.g., Archibald & Gathercole, 2006; Briscoe & Rankin, 2009) are also reported to perform poorly on tasks assessing the central executive component—typically tasks in which information is held in memory for later recall while some processing is carried out on the information. However, the central executive component has not been the focus of research with RLTs; how their central executive performance compares to that of children with SLI is not known.

Given the evidence that RLTs may continue to show delay in some areas of language and memory, Petruccelli investigated whether a subset of RLTs from the ELVS sample would perform similarly to children with typical development (TLD) on a battery of memory tasks or similarly to children who had been identified as LTs at age 2 and SLI at age 4 (Petruccelli, Bavin, & Bretherton, 2012).

Some ELVS children were not eligible to participate in this follow-up study because they were participants in another, and we did not want to overly burden families. LTs from non–English-speaking background were also excluded because of possible confounds in estimating their vocabulary using the CDI: Words and Sentence (Fenson et al., 2007) at age 2. The final sample comprised 95 children: 24 of the 43 eligible children identified as SLI at age 4 who had also been LTs at age 2; 39 of the 70 eligible RLTs; and 32 children with TLD, stratified across the LGAs. The person who tested the children was naive to their group membership. Five additional RLTs recruited were dropped from the analysis because the RLT group was found to have a significantly higher score than the two other groups on the K-BIT2 matrices subtest, used as a measure of nonverbal ability at age 4. In order to match the groups on the K-BIT2 scores, the children with the highest scores in the RLT group were excluded from analysis.

The mean scores on productive vocabulary on the CDI at age 2 were similar for the SLI and RLT groups (SLI = 55.96, RLT = 57.87). There was no significant age difference across groups; for the SLI group, the mean age was 63.29 months, for the RLT group it was 62.87 months, and for the TLD group it was 63.19 months. All families who accepted the invitation to participate were included, resulting in more girls participating than boys, particularly in the RLT group (SLI: boys = 10, girls = 14; RLT: boys = 13, girls = 26; TLD: boys = 13, girls = 19).

Of the SLI group, 33.3% were from the LGAs that represented the more disadvantaged families based on SEIFA scores, 12.5% were from the middle level, and 54.2% were from the LGAs with the least disadvantage. For the RLT group, 28.2% were recruited from the more disadvantaged group, 28.2% were from the middle level, and 43.6% were from the LGAs with the least disadvantage. For the TD group, 31.25% were from the more disadvantaged group, 21.9 % were from the middle level, and 46.9% were from the LGAs with the least disadvantage. So, the low socio-economic level was not overly represented in the SLI and RLT groups.

The children were assessed on all four memory components of Baddeley's model of working memory: phonological loop, visuospatial memory, episodic buffer, and central executive, as discussed previously. Phonological memory was assessed with Digit Recall and Word List Recall from the Working Memory Battery for Children (WMBC; Pickering & Gathercole, 2001) and The Children's Test of Nonword Repetition (CNRep; Gathercole & Baddeley, 1996). The episodic buffer task was the Recalling Sentences subtest of the Clinical Evaluation of Language Fundamentals, Fourth Edition–Australian (CELF-4; Semel, Wiig, & Secord, 2004). Two tasks from the WMBC, Picture Location and Block Recall, were used to assess visuospatial memory, and the central executive component was assessed with Backwards Digit Span from the WMBC.

Means and standard deviations for each group for each memory measure are presented in Table 1.4. With the exception of one task testing visuospatial memory, the mean scores for the RLT group fell between those of the other two groups. Analyses of the data included a combination of ANOVA, MANOVA, MANCOVA to control for nonverbal scores, and posthoc comparisons using Tukey HSD tests. For the measures of phonological short-term memory, no significant differences were found between the RLT and TLD groups, but the children with SLI scored significantly lower than the TLD and RLT groups on Digit Recall. In addition, significantly more children with SLI (29.2%) had scores of –1 $SD$ or lower on Digit Recall than children from the TLD group (6.3%). In the RLT group, 12.8% had scores of –1 $SD$ or lower, but no significant differences were found between the RLT and TLD groups or between the RLT and SLI groups. On Word List Recall, the percentage of children with SLI scoring –1 $SD$ or lower was 29.2%, whereas for the RLTs it was 17.9% and for the TLD group it was 16.1%.

**Table 1.4.** Means and standard deviations by group for the working memory tasks

| Measure | SLI | RLT | TLD |
| --- | --- | --- | --- |
| | *M* (*SD*) | *M* (*SD*) | *M* (*SD*) |
| Digit Recall | 86.87 (7.18) | 96.56 (12.94) | 101.50 (9.71) |
| Word List Recall | 90.46 (11.11) | 97.28 (18.09) | 99.39 (16.22) |
| CNRep Total score | 89.05 (15.90) | 97.78 (14.72) | 104.13 (17.86) |
| Recalling Sentences | 6.08 (2.57) | 9.33 (2.32) | 10.47 (1.92) |
| Block Recall | 86.46 (17.99) | 97.85 (16.62) | 90.56 (16.59) |
| Pictures Location | 9.12 (2.88) | 10.15 (2.59) | 9.37 (2.48) |
| Backwards Digit Recall | 82.46 (10.05) | 86.33 (12.89) | 89.72 (10.20) |

From Petruccelli, N., Bavin, E.L., & Bretherton, L. (2012). Children with specific language impairment and resolved late talkers: Working memory profile at age 5 years. *Journal of Speech, Language, and Hearing Research, 55,* 1690–1703; adapted by permission.

*Key:* SLI, specific language impairment; RLT, resolved late talkers; TLD, typical development; CNRep, The Children's Test of Nonword Repetition (Gathercole & Baddeley, 1996).

On the CNRep, the SLI group repeated significantly fewer nonwords correctly than the TLD group. This resulted from fewer of the long words (20 of the total 40) being repeated correctly, which supports previous research findings. Differences between the RLT and SLI groups and between the RLT and TLD groups were not statistically significant (mean scores: SLI = 4.33 [$SD$ = 3.44], RLT = 6.43 [$SD$ = 4.05], and TLD = 8.13 [$SD$ = 4.62]). Thus, children in the RLT group were more likely to find the task challenging than those with TLD.

For the episodic buffer task Recalling Sentences, the SLI group had significantly lower scores than the other two groups, supporting previous research findings. For the central executive task, Backwards Digit Recall, children from all groups found the task difficult. The mean score for the SLI group was lower than for the other two groups but not significantly so. However, of note is the percentage of children in each group with scores of at least 1 $SD$ below the mean. The RLT percentage (35.8%) was greater than that of the TLD group (25%) but lower than that of the SLI group (41.7%).

For the visual spatial memory tasks, Picture Location and Block Recall, when K-BIT2 scores were included as a covariate, no significant group differences were found. For all other tasks, when K-BIT2 scores were used as a covariate, the results did not change.

In summary, the RLTs showed no significant deficit in memory in that their scores were not significantly lower than those of the TLD group, although the mean scores were not as high as those of the TLD group on all measures except Block Design. On Digit Recall, a significant difference was found between the RLT and SLI groups. In contrast and in support of previous research results, the SLI group differed significantly from the TLD group on measures of phonological short-term memory and the episodic buffer—that is, Digit Recall, CNRep, and Recalling Sentences.

Immature memory could partly explain why language-related problems appear to emerge in children whose late talking seems to have resolved. It might be assumed that memory for the children with delayed language onset would not develop as well over the early school years as for typically developing children. Archibald and Gathercole (2006) tested 7- to 11-year-old children on the same Digit Recall and Word List Recall tasks as used in the current study and found that 60% of an SLI group performed at least 1 $SD$ below the mean on Digit Recall and 70% on Word List Recall. However, they did not assess RLT, nor did they indicate if their SLI sample had been LTs. Memory develops over the period from age 4 to age 8 (Luciana & Nelson, 1998), with central executive skills continuing to mature though adolescence (Best & Miller, 2010). Thus it is likely that memory was not well enough developed in the subsample recruited from ELVS to show significant group differences between the RLT and TLD groups at age 5 but that more mature memory for the children with typical development included in the study would become evident in their school years. Over time, residual effects of LT status may emerge for the RLT in the ELVS study. We did, however, find in some tasks that more individuals in the RLT group had low scores than in the TLD group.

## CONCLUSIONS

In most of the previous research on RLTs, samples have not been drawn from a large community sample as in the current study, and there has been a wide range reported for the proportion of children whose late talking has resolved in the pre-school years. Given the increasing contribution from environmental factors in language outcomes found with our age 4 ELVS sample, it is important that samples are representative. LTs are not a homogeneous group. Failing to produce words may be due to reasons other than an underlying language problem. The fact that some resolve without apparent subsequent delay suggests different reasons contribute to late talking. Research on SLI has not always reported whether children in the sample were LTs or not or whether the children had receptive and expressive language problems. As indicated by the ELVS data, a substantial number of children with SLI were not LTs at age 2; thus, late talking at age 2 is not necessary for later language problems to be identified, although it is clearly a risk factor (see also Chapter 17).

Overall, the results from ELVS support previous research that has reported family history of language problems, minority status, and low maternal education as risk factors for LT status, and LT status is a moderate risk factor for later language impairment. However, more fine-grained analysis of contributing factors and later outcomes with representative samples may help explain some of the variability in productive vocabulary at age 2 and factors that interact in determining language outcomes by early school age and beyond. Comparing at the group level does not provide information about development for individual children. A valuable contribution would be to identify developmental paths in memory for individual children whose late talking resolves and those whose late talking does not resolve.

## REFERENCES

Alloway, T.P., Gathercole, S.E., Willis, C.S., & Adams, A.-M. (2004). A structural analysis of working memory and related cognitive skills in young children. *Journal of Experimental Child Psychology, 87,* 85–170.

Archibald, L.M., & Gathercole, S.E. (2006). Short-term and working memory in specific language impairment. *International Journal of Language & Communication Disorders, 41*(6), 675–693.

Archibald, L.M., Joanisse, M.F. (2009). On the sensitivity and specificity of nonword repetition and sentence recall to language and memory impairments in children. *Journal of Speech Language and Hearing Research, 52,* 899–914.

Australian Bureau of Statistics. (2001). *Socio-economic indexes for areas.* Canberra, Australia: Author.

Australian Bureau of Statistics. (2006). *Population by age and sex, Victoria, June 2003.* Retrieved from http://www.abs.gov.au/ausstats/abs@.nsf/ProductsbyReleaseDate/B81A45749 DEEC800CA25702F0071F5F1?OpenDocument

Baddeley, A.D. (1986). *Working memory.* New York, NY: Oxford University Press.

Baddeley, A.D. (1992). Working memory. *Science, 255,* 556–559.

Baddeley, A.D. (2000). The episodic buffer: A new component of working memory. *Trends in Cognitive Science, 4,* 417–423.

Bates, E., & Goodman, J. (1997). On the inseparability of grammar and the lexicon: Evidence from acquisition, aphasia and real-time processing. *Language and Cognitive Processing, 12,* 507–584.

Bavin, E.L., Prior, M., Reilly, S., Bretherton, L., Williams, J., Eadie, P., . . . Ukoumunne, O.C. (2008). The Early Language in Victoria Study: Predicting vocabulary at age 1 and 2 years from gesture and object use. *Journal of Child Language, 35,* 687–701.

Bavin, E.L., Wilson, P.H., Maruff, P., & Sleeman, F. (2005). Spatio-visual memory of children with specific language impairment: Evidence for generalized processing problems. *International Journal of Language & Communication Disorders, 40*(3), 319–332.

Beitchman, J.H., Wilson, B., Brownlie, E.B., Walters, H., Inglis, A., & Lancee, W. (1996). Long-term consistency in speech/language profiles: II. Behavioural, emotional and social outcomes. *Journal of the American Academy of Child and Adolescent Psychiatry, 35*(6), 815–825.

Beitchman, J.H., Wilson, B., Johnson, C.J., Atkinson, L., Young, A., Adlaf, E., . . . Douglas, L. (2001). Fourteen year follow-up of speech/language impaired children and control children: Psychiatric outcome. *Journal of the American Academy of Child and Adolescent Psychiatry, 40*(1), 75–82.

Best, J.R., & Miller, P.H. (2010). A developmental perspective on executive function. *Child Development, 81,* 1641–1660.

Bishop, D.V.M. (2006). What causes specific language impairment in children? *Current Directions in Psychological Science, 15,* 217–221.

Bishop, D.V.M. (2008). Specific language impairment, dyslexia, and autism: Using genetics to unravel their relationship. In C.F. Norbury, J.B. Tomblin, & D.V.M. Bishop (Eds.), *Understanding language disorders: From theory to practice* (pp. 67–78). London, United Kingdom: Psychology Press.

Bishop, D.V., & Adams, C. (1990). A prospective study of the relationship between specific language impairment, phonological disorders and reading retardation. *Journal of Child Psychology and Psychiatry, 31,* 1027–1050.

Bishop, D.V., & Edmundson, A. (1987). Language impaired 4-year-olds: Distinguishing transient from persistent impairment. *Journal of Speech and Hearing Disorders, 52,* 156–173.

Bishop, D.V.M., North, T., & Donlan, C. (1996). Nonword repetition as a behavioural marker for inherited language impairment: Evidence from a twin study. *Journal of Child Psychology and Psychiatry, 37,* 391–403.

Botting, N., & Conti-Ramsden, G. (2000). Social and behavioural difficulties in children with language impairment. *Child Language Teaching and Therapy, 16*(2), 105–120.

Bricker, D., & Squires, J. (with assistance from Mounts, L., Potter, L., Nickel, R., Twombly, E., & Farrell, J.). (1999). *Ages & Stages Questionnaires®(ASQ): A parent-completed, child monitoring sytem* (2nd ed.). Baltimore, MD: Paul H. Brookes Publishing Co.

Briscoe, J., & Rankin, P.M. (2009). Exploration of a "double-jeopardy" hypothesis within working memory profiles for children with specific language impairment. *International Journal of Language and Communication Disorders, 44,* 236–250.

Conti-Ramsden, G., Botting, N., & Faragher, B. (2001). Psycholinguistic markers for specific language impairment (SLI). *Journal of Child Psychology and Psychiatry, 42,* 741–748.

Dale, P.S., Price, T.S., Bishop, D.V., & Plomin, R. (2003). Outcomes of early language delay, part I: Predicting persistent and transient language difficulties at 3 and 4 years. *Journal of Speech Language Hearing Research, 46,* 544–560.

Desmarais, C., Sylvestre, A., Meyer, F., Bairati, I., & Rouleau, N. (2008). Systematic review of the literature on characteristics of late-talking toddlers. *International Journal of Language and Communication Disorders, 43*(4), 361–389.

Ellis Weismer, S. (2007). Typical talkers, late talkers, and children with specific language impairment: A language endowment spectrum? In R. Paul (Ed.), *Language disorders from a developmental perspective: Essays in honor of Robin S. Chapman* (pp. 83–101). Mahwah, NJ: Lawrence Erlbaum Associates.

Ellis Weismer, S., & Evans, J. (2002). The role of processing limitations in early identification of specific language impairment. *Topics in Language Disorders, 22*(3), 15–29.

Ellis Weismer, S., Evans, J., & Hesketh, L.J. (1999). An examination of verbal working memory capacity in children with specific language impairment. *Journal of Speech, Language, and Hearing Research, 42*(5), 1249–1260.

Ellis Weismer, S., Murray-Branch, J., & Miller, J.F. (1994). A prospective longitudinal study of language development in late talkers. *Journal of Speech and Hearing Research, 36,* 1037–1062.

Ellis Weismer, S., Tomblin, J.B., Zhang, X., Buckwalter, P., Chynoweth, J.G., & Jones, M. (2000). Nonword repetition performance in school-age children with and without language impairment. *Journal of Speech, Language, and Hearing Research, 43,* 865–878.

Evans, J.L., Alibali, M., & McNeil, N. (2001). Divergence of verbal expression and embodied knowledge: Evidence from speech and gesture in children with specific language impairment. *Language and Cognitive Processes, 16,* 309–331.

Fenson, L., Dale, P.S., Reznick, J.S., Bates, E., Thal, D., & Pethick, S.J. (1994).Variability in early communicative development. *Monograph of the Society for Research in Child Development, 59,* 1–173.

Fenson, L., Marchman, V.A., Thal, D.J., Dale, P.S., Reznick, J.S., & Bates, E. (2007). *MacArthur-Bates Communicative Development Inventories (CDIs)* (2nd ed.). Baltimore, MD: Paul H. Brookes Publishing Co.

Gathercole, S., & Baddeley, A.D. (1990). Phonological memory deficits in language disordered children: Is there a causal connection. *Journal of Memory and Language, 29,* 336–360.

Gathercole, S., & Baddeley, A.D. (1996). *The Children's Test of Nonword Repetition.* London, United Kingdom: Psychological Corp.

Girolametto, L., Pearce, P.S., & Weitzman, E. (1996). Children with a history of expressive language delay: Outcomes at 5 years of age. *American Journal of Speech-Language Pathology, 10,* 358–369.

Hart, B., & Risley, T.R. (1995). *Meaningful differences in the everyday experience of young American children.* Baltimore, MD: Paul H. Brookes Publishing Co.

Hoff-Ginsburg, E. (1998). The relation of birth order and socioeconomic status to children's language experience and language development. *Applied Psycholinguistics, 19*(4), 603–629.

Hoffman, L.M., & Gillam, R.B. (2004). Verbal and spatial information processing constraints in children with specific language impairment. *Journal of Speech, Language, and Hearing Research, 47*(1), 114–125.

Kaufman, A.S., Kaufman, N.L. (2004). *Kaufman Brief Intelligence Test, Second Edition.* Bloomington, MN: Pearson, Inc.

Kessler, R., & Mroczek, D. (1994). *Non-Specific Psychological Distress Scale.* Ann Arbor, MI: Institute for Social Research.

Klee, T., Carson, D., Gavin, W., Hall, L., Kent, A., & Reece, S. (1998). Concurrent and predictive validity of an early language screening program. *Journal of Speech, Language, and Hearing Research, 41,* 627–641.

Leonard, L. (1989). Language learnability and specific language impairment in children. *Applied Psycholinguistics, 10,* 179–202.

Leonard, L. (1998). *Children with specific language impairment.* Cambridge, MA: MIT Press.

Luciana, M., & Nelson, C. (1998). The functional emergence of prefrontally-guided working memory systems in four to eight-year-old children. *Neuropsychologica, 36,* 273–293.

Manhardt, J., & Rescorla, L. (2002). Oral narrative skills of late talkers at ages 8 and 9. *Applied Psycholinguistics, 23,* 1–21.

Marton, K. (2008). Visuo-spatial processing and executive functions in children with specific language impairment. *International Journal of Language and Communication Disorders, 43,* 181–200.

Nelson, H.D., Nygren, P., Walker, M., & Panoscha, R. (2006). *Screening for speech and language delay in preschool children: Systematic evidence review for the US Preventive Services Task Force.* Retrieved from http://www.pediatrics.org/cgi/content/full/117/2/e298

Noel, M., Peterson, C., & Jesso, B. (2008). The relationship of parenting stress and child temperament to language development among economically disadvantaged preschoolers. *Journal of Child Language, 35,* 823–843.

Paul, R. (1991). Profiles of toddlers with slow expressive language development. *Topics in Language Disorders, 11,* 1–13.

Paul, R. (1993). Outcomes of early expressive language delay. *Journal of Childhood Communication Disorders, 15,* 7–14.

Paul, R., & Alforde (1993). Grammatical morpheme acquisition in 4-year olds with normal, impaired and late developing language. *Journal of Speech and Hearing Research, 36,* 1271–1275.

Paul, R., Spangle-Looney, S., & Dahm, P. (1991). Communication and socialization skills at age 2 and 3 in "late talking" young children. *Journal of Speech and Hearing Research, 34,* 858–865.

Petruccelli, N., Bavin, E.L., & Bretherton, L. (2012). Children with specific language impairment and resolved late talkers: Working memory profile at age 5 years. *Journal of Speech, Language and Hearing Research, 55,* 1–14.

Pickering, S.J., & Gathercole, S.E. (2001). *Working Memory Battery for Children.* London, United Kingdom: Psychological Corporation Europe.

Raven, J.C. (1997). *Mill Hill Vocabulary Scale.* Oxford, United Kingdom: Oxford Psychologists Press.

Reilly, S., Bavin, E.L., Bretherton, L., Conway, L., Eadie, P., Cini, E., . . . Wake, M. (2009). The Early Language in Victoria Study (ELVS): A prospective, longitudinal study of communication skills and expressive vocabulary development at 8, 12 and 24 months. *International Journal of Speech-Language Pathology, 11*(5), 344–357.

Reilly, S., Eadie, P., Bavin, E.L., Wake, M., Prior, M., Williams, J., . . . Ukoumunne, O.C. (2006). Growth of infant communication between 8 and 12 months: A population study. *Journal of Paediatrics and Child Health, 42,* 764–770.

Reilly, S., Wake, M., Bavin, E.L., Prior, M., Williams, J., Bretherton, L., . . . Ukoumunne, O. (2007). Predicting language at 2 years of age: A prospective community study. *Pediatrics, 120e,* e1441–e1449. Retrieved from http://www.pediatrics.org/cgi/content/full/120/6/e1441

Reilly, S., Wake, M., Ukoumunne, O.C., Bavin, E.L., Prior, M., Cini, E., . . . Bretherton, L. (2010). Predicting language outcomes at 4 years of age: Findings from the Early Language in Victoria Study. *Pediatrics, 126e,* e1530–e1537.

Rescorla, L. (1989). The Language Development Survey: A screening tool for delayed language in toddlers. *Journal of Speech and Hearing Disorders, 54,* 587–599.

Rescorla, L. (2002). Language and reading outcomes to age 9 in late-talking toddlers. *Journal of Speech, Language and Hearing Research, 45,* 360–371.

Resorla, L. (2005). Age 13 language and reading outcomes in late-talking toddlers. *Journal of Speech, Language, and Hearing Research, 48,* 459–472.

Rescorla, L. (2009). At 17 language and reading outcomes in late-talking toddlers. *Journal of Speech, Language, and Hearing Research, 52,* 16–30.

Rescorla, L., & Achenbach, T.M. (2002). Use of the language development survey (LDS) in a national probability sample of children 18 to 35 months old. *Journal of Speech, Language, and Hearing Research, 45,* 733–743.

Rescorla, L., Dahlsgaard, K., & Roberts, J. (2000). Late-talking toddlers: MLU and IPSyn outcomes at 3;0 and 4;0. *Journal of Child Language, 27,* 643–664.

Rescorla, L., Roberts, J., & Dahlsgaard, K. (1997). Late talker at 2: Outcome at age 3. *Journal of Speech, Language and Hearing Research, 40,* 556–566.

Roos, E.M., & Ellis Weismer, S. (2008). Language outcomes of late talking toddlers at preschool and beyond. *Perspectives on Language Learning and Education, 15,* 119–126.

Scarborough, H. (1990). Index of Productive Syntax. *Applied Psycholinguistics, 11,* 1–12.

Semel, E., Wiig, E., & Secord, W.A. (2004). *Clinical Evaluation of Language Fundamentals, Fourth Edition–Australian.* New South Wales, Australia: Harcourt Assessment.

Squires, J., & Bricker, D. (1993). *Infant/Child Monitoring Questionnaires procedures manual* (Rev. ed.). Eugene: University of Oregon.

Squires, J., Bricker, D., & Potter, L. (1997). Revision of a parent-completed developmental screening tool: Ages and Stages Questionnaires. *Journal of Pediatric Psychology, 22,* 313–328.

Squires, J., Potter, L., & Bricker, D. (1999). *The ASQ user's guide* (2nd ed.). Baltimore, MD: Paul H. Brookes Publishing. Co.

Stein, A., Malmberg, L.E., Sylva, K., Barnes, J., Leach, P., & the FCCC team. (2008). The influence of maternal depression, caregiving, and socioeconomic status in the post-natal year on children's language development. *Child: Care, Health and Development, 34,* 603–612.

Thal, D.J., & Tobias, S. (1994). Relationship between language and gesture in normal development and late-talking toddlers. *Journal of Speech, Hearing Research, 37,* 157–170.

Thal, D., Tobias, S., & Morrison, D. (1991). Language and gesture in late-talkers: A one year follow-up. *Journal of Speech, Hearing Research, 34,* 604–612.

Tomblin, J.B., Records, N.L., Buckwalter, P., Zhang, X., Smith, E., & O'Brien, M. (1997). Prevalence of specific language impairment in kindergarten children. *Journal of Speech, Language and Hearing Research, 40,* 1245–1260.

Tomblin, J.B., Records, N.L., & Zhang, Z. (1996). A system of diagnosis of specific language impairment in kindergarten children. *Journal of Speech and Hearing Research, 39,* 1284–1294.

Ukoumunne, O.C., Wake, M., Carlin, J., Bavin, E.L., Lum, J., Skeat, J., . . . Reilly, S. (2012). Profiles of language development in pre-school children: A longitudinal latent class analysis of data from the Early Language in Victoria Study. *Child: Care, Health and Development, 38,* 341–349.

Wetherby, A.M., & Prizant, B.M. (2002). *Communication and Symbolic Behavior Scales Developmental Profile™ (CSBS DP™).* Baltimore, MD: Paul H. Brookes Publishing Co.

Wiig, E.H., Secord, W.A., & Semel, E. (2006). *Clinical Evaluation of Language Fundamentals–Preschool, Second Edition–Australian.* Sydney, Australia: Harcourt Assessment.

Zubrick, S.R., Taylor, C.L., Rice, M.L., & Slegers, D.W. (2007). Late language emergence at 24 months: An epidemiological study of prevalence, predictors, and covariates. *Journal of Speech, Language, and Hearing Research, 50,* 1562–1592.

# 2

# Population and Public Health Perspectives on Late Language Emergence at 24 Months as a Risk Indicator for Language Impairment at 7 Years

Catherine L. Taylor, Stephen R. Zubrick, and Mabel L. Rice

The emergence of language during the toddler period is one of the most striking accomplishments in young children's development. Children show considerable variation in the onset of language, with some children beginning to talk much later than others. The term *late language emergence (LLE)* is used to describe toddlers with no known developmental disorders who do not meet age expectations for expressive vocabulary size and/or emergent grammar at 24 months. The term *normal language emergence (NLE)* is used to describe toddlers who do meet age expectations for expressive vocabulary size and/or emergent grammar. This chapter addresses three of the many interesting and important questions about children who are late to start talking: 1) What is the prevalence of LLE in the general population of children at 24 months? 2) What are the risks associated with LLE? and 3) What are the language outcomes of 7-year-old children with and without a history of LLE?

We begin the chapter with an overview of the timing and growth mechanisms in typical and atypical language development in early childhood. Next we consider individual differences in language acquisition from a public health perspective and discuss population-level study designs for understanding language acquisition and language impairment. We then summarize the findings from two of our population-level studies on the prevalence, predictors, and outcomes of delayed onset of

Preparation of this chapter was supported by the National Institutes of Health under Award Numbers RO1DC05226, P30DC005803, and P30HD002528; the National Health and Medical Research Council Program Grant (572742); and the Health Promotion Foundation of Western Australia (8016). The content is solely the responsibility of the authors and does not necessarily represent the official views of the National Institutes of Health. We thank the staff at the Western Australian Data Linkage Branch and the Maternal and Child Health Unit, and the children and families who participated in the studies.

language at 24 months. We finish the chapter with some observations about the theoretical and public health implications of our findings.

## TIMING AND GROWTH MECHANISMS IN
## TYPICAL AND ATYPICAL LANGUAGE DEVELOPMENT

Our overarching interest in studying the prevalence, predictors, and outcomes of LLE is to understand individual differences in language acquisition, with a particular focus on understanding the timing and growth characteristics of primary language impairment. Children with primary language impairment do not meet age expectations for language acquisition. These are children with otherwise typical development whose individual differences are largely confined to language. The term *specific language impairment (SLI)* is used to describe children with primary language impairment and otherwise typical development. The inclusionary criteria for an SLI diagnosis of include performance 1 standard deviation (*SD*) or more below the mean on at least one omnibus language assessment, along with normal hearing, normal nonverbal intelligence, and a monolingual family background. Children with developmental disorders are excluded from an SLI diagnosis (Rice, 2003). SLI can be identified reliably from 3 years of age, and there is considerable interest in the extent to which LLE at 24 months is a risk indicator for SLI (Tager-Flusberg & Cooper, 1999).

Both LLE and SLI are benchmarked to delayed language acquisition relative to a child's chronological age. A point of difference, however, is that LLE represents a normal variation in language acquisition for most children (Fenson et al., 1994), whereas the unexpected and largely unexplained variation for children with SLI persists for years (Rice, 2009). A further point of difference is that a delay model fits observations of children with LLE benchmarked to 24 months, but this model does not fit observations of children with SLI over time (Rice, 2009). A delay model predicts that the language systems of children with SLI have the same characteristics as the language systems of younger children with typical development. That is, the delay model predicts a pattern of synchronized development across all dimensions of the language system and parallel growth.

Studies of children with SLI that have used growth curve modeling have shown that a delay model does not fully specify the ways in which the language systems of children with SLI differ from children with typical development across all dimensions of language. These studies have shown that growth is actually not synchronized across all dimensions of the language system (e.g., syntax, morphosyntax, semantics) for children with SLI and that morphosyntactic development is more vulnerable than a delay model would predict. Instead, the model that fits the evidence for general immaturity in the language systems of children with SLI as well as specific vulnerability in the morphosyntactic dimension of language is the delay-within-disruption model (Rice, 2003, 2004, 2009). For children with SLI, the delay-within-disruption model captures the disruption to the expected pattern of morphosyntactic development over and above general immaturity in the syntactic and semantic dimensions of language. From a theoretical perspective, both the delay model and the delay-within-disruption model predict that children with SLI have a history of language delay at the onset of language between 12 and 24 months.

## A PUBLIC HEALTH PERSPECTIVE ON LANGUAGE ACQUISITION

In the field of public health, developmental accomplishments such as language acquisition are viewed as important outcomes in their own right as well as developmental means for literacy, education, and employment. The crucial role of oral language in enabling literacy, education, and employment means that to study language acquisition is to study one of the major pathways that support human capability formation (Sen, 1999).

The developmental achievements that accrue to individuals and populations in childhood have lasting effects on life opportunities for individuals and the productive wealth and human capability of populations (Marmot, 2010). Increasingly, early childhood (birth to 4 years) is the focus of global and national public policy frameworks for human capability expansion (Council of Australian Governments, 2009; Organisation for Economic Co-operation and Development, 2007; United Nations General Assembly, 1989).

## POPULATION-LEVEL STUDY DESIGNS FOR UNDERSTANDING INDIVIDUAL DIFFERENCES IN LANGUAGE ACQUISITION

Life span/longitudinal epidemiology is a public health approach to understanding determinants of health over the life span. Traditionally, the approach has been used to understand chronic disease epidemiology (e.g., coronary heart disease; Lynch & Davey Smith, 2005), although increasingly this approach is being used to understand human capability formation from the perspective of childhood (Zubrick et al., 2009). From a human capability perspective, a child's biology (including genetics and epigenetics) (Rice, 2012) and the multiple contexts (Bronfenbrenner, 2005) in which he or she grows up provide developmental resources or means for future capability formation, such as language acquisition, literacy, and educational achievement. This perspective argues for careful specifications of the upper and lower age boundaries of specific stages of development as part of a reliable measurement system, as essential documentation of how key abilities change over time, and as essential underpinnings of theoretical accounts of language acquisition.

Longitudinal study designs include population registers (e.g., births), administrative data collections (e.g., education), time-series studies (e.g., census), cross-sectional cohort studies, retrospective cohort studies, prospective cohort studies, and case-control studies. Each design reveals different facets of the life span and has unique strengths and limitations (Zubrick et al., 2009). The integration of different approaches builds on the strengths of individual designs and maximizes the return on the considerable resources that population-level research requires. For example, birth cohort studies that start with a cross-sectional design can become the first wave in a prospective longitudinal design. Case-control studies can be nested in a prospective longitudinal design. Prospective longitudinal studies can investigate intergenerational effects on child development using a family design or by following children into parenthood and studying children of children. Linking administrative data collections to data from longitudinal cohort studies can provide information about stages of the life span that are not within the scope of the longitudinal design.

Population-level research in language acquisition has a relatively short history. Advances in data design, analytic techniques (including molecular genetics), and measurement of language phenotypes have made it feasible to investigate individual differences in language acquisition on a large scale. For example, the PhenX toolkit for populationwide genomic studies includes measures of late language emergence LLE and SLI (Hamilton et al., 2011). These measures and other speech and language measures are available from the PhenX web site (https://www.phenxtoolkit.org).

It is standard practice for contemporary cohort studies of child development to include measures of language acquisition from the time of onset in the first 2 years of life. For example, in 2003, the Australian government initiated the Longitudinal Study of Australian Children (LSAC). This study comprises two cohorts of approximately 5,000 children in each. The infant cohort was recruited at 9 months, and the kindergarten cohort was recruited at 4–5 years (Sanson et al., 2002; Soloff, Lawrence, Misson, & Johnstone, 2005). As of 2012, there were four waves of data available for each cohort. A fifth wave of data collection is in the field with funding to continue data collection every 2 years through 2018. Language measures are collected in each wave of the study (Taylor, Maguire, & Zubrick, 2011), and a series of papers modeling trajectories in language development across childhood and early adolescence are underway.

## TWO POPULATION-LEVEL STUDIES FROM THE TWINS AND SINGLETONS WITH SPECIFIC LANGUAGE IMPAIRMENT PROJECT

In our Twins and Singletons with Specific Language Impairment project (2002–2017) funded by the National Institute on Deafness and Communication Disorders (NIDCD), we are combining the strengths of several population-level study designs, data resources, and analytic approaches to investigate individual differences in language acquisition from onset to adolescence (National Institutes of Health Research Portfolio Online Reporting Tools, 2012). In this section, we discuss two studies from this project on the prevalence, predictors, and outcomes of LLE in single-born children (Rice, Taylor, & Zubrick, 2008; Zubrick, Taylor, Rice, & Slegers, 2007).

These studies exemplify the research benefits and methods of population-level inquiry for understanding the early manifestations of language impairment, including the ability to evaluate potential predictors. For each study, we provide a summary of key methodological elements, including sources of infrastructure support, as well as the measurement systems involved. We highlight key findings as potential directions for future research and the development of comprehensive interpretive models of language impairment.

### Study 1: A Prospective Cohort Study of the Prevalence and Risks for Late Language Emergence at 24 Months in Single-Born Children

The aims of this study were to investigate the prevalence of LLE at 24 months in the general population and to identify risks for LLE from a comprehensive range of child, maternal, and family characteristics with known associations with child health, development, and well-being outcomes (Zubrick et al., 2007).

***Study Design*** The study design was a prospective cohort study. This is a classic epidemiological study design for investigating the prevalence of a health outcome (e.g., LLE) that is unknown when the study begins (e.g., at birth) and the risk exposures for the health outcome. In this design, risk exposures (e.g., pregnancy risks) are measured before the health outcome is known (Zubrick et al., 2009).

This prospective cohort study began at birth. Children born in 1995 and 1996 were selected at random from a total population frame of statutory birth notifications for the state of Western Australia 3 months postpartum. The original cross-sectional study was designed to investigate maternal and infant health in pregnancy and the first 3 months of childhood. The study did not include Australian Aboriginal infants who were selected for a concurrent study of Aboriginal maternal and infant health.

This study was conducted in Western Australia using the state's internationally renowned data linkage infrastructure, which was established in 1998. Data linkage is the bringing together of data (e.g., health and education records) routinely collected by different government and nongovernment agencies (Holman et al., 2008; Stanley, Croft, Gibbins, & Read, 1994). Since 2009, the Australian Government, in partnership with state and territory governments, universities, and research institutes, has been developing its national health and human services data linkage infrastructure. Three proof-of-concept projects are underway, and this data linkage infrastructure will be an asset for future longitudinal epidemiological studies (Population Health Research Network, 2011). One of the strengths of population-level research is that the characteristics of the study cohort can be compared with the characteristics of the total population cohort. These comparisons allow judgments to be made about the generalizability of study results based on the representativeness of the study cohort. In longitudinal research, the challenge is to retain participants over time and maintain the representativeness of the study cohort. Cohort attrition is inevitable in longitudinal research. Changes in the representativeness of the study cohort over time are determined by comparing the characteristics of participants at each wave of follow-up with the characteristics of participants at the beginning of the study. Missing data were handled using data imputation methods.

***Participants*** There were 4,007 non-Aboriginal mothers with live singleton births in 1995 and 1996 who participated in the 3-month survey. The study cohort was broadly representative of the total population except for a slight underrepresentation of young mothers younger than 20 years (3.6% of the study cohort vs. 6% in the total population) and low birth weight infants (4.7% in the study cohort vs. 5.3% in the total population). The original cross-sectional study design was enhanced to a longitudinal design with additional funding from the Health Promotion Foundation of Western Australia. To fit the budget for the longitudinal study, the original study cohort was randomly reduced by 30%. To ensure that hard-to-reach families susceptible to attrition bias were adequately represented in the longitudinal cohort study, 100 mothers excluded by random assignment were subsequently retained in the study cohort. From the original sample of 4,007 women who participated in the 3-month cross-sectional study, 2,837 mothers were selected for the longitudinal study, of whom 2,224 (78%) consented to participate.

The longitudinal study comprised annual postal surveys from 1–8 years completed by mothers within a month of the study child's birthday. At the 7-year follow-up, the study child's classroom teacher also completed a survey about the child and administered direct behavioral measures of verbal and nonverbal cognition.

There was an 85% return on the 2-year surveys (1,880 out of 2,224 mothers) and most were complete. The average amount of item missing data in the surveys was 2.2% and ranged from 0% (mother's place of birth, child gender, and age) to 7.6% (dimensions of temperament, rhythmicity–sleep). Attrition bias was investigated by comparing the child, maternal, and family characteristics of respondents to the 3-month survey with respondents to the 2-year survey. The expected pattern of attrition bias was observed, with slightly higher levels of maternal education, income, and marriage for 2-year survey respondents compared with 3-month survey respondents.

As the focus of this study was on LLE as a risk indicator for primary language impairment, two inclusion criteria were used to select children eligible for *case* (LLE) and *control* (NLE) status. The first was that the child was growing up in an English-speaking monolingual home. The second was that the child did not have any known condition (e.g., hearing loss) that would preclude a subsequent diagnosis of SLI. Of the 1,880 respondents to the 2-year survey, 1,766 children met these criteria. The study design was a case-control study nested in a cohort study (Clayton & Hills, 1996).

***Identification of Late Language Emergence***    LLE was identified using the Communication Scale in the Infant/Child Monitoring Questionnaire (IMQ), now known as the Ages & Stages Questionnaires® (ASQ) (Bricker & Squires, 1999; Squires & Bricker, 2009). The ASQ is a parent-report instrument to identify children at risk for communication, gross motor, fine motor, adaptive problem solving, and personal-social development. The ASQ Communication Scale asks parents to observe six early receptive and expressive language milestones: 1) pointing to pictures of objects on request, 2) combining words, 3) following simple instructions, 4) naming simple objects in pictures, 5) pointing to body parts on request, and 6) using personal pronouns. Parents are asked to report on each milestone using the response categories, *yes, not yet,* or *sometimes.* We used an item response theory (IRT) approach (Samejima, 1969) to create an ASQ Item Composite measure to identify children with LLE. The IRT approach used all of the items in the original ASQ Communication Scale, differentially adjusted the scale for item difficulty, handled missing data, and used a continuous estimate of communication on a scale that was not sample dependent. The IRT Item Composite provided the best discrimination (i.e., informativeness) and lowest measurement error in the ability range from $-1.0$ *SD* to $-1.5$ *SD* below the mean. We chose a cutoff point of $-1$ *SD* on the ASQ Item Composite to identify 2-year-olds with LLE. Using this cutoff point, the ASQ Item Composite identified 238 out of 1,766 (13.4%) children with LLE (i.e., the bottom 13.4% of the sample). Consistent with previous studies, males were vastly overrepresented in this sample of children with LLE (70.8%).

The concurrent validity of the ASQ Item Composite was investigated through a series of comparisons with the Language Development Survey (LDS; Rescorla, 1989). The LDS is a parent-report measure of expressive vocabulary development and emergent grammar. Expressive vocabulary is assessed with a 310-word expressive vocabulary checklist, and emergent grammar is assessed with a single question asking if the child combines two or more words. The concurrent validity of the ASQ Item Composite and the LDS was investigated in three ways. First, we calculated the correlation between the ASQ Item Composite and the LDS expressive vocabulary score. The continuous scores on these measures were moderately correlated ($r$ (886) = 0.675, n = 888, $p$ < .001). Second, we established the concordance between the ASQ and LDS questions about combining two or more words. Responses to both questions were available for 896 children. There was 100% correspondence between these items for 860 out of 896 (96%) children. Finally, we calculated mean LDS expressive vocabulary scores for children who scored above and below the –1 $SD$ cutoff -point for LLE on the ASQ Item Composite. Children who scored below –1 $SD$ on the ASQ Item Composite had significantly lower LDS expressive vocabulary scores than children who scored above the –1 $SD$ on the ASQ Item Composite ($M$ = 63, $SD$ = 53 vs. $M$ = 196, $SD$ = 71). These results support the concurrent validity of the ASQ Item Composite and the LDS.

The emergence of word combinations around 24 months is an important milestone in children's language acquisition. Children's production of 2–3 word combinations marks the transition from single words to grammar. The sole use of single words beyond 24 months is widely accepted as a screening criterion for LLE (Fenson et al., 2007). The ASQ Item Composite contained a single item asking if the child said 2–3 words together. Therefore, we were able to identify the percentage of children in our sample who were not combining words at 24 months. This single-item screening criterion identified 19.1% of the children at the single-word stage of language acquisition at 24 months. This is very similar to the estimate of 17% of children being at the single-word stage at 24 months in the Early Language in Victoria Study (ELVS; Reilly et al., 2009; see also Chapter 1).

### *Child, Maternal, and Family Level Risks for Late Language Emergence*

Guided by a bioecological model of child development (Bronfenbrenner, 2005), measures of a comprehensive range of child, maternal, and family characteristics known to influence children's health, development, and well-being were collected for the cohort, using survey methods and data linkage to the Midwives Notification System (MNS). The MNS comprises information about maternal demography, pregnancy, birth, and infant outcomes for all children born in Western Australia. There is a statutory requirement for midwives to collect these data for every birth in the state (Holman et al., 2008).

The fetal and neonatal risks in our model were male gender, fetal growth restriction (< 85% proportion of optimal birth weight), premature birth (< 36 weeks' gestation), and increased time to spontaneous respiration (> 2 minutes). Fetal growth restriction, premature birth, and increased time to spontaneous respiration also are known risks for the developing brain and central nervous system (CNS).

In recognition of the dynamic complementarity (Heckman, 2008) among different aspects of development, we also modeled risks for LLE from other domains of development, as well as the child's age. Child temperament was measured with the Revised Dimensions of Temperament Survey (DOTS-R; Windle, 1992; Windle & Lerner, 1986). The risk variables were high activity, low approach, low flexibility, low mood, low rhythmicity, and low task orientation. Child behavior was measured with the Child Behavior Checklist/1½–5 (CBCL; Achenbach & Rescorla, 2000). The

CBCL comprises 99 behavior problems. The total number of problems reported are converted to normalized $T$ scores (M = 50, SD = 10). We used the cutoff point ($T \geq 67$) for the syndrome scores and ($T \geq 60$) for Total Problems score to identify children in the borderline/clinical range (i.e., Abnormal range). The risk variables were Abnormal $T$ scores for Total Problems, Internalizing Problems, and Externalizing Problems. Milestones in gross motor, fine motor, adaptive, and personal–social development were measured with the ASQ. The risk variables were scores on or below the cutoff points on any of the scales. These scores identified children at risk for meeting these milestones (i.e., developmental lag). In addition, we modeled the child's age in months as a candidate risk for LLE.

The maternal risk variables in the model were low education, young age at child's birth, cigarette use, no paid employment, psychological distress, and dysfunctional parenting. The family risks were a positive family history of late talking, nonoriginal family structure (e.g., step/blended, sole parent), presence of one or more siblings, low Socio-Economic Indexes for Areas (SEIFA) scores, poor family functioning, and child in day care.

### Analytic Approach and Interpretation of Results

We used multivariate logistic regression (Hosmer & Lemeshow, 1989) to model child, maternal, and family risks for LLE. The associations between LLE and the risk variables were expressed as odds ratios (*OR*). The odds ratio compares the likelihood (expressed as odds) of LLE for children with and without the risk factor (e.g., males vs. females). Risk factors with statistically significant odds ratios greater than 1 indicate that the likelihood of LLE is greater for children with that risk factor (e.g., males) than children without the risk factor (e.g., females).

The odds ratio for male gender was 2.7, meaning that males were almost three times as likely as girls to be identified with LLE. Ninety-five percent confidence intervals (95% CIs) are reported for all odds ratios. The confidence interval is the range of plausible values for the odds ratio. For example, the odds ratio for the risk for LLE associated with male gender was 2.742, and the 95% confidence interval was [1.185, 3.016]. The lower boundary of the 95% confidence interval was close to 1, and the upper boundary was close to 3. This means that we can be 95% confident that this risk estimate lies within the upper and lower boundaries of the confidence interval. Odds ratios with narrow confidence intervals are more precise estimates of risk than odds ratios with wide confidence intervals (Cumming, 2012; Ellis, 2010).

In the multivariate logistic regression model, all variables (i.e., risk factors) were entered into the model in a single step. Derived estimates from this process are multivariately adjusted for the effects of other variables and reveal the unique (i.e., independent) contribution of each risk factor for LLE.

### Subtle Neurodevelopmental Risks for Late Language Emergence Were Predominant

The evidence from this study was that child risks for LLE were predominant. Some child risks were identified at birth and others at 24 months. The fetal and neonatal risks were male gender (*OR* = 2.742, 95% CI [1.185, 3.016]), fetal growth restriction (*OR* = 1.88, 95% CI [1.18, 3.01]), and prematurity (*OR* = 1.84, 95% CI [1.04, 3.25]). The developmental risks at 24 months were younger chronological age (*OR* = 0.991, 95% CI [0.986, 0.995]) and developmental lag on the ASQ Gross Motor Scale ($OR$ = 3.12, 95% CI [1.29, 7.51]), Fine Motor Scale ($OR$ = 2.39, 95% CI [1.19, 4.77]), Adaptive Scale ($OR$ = 2.64, 95% CI [0.66, 4.21]), and Personal–Social Scale ($OR$ = 5.52, 95% CI [2.05, 14.86]). Perhaps surprisingly, none of the maternal risks were associated with LLE. That is, low maternal education, young age at child's birth, cigarette use, no paid employment, psychological distress, and dysfunctional parenting were not risks for LLE in our model. We identified two family level risks with different etiological pathways. A positive family history of late talking ($OR$ = 2.11, 95% CI [1.39, 3.19]) and the presence of siblings ($OR$ = 2.07, 95% CI [1.39, 3.09]) were both associated with a twofold risk for LLE. A positive family history of late talking is a genetic risk, and the presence of siblings is a postnatal family environment risk. In our model, family type (e.g., sole parent), low SEIFA scores, poor family functioning, and child in day care were not risks for LLE.

In summary, child risks dominated our etiological model for LLE. These risks were subtle and best characterized as nonclinical neurobiological vulnerabilities. These subtle vulnerabilities were present at birth and at 24 months in physical, cognitive, psychological, and social domains. The risks for LLE, ordered from highest to lowest, were

- Developmental lag on the ASQ Personal–Social Scale
- Developmental lag on the ASQ Gross Motor Scale
- Male gender
- Developmental lag on the ASQ Fine Motor Scale
- Positive family history of LLE
- Presence of siblings
- Fetal growth restriction
- Prematurity
- Younger age of child

Although developmental lag on the ASQ Personal–Social Scale conferred the highest risk for LLE, the item that was most discriminating on the Personal–Social Scale was the use of personal pronouns. In this case, the risk variable and the outcome variable cannot be considered as completely independent. Separation of personal–social and language domains is a measurement challenge at this young age. The results support the view that linguistic, cognitive, psychological, social, and physical abilities develop synergistically, enabled (or constrained) by common and specialized brain and CNS architecture and function and shaped by the child's nurturance, social interactions, shared activities, and input from caregivers. A child's physical, cognitive, psychological, and social competencies are part of the resource mix for language acquisition (Taylor, 2010).

In our model, maternal and family environment risks for LLE were conspicuous in their absence. None of the maternal risks were associated with LLE, and the presence of siblings was the only family environment risk associated with LLE. These findings are comparable to those of Reilly and colleagues (2007), who reported a lack of association between maternal and family risks and LLE at 24 months in a large community-ascertained sample of Australian children (see also Chapter 1).

## Study 2: A Nested Case-Control Study of Language Outcomes at 7 Years for Children with and without a History of Late Language Emergence at 24 Months

This study compared children with and without a history of LLE at 24 months on multiple dimensions of language at 7 years. The study had three objectives. The first objective was to investigate the extent to which LLE was an indicator of normal variation in language acquisition and/or a risk indicator for performance in the language impairment range. The second objective was to compare the performance of children with and without a history of LLE across multiple dimensions of language to see if the patterns fit the delay model or the delay-within-disruption model. The third objective was to determine whether there were more males than females in the low range of performance at 7 years, as was the case at 24 months (Rice et al., 2008).

*Study Design*    The design for Study 2 was a case-control study nested in the prospective cohort study from Study 1. Recall that the original prospective cohort study design was used to investigate the prevalence and risks for LLE in a cohort of 1,766 children recruited at birth. In Study 1, data were collected using postal questionnaires, an efficient and cost-effective method for large-scale studies. The children with LLE and NLE in the prospective cohort study comprised all possible children with and without LLE. In Study 2, data were collected using labor intensive, face-to-face behavioral assessments of multiple dimensions of language. Collection of these data was feasible only for a subsample of the original cohort, for resource reasons and because sample attrition is inevitable in longitudinal research.

Our approach to identifying LLE and NLE in the nested case-control study was different to the approach used in the prospective cohort study. In Study 1 we identified LLE and NLE using the ASQ Item Composite that comprised expressive and receptive language criteria. In Study 2, we identified children with a history of LLE (i.e., cases) and children with a history of NLE (i.e., controls) using expressive language criteria drawn from the literature (e.g., Fenson et al., 1993; Rescorla, 1989). We used expressive language criteria because we wanted to maximize the size of the case group. We knew from Study 1 that a single expressive language screening criterion (e.g., not combining words) identified more children with LLE than the ASQ Item Composite (19.1% vs. 13.4%).

The expressive language criteria for identifying cases with LLE included a response of "not combining words" on the ASQ item, "Does your child say 2 or 3 words together?" or an expressive vocabulary score of 70 words or less on the LDS. An LDS expressive vocabulary score of 70 words or less identified children who scored below the 15th percentile in the sample of 902 children for whom LDS expressive vocabulary scores were available. The expressive language criteria for identifying controls with NLE was a response of "combining words" on the ASQ item, "Does your child say 2 or 3 words together?" and an expressive vocabulary score of more than 70 words on the LDS.

***Participants***   Sixty-six percent of children in the 2-year survey participated in the longitudinal cohort study at 7 years. Although there was sample attrition between 2 years and 7 years, there was no selective attrition of children with LLE (13.4% with LLE at 24 months vs. 14.2% with LLE at 7 years). Not all children who met the expressive language criteria for LLE and NLE at 2 years were selected as cases and controls in the language outcomes study at 7 years. To be selected as a case or a control, a child had to be a current participant in the cohort study, living in Western Australia, and younger than 8 years of age at the time of the follow-up. Additional inclusion criteria were that the child was growing up in a monolingual English-speaking home and did not have exclusionary conditions for primary language impairment, such as deafness, an intellectual disability, or an autism spectrum disorder.

We selected 185 cases who met the expressive language criteria for LLE at 2 years and the inclusion criteria. Of these 185 cases, 169 were successfully contacted and 128 (76%) agreed to participate in the language outcomes study. We selected 170 controls at random who met the expressive language criteria for NLE at 2 years and the inclusion criteria. Of these 170 controls, 131 were successfully contacted and 109 (83%) agreed to participate in the language outcomes study. Therefore, the nested case-control study comprised a sample of 237 children from the original cohort of 1,766 children in the 2-year survey. Of these 237 children, 128 cases had a history of LLE, and 109 controls had a history of NLE based on expressive language criteria.

A series of statistical tests were calculated to determine whether the case and control groups differed on child age, child gender, maternal education, maternal mental health, parenting style, maternal hours in paid employment, family type, family functioning, family income, socioeconomic area resources, and socioeconomic area disadvantages. The case and control groups differed only in gender composition and family size. The LLE group contained more boys and less only children than the NLE group. The mean age of the cases and controls was 7.25 years.

***Language Outcome Measures at Age 7***   The focus of this study was to compare the performance of the LLE and NLE groups on language outcome measures, not to identify individual children with SLI. This approach involved group comparisons of mean levels of performance on multiple dimensions of language as well as group comparisons of low levels of performance on all the language measures. Low levels of performance were defined as scores 1 *SD* or more below the mean on any language measure. We refer to this as the language impairment range. This is consistent with the criterion of 1 *SD* below the mean that is used in the growth modeling studies of SLI discussed previously (Rice, 2004), and it is close to the criterion of 1.14 *SD* below the mean used in the final definition of SLI reported by Tomblin et al. (1997). Inherent in our approach was the possibility that an individual in either group (LLE or NLE) scored in the low range of performance on one measure and within the normal range of performance on another measure.

All children in the follow-up study passed an audiogram hearing screening test. There were no significant differences between the LLE and NLE group means on the Columbia Mental Maturity Scale (CMMS; Burgemeister, Blum, & Lorge, 1972) and no significant difference in the percentage of cases and controls who scored 1 *SD* or more below the mean on the CMMS.

Language outcome measures at age 7 comprised direct behavioral assessment of speech, general language ability, syntax, morphosyntax, and semantics. Children's speech production was measured with the Goldman Fristoe Test of Articulation–Second Edition (GFTA-2; Goldman & Fristoe, 2000) and the Rice/Wexler Test of Early Grammatical Impairment (TEGI) Phonological Probe (Rice & Wexler, 2001). The TEGI Phonological Probe was used to screen children's production of phonemes that mark third-person singular –s and regular past tense –ed. The language measures included the Test of Language Development–Primary, Third Edition (TOLD-P:3; Newcomer & Hammill, 1997) for general language ability, syntax, morphosyntax, and semantics; Mean Length of Utterance in Morphemes (MLU-M) for a global measure of grammatical development, calculated from spontaneous adult–child conversations using the Systematic Analysis of Language Transcripts (SALT) program (Miller & Chapman, 1991); and the Peabody Picture Vocabulary Test-III (PPVT-III; Dunn, Dunn, & Williams, 1997) for receptive vocabulary ability. Standard scores were calculated for all speech and language outcome variables.

This study was the first to comprehensively investigate morphosyntactic outcomes for children with and without a history of LLE. Additional information about this dimension of language is detailed here to aid interpretation of the results. The TEGI is a unique test of morphosyntax for the identification of children with SLI for clinical and research purposes (Rice & Wexler, 2001), and more recently for molecular genetic studies (Rice, Smith, & Gayan, 2009). Children with SLI show delayed acquisition of grammatical tense marking from early to late childhood. This is a striking departure from the normative expectation that children will show adult-like mastery of this part of grammar by kindergarten age (Rice & Wexler, 1996; Rice, Wexler, & Cleave, 1995; Rice, Wexler, & Hershberger, 1998). TEGI is ideally suited to studies that aim to differentiate children with SLI from children with typical development in the general population. Furthermore, children's performance on TEGI can be interpreted in terms of progress toward adult grammar. This adds a growth perspective to longitudinal outcome studies, not evident from conventional language assessments that measure performance on a bell-shaped curve. TEGI has five test components. The Phonological Probe assesses children's production of phonemes that mark third-person singular –s and regular past tense –ed. The Third Person Singular Probe assesses children's use of third-person singular present tense –s verb forms with singular subjects (e.g., "A teacher teaches"). The Past Tense Probe assesses children's use of regular past tense –ed (e.g., "She skated") and irregular past tense (e.g., "He built the birdhouse") verb forms. The BE/DO Probe assesses children's use of these *be* forms: *be* copula singular and plural statements (e.g., "The kitty is hungry," "The bears are hungry") and questions (e.g., "Is the kitty hungry?" "Are the bears hungry?"), *be* auxiliary singular and plural statements (e.g., "The kitty is jumping," "The bears are jumping") and questions (e.g., "Is the kitty resting?" "Are the bears resting?"), and *do* auxiliary singular and plural questions (e.g., "Does the kitty like milk?" "Do the bears like milk?"). The Grammaticality Judgment Probe assesses children's detection of grammatical and ungrammatical simple clauses. The ungrammatical clauses contain dropped markers (e.g., "He look happy now"), agreement errors (e.g., "He am hurt"), or dropped –*ing* (e.g., "He is smile"). This probe is designed as a comprehension analogue to the production probes. Scores are available for each probe individually, for each component of the BE/DO Probe and the Grammaticality Judgment Probe, and for composites. The two composite measures are the Grammatical Composite (Third Person Singular Probe, Past Tense Probe, and BE/DO Probe) and the Screener (Third Person Singular Probe and Past Tense Probe).

**Data Analysis** We conducted four analyses for this study. First, we conducted a series of univariate $t$ calculations to compare mean levels of performance for the LLE and NLE groups on each of the language measures. Effect sizes for differences in LLE and NLE group means were calculated as Cohen's measure of sample effect size ($d$). An effect size of 0.20 is considered small; 0.50, medium; and 0.80, large (Cohen, 1988). Second, we conducted a series of Chi-square calculations to compare the groups' performance in the language impairment range on each of the language measures. Third, we grouped the children by gender and conducted a series of Chi-square calculations to compare the number of males and females in the language impairment range on each of the language measures. Fourth, we determined whether grouping children with LLE and NLE using expressive language criteria versus a combination of expressive and receptive criteria affected the results. ASQ Item Composite scores were available for 232 out of 237 children in the follow-up study. As noted previously, the ASQ Item Composite was more restrictive (i.e., yielded lower prevalence) than the expressive language criteria. That is, in this subsample, the ASQ Item Composite identified 88 children with LLE and 144 children with NLE, compared with 128 children with LLE and 109 children with NLE using the expressive language criteria. The analyses were repeated using the ASQ Item Composite grouping method, and the results were essentially the same. Therefore, only the results for the expressive language grouping method are reported here.

### Late Language Emergence and Normal Language Emergence Group Differences in Mean Levels of Performance on Multiple Dimensions of Language   The
results showed significant group differences in language outcomes for children with and without a history of LLE who had comparable maternal and family characteristics. Children with a history of LLE, compared with children with a history of NLE, had lower levels of performance on multiple dimensions of language. Speech, syntax, morphosyntax, and semantics were at lower levels for children with a positive history. Children with LLE had significantly lower performance on the GFTA-2, TOLD-P:3 Spoken Language Quotient, TOLD-P:3 Syntax Quotient, PPVT-III, TEGI Third Person Singular Probe, TEGI Past Tense Probe, TEGI BE/DO Probe (BE and DO results presented separately), TEGI Grammatical Composite (Third Person Singular Probe, Past Tense Probe, BE/DO Probe), TEGI Screener (Third Person Singular Probe and Past Tense Probe), and TEGI Grammaticality Judgment Probe (GJ-Dropped Marker, GJ-Agreement, and GJ-Dropped *–ing*). The effect sizes (Cohen's $d$) for significant group differences from highest to lowest were: TEGI Third Person Singular Probe (1.93), TEGI Grammatical Composite (0.94), TEGI Screener (0.81), TEGI BE copula and auxiliary (0.63), GFTA-2 (0.53), TEGI Past Tense Probe (0.50), TOLD-P:3 Syntactic Quotient (0.50), TEGI DO auxiliary (0.49), TEGI GJ-Dropped Marker (0.47), TOLD-P:3 Spoken Language Quotient (0.33), and PPVT-III (0.32). The dimensions of language that did not differentiate children with and without a history of LLE were MLU-M, TOLD-P:3 Semantics Quotient, TEGI GJ-Agreement, and TEGI GJ-Dropped *-ing*.

***Late Language Emergence and Normal Language Emergence Group Differences in Performance in the Language Impairment Range on Multiple Dimensions of Language***    The low performance range was defined as a score of 1 *SD* or more below the mean on any of the language measures. This is subsequently referred to as the language impairment range, consistent with other studies (Rice, 2009). Significantly more children with LLE than NLE scored in the language impairment range on seven measures: TOLD-P:3 Syntactic Quotient (18% vs. 8%), TOLD-P:3 Spoken Language Quotient (20% vs. 11%), TEGI Third Person Singular Probe (10% vs. 1%), TEGI Past Tense Probe (13% vs. 4%), TEGI GJ-Dropped Marker (23% vs. 14%), TEGI Screener (Third Person Singular Probe and Past Tense Probe; 9% vs. 2%), and GFTA-2 (7% vs. 2%). On these seven measures, most of the children in the language impairment range had a history of LLE. The percentages were TEGI Third Person Singular Probe, 93%; TEGI Screener, 85%; GFTA-2, 82%; TEGI Past Tense Probe, 80%; TOLD-P:3 Syntactic Quotient, 72%; TOLD-P:3 Spoken Language Quotient, 68%; and TEGI GJ-Dropped Marker, 66%. Once again, group differences in performance in the language impairment range were most evident on measures of syntax and morphosyntax.

There were no significant group differences in performance in the language impairment range on the TOLD-P:3 Semantic Quotient or PPVT-III. That is, performance in the low range on measures of the semantic dimension of language did not differentiate the groups. Furthermore, there were no significant gender differences in performance in the language impairment range on the language measures, with one exception: More girls than boys scored in the language impairment range on the TEGI DO Probe. Thus, the pattern of more males than females in the low range of performance at 24 months (i.e., LLE) was not evident in the low range of performance at 7 years.

***Gender Differences in Performance in the Language Impairment Range at 7 Years***    The LLE and NLE groups in our study were not matched for gender. The gender composition of the LLE group at 7 years was 74% male because more males than females were identified with LLE at 24 months. The gender composition of the NLE group was 48% male at 24 months and 50% male at 7 years. The gender composition of the NLE group in the follow-up study was equivalent to the gender composition in the general population because these children were ascertained at random from the population sample. At 7 years, there were more males (62%) than females in the follow-up sample but not significantly more males than females in the language impairment range on any of the language measures.

## CONCLUSIONS

The results of the study of the prevalence and risks for LLE at 24 months established a prevalence estimate of 13.4% LLE in the general population using the expressive plus receptive ASQ criterion. Risks for LLE were few and predominantly neurodevelopmental in nature. Low socioeconomic status was not associated with increased risk for LLE, consistent with the results from the ELVS (Reilly et al., 2007). In interpreting these results, it is important to differentiate studies of low socioeconomic status risk for language acquisition in the low range of performance (e.g., Hart & Risley, 1995) from studies of socioeconomic status influences on the full range of performance (e.g., Fenson et al., 1994). The results of studies of low socioeconomic status risk for the low range of performance do not run counter to the results of studies of socioeconomic status influences on the full range of performance because the phenomenology is different. This was elegantly illustrated in Dale et al.'s (1998) study of more than 3,000 twins at 24 months. Different patterns of genetic and environmental influences were observed for twins in the low range of language abilities compared with the full sample. Genetic influences were greater in the low range of language abilities compared with the full sample (73% vs. 25%). The pattern was opposite for shared environment influences. Shared environment influences were greater in the full sample compared with the low range of language abilities (69% vs. 18%). Large-scale studies are needed to explore the phenomenology of individual differences in language acquisition across the full range of performance.

The results of the study of language outcomes for children with and without a history of LLE at 24 months provided support for LLE as a risk indicator for performance in the language impairment range at 7 years, even though most of the children with a history of LLE did not score in the language impairment range at 7 years. On the seven measures of syntax and morphosyntax that differentiated children with and without a history of LLE, most of the children in the language impairment range had a history of LLE. This pattern of an early risk phenotype not being fully prognostic of a subsequent disorder phenotype is not unique to behaviorally defined disorders such as SLI. A similar pattern is observed in asthma, for example, whereby wheezing in the first 2 years of life is a risk indicator for asthma, but most children who wheeze do not develop asthma (Martinez et al., 1995). This phenomenon poses a major challenge to prevention efforts for conditions in which early phenotypes are not fully prognostic of future diagnoses. An added complication with LLE is that it is a risk indicator for primary language impairment (SLI) as well as for secondary language impairment associated with developmental disorders such as intellectual disability and autism.

The results also provided support for the delay-within-disruption model of language impairment from a different perspective to growth modeling studies of children with SLI. First, we observed that the LLE group had lower mean levels of performance compared with the NLE group on semantic, syntactic, and morphosyntactic dimensions of language. Second, group differentiation was greatest on measures of syntax and morphosyntax. The only large effect sizes were for group differences in mean levels of performance on TEGI measures of morphosyntax. Third, group differences in performance in the language impairment range were also most evident on measures of syntax and morphosyntax. Fourth, 66%–82% of all the children in the language impairment range on the measures that differentiated the groups were from the LLE group at 24 months.

On the TOLD-P:3 omnibus language measure, 20% of the LLE group and 11% of the NLE group scored -1 *SD* or more below the mean. On one hand, this suggests a doubled risk for performance in the language impairment range at 7 years for children with a history of LLE. On the other hand, most of the LLE and NLE children met age expectations for performance on an omnibus language measure at 7 years. Of interest is the 11% of the NLE group who did not meet age expectations. This shows that NLE is not a universal pathway to normal language acquisition.

We clearly need to know more about stability and change in growth trajectories for different dimensions of language from onset in the first 2 years of life to adult levels of mastery. We also need prospective studies that extend beyond childhood to further understand language acquisition and impairment as a developmental means for future human capability.

## REFERENCES

Achenbach, T.M., & Rescorla, L.A. (2000). *Manual for the ASEBA Preschool Forms and Profiles.* Burlington: University of Vermont, Department of Psychiatry.

Bricker, D., & Squires, J. (1999). *Ages & Stages Questionnaires®: A parent-completed child monitoring system* (2nd ed.). Baltimore, MD: Paul H. Brookes Publishing Co.

Bronfenbrenner, U. (2005). *Making human beings human: Bioecological perspectives on human development.* Thousand Oaks, CA: Sage.

Burgemeister, B.B., Blum, L.H., & Lorge, I. (1972). *Columbia Mental Maturity Scale.* San Antonio, TX: Psychological Corporation.

Clayton, D., & Hills, M. (1996). *Statistical models in epidemiology.* London, England: Oxford University Press.

Cohen, J. (1988). *Statistical power analysis for the behavioral sciences* (2nd ed.). Mahwah, NJ: Lawrence Erlbaum Associates.

Council of Australian Governments. (2009). *Investing in the early years—A national early childhood development strategy. An initiative of the Council of Australian Governments.* Retrieved from http://www.coag.gov.au/sites/default/files/national_ECD_strategy.pdf

Cumming, G. (2012). *Understanding the new statistics: Effect sizes, confidence intervals, and meta-analysis.* New York, NY: Taylor & Francis.

Dale, P.S., Simonoff, E., Bishop, D.V.M., Eley, T.C., Oliver, B., Price, T.S., . . . Plomin, R. (1998). Genetic influence on language delay in two-year-old children. *Nature Neuroscience, 1*(4), 324–328.

Dunn, L.M., Dunn, L.M., & Williams, K.T. (1997). *Peabody Picture Vocabulary Test* (3rd ed.). Circle Pines, MN: American Guidance Service.

Ellis, P. (2010). *The essential guide to effect sizes: Statistical power, meta-analysis, and the interpretation of research results.* Cambridge, United Kingdom: Cambridge University Press.

Fenson, L., Dale, P.S., Reznick, J.S., Bates, E., Thal, D., & Pethick, S.J. (1994). Variability in early communicative development. *Monographs of the Society for Research in Child Development, 59*(5), 1–173.

Fenson, L., Dale, P.S., Reznick, J.S., Thal, D., Bates, E., Hartung, J.P., . . . Reilly, J. (1993). *MacArthur Communicative Development Inventories: User's guide and technical manual.* Baltimore, MD: Paul H. Brookes Publishing Co.

Fenson, L., Marchman, V.A., Thal, D.J., Dale, P.S., Reznick, J.S., & Bates, E. (2007). *MacArthur-Bates Communicative Development Inventories: User's guide and technical manual* (2nd ed.). Baltimore, MD: Paul H. Brookes Publishing Co.

Goldman, R., & Fristoe, M. (2000). *Goldman Fristoe Test of Articulation* (2nd ed.). Circle Pines, MN: American Guidance Service.

Hamilton, C.M., Strader, L.C., Pratt, J.G., Maiese, D., Hendershot, T., Kwok, R.K., . . . Haines, J. (2011). The PhenX toolkit: Get the most from your measures. *American Journal of Epidemiology, 174*(3), 253–260. doi: 10.1093/aje/kwr193

Hart, B., & Risley, T. (1995). *Meaningful differences in the everyday experience of young American children.* Baltimore, MD: Paul H. Brookes Publishing Co.

Heckman, J. (2008). Schools, skills and synapses. *Economic Inquiry, 46*(3), 289–324.

Holman, C.D., Bass, A.J., Rosman, D.L., Smith, M.B., Semmens, J.B., Glasson, E.J., . . . Stanley, F.J. (2008). A decade of data linkage in Western Australia: Strategic design, applications and benefits of the WA data linkage system. *Australian Health Review, 32,* 766–777.

Hosmer, D.W., & Lemeshow, S. (1989). *Applied logistic regression.* New York, NY: Wiley Interscience.

Lynch, J., & Davey Smith, G. (2005). A life course approach to chronic disease epidemiology. *Annual Review of Public Health, 26,* 1–35.

Marmot, M. (2010). *Fair society, healthy lives: The Marmot review.* Retrieved from http://www.instituteofhealthequity.org/projects/fair-society-healthy-lives-the-marmot-review/fair-society-healthy-lives-full-report

Martinez, F.D., Wright, A.L., Taussig, L.M., Holberg, C.J., Halonen, M., Morgan, W.J., & The Group Health Medical Associates. (1995). Asthma and wheezing in the first six years of life. *The New England Journal of Medicine, 332*(3), 133–138.

Miller, J., & Chapman, R. (1991). *Systematic analysis of language transcripts.* Madison: University of Wisconsin Language Analysis Lab.

National Institutes of Health Research Portfolio Online Reporting Tools (NIH RePORT). (2012). *Twins and singletons with specific language impairment.* Retrieved from http://projectreporter.nih.gov/project_info_description.cfm?aid=8256059&icde=13427835&ddparam=&ddvalue=&ddsub=&cr=1&csb=default&cs=ASC

Newcomer, P.L., & Hammill, D.D. (1997). *Test of Language Development–Primary* (3rd ed.). Austin, TX: PRO-ED.

Organisation for Economic Co-operation and Development. (2007). *Human capital: How what you know shapes your life.* Retrieved from http://www.oecd.org/insights/humancapitalhowwhatyouknowshapesyourlife.htm. doi:10.1787/9789264029095-en

Population Health Research Network. (2011). *Population Health Research Network annual review 2010–2011.* Perth, Western Australia: Population Health Research Network Program Office.

Reilly, S., Bavin, E.L., Bretherton, L., Conway, L., Eadie, P., Cini, E., . . . Wake, M. (2009). The Early Language in Victoria Study (ELVS): A prospective, longitudinal study of communication skills and expressive vocabulary development at 8, 12 and 24 months. *International Journal of Speech-Language Pathology, 11*(5), 344–357.

Reilly, S., Wake, M., Bavin, E.L., Prior, M., Williams, J., Bretherton, L., . . . Okoumunne, O.C. (2007). Predicting language at 2 years of age: A prospective community study. *Pediatrics, 120,* e1441-e1449.

Rescorla, L. (1989). The Language Development Survey: A screening tool for delayed language in toddlers. *Journal of Speech and Hearing Disorders, 54,* 587–599.

Rice, M. (2003). A unified model of specific and general language delay: Grammatical tense as a clinical marker. In Y. Levy & J. Schaeffer (Eds.), *Language competence across populations* (pp. 63–95). Mahwah, NJ: Lawrence Erlbaum Associates.

Rice, M. (2004). Growth models of developmental language disorders. In M.L. Rice & S.F. Warren (Eds.), *Developmental language disorders: From phenotypes to etiologies* (pp. 207–240). Mahwah, NJ: Lawrence Erlbaum.

Rice, M. (2009). How different is disordered language. In J. Colombo, P. McCardle, & L. Freund (Eds.), *Infant pathways to language: Methods, models, and research directions* (pp. 65–80). New York, NY: Taylor and Francis Group.

Rice, M. (2012). Toward epidenetic and gene regulation models of specific language impairment: Looking for links among growth, genes, and impairments. *Journal of Neurodevelopmental Disorders, 4*(27), Advance online publication. doi: 10.1186/1866-1955-4-27

Rice, M., Smith, S., & Gayan, J. (2009). Convergent genetic linkage and associations to language, speech and reading measures in families of probands with Specific Language Impairment. *Journal of Neurodevelopment.* doi: 10.1007/s11689-11009-19031-x.

Rice, M., Taylor, C., & Zubrick, S. (2008). Language outcomes of 7-year-old children with or without a history of late language emergence at 24-months. *Journal of Speech, Language, and Hearing Research, 51*(2), 394–407.

Rice, M., & Wexler, K. (1996). Toward tense as a clinical marker of specific language impairment in English-speaking children. *Journal of Speech and Hearing Research, 39,* 1239–1257.

Rice, M., & Wexler, K. (2001). *Rice/Wexler Test of Early Grammatical Impairment.* San Antonio, TX: The Psychological Corporation.

Rice, M., Wexler, K., & Cleave, P. (1995). Specific language impairment as a period of extended optional infinitive. *Journal of Speeech, Language, and Hearing Research, 38,* 850–863.

Rice, M., Wexler, K., & Hershberger, S. (1998). Tense over time: The longitudinal course of tense acquisition in children with specific language impairment. *Journal of Speech, Language, and Hearing Research, 41*(6), 1412–1431.

Samejima, F. (1969). Estimation of latent ability using a response pattern of graded scores. *Psychometrika Monograph Supplement, 34*(4), 100–114.

Sanson, A., Nicholson, J., Ungerer, J., Zubrick, S., Wilson, K., Ainley, J., . . . Wake, M. (2002). *LSAC discussion paper no. 1: Introducing the Longitudinal Study of Australian Children.* Retrieved from http://www.aifs.gov.au/growingup/pubs/discussion/dp1/index.html

Sen, A. (1999). *Development as freedom.* Oxford, United Kingdom: Oxford University Press.

Soloff, C., Lawrence, D., Misson, S., & Johnstone, R. (2005). *LSAC technical paper no. 1: Sample design.* Retrieved from http://www.aifs.gov.au/growingup/pubs/technical/tp1.pdf

Squires, J., & Bricker, D. (2009). *Ages & Stages Questionnaires®: A parent-completed child monitoring system* (3rd ed.). Baltimore, MD: Paul H. Brookes Publishing Co.

Stanley, F., Croft, M.L., Gibbins, J., & Read, A.W. (1994). A population database for maternal and child health research in Western Australia using record linkage. *Paediatric and Perinatal Epidemiology, 8,* 433–447.

Tager-Flusberg, H., & Cooper, J. (1999). Present and future possibilities for defining a phenotype for specific language impairment. *Journal of Speech Language and Hearing Research, 42*(5), 1275–1278.

Taylor, C.L. (2010). Early motor development is part of the resource mix for language acquisition. *Journal of Child Language, 37*(2), 281–285.

Taylor, C.L., Maguire, B., & Zubrick, S.R. (2011). Children's language development. In B. Maguire & B. Edwards (Eds.), *The Longitudinal Study of Australian Children Annual Statistical Report 2010.* (pp. 107–121). Melbourne: Australian Institute of Family Studies.

Tomblin, J.B., Records, N.L., Buckwater, P., Zhang, X., Smith, E., & O'Brien, M. (1997). Prevalence of specific language impairment in kindergarten children. *Journal of Speech, Language, Hearing Research, 40,* 1245–1260.

United Nations General Assembley. (1989, November 20). Convention on the Rights of the Child. *Convention on the Rights of the Child.* Retrieved from http://treaties.un.org/doc/Publication/MTDSG/Volume%20I/Chapter%20IV/IV-11.en.pdf

Windle, M. (1992). Temperament and social support in adolescence: Interrelations with depressive symptoms and delinquent behavior. *Journal of Youth and Adolescence, 21*(1), 1–21.

Windle, M., & Lerner, R.M. (1986). Reassessing the dimensions of temperamental individuality across the lifespan: The Revised Dimensions of Temperament Survey (DOTS-R). *Journal of Adolescent Research, 1*(2), 213–230.

Zubrick, S., Taylor, C., Lawrence, D., Mitrou, F., Christensen, D., & Dalby, R. (2009). The development of human capability across the lifecourse: Perspectives from childhood. *Australian Journal of Epidemiology, 16*(3), 6–10.

Zubrick, S., Taylor, C., Rice, M., & Slegers, D. (2007). Late language emergence at 24 months: An epidemiological study of prevalence, predictors and covariates. *Journal of Speech, Language, and Hearing Research, 50,* 1562–1592.

**3**

# Danish Late Talkers

## *A First Portrait*

Dorthe Bleses and Werner Vach

Late talkers (LTs) have been defined by a variety of criteria, but delayed expressive vocabulary appears to be the most robust (Desmarais, Sylvestre, Meyer, Bairati, & Rouleau, 2008). The growing body of literature on the characteristics of LTs has demonstrated that this group of children is very heterogeneous in regard to linguistic abilities. Most studies have focused on identifying factors that predict late talking and how well late talking can predict later language problems and educational attainment. Much less attention has been given to obtaining a better understanding of the broader communicative skills of LTs. In one review, Desmarais and colleagues (2008) have attempted to characterize the communication abilities of LTs, including both linguistic and social variables. According to Desmarais et al., most studies have examined expressive language skills in LTs; in spite of its recognized importance, only a limited number of studies have analyzed comprehension skills in LTs. Because of this, these studies indicate that there are only two groups of LTs: one group of children who are characterized by having low expressive language skills but typical comprehension abilities for their age, and another group of children who are delayed in both expressive and receptive language skills. Furthermore, LTs have also been reported to be less communicative than typically developing (TD) children and to use fewer communicative acts (e.g., Paul & Shiffer, 1991; Rescorla & Merrin, 1998). Finally, studies have indicated that LTs have weaker grammatical abilities (e.g., Rescorla, Dahlsgaard, & Roberts, 2000; Rice, Taylor, & Zubrick, 2008).

In another more recent study, Desmarais et al. (2010) investigated the language profiles of 68 clinically referred children ages 18–35 months. The study included measures of expressive vocabulary and sentence complexity, comprehension, and broader communicative measures. Even though all children had expressive vocabulary scores below the 10th percentile on the MacArthur-Bates Communicative

Development Inventories (CDIs; Fenson et al., 2007), results showed that LTs differed in their language comprehension skills and their expression and engagement in communication, indicating distinguishable profiles for LTs.

Independent of specific profiles, how many children can be considered LTs? Studies have estimated this prevalence based on criteria such as percentiles or absolute numbers (e.g., fewer than 50 words). In such cases, the cutoff points are rather arbitrary. An absolute number is only suitable for a limited age range, as vocabulary typically grows fast once a child learns about 50 words. Percentiles allow comparisons across a wider age range but fix the percentage of LTs in each age group. A series of studies based on the CDIs following children learning how to speak English used a score below the 10th percentile on the expressive vocabulary subscale as the criterion for identification of LTs at 24 months (e.g., Dale, Price, Bishop, & Plomin, 2003; Reilly et al., 2007) and for LTs between 25 and 36 months (e.g., Horwitz et al., 2003). Prevalence estimates from population-based studies using the Language Development Survey (Rescorla, 1989) and a criterion of fewer than 50 words or no word combinations at 24 months have led to estimates of LTs between 10% and 20% (e.g., Klee et al., 1998; Rescorla & Alley, 2001). Based on the Ages & Stages Questionnaires®, Zubrick et al. (2007) found that 13.4% of 1,766 2-year-old children were LTs based on a combined measure of expressive vocabulary and word combinations (with 19.1% when word combinations were used as the only criterion). Based on these studies, it can be estimated that between 10% and 20% of children can be characterized as LTs.

## THE RELEVANCE OF PARENTAL EDUCATION
## FOR THE DEVELOPMENT OF LATE TALKING

Several studies have identified factors associated with both the emergence of late talking and the short- and long-term outcomes of late talking, including child characteristics (e.g., gender, birth history, perinatal status, otitis media, behavioral problems), familial and social variables (e.g., parental stress, socioeconomic status [for an overview, see Desmarais et al., 2008]), and genetic/biological factors including family history of language delay (e.g., Dale et al., 2003). Population-based studies, however, have reported varying results with respect to the variance that familial and social factors can explain. For example, a twin study by Bishop, Price, Dale, and Plomin (2003) indicated that environmental factors play the major role in causing early language delay, but it did not specify what the environmental factors were. Some Australian and Dutch studies that investigated a wide range of specific environmental factors, however, have suggested that these factors were only able to explain a limited amount of variance in language skills among LTs (Henrichs et al., 2011; Reilly et al., 2007; Zubrick et al., 2007). So, although the environment seems to play an important role in the development of late talking, the precise role is unclear.

The most studied external factor leading to late talking is the parents' socioeconomic status, which is most commonly measured by the level of parental (mainly maternal) education. Differences in socioeconomic status have been shown to have an impact on children's language development. According to Hoff (2013), the proportion of children living in poverty whose language development reflects influence of socioeconomic status is likely to be greater than 22%. Across a wide age range starting at 18 months, studies have found that children from families with low socioeconomic status have lower language skills in a variety of linguistic domains, including vocabulary, grammar, narrative and phonological development, and speed of processing (Hoff, 2013). Vocabulary appears to be the most sensitive language skill related to socioeconomic status across a variety of different methods (Hart & Risley, 1995; Hoff, 2003). Other studies have investigated the role of socioeconomic status for comprehension and production of complex sentences and found that the socioeconomic status differences are large in particular for acquisition of complex sentences (Huttenlocher, Waterfall, Vasilyeva, Vevea, & Hedges, 2010; Vasilyeva & Waterfall, 2011).

Socioeconomic effects for children have been found in the age range in which LTs are diagnosed. A study by Huttenlocher and colleagues (2010)—which was based on longitudinal video recordings of 47 parent–child pairs from diverse socioeconomic backgrounds with the children ranging in age from 14 to 42 months—revealed that socioeconomic status was a highly significant predictor of child language. Hoff (2003) has also documented socioeconomic effects with children at 24 months in a study based on naturalistic interactions between 33 mother–child pairs from high socioeconomic backgrounds and 30 mother–child pairs with mid-level socioeconomic backgrounds. According to the review by Desmarais et al. (2008), two studies have specifically investigated the effect of maternal educational level on vocabulary scores in LTs (Dale et al., 2003; Horwitz et al., 2003), and both studies indicated that the presence of a child's vocabulary delay at 24 months is correlated with the mother's low level of education.

Huttenlocher et al. (2010) also reported that the socioeconomic status effects remained constant over age for vocabulary development but increased for some measures of syntactic development. Nevertheless, the effect of socioeconomic status on different language domains in children of different ages is an issue that needs further investigation.

According to Hoff (2013), studies have pointed to differences in language experience as the primary mediator of differences in children's language development related to socioeconomic status. Mothers with less education often talk less to their children, make use of a smaller vocabulary and less complex and varied syntactic structures, and use language in a way that is less supportive of language development. The fact that studies have documented that educators can also have a positive effect on children's language acquisition suggests that there is an effect of parental input that is not simply a reflection of shared genetics between parent and child (Vasilyeva & Waterfall, 2011).

Research also suggests that attending formal child care can be a preventive means of attenuating effects of disadvantage on children's early language and literacy development. Both the quality and quantity of child care have been shown to have short- as well as long-term positive effects on cognitive and noncognitive outcomes in children (e.g., Hall et al., 2009; Melhuish et al., 2008; Vandell, Belsky, Burchinal, Steinberg, & Vandergrift, 2010). High-quality child care with high-quality, curriculum-based instruction embedded in positive and responsive interactions, then, may be necessary to improve academic outcomes such as language development for children at a socioeconomic disadvantage (Burchinal, Vandergrift, Pianta, & Mashburn, 2010). For example, Geoffroy et al. (2010) demonstrated that children of mothers with low levels of education who received formal child care obtained higher school readiness in comparison with those who were cared for by their parents.

## WHY STUDY DANISH CHILDREN?

The empirical knowledge of LTs just discussed is almost entirely based on English-speaking children, so it is important to explore LTs acquiring other languages, as the results might be different. A recent comparative study of English and Danish children ages 6–9 with language impairments found that even though both receptive vocabulary and past tense skills were compromised, as predicted, in both Danish and English children relative to controls, the Danish children's past tense skills were, contrary to expectations, significantly more compromised (Lum & Bleses, 2012).

Studying LTs acquiring other languages than English will potentially bring about new insights. Studying Danish LTs in particular would add new perspectives in two ways. First, Danish LTs are interesting to study because cross-linguistic research has suggested that children acquiring Danish are faced with a particularly difficult task of segmenting the speech input in the early phases of their language development, and in selected aspects of later development as well. Second, Danish children are reared in a way that can add new insights into the potential of child care for promoting resilience in language and literacy skills.

### Difficulty in Early Phases of Language Development

Linguistically speaking, Danish is a Germanic language, and in many ways is similar to English, with semi-restricted word order (verb second) and obligatory subject (except for imperatives), but morphologically speaking, Danish is somewhat more complex. Nouns fall in two gender classes and are inflected for number and definiteness. Like verbs in the other Germanic languages, Danish verbs fall in two main classes—weak (regular) and strong (irregular)—but there are two weak classes in Danish. Danish verbs are inflected for tense, mood, and voice. Adjectives are inflected for number, definiteness, and gender. The main mode of inflection is suffixation. The Danish lexicon is predominantly Germanic in origin, with imported words coming from a range of different source languages.

What do we know about Danish children's language development? Comprehensive studies of Danish children's language development are a relatively new undertaking. Almost 100 years passed from the first diary study of a single boy's early language development by his farther, the famous Danish linguist Otto Jespersen (1916), until large-scale population-based studies were carried out providing the first mappings of Danish children's language and communication abilities (Bleses et al., 2008a; Bleses, Lum, et al., 2011; Bleses, Vach, Jørgensen, & Worm, 2010). These studies and others have provided a general picture of Danish children's early language development by examining the developmental trajectories of early gestures, receptive and productive vocabulary, grammatical development (Bleses et al., 2008a), the characteristics of the first words spoken, and the composition of the earliest lexicon (Wehberg et al., 2007; Wehberg et al., 2008). As in other population-based investigations of early language development, the studies have revealed a substantial variability among children. The overall developmental path of Danish children up to 3 years has therefore proven very similar to that of children acquiring other Germanic languages, including the Scandinavian languages. However, the pace of Danish children's language development is apparently slower, even when compared with the Norwegian and Swedish neighbor languages (Bleses et al., 2008b; Bleses, Basbøll, & Vach, 2011), which Danish is both genetically and typologically related to. Cross-linguistic comparisons indicate that the phonetic structure of the Danish language itself may play a role for this slower development (Bleses, Basbøll, Lum, & Vach, 2010; Bleses et al., 2011). Danish is very different with respect to its sound structure, due to a combination of a complicated segmental phonology of weak vowel reduction and many nonlateral approximants.

Even though there are now descriptions of some general characteristics of Danish children with low language abilities (Bleses, Højen, Jørgensen, Jensen, & Vach, 2010; Vach, Bleses, & Jørgensen, 2010), none of the existing studies has focused on LTs, and, therefore, knowledge about LTs acquiring Danish is practically nonexistent.

What is expected of LTs acquiring Danish? Due to the overall similarity with other Germanic languages, we expect to find linguistic profiles of Danish LTs similar to those documented for English (i.e., lower language abilities in the domains of expressive vocabulary, comprehension, and communicative skills). However, findings that Danish children score low on measures of early receptive and expressive skills may imply a higher proportion of Danish LTs at 24 months than in other languages, if a fixed criterion is used. These—to some extent—conflicting hypotheses make it particularly interesting to investigate LTs acquiring Danish.

## Child Rearing

The second reason why the study of Danish LTs is interesting is the way in which Danish children are reared. Danish children grow up in families in which parents generally are well educated. Denmark falls higher than that of the Organisation for Economic Co-operation and Development (OECD; 2012) average with respect to educational attainment expressed as average numbers of years of successfully completed formal education. Only approximately 10% of parents have primary and secondary school as their highest education, 40% have a short or a vocational education, 30% have a medium postsecondary education, and 20% have a long postsecondary education based on the definitions of Statistics Denmark (a state institution under the Ministry of Economic Affairs and the Interior) (Bleses, Højen, et al., 2010). Danish children also typically grow up in families in which both parents work outside the home. Approximately 82% of mothers with children younger than 15 years are employed, which is the third highest among the 34 OECD countries (the average is 66%; OECD Family database) (see a list of OECD countries at http://www.oecd.org/about/membersandpartners). As a consequence, Denmark has the highest enrollment in child care of children ages 0–2;11 years among OECD countries (66% vs. an average of 30% (OECD, 2011), with Danish children spending approximately 35 hours per week in child care. From 3;0 to 5;0 years, on average 91% of children are enrolled in child care (ranking 11th among OECD countries). Approximately 20% of families lack sufficient social resources (Christensen, Socialforskningsinstituttet, & Arv, 2004).

Based on overall characteristics of Danish children's social context we expect that low parental education will have less of an impact on Danish children's development compared with what has been shown in existing studies in other countries. We base this expectation on the fact that a very high proportion of Danish children from families with low socioeconomic status in the available studies have been attending formal child care for at least 2 years, which has been shown to attenuate disadvantage.

## OBJECTIVES

This chapter summarizes findings from two studies, which we refer to as the CDI Late Talker Study and the National Language Assessment Study. The CDI Late Talker Study is based on the data of the population-based norming study (Bleses et al., 2008a, 2008b) of the Danish adaptation of The MacArthur-Bates CDIs (Fenson et al., 2007), which was completed by parents of more than 6,000 children ages 8–36 months. These data are limited to measuring productive vocabulary and grammar skills. We refer to children between 24 and 36 months of age in the CDI study who scored below the 10th percentile as LTs.

The National Language Assessment Study was based on data from national language assessment programs of low-performing children ages 35–40 months (Bleses, Lum, et al., 2011; Bleses, Vach, et al., 2010). We refer to children from the National Language Assessment Study who scored below the 10th percentile as low performers. In both the CDI Late Talker Study and the National Language Assessment Study, we refer to children scoring between the 10th and the 30th percentiles as slow developing (SD), and children scoring higher than the 30th percentile as TD.

The questions we address in this chapter are

1.  What is the prevalence of LTs at 24 months acquiring Danish based on three different criteria—fewer than 50 words, no combinations, or fewer than 50 words or no combinations—and how does this compare to LTs acquiring English?

2.  How does the relationship of the development of grammar to vocabulary in Danish compare among LTs, SD children, and TD children?

3.  What characterizes the language abilities of low performers acquiring Danish between 34 and 40 months, and what are the similarities and differences to LTs?

4.  How does socioeconomic status as measured by parental education influence the linguistic profiles of low performers acquiring Danish?

Questions 1 and 2 are addressed using the CDI Late Talker Study. This study allows for detailed analyses of the relation between productive vocabulary and grammatical complexity in LTs by comparing them with children at different levels of abilities and different age groups (in children from 24 to 29 months and from 30 to 36 months). The CDI Late Talker Study, however, is not an optimal dataset to consider questions of socioeconomic influences on children's language development due to an overrepresentation of parents with middle and higher education. Hence, parental education was not able to explain any of the variation among children (Bleses, Vach, & Wehberg, 2008).

Questions 3 and 4 will be addressed using the National Language Assessment Study. Here we have the opportunity to examine the role of a wider range of oral language and literacy skills in low performers—including expressive vocabulary, comprehension skills, narrative skills, pronunciation and sound discrimination skills and communicative strategies—and compare the results of low performers with children at different levels of abilities and with younger LTs. Furthermore, the assessment studies go beyond the "convenience sample" in research (Fernald, 2010) by including a proportion of children with low-income parents that is similar to that of the general child–family population in Denmark, making them appropriate for exploring effects of socioeconomic status (parental education) on a range of language skills. Even though socioeconomic status may affect children differently depending on the age of the children, the overlap in age between the CDI and the assessment studies may provide some indication of how socioeconomic status affects LTs in the earlier age range.

## THE STUDIES

The CDI Late Talker Study was a cross-sectional study based, as mentioned previously, on the Danish adaptation of the CDIs. The National Language Assessment Study was a cross-sectional study with two waves based on different versions of the Danish SI-3 assessment tool (Bleses, Højen, et al. 2010; discussed in more detail in the following section). In the age range being reviewed, there are only a few other instruments available, such as the Reynell Developmental Language Scales (Reynell, 1977). Some limited comparisons between the SI-3 and Reynell assessment are discussed.

### CDI Late Talker Study

In this study we used data from the CDI: Words and Sentences form ("CDI: Ord og Sætninger") from the MacArthur-Bates CDIs (Fenson et al., 2007), which covers productive vocabulary and how children use words (in the "Words Children Use" section), inflectional endings (part 1 and 2), word forms, and complex language (in the "Sentences and Grammar" section). This instrument is used for children between 16 months and 36 months, going later in development than most CDI: Words and Sentences adaptations. At the structural level, the Danish form is almost completely the same as the American CDI, but various linguistic and cultural modifications were applied in the Danish adaptation, reflecting the differences between Danish and American English morphology as well as cultural differences (Bleses et al., 2008a). The Danish CDI: Words and Sentences form contains 725 words (vs. 680 on the American form). Acceptable levels for both validity and reliability of the Danish CDI instrument have been found (Bleses et al., 2008a).

The CDI sample included 6,112 children. The data were collected in 2002 and 2003. Inclusion criteria were monolingual Danish children living with their parents and having no reported speech, hearing, or other serious (chronic) health problems. (Note that the occurrence of otitis media followed by tympanotomy tube or premature birth at a gestational age of 32 weeks or later did not lead to exclusion.) Information about parental education (see Table 3.1) was obtained through a questionnaire completed by the parents. (The variables of parental highest education are defined based on Statistics Denmark's definitions.)

The sample was balanced with respect to gender. The distribution of parent education was skewed in the direction of educated, middle-class families being overrepresented, which is a frequent global phenomenon in CDI studies (see Fenson et al., 2007). Approximately 85% of children were in child care, with the average amount of time spent in child care between 35 and 40 hours per week.

### National Language Assessment Study

The National Language Assessment Study was based on two versions of a broader language screening instrument developed by Denmark's Center for Child Language on behalf of government bodies as part of a nationwide language screening program. The first version of the screening tool, Screening Instrument for 3-Year-Olds

**Table 3.1.** Parental educational distribution in the CDI Late Talker Study[a]

| Basic characteristics of the population | The CDI Late Talker Study (ages 0;8–3;0) n = 6,112 | | Child–family population in Denmark[b, c] |
|---|---|---|---|
| | n | % | % |
| Basic education | 243 | 4 | 28 |
| Short further education | 2675 | 42 | 52 |
| Medium further education | 1759 | 28 | 11 |
| Long further education | 1282 | 21 | 9 |
| Missing/unknown | 153 | 5 | 0 |

*Source:* Bleses, Vach, Slott, Wehberg, Thomsen, Madsen, and Basbøll (2008a).
[a]See Bleses et al. (2008a, 2008b).
[b]This information is based on Statistics Denmark.
[c]All children at age 1;0–3;0 years in Denmark and their parents.

("Sprogvurderingsmateriale til 3-årige," SI-3, Bleses, Højen, et al. 2010), consists of seven subscales, including oral receptive and productive language skills, phonological awareness, and short-term memory, each implemented by a report to be completed by parents or a test to be administered by the child care staff. The SI-3 is administered by child care staff based on a small manual combining the tests with a short introduction, more detailed instructions, and a few examples. During the development of the SI-3, validation studies were performed comparing the scoring of the staff with those of experienced research assistants, and discrepancies were rather infrequent (Bleses, Højen, et al., 2010). Detailed descriptions of the subscales, test development, and psychometric properties of the SI-3 have previously been presented (Bleses, Højen, et al., 2010). Note that selection of items for the SI-3 aimed at obtaining a left-skewed distribution of the score to be able to distinguish reliably among children in the lower end of the distribution.

The Danish Ministry of Social Affairs then commissioned Bleses and colleagues to revise and expand the SI-3. Besides a few changes of individual items on various subscales, only two major changes were carried out: The Memory subscale was removed and a Narrative Task subscale was added (Bleses, Lum, et al., 2011). Table 3.2 summarizes the subscales included in the SI-3 and the changes made in the Revised SI-3.

For the first wave of the National Language Assessment Study, we analyzed the data of nearly 15,000 unselected children ages 34–40 months from 35 municipalities where the SI-3 was used as part of the mandatory screening. Only monolingual children were included in the dataset, and the age range was restricted to 35–40 months. After having applied the inclusion criteria, 7,197 girls and 7,644 boys remained from 32 municipalities; 972 child care centers contributed with a median number of 13 children. The 32 municipalities were equally distributed across the country covering urban and rural areas.

In the second wave of the National Language Assessment Study, we analyzed data for 1,061 unselected children aged 35–40 months from 14 municipalities where the Revised SI-3 was administered as part of the norming of the instrument. The municipalities covered both rural and urban areas of varying sizes in Denmark.

Using a service of Statistics Denmark, it was possible to obtain information on parents' highest educational level based on Statistics Denmark's definitions, as

**Table 3.2.** Subscales of the Screening Instrument for 3-Year-Olds (SI-3; Bleses, Højen, et al., 2010) and the Revised SI-3 (Bleses, Lum, et al., 2011)

| | | SI-3(2007) | Revised SI-3 (2010) | |
|---|---|---|---|---|
| Subscales | | Number of items (maximum score) | Number of items (maximum score) | Instrumentation |
| Productive language skills | | | | |
| I | Vocabulary | 100 (100) | 100 (100)[a] | Parental checklist[b] |
| II | Complex grammar | | | Parental checklist |
| | i. Inflectional endings | 3 (6) | 3 (6) | |
| | ii. Complex grammar | 7 (42) | 7 (42) | |
| III | Pronunciation of sounds | 10 (10) | 10 (10)[c] | Imitation task |
| IV | Narrative task | Not included | 24 (24) | Production task |
| Receptive language skills | | | | |
| V | Sound discrimination | 16 (16) | 16 (16)[d] | Picture identification task |
| VI | Memory | 12 (12) | Removed | Imitation task |
| VII | Comprehension of complex concepts (3 ys) | 12 | 12 | Object manipulation task Picture elicitation task |
| | i. Prepositions | (12) | (12) | |
| | ii. Abstract words | 6 (6) | 8 (8)[e] | |
| Communication skills | | | | |
| VIII | Communicative strategies | 7 | 7[f] | Staff checklist |

From Bleses, D., Vach, W., Jørgensen, R.N., & Worm, T. (2010). The internal validity and acceptability of the Danish SI-3: A language screening instrument for 3-year-olds. *Journal of Speech, Language, and Hearing Research, 53,* 490–507; adapted by permission. © 2010 American Speech-Language-Hearing Association.

[a]Seven qualitative questions about atypical development have been added (i.e., they are not included in the summary score).

[b]The word list is a short version of the CDI: Words and Sentences (cf. Vach et al., 2010).

[c]One target word was replaced.

[d]Two word pairs were replaced.

[e]The words have been changed, and two words were added.

[f]Seven qualitative questions about communication strategies have been added (i.e., they are not included in the summary score).

shown in Table 3.3. For more information, see Bleses, Lum, et al. (2011). Data from Statistics Denmark and child data were correlated (i.e., overall summary score and score on each of the subscales). The sample was evenly distributed across gender, and the educational distribution among parents matched that of the general population in Denmark. All children were in child care.

There are some limitations in the use of the SI-3 and to some extent also the Revised SI-3. It has only been possible to validate the instruments to a limited extent.

**Table 3.3.**  Parent educational distribution in the National Language Assessment Study[a]

| Basic characteristics of the population | SI-3 (Sprogvurdering.dk) (ages 2;10–3;4) n = 14,910 | | Revised SI-3 (norming study) (ages 2;10–3;4) n = 1,009 | | Child–family population in Denmark[b] |
|---|---|---|---|---|---|
| Primary school | 782 | 5 | 60 | 10 | 8 |
| Upper secondary school | 274 | 2 | 11 | 2 | 3 |
| Vocational | 5,102 | 35 | 192 | 34 | 32 |
| Short education | 1,256 | 9 | 35 | 6 | 8 |
| Medium further education | 4,461 | 31 | 173 | 30 | 29 |
| Long further education | 2,589 | 18 | 102 | 18 | 21 |
| Missing/unknown | 0 | 0 | 436 | 0 | 0 |

[a]See Bleses, Lum, et al. (2011) and Bleses, Vach, Jørgensen, and Worm (2010).
[b]This information is based on Statistics Denmark (see Bleses et al., 2008a, 2008b).

Furthermore, the psychometric properties of some subscales of the SI-3 are not fully acceptable (i.e., the measurement error may to some extent diminish our possibilities to address the two research questions we address in the paper).

## CDI LATE TALKER STUDY: LATE TALKERS ACQUIRING DANISH PREVALENCE RATE

The first research question we address is what is the prevalence rate of LTs at 24 months of age acquiring Danish, and how does this compare to LTs acquiring English? In Table 3.4, we compare the percentage of LTs based on the following three criteria for estimating prevalence: **fewer than 50 words, no combinations, or fewer than 50 words or no combinations.** (Note that the CDI Late Talker Study only includes Danish monolingual children.)

Results indicate that the prevalence rate of male LTs is approximately equivalent to the 10th percentile cutoff used in several studies when the criterion of < 50 words is used (11%). The criterion of no word combinations results in a slightly higher prevalence (14%). If we use the criterion of either <50 words *and* no word

**Table 3.4.**  Percentage of late talkers by gender based on three criteria for estimating prevalence for children at 2;0 years from the CDI Late Talker Study[a]

| | Male N = 104 | | Female N = 112 | |
|---|---|---|---|---|
| | n | % | n | % |
| < 50 words | 11 | 11 | 8 | 7 |
| No word combinations | 15 | 14 | 7 | 6 |
| < 50 words OR no word combinations | 18 | 17 | 11 | 10 |

[a]See Bleses et al. (2008a, 2008b).

combinations, 17% of male children are identified as LTs. For females, the prevalence of late talking is lower (between 7% and 10%). Altogether, the prevalence rates at 24 months are quite similar to what have been found for children acquiring English. It is worth noting that when using fixed criteria for identifying Danish LTs, in particular when using or including a grammatical indicator of late talking, the prevalence is higher than 10% and in the high end compared with findings based on English LTs. For girls, the use of a fixed cutoff point results in similar results to English-acquiring children. The fact that using productive vocabulary as an indicator results in a similar prevalence of LTs compared with English is consistent with earlier results that Danish children's early productive skills are in the low end compared with children acquiring other languages.

## Vocabulary and Grammar Development in Late Talkers

The second question we address is as follows: How does the relationship of the development of grammar to vocabulary in Danish compare among LTs, SD children, and TD children?

The CDI Late Talker Study offers an opportunity to investigate the relation between expressive vocabulary and various indicators of grammatical competences by comparing LTs, SD children, and TD children. Figures 3.1 and 3.2 illustrate the relation among three ranges of expressive vocabulary scores (LTs, SD children, and TD children) and the score on the complexity scale (33 sentence pairs that contrast in length and grammatical complexity), as well as the extent to which children sometimes or often use plural, possessive, and past tense inflectional endings, and have started to combine words by age (24–29 months or 30–26 months, respectively). The first three columns from the left indicate the summary score on the complexity scale for the three groups. The next three sets of columns indicate the frequency with which the three groups of children sometimes (S) or often (O) have started to use the three inflections, whereas the last three columns show the frequency with which the three groups of children sometimes (S) or often (O) have started to combine words.

As can be read from Figure 3.1, there is systematic variation among LTs, SD children, and TD children (as defined by expressive vocabulary) already from 24 to 29 months with respect to scores on measures of grammar and complexity. LTs are significantly behind TD children on all measures. The differences in achievement among the three groups of children are significantly different (p <.0001) for all subscales. LTs and SD children are similar in acquisitional patterns with the exception of complexity and word combinations. Almost none of the LTs have started to use inflectional endings or word combinations often, whereas this behavior is more common for SD children, though not for past tense inflections.

Turning now to the older children (30–36 months) in Figure 3.2, we find that the variance in score among the three groups of children is still substantial. For this older age group, the scores among LTs, SD children, and TD children are significantly different (p < .0001) for all subscales. LTs are significantly behind TD children on all measures. Compared with the younger age group, we have a similar picture, but with one substantial difference: For the inflectional endings, the SD children are now always closer to the TD children, and this even holds for word combinations, although a ceiling makes the judgment more difficult here. Consequently, the gap between LTs and SD children with respect to these aspects has increased.

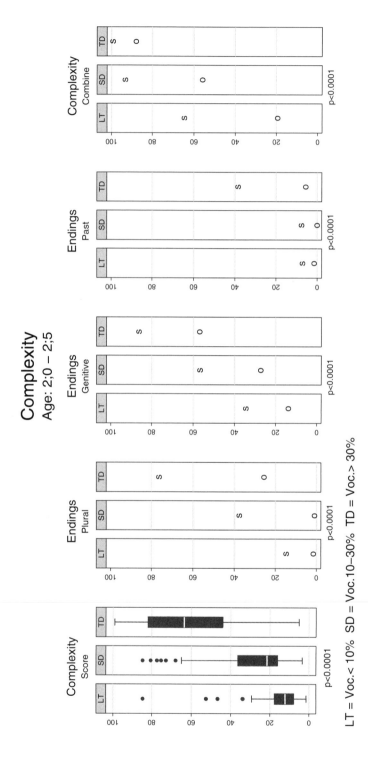

**Figure 3.1.** Productive subscales in the CDI: Words and Sentences component of the MacArthur-Bates Communicative Development Inventories (CDIs; Fenson et al., 2007) by levels of expressive vocabulary score for late talkers (LTs), slow developing (SD) children, and typically developing (TD) children from 24–29 months. Distributions of the complexity score visualized by box plots and relative frequencies of marking the single items as often (O) or as sometimes or often (S). (*Key: Voc., vocabulary.*)

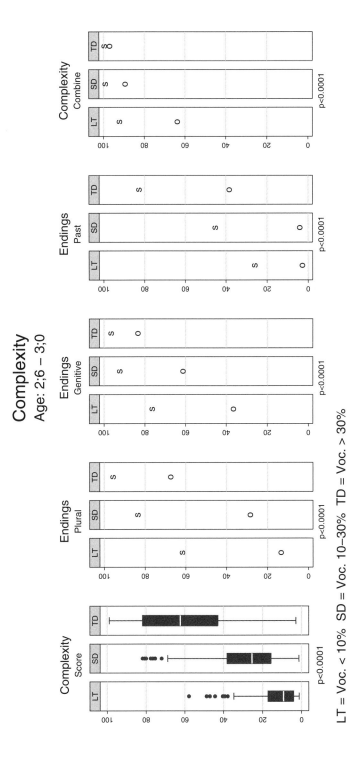

**Figure 3.2.** Productive subscales in the CDI: Words and Sentences component of the MacArthur-Bates Communicative Development Inventories (CDIs; Fenson et al., 2007) by levels of expressive vocabulary score for late talkers (LTs), slow developing (SD) children, and typically developing (TD) children from 30–36 months. Distributions of the complexity score visualized by box plots and relative frequencies of marking the single items as often (O) or as sometimes or often (S). (*Key:* Voc., vocabulary.)

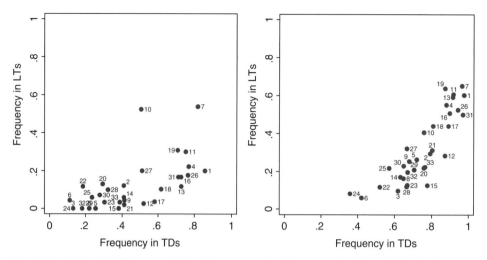

**Figure 3.3.** Scatterplot of frequency of using the more complex form, comparing for each item the frequency in late talkers (LTs) with the frequency in typically developing (TD) children in two age groups: 24–29 months (left scatterplot) and 30–36 months (right scatterplot).

To obtain more insight into the potential difficulties of LTs with the acquisition of grammar, we have attempted to identify those items of grammar on which LTs scored lowest compared with TD children. For this we made scatterplots of the frequencies of using the more complex form, comparing for each item the frequency in LTs with the frequency in TD children only (see Figure 3.3).

From the scatterplots we can conclude that LTs always score lower than TD children, with one remarkable exception, namely item 10 in the age range of 24–29 months (left scatterplot). For both TD children and LTs, the more complex form is used by about half of the children. This item compares the use of a present tense form and a regular past tense form when talking about something in the past. We can also see further differences between the items in children ages 30–36 months (right scatterplot). The items at the upper boundary of the point cloud are those that are easiest for LTs (i.e., in these items they are least behind the TD children); the items at the bottom boundary of the point cloud are those for which LTs are most behind the TD children. It is notable that several of the easiest items are related to grammatical constructs: Like item 10, item 22 compares the use of a present tense form with a regular past tense form; item 25 compares a present tense form with an irregular past tense form; item 20 compares a present tense and an irregular past tense form in a question; and items 7 and 19 check the use of the genitive -s. In contrast, the items appearing at the lower boundary with the greatest delay are not related to grammatical forms, but to the use of more complex constructions: Item 3 compares "light up" with "light up, such that I can see"; item 12 compares "cookie mother" with "cookie for mother"; item 15 compares "baby would eat" with "baby would like to eat"; and item 17 compares "this a mouse" with "this is a mouse." This pattern suggests that LTs are most hampered in grammatical development with respect to building longer and more complex forms but are slightly less hampered with respect to acquiring and using inflectional forms.

We performed a similar analysis with respect to the specific vocabulary categories of the CDI: Words and Sentences. The ranking of the categories was quite similar between LTs and TD children. One notable difference was that in the younger age group the categories "sounds," "people," and "games and routines" turned out to be relatively easy for LTs, suggesting that social relations, which are less impaired in LTs, may help them to acquire words.

When exploring the variation in children's response patterns in the section "How children use words" (i.e., use of words to refer to the past or future or to missing or absent objects or people), a consistent pattern emerged. The frequencies of affirmative responses were in all cases lower in LTs (the differences in score among the children are significantly different (p < .0001) for all five questions). LTs almost never use language that refers to absent objects, and only approximately 50% use language that refer to the past and the future.

In summary, we can observe very distinct differences in the grammar abilities of LTs compared with SD children and TD children. On the grammar scale, approximately 75% of LTs scored lower than the lower quartile in SD children, and nearly all of them scored lower than the lower 25th percentile of TD children. With respect to inflectional endings and word combinations, the discrepancy between LTs and SD children tends to increase with age. LTs seem to have slightly fewer problems with using inflectional endings (except for past tense) than with using more complex grammatical forms.

## THE NATIONAL LANGUAGE ASSESSMENT STUDY: CHARACTERISTICS OF SLIGHTLY OLDER LOW PERFORMERS' LANGUAGE DEVELOPMENT

The third question we address in this chapter is what characterizes the language abilities of low performers acquiring Danish between 34 and 40 months, and what are the similarities and differences to LTs? The two assessment studies enable examination of the relation among a wider range of language abilities including expressive vocabulary, comprehension skills, memory skills (SI-3 only), narrative skills (Revised SI-3 only), pronunciation, sound discrimination, and communicative strategies, and the comparison of low performers to SD and TD children.

Figure 3.4 compares the scores of low performers in the SI-3 to SD and TD children using expressive vocabulary as the independent measure. (Note that the pronunciation and sound discrimination subscale is a criterion-based test designed to identify very low-performing children.) Figure 3.4 documents that the systematic variation among low performers, SD children, and TD children that we observed in the CDI Late Talker Study can be found in somewhat older low performers, SD children, and TD children. The differences in scores are not so pronounced. However, all differences in achievement among the three groups of children are significantly different (p < .0001 for all subscales). Overall, low performers exhibit the same developmental patterns as SD and TD children but score at lower levels. The difference in score is most evident on the inflectional endings (same three questions as in the CDI Late Talker Study) and the complexity subscales (an index of sentence complexity ranging from single words to complex sentences), in which the 50% range of scores of low performers and TD children does not overlap. That is, low performers demonstrate a distinct delay in these two language domains at this age level, as we saw with low performers at earlier ages. Correspondingly, in relation to comprehension (prepositions) and communicative scores, we find considerable differences, as all low performers score below the median of TD children.

56

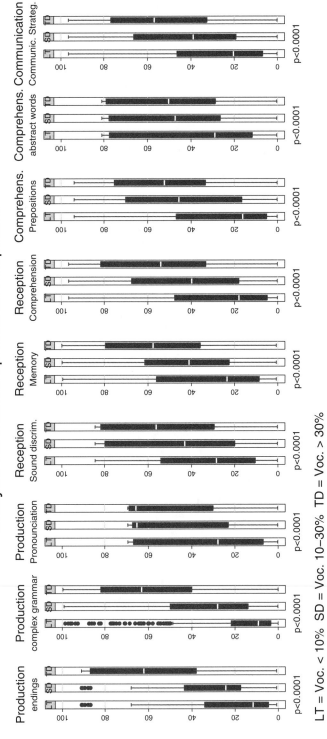

**Figure 3.4.** Percentage scores on eight subscales of the Screening Instrument for 3-Year-Olds (SI-3; Bleses, Højen, et al., 2010) by expressive vocabulary score for late talkers (LTs), slow developing (SD) children, and typically developing (TD) children. *Note:* LTs = vocabulary < 10%, SD = vocabulary 10%–30%, TD = vocabulary > 30%.

Nevertheless, these language measures appear not to be as challenging for low performers compared with grammatical complexity. In low performers, more variance can be registered in the sound pronunciation subscale than for SD and TD children. For instance, more than half of the low performers scored below the lower quartile of TD children. Also, the variation among low performers on the pronunciation subscale is very large. In summary, the low performers score lower than SD and TD children on all measures, but the differences are less marked when compared with the difference between LTs and SD and TD children in the CDI Late Talker Study.

The systematic variation between low performers and TD children is confirmed by single-item–level analyses. Such analyses can determine whether the ranking of the items with respect to the mean score or frequency is similar across the two groups of children, and the LTs just score lower. An example of this type of analysis, focused on the items of the comprehension subscale (prepositions), is illustrated in the scatterplot in Figure 3.5.

On the communicative strategy subscale, on the contrary, the ranking of the items do differ. Again, all low performers score lower than TD children, but the difference varies from item to item, even for items with similar average scores in TD children. Low performers seem to score particularly low on items related to the understanding of turn taking in conversations, talking coherently about an event, maintaining a short conversation about a topic, and using language to communicate intent.

The results from the second wave of The National Language Assessment Study (based on the Revised SI-3) basically replicate the findings from the study based on the first wave. Low performers scored consistently lower then both SD and TD children on complex grammar; inflectional endings; comprehension (prepositions); communicative strategies; and, we can now add, the narrative subscale. The difference between low performers and the other two groups of children is less pronounced on the rest of the subscales.

Finally, comparing the language profile of slightly older low performers to that of LTs, we can conclude that there are many similarities. The analyses indicate that

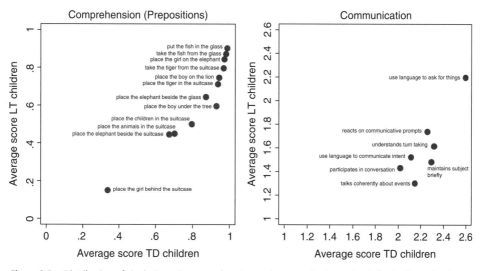

**Figure 3.5.** Distribution of single items in comprehension and communication subscale in the Screening Instrument for 3-Year-Olds (SI-3; Bleses, Højen, et al., 2010) by language status.

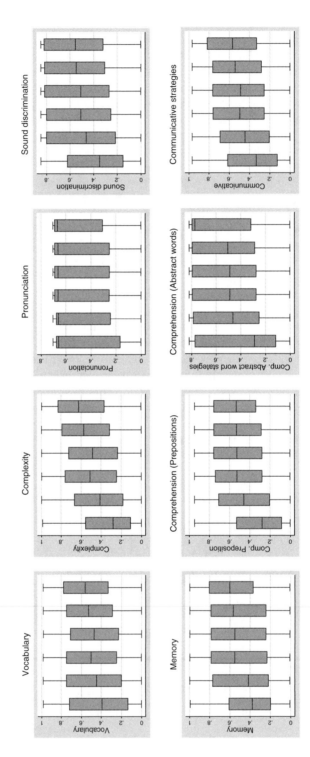

**Figure 3.6.** Distribution of scores in each of the seven subscales of the Screening Instrument for 3-Year-Olds (SI-3; Bleses, Højen, et al., 2010) by parental educational level. *Note:* From the left, bar 1 = primary school, bar 2 = vocational education, bar 3 = upper secondary school, bar 4 = short education, bar 5 = medium further education, and Bar 6 = long further education.

the median score of low performers is lower than that of SD and TD children on all of the language domains that were measured. We found that LTs in particular scored distinctly lower on grammatical complexity compared with SD and TD children. The very low scores on grammatical complexity we established in LTs, therefore, continue to characterize the linguistic profile of slightly older low performers.

## The Relation of Parental Education to the Prevalence and Nature of Late Talkers Acquiring Danish

The fourth research question we address in this chapter is how does socioeconomic status as measured by parental education influence the linguistic profiles of low performers acquiring Danish? Based on information from Statistics Denmark, six different levels of parental education can be distinguished, ranging from primary school to long education (e.g., as university master degree, dentist) Associations among children's scores and fathers', mothers', and the family's highest education have been calculated. In order to get an indication of the overall association between child outcome and parental education, the distribution of scores for the seven subscales in SI-3 by highest parental education are shown in Figure 3.6. (*Note:* Analyses using mother's education gave nearly the same results, whereas the association with father's education is less pronounced.)

Several interesting observations can be made. First, there is an association between the family's highest education and child outcome for almost all subscales in SI-3, and for most subscales the association is linear: The scores increase with increasing parental education. Even in the pronunciation and sound discrimination subscales, in which the variance among children is much reduced due to the criterion-based design, marginal differences caused by different levels of parental education can be seen. Second, the subscales that demonstrate the highest influence of education are grammatical complexity, comprehension (both prepositions and in particular abstract words), and, to a lesser extent, communicative strategies.

Table 3.5 summarizes the correlations between the family's highest education and the children's score on the SI-3 subscales. We found significant correlations for all scales, ranging between 0.09 and 0.23. The correlation with vocabulary was only 0.14, the fourth smallest value. We also analyzed the correlations separately for

**Table 3.5.** The Pearson correlation between score and educational level

|  | Correlation | $p$ | $R^2$ |
|---|---|---|---|
| Vocabulary | .14 | < .001 | 0.021 |
| Complexity | .23 | < .001 | 0.057 |
| Pronunciation | .09 | < .001 | 0.010 |
| Sound discrimination | .11 | < .001 | 0.013 |
| Memory | .13 | < .001 | 0.018 |
| Comprehension | .22 | < .001 | 0.056 |
| Communicative strategies | .16 | < .001 | 0.024 |

*Note:* This table shows the Pearson correlation between the score and the highest educational level in the family with a *p*-value of testing the null hypothesis for no correlation and adjusted $R^2$ values from a model using the educational level as a categorical covariate.

the LTs, SD children, and TD children to investigate whether LTs are less or more sensitive to the level of education. We could find significant differences only for the vocabulary score, with a correlation of 0.13 in the low performers, a correlation of 0.05 in SD children, and a correlation of $-0.02$ in TD children ($p = .002$), all of which suggests that low performers are more sensitive to socioeconomic differences with respect to vocabulary development than children with a larger vocabulary.

## THE FIRST PORTRAIT OF LATE TALKING AND LOW PERFORMING DANISH CHILDREN FROM 24 TO 40 MONTHS

LTs acquiring Danish have until now not been studied empirically. In this chapter we have provided a first, preliminary account of LTs acquiring Danish by comparing the pattern of development of LTs, SD children, and TD children based on a Danish CDI Late Talker Study including children ages 24–36 months. Furthermore, we studied the linguistic profiles of low performers ages 34–40 months and compared their profiles to those of LTs. Both studies have provided opportunities to investigate the relation between expressive vocabulary and a range of grammatical competencies; in the two assessment studies, it was possible to investigate the role of an even broader set of productive and comprehensive language skills.

We have addressed four questions in this chapter. In the CDI Late Talker Study we addressed the prevalence of LTs at 24 months acquiring Danish and how this result compared with children acquiring English. Concerning prevalence, from the outset it was not quite clear what to expect in Danish LTs because the general developmental pattern observed is similar to that of children acquiring other comparable languages, although some studies have indicated a slower developmental path overall, particularly in relation to receptive language skills (e.g., Bleses et al., 2008b). The first observation would predict similar prevalence rate of LTs, whereas the latter would predict that a higher proportion of LTs when a fixed cutoff point is used. However, the analyses of 2-year-old children showed that the prevalence of LTs acquiring Danish is comparable to studies of English-acquiring children, which have led to estimations of between 10% and 20%. Depending on the criterion and gender of the child, between 7% of girls (based on the criterion < 50 words) and 17% of boys (based on the criterion of < 50 words or no word combinations) can be categorized as LTs.

In the CDI Late Talker Study we also addressed the development of vocabulary and grammar abilities—and the relation between them—by comparing LTs acquiring Danish to SD and TD children in two age groups. We predicted that the relation among different language domains would be comparable to that of children acquiring other languages with particularly low language skills in vocabulary, comprehension, and communicative skills. Generally, these expectations were met, but several interesting differences appeared. The first is related to grammatical skills in Danish LTs. Based on an expressive vocabulary score below the 10th percentile, we find similar results for LTs independently of age—that is, LTs scored much lower than TD children on grammatical measures. The findings replicated earlier studies that established that English LTs tend to combine words later, use fewer endings, and use less-advanced sentences than other children their age (Dale et al., 2003; Rescorla et al., 2000; Rice et al., 2008; Zubrick et al., 2007). In the case of Danish LTs, however, this pattern turned out to be even more marked;

as Danish LTs at 24–29 months had not even started to combine words, they hardly used any endings at all, and their score on the complexity scale was at floor level. Similarly, LTs at age 2;0–2;5 hardly used language to refer to the past, future, or absent objects and people, indicating that decontextualized use of language has not yet emerged. These results support earlier conclusions that a child's expressive vocabulary needs to exceed a certain level before the development of more complex language occurs.

In the National Language Assessment Study, we addressed the language abilities of low performers acquiring Danish between 34 and 40 months and identified similarities and differences compared with younger LTs. It appeared that somewhat older low performers performed much worse than TD children, and that the difference is more pronounced than the one we observed at younger ages when comparing LTs and TD children. Grammatical skill was the language competence that was the most affected in LTs. Moreover, the gap between LTs and SD children tends to increase with age. Although a direct comparison with results from other languages is difficult due to differences in the definition of outcome measures and also study designs, it is our impression that the discrepancy in acquisition level of grammatical skills between Danish LTs and TD children is more pronounced than for English-speaking children. Such a more pronounced discrepancy cannot be explained by the more complex morphology of Danish compared with English. Norwegian children who are faced with the same level of inflectional morphology score significantly higher than Danish children (Kristoffersen et al., 2012). We likewise established that low performers scored lower on other productive language measures (i.e., on the narrative subscale and to a lesser extent pronunciation), though the scores were not as low as for the grammatical subscales.

In conclusion, grammatical complexity and inflectional endings appear to be a strong marker of delayed language development in Danish children at ages 24–40 months. The mastery of inflectional morphology is challenging for Danish LTs not just at 24 months. As mentioned previously, when Lum and Bleses compared 6- and 9-year-old children with diagnosed language impairments with TD children, the effect size observed for the analyses on past tense was significantly larger relative to the observed effect size examining receptive vocabulary. The difference was larger in Danish children compared with English children, suggesting that past tense forms were harder for Danish children with language impairments compared with English children with language impairments (Lum & Bleses, 2012). Even developing 4- to 8-year-old TD children score lower on past tense tasks when compared with Icelandic-, Norwegian-, and Swedish-speaking children (Bleses, Basbøll, & Vach, 2011). An apparent explanation for this pattern is that inflectional endings are particularly susceptible to the reduction processes described at the beginning of this chapter, and these results are compatible with the hypothesis that the phonetic structure of Danish poses a specific challenge to Danish children in general and children with language delays in particular.

Low performers suffer from some communication problems as well, probably due to their expressive problems. As described previously, low performers seem to have specific problems with the understanding of turn taking in conversations, talking coherently about an event, and maintaining a short conversation about a topic. A limited vocabulary and less sophisticated means of producing contextualized language, not surprisingly, negatively affects low performers' capabilities to express themselves and to maintain a conversation. This result supports conclusions from earlier research that LTs are less communicative than TD children, even though this was measured in somewhat older children at ages 2;10–3;4 (e.g., Desmarais et al., 2010; Rescorla & Merrin, 1998).

Finally, we examined the role of parental education for low performers compared with SD and TD children based on approximately 15,000 children from 34 to 40 months. The analyses demonstrated association on practically all of the linguistic domains investigated even though the $R^2$ values were not large. The pattern of increasing score with increasing parental education confirms our underpinning hypothesis that parental education is associated with children's language development. Taking into account the measurement errors of our instrument, the impact of parental education perhaps is even higher.

The impact of parental education was evident for all subscales. In contrast to the findings of others (e.g., Hoff, 2013), productive complexity as well as comprehension of complex sentences were more sensitive to differences in parental education than vocabulary. This may be related to the fact that all of our scales are constructed to obtain left-skewed distrubutions with the majority of children scoring rather high. However, ceiling was not more pronounced for vocabulary than for other scales.

Empirical studies of the home learning environment in Danish families are yet to come, but there is no reason to expect that the quality of the home learning environment in parents with less education are significantly different compared with parents in other comparable societies. Nonetheless, given that the vast majority of children with low socioeconomic status already have attended child care for 2 years, this result is still somewhat unexpected. Danish child cares in general have a high quality when compared with other countries based on standard measures of quality, and, therefore, they might have been expected to moderate the effects of parental education. The child-to-staff ratio in formal child care services for children at 0–36 months is the sixth highest, and the child-to-staff ratio in preschools is the highest among OECD countries (OECD, 2011). Similarly, the public expenditure on child care and early education services, when calculated based on the percent of gross domestic product (2007) was the highest in OECD. These indices of quality do appear to benefit children in the long run. One longitudinal study indicated that a higher number of staff members per child, a higher share of male staff, and a higher share of staff with a pedagogic education lead to significant improvements in Danish children's test results at the end of ninth grade (Bauchmüller, Gørtz, & Rasmussen, 2011).

So why do we find a discrepancy between children from families from low and high socioeconomic backgrounds that is comparable to what have been found in countries where such quality indicators appear to be lower? Following Burchinal et al. (2010), one hypothesis is that the instructional quality of Danish child cares is not sufficiently high in order to attenuate the disadvantage of low parental education. Danish child cares have traditionally focused broadly on learning and social development, and they often do not explicitly address children's development of specific language and literacy skills. Consequently, the language-supporting activities in Danish child cares may not expose children from low socioeconomic backgrounds to sufficient language-learning opportunities. Having universal enrollment in child cares is, therefore, not enough to attenuate the negative effects of economic disadvantage, these results suggest.

Taking the possible influence of poor language environment into account, the result of a rather low correlation between educational level and vocabulary may be interpreted in a way that vocabulary is rather "robust" against the poor environment. Poorer environments may still provide enough input (perhaps also from other children) to build up a basic vocabulary, but acquisition of grammar, comprehension, and pragmatic skills is not supported sufficiently. This perspective may also explain why children at 36 months have already overcome a possible delay in building up the vocabulary. Both explanations raise the question of whether "late talkers" is a useful category to identify children at risk at 36 months, or whether categories such as "late comprehenders" or "late communicators" may be more relevant.

## CONCLUSIONS

This first portrait of Danish LTs suggests a series of follow-up studies with both basic and applied significance. Due to limitations of data at present, we were not able to shed any light on how persistent the language problems are in Danish LTs. The results from this and other studies suggest that syntactic complexity and inflectional morphology may be more impaired in Danish LTs, and even TD children face problems late in acquisition. The potential role for these linguistic domains as early makers of language delays should therefore be examined in longitudinal studies. We plan to follow the 3-year-old children over the next years to be able to address the question.

Similarly, it would be very interesting to follow the natural history of language delay and relate these data to the acquisition of reading. Children from the CDI Late Talker Study have now passed second grade, and it is therefore possible to link early language development data to reading tests at the national level. Such a study is currently under development.

Finally, more studies of the quality of the home learning environment and pre-school/child care instructional quality and their potential role in language development are strongly needed. Two large intervention studies that are currently underway will provide some answers.

## REFERENCES

Bauchmüller, R., Gørtz, M., & Rasmussen, A.W. (2011). *Long-run benefits from universal high-quality pre-schooling.* Retrieved from http://www.akf.dk/udgivelser_en/container/2011/udgivelse_1098/#

Bishop, D.V., Price, T.S., Dale, P.S., & Plomin, R. (2003). Outcomes of early language delay: II. Etiology of transient and persistent language difficulties. *Journal of Speech, Language, and Hearing Research, 46,* 561–575.

Bleses, D., Basbøll, H., Lum, J., & Vach, W. (2010). Phonology and lexicon in a cross-linguistic perspective: The importance of phonetics–a commentary on Stoel-Gammon's 'Relationships between lexical and phonological development in young children'. *Journal of Child Language, 38*(1), 61–68.

Bleses, D., Basbøll, H., & Vach, W. (2011). Is Danish difficult to acquire? Evidence from Scandinavian past tense studies. *Language and Cognitive processes, 26,* 1193–1231.

Bleses, D., Højen, A., Jørgensen, R.N., Jensen, K.Ø., & Vach, W. (2010). *Sprogvurdering af 3-årige (09): karakteristika og risikofaktorer.* Retrieved from http://www.cfb.sdu.dk/DK/forsk/doc/E-print_10_2010.pdf

Bleses, D., Lum, J., Højen, A., Jørgensen, R., Iachine, I., Andersen, M.K., . . . Vach, W. (2011). *Sprogvurderingsmateriale til 3-årige, Inden skolestart og i Børnehaveklassen. Metodisk oversigt.* Retrieved from http://www.cfb.sdu.dk/DK/forsk/doc/E-print_13_2011.pdf

Bleses, D., Vach, W., Jørgensen, R.N., & Worm, T. (2010). The internal validity and acceptability of the Danish SI-3: A language screening instrument for 3-year-olds. *Journal of Speech, Language, and Hearing Research, 53,* 490–507.

Bleses, D., Vach, W., Slott, M., Wehberg, S., Thomsen, P., Madsen, T., & Basbøll, H. (2008a). The Danish Communicative Development Inventories: Validity and main developmental trends. *Journal of Child Language, 35,* 651–669.

Bleses, D., Vach, W., Slott, M., Wehberg, S., Thomsen, P., Madsen, T., & Basbøll, H. (2008b). Early vocabulary development in Danish and other languages: A CDI-based comparison. *Journal of Child Language, 35*(3), 619–650.

Bleses, D., Vach, W., & Wehberg, S. (2008). Individuelle forskelle i danske børns tidlige sprogtilegnelse: Hvad kan børne- og forældrerelaterede baggrundsfaktorer forklare? *Psyke og Logos, 2,* 512–537.

Bricker, D., & Squires, J., with Mounts, L., Potter, L., Nickel, R., Twombly, E., & Farrell, J. (1999). *Ages & Stages Questionnaires® (ASQ): A parent-completed, child-monitoring system* (2nd ed.). Baltimore, MD: Paul H. Brookes Publishing Co.

Burchinal, M., Vandergrift, N., Pianta, R., & Mashburn, A. (2010). Threshold analysis of association between child care quality and child outcomes for low-income children in pre-kindergarten programs. *Early Childhood Research Quarterly, 25*(2), 166–176.

Christensen, E., Socialforskningsinstituttet [Danish National Institute of Social Research], & Arv, S. (2004). *7 års børneliv.* Copenhagen, Denmark: Socialforskningsinstituttet.

Dale, P.S., Price, T.S., Bishop, D.V.M., & Plomin, R. (2003). Outcomes of Early Language Delay I. Predicting Persistent and Transient Language Difficulties at 3 and 4 Years. *Journal of Speech, Language, and Hearing Research, 46*(3), 544–560.

Desmarais, C., Sylvestre, A., Meyer, F., Bairati, I., & Rouleau, N. (2008). Systematic review of the literature on characteristics of late-talking toddlers. *International Journal of Language & Communication Disorders, 43*(4), 361–389. doi: 10.1080/13682820701546854

Desmarais, C., Sylvestre, A., Meyer, F., Bairati, I., & Rouleau, N. (2010). Three profiles of language abilities in toddlers with an expressive vocabulary delay: Variations on a theme. *Journal of Speech, Language, and Hearing Research, 53*(3), 699–709.

Fenson, L., Marchman, V.A., Thal, D.J., Dale, P.S., Reznick, J.S., & Bates, E. (2007). *MacArthur-Bates Communicative Development Inventories (CDIs)* (2nd ed.). Baltimore, MD: Paul H. Brookes Publishing Co.

Fernald, A. (2010). Getting beyond the "convenience sample" in research on early cognitive development. *Behavioral and Brain Sciences, 33*(2–3), 91–92.

Geoffroy, M.C., Côté, S.M., Giguère, C.É., Dionne, G., Zelazo, P.D., Tremblay, R.E., . . . Séguin, J.R. (2010). Closing the gap in academic readiness and achievement: The role of early childcare. *Journal of Child Psychology and Psychiatry, 51*(12), 1359–1367.

Hall, J., Sylva, K., Melhuish, E., Sammons, P., Siraj-Blatchford, I., & Taggart, B. (2009). The role of pre-school quality in promoting resilience in the cognitive development of young children. *Oxford Review of Education, 35*(3), 331–352.

Hart, B., & Risley, T.R. (1995). *Meaningful differences in the everyday experience of young American children.* Baltimore, MD: Paul H. Brookes Publishing Co.

Henrichs, J., Rescorla, L., Schenk, J.J., Schmidt, H.G., Jaddoe, V.W.V., Hofman, A., . . . Tiemeier, H. (2011). Examining continuity of early expressive vocabulary development: The Generation R Study. *Journal of Speech, Language, and Hearing Research, 54*(3), 854–869.

Hoff, E. (2003). The specificity of environmental influence: Socioeconomic status affects early vocabulary development via maternal speech. *Child Development, 74*(5), 1368–1378.

Hoff, E. (2013). Interpreting the early language trajectories of children from low-SES and language minority homes: Implications for closing achievement gaps. *Developmental Psychology, 49*(1), 4–14.

Horwitz, S., Irwin, J.R., Briggs-Gowan, M.J., Bosson Heenan, J.M., Mendoza, J., & Carter, A.S. (2003). Language delay in a community cohort of young children. *Journal of the American Academy of Child & Adolescent Psychiatry, 42*(8), 932–940.

Huttenlocher, J., Waterfall, H., Vasilyeva, M., Vevea, J., & Hedges, L.V. (2010). Sources of variability in children's language growth. *Cognitive Psychology, 61*(4), 343–365.

Jespersen, O. (1916). *Nutidssprog hos börn og voxne.* Copenhagen/Christiania: Gyldendal.

Klee, T., Carson, D.K., Gavin, W.J., Hall, L., Kent, A., & Reece, S. (1998). Concurrent and predictive validity of an early language screening program. *Journal of Speech, Language, and Hearing Research, 41*(3), 627–641.

Kristoffersen, K.E., Simonsen, H.G., Bleses, D., Wehberg, S., Jørgensen, R.N., Eiesland, E.L.I.A., & Henriksen, L.Y. (2012). The use of the Internet in collecting CDI data—An example from Norway. *Journal of Child Language.* Available from http://journals. cambridge.org/action/displayAbstract?fromPage=online&aid=8584096

Lum, J.A.G., & Bleses, D. (2012). Declarative and procedural memory in Danish speaking children with specific language impairment. *Journal of Communication Disorders, 45*(1), 46–58.

Melhuish, E.C., Phan, M.B., Sylva, K., Sammons, P., Siraj-Blatchford, I., & Taggart, B. (2008). Effects of the home learning environment and preschool center experience upon literacy and numeracy development in early primary school. *Journal of Social Issues, 64*(1), 95–114.

Organisation for Economic Co-operation and Development. (2011). *Enrollment in childcare and pre-schools.* Retrieved from http://www.oecd.org/els/socialpoliciesanddata/37864698.pdf

Organisation for Economic Co-operation and Development. (2012). *Educational attainment by average years spent in formal education.* Retrieved from http://www.oecd. org/els/familiesandchildren/CO3.1%20Educational%20attainment%20by%20gender%20 -%20updated%20051012.pdf

Paul, R., & Shiffer, M.E. (1991). Communicative initiations in normal and late-talking toddlers. *Applied Psycholinguistics, 12*(4), 419–431.

Reilly, S., Wake, M., Bavin, E.L., Prior, M., Williams, J., Bretherton, L., . . . Ukoumunne, O.C. (2007). Predicting language at 2 years of age: A prospective community study. *Pediatrics, 120*(6), e1441–e1449.

Rescorla, L. (1989). The Language Development Survey: A screening tool for delayed language in toddlers. *Journal of Speech and Hearing Disorders, 54*(4), 587–599.

Rescorla, L., & Alley, A. (2001). Validation of the Language Development Survey (LDS): A parent report tool for identifying language delay in toddlers. *Journal of Speech, Language, and Hearing Research, 44*(2), 434–445.

Rescorla, L., Dahlsgaard, K., & Roberts, J. (2000). Late-talking toddlers: MLU and IPSyn outcomes at 3;0 and 4;0. *Journal of Child Language, 27*(3), 643–664.

Rescorla, L., & Merrin, L. (1998). Communicative intent in late-talking toddlers. *Applied Psycholinguistics, 19,* 393–414.

Reynell, J. (1977). *Manual for the Reynell Developmental Language Scales* (Revised). Windsor, United Kingdom: National Foundation for Educational Research.

Rice, M.L., Taylor, C.L., & Zubrick, S.R. (2008). Language outcomes of 7-year-old children with or without a history of late language emergence at 24 months. *Journal of Speech, Language, and Hearing Research, 51*(2), 394–407.

Vach, W., Bleses, D., & Jørgensen, R.N. (2010). Construction of a Danish CDI short form for language screening at the age of 36 months: Methodological considerations and results. *Clinical Linguistics & Phonetics, 24*(8), 602–621.

Vandell, D.L., Belsky, J., Burchinal, M., Steinberg, L., & Vandergrift, N. (2010). Do effects of early child care extend to age 15 years? Results from the NICHD study of early child care and youth development. *Child Development, 81*(3), 737–756.

Vasilyeva, M., & Waterfall, H. (2011). *Variability in language development: Relation to socioeconomic status and environmental input.* In S. Neuman & D. Dickinson (Eds.), *Handbook of early literacy research* (Vol. 3). New York, NY: Guildford Press.

Wehberg, S., Vach, W., Bleses, D., Thomsen, P., Madsen, T.O., & Basbøll, H. (2007). Danish children's first words: Analysing longitudinal data based on monthly CDI parental reports. *First Language, 27*(4), 361–383.

Wehberg, S., Vach, W., Bleses, D., Thomsen, P., Madsen, T.O., & Basbøll, H. (2008). Girls talk about dolls and boys about cars? Analyses of group and individual variation in Danish children's first words. *First Language, 28*(1), 71–85.

Zubrick, S.R., Taylor, C.L., Rice, M.L., & Slegers, D.W. (2007). Late language emergence at 24 months: An epidemiological study of prevalence, predictors, and covariates. *Journal of Speech, Language, and Hearing Research, 50,* 1562–1592.

# 4

# Distinguishing the Bilingual as a Late Talker from the Late Talker Who Is Bilingual

Barbara Zurer Pearson

In the folk-wisdom on the subject, bilingual input to an infant is considered a reason for late emergence of language. If a bilingual-learning child appears to be late in producing first words, for example, it is common to hear, "But of course, she (or he) is bilingual." This chapter digs for the kernel of truth in this widespread opinion but also questions whether bilingual input by itself can be a cause for slowing down the universal process of learning to talk. What are the issues that need to be resolved in order to identify late talkers among children growing up in bilingual environments? What factors make it harder to differentiate genuine late talkers among bilinguals than among children growing up monolingually? How can difficulties in assessment be overcome, or at least taken into account, so that typical bilingual development will not be confused with language deficit or delay while children from bilingual homes who would benefit from intervention are not overlooked?

## TWO MEANINGS OF *EMERGENCE:* ONSETS AND INVENTORIES

First, recall that the focus of this book is language *emergence* and what we can learn about children whose *first* steps in language come later than their peers'. Because the large majority of children are using language—producing words and sentences and engaging in conversations—by age 3, the focus of this discussion will be children who have regular exposure to two (or more) languages during their first 3 years. Such children are generally considered *simultaneous* or *infant* bilinguals, although there is opportunity even by age 3 for one of the languages to be established before the other. Therefore, even in this young age range, there may be a subgroup one could call *sequential bilinguals* or *early second language learners* (Pearson & Fernández, 1994).

Clarifying what can be meant by *emergence* and how its different meanings can inform our discussion of bilingual timetables is more complex. In one sense of the term, language acquisition is marked by a series of *qualitative* changes, or *onsets,* experienced as category shifts. For example, before children start producing mature syllables consisting of a well-formed consonant and a vowel, such as [da] or [baba], their overall phonetic output can be described, using Oller's terms, as mostly quasi-vocalic or vocalic, with transitions between proto-consonants and vowels that are slower than in adult speech, as in the difference between [b-waa] and [ba] (Oller, 1980). A careful observer can pinpoint the day when a child's vocalizations first fulfill the physical parameters of pitch and duration that characterize mature syllables, also called canonical syllables, which are the building blocks for words in all of the world's languages (Oller, 2000). The older precanonical vocalizations continue to coexist with the newer ones, even in adult speech to a lesser extent. But we call the shift "qualitative" because the new behavior, canonical babbling, is not an added instance of the prior skill; it is a new skill added to the child's repertory. With allowances for imprecision in our observations, qualitative changes in children's vocal and symbolic behavior are either observed, or they are not observed. Relative timetables can be determined based on average onsets across groups, and judgments can be made of whether the child is meeting expectations.

By contrast, other changes in linguistic behavior are measured *quantitatively,* and progress is generally described in terms of the size of the child's *inventories* of language units, such as the number of different syllable types, or the number of different words or word endings (morphosyntax). Comparisons between children or within the same child in different languages and/or at different times can be made in terms of inventory size. For example, one child might have 10 words at a given age while another child has 100 words, or one child's longest utterance might comprise four morphemes at one age point and six morphemes at a later age point.[1]

Bilingual input does not appear to impair the ability to learn and use language. As many researchers have noted, when taking children's achievements across two languages into account, the combined inventories of bilingual children's two languages show parity with monolingual benchmarks (Hoff et al., 2012; Pearson, Fernández, & Oller, 1993; Petitto et al., 2001). As long as both languages combined are taken into account, bilinguals typically need no different measures for either onsets or inventories to reflect their full language knowledge. However, when single-language measures are the focus, there is a potential for smaller inventories in at least one language for children whose total input and output are divided among two or more languages. Furthermore, many linkages between developments have been shown to rely on language-specific learning, so increasingly, quantitative precursors in a language are linked to growth *in that same language* (Conboy & Thal, 2006; Marchman, Fernald, & Hurtado, 2010; Marchman, Martínez-Sussmann, & Dale, 2004; Simon-Cereijido & Gutiérrez-Clellen, 2009). For these reasons, expectations for inventory sizes may differ between monolinguals and bilinguals, and the determination of "on-time emergence" will depend on the standard used to establish what is "average."

---

[1]The qualitative-quantitative distinction is not a complete dichotomy. One example of the fuzziness of the distinction is seen with inventories of early vocabulary, in which there are words within the inventories that are qualitatively different—content words that are chiefly names for things and events are less complex in their usage than are function words (e.g., prepositions, determiners, conjunctions). But, typically, quantitative measures count units equally.

## EXTERNAL VERSUS INTERNAL FACTORS
## AFFECTING LINGUISTIC DEVELOPMENT

In considering the basis for appropriate timetables for monolingual and bilingual development, we distinguish the effects of external and internal influences. Factors *external* to children involve children's environments and the extent to which others do or do not support their linguistic development, whereas *internal* factors derive from facts about children themselves and their abilities. If the source of an apparent delay can be traced to factors external to the child (e.g., in the characteristics of their input), it will be important not to use a pattern of slower emergence in one or even two languages as a basis to infer lesser linguistic capabilities for the child. For reasons that are discussed in the second part of this chapter, language sciences have not yet succeeded in establishing normative timetables calibrated on the bilingual experience. All language development—qualitative and quantitative—is based on the learner's language experience, but this chapter proposes to show that quantitative measures are more sensitive than qualitative changes to variations of input in typical experiences. Therefore, greater impact is expected of bilingual input on language outcomes measured quantitatively—that is, on inventories rather than onsets.

Especially vexing, as discussed later in this chapter, is the inadequacy of current norms to capture the complexity of the bilingual experience. Monolingual norms are almost always used to evaluate bilinguals, with no consideration for how the task being measured may be different for monolingual and bilingual speakers (Pearson, 1998). Also as discussed next, in a few cases in which bilingual performance was taken as the measurement standard, it was the monolinguals who fell short. Therefore, for many aspects of language, the suitability of the norms must be questioned. Also, monolingual–bilingual differences may be lesser or greater at different stages of development (Gathercole, 2002a, 2002b, 2002c; Golberg, Paradis, & Crago, 2008), so length of exposure to a language may be a better basis for determining expected levels of performance than the more typical practice of using chronological age. (It is a separate question whether the average bilingual timetable warrants intervention in some academic contexts.)

## THE GOALS OF THIS CHAPTER

In this chapter, we consider 1) the qualitative and quantitative senses of language emergence separately and examine how they unfold in various bilingual environments[2] as well as 2) some added difficulties the additional language(s) of bilingual speakers pose for assessment, complicating the choice of what should be tested and who the appropriate comparison group should be. Finally, we make suggestions for identifying and treating delayed bilingual language learners from birth to 3 years.

---

[2]In considering bilingual environments as having less input of a given language than a monolingual environment, we are not saying that all bilinguals have less single-language input than all monolinguals— merely that a given bilingual with input in two or more languages has less input in a language than he or she would were all the input in that language.

## QUALITATIVE STEPS IN LANGUAGE EMERGENCE: ONSET MILESTONES

By around age 3, most children have reached at least three major onset milestones: the emergence of syllables, words, and two-word combinations. Mature syllables appear in babble around the same time as teeth, at about 6 or 7 months; words appear, like first steps, around the first birthday; and children form their first two-word combinations around 18–30 months, as they move beyond toddlerhood. Like the physical and motor developments that are observed in all human societies on a universal timetable, linguistic onset times are relatively fixed, but there are wide ranges around the averages, almost as large as the intervals between stages.

### External and Internal Factors Affecting Onsets

An extreme example of an external factor influencing onsets would be the absence of human language in the child's environment. Thus, in the case of *feral* children, who somehow survive in a world without human caregivers, the child has no language models and there is no onset of even one language (Curtiss, 1988). A bilingual timetable is moot, as there can be no bilingual learning in circumstances that do not support learning even one language. In less drastic contexts, the timetable for development will depend less on the characteristics of the individual learner than on the environment. However, it is still not known with any precision how little of a second language directed to the child would nonetheless be sufficient to initiate and support fluency in the second language for linguistically typical children.

Among internal factors affecting language onsets, the most obvious is a hearing loss, which prevents the child from making use of adequate auditory language stimuli that are almost always present in children's environment (Pinker, 1994). Profound cognitive impairments that prevent children from processing the input they hear can be another child factor preventing on-time language emergence. Some cognitive conditions with consequences for language acquisition are well diagnosed. For example, Down syndrome or other forms of intellectual disability delay the development of language and restrict its scope (Oller, Eilers, Steffens, Lynch, & Urbano, 1994). Other neurological abnormalities may go undetected until language development is at issue. For example, as Oller, Eilers, Neal, and Schwartz (1999) found in an epidemiological study of 11-month-olds identified at birth with risk factors (e.g., prematurity, low birth weight, fetal exposure to drugs), failure to develop language in a timely manner was in some cases the first indicator for such abnormalities.

Internal factors such as deafness or other neurological impairments that may delay language onsets can, and do, co-occur with bilingual input. However, they are no more prevalent among bilinguals than other subgroups. Therefore, one has no reason to expect bilingual learners to show later emergence due to neurological conditions any more than among other subgroups. An exception to this claim might be a tendency for stuttering, which for a time was considered to be exacerbated by bilingual input, but that hypothesis has not been supported empirically (Bernstein Ratner, 2011; Van Borsel, Maes, & Foulon, 2001). In fact, no handicapping conditions unique to bilingual learners are suspected, and none have been observed. Not surprisingly, then, as demonstrated next, bilingual-learning children achieve onset milestones within the same broad but fairly rigid windows as monolingual-learning children.

## Major Onset Milestones

**Syllables**    *Canonical babbling,* or the production of mature syllables, around 5–7 months postnatally is the first evidence of language emergence in production (Oller, 2000). Among monolingual children, conditions that significantly reduce the amount of language addressed to the child, such as low socioeconomic status or extreme poverty, have effects that are seen in inventories of language units (Gathercole & Hoff, 2007; Hoff, 2006) but appear to have little or no effect on the quality of canonical babbling nor the timing of its onset (Oller, Eilers, Basinger, Steffens, & Urbano, 1995). Similarly, the potential neurological immaturity seen with premature birth, which might be expected to delay babbling, is balanced by greater auditory experience. So without a correction for gestational age, premature children babble at the same average age as full-term infants, and, when an age correction is applied, they are more advanced (Eilers et al., 1993), but both measures of the onsets fall within normal limits.

Deafness has more serious effects on canonical babbling. Even profoundly deaf children vocalize spontaneously, and until the 1970s, following Lenneberg, Rebelsky, and Nichols (1965), they were considered to babble like hearing children. However, Oller (1980) proposed a conceptual framework that permitted a more precise description of canonical syllables with which deaf children's vocalizations could be distinguished qualitatively from true canonical babbling. Oller and his colleagues (reported in Oller, 2000) observed that among their study participants with diagnosed profound hearing loss, none achieved canonical babbling before 11 months of age, so they posited 11 months as a cutoff for typical development. Using that criterion, bilinguals are in no way late babblers, and in fact, the average onset for the bilingual subgroup in Oller, Eilers, Urbano, and Cobo-Lewis' (1997) studies was 26.7 weeks, 4 days earlier than the monolingual average and well before the 11-month mark at which one would have cause to worry.

**First Words**    Once children have mastered syllables, which they first use primarily in vocal play (Oller, 2000), it takes as much as another 6 months or more to attach consistent meanings to the syllables and then build them into words (Oller, Levine, Cobo-Lewis, Eilers, & Pearson, 1998). Children's first words are typically the focus of parents' attention, and they have also been examined by several research groups. It is quite well established that bilingual children produce their first words within the same time window as monolingual-learning children, between 8 and 24 months (Pearson, 1998; Petitto et al., 2001).

There is sometimes difficulty distinguishing when a child has achieved true referential words as distinct from prelinguistic vocalizations. For example, some proto-words are more action than symbol: A child's vocalization may be a turn in a specific routine (Nelson, 1985), as when a mother says, "ready, set," and the child adds, "go." The *go* has no meaning outside that phrase and is not used flexibly in other contexts. Thus, it is not a true word. Or, one parent might erroneously count a repetition as a word, whereas another may withhold calling a child's consistent vocalization a word until it sounds like the adult target. In fact, the actual syllables used are less important than the establishment of joint attention around their production. By means of joint attention, a symbolic value is assigned to the vocal (or hand) gesture—the word—and communicated to a hearer.

Anecdotal reports that acquisition of first words was later for a bilingual child may stem from the greater difficulty parents of bilinguals could have in recognizing children's words when they say them. Although some accounts posit lower accuracy in pronunciation for bilinguals (Fabbiano-Smith & Goldstein, 2010), these reports are not consistent with a more focused test of intelligibility by Navarro (1998). Navarro excerpted early words and phrases from tapes of spontaneous speech of monolingual and bilingual toddlers, and she played the excerpts without any context for bilingual listeners. In this format, listeners had to identify the words on the basis of their phonetic form alone. Even from 26-month-old children, well past their first words, listeners could identify the meaning of children's words in Navarro's stimuli only 24% of the time for either language group, compared with 94% for adult utterances in both languages from the same recordings (Navarro, Pearson, Cobo-Lewis, & Oller, 2005). Monolinguals' and bilinguals' utterances without disambiguating context were equally unintelligible.

Thus, in both cases, listeners relied heavily on context to help identify what a child was attempting to say (Navarro et al., 2005). For the monolingual child, listeners' expectations are limited to a single language context, whereas parents of bilinguals have a larger set of possibilities to consider. For example, in interviews about early bilingual language emergence, several parents reported being so focused on a minority language that they did not notice a word in the majority language for several weeks after it appeared (Pearson, 2008).

***Two-Word Combinations***   The third crucial onset in early language development is the beginning of syntax, or two-word combinations. The difference between children's three-word and four-word phrases or sentences is counted here as a quantitative development. So, why do we consider the step from one-word utterances to two-word phrases to be a qualitative shift? As Roeper (2007) explains in his book about the emergence of grammar, it is adding that second word in the combination that propels the child into syntax. The second word requires children to add not just another atomic concept to their utterance, but they must also add a relationship *between the words*. Even in the one-word stage, children show understanding of relationships *between concepts* (Roeper, 2007; see also Anisfeld, Rosenberg, Hoberman, & Gasparini, 1998). For example, when a child says "coat" while pointing to the door, she or he can be commenting on the association between wearing a coat and going outdoors, or may be asking to go outdoors. Dogs, too, show this ability using nonverbal "words," such as carrying a frisbee to the door and whining to be taken out to play. But when children use two words, such as "Mommy coat," they are not only expressing the relationship between Mommy and a coat, but they are also assigning structure to the words used to express the relationship. Just as a *watch pocket* is a kind of pocket and a *pocket watch* is a kind of watch, children's earliest combinations, such as "Mommy sock" or "throw Daddy," assign one word as the head of the combination and the other as its dependent. So from this point, each word in a string of words carries a meaning *in the world* and a structural role *in the utterance*.

Not all multiword utterances indicate that the child has crossed the threshold into the realm of syntax, however. Very commonly, a child (or even an adult second language learner) might use a multiword utterance because she or he failed to segment it into its parts. So, "I like it" could be used as one word without taking its separate elements into consideration. This becomes evident later when the learner uses the "phrase" in combination with other words, such as "I-like-it swing." But saying "Mommy sock" when the child also says "Adam sock" shows that the elements are independent of each other for the child, and a word can be combined with whole categories of other words, not just one (Bloom, 1971). True two-word utterances are a giant step.

Less attention has been devoted to the relative timing of the onset of two-word combinations in bilingual children. Unlike vocabulary, which is universally agreed to depend on both the quantity and quality of input, the development of syntax has been considered innate, and much less dependent on environmental factors (Chomsky, 1965; Lenneberg et al., 1965). More recent theories of language emergence, such as usage-based theories (Tomasello, 2003) or emergentism (e.g., MacWhinney, 1999), may challenge the view of language as innately hard-wired in the brain, but they have not changed the timetable: Canonical babbling is still expected during the first year, first words during the second year, and first phrases by the middle of the third year (Fenson et al., 1994). However, recent papers, such as those by Hoff et al. (2012) and Thordardottir, Rothenberg, Rivard, and Naves (2006), have suggested that a bilingual delay can be observed in the emergence of syntax (e.g., a slower developmental trend in the onset of two-word phrases among children with bilingual input). In Hoff et al.'s study (2012), a group of bilingual 22- to 30-month-olds with a range of different patterns of balance between the languages in their input were shown to be later relative to English monolingual controls in combining words in English and in Spanish. On closer inspection, however, the apparent delay in this milestone disappeared when combining in either language was considered. The numbers of monolingual and bilingual children credited with word combinations at each age (1;10 and 2;2) were the same.

Thordardottir et al. (2006) used a version of the same parent report instruments as in Hoff et al.'s (2012) study to measure children's early vocabulary and syntax but, in their case, for children learning English and French. Unlike Hoff et al. (2012), Thordardottir's study selected a bilingual group that had relatively equal, or balanced, input between the two languages. Furthermore, the bilinguals were compared with both monolingual controls in English and monolingual controls in French. Consistent with Hoff et al.'s findings, even this balanced bilingual group was significantly lower than the English monolinguals with respect to both vocabulary size and a measure of sentence complexity in English. However, the bilingual learners were not reliably different in French from the French monolinguals in either vocabulary or grammar. So, one cannot make a categorical statement about the bilingual group's skills relative to monolinguals in general. Comparisons must be more nuanced and should take possible cross-linguistic differences in languages and language socialization into account.

Indeed, if bilingual input delayed the onset of two-word utterances, parents might choose—if they had a choice—to withhold exposure to a second language until after novel two-word combinations had been observed in the first language. As Hoff et al.'s (2012) data show, however, that precaution is not necessary. When progress in *either* of the children's languages was taken into account, all the bilingual children had made the same syntactic move as the monolinguals at the same ages. However, very few had made it in both languages. Thus, even if we have measured the bilingual child in both languages but consider the languages only one at a time, we would miss the important fact that at the expected age the child produced an utterance with a syntactic description—both a meaning and a structural representation—in at least one language, just as a monolingual child had produced a syntactic utterance in just one language.

## QUANTITATIVE STEPS IN LANGUAGE EMERGENCE: INVENTORIES

The three universal milestones of language emergence discussed so far are category changes: They bring children to a different stage of development, and they appear more paced by maturation than experience (Lidz, 2007; Petitto et al., 2001). By contrast, many incremental changes are also taking place within stages in the process of language emergence. Laboratory techniques developed since the 1970s have been able to demonstrate infants' sophisticated linguistic learning from even before birth, which contributes to inventories of linguistic units. Well before first words, children have been shown to analyze their input for statistical patterns that help them uncover the phonemes of their languages (Aslin, Saffran, & Newport, 1998). In toddlers, the relationship between quantity of words in the child's input and quantity of the child's language output is tight even for monolinguals (Hart & Risley, 1999). For many such quantitative changes, average bilinguals,[3] whose input and output are divided between two or more languages, will often show smaller inventories and later development within the stages defined by the qualitative shifts.

### Variations in Patterns of Input

Consistent with the framework articulated by Pearson et al. (1993), Hoff and her colleagues (2012) sharpen our view of the difference between children's *total* stock of words as opposed to their inventories in each language alone, English in one list and Spanish in another. In Hoff and her colleagues' study, the pattern of single-language results differed among three subgroupings within the bilingual group. The children with the least input in English were on average significantly behind their monolingual peers in English receptive vocabulary. By contrast, the bilinguals with the most input in English had receptive measures that were within around 10% of the monolingual control group's measures—differences that were for the most part not statistically significant. (See also Pearson et al., 1993, and Thordardottir et al., 2006, for French). However, unlike Hoff et al., most studies do not show results separately for bilingual subgroups according to levels of input, such as "Spanish dominant," "English dominant," or "balanced bilingual." Rather, they present a mean for all bilinguals together on the idea that uneven levels of language exposure are randomly distributed, and in a large enough group, input differences will even out (e.g., Bialystok, Luk, Peets, & Yang, 2010). With one mean for the total group, low-input children balance out high-input children, and the pattern for the children with adequate input is obscured. Thus, even when the bilingual subgroup with high levels of input shows no delay, evidence of their adequate performance is not apparent when their data are aggregated with the low-input group's data. The inference

---

[3]*Average bilingual* is a problematic concept, as will be discussed later. Here it is used in a very general sense.

is often drawn that all bilinguals are delayed, even when, as Hoff et al. show, some bilingual subgroups are not. (See also Navarro et al., 2005; Pearson, 2002.)

## Monolingual–Bilingual Differences in Quantitative Measures

***Dynamic Word-Learning Measures***   One domain where bilinguals have been shown to exhibit a delay of several months relative to monolinguals is in the child's ability to use fine-grained phonetic information to aid in word learning. This could easily translate into a slower increase in vocabulary size for children who were poorer at this skill. Stager and Werker (1997) used the *switch paradigm* to discover when children were able to make a new association between a novel sound and a novel object presented to them in a 20-second training video. In the habituation phase of the switch experiment, the child is shown two different videos— for example, one of a molecule model moving from side to side and one of a waterwheel spinning—while words naming the objects are repeated several times. In the test phase, the critical trial comes when the pairing is switched and an auditory stimulus is heard with the wrong object. If the child looks longer at the switched events than the non-switched ones, she or he is credited with having first made the expected association and then noticing that the expectation was not met.

Typically developing (TD) monolingual children showed that they could pair novel labels with novel objects in the context of the experiment at age 14 months if the object labels were phonetically dissimilar (Stager & Werker, 1997). However, when the labels varied by just one phoneme (e.g., a minimal pair such as *bih* and *dih*), 14-month-olds failed, but 17-month-olds were successful (Werker, Fennell, Corcoran, & Stager, 2002). Among bilingual-learning children, the analogous ages were 17 months for dissimilar labels and 20 months for minimal pairs, indicating a 3-month delay (Fennell, Byers-Heinlein, & Werker, 2007).

To confirm whether the apparent delay represented a specific weakness in bilinguals not found in monolinguals, Mattock, Polka, Rvachew, and Krehm (2010) created a bilingual version of the switch experiment. Instead of training the children to make the label-to-object association using monolingual auditory stimuli, they used bilingual stimuli taken from the children's two languages, French and English, spoken by a single bilingual speaker. Half of the training tokens were extracted from a recording in which a nonsense word was embedded in an English carrier phrase: "Look at the *bowce*. That's a great *bowce*" [or *gowce*]). The other half were taken from a tape in which the same nonsense words were embedded in a French carrier phrase: "Regarde la *bowce*. C'est une bonne *bowce*" [or *gowce*]). With bilingual training tokens, the 17-month-old bilingual children made the required associations and learned the labels, whereas the monolinguals of the same age were unable to do so. In follow-up experiments, as expected from previous work, the monolinguals could do the task successfully when the labels were distinguished by a contrast in their own language, but not from the mixed stimuli, nor from a contrast that was phonemic in a different language. The authors interpreted this different timetable as showing bilinguals' greater facility learning from mixed language input. For the monolinguals, the bilingual presentation increased phonetic variability and introduced sounds that did not match the input they were experiencing in their environment. These factors made it harder for them to learn what bilingual children were able to learn. So, advantage was relative. Each group showed superior performance on tasks that were suited to the language-learning challenges that faced them outside the laboratory.

**Phoneme Discrimination**    As shown above, language input trains children's perceptual skills to specific characteristics of the languages to be learned. This *perceptual tuning* has been demonstrated as early as the second half of the first year of life (Werker, Gilbert, Humphrey, & Tees, 1981). Progress in most types of learning comes from adding new skills, but some major early advances in perceptual tuning are inhibitory, so "learning" those things means learning to ignore them. Thus, a corollary of learning the inventory of phoneme contrasts in one's ambient language is learning to ignore differences that are not phonemic in that language. The classic illustration by Werker and her colleagues (1981) is of the child's move away from having a "universal ear" to training an "English ear" or a "Hindi ear." In their experiment, infants at 6–8 months from monolingual English environments could show through a conditioned head-turn response that they distinguished a non-English, Hindi sound contrast that English-speaking adults did not discriminate. In follow-up work with contrasts from Hindi and also the Native American language Salish, Werker and Tees (1984) established that by 10–12 months children had begun to specialize: Monolingual learners had tuned their perception to their native language and, like the adult participants, no longer distinguished nonnative contrasts in this task.

When these phenomena were studied in bilinguals (Bosch & Sebastián-Gallés, 2003), the bilingual-learning children were shown to be later than monolinguals in similarly streamlining the set of phonemic contrasts to which they attended. The bilingual pattern of development was more complex, and so monolinguals' language perception and interpretation appeared to be more efficient. For example, by 4 months of age, monolingual Spanish, monolingual Catalan, and bilingual Spanish and Catalan learners could all distinguish both a Spanish-only and a Catalan-only vowel contrast. By 9 months, the Spanish children had advanced to the point where they no longer responded to the Catalan contrast as a difference, and the Catalan children no longer distinguished the Spanish-only phonemes, but the Spanish-Catalan bilinguals still distinguished both sets (Albareda-Castellot, Pons, & Sebastián-Gallés, 2011). So, as with Mattock et al.'s (2010) experiment, progress in these skills was meaningful only in light of the learners' goal.

**Phonological Memory**    Yet another comparison shown to favor monolinguals involves phonological memory, which also appears to be enhanced by amount of phonological experience (S. Gathercole, 2006; Hoff, Core, & Bridges, 2008). Thus, children who have had adequate exposure to the sounds of a language are able to make stronger phonological representations of those sounds and will have better memory for them than children with weaker representations. Memory performance with nonwords is superior when the nonwords are consistent with the phonological structure of one's language (Thorn & S. Gathercole, 1999). Among bilingual learners, for example, children with less exposure to a language than monolingual peers were less able to repeat nonwords based on that language (Parra, Hoff, & Core, 2011). To be sure, some of their relevant experience was language-general and explained variance in both languages. But when shared variance was controlled for, the authors still found language-specific effects that explained 27% of the variance for English and 20% of the variance for Spanish. The implication is that bilinguals will have smaller single-language vocabularies and will have poorer phonological memories to bring to the task of learning more words in that language. Not surprisingly, in S. Gathercole's (2006) and Parra et al.'s (2011) experiments, children with less well-developed phonological memories also had smaller single-language vocabularies, regardless of whether they were monolingual or bilingual.

**Processing Speed**    Another potential advantage for a word learner in either one or two languages is faster speed in processing language input, shown in comprehension tasks. Fernald, Perfors, and Marchman (2006) demonstrated with monolingual learners that a larger vocabulary was associated with faster response times in tests of word comprehension. (See Chapter 8.) But, which came first, the faster processing or the larger vocabulary? It would seem logical to assume that a larger vocabulary is the *consequence* of individual differences in phonological memory or processing speed: that faster and more accurate processing leads over time to a larger vocabulary and slower processing leads to a smaller vocabulary. However, experiments by Fernald and her colleagues (2006) suggested the opposite: They argue that larger vocabularies *enable* faster processing speeds. Fernald's lab used the *looking-while-listening* task to explore this question. Children were shown a display of two pictures—for example, a car and a dog. Then a word was spoken naming one of them. "Look at the____." The child's eye movements after the onset of the label were measured. Trials in which the child was already looking at the picture named when the word was spoken were not counted. The crucial measure was how many milliseconds it took for the child to *switch* his or her gaze to the picture being referred to. Average response times (RTs) to switch one's gaze to the target ranged from 300 to 1,800 milliseconds. Older children and those with larger vocabularies at each age tested had faster response times, and children with smaller vocabularies had slower response times.

Using this method with bilingual children, Marchman, Fernald, and Hurtado (2010) were able to demonstrate that the direction of the influence went from greater vocabulary to increased speed. Forty-nine Spanish- and English-learning children between ages 1;3 and 3;1 did the looking-while-listening task in English and Spanish on separate days about a week apart. The researchers found that RT measures to turn to the target in each language were not associated with each other or with total vocabulary measures (i.e., measures that incorporated Spanish and English in one variable). The only significant correlations were those between RT and vocabulary size *in the same language.* The first-order correlations were almost unchanged in partial correlations that controlled for RT and vocabulary size in the other language, indicating that the relationship observed was independent of individual differences in the other language.

A further analysis, done in each language separately, split children into subgroups of those above and below the median split for vocabulary size in that language. The subgroup analysis within language showed even more clearly the crucial contribution of existing vocabulary to processing speed, as the children with higher vocabularies were significantly faster and more accurate than the low-vocabulary group in the same language. Crucially, *RT was different for the same child in her two languages.* Individual children were faster in the language where they had the larger vocabulary. So, it appears that difference in response time was not just an individual difference, independent of the child's language knowledge. Rather, the child with the larger vocabulary was, perhaps by virtue of the larger vocabulary, better equipped to learn new words more quickly than peers with smaller vocabularies. The more children learned, the more they created a better foundation for learning more.

### Transitory Advantage

At the outset of word learning, skills such as better phonological memory for syllables and faster speech processing for words may be a cause, not a consequence, in that they could provide earlier entrée into the word-learning process. Then, as the child learned more words, the initial advantage would continue to grow in that language, but not for stimuli from another language. This dynamic would soon translate into bilingual children with smaller average single-language vocabularies being outpaced by monolinguals whose single-language vocabularies were larger on average and growing more quickly. Fortunately, we know from studies at later ages that many gaps between monolinguals and bilinguals, such as the one in vocabulary size (Oller & Eilers, 2002), and other syntactic and morphosyntactic learning tend to narrow (Gathercole, 2002a, 2002b, 2002c). So, there must be a mechanism to attenuate the effect.

The mechanism proposed that would allow bilinguals' inventories to eventually be equivalent to monolingual peers' inventories, despite a lesser amount of input, is a *threshold.* Below a threshold, the amount of input will matter, but once a critical mass has been reached and the feature acquired, the amount of input would no longer be crucial (Gathercole, 2002a). The threshold for different language features will be different depending on factors that shift for different constructions, such as opacity of the form-function mappings or segmentation difficulties, as discussed by Gathercole and Hoff (2007). At present, however, the field lacks a means to determine when one might expect a threshold to be reached in different languages for different constructions that display varying degrees of complexity. For example, gender in Spanish is simpler and more quickly acquired than gender in Welsh, where a system of phonological changes, or *mutations,* makes recognition of the forms more difficult (Gathercole & Thomas, 2005). Thus, one can predict that it will take more input to reach the threshold for learning gender in Welsh compared with Spanish. For the most part, we can only speculate about where and when one would expect parity between measures among bilingual and monolingual groups, and where differences would be predicted.

## ASSESSMENT OF BILINGUAL LEARNERS

Even without more precise details for other phenomena, studies such as Gathercole's (2002a, 2002b, 2002c) have established that bilinguals will likely be different on many quantitative measures—that is, inventories of linguistic units in production or of different constructions comprehended. More specifically, in a language in which they have not reached a threshold of sufficient input, bilinguals will have lower scores than monolinguals—to the point that TD bilingual groups have been thought to resemble monolingual children with language impairment (LI; Orgassa & Weerman, 2008; Paradis, 2010). It becomes imperative, then, to locate the boundary between late and on-time emergence. If one does not take the effect of different amounts of input on quantitative measures into account, then bilinguals will be overidentified for language services. Up to what point can parents and professionals be confident that apparent delay is transitory, and after what point should they worry and begin to intervene?

## Boundary Between Typical and At-Risk Development

This section explores efforts in the field of communication disorders to find a means of distinguishing a temporary delay among bilingual learners from a true language delay. Furthermore, if a delay is temporary, can it be predicted how long it will last? Although the focus of this chapter is on simultaneous or very early sequential bilinguals, this section looks at sequential bilinguals at slightly older ages, when long-term patterns will have had time to reveal themselves. Studying older children, we will also be able to see relationships among skills that might not have developed during early language emergence. Thus, we will be able to see which effects of reduced input in bilinguals correlate with other language and cognitive processes and can be used as proxies for measures of those other skills, and which have only local effects and do not generalize to other skills (Oller, Pearson, & Cobo-Lewis, 2007). We propose that many principles derived from children who started learning their second language later than age 3 will nonetheless be applicable to children before age 3, especially for children with very little input in a language, who may be like beginners in that language.

Early on, with very little exposure to a new language, a given bilingual will not have reached the same thresholds in the second language, L2, that she or he would have had there been either more input or earlier input in the new language. (See Footnote 2 in this chapter.) Golberg, Paradis, and Crago (2008) introduced age as "length of time with regular L2 input," rather than time since birth. So, for various quantitative measures, the question becomes, what is the "language age" we expect an emerging bilingual will need in a new language in order to catch up to the monolingual child who has had consistent and exclusive input in that language since birth?

Golberg and her colleagues (2008) asked this question about 5-year-olds because arrival at school at age 5 is for large numbers of children their first exposure to the community language in which they will receive their education and will be most frequently measured. In their western Canadian context, Golberg and her colleagues' bilingual-learning participants achieved standardized scores in receptive vocabulary in the average range by 18 months of English exposure (MOE) and were close to parity with monolinguals by 34 MOE. Language samples from monolingual controls were not available for catch-up measures in expressive vocabulary, but by 34 MOE, the bilingual children were well ahead of monolingual 39-month-olds in a comparison group reported in a different study. Also, they had almost eliminated the difference between their scores and the scores of the monolingual comparison children that existed at age 5 when they had 9 MOE. The researchers' measure of contextually appropriate uses of the word *do* as opposed to its overuse as a general all-purpose verb also showed meaningful progress by 21 MOE.

Paradis (2010) asked the normative question in a more detailed way for syntactic measures. She distinguished a different timetable for structures that are more vulnerable to impairment in monolinguals compared with those that are generally less vulnerable. In her example for TD bilinguals, tense morphemes, especially past /-ed/, which are considered markers for impairment in English (Rice & Wexler, 1996), as opposed to nontense markers (e.g., plural –s and aspectual –ing), showed different timetables of development relative to monolinguals. Both tense and non-tense markers were equally delayed for the young sequential bilinguals at the time of their earliest exposure to the new language. However, the bilinguals' nontense markers surpassed levels for *monolingual children with LI* within 23 months (and hence were no longer in danger of being confused for monolinguals with LI on that structure), whereas the tense markers had improved by 23 MOE but were still well behind nontense markers even at 34 MOE, their last observation point.

In defining the boundary of typical development, then, Paradis (2010) proposed that one must distinguish which elements of the language are vulnerable to impairment among monolingual speakers of that language and expect that bilinguals will also find those structures challenging. Thus, there will be a different set of expectations for those features in particular. A generally applicable strategy proposed by Paradis is to make separate comparisons: comparing TD monolinguals to monolinguals with LI and then comparing TD monolinguals and TD bilinguals to each other. Paradis suggests not comparing the child to be evaluated with either monolinguals with TD or LI but to focus on *the time interval* between monolinguals with LI and TD as a guideline for evaluating delay in bilinguals. That is, one would not conclude that a bilingual child was delayed until the gap between the target child and TD bilingual children was at least as large as the gap observed between TD and LI scores in *monolingual* populations.

## Difficulty Constructing Bilingual Norms

As seen with Hoff et al. (2012), patterns of development were very different for bilinguals depending on the division of input they heard in their two languages. Paradis (2010) added more variability based on geographic context and the relative prestige of the child's first language in different communities. (See also Eilers, Pearson, and Cobo-Lewis, 2006.) Similarly, Scheele, Leseman, and Mayo (2010) pointed to differences attributed to literacy differences between Dutch learners from Turkish homes compared with Dutch learners from Berber-speaking homes. In that case, they argued, the crucial difference was between Turkish, as a written language with a strong literature, and Berber, which is not a written language. In this confusing array of possibilities, who can we adopt as the "standard bilingual"? The simultaneous bilingual in an advantageous environment? Or the sequential bilingual whose first language (L1) carries a stigma and receives no support for its further development? Or a child representing any one of the 1,024 (or $2^{10}$) possible permutations for ten of the most basic parameters of bilingual circumstances which, like *simultaneous* versus *sequential,* vary in just two dimensions (Pearson, 2008; Romaine, 1995)? And in which language should the child be tested? At what point in development (Golberg et al., 2008)?

## Proposals for Bilingual Measures

Feasibility limits proposals for the choice of a reference group and for the methods of making appropriate comparisons. There have been some improvements in terms of recommendations for special bilingual, or *conceptual,* scoring that combines the child's knowledge of two languages—taken from two instruments—into one score (Pearson, 1998). Most recently, researchers like O'Toole and Fletcher (2008; O'Toole, in press) have gone a step further and combined analogous tests in each language into one comprehensive instrument—in their case, the MacArthur-Bates Communicative Development Inventories (CDIs) in Irish and English. They have also taken steps toward establishing a range of bilingual norming groups based on the division of languages in the children's environment, following a practice pioneered by Gathercole, Thomas, and Hughes (2008) in Wales. That is, O'Toole and her colleagues created different norms for children with 1) only the minority language in the home, 2) both minority and majority languages in the home, and 3) only the majority language in the home. As in Wales, the children in O'Toole's community are taught in the minority language in the school and use the majority language in the broader community. In addition, all potential examiners are bilingual, as there are no monolingual Welsh or Irish speakers.

Other efforts have also aimed to develop a bilingual norming group for some skills (e.g. Brownell, 2001), but, as we have argued, one set of norms for a range of bilinguals is still problematic. Peña et al. (n.d.) have been working since the late 1990s to make a standardized test with only one set of norms that can diagnose language delay in a wide spectrum of bilingual 4- to 6-year-olds learning Spanish and English—the Bilingual English-Spanish Assessment, or BESA. (As of this writing, the authors report that the test is essentially complete but it is still not in the public domain.) The BESA adopts a language-neutral approach for testing children in their two languages. Peña et al. propose that all children be tested in the two languages and then the cutoff for a diagnosis of risk for LI be defined with respect to either language. Of four subtests, two in English and two in Spanish, children would be identified as at risk only if they failed at least three parts (i.e., they were slower in both languages compared with the BESA's TD *bilingual*—not monolingual—reference groups).

Gutiérrez-Clellen, a member of the BESA development group, and Simon-Cereijido (2010) established further that nonword repetition (NWR) tests, often considered to be language and dialect-neutral (Dollaghan & Campbell, 1998), also require a bilingual administration. First, such tests are not completely language neutral, in that each language (or dialect, per Seymour, Roeper, & de Villiers, 2003) needs a version of the test that respects its phonological structure (Gutiérrez-Clellen & Simon-Cereijido, 2010). Gutiérrez-Clellen and Simon-Cereijido showed that scores on NWR tests in either language individually were inadequate to identify LI among bilinguals, but in combination—if children failed both the English *and* the Spanish version of the test—the two tests would give reasonable sensitivity, specificity, and likelihood ratios, all standard measures of test adequacy (Dollaghan & Horner, 2011).

## CLINICAL IMPLICATIONS

As Hoff et al. (2012) reported, there are claims in both the scholarly and popular literatures that balanced bilinguals (those with approximately equal input in each language) should be equivalent to monolinguals in every aspect of language development in each language. To the contrary, we see, even in this very short overview, that there are many aspects of language for which such claims will not be true.

That is, many quantitative comparisons between monolinguals and bilinguals will favor the monolinguals. It is important to remember, however, that the terms of such comparisons are generally based on a monolingual norm. For these developments, it will be important to analyze the evidence of linguistic progress in a way that takes the child's bilingual experience into account, as previously discussed, for example, when we saw instances in which the bilingual pattern for specific linguistic skills was used as the reference, and the monolinguals were disadvantaged relative to bilinguals.

Recognizing that there is much more to be accomplished to achieve adequate standards for bilinguals at any age, we nonetheless present the following principles to keep in mind when interpreting results from assessing bilinguals birth to 3 years (and beyond):

1.  When making the determination of late emergence, one needs to clarify what skill or skills are being assessed—whether they are onset milestones or quantitative inventories. Low inventory measures will most likely be transitory, whereas late onsets are more likely to represent a serious problem.

2.  For onset phenomena, counting progress in either language, as with total conceptual scoring (Pearson, 1998), provides an approximation of typicality relative to monolingual standards in which all growth is in one language. Thus, there would be cause for concern if a 30-month-old bilingual child was not combining words in either single language or in mixed utterances.

3.  For inventories of linguistic units, the bilinguals' language history (e.g., *language age* in each language) should be taken into account, and appropriate levels of expectation should be used (Golberg et al., 2008).

4.  If one makes comparisons to monolinguals, such comparisons must be made to monolinguals in each language, as there may be cross-linguistic differences that will lead to different conclusions based on different standards in the different languages (Thordardottir et al., 2006).

5.  Especially when comparing bilingual children's performance on language elements known to be markers of LI in the language being tested, one should follow Paradis' (2010) proposal to calibrate risk for impairment on known gaps between TD and LI monolingual groups.

6.  Because monolingual norms are all that is available, researchers and clinicians will inevitably end up using them with bilinguals, but must do so cautiously. It may be useful to use them descriptively, not prescriptively, following a suggestion by Wyatt (2002).

7.  Generalizing from one skill to general ability should be avoided with bilinguals even when correlations among monolinguals show that one skill may be a reasonable proxy for another. The correlations between subskills is different for bilinguals (Oller et al., 2007). For example, low scores on vocabulary for monolinguals predict low scores on other measures, whereas different measures exhibit fewer interrelationships among bilinguals.

## Balancing Attention to L1 and L2

Looking beyond the stage of language emergence to school entry, one can see that bilingual background, especially when coupled with poverty and low levels of maternal education (Hoff, 2006), can lead to lower scores on single-language vocabulary and grammatical measures. When predictable monolingual/bilingual differences are not taken into account in planning educational programs, dual-language learners can face academic handicaps in monolingual programs (Hoff, 2013). Should bilingual background, then, be considered a qualifying factor for language intervention? If so, what form should interventions for dual-language learners take?

Language enrichments that help parents and teachers optimize their interactions with language learners, such as those from The Hanen Centre (http://www. hanen.org), are helpful in any context. Similarly, interventions and academic programs that capitalize on bilingual children's strengths, such as those by Carlo et al. (2004) or Tabors (2008), have only an upside and little downside. Too often, however, the solution for counteracting reduced input in the majority language is to subtract the child's L1 and focus only on providing input in the L2-majority language.

The dangers of subtractive environments created by an exclusive focus on the L2 have been acknowledged since they were first identified by Lambert (1977). Now, in the face of political movements that distort educational options for dual-language learners, more recent research explores the dangers of *serial monolingualism,* that is, going from being monolingual in one language to being monolingual in another language (Crago, 2006, citing Snow). So-called "L2-monolinguals" (Han, 2010) are neither monolinguals nor bilinguals; they appear to have the disadvantages of both groups and the advantages of neither. They do not have superior academic outcomes in the L2 as Collier and Thomas (2004) and Oller and Eilers (2002) have shown are possible, and they risk worse social outcomes than true bilinguals (Han, 2010; Wong-Fillmore, 1991). Plus, one loses an opportunity for the child to become truly bilingual.

## CONCLUSIONS

Because the human language faculty, or Multilingual Acquisition Device, or "MAD" (Crystal, 2002), is capable of learning many languages, bilingual and monolingual children are equally prepared for the pursuit of multilingualism when they are born. But monolingual children appear to drop back to a monolingual goal by the second half of the first year of life when they cast off their sensitivity to sounds they have not yet heard. By contrast, at the same ages, bilingual-learning children are seen to hold on to their early skills and commit less completely to single-language norms. Therefore, by shutting out evidence that does not make a case in the single language they are learning, monolingual learners may achieve short-term gains through increased efficiency of processing. However, it becomes harder for them later in life when they need to join the multilingual majority in our increasingly globalized world. Early second language learners and some older individuals can overcome the monolingual handicap by learning another language, but the task is more effortful and ultimate attainment generally lower, especially for adults. So many monolinguals never catch up with their bilingual peers in this respect.

# REFERENCES

Albareda-Castellot, B., Pons, F., & Sebastián-Gallés, N. (2011). The acquisition of phonetic categories in bilingual infants: New data from an anticipatory eye movement paradigm. *Developmental Science, 14*(2), 395–401.

Anisfeld, M., Rosenberg, E.S., Hoberman, M.J., & Gasparini, D. (1998). Lexical acceleration coincides with the onset of combinatorial speech. *First Language, 18,* 165–184.

Aslin, R.N., Saffran, J.R., & Newport, E.L. (1998). Computation of conditional probability statistics by human infants. *Psychological Science, 9,* 321–324.

Bernstein Ratner, N. (2011). Fluency. In B.A. Goldstein (Ed.), *Bilingual language development and disorders in Spanish-English speakers* (2nd ed., pp. 311–333). Baltimore, MD: Paul H. Brookes Publishing Co.

Bialystok, E., Luk, G., Peets, K.F., & Yang, S. (2010). Receptive vocabulary differences in monolingual and bilingual children. *Bilingualism: Language and Cognition, 13,* 525–531.

Bloom, L. (1971). Why not pivot grammar? *Journal of Speech and Hearing Disorders, 36,* 40–50.

Bosch, L., & Sebastián-Gallés, N. (2003). Simultaneous bilingualism and the perception of a language-specific vowel contrast in the first year of life. *Language and Speech, 46*(2–3), 217–243.

Brownell, R. (2001). *Spanish-Bilingual Edition: Expressive One-Word Picture Vocabulary Test manual.* Novato, CA: Academic Therapy Publications.

Carlo, M., August, D., McLaughlin, B., Snow, C., Dressler, C., Lipman, D., . . . White, C. (2004). Closing the gap: Addressing the vocabulary needs of English language learners in bilingual and mainstream classrooms. *Reading Research Quarterly, 39*(2), 188–215.

Chomsky, N. (1965). *Aspects of the theory of syntax.* Cambridge, MA: The MIT Press.

Collier, V.P., & Thomas, W.P. (2004). The astounding effectiveness of dual language education for all. *NABE Journal of Research and Practice, 2*(1), 1–19.

Conboy, B.T., & Thal, D.J. (2006). Ties between the lexicon and grammar: Cross-sectional and longitudinal studies of bilingual toddlers. *Child Development, 77,* 712–735.

Crago, M. (2006). Multiple perspectives on research on childhood bilingualism. In P. McCardle & E. Hoff (Eds.), *Childhood bilingualism* (pp. 149–156). Clevedon, United Kingdom: Multilingual Matters.

Crystal, D. (2002). *The language revolution.* Cambridge, United Kingdom: Polity Press.

Curtiss, S. (1988). Abnormal language acquisition and the modularity of language. In F.J. Newmeyer (Ed.), *Linguistics: The Cambridge Survey* (pp. 96–116). Cambridge, United Kingdom: Cambridge University Press.

Dollaghan, C., & Campbell, T. (1998). Nonword repetition and child language impairment. *Journal of Speech and Hearing Research, 41,* 1136–1146.

Dollaghan, C.A., & Horner, E.A. (2011). Bilingual language assessment: A meta-analysis of diagnostic accuracy. *Journal of Speech, Language, and Hearing Research, 54,* 1077–1088. doi:10.1044/1092-4388(2010/10–0093

Eilers, R.E., Oller, D.K., Levine, S., Basinger, D., Lynch, M., & Urbano, R. (1993). The role of prematurity and socioeconomic status in the onset of canonical babbling in infants. *Infant Behavior and Development, 16*(3), 297–315.

Eilers, R.E., Pearson, B.Z., & Cobo-Lewis, A.B. (2006). The social circumstances of childhood bilingualism: The Miami experience. In P. McCardle & E. Hoff (Eds.), *Childhood bilingualism* (pp. 68–90). Clevedon, United Kingdom: Multilingual Matters.

Fabbiano-Smith, L., & Goldstein, B.A. (2010). Phonological acquisition in bilingual Spanish–English speaking children. *Journal of Speech, Language, and Hearing Research, 53,* 160–178.

Fennell, C.T., Byers-Heinlein, K., & Werker, J.F. (2007). Using speech sounds to guide word learning: The case of bilingual infants. *Child Development, 78*(5), 1510–1525.

Fenson, L., Dale, P.S., Reznick, J.S., Bates, E., Thal, D.J., & Pethick, S.J. (1994). Variability in early communicative development. *Monographs of the Society for Research in Child Development, 59*(5), 1–185. Retrieved from http://www.jstor.org/stable/1166093

Fernald, A., Perfors, A., & Marchman, V.A. (2006). Picking up speed in understanding: Speech processing efficiency and vocabulary growth across the second year. *Developmental Psychology 42*(1), 98–116.

Gathercole, S.E. (2006). Nonword repetition and word learning: The nature of the relationship. *Applied Psycholinguistics, 27,* 513–543.

Gathercole, V.M. (2002a). Command of the mass/count distinction in bilingual and monolingual children: An English morphosyntactic distinction. In D.K. Oller & R.E. Eilers (Eds.), *Language and literacy in bilingual children* (pp. 175–206). Clevedon, United Kingdom: Multilingual Matters.

Gathercole, V.M. (2002b). Grammatical gender in bilingual and monolingual children: A Spanish morphosyntactic distinction. In D.K. Oller & R.E. Eilers (Eds.), *Language and literacy in bilingual children* (pp. 207–219). Clevedon, United Kingdom: Multilingual Matters.

Gathercole, V.M. (2002c). Monolingual and bilingual acquisition: Learning different treatments of *that*—Trace phenomena in English and Spanish. In D.K. Oller & R.E. Eilers (Eds.), *Language and literacy in bilingual children* (pp. 220–254). Clevedon, United Kingdom: Multilingual Matters.

Gathercole, V.M., & Hoff, E. (2007). Input and the acquisition of language: Three questions. In E. Hoff & M. Schatz (Eds.), *Blackwell handbook of language development* (pp. 107–127). Malden, MA: Blackwell.

Gathercole, V.M., & Thomas, E. (2005). Minority language survival: Input factors influencing the acquisition of Welsh. In J. Cohen, K.T. McAlister, K. Rolstad, & J. MacSwan (Eds.), *ISB4: Proceedings of the 4th International Symposium on Bilingualism* (pp. 852–874). Somerville, MA: Cascadilla Press.

Gathercole, V.C.M., Thomas, E.M., & Hughes, E. (2008). Designing a normed receptive vocabulary test for bilingual populations: A model from Welsh. *International Journal of Bilingual Education and Bilingualism, 11(*6), 678–720.

Golberg, H., Paradis, J., & Crago, M. (2008). Lexical acquisition over time in minority first language children learning English as a second language. *Applied Psycholinguistics, 29,* 1–25.

Gutiérrez-Clellen, V.F., & Simon-Cereijido, G. (2010). Using nonword repetition tasks for the identification of language impairment in Spanish-English-speaking children: Does the language of assessment matter? *Learning Disabilities Research & Practice,* 25(1), 48–58.

Han, W.J. (2010). Bilingualism and socioemotional well-being. *Children and Youth Services Review, 32,* 720–731. doi:10.1016/j.childyouth.2010.01.009

Hart, B., & Risley, T. (1999). *The social world of children learning to talk.* Baltimore, MD: Paul H. Brookes Publishing Co.

Hoff, E. (2006). How social contexts support and shape language development. *Developmental Review, 26,* 55–88.

Hoff, E. (2013). Interpreting the early language trajectories of children from low-SES and language minority homes: Implications for closing achievement gaps. *Developmental Psychology, 49*(1), 4–14.

Hoff, E., Core, C., & Bridges, K. (2008). Non-word repetition assesses phonological memory and is related to vocabulary development in 20- to 24-month-olds. *Journal of Child Language, 35,* 903–916.

Hoff, E., Core, C., Place, S., Rumiche, R., Señor, M., & Parra, M. (2012). Dual language exposure and early bilingual development. *Journal of Child Language, 39,*1–27. doi:10.1017/S0305000910000759

Lambert, W.E. (1977). Effects of bilingualism on the individual: Cognitive and sociocultural consequences. In P.A. Hornby (Ed.), *Bilingualism: Psychological, social, and educational implications* (pp. 15–28). New York, NY: Academic Press.

Lenneberg, E., Rebelsky, F.G., & Nichols, I.A. (1965). The vocalizations of infants born to deaf and hearing parents. *Vita Humana (Human Development), 8,* 23–37.

Lidz, J. (2007). The abstract nature of syntactic representations. In E. Hoff & M. Shatz (Eds.), *Blackwell handbook of language development* (pp. 277–303). Malden, MA: Blackwell.

MacWhinney, B. (Ed.). (1999). *The emergence of language.* Mahwah, NJ: Lawrence Erlbaum Associates.

Marchman, V.A., Fernald, A., & Hurtado, N. (2010). How vocabulary size in two languages relates to efficiency in spoken word recognition by young Spanish–English bilinguals. *Journal of Child Language, 37*(4), 817–840. doi:10.1017/S0305000909990055

Marchman, V.A., Martínez-Sussmann, C., & Dale, P.S. (2004). The language-specific nature of grammatical development: Evidence from bilingual language learners. *Developmental Science, 7,* 212–224.

Mattock, K., Polka, L., Rvachew, S., & Krehm, M. (2010). The first steps in word learning are easier when the shoes fit: Comparing monolingual and bilingual infants. *Developmental Science, 13*(1), 229–243. doi:10.1111/j.1467-7687.2009.00891.x

Navarro, A. (1998). *Phonetic effects of the ambient language in early speech: Comparisons of monolingual- and bilingual-learning children* (Unpublished doctoral dissertation). Coral Gables, FL: University of Miami.

Navarro, A., Pearson, B.Z., Cobo-Lewis, A.B., & Oller, D.K. (2005). Differentiation in early phonological adaptation? In J. Cohen, K. McAlister, K. Rolstad, & J. MacSwan (Eds.), *ISB4: Proceedings of the 4th International Symposium on Bilingualism* (pp.1690–1702). Somerville, MA: Cascadilla Press.

Nelson, K. (1985). *Making sense: The acquisition of shared meaning.* New York, NY: Academic Press.

Oller, D.K. (1980). The emergence of the sounds of speech in infancy. In G. Yeni-Komshian, J. Kavanagh, & C. Ferguson (Eds.), *Child phonology, Volume 1: Production* (pp. 93–112). New York, NY: Academic Press.

Oller, D.K. (2000). *The emergence of the speech capacity.* Mahwah, NJ: Lawrence Erlbaum Associates.

Oller, D.K., & Eilers, R. (Eds.). (2002). *Language and literacy in bilingual children.* Clevedon, United Kingdom: Multilingual Matters.

Oller, D.K., Eilers, R.E., Basinger, D., Steffens, M.L., & Urbano, R. (1995). Extreme poverty and the development of precursors to the speech capacity. *First Language, 15,* 167–188.

Oller, D.K., Eilers, R.E., Neal, A.R., & Schwartz, H.K. (1999). Precursors to speech in infancy: The prediction of speech and language disorders. *Journal of Communication Disorders, 32*(4), 223–246.

Oller, D.K., Eilers, R.E., Steffens, M., Lynch, M., & Urbano, R. (1994). Speech-like vocalizations in infancy: An evaluation of potential risk factors. *Journal of Child Language, 21,* 33–58.

Oller, D.K., Eilers, R.E., Urbano, R., & Cobo-Lewis, A.B. (1997). Development of precursors to speech in infants exposed to two languages. *Journal of Child Language, 27,* 407–425.

Oller, D.K., Levine, S., Cobo-Lewis, A.B., Eilers, R.E., & Pearson, B.Z. (1998). Vocal precursors to linguistic communication: How babbling is connected to meaningful speech. In R. Paul (Ed.), *Exploring the speech–language connection* (pp. 1–23). Baltimore, MD: Paul H. Brookes Publishing Co.

Oller, D.K., Pearson, B.Z., & Cobo-Lewis, A.B. (2007). Profile effects in early bilingual language and literacy. *Applied Psycholinguistics, 28,* 191–230.

Orgassa, A., & Weerman, F. (2008). Dutch gender in specific language impairment and second language acquisition. *Second Language Research, 24,* 333–364.

O'Toole, C. (in press). Using parent report to assess bilingual vocabulary acquisition: A model from Irish. In V.C. Mueller Gathercole (Ed.), *Bilinguals and assessment: State of the art guide to issues and solutions from around the world.* Clevedon, United Kingdom: Multilingual Matters.

O'Toole, C., & Fletcher, P. (2008). Developing assessment tools for bilingual and minority language acquisitions. *Journal of Clinical Speech and Language Studies, 16,* 12–27.

Paradis, J. (2010). The interface between bilingual development and specific language impairment. (Keynote article). *Applied Psycholinguistics, 31,* 227–252. doi:10.1017/S0142716409990373

Parra, M., Hoff, E., & Core, C. (2011). Relations among language exposure, phonological memory, and language development in Spanish–English bilingually-developing two-year-olds. *Journal of Experimental Child Psychology, 108,* 113–125.

Pearson, B.Z. (1998). Assessing lexical development in bilingual babies and toddlers. *International Journal of Bilingualism, 2,* 347–372.

Pearson, B.Z. (2002). Narrative competence among monolingual and bilingual school children in Miami. In D.K. Oller & R.E. Eilers (Eds.), *Language and literacy in bilingual children* (pp. 135–174). Clevedon, United Kingdom: Multilingual Matters.

Pearson, B.Z. (2008). *Raising a bilingual child.* New York, NY: Random House.

Pearson, B.Z., & Fernández, S.C. (1994). Patterns of interaction in the lexical growth in two languages of bilingual infants and toddlers. *Language Learning, 44,* 617–653.

Pearson, B.Z., Fernández, S.C., & Oller, D.K. (1993). Lexical development in bilingual infants and toddlers: Comparison to monolingual norms. *Language Learning, 43,* 93–120.

Peña, E.D., Gutiérrez-Clellen, V.F., Iglesias, A., Goldstein, B., & Bedore, L.M. (n.d.). *Bilingual English Spanish Assessment (BESA).* Unpublished manuscript.

Petitto, L.A., Katerelos, M., Levy, B.G., Gauna, K., Tetrealt, K., & Ferraroi, V. (2001). Bilingual signed and spoken language acquisition from birth: Implications for the mechanisms underlying early bilingual language acquisition. *Journal of Child Language, 28,* 453–496.

Pinker, S. (1994). *The language instinct.* New York, NY: Harper Perennial.

Rice, M.L., & Wexler, K. (1996). Toward tense as a clinical marker of specific language impairment. *Journal of Speech, Language, and Hearing Research, 39,* 1236–1257.

Roeper, T. (2007). *Prism of grammar.* Cambridge, MA: The MIT Press.

Romaine, S. (1995). *Bilingualism.* Oxford, United Kingdom: Blackwell.

Scheele, A.F., Leseman, P., & Mayo, A.Y. (2010). The home language environment of monolingual and bilingual children and their language proficiency. *Applied Psycholinguistics, 31,*117–140. doi:10.1017/S0142716409990191

Seymour, H., Roeper, T., & de Villiers, J. (2003). *Diagnostic Evaluation of Linguistic Variation, Screening Test.* San Antonio, TX: Harcourt Assessments.

Simon-Cereijido, G., & Gutiérrez-Clellen, V.F. (2009). A cross-linguistic and bilingual evaluation of the interdependence between lexical and grammatical domains. *Applied Psycholinguistics, 30,* 315–338.

Stager, C.L., & Werker, J. (1997). Infants listen for more phonetic detail in speech perception than in word-learning. tasks. *Nature, 388,* 381–382.

Tabors, P. (2008). *One child, two languages: A guide for early childhood educators of children learning English as a second language* (2nd ed). Baltimore, MD: Paul H. Brookes Publishing Co.

Thordardottir, E., Rothenberg, A., Rivard, M., & Naves, R. (2006). Bilingual assessment: Can overall proficiency be estimated from separate measurement of two languages? *Journal of Multilingual Communication Disorders, 4,* 1–21.

Thorn, S.C., & Gathercole, S.E. (1999). Language-specific knowledge and short-term memory in bilingual and non-bilingual children. *Quarterly Journal of Experimental Psychology: Human Experimental Psychology, 52*(2), 303–324.

Tomasello, M. (2003). *Constructing a language: A usage-based theory of language acquisition.* Cambridge, MA: Harvard University Press.

Van Borsel, J., Maes., E., & Foulon, S. (2001). Stuttering and bilingualism: A review. *Journal of Fluency Disorders, 26,* 179–206.

Werker, J.F., Fennell, C.T., Corcoran, K.M., & Stager, C.L. (2002). Infants' ability to learn phonetically similar words: Effects of age and vocabulary size. *Infancy, 3*(1), 1–30.

Werker, J.F., Gilbert, J., Humphrey, H., & Tees, R.C. (1981). Developmental aspects of cross-language speech perception. *Child Development, 52,* 349–355.

Werker, J.F., & Tees, R.C. (1984). Cross-language speech perception: Evidence for perceptual reorganization during the first year of life. *Infant Behavior and Development,7*(1), 49–63. doi:10.1016/S0163–6383(84)80022–3

Wong-Fillmore, L. (1991). When learning a second language means losing the first. *Early Childhood Research Quarterly, 6,* 323–346.

Wyatt, T.A. (2002). Assessing the communicative abilities of clients from diverse cultural and language backgrounds. In D.E. Battle (Ed.), *Communication disorders in multicultural populations* (3rd ed., pp. 415–459). Boston, MA: Butterworth-Heinemann.

# Characteristics
# and Causes

# 5

# Late Talker as a Clinical Category

*A Critical Evaluation*

Christine Dollaghan

T o begin this chapter, we invite you to make a prediction using the data shown in Table 5.1, which came from a large sample of children participating in a research study. The leftmost column of this table lists parent-reported expressive vocabulary sizes for 10 children at 36 months of age obtained using the Language Development Survey (LDS; Rescorla, 1989). To provide some context, both Rescorla and Alley (2001) and Klee et al. (1998) reported that the average vocabulary size on the LDS for children a year younger than those shown in Table 5.1 was more than 175 words, with a standard deviation of about 82 words.

As shown in the middle column, five of the children had significant deficits in receptive vocabulary, defined as standard scores below 80 (approximately the 10th percentile) on the Peabody Picture Vocabulary Test–Revised (PPVT; Dunn & Dunn, 1981); the other five children had PPVT scores of 82 or higher. Note that the PPVT scores from the 10 children are listed from lowest to highest rather than being linked to the list of LDS scores. Your task is to predict which LDS scores go with which PPVT scores.

You could approach this task by random guessing, but you are more likely to seek a pattern in the LDS scores that might suggest which children are likely to have poor PPVT scores. Ranking the LDS scores from lowest to highest, as shown in the right-hand column, immediately reveals a subgroup of five children whose LDS scores are abnormally low, even when compared with children a full year younger. It would be a reasonable strategy to use this pattern as the basis for predicting that the five children with abnormally low LDS scores would be the same five who have low PPVT scores.

The chapter author is grateful to Blair Miller and Melissa Sherman for checking scores included in these analyses.

**Table 5.1.**  Scores from ten 36-month-old children on the Language Development Survey (LDS; Rescorla, 1989) and the Peabody Picture Vocabulary Test–Revised (PPVT; Dunn & Dunn, 1981)

| LDS words | PPVT scores (lowest to highest) | LDS words (lowest to highest) |
|---|---|---|
| 64 | 45 | 47 |
| 56 | 46 | 48 |
| 47 | 59 | 56 |
| 168 | 63 | 64 |
| 77 | 63 | 77 |
| 48 | 82 | 168 |
| 244 | 83 | 171 |
| 171 | 85 | 244 |
| 290 | 87 | 254 |
| 254 | 91 | 290 |

In fact, however, using this pattern would give you an accuracy rate of zero: All five children with low LDS scores had PPVT scores in the normal range, and the five children with higher LDS scores had abnormally low PPVT scores. Random guessing would probably have resulted in a higher accuracy rating than using an apparent subgroup that caught your eye when you organized the data set in a particular way.

This example is intended to illustrate how natural it is for human beings to categorize when faced with a need for prediction; creating categories in the face of uncertainty almost seems to be a basic human need. There is no doubt that categorizing is crucial for both theoretical and clinical endeavors. Bailey (1994, p. 15) noted, "Theory cannot explain much if it is based on an inadequate system of classification"; Haslam and Beck (1994, p. 692) pointed out that valid clinical categories offer "stronger possibilities for determining etiology, mechanism, and differential treatment." Proposing category distinctions, however, is far easier than testing their validity, and the history of science is littered with categories that seemed sensible at the time but ultimately had to be discarded. Meehl (1997), for example, noted that *witch* was an important diagnostic category for Europeans living in the 1400s. More recent years have seen the demise of some categories (e.g., neurasthenia) and the parsing of others (e.g., cancer) into subtypes linked to specific etiologies, treatments, and prognoses (Mukherjee, 2010).

The validity of categories whose primary functions are theoretical may not be considered until contradictory or uninterpretable findings force the development of a new classification scheme. Evaluating the validity of clinical categories, however, is a greater concern (Meehl, 1997) because such categories provide a rationale for treating category members differently from other people, in ways that, however well-intentioned, may be harmful as well as beneficial. For this reason, testing the validity of clinical categories assumes an ethical force that is not present when categories are of purely theoretical interest.

*Late Talker* is an example of a clinical category; it originated in scientific studies of typical language acquisition as a label for otherwise typical children whose parent-reported language skills placed them at the lower end of a normal distribution. A number of terms have been used to characterize such children over the years, including *specific expressive language delay* (Rescorla, 1989), *slow expressive language development* (Paul & Smith, 1993), *expressive type-specific language impairment* (Rescorla, Roberts, & Dahlsgaard, 1997), *expressive language delay* (Rescorla & Alley, 2001), *early language delay* (Dale, Price, Bishop, & Plomin, 2003), *late language emergence* (Zubrick, Taylor, Rice, & Slegers, 2007), and *slow expressive development* (Fasolo, Majorano, & D'Odorico, 2008). Late-talking children who move into the typical range of language performance within a few years have been referred to as late bloomers (Paul & Smith, 1993) or children with a history of expressive language delay (Paul, Murray, Clancy, & Andrews, 1997).

Late talking sometimes has been viewed as a clinical diagnosis warranting direct language intervention; a 2011 draft of the *Diagnostic and Statistical Manual of Mental Disorders, Fifth Edition* (*DSM-5*), posted on the American Psychiatric Association's *DSM-5* web site at that time included a new neurodevelopmental disorder, Late Language Emergence, for which Late Talking was listed as a synonym. Late talking has also been viewed as a provisional diagnosis warranting either indirect clinical service in the form of surveillance, close monitoring, or watchful waiting (Paul, 2000) or direct treatment intended to prevent or lessen the effect of deficits that are anticipated at later ages.

This chapter considers the origins and evolution of the view that *Late Talker* defines a category of clinical concern, and critically evaluates the strength of the evidence supporting this view. In keeping with its status as a category label the phrase, *Late Talker* is capitalized throughout the chapter, but the more general, purely descriptive phrase *late talking* is not.

## ORIGINS OF *LATE TALKER* AS A CLINICAL CATEGORY

Definitions of late talking children have varied somewhat over the years, but all definitions include a small parent-reported expressive vocabulary and an absence of cognitive, perceptual, or other deficits that could explain it. The latter exclusionary criterion is shared with definitions of specific language impairment, specific reading disability, and specific learning disability, all of which stipulate that the child's difficulties be unexpected and/or unexplained by problems in other areas of development. Expressive vocabulary has virtually always been measured using a version of either the LDS (Rescorla, 1989) or the MacArthur Communicative Development Inventories (CDIs; Fenson et al., 1993; later renamed the MacArthur-Bates CDIs; Fenson et al., 2007). Both of these instruments solicit parental recognition judgments (Dale, Bates, Reznick, & Morisset, 1989) concerning several hundred words presented in categorized lists; a 100-word short form of the CDIs has also been employed in some investigations (e.g., Bishop, Price, Dale, & Plomin, 2003; Dale et al., 2003). In addition to judgments concerning expressive vocabulary items, the LDS elicits the parent's recall of up to three of the child's longest spoken multiword utterances, and the CDIs, depending on the child's age, solicit judgments concerning word comprehension, use of gestures, or morphosyntactic constructions (including the three longest spoken utterances). In some studies, information on receptive vocabulary and/or multiword combinations has been incorporated with expressive vocabulary size in setting criteria for late talking.

Initial studies with the CDIs and the LDS in young children who were not suspected of any developmental problems revealed an enormous range of vocabulary sizes. For example, Fenson et al. (1993) reported that 16-month-old girls at the 10th percentile for vocabulary production had just 6 words, whereas those at the 90th percentile had 144 words. Such heterogeneity seems to invite efforts to identify subgroups (Haslam & Beck, 1994), and children falling at the lower end of the normal distribution began to be referred to as Late Talkers (LTs). Assigning a label to a group of individuals that sets them apart from others, even if only by virtue of their location relative to an arbitrary cutoff on a normal distribution, seems to foster an assumption that these groups must differ in other nonarbitrary ways. This assumption in turn motivates studies aimed at identifying other differences between the groups, as well as studies of the associations between the measure used to distinguish the groups and measures of other skills.

Many such studies can be found in the literature on LTs. Statistically significant group mean differences between children below and above the late talking cutoff have been reported on many measures of linguistic, communicative, cognitive, emotional, and other characteristics, assessed concurrently or after intervals ranging from a few weeks to more than 15 years. Differences have generally been found irrespective of the parent-report instrument employed (LDS, CDI, or a combination of these and other measures, e.g., Rice, Taylor, & Zubrick, 2008), the specific threshold for low performance (e.g., ≤ 10th percentile, ≥ −1 standard deviation), or the age at which late talking was identified. (See Desmarais, Sylvestre, Meyer, Bairati, & Rouleau, 2008, for a summary of such findings from studies of LTs identified at age 2.) Similarly, many correlational and regression-based analyses reflecting associations across entire distributions of scores have shown statistically significant relationships between parent-reported expressive vocabulary size and a variety of other measures (e.g., Jones Moyle, Ellis Weismer, Evans, & Lindstrom, 2007; Paul, 2000; Reese & Read, 2000; Rescorla & Achenbach, 2002; Rescorla, Mirak, & Singh, 2000; Rescorla et al., 1997; Whitehurst, Smith, Fischel, Arnold, & Lonigan, 1991; Zubrick et al., 2007).

## LIMITATIONS OF EVIDENCE FROM GROUP-LEVEL ANALYSES

Correlational, regression-based, and group mean comparison studies of LTs can all be thought of as *group-level* analyses, as they concern measures of central tendency and association calculated over a sample that generally includes children along a broad continuum of performance. Such studies unquestionably are of scientific interest, but evidence from group-level analyses has limited relevance with respect to evaluating the validity of a category distinction as applied to individual children. For one thing, because correlations among measures of cognitive skills appear to be the rule rather than the exception (Lykken, 1991), it is not unexpected to find significant links between expressive vocabulary size and scores on other measures that reflect, depend on, or relate to vocabulary skills. Second, as Meehl (1992) noted, when two measures have a nonzero correlation, selecting groups to represent relatively higher and lower scores on one of the measures is virtually guaranteed to result in a group mean difference on the other. Results of the systematic review reported by Desmarais et al. (2008) may illustrate this point. When groups of LTs and controls were compared on measures of early phonological skills, which are strongly associated with early lexical skills, significant group mean differences were found on 11 of 12 contrasts. However, on measures of communication and behavior less directly linked to expressive vocabulary, the groups differed significantly on fewer than half of the comparisons.

## INDIVIDUAL-LEVEL ANALYSES OF CLASSIFICATION ACCURACY

In short, although correlational, regression-based, and group mean comparison studies can provide preliminary evidence concerning a proposed category distinction, such evidence does not address the most fundamental question about a category used for clinical purposes—that is, the extent to which individuals are classified correctly as category members or nonmembers. Evidence on this question requires not group-level analyses, but rather *individual-level* studies in which binary classification decisions according to different measures administered to each individual in a sample are compared directly. One measure, known as the reference standard, is taken to reflect each individual's true status (affected/positive vs. unaffected/negative) with respect to the disorder or deficit of interest. The accuracy of the other measure, known as the index test, is determined by comparing its category assignment for each individual to his or her category assignment according to the reference standard. To avoid the potential for subjective bias, the two measures ideally should be administered to each individual by different examiners, blinded to other sources of information concerning the individual's category assignment.

Results from such individual-level analyses of classification accuracy conventionally are presented in a 2 × 2 contingency table, with the upper left cell containing the number of true positive cases, the upper right cell containing the number of false positive cases, the lower left cell containing the number of false negative cases, and the lower right cell containing the number of true negative cases. Comparisons between binary category assignments of the index and reference measure can be reported using a variety of accuracy metrics, including odds ratios, relative risk ratios, sensitivity and specificity values, positive and negative predictive values, and positive and negative likelihood ratios (LRs; Bossuyt et al., 2003). Point estimates for these values should be accompanied by surrounding confidence intervals (CIs), reflecting the range within which the true accuracy value can be predicted to fall with a specified degree of probability (conventionally 95%). In addition, because accuracy values can vary substantially depending on the nature of the sample for which they are calculated (e.g., the ratio of affected to unaffected individuals in the sample, the severity of those affected, the representativeness of those unaffected), evidence concerning accuracy is best derived from a synthesis across different studies, facilities, and samples.

### Classification Accuracy: Late-Talking Status and Concurrent Language Performance

A relatively small number of investigators (Klee et al., 1998; Paul, Spangle Looney, & Dahm, 1991; Rescorla, 1989; Rescorla & Alley, 2001) have reported on the accuracy of late talking status based on parent report and language performance measured concurrently and directly, at a single point in time. Reference standards in these studies have included a clinical evaluation by a speech-language pathologist and items or sections from tests such as the Reynell Expressive and Receptive Language Scales (Reynell, 1977), the Preschool Language Scale (Zimmerman, Steiner, & Pond, 1992), the Bayley Scales of Infant Development (Bayley, 1969), the Stanford-Binet Intelligence Scale (Terman & Merrill, 1960), and the Vineland Adaptive Behavior Scales (Sparrow et al., 1984). The resulting concurrent accuracy metrics, when reported, have most often been characterized as excellent based on point estimates of sensitivity and specificity exceeding 85% (Klee et al., 1998; Rescorla, 1989; Rescorla & Alley, 2001).

## Classification Accuracy: Late-Talking Status and Subsequent Language Performance

The greatest clinical impetus for identifying children as LTs, however, is the prevention or amelioration of future language-related deficits. In this situation the relevant evidence concerning classification accuracy comes from studies comparing each child's status (LT or not) on an index measure at one age with his or her status (impaired or not) on a reference measure of language obtained at a later age. A number of such investigations have been conducted (e.g., Dale et al., 2003; Heilmann, Ellis Weismer, Evans, & Hollar, 2005; Henrichs et al., 2011; Klee et al., 1998; Westerlund, Berglund, & Eriksson, 2006), but accuracy metrics have varied across investigations, and CIs have rarely been reported. In addition, conclusions about the accuracy with which late talking predicts later outcomes have varied widely, being characterized by some investigators as excellent and effective (e.g., Heilmann et al., 2005; Klee et al., 1998) and by other investigators as disappointing or inadequate (e.g., Dale et al., 2003; Thal, Bates, Goodman, & Jahn-Samilo, 1997; Zubrick et al., 2007). In such a situation, a synthesis of the existing evidence can be very useful (Dollaghan & Horner, 2011).

## A SYNTHESIS OF THE EVIDENCE ON PREDICTIVE CLASSIFICATION ACCURACY

Accordingly, we examined the literature to identify studies providing data that could be used to calculate consistent accuracy metrics and CIs for comparisons between individual children's late talking status at one age and their language performance at least 6 months later. Because we undertook this analysis as an exploration of the available evidence on binary classification accuracy, not as a formal meta-analysis, studies were not excluded if they failed to meet all quality criteria (e.g., blinding of examiners); all studies providing the necessary data were included. The requisite data could take one of two forms: 1) cell frequencies (i.e., the number of true positive, false positive, false negative, and true negative cases) from a 2 × 2 contingency table reflecting binary status on an index measure (LT or not) and binary status on a reference measure of later language (impaired or not); or 2) sample sizes, values for sensitivity and specificity, and/or percentages of children in each group scoring in the affected or unaffected range that could be used to calculate the four cell frequencies. We identified 13 published studies and 1 unpublished investigation providing such data. These studies included a total of 45 comparisons between an index measure of late talking and a language or language-related reference (outcome) measure obtained at a later age. We used these data to generate consistent accuracy metrics and CIs that could be displayed graphically on a forest plot. The two accuracy metrics selected for these analyses were the positive LR and the negative LR.

## Likelihood Ratios

As described by Sackett, Haynes, Guyatt, and Tugwell (1991), an LR expresses the odds that a given index test result (i.e., positive/affected or negative/unaffected) would be expected in an individual who is affected, as opposed to not affected, by the target disorder according to the reference standard. The LR for a positive index test result (also known as the positive LR) is the ratio of the odds of a positive test result in people with the disorder as compared with those without the disorder. In brief, if the positive LR for an index measure is high, a person who obtains a positive score on it is very likely to have the disorder. Of several ways to characterize and calculate the positive LR, the simplest is the following formula: sensitivity/(1-specificity). Conversely, the LR for a negative (unaffected) index test result (also known as the negative LR) is the ratio of the odds of a negative test result in affected individuals as compared with unaffected individuals. If the negative LR for an index measure is low, a person with a negative score on the index test is very unlikely to have the disorder. A simple way to calculate the negative LR is with the following formula: (1-sensitivity)/specificity.

Descriptive guidelines for interpreting LRs have been proposed (e. g., Sackett et al., 1991). For example, when an index measure has a positive LR of 10 or more, a person scoring in the affected range on the index measure is highly likely to be affected on the reference test as well. Conversely, when an index measure has a negative LR of 0.10 or lower, a person scoring in the unaffected range on the index measure is highly likely to be free of the disorder according to the reference test. Positive LR values around 3 and negative LR values around 0.30 have been characterized as somewhat suggestive of the person's status as affected or as unaffected, respectively, but additional testing is required in order to classify the person with confidence. Finally, for both positive and negative LRs, values near 1 indicate that the index measure's classification accuracy is too poor for it to be useful in efforts to categorize a person as being a member of the affected group or as a member of the unaffected group according to the reference measure.

The point estimates for positive and negative LRs provide a starting point for evaluating accuracy, but information about their respective CIs is crucial when considering their potential clinical utility. CIs reflect the precision of a point estimate. If the CI is narrow, the obtained accuracy value is likely to be similar to the true accuracy value; if the CI is wide, there is greater potential for the obtained metric to diverge considerably from the true value. For a positive LR, the important value is the lower bound of the 95% CI, which would ideally be 10 or higher; for a negative LR, the relevant value is the upper bound of the 95% CI, which would ideally be 0.10 or lower.

## Studies and Measures Included in the Synthesis of Evidence

Information on the 14 eligible investigations and the 45 language outcomes to which earlier late talking status was compared is summarized in Table 5.2, which shows for each study the index measure used to define late talking, the reference measure or measures used to define later language deficits, the approximate ages

**Table 5.2.** Studies with their index measure of late talking (LT), reference measure(s) of later language deficits (LD), approximate ages at which LT and LD measures were administered, frequency of true positive (TP), false positive (FP), false negative (FN), and true negative (TN) cases, and sensitivity and specificity values with 95% confidence intervals.

| Study | Index (LT) | Reference (LD) | Age of LT, LD | TP | FP | FN | TN | Sensitivity | Specificity |
|---|---|---|---|---|---|---|---|---|---|
| Dale et al. (2003) – 1 | ≤ 15 words, MCDI:UKSF | ≤ 15th percentile on 2 of 3 measures | 2, 3 years | 326 | 414 | 448 | 5,821 | .42 (.39, .46) | .93 (.93, .94) |
| Dale et al. (2003) – 2 | Same | ≤ 15th percentile on two of three measures | 2, 4 years | 250 | 372 | 514 | 5,536 | .33 (.29, .36) | .94 (.93, .94) |
| Dollaghan (n.d.) – 1 | –1.5 SD, LDS vocabulary | –1.5 SD, PPVT | 3, 4 years | 20 | 50 | 32 | 614 | .38 (.25, .53) | .92 (.90, .94) |
| Dollaghan (n.d.) – 2 | Same | –1.5 SD, PPVT | 3, 6 years | 15 | 54 | 20 | 618 | .43 (.26, .61) | .92 (.90, .94) |
| Ellis Weismer (2007) – 1 | ≤ 10th percentile, MCDI expressive vocabulary | ≥ –1.0 SD, TOLD: P3 speaking quotient | 2.5, 5.5 years | 3 | 37 | 0 | 43 | 1.0 (.29, 1.0) | .54 (.42, .65) |
| Ellis Weismer (2007) – 2 | Same | ≥ –1.0 SD, TOLD: P3 listening quotient | Same | 0 | 40 | 0 | 43 | — | — |
| Heilmann et al. (2005) | ≤ 10th percentile, CDI expressive vocabulary | ≥ –1.0 SD, PLS expressive and MLUm | 2, 2.5 years | 30 | 8 | 7 | 55 | .81 (.65, .92) | .87 (.76, .94) |
| Henrichs et al. (2011) | < 10th percentile, MCDI:NSF expressive vocabulary | < 10th percentile, Dutch LDS vocabulary | 18, 30 months | 96 | 232 | 227 | 3,204 | .30 (.25, .35) | .93 (.92, .94) |
| Klee et al. (1998) | LDS Delay 3 | Clinical SLP evaluation | 2, 3 years | 4 | 3 | 2 | 27 | .67 (.22, .96) | .90 (.74, .98) |
| Paul (2000) | < 50 LDS words | < 10th percentile, DSS for age 6:6 | 2 years, Grade 2 | 5 | 27 | 0 | 27 | 1.0 (.48, 1.0) | .50 (.36, .64) |
| Paul et al. (1997) – 1 | < 50 LDS words | < 10th percentile, DSS for age 6:6 | 2 years, Grade 2 | 5 | 27 | 0 | 27 | 1.0 (.48, 1.0) | .50 (.36, .64) |
| Paul et al. (1997) – 2 | Same | < 10th percentile, TOLD speaking quotient | Same | 3 | 29 | 0 | 27 | 1.0 (.29, 1.0) | .48 (.35, .62) |
| Paul et al. (1997) – 3 | Same | < 10th percentile, TOLD oral vocabulary | Same | 1 | 31 | 0 | 27 | 1.0 (.02, 1.0) | .47 (.33, .60) |

| Study | | | | | | | | | |
|---|---|---|---|---|---|---|---|---|---|
| Paul et al. (1997) – 4 | Same | Same | < 10th percentile, TOLD sentence imitation | 4 | 28 | 0 | 27 | 1.0 (.40, 1.0) | .49 (.35, .63) |
| Paul et al. (1997) – 5 | Same | Same | < 10th percentile, TOLD grammatical completion | 1 | 31 | 1 | 26 | .50 (.01, .99) | .46 (.32, .59) |
| Paul et al. (1997) – 6 | Same | Same | < 10th percentile, TOLD word articulation | 10 | 22 | 3 | 24 | .77 (.46, .95) | .52 (.37, .67) |
| Paul et al. (1997) – 7 | Same | Same | < 10th percentile, TOLD listening quotient | 0 | 32 | 0 | 27 | — | — |
| Paul et al. (1997) – 8 | Same | Same | < 10th percentile, PIAT reading recognition | 0 | 31 | 1 | 26 | .50 (.01, .99) | .46 (.32, .59) |
| Paul et al. (1997) – 9 | Same | Same | < 10th percentile, PIAT reading comprehension | 1 | 31 | 0 | 27 | 1.0 (.02, 1.0) | .47 (.33, .60) |
| Paul et al. (1997) – 10 | Same | Same | < 10th percentile, PIAT spelling | 0 | 32 | 0 | 27 | — | — |
| Paul et al. (1997) – 11 | Same | Same | < 10th percentile, LAC | 2 | 30 | 0 | 27 | 1.0 (.16, 1.0) | .47 (.34, .61) |
| Paul & Smith, 1993 | LDS Delay 3 | 2, 4 years | < 10th percentile, DSS | 13 | 10 | 0 | 22 | 1.0 (.75, 1.0) | .69 (.50, .84) |
| Paul et al. (1991) – 1 | ≤ 10 LDS words, 18–23 months; Delay 3, 24–34 months | 2, 3 years | > –1 SD, VABS expressive language | 10 | 11 | 0 | 21 | 1.0 (.69, 1.0) | .66 (.47, .81) |
| Paul et al. (1991) – 2 | Same | Same | > –1 SD, VABS socialization | 10 | 11 | 0 | 21 | 1.0 (.69, 1.0) | .66 (.47, .81) |
| Paul et al. (1991) – 3 | Same | Same | > –1 SD, VABS receptive | 7 | 14 | 0 | 21 | 1.0 (.59, 1.0) | .60 (.42, .76) |
| Perry Carson et al. (2003) | LDS Delay 3 | 2, 3 years | > –1.0 SD, LEO, LRO, or MLUm | 4 | 2 | 0 | 7 | 1.0 (.40, 1.0) | .78 (.40, .97) |
| Rescorla et al. (1997) – 1 | LDS Delay 3 | 2, 3 years | > –1 SD, EOWPVT | 7 | 27 | 0 | 21 | 1.0 (.59, 1.0) | .44 (.30, .59) |

*(continued)*

**Table 5.2.** *(continued)*

| Study | Index (LT) | Reference (LD) | Age of LT, LD | TP | FP | FN | TN | Sensitivity | Specificity |
|---|---|---|---|---|---|---|---|---|---|
| Rescorla et al. (1997) – 2 | Same | > –1 *SD*, Reynell expressive scale | Same | 14 | 20 | 0 | 21 | 1.0 (.77, 1.0) | .51 (.35, .67) |
| Rescorla et al. (1997) – 3 | Same | > –1 *SD*, MLU | Same | 22 | 12 | 0 | 21 | 1.0 (.85, 1.0) | .64 (.45, .80) |
| Rescorla et al. (1997) – 4 | Same | > –1 *SD*, IPSyn | Same | 26 | 8 | 0 | 21 | 1.0 (.87, 1.0) | .72 (.53, .87) |
| Rice et al. (2008) – 1 | < 70 LDS words or no ASQ word combinations | ≥ –1 *SD*, PPVT-III | 2, 7 years | 6 | 122 | 4 | 105 | .60 (.26, .88) | .46 (.40, .53) |
| Rice et al. (2008) – 2 | Same | ≥ –1 *SD*, TOLD: P3 spoken quotient | Same | 26 | 102 | 12 | 97 | .68 (.51, .82) | .49 (.42, .56) |
| Rice et al. (2008) – 3 | Same | ≥ –1 *SD*, TOLD: P3 syntax quotient | Same | 23 | 105 | 9 | 100 | .72 (.53, .86) | .49 (.42, .56) |
| Rice et al. (2008) – 4 | Same | ≥ –1 *SD*, TOLD: P3 semantics quotient | Same | 24 | 104 | 17 | 92 | .58 (.42, .74) | .47 (.40, .54) |
| Rice et al. (2008) – 5 | Same | ≥ –1 *SD*, MLU | Same | 28 | 97 | 25 | 84 | .53 (.39, .67) | .46 (.39, .54) |
| Rice et al. (2008) – 6 | Same | ≥ –1 *SD*, TEGI 3rd singular | Same | 13 | 114 | 1 | 108 | .93 (.66, 1.0) | .49 (.42, .55) |
| Rice et al. (2008) – 7 | Same | ≥ –1 *SD*, TEGI past tense | Same | 16 | 111 | 4 | 105 | .80 (.56, .94) | .49 (.42, .56) |
| Rice et al. (2008) – 8 | Same | ≥ –1 *SD*, TEGI *BE* copula, auxiliary | Same | 24 | 103 | 14 | 95 | .63 (.46, .78) | .48 (.41, .55) |

| | | | | | | | | |
|---|---|---|---|---|---|---|---|---|
| Rice et al. (2008) –9 | Same | ≥ –1 SD, TEGI DO auxiliary | 19 | 107 | 11 | 97 | .63 (.44, .80) | .48 (.40, .55) |
| Rice et al. (2008) –10 | Same | ≥ –1 SD, TEGI grammatical composite | 14 | 113 | 6 | 103 | .70 (.46, .88) | .48 (.41, .55) |
| Rice et al. (2008) –11 | Same | ≥ –1 SD, TEGI screener composite | 11 | 116 | 2 | 107 | .85 (.55, .98) | .48 (.41, .55) |
| Rice et al. (2008) –12 | Same | ≥ –1 SD, TEGI dropped marker judgment | 29 | 99 | 15 | 94 | .66 (.50, .80) | .49 (.42, .56) |
| Rice et al. (2008) –13 | Same | ≥ –1 SD, TEGI agreement marker judgment | 25 | 103 | 14 | 95 | .64 (.47, .79) | .48 (.41, .55) |
| Rice et al. (2008) –14 | Same | ≥ –1 SD, TEGI dropped –ing judgment | 15 | 113 | 9 | 100 | .62 (.41, .81) | .47 (.40, .54) |
| Thal et al. (1997) | ≤ 10th percentile, CDI expressive vocabulary | ≤ 10th percentile, CDI expressive vocabulary | 2, 2.5 years | 1 | 4 | 0 | 23 | 1.0 (.02, 1.0) | .85 (.66, .96) |

*Note:* Different reference measures from a single study are identified by the number after the publication date, which also identifies that reference measure in Figures 5.1 and 5.2.

*Key:* ASQ, Ages & Stages Questionnaires® (Bricker & Squires, 1999); CDI, MacArthur-Bates Communicative Development Inventory (Fenson et al., 1993); DSS, Developmental Sentence Score (Lee, 1974); EOWPVT, Expressive One-Word Picture Vocabulary Test (Gardner, 1981); IPSyn, Index of Productive Syntax (Scarborough, 1990); LAC, Lindamood Auditory Conceptualization Test (Lindamood & Lindamood, 1979); LDS, Language Development Survey (Rescorla, 1989); LEO, Language Expressive Organization subtest, Mullen Scales of Early Language (Mullen, 1993); LRO, Language Receptive Organization subtest, Mullen Scales of Early Language (Mullen, 1993); MCDI, MacArthur Communicative Development Inventories (Fenson et al., 1993); MCDI:NSF, Dutch version of the MacArthur Short Form Vocabulary Checklist (Zink & Lejaegere, 2003); MCDI:UKSF, MacArthur Communicative Inventory: U.K. Short Form (Dionne, Dale, Boivin, & Plomin, 2003); MLUm, Mean length of utterance in morphemes; PIAT, Peabody Individual Achievement Test (Dunn & Markwardt, 1970); PLS, Preschool Language Scale–Third Edition (Zimmerman, Steiner, & Pond, 1992); PPVT, Peabody Picture Vocabulary Test–Revised (Dunn & Dunn, 1981); PPVT-III, Peabody Picture Vocabulary Test–III (Dunn, Dunn, & Williams, 1997); Reynell, Reynell Developmental Language Scales (Reynell, 1977); TEGI, Rice/Wexler Test of Early Grammatical Impairment (Rice & Wexler, 2001); TOLD, Test of Language Development–Primary (Newcomer & Hammill, 1988); TOLD:P3, Test of Language Development–3 (Primary) (Newcomer & Hammill, 1997); VABS, Vineland Adaptive Behavior Scales (Sparrow et al., 1984).

at which the index and reference measures were administered, and values for cells in the contingency table. The four cell frequencies for each measure were entered into Meta-DiSc software (Zamora, Abraira, Muriel, Khan, & Coomarasamy, 2006), which calculated the sensitivity, specificity, and their corresponding 95% CIs for 42 measures; meaningful sensitivity and specificity values could not be calculated for 3 measures in which two of the four contingency table cells were empty. It is important to consider the sensitivity and specificity values shown in Table 5.2 in conjunction with the lower bounds of their CIs—depending on the size, variability and base rate of affected children in a sample the true values for sensitivity and specificity could be considerably poorer than the observed values. For example, Table 5.2 contains a number of seemingly perfect values (1.00) for sensitivity, but many of these have lower bounds well below 0.50, the level that corresponds to chance agreement for a binary classification task. The point estimates and lower bounds for specificity shown in the table are generally higher, but this is a predictable mathematical feature of samples that contain many more unaffected than affected participants, a common occurrence in studies of late talking given its estimated prevalence of 10%–15%. Indeed, one of the reasons that LR values are preferred as accuracy metrics is that they vary relatively less than do sensitivity and specificity over samples with different base rates (Sackett et al., 1991).

### Forest Plots for Likelihood Ratios

The Meta-DiSc software (Zamora et al., 2006) also calculated positive and negative LRs with their 95% CIs for the 42 measures in Table 5.2 that had sensitivity and specificity values. Note that different reference measures from a single study are identified by numbers corresponding to those shown in Table 5.2. Figure 5.1 shows the results for positive LRs; Figure 5.2 shows results for negative LRs. In addition to numerical values for LRs and CIs, each figure includes a forest plot showing each LR as a closed circle through which a horizontal line corresponding to its 95% CI is drawn. The bottom of each forest plot also shows a pooled LR value (filled diamond) with its 95% CI (vertical dashed lines). However, the pooled value in both instances is associated with a significant Cochran-Q test and a high Inconsistency (I-square) value indicating significant nonrandom variation among measures. Accordingly, the pooled values cannot be interpreted with confidence, and they will not be discussed further (see Higgins & Thompson, 2002).

Turning first to Figure 5.1, recall that a positive LR ideally would have a lower bound of at least 10, the level at which children who are LTs are virtually certain to have later language deficits. Lower bounds around 3 provide some suggestion that LTs might have later language deficits, but additional testing would be needed. Finally, lower bounds around 1 indicate that LTs are no more likely to have later deficit than children who are not LTs, who will be referred to here as Timely Talkers. As Figure 5.1 shows, only six measures had positive LR values with lower bounds greater than 3, and none had a lower bound as high as 6. Lower bounds for many of the remaining measures were near 1, indicating that flipping a coin would be about as accurate as LT status for predicting whether a child would have a language deficit in the future.

For Figure 5.2, recall that a negative LR ideally would have an upper bound no higher than 0.10, the level at which children who are Timely Talkers at an earlier age are virtually certain to have typical language skills later in development.

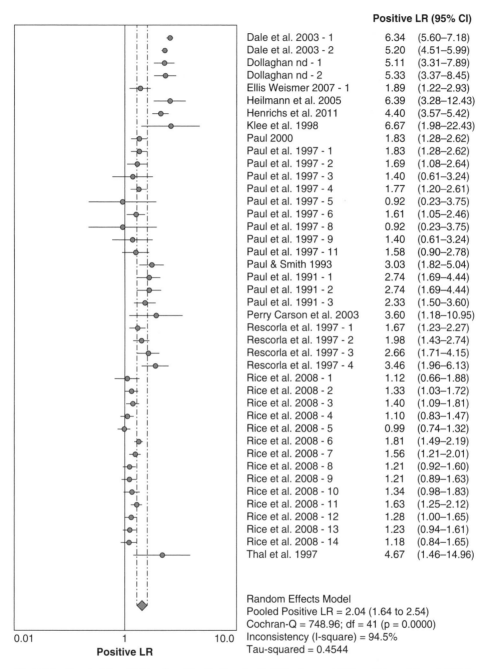

**Figure 5.1.** Forest plot and table of positive likelihood ratio (LR) values and 95% confidence intervals (CIs) for studies and reference measures listed in Table 5.2. Note that meaningful values could not be calculated for 3 of the 45 measures due to empty cells in contingency tables.

Upper bounds around 0.30 can be viewed as somewhat suggestive of typical language outcomes for Timely Talkers, whereas upper bounds around 1 indicate that Timely Talkers are no more likely to have typical language outcomes than are LTs. Figure 5.2 shows that no measure had a negative LR with an upper bound as low as

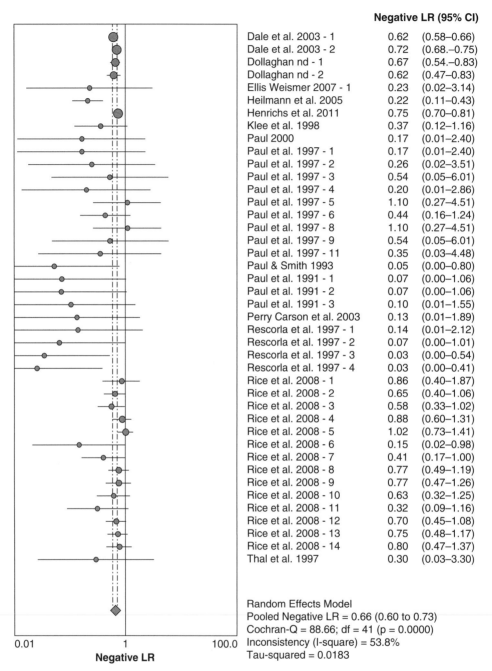

**Negative LR (95% CI)**

| Study | Negative LR | (95% CI) |
|---|---|---|
| Dale et al. 2003 - 1 | 0.62 | (0.58–0.66) |
| Dale et al. 2003 - 2 | 0.72 | (0.68.–0.75) |
| Dollaghan nd - 1 | 0.67 | (0.54.–0.83) |
| Dollaghan nd - 2 | 0.62 | (0.47–0.83) |
| Ellis Weismer 2007 - 1 | 0.23 | (0.02–3.14) |
| Heilmann et al. 2005 | 0.22 | (0.11–0.43) |
| Henrichs et al. 2011 | 0.75 | (0.70–0.81) |
| Klee et al. 1998 | 0.37 | (0.12–1.16) |
| Paul 2000 | 0.17 | (0.01–2.40) |
| Paul et al. 1997 - 1 | 0.17 | (0.01–2.40) |
| Paul et al. 1997 - 2 | 0.26 | (0.02–3.51) |
| Paul et al. 1997 - 3 | 0.54 | (0.05–6.01) |
| Paul et al. 1997 - 4 | 0.20 | (0.01–2.86) |
| Paul et al. 1997 - 5 | 1.10 | (0.27–4.51) |
| Paul et al. 1997 - 6 | 0.44 | (0.16–1.24) |
| Paul et al. 1997 - 8 | 1.10 | (0.27–4.51) |
| Paul et al. 1997 - 9 | 0.54 | (0.05–6.01) |
| Paul et al. 1997 - 11 | 0.35 | (0.03–4.48) |
| Paul & Smith 1993 | 0.05 | (0.00–0.80) |
| Paul et al. 1991 - 1 | 0.07 | (0.00–1.06) |
| Paul et al. 1991 - 2 | 0.07 | (0.00–1.06) |
| Paul et al. 1991 - 3 | 0.10 | (0.01–1.55) |
| Perry Carson et al. 2003 | 0.13 | (0.01–1.89) |
| Rescorla et al. 1997 - 1 | 0.14 | (0.01–2.12) |
| Rescorla et al. 1997 - 2 | 0.07 | (0.00–1.01) |
| Rescorla et al. 1997 - 3 | 0.03 | (0.00–0.54) |
| Rescorla et al. 1997 - 4 | 0.03 | (0.00–0.41) |
| Rice et al. 2008 - 1 | 0.86 | (0.40–1.87) |
| Rice et al. 2008 - 2 | 0.65 | (0.40–1.06) |
| Rice et al. 2008 - 3 | 0.58 | (0.33–1.02) |
| Rice et al. 2008 - 4 | 0.88 | (0.60–1.31) |
| Rice et al. 2008 - 5 | 1.02 | (0.73–1.41) |
| Rice et al. 2008 - 6 | 0.15 | (0.02–0.98) |
| Rice et al. 2008 - 7 | 0.41 | (0.17–1.00) |
| Rice et al. 2008 - 8 | 0.77 | (0.49–1.19) |
| Rice et al. 2008 - 9 | 0.77 | (0.47–1.26) |
| Rice et al. 2008 - 10 | 0.63 | (0.32–1.25) |
| Rice et al. 2008 - 11 | 0.32 | (0.09–1.16) |
| Rice et al. 2008 - 12 | 0.70 | (0.45–1.08) |
| Rice et al. 2008 - 13 | 0.75 | (0.48–1.17) |
| Rice et al. 2008 - 14 | 0.80 | (0.47–1.37) |
| Thal et al. 1997 | 0.30 | (0.03–3.30) |

Random Effects Model
Pooled Negative LR = 0.66 (0.60 to 0.73)
Cochran-Q = 88.66; df = 41 (p = 0.0000)
Inconsistency (I-square) = 53.8%
Tau-squared = 0.0183

0.01                    1                    100.0

**Negative LR**

**Figure 5.2.** Forest plot and table of negative likelihood ratio (LR) values and 95% confidence intervals (CIs) for studies and reference measures listed in Table 5.2. Note that meaningful values could not be calculated for 3 of the 45 measures due to empty cells in contingency tables.

0.30, and only two had upper bounds below 0.50. Many of the remainder had upper bounds at or above 1.0, indicating that Timely Talkers were no more likely than LTs to have typical-range language skills at a later date.

This synthesis of the evidence across varying index tests, outcome measures, and ages shows that the predictive accuracy from early status as a LT or a Timely

Talker to adequate or inadequate language skills even 6 months later is quite poor. This will not surprise the many investigators who have concluded from their individual studies of late talking that there is "no evidence of ability to predict outcome for individual children" (Thal et al., 1997, p. 239; see also Bishop et al., 2003; Dale et al., 2003; Paul, 2000). However, when coupled with previous conclusions, the present findings force us to ask why late talking has continued to command so much attention from researchers and clinicians for so many years. We speculate that several forces might be at work here.

## Potential Reasons for the Persistence of *Late Talker* as a Clinical Category

One such factor seems to be the weight of psychometric tradition, in which, despite numerous caveats (e.g., Freberg, Vandiver, Watkins, & Canivez, 2008; Wechsler, 1991), predictive accuracy has usually been defined in terms of group-level correlations between test scores at different ages rather than in terms of binary classification accuracy at the level of individual children assessed at different points in time. As noted earlier, the correlation between the full distributions of scores obtained at two different ages may be large and statistically significant, such that knowing a person's score at one age enables his or her score at the other age to be broadly predicted with some degree of confidence. However, because correlational analyses do not zero in on the more specific portion of the distribution defined by a binary cutoff value, they provide no evidence concerning binary classification accuracy. And when classification accuracy is assessed directly, late talking is not the only measure from young children for which the evidence is disappointing at best. Dollaghan and Campbell (2009) reported several other language and intelligence measures for which scores at ages 3, 4, and 6 years were significantly and strongly correlated at the group level, but for which binary classification accuracy was quite poor. It appears that additional studies of classification accuracy are urgently needed, not only for late talking but also for other measures of early communication development.

A related factor may be that many developmental behavioral disorders are defined according to a Gaussian model, in which the boundary between normal and abnormal can only be set according to a threshold on a continuous distribution of scores. As discussed by Sackett et al. (1991), such a definition necessarily "medicalizes" all of the individuals falling below the cutoff, whether or not they are distinguished as a group from individuals above the cutoff in some clinically meaningful way. Rescorla (2009), Tomblin (2011), and Dollaghan (2004, 2011) are among the investigators who have suggested that children with specific language impairment do not constitute a qualitatively distinct group but rather represent those at the lower end of a continuous distribution of language skill. Another unfortunate result of using a Gaussian definition of normalcy is the tendency to identify individuals whose scores fall at or just below the cutoff as "borderline cases." Wilson and Jungner (1968) argued that if individuals who obtain borderline scores on a test are informed of their results at all, they should be told that they scored within the normal range, but it appears that the opposite conclusion is often drawn about such individuals in much of the literature on language impairment. Although a lack of responsiveness to adequate instruction, rather than an arbitrary threshold on the normal curve, is increasingly used to distinguish school-age children developing typically from those with specific learning disabilities, the Gaussian tradition continues to dominate in the literature concerning younger children.

## Early Identification and Screening: Balancing Benefits and Harms

A final potential factor contributing to the persistence of the view that late talking is a category of clinical interest might be the assumption that the benefits of early identification efforts will outweigh their harms. With few exceptions (e.g., Klee, Pearce, & Carson, 2000; Paul, 2000) the question of whether early identification efforts might be harmful rarely arises in the literature on developmental communication disorders. Probably not coincidentally it appears that empirical evidence concerning the adverse effects of screening is virtually nonexistent. For example, in a systematic review of the evidence from more than 700 studies of brief (≤ 10 min) screening protocols for identifying speech and language delay in preschoolers free of comorbid conditions such as hearing or neurological impairments, Nelson, Nygren, Walker, and Panoscha (2006) found limited evidence concerning accuracy or benefits of screening and no studies addressing its adverse effects.

The situation is different in medicine, in which the balance of benefits and harms associated with a clinical classification test is often evaluated using factors such as the test's accuracy and cost, the availability of effective treatments, and whether testing was sought by the individual or was mandated by the public health system (Juth & Munthe, 2012). The evaluation of benefits and harms is especially complicated, and evidence concerning accuracy is especially important, for screening tests administered to identify future cases of disease among asymptomatic or latent-stage individuals who consider themselves healthy. If early detection efforts are perfectly accurate, benefits of screening should certainly outweigh harms for true positive cases if it enables such individuals to receive effective treatment more promptly than they would have otherwise. When a screening test for asymptomatic individuals is inaccurate, however, potential harms to misclassified individuals are obvious. False positive cases might incur unnecessary emotional distress, clinical procedures, and financial obligations (e.g., Shickle & Chadwick, 1994); false negative cases might not be treated as promptly as would be ideal.

Concerns about the special ethical issues surrounding early detection efforts led Wilson and Jungner (1968, pp. 26–27) to propose the following 10 criteria as a way to stimulate discussion about benefits and harms prior to a decision to implement a screening program:

1. The condition sought should be an important health problem.

2. There should be an accepted treatment for patients with recognized disease.

3. Facilities for diagnosis and treatment should be available.

4. There should be a recognizable latent or early symptomatic stage.

5. There should be a suitable test or examination.

6. The test should be acceptable to the population.

7. The natural history of the condition, including development from latent to declared disease, should be adequately understood.

8. There should be an agreed policy on whom to treat as patients.

9. The cost of case-finding (including diagnosis and treatment of patients diagnosed) should be economically balanced in relation to possible expenditure on medical care as a whole.

10. Case-finding should be a continuing process and not a "once and for all" project.

Shickle and Chadwick (1994) noted that no screening program is likely to meet all of these criteria, nor has a system for ranking their importance been proposed. Nonetheless, these "ten commandments of screening" (Juth & Munthe, 2012, p. 4) have often been endorsed over the ensuing years. For example, in a white paper on the ethics of newborn screening, the President's Council on Bioethics (2008, p. 105) concluded that screening programs that fail to meet the Wilson and Jungner criteria should not be mandatory but that such programs may be offered to parents under a research paradigm, "presented forthrightly as pilot studies, whose benefits and risks to the infant are not certain, and for which IRB approval should be obtained."

The Wilson and Jungner (1968) criteria seem rarely to have been discussed with respect to early detection of developmental behavioral disorders, including language impairment, and it is worth examining the extent to which the effort to identify LTs as a clinical category would meet them. There seems to be little doubt that language impairment is an important health problem, and measures of late talking certainly seem to be acceptable based on their widespread use around the world. There also exists considerable evidence that treatment to increase the size of children's spoken vocabularies is effective, although whether such early treatment actually changes the course of the disorder (Wilson & Jungner, 1968) remains unknown. Evidence is also needed concerning economics of providing clinical services in the form of increased surveillance, follow-up testing, or direct treatment for children identified as LTs, particularly in relation to children with other health care needs who must compete for finite health care resources. With respect to criteria number 4 and number 7, it is difficult at present to argue that we fully understand the progression from late talking to frank language impairment or that we can recognize the disorder in its latent or early symptomatic stage. Finally, the evidence presented here indicates that the existing measures of late talking are not suitable due to their poor prediction of outcomes. Wilson and Jungner suggested that a fairly high false positive rate might be an acceptable price to pay for a fast, easy, inexpensive screening test, but they argued that "the false negative rate should be very low since missed cases may lead to individual disasters" (p. 31). Clearly this is not the case for measures of late talking examined here, which failed to identify many children who were found to have language difficulties at a later age.

## LATE TALKING AS A CLINICAL CATEGORY: A MODEST PROPOSAL

If the idea that LTs should be identified and followed clinically is an example of something that "we do know, that isn't so," what, if anything, should be done about it? Questioning the validity of extant clinical categories is scientifically and politically fraught, as can be seen in the lengthy and contentious debates over proposed revisions of clinical taxonomies or nosologies such as the American Psychiatric

Association's *DSM* and World Health Organization's *International Classification of Diseases (ICD)* during the past decades. However, the evidence presented here, coupled with the Wilson and Jungner (1968) criteria and the thoughtful discussion of the ethics of early detection and screening by Juth and Munthe (2012), make it reasonable to propose a moratorium on using measures of late talking to identify young children who should receive clinical services.

Such a moratorium would not prevent additional research into the predictive accuracy of late talking status, although the weight and consistency of the findings of poor predictive accuracy across the studies and samples reviewed here suggests that those findings are reasonably robust. In addition, the kinds of studies that would be needed to show that late talking status predicts future status accurately, or that the benefits of identifying LTs exceed harms, are likely to be quite costly. The best evidence in this regard would come from well-designed and rigorously implemented randomized trials in which otherwise healthy children are randomized either to a group to be screened for late talking or to an unscreened group, with both groups then followed prospectively to determine the extent to which screening resulted in better outcomes. In the current funding climate it seems doubtful that the resources required for such studies will be forthcoming in the near future.

A moratorium on using late talking as a clinical category would not preclude ongoing efforts (e.g., Choudhury & Benasich, 2011; Fernald & Marchman, 2012; Marchman & Fernald, 2008) to develop more accurate measures than parent-reported vocabulary for the early identification of children who will experience deficits in language and language-related skills at later ages. Of course, any alternative measures that are proposed to be clinically meaningful must be held to the same standards and considerations described earlier, including evidence of their binary predictive classification accuracy at the level of individual children, rather than just evidence from group mean comparison, correlational, and regression-based studies.

A moratorium on using *Late Talker* as a clinical category also would not prevent its use as a category of theoretical interest. Consistent with the approach described earlier (President's Council on Bioethics, 2008), parents from whom informed consent had been obtained under an institutional review board (IRB) protocol could be offered the opportunity to complete a measure of late talking as part of a research study, but it would be important to avoid the implication that the child's performance on the measure has implications for his or her future language skills.

Finally, a moratorium on using *Late Talker* for clinical purposes might motivate additional critical analyses of the reasons for the relationships between expressive vocabulary size and other aspects of early language development. Lexical knowledge appears to be one of the most readily malleable aspects of the linguistic system (e.g., Friedrich & Friederici, 2011; Marulis & Neuman, 2010; Shtyrov, 2011), and frequency of exposure to words, strongly associated with word learning, differs significantly for children from different backgrounds. A better understanding of the causal factors underpinning these associations, validated by strong empirical evidence, should facilitate the search for measures that might be more successful than early vocabulary size in identifying the children at greatest risk for future language deficits.

Tufte described "a persistent *rage to conclude* that denies the implications, complexities and uncertainties of primary evidence" (2006, p. 154). The present chapter represents an effort to avoid a similar *rage to categorize* that could prevent researchers from acknowledging the strengths, weaknesses, and gaps in the evidence concerning the benefits and harms of using Late Talker as a clinical category.

## REFERENCES

American Psychiatric Association. (n.d.). *Diagnostic and statistical manual of mental disorders (DSM-5)*. Retrieved from http://www.dsm5.org/

Bailey, K.D. (1994). *Typologies and taxonomies: An introduction to classification techniques.* Thousand Oaks, CA: Sage.

Battaglia, M., Bucher, H., Egger, M., Grossenbacher, F., Minder, C., & Pewsner, D. (2002). *The Bayes library of diagnostic studies and reviews* (2nd ed.). Basel, Switzerland: Division of Clinical Epidemiology and Biostatistics, Institute of Social and Preventive Medicine, University of Berne, and Basel Institue for Clinical Epidemiology, University of Basel.

Bayley, N. (1969). *Bayley Scales of Infant Development.* New York: Psychological Corporation.

Bishop, D.V.M., Price, T.S., Dale, P.S., & Plomin, R. (2003). Outcomes of early language delay: II. Etiology of transient and persistent language difficulties. *Journal of Speech, Language, and Hearing Research, 46*, 561–575.

Bossuyt, P.M., Reitsma, J.B., Bruns, D.E., Gatsonis, C.A., Glasziou, P.P., Irwig, L.M., . . . Lijmer, J.G. (2003). The STARD statement for reporting studies of diagnostic accuracy: Explanation and elaboration. *Clinical Chemistry, 49*, 7–18.

Bricker, D., & Squires, J., with Mounts, L., Potter, L., Nickel, R., Twombly, E., & Farrell, J. (1999). *Ages & Stages Questionnaires®: A parent-completed, child-monitoring system* (2nd ed.). Baltimore, MD: Paul H. Brookes Publishing Co.

Choudhury, N., & Benasich, A. (2011). Maturation of auditory evoked potentials from 6 to 48 months: Prediction to 3 and 4 year language and cognitive abilities. *Clinical Neurophysiology, 122*, 320–338.

Dale, P.S., Bates, E., Reznick, J.S., & Morisset, C. (1989). The validity of a parent report instrument of child language at twenty months. *Journal of Child Language, 16*, 239–249.

Dale, P.S., Price, T.S., Bishop, D.V.M., & Plomin, R. (2003). Outcomes of early language delay: I. Predicting persistent and transient language difficulties at 3 and 4 years. *Journal of Speech, Language, and Hearing Research, 46*, 544–560.

Desmarais, C., Sylvestre, A., Meyer, F., Bairati, I., & Rouleau, N. (2008). Systematic review of the literature on characteristics of late-talking toddlers. *International Journal of Language and Communication Disorders, 43*, 361–389.

Dionne, G., Dale, P.S., Boivin, M., & Plomin, R. (2003). Genetic evidence for bidirectional effects of early lexical and grammatical development. *Child Development, 74*, 394–412.

Dollaghan, C.A. (2004). Taxometric analysis of specific language impairment in 3- and 4-year-old children. *Journal of Speech, Language, and Hearing Research, 47*, 464–475.

Dollaghan, C. (2011). Taxometric analyses of specific language impairment in 6-year-old children. *Journal of Speech, Language, and Hearing Research, 54*, 1361–1371.

Dollaghan, C. (n.d.). *Predictive accuracy of early expressive vocabulary to language skills at ages 3 and 4 years.* Manuscript in preparation.

Dollaghan, C.A., & Campbell, T.F. (2009). How well do poor language scores at ages 3 and 4 predict poor language scores at age 6? *International Journal of Speech-Language Pathology, 11*, 358–365.

Dollaghan, C.A., & Horner, E.A. (2011). Bilingual language assessment: A meta-analysis of diagnostic accuracy. *Journal of Speech, Language, and Hearing Research, 54*, 1077–1088.

Dunn, L., & Dunn, L. (1981). *Peabody Picture Vocabulary Test–Revised.* Circle Pines, MN: American Guidance Service.

Dunn, L.M., Dunn, L.M., & Williams, K.T. (1997). *Peabody Picture Vocabulary Test–III.* Circle Pines, MN: American Guidance Service.

Ellis Weismer, S. (2007). Typical talkers, late talkers, and children with specific language impairment: A language endowment spectrum? In R. Paul (Ed.), *Language disorders from a developmental perspective: Essays in honor of Robin S. Chapman* (pp. 83–101). Mahwah, NJ: Lawrence Erlbaum Associates.

Fasolo, M., Majorano, M., & D'Odorico, L. (2008). Babbling and first words in children with slow expressive development. *Clinical Linguistics & Phonetics, 22,* 83–94.

Fenson, L., Dale, P.S., Reznick, J.S., Thal, D., Bates, E., Hartung, J.P., . . . Reilly, J.S. (1993). *MacArthur Communicative Development Inventories: User's guide and technical manual.* Baltimore, MD: Paul H. Brookes Publishing Co.

Fenson, L., Marchman, V.A., Thal, D.J., Dale, P.S., Reznick, J.S., & Bates, E. (2007). *MacArthur-Bates Communicative Development Inventories (CDIs)* (2nd ed.). Baltimore, MD: Paul H. Brookes Publishing Co.

Fernald, A., & Marchman, V.A. (2012). Individual differences in lexical processing at 18 months predict vocabulary growth in typically developing and late-talking toddlers. *Child Development, 83,* 203–222.

Freberg, M.E., Vandiver, B.J., Watkins, M.W., & Canivez, G.L. (2008). Significant factor score variability and the validity of the WISC-III full scale IQ in predicting later academic achievement. *Applied Neuropsychology, 15,* 131–139.

Friedrich, M., & Friederici, A.D. (2011). Word learning in 6-month-olds: Fast encoding-weak retention. *Journal of Cognitive Neuroscience, 23,* 3228–3240.

Gardner, M.F. (1981). *Expressive One-Word Picture Vocabulary Test.* Novato: CA: Academic Therapy Publications.

Haslam, N., & Beck, A.T. (1994). Subtyping major depression: A taxometric analysis. *Journal of Abnormal Psychology, 103,* 686–692.

Heilmann, J., Ellis Weismer, S., Evans, J., & Hollar, C. (2005). Utility of the MacArthur-Bates Communicative Development Inventory in identifying language abilities of late-talking and typically developing toddlers. *American Journal of Speech-Language Pathology, 14,* 40–51.

Henrichs, J., Rescorla, L., Schenk, J.J., Schmidt, H.G., Jaddoe, V.W.V., Hofman, A., . . . Tiemeier, H. (2011). Examining continuity of early expressive vocabulary development: The generation R study. *Journal of Speech, Language, and Hearing Research, 54,* 854–869.

Higgins, J.P.T., & Thompson, S.G. (2002). Quantifying heterogeneity in a meta-analysis. *Statistics in Medicine, 21,* 1539–1558.

Jones Moyle, M., Ellis Weismer, S., Evans, J.L., & Lindstrom, M.J. (2007). Longitudinal relationships between lexical and grammatical development in typical and late-talking children. *Journal of Speech, Language, and Hearing Research, 50,* 508–528.

Juth, N., & Munthe, C. (2012). *The ethics of screening in health care and medicine.* New York, NY: Springer.

Klee, T., Carson, D.K., Gavin, W.J., Hall, L., Kent, A., & Reece, S. (1998). Concurrent and predictive validity of an early language screening program. *Journal of Speech, Language, and Hearing Research, 41,* 627–641.

Klee, T., Pearce, K., & Carson, D.K. (2000). Improving the positive predictive value of screening for developmental language disorder. *Journal of Speech, Language, and Hearing Research, 43,* 821–833.

Lee, L. (1974). *Developmental sentence analysis.* Evanston, IL: Northwestern University Press.

Lindamood, C., & Lindamood, P. (1979). *Lindamood Auditory Conceptualization Test.* Allen, TX: DLM.

Lykken, D.T. (1991). What's wrong with psychology anyway? In D. Cicchetti & W.M. Grove (Eds.), *Thinking clearly about psychology* (Vol. 1., pp. 3–39). Minneapolis: University of Minnesota Press.

Marchman, V.A., & Fernald, A. (2008). Speed of word recognition and vocabulary knowledge in infancy predict cognitive and language outcomes in later childhood. *Developmental Science, 11,* F9–F16. doi:10.1111/j.1467–7687.2008.00671.x

Marulis, L.M., & Neuman, S.B. (2010). The effects of vocabulary intervention on young children's word learning: A meta-analysis. *Review of Educational Research, 80,* 300–335.

Meehl, P.E. (1992). Factors and taxa, traits and types, differences of degree and differences in kind. *Journal of Personality, 60,* 117–174.

Meehl, P.E. (1997). Credentialed persons, credentialed knowledge. *Clinical Psychology: Science and Practice, 4,* 91–98.

Mukherjee, S. (2010). *The emperor of all maladies.* New York, NY: Scribner.

Mullen, E. (1993). *Mullen Scales of Early Language: AGS edition.* Circle Pines, MN: American Guidance Service.

Nelson, H.D., Nygren, P., Walker, M., & Panoscha, R. (2006). Screening for speech and language delay in preschool children: Systematic evidence review for the US Preventive Services Task Force. *Pediatrics, 117,* e298. doi:10.1542/peds.2005-1467

Newcomer, P., & Hammill, D. (1988). *Test of Language Development–Primary.* Austin, TX: PRO-ED.

Newcomer, P., & Hammill, D. (1997). *Test of Language Development–3 (Primary).* Austin, TX: PRO-ED.

Paul, R. (2000). Predicting outcomes of early expressive language delay: Ethical implications. In D.V.M. Bishop & L.B. Leonard (Eds.), *Speech and language impairments in children: Causes, characteristics, intervention and outcome* (pp. 195–209). Philadelphia, PA: Taylor & Francis.

Paul, R., Murray, C., Clancy, K., & Andrews, D. (1997). Reading and metaphonological outcomes in late talkers. *Journal of Speech, Language, and Hearing Research, 40,* 1037–1047.

Paul, R., & Smith, R.L. (1993). Narrative skills in 4-year-olds with normal, impaired, and late-developing language. *Journal of Speech and Hearing Research, 36,* 592–598.

Paul, R., Spangle Looney, S., & Dahm, P.S. (1991). Communication and socialization skills at ages 2 and 3 in "late-talking" young children. *Journal of Speech and Hearing Research, 34,* 858–865.

Perry Carson, C., Klee, T., Carson, D.K., & Hime, L.K., (2003). Phonological profiles of 2-year-olds with delayed language development: predicting clinical outcomes at age 3. *American Journal of Speech-Language Pathology, 12,* 28–39.

President's Council on Bioethics. (2008, December). *The changing moral focus of newborn screening: An ethical inquiry by the President's Council on Bioethics.* Washington, DC: Author. Retrieved from http://bioethics.georgetown.edu/pcbe

Reese, E., & Read, S. (2000). Predictive validity of the New Zealand MacArthur Communicative Development Inventory: Words and sentences. *Journal of Child Language, 27,* 255–266.

Rescorla, L. (1989). The Language Development Survey: A screening tool for delayed language in toddlers. *Journal of Speech and Hearing Disorders, 54,* 587–599.

Rescorla, L. (2009). Age 17 language and reading outcomes in late-talking toddlers: Support for a dimensional perspective on language delay. *Journal of Speech, Language, and Hearing Research, 52,* 16–30.

Rescorla, L., & Achenbach, T.M. (2002). Use of the Language Development Survey (LDS) in a national probability sample of children 18 to 35 months old. *Journal of Speech, Language, and Hearing Research, 45,* 733–743.

Rescorla, L., & Alley, A. (2001). Validation of the Language Development Survey (LDS): A parent report tool for identifying language delay in toddlers. *Journal of Speech, Language, and Hearing Research, 44,* 434–445.

Rescorla, L., Mirak, J., & Singh, L. (2000). Vocabulary growth in late talkers: Lexical development from 2;0 to 3;0. *Journal of Child Language, 27,* 293–311.

Rescorla, L., Roberts, J., & Dahlsgaard, K. (1997). Late talkers at 2: Outcome at age 3. *Journal of Speech, Language, and Hearing Research, 40,* 556–566.

Reynell, J. (1977). *Reynell Developmental Language Scales.* Windsor, United Kingdom: NFER.

Rice, M.L., Taylor, C.L., & Zubrick, S.R. (2008). Language outcomes of 7-year-old children with or without a history of late language emergence at 24 months. *Journal of Speech, Language, and Hearing Research, 51,* 394–407.

Rice, M.L., & Wexler, K. (2001). *Rice/Wexler Test of Early Grammatical Impairment.* San Antonio, TX: Psychological Corporation.

Sackett, D.L., Haynes, R.B., Guyatt, G.H., & Tugwell, P. (1991). *Clinical epidemiology: A basic science for clinical medicine* (2nd ed.). Boston, MA: Little, Brown.

Scarborough, H.S. (1990). Index of Productive Syntax. *Applied Psycholinguistics, 11,* 1–12.

Shickle, D., & Chadwick, R. (1994). The ethics of screening: Is "screeningitis" an incurable disease? *Journal of Medical Ethics, 20,* 12–18.

Shtyrov, Y. (2011). Fast mapping of novel word forms traced neurophysiologically. *Frontiers in Psychology, 2,* article 340, 1–9, doi:10.3389/fpsyg.2011.00340

Sparrow, S.S., Balla, D.A., & Cicchetti, D.V. (1984). *Vineland Adaptive Behavior Scales (Survey Form).* Circle Pines, MN: American Guidance Service.

Terman, L., & Merrill, M. (1960). *Stanford-Binet Intelligence Scale.* Boston, MA: Houghton Mifflin.

Thal, D.J., Bates, E., Goodman, J., & Jahn-Samilo, J. (1997). Continuity of language abilities: An exploratory study of late- and early-talking toddlers. *Developmental Neuropsychology, 13,* 239–273.

Tomblin, B. (2011). Co-morbidity of autism and SLI: Kinds, kin and complexity. *International Journal of Language and Communication Disorders, 46,* 127–137.

Tufte, E. (2006). *Beautiful evidence.* Cheshire, CT: Graphics Press.

Wechsler, D. (1991). *Wechsler Intelligence Scale for Children* (3rd ed.). San Antonio, TX: Psychological Corporation.

Westerlund, M., Berglund, E., & Eriksson, M. (2006). Can severely language delayed 3-year-olds be identified at 18 months? Evaluation of a screening version of the MacArthur-Bates Communicative Development Inventories. *Journal of Speech, Language, and Hearing Research, 49,* 237–247.

Whitehurst, G.J., Smith, M., Fischel, J.E., Arnold, D.S., & Lonigan, C.J. (1991). The continuity of babble and speech in children with specific expressive language delay. *Journal of Speech and Hearing Research, 34,* 1121–1129.

Wilson, J.M.G., & Jungner, G. (1968). *Principles and practice of screening for disease.* Retrieved from http://whqlibdoc.who.int/php/WHO_PHP_34.pdf

World Health Organization. (n.d.). *International classification of diseases (ICD).* Retrieved from http://apps.who.int/classifications/icd/en

Zamora, J., Abraira, V., Muriel, A., Khan, K., & Coomarasamy, A. (2006). Meta-DiSc: A software for meta-analysis of test accuracy data. *BMC Medical Research Methodology, 6*(31). Retrieved from http://www.biomedcentral.com/1471–2288/6/31

Zimmerman, I., Steiner, V., & Pond, R. (1992). *Preschool Language Scale–Third Edition.* Chicago, IL: Psychological Corporation.

Zink, I., & Lejaegere, M. (2003). *N-CDIs: Korte vormen, aanpassing en hernormering van de MacArthur Short Form Vocabulary Checklists van Fenson et al.* [N-CDIs: Short forms, adaptations and norms of the Dutch version of the short form of the MacArthur Vocabulary Checklists of Fenson et al.]. Leuven, Belgium: Acco.

Zubrick, S.R., Taylor, C.L., Rice, M.L., & Slegers, D.W. (2007). Late language emergence at 24 months: An epidemiological study of prevalence, predictors, and covariates. *Journal of Speech, Language, and Hearing Research, 50,* 1562–1592.

# 6

# Phonology and the Lexicon in Late Talkers

Michelle MacRoy-Higgins and Richard G. Schwartz

There is a bidirectional relationship between phonology and lexical development in children who are developing language typically (for a review, see Stoel-Gammon, 2011). For example, early vocalizations and babbling are related to children's first words and syllable shapes. If *bababa* is observed frequently in an infant's babble, then it is likely that an early word in his or her lexicon would consist of similar phonemes and syllable structure, such as *baba* for *bottle*. This relationship between phonology is especially apparent during the period of the first 50 words, with phonology influencing the words acquired in production vocabulary. This influence of phonology on vocabulary acquisition has been identified as one factor underlying the rapid vocabulary development at the end of this period (e.g., Metsala, 1999; Werker, Fennell, Corcoran, & Stager, 2002). This chapter reviews these early relations between phonology and lexical development in typically developing (TD) children, late talkers (LTs), and children with specific language impairment (SLI). We also consider the relations among phonology and other language domains in children with SLI. Finally, we focus on the effects of phonotactic probability on novel word learning in LTs.

Among the questions we address in this chapter are the following: 1) Do children with delayed expressive vocabulary development demonstrate a similar bidirectional relationship between their phonological and lexical systems? 2) Is this relationship present but delayed? 3) Or does an underlying impairment in either system contribute to toddlers' early expressive language delay? These questions are particularly relevant to LTs, who are usually identified around 2 years of age when they produce fewer than 50 words and do not combine words (Rescorla, 1989). However, LTs manifest differences in their linguistic development well before they begin producing words. As discussed in more detail in the Babbling and Early Vocalizations in Late Talkers section, LTs exhibit delays in the phonology of their early vocalizations in addition to a general delay in expressive language development.

## SPEECH PERCEPTION, BABBLING, AND EARLY VOCALIZATIONS IN TYPICALLY DEVELOPING INFANTS

Young infants display a wide range of sophisticated speech perception skills at a very young age, long before their production of true words (e.g., Eimas, Siqueland, Jusczyk, & Vigorito, 1971). For instance, 1-month-old infants demonstrate categorical perception for voicing contrasts (Eimas et al., 1971), and 3-month-old infants can detect differences in place and manner in speech sounds (Jusczyk, 1992).

Early experience with speech sounds is essential for other aspects of language as well as for speech processing. For example, perceptual abilities are important for language development, as a positive correlation has been observed between 6-month-old infants' perceptual abilities and later expressive vocabulary at 13, 16, and 24 months of age (Trehub, 1976; Tsao, Liu, & Kuhl, 2004). Very young infants have the ability to perceive phonemic contrasts in other languages as well as in their native language (Polka & Werker, 1994; Werker & Tees, 2002). Infants' speech perception abilities change as they have increased experience with the language and phonology of their environment. By 6–8 months of age, infants are less sensitive to nonnative vowel contrasts than to native contrasts (Polka & Werker, 1994). At 10–12 months of age, infants are less sensitive to nonnative consonant contrasts as compared with younger infants (Werker & Tees, 2002). By this age, infants have developed phonemic categories that are consistent with their native language, and there is a decline in their abilities to perceive speech sounds that are not important for the development of a phonological system in the language to which they are exposed.

Although there is some degree of variation among infants, those that develop language in a typical manner generally follow a common pattern of prelinguistic vocalization. After a period of *reflexive cries and vegetative sounds* (0–2 months), *cooing and laughter* (2–4 months), and *vocal play* (4–6 months), infants begin to demonstrate *canonical babbling* (6 months and older), followed by *jargon* (10 months and older). A hierarchy of babble complexity has been described by Oller (1980). Level I utterances consist of a vowel, syllabic consonant, or glottal stop (not a true consonant, similar to vocal play; e.g., [i]). Level II utterances consist of vowel, consonant (VC) or consonant, vowel (CV) structures with a single consonant type (*canonical babbling;* e.g., *ba or ma*). Level III utterances consist of syllables with at least two true consonants, differing in place or manner of articulation (*variegated babbling;* e.g., *badaba*). The consonant-like sounds and syllables that have been observed in babble and jargon are fairly consistent among TD infants, with open syllables (CV, CVCV) consisting of stops, nasals, and glides (i.e., [d], [b], [m], [t], [g], and [w]) observed frequently (Locke, 1983).

Infant babble and lexical development are related. The sounds and syllable shapes observed in babble are frequently observed in early word productions, the number of phonemes observed during an infant's babble is positively correlated to later lexicon size, and the age of onset of meaningful speech (i.e., emergence from babbling) is negatively correlated to later lexicon size (Stoel-Gammon, 1991). In addition, the complexity of babble in TD infants is related to vocabulary size. Stoel-Gammon (1991) observed that the complexity of babble increases (fewer Level I utterances, more level II and III utterances) as age and vocabulary increase, suggesting that as an infant enters the *meaningful speech stage*—defined as production of at least 10 different true words—the complexity of babble shows a regular and systematic change such that it comes to closely resemble true words.

Both early speech perception and production are essential skills that are needed to establish a foundation upon which oral language develops. Compromised speech perception or compromised early speech production can negatively influence the typical course of development of oral language.

## BABBLING AND EARLY VOCALIZATIONS IN LATE TALKERS

Toddlers who are LTs exhibit babbling patterns that are both delayed and different from those of their TD peers (Fasolo, Majorano, & D'Odorico, 2008; Oller, Eilers, Neal, & Schwartz, 1999; Stoel-Gammon, 1989; Whitehurst, Smith, Fischel, Arnold, & Lonigan, 1991). Specifically, toddlers who are LTs show a delay in the onset of canonical babbling (Oller et al., 1999), and once they regularly produce babble, the complexity is not comparable to that of their peers (Fasolo et al., 2008). Babble complexity is noteworthy because it has shown to predict lexical growth (Whitehurst et al., 1991).

In an early investigation, Stoel-Gammon (1989) examined speech development in a group of 34 children from 9 to 24 months of age to observe patterns of babbling and early word productions. Two of the 34 toddlers from this group demonstrated delayed lexical development at 24 months. Although both toddlers were in the meaningful speech stage, their babbling was markedly different than their peers who demonstrated typical lexical growth. One toddler showed little change in complexity of her utterances and produced only Level I vocalizations at 24 months of age. The other toddler who was a late talker did produce more complex babble (Level II) containing a true consonant, but the consonant was an unusual one (velar [g]). Also, this consonant was not represented in his early lexical development, unlike the pattern usually observed in toddlers with typical language development.

A subsequent study also found that the complexity of toddlers' vocalizations was related to their lexical development (Whitehurst et al., 1991). In a large sample (37 two-year-olds) with delayed lexical development, the type of babble produced at age 2 was predictive of language skills 5 months later. Those toddlers who produced more consonant babble (Levels II and III) had higher language outcomes than those who engaged in vowel babble and other vocalizations (Level I babble), suggesting that language outcomes can be predicted at an early age by examination of babble complexity.

The age at which consonant babbling (Level II) is first observed is also predictive of later productive vocabulary (Oller et al., 1999). Infants who produced less canonical babbling (Level II) between 10 and 12 months had smaller productive vocabularies at 18, 24, and 30 months of age than peers who produced canonical babbling at expected ages (Oller et al., 1999).

Delays in babbling and subsequent lexical development have also been observed in children exposed to languages other than English. Babbling complexity was predictive of lexical development in a group of 20-month-old infants who were exposed to Italian (Fasolo et al., 2008). The infants with delayed lexical development produced more Level I babble than their TD peers, who produced Level II and Level II babble more frequently (Fasolo et al., 2008), consistent with findings from infants exposed to English.

Receptive language, cognition, and hearing were all reported to be normal in these investigations. Therefore, the differences observed in consonant babble in toddlers who are LTs may indicate that the underlying impairment is related to their phonological ability, which later is reflected in language production, but not necessarily in language comprehension. Oller and colleagues (1999) argued that the relationship between delays in canonical babbling and consequent delays in expressive language skills could represent either an underlying difficulty in speech sound production or an underlying impairment in a child's ability to retrieve phonological representations needed to perform production tasks.

In summary, the few studies examining early babbling in LTs have found that features of their babbling were correlated with the size of their lexicon. The overall frequency of babbling (how often they vocalized) did not seem to be as important for later lexical development as the complexity of babble (Level, I, II, or III). This suggests that early vocalizations are important in establishing a productive vocabulary, and therefore babbling should be considered when identifying children at risk for lasting language difficulties. Because LTs show differences in early vocalizations as young as 10–12 months, infants at risk for language delay may be identified early. It is important to consider the type of babble infants produce when determining eligibility for intervention; those that show limited consonant babble (Level II or III) would benefit most from intervention, as they are likely to show lexical delay.

## PHONOLOGICAL CHARACTERISTICS OF EARLY WORDS IN LATE TALKERS

LTs continue to demonstrate phonological delays once they begin to produce their first words. This leads us to ask whether they are merely delayed in their phonological skills, resembling younger TD children, or whether they have atypical phonologies. Some studies suggest that the phonological characteristics observed in LTs' speech are characteristic of younger, TD children, whereas other studies suggest that LTs show disordered phonological patterns.

Compared with their age-matched controls, studies have found that toddlers who are LTs show delays in syllable structure, the percentage of consonants correct (PCC), the number of consonant types produced, phonemic inventory (including vowels and consonants), the total number of vocalizations, and the number of consonants produced in the medial and final word positions (Mirak & Rescorla, 1998; Paul & Jennings, 1992; Rescorla & Ratner, 1996; Schwartz, Leonard, Folger, & Wilcox, 1980; Thal, Oroz, & McCaw, 1995).

Schwartz and colleagues (1980) compared three young children (2;7–3;7) with language delay and three TD younger children (1;7–1;9), and matched them for production vocabulary size, nonverbal cognitive skills, and mean length of utterance (MLU; 1.01–1.4). A detailed comparison of their phonologies revealed similarities between the two groups in phonetic inventory sizes, productivity, variability, contrast, and error patterns. Similar results were found in subsequent studies examining the relationship between phonology and overall language development (Paul & Jennings, 1992; Thal et al., 1995). Paul and Jennings (1992) found that LTs resembled younger TD peers in their production of early developing consonant classes and canonical syllable shapes. Similarly, Thal and colleagues (1995) found that phonemic inventory and syllable structure in toddlers who were LTs resembled those of younger peers with similar vocabulary size. Results from these studies suggest that the phonological characteristics of LTs are delayed rather than atypical.

Although early phonology in LTs appears to be delayed rather than deviant, some research suggests that LTs do not exhibit a normal progression of phonological development from this point on. That is, atypical patterns seem to appear longitudinally. Williams and Elbert (2003) monitored phonology and language skills over the course of 1 year for five children identified as LTs. After this period of time, three children demonstrated average language abilities, but two children continued to show language delays. At age 3, the phonologies of the three children who had caught up resembled younger TD children; the children who did not catch up displayed different phonological patterns. They showed persistent syllable structure differences, and more atypical speech sound errors such as d/h and dʒ/t were observed, whereas the children who caught up produced more typical substitutions such as w/l (gliding) or d/g (fronting). The LTs who did not catch up showed little change in accuracy as measured by PCC over time, and greater sound variability was observed. For example, one child attempted to produce /t/ as [t, w, ts, d, dz]. Furthermore, that child did not add new phonemes to his repertoire in a typical fashion. Specifically, this late talker's early phonemic repertoire consisted of nasals (in word-initial and word-final positions) and glides (in word-initial position). Over the course of several months, he added stops to his repertoire, which are typically observed in babbling and in first word productions.

Although all five LTs met the same initial criteria, those whose phonological skills did not resemble younger TD children did not exhibit as much linguistic growth. These LTs continued to demonstrate linguistic impairments during their preschool years, suggesting LTs whose phonologies are disordered are at particular risk for lasting language impairment.

Other investigations have shown phonology to be a predictor of continued language delay in LTs. Phonological skills in a group of toddlers who were LTs at age 2 were correlated with MLU and expressive vocabulary at age 3 (Carson, Klee, Carson, & Hime, 2003). The following risk factors were associated with continued language delay at age 3: limited attempts to produce phonemes from a variety of classes, a limited phonemic inventory, and limited syllable shapes. Stoel-Gammon (1991) suggested that 24-month-olds exhibiting atypical phonological patterns (e.g., numerous vowel errors, deletion of initial consonants, production of glottal consonants, substitution of back consonants for front consonants, lack of final consonants) are likely to have difficulties with lexical development. Overall, the more delayed or disordered the phonological system is at age 2, the more the child is at risk for continued and more general language delays.

To summarize, LTs have less complex and less systematic phonologies compared with their peers, which is demonstrated in their babble, continues to be observed in their phonological systems once they begin producing words, and continues as their lexicons grow. Therefore, when identifying a toddler as a late talker, it is not only important to consider the number of expressive vocabulary words in his or her lexicon but also to consider his or her phonological skills. Phonological characteristics may predict whether a late talker will later resemble a child with typical language development or a child with SLI.

## PHONOLOGY AND WORD LEARNING IN TYPICALLY DEVELOPING CHILDREN

In TD children, phonological regularities within a language influence infants' and children's abilities to perceive, acquire, and produce new words. For example, TD infants in their first year of life show sensitivity to *phonotactic probability,* which is the likelihood of occurrence of a particular sound sequence (Jusczyk, Luce, & Charles-Luce, 1994). Jusczyk and colleagues (1994) used a head-turn procedure to examine 6- and 9-month-old infants' preference for common versus rare sound sequences. Nine-month-old infants attended longer to nonsense words consisting of common sound sequences than to nonsense words consisting of rare sound sequences; 6-month-old infants did not show this preference. Thus, infants as young as 9 months of age were sensitive to the phonological regularities of words in the language to which they are exposed.

The phonotactic structure of a word also has a facilatory affect on how willingly and accurately young children (20- to 28-month-olds) produce that word. For example, they are more likely to imitate phonemes correctly in common sound sequences as compared with rare sound sequences, in both real and nonsense forms (Zamuner, Gerken, & Hammond, 2004). Similar results were observed in older children (3–8 years); rare sound sequences are produced with less accuracy than common sound sequences (Edwards, Beckman, & Munson, 2004).

Phonotactic probability also influences the acquisition of new words (Storkel, 2001, 2003, 2004; Storkel & Maekawa, 2005). Children ages 3–6 years learn the labels (nonsense forms) for new nouns and verbs that have common sound sequences more easily than words with rare sound sequences (Storkel, 2001, 2003). An advantage for acquiring words with common sound sequences has been replicated in younger, TD 24-month-olds (MacRoy-Higgins, Schwartz, Shafer, & Marton, 2012). These results suggest that when exposed to new lexical items, toddlers and children use regularities observed in their language (e.g., phonotactic probability) to store, access, and produce the phonological forms needed to represent these words.

Another aspect of phonology that contributes to lexical growth in TD children is *phonological selectivity.* Ferguson and Farwell (1975) first observed that during the period of the first 50 words, children are individually selective in the words they include in their production vocabularies. A series of studies conducted by Leonard, Schwartz, and colleagues demonstrated that the lexical items that toddlers and young children preferentially add to their productive vocabulary are related to their established phonological systems. TD toddlers are more likely to add new words to their lexicons when they contain phonemes that they produce accurately (IN words) in spontaneous speech, as compared with words that contain phonemes not in their productive vocabularies (OUT words; Leonard, Schwartz, Morris, & Chapman, 1981; Leonard, Schwartz, Swanson, & Frome Loeb, 1987; Schwartz et al., 1980). In addition, productive phonological skills correlate with overall language production skills such as MLU (e.g., Schwartz et al., 1980). These studies demonstrated that Ferguson and Farwell's findings were not due simply to individual differences in input; that is, a child who was exposed to more words containing fricatives than another child might have more words with fricatives in the first 50 words than a child who was exposed to fewer words with fricatives based simply on frequency. Instead, the early vocabularies of TD toddlers are related to their established phonological system.

Storkel (2005, 2006) examined this relationship between phonological knowledge and lexical acquisition in older children (3–5 years old) with typical language development. She found the opposite pattern; preschool children acquired words containing OUT sounds more easily than words containing IN sounds in a brief word-learning period. This opposite finding might reflect the differing salience of IN versus OUT sounds at these two points in development. Alternatively, these apparently conflicting findings might reflect methodological differences in definition of OUT words (i.e., *not attempted and not produced* in Schwartz et al. vs. *not produced accurately* in Storkel) or may reflect differences in word-learning procedures (i.e., focused stimulation in Schwartz et al. vs. a story context in Storkel). In the first of these studies, Storkel used two consonants to form words in each category, but in the second study, she treated sounds comprising OUT words as falling along a continuum of accuracy. By treating phonological knowledge continuously rather than categorically, Storkel was able to demonstrate an inverse continuous relationship between knowledge and word learning; most knowledge yielded the poorest word learning, and least knowledge yielded the best word learning. In these preschool children, established phonological knowledge had little positive effect on word learning. Rather, emerging knowledge facilitated word learning, whereas limited knowledge inhibited word learning. This is a topic that bears further investigation in younger children with better and broader specification of phonological knowledge beyond production accuracy.

There is ample empirical support to suggest a phonological basis for the acquisition of vocabulary in TD children, especially during early lexical acquisition. Children recognize phonological regularities in the language to which they are exposed and use these regularities or patterns in acquiring new words. Because LTs do not have phonologies that are as well developed as their peers, they are at a disadvantage for acquiring a lexicon in the same manner. Because many toddlers who are LTs are later diagnosed with SLI and demonstrate pervasive difficulties with language (Leonard, 2000), it is worth considering the more developed SLI literature concerning phonology and language impairments in other domains.

## PHONOLOGY AND OTHER LANGUAGE DOMAINS IN LANGUAGE IMPAIRMENT

A significant number of children with SLI demonstrate phonological impairments, measured by production, perception, metalinguistic awareness, and working memory performance. Furthermore, impairments in other areas of language, such as morphosyntax or lexical access, may derive to some extent from phonological factors. As such, the phonological limitations observed in toddlers identified as LTs may represent an early manifestation of the relations between these limitations and language acquisition more generally. It is worth noting that two models of SLI

(Chiat, 2001; Joanisse & Seidenberg, 1998) identify the causal locus of SLI and its associated impairments as deficient phonological representations or processing.

We can consider the role that phonological factors play in SLI from several perspectives. One is the overlap between children with phonological disorders and children with language impairments in other domains. Researchers have long questioned the independence of speech (presently classified as phonology) disorders (Pollack & Rees, 1972; Shriner, Halloway, & Daniloff, 1969). Menyuk and Looney (1972) first observed that children with language impairments made phonological errors in sentence repetitions along with expected syntactic errors. Several more recent studies have attempted to provide more information about phonological disorders and more general language disorders. For instance, one study found that one third of children with speech delays of unknown origin had significant impairments in language comprehension, and language production abilities were deficient in almost 80% of these children (Shriberg & Kwiatkowski, 1994). Furthermore, a child's cognitive-linguistic status proved to be highly predictive of short-term and long-term resolution of phonological disorders (Shriberg, Gruber, & Kwiatkowski, 1994; Shriberg, Kwiatkowski, & Gruber, 1994). Clearly these populations overlap, but the specific cognitive-linguistic mechanisms underlying the patterns of co-occurrence remain undetermined. A detailed review of the diagnostic, cognitive, and etiological overlaps among speech sound disorders, language impairment, and reading disability by Pennington and Bishop (2009) found most existing models lacking. A model that includes multiple cognitive impairments/risk factors seems necessary to explain the co-morbidity of these disorders. Such a model predicts impairments that are common to all three disorders and some that are disorder specific. It also means that an impairment in one underlying cognitive-linguistic ability may not lead to an overt disorder unless one or more of the other disorders are present. As Pennington and Bishop noted, one limitation in available data is that researchers often exclude children with multiple disorders. Another limitation in the understanding of these overlaps is the clinical instruments (i.e., language, articulation, and reading tests) we use. Virtually all are off-line; the results are endpoint responses that do not provide information about the processing leading to those responses. Also, most are synchronic, therefore providing only snapshot of performance rather than longitudinal or learning processes, and many are poorly informed linguistically.

This general relationship between phonological and language impairments can be further illuminated by considering error patterns. For example, children with language impairments exhibit phonological error patterns that are less consistent, persist longer, and are rarely observed in children without language impairments (Ingram, 1974, 1976). Some error patterns, such as final consonant deletion, seem to be more strongly associated with more general language impairments (e.g., Ingram, 1974, 1976; Panagos, 1974). A review of unusual and subtle patterns in children with phonological disorders suggested that these error patterns are consistent with typical phonologies but represent ways to deal with severe output constraints (Leonard, 1985).

There are a number of other issues concerning the impact of phonological impairments on the lexicon in children with language impairments, including phonological working memory, speech perception, and lexical access. Nonword repetition, which has been widely employed as a measure of phonological working memory (e.g., Dollaghan, Biber, & Campbell, 1995; Dollaghan & Campbell, 1998; Gathercole & Baddeley, 1990), is deficient in children with SLI. The typical finding is that they produce one- and two-syllable words accurately but perform more poorly than their TD peers (age-matched and younger) on nonwords that are three syllables or longer (Archibald & Gathercole, 2006; Botting & Conti-Ramsden, 2001; Dollaghan & Campbell, 1998; Gathercole & Baddeley, 1990; Montgomery, 1995). Nonword repetition scores are correlated with vocabulary growth and development (Gathercole, 2006). To some extent, this deficit may simply reflect a lack of familiarity with less frequent, multisyllabic words rather than weak working memory abilities. Impairments in speech perception, particularly categorical perception, may also affect nonword repetition. Poor performance may simply reflect phonological impairments and, in some respects, may be a more accurate measure of phonological abilities than working memory. Findings from lexical decision tasks with and without priming (Edwards & Lahey, 1996; Velez & Schwartz, 2011) have been interpreted as indicating impairments in phonological representations. In contrast, a cross-modal picture-naming interference task (the child names a picture while hearing a word that is either related to or unrelated to the picture) revealed a similar time course for the availability of phonological information (rhymes) in picture naming for children with SLI and their peers when the words were highly familiar (Seiger-Gardner & Schwartz, 2008). Less familiar words might have revealed group differences, however. When the same paradigm was used to compare naming performance with an interfering stimulus that shared a rhyme or an onset with the target, only onsets (e.g., an auditory stimulus of *book*) had an effect on picture naming (e.g., *bat*) times, and children with SLI exhibited phonological interference (Seiger-Gardner & Brooks, 2008). When children with SLI access a cohort of words (all beginning with the same sound) they experience interference from nontarget words that delays their production of the target. This may account for word-finding difficulties observed in children with SLI, and it may reflect an atypical organization of the mental lexicon stemming from earlier development.

Impairments in the production of morphosyntactic inflections and function words may also be attributed to phonological factors (e.g., Gallon, Harris, & van der Lely, 2007; Joanisse & Seidenberg, 1998; Leonard, Davis, & Deevy, 2007; Marshall & van der Lely, 2006, 2007). Children with SLI were less likely to produce past tense *-ed* in English when the word stem was low in its phonotactic probability (Leonard et al., 2007) and less likely to produce the past tense when *-ed* formed a consonant cluster that does not occur in uninflected English words (Marshall & van der Lely, 2006). Inflection and function word production are also influenced by word and phrase prosodic structure (e.g., McGregor & Leonard, 1994); unstressed syllables are omitted when they do not fit an English trochaic pattern.

A final facet of phonological impairments in SLI is the long-standing finding regarding perceptual impairments in children with SLI (see Schwartz, 2009, for a review). Several studies using subgroups from a large-scale study of children at risk for language impairment (Marinis, 2011) point to a relation between early speech perception and later language impairments. One study revealed perceptual impairments in differential brain responses to trochaic and iambic syllable sequences at 5 months of age that were related to more limited word production and risk for SLI at later ages. Another study revealed a strong relationship between poor perceptual performance in the at-risk toddlers using a preferential-looking paradigm relating sensitivity to mispronunciations at 19 months to language abilities at 30 months. A final study examined brainstem-evoked response latencies at 6 months as a predictor of later parent questionnaires and standardized language tests. Although there was a relationship between inter-peak latencies at 6 months and language abilities, later brainstem-evoked measures showed that the children with poor language outcomes caught up in their basic auditory abilities. These findings led Marinis to argue that there is evidence for an auditory-perceptual or phonological perceptual basis for SLI that reflects some basic impairment in the integration between phonological or auditory abilities and other aspects of language (see Jakubowicz, 2003). Later in development, though, when some of these impairments can no longer be detected, the varied impairments characteristic of SLI may remain.

Leonard and Schwartz and colleagues (e.g., Leonard, Schwartz, Folger, & Wilcox, 1978; Schwartz, 1988; Schwartz & Leonard, 1982, 1985; Schwartz, Leonard, Messick, & Chapman, 1987) extended their initial work on TD children to examine the influence of phonological and other factors on word learning in young children with SLI who all had a history of being LTs. In these studies, novel words or low-frequency, unfamiliar real words representing unfamiliar objects or actions were presented via focused stimulation (e.g., "Here's a _____") to children over the course of 8–10 training sessions. Comprehension and production of these newly taught words were tested. The phonological condition of interest in these studies was whether the experimental word contained sounds that the child had produced accurately in an initial language sample (IN words) or whether the experimental word contained sounds that the child never produced and never were in the adult targets the child produced in the language sample (OUT words). In some studies, a third category of words including sounds that the child attempted but never produced accurately (ATTEMPTED words). In general, the groups were similar in that they acquired more IN words over fewer sessions and produced them more accurately than OUT words. Attempted words were acquired similarly to OUT words by both groups, but children with SLI were much more likely to produce these words with uncommon errors that were not the same as the errors they made producing corresponding real words in their language sample. This suggested that the children with SLI did not relate novel words to their existing phonological representations of word production. The implication of these findings is that children with SLI do not have the same advantage available as their peers of using existing phonological knowledge to acquire new words. The children with SLI were also less likely to extend the experimental words to novel exemplars of the original referent in posttesting than their TD peers. This suggests that the integration of new words to their vocabularies may have conceptual and phonological components that are deficient in children with SLI.

Storkel (2005) examined this relationship between existing phonological knowledge and novel word learning in preschool children diagnosed with phonological disorders. She found that children with phonological disorders performed more poorly in learning words with more common sound sequences than with less common sequences, whereas TD, phonologically matched peers showed a common sound sequence advantage. This suggests that preschool children diagnosed with phonological impairments, similar to those diagnosed with SLI, do not use the same phonological cues when learning new words as their TD peers. The still emerging understanding of the interaction between phonology and more general language impairments in children with SLI suggests a need to examine the influence of phonology on lexical acquisition in LTs in greater detail.

## PHONOTACTIC PROBABILITY AND WORD LEARNING IN LATE TALKERS

As noted previously, there is a general relationship between expressive vocabulary size and phonological abilities; toddlers with small expressive vocabularies have more limited phonologies than toddlers with large vocabularies. The same is true of LTs: Those with more than 10 words had more advanced phonology skills, as measured by the number of intelligible utterances and the complexity of utterances, than LTs with fewer than 10 words in their production vocabularies (Thal et al., 1995). The LTs with more advanced lexical skills had more advanced phonology skills, as measured by the number of intelligible utterances and the complexity of utterances.

Even though there is a clear relation between phonology and vocabulary in LTs, its direction and causal nature cannot be assumed. We are not sure whether initial delays in phonology are responsible for slow vocabulary growth, or whether some impairment in lexical acquisition limits the development of the phonological system. Ellis Weismer and Evans (2002) suggested the former relationship. They examined word learning via a fast mapping paradigm in a group of LTs and their age-matched peers. The LTs demonstrated similar comprehension of familiar words but performed more poorly on comprehension and production of newly learned words compared with their TD, age-matched peers. The underlying cause of this lexical learning impairment could be due to inefficient phonological coding, which is needed to map new phonological information to lexical items (Ellis Weismer & Evans, 2002).

Stokes (2010) suggested that LTs' expressive language delay was related to an inability to extract statistical properties from their ambient language. When Stokes examined the words that LTs said, a different relationship of vocabulary size to *neighborhood density* (the number of words in the English lexicon that are phonologically similar to the target word) and *word frequency* was observed than was seen in their peers. The vocabularies of toddlers with limited vocabularies consisted of words with high neighborhood density and low frequency. Thus, their vocabularies contained words that had many phonological neighbors and that were not frequently produced in the ambient language. Toddlers with large vocabularies showed the opposite pattern. That is, they said words that did not have many phonological neighbors and that were frequently produced in the ambient language. These results suggest that LTs extract the statistical properties of language in a manner that is different than their peers, which may be contributing to their early and continued lexical delay.

A recent study specifically examined the causal relationship between phonology and lexical acquisition in a group of 24-month-olds who were either LTs or had typical language development. The toddlers were taught 12 novel words over the course of 10 training sessions through focused stimulation procedures (MacRoy-Higgins et al., 2012). The novel words differed in phonotactic probability (high vs. low) and the LTs were matched to their peers with typical language development for age, gender, socioeconomic status, and cognitive abilities. After the training sessions, word learning was tested through comprehension, production, and toddlers' ability to detect mispronunciations of the newly learned words, using a preferential looking paradigm.

TD toddlers performed better than the LTs on all tasks. They also showed a preference for high phonotactic probability words on measures of word naming, speech sound accuracy, and the detail of phonological representations (measured using the preferential looking paradigm), suggesting that they are sensitive to statistical properties of phonology. In contrast, LTs did not show a difference for words containing high versus low phonotactic probability. These results indicate that toddlers who are LTs do not use the same phonological cues as their TD peers when learning new words. The authors concluded that the underlying impairment in toddlers who are LTs could be an early inability to detect regularities in the phonological system of the language that they are exposed to, which in turn inhibits their ability to store the phonological forms needed to acquire lexical items.

The implications of these results for intervention remain unclear. Lexical intervention has a positive effect on LTs' productive phonology skills (Girolametto, Pearce, & Weitzman, 1997). After they engaged in a brief period of treatment (11 weeks) with a parent-centered intervention program focused on improving vocabulary production, toddlers who were LTs also made gains in two areas of phonology that were not directly targeted: syllable structure and consonant inventory. However, the long-term benefits of intervention are unknown in LTs. We do not know if targeting early perception and production has a lasting and beneficial result on higher-order language abilities. More intervention studies are needed to determine what untrained phonological gains may occur as a result of lexical intervention and vice versa. Perhaps an integrated approach may prove to be the most effective.

## CONCLUSIONS

The primary interactions among speech perception, phonology, and the lexicon in infancy (e.g., Jusczyk, 2000) form the cognitive-linguistic base on which sentence comprehension and production are built. Infants who demonstrate early differences in speech perception and production are likely to show impairments in lexical development as toddlers, which in turn negatively influence their morphosyntactic and syntactic development. There appears to be an early synergy among the components of language development in children developing typically and atypically. Any one component may lead or lag behind other components and either pull other components along or exert a drag on the development of other components. With development, the general synergy may weaken, leaving behind more specific relations among components. Furthermore, when impairments in one domain (e.g., speech perception) partially or completely resolve themselves with development, the causal links are more distant, more complex, and not easily specified. Thus, tracing the impairments in the base to impairments in particular language components presents a great challenge. Furthermore, the linking of impairments across less directly related language components (e.g., phonology and sentence processing) presents empirical and conceptual challenges.

For LTs, there continue to be significant research needs, including more intervention studies that examine cross-language domain outcomes and the development of integrated phonological and lexical approaches. Longitudinal approaches that identify earlier risk factors in speech production and perception would also be useful in understanding this relationship. Finally, more dynamic learning and processing measures are critical to our understanding of the relationship between phonology and other language domains.

## REFERENCES

Archibald, L.M.D., & Gathercole, S.E. (2006). Short-term memory and working memory in specific language impairment. In T.P. Alloway & S.E. Gathercole (Eds.), *Working memory and neurodevelopmental disorders* (pp. 139–160). New York, NY: Psychology Press.

Botting, N., & Conti-Ramsden, G. (2001). Non-word repetition and language development in children with specific language impairment (SLI). *International Journal of Language & Communication Disorders, 36*(4), 421–432.

Carson, C.P., Klee, T., Carson, D.K., & Hime, L.K. (2003). Phonological profiles of 2-year-olds with delayed language development: Predicting clinical outcomes at age 3. *American Journal of Speech-Language Pathology, 12,* 28–39.

Chiat, S. (2001). Mapping theories of developmental language impairment: Premises, predictions and evidence. *Language and Cognitive Processes, 16,* 113–142.

Dollaghan, C., Biber, M., & Campbell, T. (1995). Lexical influences on nonword repetition. *Applied Psycholinguistics, 16,* 211–222.

Dollaghan, C., & Campbell, T.F. (1998). Nonword repetition and child language impairment. *Journal of Speech, Language, and Hearing Research, 41*(5), 1136–1146.

Edwards, J., Beckman, M.E., & Munson, B. (2004). The interaction between vocabulary size and phonotactic probability effects on children's production accuracy and fluency in nonword repetition. *Journal of Speech, Language, and Hearing Research, 47,* 421–436.

Edwards, J., & Lahey, M. (1996). Auditory lexical decisions of children with specific language impairment. *Journal of Speech and Hearing Research, 39,* 1263–1273.

Eimas, P.D., Siqueland, E.R., Jusczyk, P., & Vigorito, J. (1971). Speech perception in infants. *Science, 171,* 303–306.

Ellis Weismer S., & Evans, J.L. (2002). The role of processing limitations in early identification of specific language impairment. *Topics in Language Disorders, 3,* 15–29.

Fasolo, M., Majorano, M., & D'Odorico, L. (2008). Babbling and first words in children with slow expressive development. *Clinical Linguistics and Phonetics, 22*(2), 83–94.

Ferguson, C.A., & Farwell, C. (1975). Words and sounds in early language acquisition: English initial consonants in the first fifty words. *Language, 51,* 419–439.

Gallon, N., Harris. J., & van der Lely, H.K.J. (2007). Non-word repetition: An investigation of phonological complexity in children with Grammatical SLI. *Clinical Linguistics and Phonetics, 21,* 435–455.

Gathercole, S.E., (2006). Nonword repetition and word learning: The nature of the relationship. *Applied Psycholinguistics, 27,* 513–543.

Gathercole, S.E., & Baddeley, A.D. (1990). Phonological memory deficits in language disordered children: Is there a causal connection? *Journal of Memory and Language, 29*(3), 336–360.

Girolametto, L., Pearce, P., & Weitzman, E. (1997). The effects of lexical intervention on the phonology of late talkers. *Journal of Speech, Language, and Hearing Research, 40,* 338–348.

Ingram, D. (1974). Phonological rules in young children. *Journal of Child Language, 1,* 49–64.

Ingram, D. (1976). *Phonological disability in children.* New York, NY: Elsevier.

Jakubowicz, C. (2003). Computational complexity and the acquisition of functional categories by French-speaking children with SLI. *Linguistics, 41,* 175–211.

Joanisse, M., & Seidenberg, M. (1998). Specific language impairment: A deficit in grammar or processing? *Trends in Cognitive Sciences, 2,* 240–247.

Jusczyk, P.W. (1992). Developing phonological categories from the speech signal. In C.A. Ferguson, L. Menn, & Stoel-Gammon, C. (Eds.), *Phonological development: Models, research, implications* (pp. 17–64). Parkton, MD: York Press.

Jusczyk, P.W. (2000). The discovery of spoken language. Cambridge, MA: The MIT Press.

Jusczyk, P.W., Luce, P.A., & Charles-Luce, J. (1994). Infant's sensitivity to phonotactic patterns in the native language. *Journal of Memory and Language, 33,* 630–645.

Leonard, L.B. (1985). Unusual and subtle phonological behavior in the speech of phonologically disordered children. *Journal of Speech and Hearing Disorders, 50,* 4–13.

Leonard, L.B. (2000). *Children with specific language impairment.* Cambridge, MA: The MIT Press.

Leonard, L.B, Davis, J., & Deevy, P. (2007). Phonotactic probability and past tense use by children with specific language impairment and their typically developing peers. *Clinical Linguistics and Phonetics, 21,* 747–758.

Leonard, L.B., Schwartz, R.G., Folger, M.K., & Wilcox, M.J. (1978). Some aspects of child phonology in imitative and spontaneous speech. *Journal of Child Language, 5,* 403-416.

Leonard, L.B., Schwartz, R.G., Morris, B., & Chapman, K. (1981). Factors influencing early lexical acquisition: Lexical orientation and phonological composition. *Child Development, 52,* 882–887.

Leonard, L.B., Schwartz, R.G., Swanson, L., & Frome Loeb, D. (1987). Some conditions that promote unusual phonological behavior in children. *Journal of Clinical Linguistics and Phonetics, 1,* 23-34.

Locke, J.L. (1983). *Phonological acquisition and change.* Orlando, FL: Academic Press.

MacRoy-Higgins, M., Schwartz, R.G., Shafer, V.L., & Marton, K. (2012). Influence of phonotactic probability/neighbourhood density on lexical learning in late talkers. *International Journal of Language & Communication Disorders.* doi: 10.1111/j.1460–6984.2012.00198.x

Marinis, T. (2011). On the nature and cause of specific language impairment: A view from sentence processing and infant research. *Lingua, 121*(3), 463–475.

Marshall, C., & van der Lely, H. (2006). A challenge to current models of past tense inflection: The impact of phonotactics. *Cognition, 100*(2), 302–320.

Marshall C.R., & van der Lely, H.K.J. (2007). Derivational morphology in children with grammatical-specific language impairment. *Clinical Linguistics and Phonetics, 42,* 71–91.

McGregor, K.K., & Leonard, L.B. (1994). Subject pronoun and article omissions in the speech of children with specific language impairment: A phonological interpretation. *Journal of Speech and Hearing Research, 37,* 171–181.

Menyuk, P., & Looney, P. (1972). Relationships among components of the grammar in language disorder. *Journal of Speech and Hearing Research, 15,* 395–406.

Metsala, J.L. (1999). Young children's phonological awareness and nonword repetition as a function of vocabulary. *Journal of Educational Psychology, 1,* 3–19.

Mirak, J., & Rescorla, L. (1998). Phonetic skills and vocabulary size in late talkers: Concurrent and predictive relationships. *Applied Psycholinguistics, 19,* 1–17.

Montgomery, J.W. (1995). Sentence comprehension in children with specific language impairment: The role of phonological working memory. *Journal of Speech and Hearing Research, 38*(1), 187–199.

Oller, D.K. (1980). The emergence of the sounds of speech in infancy. In G. Yeni-Komshian, J. Davanagh, & C.A. Ferguson (Eds.), *Child phonology: Volume I: Production* (pp. 93–112). New York, NY: Academic Press.

Oller, D.K., Eilers, R.E., Neal A.R., & Schwartz, H.K. (1999). Precursors to speech in infancy: The prediction of speech and language disorders. *Journal of Communication Disorders, 32,* 223–245.

Panagos, J., (1974). Persistence of the open syllable reinterpreted as a symptom of language disorder. *Journal of Speech and Hearing Disorders, 39,* 23–31.

Paul, R., & Jennings, P. (1992). Phonological behavior in toddlers with slow expressive language development. *Journal of Speech and Hearing Research, 35*(1), 99–105.

Pennington, B.F., & Bishop, D.V.M. (2009). Relations among speech, language, and reading disorders. *Annual Review of Psychology, 60,* 283–386.

Pollack, E., & Rees, N. (1972). Disorders of articulation: Some clinical applications of distinctive feature theory. *Journal of Speech and Hearing Disorders, 37,* 451–461.

Polka L., & Werker, J.F. (1994). Developmental changes in perception of nonnative vowel contrasts. *Journal of Experimental Psychology: Human Perception and Performance, 20*(2), 421–435.

Rescorla, L. (1989). The language development survey: A screening tool for delayed language in toddlers. *Journal of Speech and Hearing Disorders, 54,* 587–599.

Rescorla, L., & Ratner, N.B. (1996). Phonetic profiles of toddlers with specific expressive language impairment (SLI-E). *Journal of Speech and Hearing Research, 39,* 153–165.

Schwartz, R.G. (1988). Phonological factors in early lexical acquisition. In M. Smith & J. Locke (Eds.), *The emergent lexicon* (pp. 185–222). New York, NY: Academic Press.

Schwartz, R.G. (2009). Specific language impairment. In R.G. Schwartz (Ed.), *The handbook of child language disorders.* New York, NY: Psychology Press.

Schwartz, R.G., & Leonard, L.B. (1982). Do children pick and choose? Phonological selection and avoidance in early lexical acquisition. *Journal of Child Language, 9,* 319–336.

Schwartz, R., & Leonard, L. (1985). Lexical imitation and acquisition in language impaired children. *Journal of Speech and Hearing Disorders, 50,* 141–149.

Schwartz, R.G., Leonard, L.B., Folger, M.K., & Wilcox, M.J. (1980). Early phonological behavior in normal and language disordered children: Evidence for a synergistic view of language disorders. *Journal of Speech and Hearing Disorders, 45,* 357–378.

Schwartz, R.G., Leonard, L.B., Messick, C., & Chapman, K. (1987). Acquisition of object names in children with specific language impairment: Action context and word extension. *Applied Psycholinguistics, 8,* 233–244.

Seiger-Gardner, L., & Brooks, P.J. (2008). Effects of onset- and rhyme-related distractors on phonological processing in children with specific language impairment. *Journal of Speech, Language, and Hearing Research, 51,* 1263–1281.

Seiger-Gardner, L., & Schwartz, R.G. (2008). Lexical access during word production in school-aged children with and without SLI. *International Journal of Language and Communication Disorders, 43,* 1–23.

Shriberg, L.D., Gruber, F.A., & Kwiatkowski, J. (1994). Developmental phonological disorders: III. Long-term speech-sound normalization. *Journal of Speech and Hearing Research, 37*(5), 1151–1177.

Shriberg, L.D., & Kwiatkowski, J. (1994). Developmental phonological disorders: I. A clinical profile. *Journal of Speech and Hearing Research, 37*(5), 1100–1126.

Shriberg, L.D., Kwiatkowski, J., & Gruber, F.A. (1994). Developmental phonological disorders: II. Short-term speech-sound normalization. *Journal of Speech and Hearing Research, 37*(5), 1127–1150.

Shriner, T.H., Halloway, M.S., & Daniloff, R.G. (1969). The relationship between articulatory deficits and syntax in speech defective children. *Journal of Speech and Hearing Research, 12,* 319–325.

Stoel-Gammon, C. (1989). Prespeech and early speech development of two late talkers. *First Language, 9,* 207–224.

Stoel-Gammon, C. (1991). Normal and disordered phonology in two-year-olds. *Topics in Language Disorders, 11,* 21–32.

Stoel-Gammon, C. (2011). Relationships between lexical and phonological development in young children. *Journal of Child Language, 38,* 1–34.

Stokes, S.F. (2010). Neighborhood density and word frequency predict vocabulary size in toddlers. *Journal of Speech, Language, and Hearing Research, 53,* 670–683.

Storkel, H.L. (2001). Learning new words: Phonotactic probability in language development. *Journal of Speech, Language, and Hearing Research, 44,* 1321–1337.

Storkel, H.L. (2003). Learning new words II: Phonotactic probability in verb learning. *Journal of Speech, Language, and Hearing Research, 46,* 1312–1323.

Storkel, H.L. (2004). The emerging lexicon of children with phonological delays: Phonotactic constraints and probability in acquisition. *Journal of Speech, Language, and Hearing Research, 47,* 1194–1212.

Storkel, H.L. (2005). The emerging lexicon of children with phonological delays: Phonotactic constraints and probability in acquisition. *Journal of Speech, Language, and Hearing Research, 47,* 1194–1212.

Storkel, H.L. (2006). Do children still pick and choose? The relationship between phonological knowledge and lexical acquisition beyond 50 words. *Clinical Linguistics and Phonetics, 20*(7–8), 523–529.

Storkel, H.L., & Maekawa, J. (2005). A comparison of homonym and novel word learning: The role of phonotactic probability and word frequency. *Journal of Child Language, 32,* 827–853.

Thal, D.J., Oroz, M., & McCaw, V. (1995). Phonological and lexical development in normal and late-talking toddlers. *Applied Psycholinguistics, 16,* 407–424.

Trehub, S.E. (1976). The discrimination of foreign speech contrasts by infants and adults. *Child Development, 47,* 466–472.

Tsao, F.-M., Liu H.-M., & Kuhl, P. (2004). Speech perception in infancy predicts language developing in the 2nd year of life: A longitudinal study. *Child Development, 75,* 1067–1084.

Velez, M., & Schwartz, R.G. (2011). Spoken word recognition in school-age children with SLI: Semantic, phonological, and repetition priming. *Journal of Speech, Language, and Hearing Research, 53,* 1616–1628.

Werker, J.R., Fennell, C.T., Corcoran, K.M., & Stager, C.L. (2002). Infants' ability to learn phonetically similar words: Effects of age and vocabulary size. *Infancy, 3,* 1–30.

Werker, J.F., & Tees, R.C. (2002). Cross-language speech perception: Evidence for perceptual reorganization during the first year of life. *Infant Behavior & Development, 25,* 121–133.

Williams, A.L., & Elbert, M. (2003). A prospective longitudinal study of phonological development in late talkers. *Language, Speech and Hearing Services in Schools, 34,* 138–153.

Whitehurst, G.J., Smith, M., Fischel, J.E., Arnold, D.S., & Lonigan, C.J. (1991). The continuity of babble and speech in children with specific expressive language delay. *Journal of Speech and Hearing Research, 34,* 1121–1129.

Zamuner, T.S., Gerken, L., & Hammond, M. (2004). Phonotactic probabilities in young children's speech production. *Journal of Child Language, 31,* 515–536.

# 7

# Using Fluency to Measure Formulation Effort in Late Talkers

Nan Bernstein Ratner

C hild language and adult language researchers have tended to view production data in somewhat different ways over the years (McKee, Rispoli, McDaniel, & Garrett, 2006). Because young children's early language production attempts diverge so obviously from adult forms, the majority of analyses of children's utterances emphasize the growth of lexical and phonological inventories, evolution of syntactic structures, and typical errors made by young language learners. Researchers who study adult language production have fewer opportunities to observe true errors or omissions in typical adult (intact users') utterances. Thus, in addition to the study of those few types of errors or "slips" that occur in children's speech, there has been a robust history of research into the time course of language production in adult speakers, using evidence from hesitations, disfluencies, and retracings (sometimes called mazes) to inform the processes by which a competent language user appears to assemble output "on the fly" during verbal tasks. This large and well-developed body of research, starting with the ground-breaking observations of Maclay and Osgood (1959) and deeply elaborated by Goldman-Eisler (1968) and others, has demonstrated that people do not fully preplan what they will say; rather, they are engaged in constituent planning of upcoming elements as they articulate initial parts of the utterance.

Disfluencies (including silent and filled pauses; repetitions of sounds, syllables, and words; mazes; and retraces) all provide evidence of the speaker's ongoing work in assembling words and phrases. We now know that production of longer and more difficult utterances will provoke higher levels of disfluency (e.g., Bock & Levelt, 1994; Chafe, 1985; Rochester & Gill, 1973, to cite only a few examples of this robust body of research). Furthermore, even the type of disfluency (e.g., filled vs. silent pauses, or the use of "um" versus "uh") tends to be relatively predictable, based on the specific challenges faced by speakers during ongoing production (e.g., Clark & Fox Tree, 2002). It is not the goal of this chapter to summarize comprehensively this large and well-articulated body of research. However, it is important to note that the study of disfluency has in fact played a major role in the development of all extant models of speech production because it informs the processes by which the general frames of utterances are developed by speakers and then gradually "fleshed out" (Bock & Levelt, 1994).

Given the evidence that even fully mature language users face challenges during the ongoing task of speaking, it is not surprising that researchers have investigated disfluency in the speech of a wide variety of individuals with language impairments (e.g., individuals with aphasia [Horner, 1987] or dementia [Gayraud, Hye-Ran, & Barkat-Defradas, 2011; Pakhomov et al., 2011]), adults with attention-deficit/hyperactivity disorder [ADHD; Engelhardt, Ferreira, & Nigg, 2011]; second language learners or those whose first languages are attriting [see Schmid & Fägersten, 2010]). An enormous body of research has studied the interaction between language demand and stuttering, in both typical school-age children and adult speakers (see Hall, Wagovich, & Bernstein Ratner, 2007, for review).

However, a much smaller body of research has examined speech disfluency and errors in the speech of typical beginning language learners, and even fewer studies have examined the speech of young language learners who are delayed or impaired in their trajectory of language development. Like adults, young language learners appear to speak before they have fully planned out what they will say, and they appear to retrieve and assemble later constituents even as they articulate the earlier parts of their utterances (Bernstein, 1981; McDaniel, McKee, & Garrett, 2010; Rispoli & Hadley, 2001; Rispoli, Hadley, & Holt, 2008; Wijnen, 1990). They also appear to experience elevated disfluency on emerging or difficult linguistic structures (Bernstein, 1981; Bernstein Ratner & Sih, 1987; Colburn & Mysak, 1982; Yairi, 1993). Although there are some qualitative differences between adult and child profiles of disfluency in speech production, one major distinction is in how *much* disfluency children demonstrate during early syntactic development. McDaniel et al. succinctly note that

> [T]he architecture of the child and adult formulators are very much the same. Sentences are planned in similar ways and the planning points are the same. The difference between children and adults lies in the amount of advance planning they undertake, and possibly in the levels of advance planning they can sustain during sentence formulation. A good analogy is the process of crossing a creek by jumping from stone to stone. Children and adults land on stones that are positioned in the same places. But adults figure out a path before starting across, whereas children do some of the figuring on the way. (2010, p. 92)

Findings from typically developing (TD) children also suggest that the rate of productive words per minute (which removes mazing and disfluency behavior) is a highly predictive measure of language proficiency in children from kindergarten through third grade; during this period it correlates positively and well with standardized oral language measures (Tilstra & McMaster, 2007). Given the fact that TD children face more challenges maintaining fluency during speech production than do many adults, and show developmentally predictable profiles, it is not surprising that a small but growing body of work shows that a variety of childhood communication conditions are accompanied by elevated levels of disfluency in conversational or elicited speech.

For example, children with specific language impairment (SLI) show a higher-than-normal frequency of disfluency and, in particular, stutter-like disfluencies (SLDs). These disfluencies may be defined as monosyllabic word repetitions, sound repetitions, prolongations of sounds, and blocks (postural fixations while speaking or attempting to initiate speech; Boscolo, Bernstein Ratner, & Rescorla, 2002; Finneran, Leonard, & Miller, 2009; Guo, Tomblin, & Samelson, 2008; Hall, 1996; Hall, Yamashita, & Aram, 1993; Hodge, Bernstein Ratner, & Rescorla, 1999; Nettelbladt & Hansson, 1999; Redmond, 2004). However, it is important to note that even though these disfluencies can be labeled as stutter-like in form, they are not at all stutter-like in quality. True stuttering events are typically characterized by a level of awareness, struggle, and reactivity that are not reported in nonstuttering children. This issue is revisited later, when discussing factors that lead to fluency breakdown in different cohorts of children. Finneran et al. (2009) commented that children with SLI are more disfluent than TD peers, even when they are grammatically accurate in their production. They conclude that "school-age children with specific language impairment may demonstrate subtle but persistent language formulation difficulties even on simple language tasks" (p. 272).

The fluency of expressive language in children with SLI shows more hesitations and more repetitions of function words during conversation and narrative than do peers with typical language skills (Navarro-Ruiz & Rallo-Fabra, 2001). Although some studies comparing oral language samples from children with SLI have found no significant differences in disfluency rate from TD peers (e.g., Newman & McGregor, 2006), other researchers report findings of elevated rates of disfluency in different cohorts of children with other communicative disorders or conditions that impact language production skills: bilingual children (Carias & Ingram, 2006), children who clutter or have learning disabilities (van Zaalen-Op't Hof, Wijnen, & Dejonckere, 2009), children with ADHD (Redmond, 2004), and children with temporal lobe seizures (Steinberg, Bernstein Ratner, Berl, & Gaillard, in press). Although typically touted as highly verbal, with intact language ability despite severe intellectual impairment, individuals with Williams syndrome are significantly more disfluent than mental age–matched peers during oral narratives, presumably because of the cognitive and linguistic load during narrative generation (Rossi, Sampaio, Gonçalves, & Giacheti, 2011). Speakers with Williams syndrome also demonstrate more SLDs than do TD peers. Finally, subtle variability in children's hesitation patterns can be reliably associated with proficiency in specific linguistic probes, such as a word derivation task (Edrington, Buder, & Jarmulowicz, 2009). For example, when asked to change a word into a different form by adding the suffix –*ity*, children with poorer ability to assign stress to the resulting word also showed significantly more disfluency, sometimes stopping to pause mid-word. These last two reports emphasize how informative fluency analysis can be in discriminating very subtle differences in language performance within a cohort of children.

Boscolo et al. (2002; see also Chapter 11) reported fluency characteristics of a cohort of 9-year-old children, studied longitudinally since age 2. Half of these children were diagnosed as late talkers (LTs), the remainder were TD peers. By age 9, group differences in language ability were evident on standardized testing, although no child in the late talker group was receiving services for clinical language impairment. Nonetheless, disfluency rates in the spontaneous language of the late talking children were roughly twice those seen in their TD peers, as was the rate of SLDs. These results appear to confirm a view that fluency of output might function as a measure of language proficiency or as a measure of formulation difficulty in children with either concurrent or past history of language delay or impairment.

The majority of the reports summarized in this section have analyzed fluency profiles in school-age children. Relatively few reports exist for younger children, with the well-known exceptions of Colburn and Mysak (1982), Wijnen (1990), Hall (1996), and Rispoli and colleagues (2008). In addition, most studies have tracked fluency behaviors alone, or have described only broad relationships between fluency and language profiles. To date, however, multiple concurrent skill areas, such as fluency, linguistic development, and phonological/speech motor abilities have not been appraised within a single population of preschool-age children to examine whether strengths and weaknesses in any of these domains interact in a principled way with the other domains. That is, are strengths or weaknesses in one skill area, such as language or phonological proficiency, predictive of strengths or weaknesses in another, such as fluency? Children at the onset of linguistic, phonological, and speech development present an interesting test case for the strength of such dependencies. If fluency is highly dependent upon maturation or stability of the linguistic, articulatory, or phonological systems, we might expect to find a strong relationship among levels of performance in language, articulation and phonology, and fluency, particularly in the frequency of stutter-like behaviors.

We have been exploring a large collection of language data taken from typically developing and expressively language-impaired children at 3 years of age (Rescorla, 1990; Rescorla & Bernstein Ratner, 1996; see also Chapter 11). These data are similar in nature (naturalistic mother–child interaction) to another set of data taken from 3-year-old children who stutter (CWS) and their TD peers (Bernstein Ratner & Silverman[1], 2000). We have used these spoken language data to conduct an initial, exploratory comparison of possible dependencies or relationships among domains of speech and language behavior in children who present with typical communication development, atypical language development, and atypical speech fluency development.

## LINKAGES AMONG FLUENCY, LANGUAGE, AND SPEECH IN 3-YEAR-OLD CHILDREN WITH A HISTORY OF LATE TALKING

Using the collection of data just described, this chapter takes an exploratory look at the relationships among linguistic skills (morphology, syntax, lexicon), fluency, and phonological/speech motor skills (phonological inventory, speech rate) in 32 young children. The first cohort consisted of 8 pairs of children matched for age, gender, and socioeconomic status, half of whom had delayed emergence of meaningful expressive language (LTs), despite typical language comprehension and intelligence, and half of whom had TD language profiles. These children were randomly selected from a larger cohort of 32 pairs of children followed in a longitudinal study of children with delayed and typical language development by Rescorla and her colleagues (Mirak & Rescorla, 1998; Rescorla, 1990; Rescorla & Bernstein Ratner, 1996; Rescorla & Schwartz, 1990). The LTs were selected on a number of criteria and, importantly, demonstrated language comprehension (as opposed to production) within normal limits. The second cohort consisted of 8 pairs of children

---

[1]Now publishing as Wagovich

matched for age, gender, and socioeconomic status, half of whom were selected for typical fluency development and half of whom were assessed within 3 months of the emergence of stuttering symptoms (CWS). These children who stuttered represent a subset, matched by age, to the children in the Rescorla database from a larger cohort of 15 pairs of children studied in our laboratory (Bernstein Ratner, 1998; Bernstein Ratner & Silverman, 2000; Miles & Bernstein Ratner, 2001) near onset of stuttering symptoms and their typically fluent peers. Our final yield is, therefore, 16 TD children, 8 LTs, and 8 CWS.

## Measures

We analyzed the children's development across the following domains both within and across groups: linguistic development (mean length of utterance [MLU]), type-token ratio (TTR) expressed as VOCD (a statistically corrected TTR resistant to sample size variation [Malvern & Richards, 2002]), phonology (percentage of consonants correct [PCC] for known targets), and speech/fluency (articulatory rate and fluency, which we appraised for the frequency of stutter-like behaviors [i.e., SLDs]).

All measures were based on samples from spontaneous play sessions between children and their mothers. MLU and VOCD were computed directly from coded transcripts using CLAN utilities (MacWhinney, 2000). PCC was derived from earlier work by Pharr, Bernstein Ratner, and Rescorla (2000) for the Rescorla cohort, and computed by hand for the Bernstein Ratner cohort. Speech rate was computed for a minimum of 25 utterances having a minimum length of 3 words, using a digital stop watch. The following behaviors were classified as SLDs: sound, syllable, and whole-word repetitions; prolongations; blocks; and broken words.

Analyses included comparisons for mean frequency of each behavior across groups, and correlations among measures both among and within groups. In all, we appraised the five speech measures (PCC, speech rate, fluency, MLU, and VOCD) among the three groups of children, classified by diagnostic status; comparisons were generated, as well as four 5 x 5 correlation matrices (one per diagnostic group and one for the sample of children as a whole).

## Findings

Results can be found in Table 7.1. The following sections present data for each speech/fluency domain comparison among groups and then discuss observed relationships among domains for all children and the diagnostic subgroups of children.

**Table 7.1.**   Mean speech and language variables for all groups

| Group | SLD rate | MLU | VOCD | PCC | Speech rate |
|---|---|---|---|---|---|
| TD children | 4.14 | 3.656 | 53.4 | 87 | 3.69 |
| LTs | 4.996 | 2.418 | 47.4 | 74.3 | 3.685 |
| CWS | 10.9 | 3.541 | 47.3 | 82.9 | 3.0625 |

*Key:* TD, typically developing; LTs, late talkers; CWS, children who shutter; SLD, stutter-like disfluencies; MLU, mean length of utterance; PCC, percentage of consonants correct.

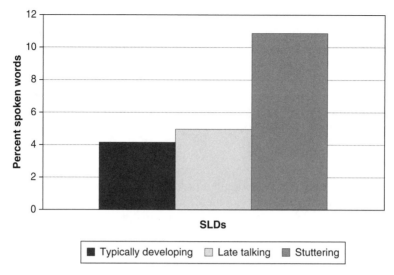

**Figure 7.1.** Percentage of stutter-like disfluencies (SLDs) among typically developing children, late talking children, and children who stutter.

***Fluency (Stutter-Like Disfluencies)***    As shown in Figure 7.1, the CWS group was most disfluent (as might be expected) and TD children were least disfluent in their frequency of SLDs. LTs fell mid-way between the other two profiles. Statistical analysis of differences among the groups set a criterion of $p = .016$ to control for multiple comparisons (Bonferroni MCT) and indicated that CWS were significantly more disfluent than TD children but not than LTs ($p = .009$). In other words, fluency rates of LTs and children who were clinically diagnosed as stuttering were statistically indistinguishable.

Also as expected, LTs had the shortest MLU values, whereas TD children had the longest utterances (see Figure 7.2). CWS fell slightly below TD children in

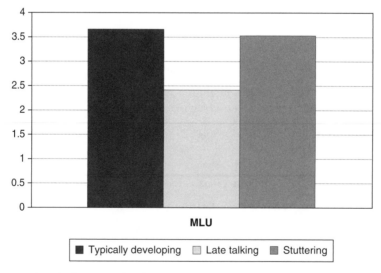

**Figure 7.2.** Mean length of utterance (MLU) among typically developing children, late talking children, and children who stutter.

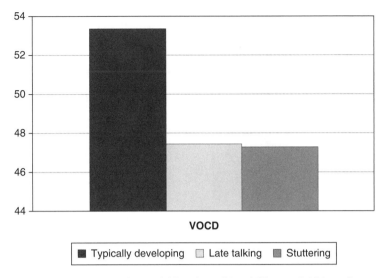

**Figure 7.3.** VOCD among typically developing children, late talking children, and children who stutter.

MLU values, but well above those for children with delayed language (for group, $p = .007$; LTs significantly different from TD children, CWS by Bonferroni MCT). These results are consistent with numerous reports showing minor, nonclinical language depression in young CWS (Hall et al., 2007).

No significant group differences were found for VOCD/TTR, although both the CWS and LT groups scored lower on $d$ (the diversity measure) than did TD children (see Figure 7.3).

No significant group differences were observed for speech rate in syllables per second. TD children and LTs demonstrated virtually identical speech rate. However, speech rate for the CWS group was slower than for the other two groups (see Figure 7.4).

Articulation (PCC) resembled the pattern seen for MLU, in which LTs performed significantly more poorly than their TD peers, whereas CWS fell into an intermediate profile, as shown in Figure 7.5 (group significant at $p < .02$, LT significantly different from TD by Bonferroni MCT.) This analysis is consistent with earlier reports of the LTs and TD children studied here (Pharr et al., 2000; Rescorla & Bernstein Ratner, 1996).

As expected, the TD children scored higher in all skill areas: They had the highest levels of fluency, utterance length, lexical diversity, and articulation accuracy. Their speech rates were higher than those of stuttering children but not distinguishable from those of LTs.

As also expected, LT children showed depressed utterance length and diminished lexical diversity. Less predictably, having been identified on the basis of slower-than-expected growth in language skills, they also showed a higher level of SLDs. This finding has been noted elsewhere and is generalizable throughout the Rescorla cohort at multiple ages (Boscolo et al., 2002); although we have not specifically followed individual children's trajectories, when considered as a group, LT children show a higher incidence of SLDs at ages 3, 5, and 9. As noted in prior

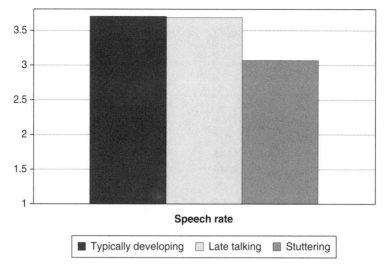

**Figure 7.4.** Speech rate among typically developing children, late talking children, and children who stutter.

studies, children with poor language skills for their age are more disfluent than TD children, suggesting an observable impact of language ability on children's fluency. LT children also showed significantly depressed phonological abilities compared with TD children, but speech rates were indistinguishable.

It is interesting that CWS show both lower phonological accuracy and speech rate, whereas LT children show poorer speech sound articulation but at a typical rate, suggesting potentially different relationships between these areas across groups.

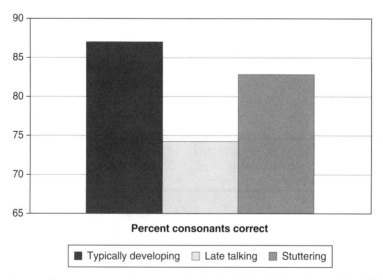

**Figure 7.5.** Percent of consonants correct among typically developing children, late talking children, and children who stutter.

***Children's Skills Across Domains***    A series of correlations were run to determine whether a given child's spontaneous language production ability in one area at 3 years of age was related to those in other areas. Correlations were run for the group of 32 children as a whole, and within each diagnostic group. Because this was an exploratory venture, we set $p < .05$.

For the group as a whole ($N = 32$), only two significant correlations were detected: 1) MLU was positively correlated with PCC ($r = .608, p < .0002$), indicating that children producing the longest utterances showed the highest articulation accuracy, and 2) speech rate was positively correlated with PCC ($r = .365, p < .04$), indicating that children with more rapid speech rates showed higher phonological accuracy. No other correlations even remotely approached significance. A body of research suggests that as utterances become longer speech rate increases (e.g., Ferreira, 1993; Malecott, Johnston, & Kizziar, 1972) We did *not* find a correlation we expected, given previous research, between utterance length and speech rate; however, this analysis did not address intraspeaker variation in rate as a function of utterance length, it merely asked whether children with the longest utterances were the most rapid speakers.

In TD children ($n = 16$), only two correlations met a test of $p < .05$: 1) speech rate correlated with PCC ($r = .688, p < .003$), suggesting that for TD children, those with the most rapid speaking rates had the highest speech sound accuracy, and 2) VOCD correlated with MLU, suggesting that the children using longer utterances displayed greater lexical diversity in spontaneous conversation ($r = .496$, $p = .05$). This relationship was absent in the other two groups.

In children with a history of late talking ($n = 8$), no correlations met a generous standard of $p < .05$, and only two even remotely approached significance: 1) MLU correlated with disfluency rate ($r = .69; p = .058$), suggesting that LTs who produced the longest utterances were the most disfluent, potentially overreaching their linguistic capacity, and 2) MLU correlated with PCC ($r = .638, p = .089$), suggesting that LTs who produced the longest utterances showed the best articulation within their group. In other words, utterance formulation skill appeared positively correlated with segmental articulation ability but appeared to stress the ability to execute output fluently. One set of relationships might be considered indices of language knowledge (sentence formation and phonological skills), whereas the other reflects language processing (sentence formation and ability to maintain fluency).

Finally, in the CWS group ($n = 8$), no correlations met a generous standard of $p < .05$, and as with the LTs, only two even approached significance: 1) MLU correlated with PCC ($r = .667, p = .07$), suggesting that stuttering children who produced the longest utterances showed the highest phonological accuracy. There was also a nonsignificant negative trend ($r = -.60, p = .11$) for CWS with the highest rates of SLDs to have lower profiles of articulation accuracy. Speech rate showed a negative, nonsignificant correlation with disfluency rate ($-.30$), suggesting that mean frequency of stuttering was *lower* for children who spoke more *rapidly* within this group.

The strongest correlation (for all children, and within the LTs and CWS group) was observed between MLU and PCC, suggesting that children (particularly those with these diagnoses) who produced the longest utterances demonstrated the highest level of articulation accuracy, and vice versa. These results add to a growing literature that suggest that aspects of grammatical and phonological development develop in tandem, and that some early expressive language delays may be related to phonological or articulatory constraints (Rescorla & Bernstein Ratner, 1996). Intervention studies in toddlers suggest that intervention to improve one area can result in improvements to the other (Girolametto, Pearce, & Weitzman, 1997).

For TD children, phonological accuracy and speech rate are highly correlated, suggesting either a common motor basis or the facilitating effects of more highly developed phonological inventories on speech planning and execution. In retrospect, and in terms of conducting future analyses, it would have been interesting to have contrasted a group of children chosen solely for articulation delay with our other three groups; it might also have been interesting to examine typical disfluency patterns across the groups, rather than only SLDs.

## What Factors Influence Fluency Breakdown?

Clearly, language plays some role, given the literature on CWS and the emerging literature on LTs. Both groups also show depressed phonology, but phonological skill does not correlate with SLD frequency.

The CWS group in this study had an array of subtle deficiencies in speech and language performance when compared with TD peers (Bernstein Ratner & Silverman, 2000). They were also most likely to stutter when trying to produce linguistically complex utterances. It was not possible to predict the frequency of SLDs in our study children from any of the variables we examined. A single exception was seen in the LTs; those who used longer utterances were more disfluent. In some respects (see Figure 7.3), LTs look as much like children at the onset of stuttering as they do TD children. Some factors thought to produce symptoms of language delay including SLI (e.g., generalized slowing; Kail, 1994) may have a role in aberrant fluency development across children with different profiles of expressive language impairment.

Language ability and task demand do seem to play some role in predicting disfluency, but the *quality* of SLDs is noticeably and critically different in CWS. LTs (and even TD children) repeated sounds and syllables, but never with the associated tension and awareness seen in CWS. As noted elsewhere (Bernstein Ratner, 1997), it is much easier to predict conditions that impair fluency in general than to model the exact properties of stutter-like events that clearly distinguish themselves from typical fluency breakdown. Some mechanism that explains this exceptional awareness of and reaction to moments of speech production failure must be identified. One candidate is auditory self-monitoring, still very poorly understood in preschool-age children. Given a very old literature that suggests that auditory self-monitoring is an emerging capacity in the age range being discussed, it may be that CWS are somewhat more precocious in monitoring their own verbal output than TD children (Razzak & Bernstein Ratner, 1999). This, in turn, could lead to a multifactorial model of stuttering onset in which potentially fragile linguistic and/or speech motor variables combine to create fluency breakdown. This breakdown in fluency may be closely monitored and responded to with tension in the children whose disfluencies develop the struggled quality that distinguishes stuttering from typical disfluency (Bernstein Ratner, 1998).

## CONCLUSIONS

There is an urgent need to incorporate research with young children in the development of speech production models (McKee et al., 2006). So many of the components embedded in contemporary models of the adult language production process are frank unknowns during the early course of development. We know very little about the stages of utterance assembly, lexical retrieval, lemma and lexeme representations, and general encoding constraints that operate to shape language output in children between the ages of 1 and 5 years. Other dynamic components of language production models, such as self-monitoring, are likewise poorly specified in child speakers. However, as with adult speakers, some traces of sentence assembly and lexical retrieval processes, as well as self-monitoring and self-correction, can be garnered from observation of disfluencies that arise in the course of speech production.

Much of the energy in tracking LTs has been spent on what might be called "absent features" of their productions: missing grammatical structures or categories, limited lexical and phonological inventories, and so forth. However, the adult literature on speech production and an emerging companion literature in both TD children and children with impairments suggest a potentially fruitful contribution of disfluency analysis in tracking emerging or challenging aspects of a child's language system. For example, in a child just beginning to master auxiliary verb use, one might find increased levels of disfluency in spontaneous utterances requiring or using auxiliary verbs. In the same sense that a language sample provides information about expressive language skills not provided by standardized testing, a language sample analysis that includes measures of fluency/disfluency may show what kinds of grammatical constructions are well-mastered or emerging, or reveal difficulty in lexical retrieval not as easily seen in confrontation naming tasks. Based on research on the determinants of type and location of fluency breakdown in adults and older children, we can infer what aspect of an utterance has caused a child to "stall" (Rispoli et al., 2008) during production. This information would be relevant both for understanding the specific problems of children with differing patterns of communicative delays or disorders, and for tracking skill growth within individual children. For example, children have been seen to be more disfluent when first mastering stages of negative and question formation, moving to complex sentence types, and so forth. As an added feature of their communicative attempts, fluency thus marks an aspect of formulation effort, which potentially can mark an intermediate stage of mastery (as in a progression from an immature syntactic form, to a disfluent production of an intermediate form closer to the adult target, through to fluent and correct adult-like production). In fact, a study by Hall (2011) found speech-language pathologists reporting increased disfluency rates in the speech of children being treated for language delay as they began to use structures targeted in therapy.

When we first embarked on studying disfluency in children who do *not* stutter, it was partially in response to requests for therapy planning advice that I often received from fellow speech-language pathologists regarding children who they judged both stuttered and had language formulation problems. The more that some of my colleagues and I listened to such case reports and asked very targeted questions about the nature of the disfluencies of concern, the more apparent it became that these children were in fact quite disfluent, but were not stuttering in the formal definition of the word (e.g., breakdown accompanied by tension, effort, and awareness). Rather, they seemed to be on an extreme tail end of typical disfluency, which made sense, given their language impairments and what we know about linguistic stressors of fluency in both children and adults. Since then, a growing body of literature has confirmed this judgment, which has at least one very practical clinical extension: Because these children do not stutter, traditional stuttering therapy is not advised for them, and would in fact take valuable time away from their major clinical problem—limited language proficiency.

It is also possible that fluency analyses of children who are late to talk or who are diagnosed with SLI at later ages can help us with another vexing problem in the categorization of SLI across languages. Leonard (2009) noted that the linguistic features of SLI vary considerably across languages. What specifically children with language impairments find difficult to acquire in one language may not look much like what a peer struggles with in another language. Because of this, many researchers have expressed a desire to see measures other than typical standardized test scores used to define the population of children with SLI across communities, such as measures of phonological working memory (e.g., nonword repetition tasks). One potential augmentative measure is some assessment of the fluency of speech production, given the growing body of data showing differences in the fluency of LTs and children with SLI, across a number of language communities.

Furthermore, the group of LTs from whom the children analyzed for this chapter were drawn continued to demonstrate statistically weaker language skills than their TD peers through age 17 (see Chapter 11), despite scoring in the typical range on all language measures. The fluency profiles seen here for very young children and reported on elsewhere for older children with SLI persuasively argue that fluency can be viewed as a marker of "underlying lexical and syntactic immaturity" (Guo et al., 2008, p. 735). Long after children appear to have mastered the ability "to produce adult-like grammatical sentences . . . language difficulties may remain, but may appear in subtle forms such as reduced fluency in sentence production" (Finneran et al., 2009, p. 272). Both sets of authors have suggested that fluency may be used as a functional marker of language proficiency in school-age children; our work suggests that fluency is an accompanying feature of language delays or disorders from the toddler years forward.

## REFERENCES

Bernstein, N. (1981). Are there constraints on childhood dysfluency? *Journal of Fluency Disorders, 6,* 341–350.

Bernstein Ratner, N. (1997). Stuttering: A psycholinguistic perspective. In R. Curlee & G. Siegel (Eds.), *Nature and treatment of stuttering: New directions* (2nd ed., pp. 99–127). Needham, MA: Allyn & Bacon.

Bernstein Ratner, N. (1998). Linguistic and perceptual characteristics of children at stuttering onset. In E.C. Healey & H.F.M. Peters (Eds.), *Proceedings of the Second World Congress on Fluency Disorders* (pp. 3–6). Nijmegen, The Netherlands: Nijmegen University Press.

Bernstein Ratner, N., & Sih, C.C. (1987). The effects of gradual increases in sentence length and complexity on children's dysfluency. *Journal of Speech and Hearing Disorders, 52*(3), 278–287.

Bernstein Ratner, N., & Silverman, S. (2000). Parental perceptions of children's communicative development at stuttering onset. *Journal of Speech, Language, and Hearing Research, 43*(5), 1252–1263.

Bock, K., & Levelt, W. (1994). Language production: Grammatical encoding. In M.A. Gernsbacher (Ed.), *Handbook of psycholinguistics* (pp. 945–984). London, United Kingdom: Academic Press.

Boscolo, B., Bernstein Ratner, N., & Rescorla, L. (2002). Fluency characteristics of children with a history of specific expressive language impairment (SLI-E). *American Journal of Speech-Language Pathology, 11*, 41–49.

Carias, S., & Ingram, D. (2006). Language and disfluency: Four case studies on Spanish-English bilingual children. *Journal of Multilingual Communication Disorders, 4*(2), 149–157.

Chafe, W. (1985). Some reasons for hesitating. In D. Tannen & M. Saville-Troike (Eds.), *Perspectives on silence* (pp. 21–30). Norwood, NJ: Ablex.

Clark, H., & Fox Tree, J. (2002). Using *uh* and *um* in spontaneous dialog. *Cognition, 84*, 73–111.

Colburn, N., & Mysak, E. (1982). Developmental disfluency and emerging grammar: Disfluency characteristics of early syntactic utterances. *Journal of Speech and Hearing Research, 25*, 414–420.

Edrington, J., Buder, E., & Jarmulowicz, L. (2009). Hesitation patterns in third grade children's derived word productions. *Clinical Linguistics & Phonetics, 23*(5), 348–374.

Engelhardt, P.E., Ferreira, F., & Nigg, J.T. (2011). Language production strategies and disfluencies in multi-clause network descriptions: A study of adult attention-deficit/hyperactivity disorder. *Neuropsychology, 25*(4), 442–453.

Ferreira, F. (1993). Effects of length and syntactic complexity on initiation times for prepared utterances. *Journal of Memory and Language, 30*, 210–233.

Finneran, D., Leonard, L., & Miller, C. (2009). Speech disruptions in the sentence formulation of school-aged children with specific language impairment. *International Journal of Language and Communication Disorders, 44*, 271–286.

Gayraud, F., Hye-Ran, L., & Barkat-Defradas, M. (2011). Syntactic and lexical context of pauses and hesitations in the discourse of Alzheimer patients and healthy elderly subjects. *Clinical Linguistics & Phonetics, 25*(3), 198–209.

Girolametto, L., Pearce, P., & Weitzman, E. (1997). Effects of lexical intervention on the phonology of late talkers. *Journal of Speech, Language, and Hearing Research, 40*, 338–348.

Goldman-Eisler, F. (1968). *Pyscholinguistics: Experiments in spontaneous speech.* New York, NY: Academic Press.

Guo, L., Tomblin, J., & Samelson, V. (2008). Speech disruptions in the narratives of English-speaking children with specific language impairment. *Journal of Speech, Language, and Hearing Research, 51*(3), 722–738.

Hall, N.E. (1996). Language and fluency in child language disorders: Changes over time. *Journal of Fluency Disorders, 21*, 1–32.

Hall, N. (2011). Emergence of stuttering-like disfluencies during therapy: An exploratory study. *Perspectives on School-Based Issues, 12*, 18–25.

Hall, N., Wagovich, S., & Bernstein Ratner, N. (2007). Language considerations in childhood stuttering. In E. Conture & R. Curlee (Eds.), *Stuttering and related disorders of fluency* (3rd ed., pp.153–167). New York, NY: Thieme.

Hall, N.E., Yamashita, T.S., & Aram, D.M. (1993). Relationship between language and fluency in children with language disorders. *Journal of Speech and Hearing Research, 36*, 568–579.

Hodge, G., Bernstein Ratner, N., & Rescorla, L. (1999, November). *Fluency in toddlers with SLI: A preliminary investigation.* Paper presented at the American Speech-Language-Hearing Association Annual Convention, San Francisco, CA.

Horner, J. (1987). Pause, planning, and paraphasia in expressive language disorders. *Topics in Language Disorders, 8*(1), 24–33.

Kail, R. (1994). A method of studying the generalized slowing hypothesis in children with specific language impairment. *Journal of Speech and Hearing Research, 37*, 418–421.

Leonard, L.B. (2009). Some reflections on the study of children with specific language impairment. *Child Language Teaching & Therapy, 25*(2), 169–171.

Maclay, H., & Osgood, C. (1959). Hesitation phenomena in spontaneous English speech. *Word, 15,* 19–44.

MacWhinney, B. (2000). *The Childes Project: Tools for analyzing talk* (3rd ed.). Mahwah, NJ: Lawrence Erlbaum Associates.

Malecott, A., Johnston, R., & Kizziar, P. (1972). Syllabic rate and utterance length in French. *Phonetica, 26,* 235–251.

Malvern, D., & Richards, B. (2002). Investigating accommodation in language proficiency interviews using a new measure of lexical diversity. *Language Testing, 19,* 85–104.

McDaniel, D., McKee, C., & Garrett, M. (2010). Children's sentence planning: Syntactic correlates of fluency variations. *Journal of Child Language, 37,* 59–94.

McKee, C., Rispoli, M., McDaniel, D., & Garrett, M. (2006). How do children become adult sentence producers? *Applied Psycholinguistics, 27*(1), 74–81.

Miles, S., & Bernstein Ratner, N. (2001). Language input to children at stuttering onset. *Journal of Speech, Language, and Hearing Research, 44,* 1116–1130.

Mirak, J., & Rescorla, L. (1998). Phonetic skills and vocabulary size in late talkers: Concurrent and predictive relationships. *Applied Psycholinguistics, 19,* 1–19.

Navarro-Ruiz, M.I., & Rallo-Fabra, L. (2001). Characteristics of mazes produced by SLI children. *Clinical Linguistics & Phonetics, 15,* 63–66.

Nettlebladt, U., & Hansson, K. (1999). Mazes in Swedish pre-school children with specific language impairment. *Clinical Linguistics & Phonetics, 13,* 483–497.

Newman, R., & McGregor, K. (2006). Teachers and laypersons discern quality differences between narratives produced by children with or without SLI. *Journal of Speech, Language, and Hearing Research, 49,* 1022–1036.

Pakhomov, S.S., Kaiser, E.A., Boley, D.L., Marino, S.E., Knopman, D.S., & Birnbaum, A.K. (2011). Effects of age and dementia on temporal cycles in spontaneous speech fluency. *Journal of Neurolinguistics, 24*(6), 619–635.

Pharr, A., Bernstein Ratner, N., & Rescorla, L. (2000). Syllable structure development of toddlers with specific expressive language impairment (SLI-E). *Applied Psycholinguistics, 21,* 429–449.

Razzak, L., & Bernstein Ratner, N. (1999). *Auditory feedback responses of young fluent and stuttering children.* Presentation at the American Speech-Language-Hearing Association Annual Convention, San Francisco, California.

Redmond, S.M. (2004). Conversational profiles of children with ADHD, SLI and typical development. *Clinical Linguistics & Phonetics, 18*(2), 107–125.

Rescorla, L. (1990). The Language Development Survey: A screening tool for delayed language in toddlers. *Journal of Speech and Hearing Disorders, 54,* 587–599.

Rescorla, L., & Bernstein Ratner, N. (1996). Phonetic profiles of toddlers with specific expressive language impairment (SLI–E). *Journal of Speech and Hearing Research, 39,* 153-165.

Rescorla, L., & Schwartz, E. (1990). Outcome of toddlers with specific expressive language delay. *Applied Psycholinguistics, 11*(4), 393–408.

Rispoli, M., & Hadley, P. (2001). The leading-edge: The significance of sentence disruptions in the development of grammar. *Journal of Speech, Language, and Hearing Research, 44*(5), 1131–1143.

Rispoli, M., Hadley, P., & Holt, J. (2008). Stalls and revisions: A developmental perspective on sentence production. *Journal of Speech, Language, and Hearing Research, 51,* 953–966.

Rochester, S., & Gill, J. (1973). Production of complex sentences in monologues and dialogues. *Journal of Verbal Learning and Verbal Behavior, 12,* 203–210.

Rossi, N., Sampaio, A., Gonçalves, Ó.F., & Giacheti, C. (2011). Analysis of speech fluency in Williams syndrome. *Research in Developmental Disabilities, 32*(6), 2957–2962.

Schmid, M., & Fägersten, K. (2010). Disfluency markers in L1 attrition. *Language Learning, 60,* 753–791.

Steinberg, M., Berstein, Ratner, N., Berl, M., & Gaillard, W. (in press). Fluency patterns in narratives from children with localization-related epilepsy. *Journal of Fluency Disorders.*

Tilstra, J., & McMaster, K. (2007). Productivity, fluency and grammaticality measures from narratives. *Communication Disorders Quarterly, 29,* 43–53.

van Zaalen-Op't Hof, Y., Wijnen, F., & Dejonckere, P. (2009). Language planning disturbances in children who clutter or have learning disabilities. *International Journal of Speech-Language Pathology, 11*(6), 496–508.

Wijnen, F. (1990). The development of sentence planning. *Journal of Child Language, 17,* 651–675.

Yairi, E. (1993). The early months of stuttering: A developmental study. *Journal of Speech and Hearing Research, 36,* 521–528.

# 8

# Variability in Real-Time Spoken Language Processing in Typically Developing and Late-Talking Toddlers

Virginia A. Marchman and Anne Fernald

Many joyful moments for parents are inspired by their child's "firsts"—a first smile, a first step, or a first word. As language researchers, we too celebrate those firsts but also appreciate that learning a language involves the gradual mastery of a wide range of skills over an extended developmental period. A major challenge, though, is that the course of language development is highly variable across children (e.g., Bates, Bretherton, & Snyder, 1988). For many children, first recognizable words emerge around their first birthday, and vocabulary grows rapidly over the next several years. For late talkers (LTs), word learning appears to be more of a struggle, signaled by delayed onset of first words and a slower rate of vocabulary growth. Although many researchers have tended to focus more on common patterns than on variability in early language growth, other researchers—including many represented in this book—have embraced the study of individual differences as a window into the endogenous and exogenous factors that shape how children begin to construct a working linguistic system.

A central question, of course, is which of these early individual differences really matter? For some LTs a delay in expressive language foreshadows weaker language skills at later ages (Rescorla, 2002, 2009). For others, the early delays are short lived, as many LTs move into the normal range in vocabulary before they

We are grateful to the children and parents who participated in this research. Special thanks to Nereyda Hurtado, Kyle MacDonald, Katherine Adams, Adriana Weisleder, Ana Luz Portillo, Poornima Bhat, Christine Potter, Amber MacMillan, Christina Branom, Rebecca Wedel, Renate Zangl, and the staff of the Center for Infant Studies at Stanford University. This work was supported by grants from the National Institutes of Health to Anne Fernald (HD 42235, DC 008838).

enter preschool. In spite of several heroic efforts to identify the factors that can reliably distinguish between transient and persistent delays, most studies report disappointingly low predictive validity from infancy to later childhood (e.g., Dale, Price, Bishop, & Plomin, 2003; Law, Boyle, Harris, Harkness, & Nye, 2000; Zubrick, Taylor, Rice, & Slegers, 2007). In this chapter, we present experimental evidence that children's skills in real-time spoken language understanding offers promise as an early marker of risk for later language outcomes. Such work not only reveals the remarkable facility with which even young language learners comprehend language as it unfolds in time but also demonstrates that variation in early online speech processing is fundamentally related to children's developing linguistic knowledge.

The chapter is organized in five sections. First, we review how variation has traditionally been conceptualized for language researchers, highlighting some of the factors that have curtailed the examination of individual differences in studies of how children learn language. We then point to some recent trends that have prompted a shift toward a greater appreciation of the significance of variation, citing analogous trends in the fields of language disorders and adult psycholinguistics. In the second section, we give an overview of the looking-while-listening (LWL) task, a child-friendly experimental procedure that provides reliable, valid estimates of young children's skill at comprehending language in real-time in infants and toddlers as young as 15 months. We next summarize a program of research with typically developing English- and Spanish-learning children, revealing that individual variation in early real-time language comprehension predicts children's trajectories of vocabulary development and subsequent language and cognitive outcomes. In the fourth section, we present our most recent extension of this work to children who are late to begin talking, showing links in LTs that are parallel to those previously shown in typically developing (TD) children. The final sections review other questions regarding individual differences and conclude with suggestions for further research.

## THE SIGNIFICANCE OF INDIVIDUAL DIFFERENCES

A textbook account of language development typically goes something like this: Early signs of language comprehension are observed during the first year, and many children begin to spontaneously produce their first words a few months later. Over the next several months, vocabulary growth continues at a slow pace but then accelerates as children begin to produce simple word combinations. Although these general statements characterize the timing and sequence of events on the average, a more realistic picture reveals massive variation in both when and how children move through these important language milestones (Bates, Dale, & Thal, 1995; Bates et al., 1988; Bloom, Lightbown, & Hood, 1975; Fenson et al., 2007; Goldfield & Snow, 1985; Nelson, 1973). Although there have been several important studies that focus on individual variation (e.g., Bates et al., 1988), the causes and consequences of variation have generally not been assumed to be highly relevant for understanding the basic mechanisms underlying the construction of language in children.

The predilection for theories that highlight what is common across children rather than what is variable has been shaped by at least three factors. First, child language research has been dominated since the middle of the 20th century by theoretical approaches that propose that learning is guided by a universal set of innate, specifically linguistic mental structures (Chomsky, 1975). The goal for researchers in this tradition is to outline the linguistic representations that all children possess and that delimit which subset of the phonological, semantic, and morphosyntactic universals characterize their particular native language. Variation among children, although acknowledged, is uninteresting from a theoretical standpoint and is viewed simply as "constrained variations on a universal theme" (Bloom, 2001, p. 1098).

Second, much of what is known about early language is derived from small-scale studies, typically involving naturalistic speech. Language sampling is a popular way for researchers to collect data in a child-friendly, play-like environment, although this technique requires considerable time and substantial training for recording, transcription, and analysis. Roger Brown's (1973) seminal work *A First Language: The Early Stages,* initiated just as Chomsky's generative approach was taking hold in linguistics, is a classic example of this approach. Taking advantage of the small, portable audio-recorders that had only recently become available, this study comprehensively documented common patterns of syntactic development in three young learners. Although Brown was careful to point out that the children achieved developmental milestones at substantially different rates, the focus of this and hundreds of subsequent studies was on universal patterns and sequences, rather than on differences among the children.

Third, as experimental research on infant abilities flourished after the 1960s, an emphasis on universals persisted with the popularity of controlled experimental methods. Citing findings based on techniques such as habituation and conditioned head turn, textbooks abounded with generalizations about the stunning skills of young infants, to the effect of "infants can discriminate phonetic contrasts categorically by 1 month of age" and "infants use knowledge of phonotactics to segment words by 7.5 months." However, these methods favored between-group comparisons of infants at different ages, with limited attention to variability *within* an age group (Fernald, 2010). And although their conclusions accurately reflected the performance of the particular children in those studies *on average,* the implicit assumption was that these findings should characterize *all* children of that age, with little acknowledgement of the variation around the group mean. Compounding this is the fact that many of these studies relied almost exclusively on monolingual English-speaking children from middle- and upper-middle-class families (Bloom, 2000), creating selection biases that masked many sources of potentially meaningful variation. The result was that variability in developmental patterns was considered to have little theoretical significance, and findings based on a small set of middle-class infants were assumed to be generalizable to all human children (Arnett, 2008; Fernald, 2010; Fernald & Weisleder, 2011).

Fortunately, there are signs that priorities in the language development literature are shifting away from universal trends and toward studies that document and seek to explain developmental variation. One early impetus was the development of data collection methods that relied on parent report rather than naturalistic observation, for example, the MacArthur-Bates Communicative Development Inventories (CDIs; Fenson et al., 2007) and the Language Development Survey (Rescorla, 1989). Parent reports take advantage of a caregiver's extensive knowledge of his or her child's behaviors across a variety of settings, and thus can provide a potentially more representative snapshot of a child's skill than laboratory-based experimental or naturalistic assessments. Part of the success of this technique is its recognition format, offering parents checklists of words, phrases, or activities on which they make judgments of their child's current behaviors. Although some have voiced concerns that parents may lack an accurate frame of reference or be prone to bias, the technique has been shown to provide reliable and valid snapshots of young children's current linguistic levels that are appropriate for most research and screening applications (Fenson et al., 2007; Law & Roy, 2008). Caution is generally recommended when assessing early comprehension skills, especially in populations of lower socioeconomic status (Arriaga, Fenson, Cronan, & Pethick, 1998), although some studies have demonstrated moderate to good validity with these groups as well (Furey, 2011; Pan, Rowe, Spier, & Tamis-LeMonda, 2004).

The refinement of the parent-report methodology made it feasible to document the extent of individual variation using larger and more diverse samples than those typically included in studies of child language (e.g., Arriaga et al., 1998). Research with the original versions of the CDIs, for example, enabled researchers to examine continuity of individual differences across various communicative skills in hundreds of children, including across vocabulary comprehension and production, gesture use and vocabulary, and vocabulary and morphosyntax (e.g., Bates et al., 1994; Marchman & Bates, 1994). However, there has been an increasing demand for shorter versions of the inventories (e.g., Fenson et al., 2000; Jackson-Maldonado, Marchman, & Fernald, 2012) that focus primarily on vocabulary, and hence provide less detail than the long forms, but that are more conducive for use in large-scale studies, such as the Twins Early Developmental Study (e.g., Dale et al., 2003; Eley, Dale, Bishop, Price, & Plomin, 2001).

The popularity of parent report in the United States was quickly followed by adaptations into many languages other than English, offering the opportunity to examine early variation from a cross-linguistic perspective (e.g., Caselli, Casadio, & Bates, 1999; Jackson-Maldonado et al., 2003; Junker & Stockman, 2002; Maitel, Dromi, Sagi, & Bornstein, 2000; Papaeliou & Rescorla, 2011) and in children learning two languages at the same time (e.g., Marchman & Martínez-Sussmann, 2002; Pearson, Fernández, & Oller, 1993; Place & Hoff, 2011). It came as no surprise that many of the local details of acquisition are dictated by the particular language that a child is learning. What was revealing, however, was that the research consistently demonstrated remarkable similarities across languages in the *extent* of the variation observed across children within different language communities. Commenting on their comparative data of Spanish, English, and Italian, Bornstein and Cote noted a strikingly similar range of vocabulary knowledge in children from these different language communities, leading these authors to conclude that "individual variability is probably a universal feature of early language acquisition" (2005, p. 311).

A heightened appreciation for variability also stems from the proliferation of large-scale research efforts that recruit substantial numbers of families from different racial and ethnic backgrounds—for example, the Early Childhood Longitudinal Study-Kindergarten Cohort (Lee & Burkum, 2002) or the National Institute of Child Health & Human Development Study of Early Child Care and Youth Development (e.g., Burchinal et al., 2011). A major goal of these efforts was to describe early developmental patterns across a variety of cognitive, social, and linguistic domains using designs that have greater internal and external validity than smaller-scale efforts. Generally adopting a perspective on development that is broader and more multifaceted than traditional experimental or naturalistic approaches, these studies examined not only what children can do with language but also which features of their home or school environments support learning. Studies in this tradition connect well with several seminal developmental studies that applied fine-grained analyses of mother–child interactions to determine which features of maternal speech predict vocabulary development (e.g., Hart & Risley, 1995; Hoff, 2003; Huttenlocher, Haight, Bryk, Seltzer, & Lyons, 1991), as well as those conducted in more applied contexts that explore the benefits of, for example, book reading at home (Scarborough & Dobrich, 1994) or exposure to rich vocabulary in daily conversations (Weizman & Snow, 2001).

Of course, the causes and consequences of variability have long been a central issue for researchers within the field of language disorders. The focus on children who are slower and less successful overall in learning language than their peers necessarily highlights the differences among children. At the same time, the practical issue of needing to define cutoffs to determine eligibility for services encouraged the establishment of distinct categories of children. As a result, it is tempting to treat all children falling below some criterion level as a homogeneous subgroup of the larger population, qualitatively distinct from those children within the normal range. Since the early 1990s, however, many clinical researchers have begun to blur distinctions between "impaired" and "typical development, opting for a dimensional view in which children with impairments are simply more likely than their TD peers to fall in the lower extremes of one or more continuous dimensions of receptive and expressive language skills (Karmiloff-Smith, 2007; Leonard, 1991; Rescorla & Roberts, 2000; Rescorla, 2009; Shaywitz, Escobar, Shaywitz, Fletcher, & Makuch, 1992). Moreover, as noted by Tomblin and colleagues, children from so-called atypically developing groups display patterns of *variation* similar to those of other children, revealing "no strong support for a clear distinction between language impairment and normal ranges of language function" (2004, p. 72). Finally, the heterogeneity of profiles *within* disorder categories is also increasingly acknowledged, as is the complexity of endogenous and exogenous factors that influence developmental trajectories (Bishop, 2006). Although conventional cutoffs are still widely applied in clinical practice and in some research designs (e.g., McMurray, Samelson, Lee, & Tomblin, 2010), both researchers and clinicians are appreciating that diverse risk factors operate in a probabilistic, rather than an absolute, fashion and affect children across the full range of levels to a greater or lesser degree (Thal & Katich, 1996).

Finally, there is increasing recognition that meaningful individual differences exist even within expert populations (i.e., adults who represent proficient users of the lexicon and grammar of their native language). Research on individual differences in adult comprehension is gaining influence in constraining models of adult psycholinguistics, a view that is consistent with proposals that language skills vary along multiple continuous dimensions. Several studies using behavioral measures of sentence comprehension reveal substantial variation in adult performance (e.g., Dąbrowska & Street, 2006; King & Just, 1991; Street & Dąbrowska, 2010). Moreover, those adults who were more proficient in language displayed different patterns of brain responses involved in lexical access (Weber-Fox, Davis, & Cuadrado, 2003) as well as syntactic processing (Pakulak & Neville, 2010) compared with adults with lower proficiency scores. One proposal is that such variability derives from individual differences in fixed cognitive capacities such as working memory (e.g., Caplan & Waters, 1999; Just & Carpenter, 1992), although other evidence suggests that differences are explained by experience-based factors rather than capacity limits (e.g., Misyak, Christiansen, & Tomblin, 2010; Wells, Christiansen, Race, Acheson, & MacDonald, 2009).

An increasing focus on the causes and consequences of variation in language acquisition is paralleled by trends in several fields, ranging from large-scale studies addressing applied questions to experimental studies of adult psycholinguistics and communication disorders. Supporting these efforts is the increasing popularity of techniques and experimental designs that enable the documentation of the extent of variation across individuals and the exploration of the features of learning environments that could account for that variation. With these studies as a backdrop to our efforts, we turn to our research using the LWL task, which documents a substantial role for early information processing skills in language learning for both TD children and LTs. More generally, these studies seek to understand the causes and consequences of individual differences in real-time language comprehension in infancy, contributing to the emerging view that variation across language users is an intriguing and critical topic in the psychological sciences.

## USING REAL-TIME MEASURES TO ASSESS THE DEVELOPMENT OF FLUENCY IN UNDERSTANDING

Because children's understanding can only be inferred indirectly from their behavior in a particular context, the development of receptive skills is less accessible to observation than expressive language and thus poses many unique challenges to researchers. Standard methods, such as pointing to a picture book, require that a young child pay attention, follow instructions, and execute a response—task demands that limit their applicability for children younger than 2 years. Although asking parents to report on their impressions can provide many useful insights into children's language accomplishments, parent-report measures may be less valid for comprehension than for production (Eriksson, Westerlund, & Berglund, 2002; Feldman et al., 2000). In addition, offline measures do not reflect the dynamic nature of language understanding and thus reveal little about the child's efficiency in interpreting familiar words in fluent speech.

With recent refinements in experimental online methods, researchers now have the tools to chart the time course of language comprehension by young language learners. The LWL task is a child-friendly method for assessing early lexical understanding in young children that has shown to be both reliable and ecologically valid (Fernald, Zangl, Portillo, & Marchman, 2008). The task is low in task demands and does not require children to execute a behavioral response beyond moving their eyes in response to a simple stimulus sentence (e.g., "Where's the baby?"). By monitoring the eye movements of the children frame by frame, the technique provides a fine-grained look at the time course of language comprehension moment by moment, as the speech unfolds in real time.

In this procedure, infants sit on their caregiver's lap in a sound-attenuated booth and look at pairs of pictures while listening to speech naming one of the

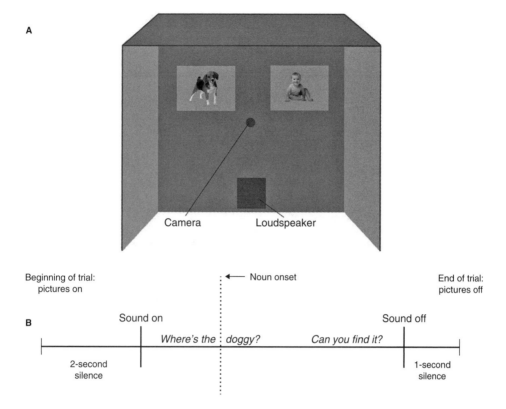

**Figure 8.1.** A) Configuration of test booth with rear-projection screen used in the looking-while-listening procedure; B) schematic time line for a typical trial. (From Fernald, A., Zangl, R., Portillo, A.L., & Marchman, V.A. [2008]. Looking while listening: Using eye movements to monitor spoken language comprehension by infants and young children. In I. Sekerina, E.M. Fernández, & H. Clahsen [Eds.], *Developmental psycholinguistics: Online methods in children's language processing* [pp. 97–135]. Amsterdam, Netherlands: John Benjamins Publishing Company. Adapted by kind permission of John Benjamins Publishing Company, Amsterdam/Philadelphia. www.benjamins.com)

pictures. A video camera situated at eye level between the pictures records the child's face (see Figure 8.1A). The video recordings are later coded frame by frame to reveal patterns of eye movements that are then time-locked to relevant points in the speech. In psycholinguistic studies with adults, reaction time (RT) is frequently used to index speed of lexical access or sentence interpretation. Analogously, in the LWL procedure, infants' gaze patterns are revealing as an experimental measure of the speed of spoken language comprehension. In particular, RT is defined as the mean latency with which the infant shifts away from the incorrect distractor picture toward the target picture, time-locked to a critical point in the stimulus sentence, such as noun onset (see Figure 8.1B).

The first cross-sectional study using this technique (Fernald, Pinto, Swingley, Weinberg, & McRoberts, 1998) assessed speed of spoken word recognition in 15-, 18-, and 24-month-old infants, spanning an age period when most children show substantial increases in vocabulary production. Figure 8.2 shows mean RTs for infants in these three age groups. Although on average 15-month-olds responded slowly and inconsistently, waiting until after the acoustic offset of the target noun to initiate a shift from distractor to target picture, 24-month-olds more consistently

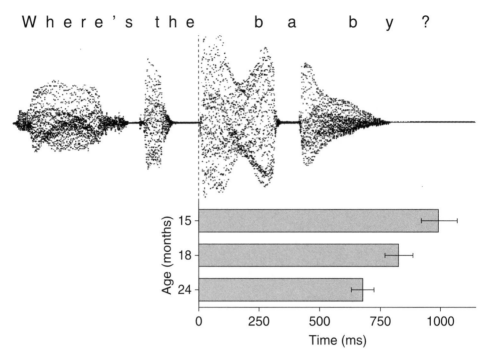

**Figure 8.2.** Mean latencies to initiate a shift in gaze from the distractor to the target picture, measured from the beginning of the spoken target word, for 15-, 18-, and 24-month-old infants. This analysis included only shifts occurring on distractor-initial trials—that is, those trials in which the infant was initially looking at the incorrect picture and then shifted to the correct picture within 1,800 milliseconds (ms) of target-word onset. (From Fernald, A., Pinto, J.P., Swingley, D., Weinberg, A., & McRoberts, G.W. [1998]. Rapid gains in speed of verbal processing by infants in the second year. *Psychological Science, 9,* 72–75; reprinted by permission of SAGE Publications, Inc.)

shifted to the correct referent before the target word was completed, based on partial phonetic information. These results revealed dramatic gains in receptive language processing over this important time in development, with infants increasing the speed with which they identify familiar words and match them with the appropriate referent in the visual scene. These developmental findings have been replicated with Latino infants from monolingual Spanish-speaking families in the United States (Hurtado, Marchman, & Fernald, 2007) and also in longitudinal samples with English-learning infants (Fernald & Marchman, 2012; Fernald, Perfors, & Marchman, 2006).

Experimental studies using the LWL procedure have shown that very young listeners, like adults, are able to take advantage of contextual information to facilitate incremental interpretation of spoken language from moment to moment. For example, Fernald, Thorpe, and Marchman (2010) showed that English-speaking 3-year-olds were more efficient at identifying the referent of "Where's the red ball?" in the presence of a red ball and a blue ball than when the color adjective is not informative. Moreover, children become increasingly adept at integrating these types of cues from the linguistic and nonlinguistic context in order to more efficiently interpret the speech that they hear. Thus, children's developing processing efficiency reflects not only increasing skill at identifying the referents of single words but also substantial improvement in their ability to interpret more complex sentence structures.

A second example that illustrates young children's skill at incremental language processing comes from our studies of Spanish-learning children. Although in English an article such as *the* reveals little information about the following noun, in languages such as Spanish, all nouns are obligatorily marked for grammatical gender in the preceding articles (e.g., "la" and "el" for "the"). For adult native speakers, hearing "la" or "el" can help the listener narrow down the set of possible referents of the upcoming noun and, in some contexts, help them identify the referent even before the noun is spoken (Dahan, Swingley, Tanenhaus, & Magnuson, 2000). But can young Spanish learners exploit this cue during real-time language processing? Using the LWL task, Lew-Williams and Fernald (2007) showed Spanish-learning 2- and 3-year-olds pictures of objects with names that were either the same (e.g., "la pelota," "ball"; "la galleta," "cookie") or different (e.g., "la pelota," "ball"; "el zapato," "shoe") in grammatical gender. Participants then heard a sentence naming one of the pictures (e.g., "Encuentra la pelota," "Find the ball"). Like adults, Spanish-speaking children were faster to orient to the correct picture when the article was potentially informative, namely on different-gender trials, than on same-gender trials, when it was not. These results demonstrate that even very young Spanish-learners can take advantage of a morphosyntactic cue such as gender-marking on articles to help them more efficiently establish reference.

## INDIVIDUAL DIFFERENCES IN FLUENCY OF UNDERSTANDING BY INFANTS AND YOUNG CHILDREN

Although the work reviewed so far highlights a few of the developmental achievements in language processing skills seen during the first years of life, a principal goal of this research program is to examine the causes and consequences of individual differences in these skills. To address this goal, we must establish that efficiency in real-time language comprehension reflects information processing skills that are directly relevant to language learning. Is it the case that young children who are faster on average to identify familiar words during real-time comprehension are also those who respond relatively more quickly at later ages? And how are these differences among children related to their lexical and grammatical knowledge, both concurrently and at later ages? Can we establish that speed and accuracy in real-time interpretation of spoken language in infancy have long-term links to language and cognitive outcomes later in childhood?

Our first study to address these questions was a longitudinal study of English-learning infants using the LWL procedure at four time points from 15 to 25 months (Fernald et al., 2006). As expected based on earlier cross-sectional findings (Fernald et al., 1998), children's efficiency in familiar word recognition improved significantly over this period. Moreover, processing skill was moderately stable from one age to the next, revealing evidence for continuity across ages in children's efficiency of spoken language understanding. Most notably, this study revealed robust relations between speed and accuracy of online speech processing and children's language knowledge. For example, we found that children's response speed and accuracy at 25 months were related not only to concurrent reported vocabulary size but also to almost all prior measures of language from the age of 12 months. Similarly strong concurrent relations were also observed

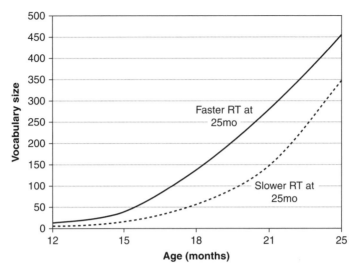

**Figure 8.3.** Trajectories of vocabulary development from 12 to 25 months in typically developing children with faster or slower response times (RTs) in the looking-while-listening (LWL) task at 25 months. (*Note:* Vocabulary size determined by the number of words produced as reported on the MacArthur-Bates Communicative Development Inventories [CDI].) (From Fernald, A., Perfors, A., & Marchman, V.A. [2006]. Picking up speed in understanding: Speech processing efficiency and vocabulary growth across the second year. *Developmental Psychology, 42,* 98–116; adapted by permission.)

when vocabulary knowledge was assessed using the Peabody Picture Vocabulary Test–Revised (Dunn & Dunn, 1981), a standardized measure of vocabulary comprehension.

However, these analyses did not take advantage of the longitudinal nature of these data, and revealed little regarding how individual children changed over time. Thus, we applied growth curve modeling to explore the degree to which individual trajectories of vocabulary growth were related to skill in online processing. Using three modeling parameters, we obtained an average starting point in vocabulary (i.e., intercept at 12 months) and the average rate of change (i.e., linear) and acceleration (i.e., quadratic) in vocabulary growth from 12 to 25 months. Then, in the second stage of this analysis, we examined whether individual differences in these parameters were related to individual differences in speed and accuracy of online language comprehension. The results indicated that features of children's vocabulary growth were indeed associated with RT and accuracy in word recognition at the end of the second year. Figure 8.3 illustrates one such relation. Here, children who were faster to recognize a familiar word during real-time language comprehension at 25 months were those children who had faster and more accelerated vocabulary growth from 12 to 25 months.

We next asked to what extent these individual differences in early processing efficiency are predictive of *long-term* outcomes. About half of the children from the original Fernald et al. (2006) longitudinal sample were tested again using standardized assessments of cognitive and language skills when the children were 8 years old (Marchman & Fernald, 2008). Because skill at spoken language comprehension has been linked to working memory in older children and adults (e.g., Gathercole & Baddeley, 1990), we specifically explored relations between early processing speed and a working memory task administered at 8 years. Although vocabulary size and RT at 25 months were both correlated with later cognitive and language skills, each made a significant unique contribution to outcomes, together accounting for nearly 58% of the variance in working memory at 8 years. Thus, measures of real-time language processing efficiency at 2 years have substantial predictive validity for outcomes in later childhood.

## EARLY PROCESSING EFFICIENCY AS A PREDICTOR OF OUTCOMES IN LATE TALKERS

These findings offer impressive evidence that individual differences in early language processing are robustly linked to variation in language outcomes in TD children. Do we see the same relations in children who show delays in the onset of productive vocabulary—that is, LTs? We use the term *late talker* descriptively, referring to children who fall at the low end of the continuum in language production, in the absence of any neurological, sensory, or cognitive impairment (Desmarais, Sylvestre, Meyer, Bairati, & Rouleau, 2008). Although children are most often labeled as LTs at 24 months, for our purposes, we defined children based on low vocabulary production at 18 months. Studies using parent report often define LTs as falling below the 10th percentile; however, here we used the more liberal cutoff of the 20th percentile (see also Jones, 2003).

Because many LTs will move into the normal range of language skills by kindergarten (e.g., Ellis Weismer, Murray-Branch, & Miller, 1994), an important question is why do some LTs overcome their early delays while others do not? Dale et al. (2003) concluded that lexical production alone—that is, when severity of vocabulary delay is used as the sole measure of language level—has poor practical utility in distinguishing transient from persistent delay in children younger than 2 years. Even when other predictors are also considered, such as male gender, family history of language delays, parental concern, or prematurity (e.g., Zubrick et al., 2007), they typically account for only a small portion of the variance and are not likely to be useful for early screening of vocabulary delays in children younger than 2 years (Feldman et al., 2005; Reilly et al., 2007). Persistent language delays have also been linked to maternal education and birth order (Bishop, Price, Dale, & Plomin, 2003; Hoff-Ginsberg, 1998), which may influence the early language environment of the child. Quantitative and qualitative features of the language children hear from caregivers are linked to variation in lexical growth (Hart & Risley, 1995; Hoff, 2003), and relations between maternal talk and vocabulary outcomes may also be influenced by factors such as maternal literacy levels, depression, knowledge of child development, and parenting practices (Pan, Rowe, Singer, & Snow, 2005; Rowe, 2007).

One important correlate of later expressive language outcomes is early skill in comprehension. For example, studies have shown that LTs who have receptive delays are at even greater risk for poor outcomes than LTs with normal-range comprehension (Thal, Tobias, & Morrison, 1991; cf. Paul, 1991). Lyytinen, Eklund, and Lyytinen (2005) found that Finnish-speaking 2-year-olds who were delayed in both receptive and expressive language performed significantly worse on school-age language and literacy assessments than LTs with normal-range receptive skills. Yet finding appropriate methods for assessing early comprehension has been a challenge for researchers because many picture-pointing tasks may be particularly

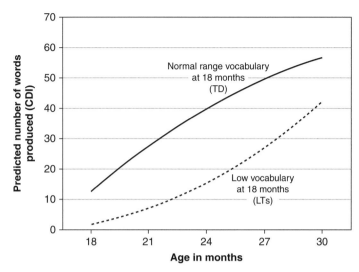

**Figure 8.4.** Predicted mean trajectories of quadratic growth in vocabulary from 18 to 30 months for typically developing (TD) children (solid line) and late talkers (LTs; dashed line). (*Key:* CDI: MacArthur-Bates Communicative Development Inventories.) (From Fernald, A., & Marchman, V.A. [2012]. Individual differences in lexical processing at 18 months predict vocabulary growth in typically developing and late-talking toddlers. *Child Development, 83,* 203–222; adapted by permission.)

difficult for young children, especially those who are experiencing developmental delays, and concerns have been raised about the reliability and validity of techniques such as parent report (Feldman et al., 2000; Tomasello & Mervis, 1994). Therefore, in Fernald and Marchman (2012), we asked whether language comprehension skills assessed using an *online* procedure with minimal task demands such as the LWL task would be predictive of later lexical development in LTs. All children participated in the LWL task at 18 months, and parents completed CDIs when their child was 18, 21, 24, and 30 months. Children were grouped into two categories based on vocabulary production at 18 months: 1) TD children ($n = 46$) with CDI scores falling above the 20th percentile, and 2) LTs ($n = 36$) with CDI scores at or below the 20th percentile. As in Fernald et al. (2006), we applied growth modeling techniques to chart individual differences in the trajectories of vocabulary growth using three parameters: vocabulary size at 30 months (i.e., intercept), rates of change from 18 to 30 months (i.e., linear growth), and rates of acceleration from 18 to 30 months, (i.e., quadratic growth). Note that because the TD children and LTs were by definition different at 18 months, these analyses set the intercept at the end point (i.e., 30 months) rather than the initial time point so that we could explore the predictors of variation in vocabulary *outcome* in these two groups of children.

In general, a comparison of growth parameters in children classified as LTs with those of children classified as TD at 18 months reveals information regarding the degree to which both the *shape* and *outcome* of development in vocabulary between 18 and 30 months is similar in LTs and TD children. Figure 8.4 shows the predicted average trajectory of vocabulary growth for each group of children. Looking first at 30-month outcomes, LTs had fewer words in their production vocabularies, on average, than TD children. Thus, the early vocabulary delays seen in the LTs at 18 months tended to persist as late as 30 months. Indeed, of the 18 children

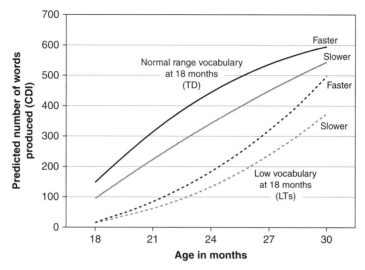

**Figure 8.5.** Predicted mean trajectories of quadratic growth in vocabulary from 18 to 30 months as a function of typically developing (TD) children (solid lines) and late talkers (LTs; dashed lines) and faster (+1 standard deviation, dark lines) versus slower (–1 standard deviation, gray lines) mean RTs at 18 months. (*Key:* CDI: MacArthur-Bates Communicative Development Inventories.) (From Fernald, A., & Marchman, V.A. [2012], Individual differences in lexical processing at 18 months predict vocabulary growth in typically developing and late-talking toddlers. *Child Development, 83,* 203–222; adapted by permission.)

who showed delays at 30 months, 14 came from the LT group, whereas only 4 had vocabulary scores above the 20th percentile at 18 months. At the same time, the LTs showed more accelerated rates of growth from 18 to 30 months than the TD children, indicating an overall trajectory of learning that suggested many of these children were catching up. Indeed, nearly two thirds of the children with early delays made greater-than-average gains in vocabulary around their second birthdays, moving into the normal range by 30 months. Note that the slower rates of growth for the TD children are a reflection of the fact that many TD children were reaching vocabulary levels at or near the ceiling of the CDIs between 24 and 30 months of age, suggesting that these models are underestimating their true vocabulary levels.

Our main goal was to determine whether children's early online language comprehension could differentiate children's trajectories of vocabulary growth. Does speed of familiar word recognition at 18 months predict variation in rate and acceleration of vocabulary development from 18 to 30 months? Most important, does skill in the efficiency of verbal processing at 18 months distinguish those LTs who move into the normal range in vocabulary over the following year from those who show continued delays? The results shown in Figure 8.5 indicate that the answers to these questions are yes. For both the LTs and TD children, the solid and dashed lines reflect the average trajectories of vocabulary development in children classified as "faster" versus "slower," respectively, in RT at 18 months in the LWL task. For children in both groups, skill in interpreting familiar words in real time was a significant predictor of the rate and shape of lexical growth. Those LTs who were faster at identifying familiar words at 18 months showed more accelerated vocabulary growth from 18 to 30 months compared with those LTs who were less efficient in online comprehension. Differences in the shape of

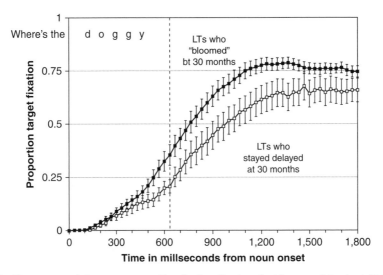

**Figure 8.6.** Time course of the mean proportion fixating the target picture on distractor-initial trials at 18 months as a function of vocabulary outcomes at 30 months. Dark squares indicated those late talkers (LTs) who "bloomed"; open squares indicate those LTs who remained delayed at 30 months. Error bars represent standard errors (SE) of the mean. (From Fernald, A., & Marchman, V.A. [2012], Individual differences in lexical processing at 18 months predict vocabulary growth in typically developing and late-talking toddlers. *Child Development, 83,* 203–222; adapted by permission.)

the vocabulary trajectories also resulted in the faster LTs having better outcomes at 30 months than LTs who were less efficient at 18 months. Analogously, stronger processing skills in TD children were associated with initially steeper trajectories, followed by a slowing of vocabulary growth over the same period compared with those TD children who were slower at 18 months. Thus, the TD children who were also faster in real-time language comprehension were also those children who were more likely than less-efficient TD children to score near the ceiling of the CDIs at the later age points. Indeed, nearly half of the TD children scored more than 600 words at 30 months, placing them at or near the 680-word limit of the instrument.

Another way to explore the relation between early skill in online comprehension and language outcomes is to look at these data *retrospectively.* We can further subgroup the LTs into two groups: 1) those LTs who "bloomed"—that is, who moved into the normal range in vocabulary by 30 months, and 2) those LTs who remained delayed in vocabulary at 30 months. Were there differences in speed of online comprehension at 18 months in those LTs who bloomed by 30 months compared with those children who did not? Again, Figure 8.6 suggests that there were. Here, we plot the time course of shifting from the distractor to the target picture in the 14 LTs who remained delayed at 30 months, compared with the 22 LTs who had bloomed. Note that the time course of shifting from distractor to target at 18 months is steeper and reaches a higher asymptote in those children who bloomed, compared with those LTs with persistent delays.

In sum, less efficient performance in the LWL task by LTs at 18 months was associated with increased risk for poor language outcomes at 30 months, as compared with LTs with more efficient processing skills. Of the 18 children from either group who were delayed in vocabulary scores (< 20th percentile) at

30 months, 11 were children with low vocabulary scores at 18 months—that is, LTs, who also had mean RT scores falling in the lower half of the distribution for all children. This very liberal cutoff for clustering children as slower versus faster yielded moderate sensitivity (61%) in predicting 30-month delays based on a combination of late talking status and processing speed. Note, however, that there were also 9 LTs with slower RTs at 18 months who showed improvements in vocabulary by 30 months, indicating that the combination of slow RT and late-onset vocabulary still does not guarantee continued delays. Nevertheless, taking both LT status and RT into account increased the positive predictive value to 55% (11 out of 20), compared with 39% when low vocabulary is considered alone. In a parallel analysis when the children were 24 months old, the age when LTs are most commonly identified, the positive predictive value increased further (8 of 12, 66%) when processing speed and vocabulary status at this later age were used as predictors. Although there is clearly more work to be done, these results converge nicely with the Fernald et al. (2006) longitudinal results with TD children and suggest that real-time measures of early language comprehension offer significant promise for identification of children at risk for persistent language disorders.

## WHY FASTER AND MORE EFFICIENT PROCESSING IN INFANCY IS ADVANTAGEOUS FOR LANGUAGE LEARNING

We conclude by considering three questions regarding the implications of these predictive relations. First, it is important to ask whether our online processing measures capture differences among children in abilities specifically related to language, or whether the task demands of the LWL procedure draw on more general abilities not unique to speech processing. When an infant quickly and consistently orients to the named picture in this paradigm, that child is demonstrating skill in understanding language, but this capacity is also linked to many perceptual, cognitive, and motor processes that extend beyond language, including selective attention, visual encoding, auditory/visual integration, and sound-form memory. Differences among children in one or more of these component processes could result in different profiles of language proficiency that manifest themselves in both language production and online language processing, consistent with the dimensional approach to language disorders (Leonard, 1991; Rescorla, 2009). Unfortunately, it is likely to be difficult to isolate the contribution of any single skill that might lie at the heart of difficulties with language processing for a given child. At the same time, it is precisely this array of cognitive processes that is essential to infants' success at comprehension in the context of daily interactions. Thus, the most compelling evidence for the ecological validity of real-time processing as measured by the LWL task is its consistent relation with other language and cognitive skills in children from diverse backgrounds (Fernald et al., 2006; Hurtado et al., 2007; Marchman & Fernald, 2008) and a range of language abilities (Fernald & Marchman, 2012).

A second question asks how the skills that contribute to reliable and rapid word recognition at 18 months could facilitate vocabulary learning. If faster RTs are associated with increases in cognitive capacity (e.g., Salthouse, 1996), the infant who identifies familiar words more quickly may have more resources available for attending to subsequent words or for processing information in the visual scene that would facilitate comprehension. This increased capacity could offer an advantage when the child encounters an unfamiliar word later in the sentence or facilitate the encoding of the distributional relations across words that form the basis for morphology and grammar. More efficient processing could also enable the child to process more of the input he or she hears in everyday speech—parsing it better and forming more complete phonological representations, which in turn could facilitate word learning. And because children rely on familiar words to infer meanings of unfamiliar words (Goodman, McDonough, & Brown, 1998), an edge in the efficiency of familiar word recognition could enable faster growth in vocabulary, which in turn could lead to increases in subsequent receptive language and grammatical development (Elman et al., 1996).

Children who are less efficient at identifying the referent of a familiar word, however, could have difficulties with learning that may have short- as well as long-term implications. Being slow to identify the referent of a known word could interfere with lexical activation and limit success in tracking distributional regularities or managing attention in real time (Evans, Saffran, & Robe-Torres, 2009; Montgomery, Evans, & Gillam, 2009). These difficulties would also have implications for children's ability to recruit existing lexical knowledge in learning new words (Ellis Weismer & Evans, 2002; Gershkoff-Stowe & Hahn, 2007), which could contribute to the links observed here between reduced processing efficiency and slower vocabulary growth in those LTs who remained delayed at 30 months.

The findings presented here and elsewhere are consistent with a model of cascading relations between early efficiency in speech processing speed and increased vocabulary knowledge. Although most children make impressive gains in spoken language processing as their rate of vocabulary learning increases over the second and third years, some 18-month-olds are faster and more reliable in lexical access than others. It was those children with more efficient processing skills who appeared to be able to learn new words more quickly. Our findings show that individual differences in these capacities are already evident in infancy and suggest that this variability is likely to have consequences for subsequent language outcomes.

Because speed of processing in adults correlates with measures of fluid intelligence, memory, reasoning, and language, several researchers have argued that gradual increases in processing speed can account for age-related growth in cognitive and language functioning (e.g., Fry & Hale, 1996; Salthouse, 1996). Correlations between infants' early vocabulary and their progress in grammar led Bates and colleagues to conclude that lexical learning is fundamental for continued linguistic and cognitive development (Bates & Goodman, 1999). Vocabulary knowledge also serves as a building block for later reading development (Lonigan, Burgess, & Anthony, 2000), and language function in the preschool years is ultimately predictive of high school dropout or graduation (Alexander, Entwisle, & Horsey, 1997). Although more research is needed to further specify developmental changes in these skills, the individual differences in processing speed we observed across TD children and LTs may begin to explain both the short- and long-term consequences of early vocabulary accomplishments in young language learners.

Third, having considered some possible consequences of differences among children in early processing efficiency and vocabulary learning, a final question is where these individual differences come from. Clearly, some individual differences in language processing skill are likely to result primarily from factors that are endogenous to the individual learners. Language disorders such as SLI are more concentrated in some families than others, and numerous studies have explored possible genetic bases for variation in linguistic proficiency. At the same time, heritability estimates for SLI have been inconsistent (Bishop, 2006), suggesting that language impairments have multiple causes (Tomblin & Buckwalter, 1998). Research also shows that genetic factors account for individual differences in the speech of TD children as well as those with SLI (Hayiou-Thomas, 2008), consistent with the view that children vary in language proficiency along multiple continuous dimensions.

There is also evidence that variability in early experience may be a key contributor to differences in cognitive and language proficiency. A study of predictors of poor language outcomes in monozygotic and dizygotic twins found that shared environmental factors were much more powerful than genetic factors in accounting for similarities in language development between twins in the same family (Oliver, Dale, & Plomin, 2004). Moreover, detailed longitudinal studies have shown that parent–child interaction varies substantially among families, and that differences in the amount and quality of child-directed speech predict developmental outcomes such as vocabulary growth (Huttenlocher et al., 1991) and children's later academic achievement (Walker, Greenwood, Hart, & Carta, 1994). Hoff (2003) has shown that the well-established relation between socioeconomic status and vocabulary knowledge is mediated by differences among mothers in the lexical diversity and grammatical complexity of their speech to children.

Could variation in early language experience also contribute to the individual differences observed in infants' real-time processing efficiency and vocabulary growth? In a longitudinal study with Spanish-speaking mothers and children, Hurtado, Marchman, and Fernald (2008) explored this question, examining links between maternal talk and children's processing efficiency and lexical development. As in other studies with English-learning children, those infants whose mothers had talked with them more during a play session at 18 months were those who had learned more vocabulary by 24 months. However, the most striking finding was that those infants who had experienced more and richer language were also faster in lexical access in the LWL task 6 months later than those who had heard less maternal talk, even after controlling for RT at 18 months. Thus, the opportunity for engagement with rich and varied language from an attentive caregiver provides the infant with models for language learning and also with practice in interpreting language in real time.

## CONCLUSIONS

Most research on language has focused on characterizing modal patterns of developmental change in linguistic proficiency, with much less attention to the differences among individuals that exist at every age. The research presented in this chapter demonstrated that meaningful individual differences in language-related abilities can be identified early in infancy and that efficiency of real-time language processing predicts subsequent vocabulary development in comparable ways for children in the normal range as well as LTs falling at the low end of the vocabulary distribution. One promising clinical implication of this research is that time course measures of comprehension may ultimately prove useful in improving early identification of children at risk for persistent language disorders. We also propose that it may be fruitful to conceptualize such links between variation in processing skills and vocabulary outcomes as continuous with the individual differences observed in older children and adults (e.g., Street & Dąbrowska, 2010) and children with language disorders (McMurray et al., 2010; Rescorla, 2009). To be sure, it remains a challenge to empirically distinguish among the multiple endogenous and experiential factors that could contribute to individual differences in TD children and LTs. By calling attention to the consistent relations between individual variation in processing skills and vocabulary development, and the possible causes and consequences of that variation, we hope that we have inspired the continued exploration of what that variation might reveal about the mechanisms guiding language development in both TD children and LTs at risk for more persistent delays.

## REFERENCES

Alexander, K., Entwisle, D., & Horsey, C. (1997, April). From first grade forward: Early foundations of high school dropout. *Sociology of Education, 70,* 87–107.

Arnett, J.J. (2008). The neglected 95%: Why American psychology needs to become less American. *American Psychologist, 63,* 602–614.

Arriaga, R.I., Fenson, L., Cronan, T., & Pethick, S.J. (1998). Scores on the MacArthur Communicative Development Inventory of children from low- and middle-income families. *Applied Psycholinguistics, 19,* 209–223.

Bates, E., Bretherton, I., & Snyder, L. (1988). *From first words to grammar: Individual differences and dissociable mechanisms.* New York, NY: Cambridge University Press.

Bates, E., Dale, P.S., & Thal, D.J. (1995). Individual differences and their implications for theories of language development. In P. Fletcher & B. MacWhinney (Eds.), *Handbook of child language* (pp. 96–151). Oxford, United Kingdom: Blackwell.

Bates, E., & Goodman, J. (1999). On the emergence of grammar from the lexicon. In B. MacWhinney (Ed.), *The emergence of language* (pp. 29–70). Mahwah, NJ: Lawrence Erlbaum Associates.

Bishop, D.V.M. (2006). What causes specific language impairment in children? *Current Directions in Psychological Science, 15*(5), 217–221.

Bishop, D.V., Price, T.S., Dale, P.S., & Plomin, R. (2003). Outcomes of early language delay: II. Etiology of transient and persistent language difficulties. *Journal of Speech, Language, and Hearing Research, 46*(3), 561–575.

Bloom, L., Lightbown, P., & Hood, L. (1975). Structure and variation in child language. *Monographs of the Society for Research in Child Development, 40*(2), 1–97.

Bloom, P. (2000). *How children learn the meanings of words.* Cambridge, MA: MIT Press.

Bloom, P. (2001). Précis of *How Children Learn the Meanings of Words. Behavioral and Brain Sciences, 24,* 1095–1103.

Bornstein, M.H., & Cote, L.R. (2005). Expressive vocabulary in language learners from two ecological settings in three language communities. *Infancy, 7*(3), 299–316.

Brown, R. (1973). *A first language: The early stages.* Cambridge, MA: Harvard University Press.

Burchinal, M., McCartney, K., Steinberg, L., Crosnoe, R., Friedman, S.L., McLoyd, V., . . . NICHD Early Child Care Research Network. (2011). Examining the Black-White achievement gap among low-income children using the NICHD Study of Early Child Care and Youth Development. *Child Development, 82,* 1404–1420.

Caplan, D., & Waters, G.S. (1999). Verbal working memory and sentence comprehension. *Behavioral and Brain Sciences, 22,* 77–126.

Caselli, M.C., Casadio, P., & Bates, E. (1999). A comparison of the transition from first words to grammar in English and Italian. *Journal of Child Language, 26,* 69–111.

Chomsky, N. (1975). *Reflections on language.* New York, NY: Pantheon Books.

Dąbrowska, E., & Street, J. (2006). Individual differences in language attainment: Comprehension of passive sentences by native and non-native English speakers. *Language Sciences, 28*(6), 604–615.

Dahan, D., Swingley, D., Tanenhaus, M.K., & Magnuson, J.S. (2000). Linguistic gender and spoken-word recognition in French. *Journal of Memory & Language, 42,* 465–480.

Dale, P.S., Price, T.S., Bishop, D.V.M., & Plomin, R. (2003). Outcomes of early language delay: I. Predicting persistent and transient language difficulties at 3 and 4 years. *Journal of Speech, Language, and Hearing Research, 46,* 544–560.

Desmarais, C., Sylvestre, A., Meyer, F., Bairati, I., & Rouleau, N. (2008). Systematic review of the literature on characteristics of late-talking toddlers. *International Journal of Language & Communication Disorders, 43,* 361–389.

Dunn, L.M., & Dunn, L.M. (1981). *Peabody Picture Vocabulary Test–Revised.* Circle Pines, MN: American Guidance Service.

Eley, T.C., Dale, P.S., Bishop, D.V.M., Price, T.S., & Plomin, R. (2001). Longitudinal analysis of components of cognitive delay: Examining the aetiology of verbal and performance aspects of cognitive delay. *Journal of Educational Psychology, 93,* 698–707.

Ellis Weismer, S., & Evans, J.L. (2002). The role of processing limitations in early identification of specific language impairment. *Topics in Language Disorders, 22*(3), 15–29.

Ellis Weismer, S., Murray-Branch, J., & Miller, J.F. (1994). A prospective longitudinal study of language development in late talkers. *Journal of Speech and Hearing Research, 37,* 852–867.

Elman, J., Bates, E.A., Johnson, M.H., Karmiloff-Smith, A., Parisi, D., & Plunkett, K. (1996). *Rethinking innateness: A connectionist perspective on development.* Cambridge, MA: The MIT Press.

Eriksson, M., Westerlund, M., & Berglund, E. (2002). A screening version of the Swedish communicative development inventories designed for use with 18-month-old children. *Journal of Speech, Language, and Hearing Research, 45,* 948–960.

Evans, J.L., Saffran, J.R., & Robe-Torres, K. (2009). Statistical learning in children with specific language impairment. *Journal of Speech, Language, and Hearing Research, 52,* 321–335.

Feldman, H.M., Dale, P.S., Campbell, T.F., Colborn, D.K., Kurs-Lasky, M., & Rockette, H.E (2005). Concurrent and predictive validity of parent reports of child language at ages 2 and 3 years. *Child Development, 76,* 856–868.

Feldman H.M., Dollaghan, C.A., Campbell, T.F., Kurs-Lasky, M., Janosky, J.E., & Paradise, J.L. (2000). Measurement properties of the MacArthur Communicative Development Inventories at ages one and two years. *Child Development, 71,* 310–322.

Fenson, L., Marchman, V.A., Thal, D.J., Dale, P.S., Reznick, J.S., & Bates, E. (2007). *MacArthur-Bates Communicative Development Inventories (CDIs)* (2nd ed.). Baltimore, MD: Paul H. Brookes Publishing Co.

Fenson, L., Pethick, S., Renda, C., Cox, J.L., Dale, P.S., & Reznick, J.S. (2000). Short-form versions of the MacArthur Communicative Development Inventories. *Applied Psycholinguistics, 21,* 95–115.

Fernald, A. (2010). Getting beyond the "convenience sample" in research on early cognitive development. *Behavioral and Brain Sciences, 33,* 91–92 doi:10.1017/S0140525X10000294

Fernald, A., & Marchman, V.A. (2012). Individual differences in lexical processing at 18 months predict vocabulary growth in typically developing and late-talking toddlers. *Child Development, 83,* 203–222.

Fernald, A., Perfors, A., & Marchman, V.A. (2006). Picking up speed in understanding: Speech processing efficiency and vocabulary growth across the second year. *Developmental Psychology, 42,* 98–116.

Fernald, A., Pinto, J.P., Swingley, D., Weinberg, A., & McRoberts, G.W. (1998). Rapid gains in speed of verbal processing by infants in the second year. *Psychological Science, 9,* 72–75.

Fernald, A., Thorpe, K., & Marchman, V.A. (2010). Blue car, red car: Developing efficiency in online interpretation of adjective-noun phrases. *Cognitive Psychology, 20,* 190–217.

Fernald, A., & Weisleder, A. (2011). Early language experience is vital to developing fluency in understanding. In S. Neuman & D. Dickinson (Eds.), *Handbook of early literacy research: Vol. 3* (pp. 3–19). New York, NY: Guilford Publications.

Fernald, A., Zangl, R., Portillo, A.L., & Marchman, V.A. (2008). Looking while listening: Using eye movements to monitor spoken language comprehension by infants and young children. In I. Sekerina, E.M. Fernández, & H. Clahsen (Eds.), *Developmental psycholinguistics: Online methods in children's language processing* (pp. 97–135). Amsterdam, Netherlands: John Benjamins Publishing Company.

Fry, A.F., & Hale, S. (1996). Processing speed, working memory and fluid intelligence: Evidence for a developmental cascade. *Psychological Science, 7,* 237–241.

Furey, J.E. (2011). Production and maternal report of 16- and 18-month-olds' vocabulary in low- and middle-income families. *American Journal of Speech-Language Pathology, 20,* 38–46.

Gathercole, S.E., & Baddeley, A.D. (1990). Phonological memory deficits in language disordered children: Is there a causal connection? *Journal of Memory & Language, 29,* 336–360.

Gershkoff-Stowe, L., & Hahn, E. (2007). Fast mapping skills in the developing lexicon. *Journal of Speech, Language, and Hearing Research, 50,* 682–697.

Goodman, J., McDonough, L., & Brown, N. (1998). Learning object names: The role of semantic context and memory in the acquisition of novel words, *Child Development, 69,* 1330–1344.

Goldfield, B., & Snow, C. (1985). Individual differences in language acquisition. In J.B. Gleason (Ed.), *Language development* (pp. 307–330). Columbus, OH: Merrill Publishing Co.

Hart, B., & Risley, T.R. (1995). *Meaningful differences in the everyday experience of young American children.* Baltimore, MD: Paul H. Brookes Publishing Co.

Hayiou-Thomas, M.E. (2008). Genetic and environmental influences on early speech, language and literacy development. *Journal of Communication Disorders, 41,* 397–408.

Hoff, E. (2003). The specificity of environmental influence: Socioeconomic status affects early vocabulary development via maternal speech. *Child Development, 74,* 1368–1878.

Hoff-Ginsberg, E. (1998). The relations of birth order and socioeconomic status to children's language experience and language development. *Applied Psycholinguistics, 19,* 603–629.

Hurtado, N., Marchman, V.A., & Fernald, A. (2007). Spoken word recognition by Latino children learning Spanish as their first language. *Journal of Child Language, 34,* 227–249.

Hurtado, N., Marchman, V.A., & Fernald, A. (2008). Does input influence uptake? Links between maternal talk, processing speed and vocabulary size in Spanish-learning children. *Developmental Science, 11*(6), F31–F39.

Huttenlocher, J., Haight, W., Bryk, A., Seltzer, M., & Lyons, T. (1991). Vocabulary growth: Relation to language input and gender. *Developmental Psychology, 27,* 236–248.

Jackson-Maldonado, D., Marchman, V.A., & Fernald, L.C.H. (2012). Short form versions of the Spanish MacArthur-Bates Communicative Development Inventories. *Applied Psycholinguistics.* doi:10.1017/S0142716412000045

Jackson-Maldonado, D., Thal, D.J., Fenson, L., Marchman, V.A., Newton, T., & Conboy, B.T. (2003). *MacArthur Inventarios del Desarrollo de Habilidades Comunicativas: User's guide and technical manual.* Baltimore, MD: Paul H. Brookes Publishing Co.

Jones, S.S. (2003). Late talkers show no shape bias in a novel name extension task. *Developmental Science, 6,* 477–483.

Junker, D.A., & Stockman, I.J. (2002). Expressive vocabulary of German-English bilingual toddlers. *American Journal of Speech-Language Pathology, 11*(3), 381–394.

Just, M.A., & Carpenter, P.A. (1992). A capacity theory of comprehension: Individual differences in working memory. *Psychological Review, 99,* 122–149.

Karmiloff-Smith, A. (2007). Atypical epigenesis. *Developmental Science, 10,* 84–88.

King, J., & Just, M.A. (1991). Individual differences in syntactic processing: The role of working memory. *Journal of Memory and Language, 30,* 580–602.

Law, J., Boyle, J., Harris, F., Harkness, A., & Nye, C. (2000). Prevalence and natural history of primary speech and language delay: Findings from a systematic review of the literature. *International Journal of Language and Communication Disorders, 35,* 165–188.

Law, J., & Roy, P. (2008). Parental report of infant language skills: A review of the development and application of the Communicative Development Inventories. *Child and Adolescent Mental Health, 13*(4), 198–206.

Lee, V.E., & Burkam, D.T. (2002). *Inequality at the starting gate: Social background differences in achievement as children begin school.* Washington, DC: Economic Policy Institute.

Leonard, L.B. (1991). Specific language impairment as a clinical category. *Language, Speech, and Hearing Services in the Schools, 22,* 66–68.

Lew-Williams, C., & Fernald, A. (2007). Young children learning Spanish make rapid use of grammatical gender in spoken word recognition. *Psychological Science, 18,* 193–198.

Lonigan, C.J., Burgess, S.R., & Anthony, J.L. (2000). Development of emergent literacy and early reading skills in preschool children: Evidence from a latent variable longitudinal study. *Developmental Psychology, 36,* 596–613.

Lyytinen, P., Eklund, K., & Lyytinen, H. (2005). Language development and literacy skills in late-talking toddlers with and without familial risk for dyslexia. *Annals of Dyslexia, 55,* 166–192.

Maitel, S.L., Dromi, E., Sagi, A., & Bornstein, M.H. (2000). The Hebrew Communicative Development Inventory: Language specific properties and cross-linguistic generalizations. *Journal of Child Language, 27,* 43–67.

Marchman, V.A., & Bates, E. (1994). Continuity in lexical and morphological development: A test of the critical mass hypothesis. *Journal of Child Language, 21*(2), 339–366.

Marchman, V.A., & Fernald, A. (2008). Speed of word recognition and vocabulary knowledge in infancy predict cognitive and language outcomes in later childhood. *Developmental Science, 11,* F9–F16.

Marchman, V.A., & Martínez-Sussmann, C. (2002). Concurrent validity of caregiver/parent report measures of language for children who are learning both English and Spanish. *Journal of Speech, Language, and Hearing Research, 45*(5), 993–997.

McMurray, B., Samelson, V.M., Lee, S.H., & Tomblin, J.B. (2010). Individual differences in online spoken word recognition: Implications for SLI. *Cognitive Psychology, 60,* 1–39.

Misyak, J.B., Christiansen, M.H., & Tomblin, J.B. (2010). Sequential expectations: The role of prediction-based learning in language. *Topics in Cognitive Science, 2,* 138–153. doi:10.1111/j.1756–8765.2009.01072.x

Montgomery, J.W., Evans, J., & Gillam, R. (2009). Relation of auditory attention on complex sentence comprehension in children with specific language impairment: A preliminary study. *Applied Psycholinguistics, 30,* 123–151.

Nelson, K. (1973). Structure and strategy in learning to talk. *Monographs of the Society for Research in Child Development, 38*(1–2), 1–135.

Oliver, B., Dale, P.S., & Plomin, R. (2004). Verbal and nonverbal predictors of early language problems: An analysis of twins in early childhood back to infancy. *Journal of Child Language, 31,* 609–631.

Pakulak, E., & Neville, H. (2010). Proficiency differences in syntactic processing of monolingual native speakers indexed by event-related potentials. *Journal of Cognitive Neuroscience, 22,* 2729–2744.

Pan, B.A., Rowe, M.L., Singer, J.D., & Snow, C.E. (2005). Maternal correlates of growth in toddler vocabulary production in low-income families. *Child Development, 76,* 763–782.

Pan, B.A., Rowe, M., Spier, E., & Tamis-LeMonda, C. (2004). Measuring productive vocabulary of toddlers in low-income families: Concurrent and predictive validity of three sources of data. *Journal of Child Language, 31,* 587–608.

Papaeliou, C.F., & Rescorla, L.A. (2011). Vocabulary development in Greek children: A cross-linguistic comparison using the Language Development Survey. *Journal of Child Language, 38*(4), 861–887.

Paul, R. (1991). Profiles of toddlers with slow expressive language development. *Topics in Language Disorders, 11,* 1–13.

Pearson, B.Z., Fernández, S.C., & Oller, D.K. (1993). Lexical development in bilingual infants and toddlers: Comparison to monolingual norms. *Language Learning, 43,* 93–120.

Place, S., & Hoff, E. (2011). Properties of dual language exposure that influence two-year-olds' bilingual proficiency. *Child Development, 82*(6), 1834–1849.

Reilly, S., Wake, M., Bavin, E.L., Prior, M., Williams, J., Bretherton, L., . . . Ukoumunne, O.C. (2007). Predicting language at 2 years of age: A prospective community study. *Pediatrics, 120,* 1441–1449.

Rescorla, L. (1989). The Language Development Survey: A screening tool for delayed language in toddlers. *Journal of Speech and Hearing Disorders, 54,* 578–599.

Rescorla, L. (2002). Language and reading outcomes to age 9 in late-talking toddlers. *Journal of Speech, Language, and Hearing Research, 45,* 360–371.

Rescorla, L. (2009). Age 17 language and reading outcomes in late-talking toddlers: Support for a dimensional perspective on language delay. *Journal of Speech, Language, and Hearing Research, 52,* 16–30.

Rescorla, L., & Roberts, J. (2002). Nominal versus verbal morpheme use in late talkers at ages 3 and 4. *Journal of Speech, Language and Hearing Research, 45,* 1219–1231.

Rowe, M.L. (2008). Child-directed speech: Relation to socioeconomic status, knowledge of child development and child vocabulary skill. *Journal of Child Language, 35,* 185–205.

Salthouse, T. (1996). The processing-speed theory of adult age differences in cognition. *Psychological Review, 103,* 403–428.

Scarborough, H.S., & Dobrich, W. (1994). On the efficacy of reading to preschoolers. *Developmental Review, 14*(3), 245–302.

Shaywitz, S.E., Escobar, M.D., Shaywitz, B.A., Fletcher, J.M., & Makuch, R. (1992). Evidence that dyslexia may represent the lower tail of a normal distribution of reading ability. *New England Journal of Medicine, 326,* 145–150.

Street, J.A., & Dąbrowska, E. (2010). More individual differences in language attainment: How much do adult native speakers of English know about passives and quantifiers? *Lingua, 120,* 2080–2094.

Thal, D., & Katich, J. (1996). Predicaments in early identification of specific language impairment: Does the early bird always catch the worm? In K.N. Cole, P.S. Dale, & D. Thal (Eds.), *Assessment of communication and language* (pp. 1–28). Baltimore, MD: Paul H. Brookes Publishing Co.

Thal, D., Tobias, S., & Morrison, D. (1991). Language and gesture in late talkers: A 1-year follow-up. *Journal of Speech and Hearing Research, 34,* 604–612.

Tomasello, M., & Mervis, C.B. (1994). The instrument is great, but measuring comprehension is still a problem. *Monographs of the Society for Research in Child Development, 59,* 174–179.

Tomblin, J.B., & Buckwalter, P. (1998). The heritability of poor language achievement among twins. *Journal of Speech and Hearing Research, 41,* 188–199.

Tomblin, J.B., Zhang, X., Weiss, A., Catts, H., & Ellis Weismer, S. (2004). Dimensions of individual differences in communication skills among primary grade children. In M.L. Rice, & S.F. Warren (Eds.), *Developmental language disorders: From phenotypes to etiologies* (pp. 53–76). Mahwah, NJ: Lawrence Erlbaum Associates.

Walker, D., Greenwood, C., Hart, B., & Carta, J. (1994). Prediction of school outcomes based on early language production and socioeconomic factors. *Child Development, 65,* 606–621.

Weber-Fox, C., Davis, L.J., & Cuadrado, E. (2003). Event-related brain potential markers of high-language proficiency in adults. *Brain and Language, 85,* 231–244.

Weizman, Z.O., & Snow, C.E. (2001). Lexical output as related to children's vocabulary acquisition: Effects of sophisticated exposure and support for meaning. *Developmental Psychology, 37,* 265–279.

Wells, J.S., Christiansen, M.H., Race, D.S., Acheson, D.J., & MacDonald, M.C. (2009). Experience and sentence processing: Statistical learning and relative clause comprehension. *Cognitive Psychology, 58,* 250–271.

Zubrick, S.R., Taylor, C.L., Rice, M.L., & Slegers, D.W. (2007). Late language emergence at 24 months: An epidemiological study of prevalence, predictors, and covariates. *Journal of Speech, Language, and Hearing Research, 50,* 1562–1592.

# Longitudinal Course/ Outcomes

# 9

# Late-Talking Toddlers

*Characterization and*
*Prediction of Continued Delay*

Donna J. Thal, Virginia A. Marchman, and J. Bruce Tomblin

In the mid-1980s, parental concern about delayed onset of language in otherwise typically developing (TD) 2-year-olds, combined with the enactment of amendments to the Education for All Handicapped Children Act (PL 99–457)—which mandated appropriate evaluation and treatment of children from birth to 3 years who are at risk for developmental disorders—motivated a number of important studies of early risk for clinically significant language impairment. The research described in this chapter was among the studies that were started at that time. Several of them (Paul, 1993; Rescorla, 1989; Rescorla & Schwartz, 1990; Whitehurst & Fischel, 1994) used standardized tests of language to identify children around their second birthday who were delayed in early language development and followed their language growth over time. The children were classified by low expressive language development and were called *late talkers* (LTs). The research described in this chapter also identified LTs with a standardized measure and followed them over time, but in addition, this project was conceptualized within a theoretical model (the local homology model, discussed in the next section) that explored the nonlinguistic correlates of language development (Bates, Benigni, Bretherton, Camaioni, & Volterra, 1979; Bates, Bretherton, & Snyder, 1988). The overarching hypothesis was that understanding the contributions of nonlinguistic skills to the achievement of early language milestones would make a significant contribution to

The research described in this chapter was supported by Grant DC000482 from the National Institute on Deafness and other Communicative Disorders (principal investigator Donna Thal). We wish to express our heartfelt gratitude to the many families who were willing to share so many hours of their lives over so many years. Thanks to their dedication, it was possible to develop this rich, longitudinal picture of the differential development of language from infancy to school age.

early identification of clinically significant language delay by extending our understanding of the nature and course of early language development and delay.

This longitudinal research program was conducted in four phases over more
than 20 years. In Phase I, the use of language and gesture in children between 18
and 32 months was explored. It was during this same period that the MacArthur-
Bates Communicative Development Inventories (CDIs) were finalized, normed, and
validated (Bates et al., 1994; Fenson et al., 1993). These parent-report instruments
offered convenient and cost-effective tools with which to explore relations between
language and gesture, and among components of language, in larger samples of children than had been feasible in previous efforts. Thus, in the second phase of the program, a large research cohort was established that would provide a reliable sample
for predicting both short- and long-term language outcomes. The goals of Phase II
were to replicate and extend, with a very large number of participants, the results
found in Phase 1, and to evaluate the effectiveness of using parent report to identify significant language delay prior to 2 years of age. In Phase III, the goals were to
measure the language and cognitive skills of children who had been classified as LTs
at 16 months of age when they were 4–7-years of age with clinical measures typically used to identify and/or characterize children with specific language impairment
(SLI). Finally, in Phase IV, the ability to predict language delay from 10 months to 16
and 28 months of age and to predict which children would have a clinical diagnosis
of SLI at 4–7 years of age from measures collected from 10 months to 28 months of
age was tested.

## PHASE I

In the 1970s, building on and refining the earlier theories of Piaget (1952, 1962)
and Werner and Kaplan (1963), Bates proposed what she called a "local homology" model. Using this model, she documented normal variations in the earliest stages of language development and relations within and between cognitive
and linguistic domains in children from about 8 months to 3 years of age. The
local homology model was distinctly different from the models of early language
development that were being used at that time. Deriving from the prevailing uni-
versalist perspectives in linguistics, those models focused on the "modal child,"
documenting the similarities in sequences of development that were obtained
across children, and largely ignoring normal variation. Models of the modal child
were helpful because they provided, for the first time, guidelines for the average
age of onset for critical language skills. They fell short, however, by ignoring the
fact that language, like every other skill acquired by humans, is distinguished by
variation. They also ignored any nonlinguistic skills that might be important to
early language development. Without clear guidelines to characterize the normal
*range* of age of appearance of specific linguistic skills and the related parallel
developments in cognition, accurate diagnosis of clinically significant language
delay was not possible. The variations in TD children documented by Bates and
other researchers (Bates et al., 1979, 1988) described the range of normal in the
linguistic domain and some nonlinguistic correlates of that development. That,
in turn, provided the opportunity to explore in greater depth how clinically significant delay could be defined in early language development, not only in terms
of onset of specific aspects of language comprehension and production but also
in terms of the relationship between components of language and nonlinguistic
cognition.

In order to clearly describe the studies carried out in Phase I, a brief review of the local homology model, including findings from TD children that support the model, is presented first. This is followed by descriptions of four studies in which the model was used to explore the development of toddlers with language delay.

## The Local Homology Model

The local homology model was developed by researchers with an interactionist perspective as a response to modular views of language development (e.g., Chomsky, 1980; Fodor, 1983; Pinker, 1981, 1982, 1987). Building from Piagetian perspectives, such researchers argued that language is "an interactive system that depends crucially on processes and representations from a variety of cognitive domains" (Bates et al., 1988, p. 11). According to this view, it is the emergence of critical cognitive systems, such as those used for perception, storage, recognition, and retrieval of information, which shapes and times the early language acquisition process. Language is not a separate, self-encapsulated module that develops independently of other systems (see Bates et al., 1988, for a more thorough discussion of this theoretical issue).

The local homology model predicts that specific relationships between language and nonlinguistic cognition will occur only at specific points in time, when each draws on the same underlying cognitive mechanisms, rather than developing in a continuous manner, as originally proposed by Piaget (1952, 1962) and Werner and Kaplan (1963). It also predicts that different aspects of language (e.g., comprehension, production) may be dissociated in the very early stages of language development because they rely on different cognitive processing mechanisms for their early development. As a result, associations between language and nonlinguistic cognitive abilities (or among different components of language) found at one point in time may not be identified earlier and may not be found again at a later point. When the earliest studies described in this chapter were designed, many associations and dissociations between language and gesture, and among components of language, had been reported in studies of TD children, providing solid guidelines for application to LTs (see Bates et al., 1988; Bates & Thal, 1991; Bates, Thal, Whitesell, Fenson, & Oakes, 1989; Shore, Bates, Bretherton, Beeghly, & O'Connell, 1990; and Thal & Bates, 1990 for more detailed discussions).

***Language and Gesture*** Four distinct (but overlapping) stages of communicative development in which there are strong associations between language and gesture have been described (see Table 9.1). The first begins between 8 and 10

**Table 9.1.** Language and gesture milestones between 8 and 30 months of age

| Age in months | Language milestones | Gesture milestones |
| --- | --- | --- |
| 8–10 | Word comprehension | Presymbolic deictic gestures and gestural routines |
| 11–13 | Word production (naming) | Recognitory or symbolic gestures (gesture naming) |
| 18–20 | Word combinations | Gesture–word and gesture–gesture combinations |
| 24–30 | Grammaticization | Sequences of 3–5 arbitrarily ordered gestures |

From Bates, E., Thal, D., Finlay, B.L., & Clancy, B. (2003). Early language development and its neural correlates. In S. Segalowitz & I. Rapin (Eds.), *Handbook of Neuropsychology* (2nd ed., p. 538). New York, NY: Elsevier. Copyright Elsevier 2003.

months of age when first signs of language comprehension are observed and the very first attempts at intentional communication occur in both the vocal and the gestural modality. In the period between 8 and 13 months of age, the typical child engages in presymbolic communication, indicating her or his intentions to request or to draw attention to something with the gestures of giving, pointing, or showing and/or nonlinguistic vocalizations. All of these communicative means are presymbolic in that they have no referential content of their own; the referent is present in the communicative context.

However, around 12 months of age for most children, word production begins in the oral modality, paralleled by the use of recognitory gestures. Recognitory gestures are movements such as making a drinking gesture to indicate a cup or opening and closing the jaw and lips to indicate a fish. These gestures are seen as having the same level of representation as early words and have been referred to as *gestural labels* or *gestural names* (Bates et al., 1979), *enactive naming* (Escalona, 1973), and *gestural depiction* (Werner & Kaplan, 1963). It was children's use of these kinds of gestures that was the focus of the LT studies that follow. In this period, the evidence suggested that both words and gestures serve the function of naming, and both move from being context-bound to being used without a specific supportive context. Such findings suggested a common reliance on a newly developed ability to represent objects mentally (Bates et al., 1979; Bates, Bretherton, Shore, & McNew, 1983; Bretherton et al., 1981; Snyder, Bates, & Bretherton, 1981). In this period, children have also been observed to use communicative gestures spontaneously in their daily communicative interactions, although there is wide variability (Acredolo & Goodwyn, 1988, 1990). Acredolo and Goodwyn suggested that the children who use gestures do so to bypass a temporary obstacle to oral language development.

At about 18–20 months, an increased rate of spoken vocabulary growth is typically observed. As children have access to greater numbers of words, they also begin to combine those words to produce simple two- and three-word combinations and then multiword utterances. It is during this same period that children also begin to produce multischeme gestural combinations in play (e.g., stirring and then drinking from a cup with a continuous action sequence; Iverson & Goldin-Meadow, 1998; Shore, O'Connell, & Bates, 1984). In this period, parallels in the language and gestural modalities suggest a common underlying cognitive mechanism that supports children's ability to combine symbolic representations (Brownell, 1988; Fenson & Ramsay, 1981; McCune-Nicolich, 1981; McCune-Nicolich & Bruskin, 1982; Nicolich, 1977; Shore, 1986).

Between 24 and 30 months, the utterances that most children produce become increasingly longer and more complex. Important developments in grammar in terms of both syntax and morphological inflection are seen. In this same period, children begin to use gestures in conventional order in familiar routines acted out with toys and also in elicited experimental procedures (McCune-Nicolich, 1981; McCune-Nicolich & Bruskin, 1982; O'Connell & Gerard, 1985; Shore, 1986; Shore et al., 1984). These sequences of communicative gestures may be seen as a counterpart to the syntactic, ordering component of grammar (usually measured by mean length of utterance [MLU] in studies of language development).

**Dissociations and Associations within Language**      Although this characterization of these developmental periods indicates strong associations between language and gesture, there is also evidence for an especially interesting dissociation *within* language. Research has shown that language comprehension and language production do not proceed in a parallel manner in the early stages of development. This dissociation is observed as a wide range of word comprehension relative to production: Although the average child understands more words than he or she says, many children have a very large receptive vocabulary but produce very few words, whereas others appear to produce almost all the words that they understand. Interestingly, comprehension and production are each associated with a different aspect of gesture (Bates, Bretherton, Snyder, Shore, & Volterra, 1980; Bates et al., 1988). Word comprehension at this early age is associated with single and multiple gesture productions in a familiar script (e.g., putting a doll to bed, feeding a doll) and demonstrates production related to lexical-conceptual analysis. Word production is associated with single recognitory gesture production and reflects rote production (Bates et al., 1988). Thus, *language and gesture are associated in different ways, depending on whether the linguistic focus is comprehension or production.*

In contrast to this striking dissociation within the lexicon, there is also evidence for a strong association between lexical development and grammar. For example, Bates et al. (1988) reported that correlations between vocabulary production at 20 months of age and MLU at 28 months of age were .83 (when based on parent report) and .73 (when based on spontaneous production). This is compared with a correlation of .48 between two measures of grammar: 20- and 28-month MLU. Similarly, in the norming study of the CDI: Words and Sentences (Fenson et al., 1994), expressive vocabulary size was strongly correlated with the grammatical complexity score ($r = .85$). These correlations provide evidence of an important connection between lexical and grammatical development in this early period, with some "critical mass" of lexical units required before grammatical generalizations can arise (Bates, Dale, & Thal, 1995; Bates et al., 1988; Marchman & Bates, 1994). If, as was strongly claimed at the time, grammar is an encapsulated module that develops outside of any other cognitive input, then this strong association between 20-month vocabulary and 28-month MLU would not be expected. Instead, the strong association suggested that grammatical development depends on the establishment of a critical lexical base (e.g., Marchman & Bates, 1994; Thal, Bates, & Goodman, 1997).

Taken together, these studies suggested that the skills that "hang together" over the course of early acquisition, even though they may not align with traditional domains of linguistic skill, reflect common underlying mechanisms of learning. Specifically, the links between early language use and the presence of symbolic gestures indicate the ability to represent knowledge symbolically (Acredolo & Goodwyn, 1988, 1990; Bates et al., 1979, 1988), and as such, could provide a window into the representational abilities of LTs. If that were the case, then perhaps a measure of early language comprehension and/or symbolic gesture use could help identify LTs who were at risk for SLI. It was this reasoning that motivated the studies of LTs described in the next section.

## Late-Talker Studies

In the first phase of this research program, four studies of LTs were carried out. In all of them, gesture tasks were designed to break symbolic play into units that were comparable to those typically used to describe language in this age range. Three of the studies (Thal & Bates, 1988; Thal & Tobias, 1992; Thal, Tobias, & Morrison, 1991) used the same cohort of 30 children selected when they were between 18 and 35 months of age. All of the LT participants were in the lowest 10% of the normal expressive vocabulary range for their age based on a parent report of vocabulary on the Language and Gesture Inventory,[1] a precursor to the CDI: Words and Gestures, and none of them produced word combinations. Their cognitive, behavioral, medical, and auditory developmental levels were all within the typical range. Each LT was individually matched to two TD children, one for age and one for expressive vocabulary. Expressive vocabulary was measured using both parent report and approximately 1 hour of spontaneous language that was sampled in three different contexts. Language comprehension was also sampled using two measures: parent report and a two-way forced choice picture identification task that was similar to the Peabody Picture Vocabulary Test (Dunn & Dunn, 1981) but modified for use with children younger than 2 years of age. The expressive vocabulary–matched children were significantly younger than the LTs and the age-matched (AM) controls. The comprehension vocabulary of the LT group was, on average, significantly higher than that of the language-matched (LM) controls, but there was substantial variability within the LT group. The scores of some LT children were close to those of the LM controls, whereas the scores of others were considerably higher.

Use of symbolic gestures was explored with two experimental tasks in which gestures were elicited through modeling and imitation in Studies 1 and 2. This choice was made for three reasons: 1) the tasks had been shown to provide more reliable estimates of the behaviors of interest at younger ages than did free play (Fenson & Ramsay, 1981), 2) they made it easier for the experimenters to clearly operationalize the behaviors to be scored, and 3) they allowed the researchers to make direct comparisons to earlier studies of TD children in which those tasks had been used (Shore, 1981, 1986; Shore et al., 1984; Shore & Bauer, 1983). In Study 3, gesture use in spontaneous communication was examined.

In Study 4 (Thal & Tobias, 1994), 17 LTs with specific *expressive* language delay participated, making this cohort directly comparable to those of Rescorla and Schwartz (1990) and Paul (1993). That is, the LTs were delayed in expressive vocabulary but not in receptive vocabulary. They were, however, identified at a younger age (16 months as opposed to around 2 years) and with somewhat different criteria. Rescorla and Schwartz, and Paul used a criterion of 6-months delay on the Reynell Expressive Language Scale (Reynell, 1977) and no word combinations at approximately 2 years of age. Thal and Tobias used a criterion of at or below the 10th percentile on expressive vocabulary and at or above the 11th percentile on receptive vocabulary on the CDIs. As in the previous 3 studies, two control groups were individually matched to the LTs, one for age and the other for expressive vocabulary. In addition, the AM controls were also matched to LTs for comprehension vocabulary. Because the CDIs were now available and normed (Fenson et al., 1993, 1994), they were used to select the experimental groups.

---

[1]This instrument was never published, but a summary of it may be found in Fenson et al. (1994).

Analysis of variance techniques and $t$-tests with a $p$ of .05 were used to evaluate the results in all four studies. In addition, when the comparison groups were very small, a statistical measure that does not require the assumption of a normal distribution (randomization test; Siegel, 1956) was used.

***Study 1: Do Late Talkers Use Representational Gestures?***   In this study the same experimental tasks used to explore gesture use in TD children (Bates, Benigni, Bretherton, Camaioni, & Volterra, 1977; Bates et al., 1979, 1980, 1983; O'Connell & Girard, 1985; Shore et al., 1984; 1990) were used to examine use of single gestures and gesture sequences in the communicative interactions of LTs. LTs and AM controls were between 18 and 32 months of age; the LM controls were somewhat younger.

***Single Representational Gestural Schemes***   The use of gesture labels, and whether those gestures were produced as abstract representations or only with realistic contextual support, was explored with this task. Each child was asked to produce a gesture that was modeled by the experimenter within the context of an imitative game. The experimenter produced the gestures with either a realistic toy object or with a placeholder (a block that had no shape resemblance to the object), and he or she used language that was supportive (actually naming the object), contradictory (using the name of a different object), or neutral (using the word *this*).

In this gesture vocabulary task, LTs performed like LM controls (who had the same size expressive vocabulary), and both of those groups performed significantly more poorly than the AM controls (who had a significantly larger expressive vocabulary). All three groups did better when the model was provided with a real object than with a placeholder, and there were no significant effects of language support. Thus, an association between expressive spoken vocabulary and gesture naming was found—a finding that is consistent with the studies of TD children in the single-word stage of language development.

***Sequencing of Representational Gestures***   The second experimental task was designed to examine use of the gestural analogue of syntactic structure by asking the child to imitate a sequence of gestural schemes within a common cultural script (e.g., putting a teddy bear to bed, feeding the teddy bear). Each script had four gestural schemes, and they were modeled with appropriate linguistic content. For this measure, the number of different schemes, number of schemes produced in modeled order, and the number of schemes in the longest uninterrupted sequence were measured.

LTs fell between LM (who produced the fewest schemes) and AM controls (who produced the most schemes) on the total number of schemes produced and the total number of schemes in the longest chain. On the number of different schemes in modeled order (a measure of sequence production, the gestural analogue of MLU), LTs performed significantly better than LM controls and did not differ from AM controls, demonstrating a dissociation between spoken language and gesture production. Thus, the ability to sequence gestural symbols was in advance of the spoken vocabulary skills of the LTs and associated instead with vocabulary comprehension—a finding that is consistent with those from TD children around 13 months of age (Bates et al., 1979).

***Study 2: Do Gesture Use and Vocabulary Comprehension Predict Expressive Language Level 1 Year Later?***    In the second study, the results of the first were combined with the additional information about whether any of the LTs had changed status over a period of 1 year (Thal et al., 1991). However, the parent report measure used was the Early Language Inventory,[2] a precursor to the CDI: Words and Sentences, instead of the Language and Gesture Inventory.

At the follow-up, six LTs had made significant gains in language development, moving well into the normal range. These "late bloomers" had reached the ceiling on the parent report instrument, making gains that were greater than those generally made by TD children (Fenson, Vella, Flynn, & Thal, 1988; Fenson, Flynn, Omens, Burgess, & Hartung, 1989), and their MLU was within the normal range (Miller & Chapman, 1981), ranging from Stage III to Stage V. The four other LTs were still delayed. At 30–35 months of age, their age equivalence on the parent report measure was between 12 and 22 months, and their MLU was still in Stage I, well below what is normal for their chronological age.

An analysis of the data from the year before revealed that none of the expressive measures differentiated the children who caught up from those who remained delayed. However, the children who remained delayed had performed significantly more poorly than the late bloomers on both of the language *comprehension* measures. The truly delayed children had also performed significantly worse than the late bloomers on *all* of the gesture production tasks. This finding clearly demonstrated an association between comprehension and gesture production in LTs. It also indicated that expressive language measures were not reliable predictors of performance 1 year later and suggested that comprehension and/or communicative use of symbolic gestures might predict later expressive language level more reliably.

***Study 3: Do Late Talkers Use Representational Gestures in Spontaneous Communication?***    The next obvious question was whether the relationships between language and gesture, and the differences between late bloomers and truly delayed LTs that were found using elicited imitation, were also present in spontaneous communication (Thal & Tobias, 1992). If use of representational gestures for communicative purposes indicates achievement of a level of cognitive development that is important for language acquisition, and their absence indicates the lack of or underdevelopment of some critical component, then the use of those gestures in spontaneous communication would occur in late bloomers but not in LTs who were truly delayed. To examine this hypothesis, use of communicative gestures from approximately 1 hour of spontaneous communication in structured and unstructured play from the first data point was analyzed. The gestures were categorized as either representational (symbolic or conventional) or nonrepresentational. They were further classified by their use to communicate (either spontaneously or as an answer), whether they were imitations, or whether they were elicited. Vocalizations were further divided into nonwords and words.

Late bloomers used significantly more communicative gestures of both types, and used them more frequently for spontaneous communication, than did

---

[2]This instrument was never published, but a summary of it may be found in Fenson et al. (1994).

truly delayed LTs and both of the normal control groups. They also used gestures as answers more frequently than did the truly delayed LTs and LM controls, but they did not differ from AM controls. The gestures of both groups of LTs and the LM controls were accompanied by significantly more nonlinguistic sounds than words, whereas those of the AM controls were accompanied by a greater proportion of words. Thus, although expressive language of late bloomers and truly delayed LTs was equally delayed in spontaneous communication, late bloomers (but not truly delayed LTs) demonstrated their ability to represent information symbolically and used it to communicate with others using the gestural modality. This provided further support for the previously observed relation between use of representational gestures and vocabulary comprehension and for the hypothesis that use of symbolic gestures might differentiate truly delayed LTs from late bloomers.

### Study 4: Gesture Use in Children with Specific Expressive Language Delay
Both single gesture use and production of gesture sequences were examined in this study, as in the first three studies. The difference between this study and the first three was that the LTs all had only expressive vocabulary delays, and the AM controls were also matched to the LTs for vocabulary comprehension. In addition, the sample size of 51 children was larger, with 17 children in each group. Although samples of this size have not been the norm in language acquisition studies because of the labor-intensive nature of data collection, one advantage of the larger sample size in this study was greater statistical power to detect group differences.

In the imitated single gesture production task, LTs and AM/comprehension-matched controls produced significantly more gestures than the expressive LM controls, and they did not differ from each other, demonstrating an association between vocabulary *comprehension* and gesture production in a situation that was comparable to standardized language tests.

In the gesture sequencing task, LTs did not differ from AM/comprehension-matched controls on the number of different schemes produced or on the number of different pairs of schemes produced in the typical order (for the spontaneous task) or the modeled order. Both produced significantly more than the expressive LM controls, providing additional support for the close relation between gesture vocabulary and spoken vocabulary *comprehension*.

The CDI: Words and Gestures measure of gestures is composed of five different categories, two of which ask parents about the representational/symbolic gestures used by young children. The results using this parent report instrument was the same as that for single-gesture imitation and both spontaneous and imitated sequences of gestures: LTs were reported to produce the same number of different representational/symbolic gestures as AM/comprehension-matched controls and significantly more than LM controls (who were matched only on expressive vocabulary).

Taken together, these studies provided the necessary support for creating the larger longitudinal studies that followed. First, there was a consistent relationship across cognitive domains: Use of representational gestures was consistently related to children's level of word comprehension. Second, the level of comprehension and gesture production appeared to be a more reliable predictor of which children remained delayed over a 1-year period. Third, the same results were found using both laboratory and parental report methods of data collection and from both elicited and spontaneous communication samples. This was particularly important for designing a large-scale study in which it would be impossible to sample the communication skills of every child in a laboratory or clinical setting.

## PHASE II

In this period, the CDIs were used to carry out a set of population-based, prospective longitudinal studies. Children were entered into the study when they were 10 months of age and were followed at predetermined intervals from 10 months to 3 years of age. The goals of the project were to push back the age of identification of LTs to 16 months (or earlier); to systematically explore the effects of language comprehension, language production, use of representational gestures, and other cognitive and family history factors on language development; and to describe the development of this large cohort of children from 10 months to 3 years of age. To achieve this goal, 1,500 children were enrolled at 10 months of age. In order to participate in the study, children were required to have had a 5-minute Apgar score of at least 7, no medical problems since birth, and to be from English-speaking families. Family history variables included gender; ethnicity; primary caregiver; family income; parental education; and documentation of any first-degree relatives with a history of learning or reading disabilities, speech or language disorders, or neurological disorders.

Parents filled out the CDI: Words and Gestures at 10, 13, and 16 months and the CDI: Words and Sentences at 16 and 28 months. A smaller number of parents also completed the CDI: Words and Sentences at 20, 24, and 36 months. In addition, 150 of the families agreed to come into the laboratory to participate in experimental and standardized measures of language development. At 10 months, parents also completed a detailed family and medical history questionnaire that was updated each time they filled out another CDI. When the participants reached 16 months of age, the CDI: Words and Gestures norms were used to identify three experimental cohorts from the 1,107 families that had completed CDIs at 10, 13, and 16 months. They were: children with typical language development (TD), children with typical comprehension but delayed production (late producers [LPs]), and children with delayed comprehension and production (late comprehenders [LCs]). TD children ($n = 863$) had scores above the 10th percentile on vocabulary comprehension and production. LPs ($n = 154$) scored at or below the 10th percentile for production but above the 10th percentile on comprehension. Finally, LCs ($n = 90$) scored at or below the 10th percentile for comprehension and production. The CDI-based cohort classifications were validated with the 150 children who came into the laboratory using the Preschool Language Scale–3 (PLS-3; Zimmerman, Steiner, & Pond, 1992). Normal cognitive development was documented for those children using the Bayley Scales of Infant Development (Bayley, 1993).

The research described here is primarily focused on comparisons among the three language groups when they were both younger and older than 16 months. In Studies 1 and 2, MANOVA, ANOVA, and Tukey tests with the significance level set at $p < .05$ were used to compare the groups. Partial eta squared was used to examine the amount of variance accounted for by each significant result. In Study 3, the chi square test ($p < .05$) was used to determine significant differences among the groups on whether or not they combined words into phrases and whether the longest utterances used were simple or complex. ANOVA ($p < .05$) was used to determine differences in the mean of the three longest utterances (M3L) reported on the CDI: Words and Sentences. Together these studies demonstrated continuity of language and gesture status based on the 16-month classificatory criteria of TD children, LPs, and LCs from 10 through 36 months of age, and different developmental trajectories for all three groups.

## Study 1: Group Differences in Early Gesture and Word Comprehension/Production

In this study, the goal was to determine if the differences in word comprehension and word production used to establish the groups at 16 months of age were also measurable at younger ages, and whether differences among the groups would be found in use of gestures at all three ages. To that end, the groups were compared on the number of words understood, words produced, and gestures produced at 10, 13, and 16 months of age as reported on the CDI: Words and Gestures.

*Receptive Vocabulary*   TD children understood significantly more words than *both* LPs and LCs, and LPs understood significantly more words than LCs (see Table 9.2). In addition, the comprehension vocabulary of LCs grew more slowly than that of the other two groups during this period. The increase in number of words understood from 10 to 13 months was 88.5 for TD children and 74.9 for LPs, compared with only 18.4 for LCs. The increase from 13 to 16 months was 89.7 for TD children and 90.8 for LPs, compared with 35.1 for LCs. At these ages, TD children scored between the 55th and 65th percentiles, LPs scored between the 45th and 55th percentiles, and LCs scored between the 10th and 15th percentiles. There were no significant gender effects for receptive vocabulary. Finally, the amount of variance accounted for by group status also increased from 5% at 10 months to 16% at 13 months and 30% at 16 months. Thus, significant differences in vocabulary *comprehension* among the three groups were *identified as early as 10 months of age* using parent report. They were consistently different, and accounted for more of the variance with increasing age, through 16 months. However, the power to differentiate among the groups was best at 16 months.

*Expressive Vocabulary*   Because of floor effects, statistical analyses were not carried out for the number of words produced. Descriptively, however, increases of 15.2 and 44.6 words produced from 10 to 16 months of age by TD children compared with only 2.6 and 3.6 for LPs and 2.2 and 4.8 for LCs were observed (see Table 9.2). The expressive vocabulary of both LPs and LCs grew much more slowly than that of TD children.

*Gestures*   Gesture analyses were separated into early gestures (communicative but not symbolic), later gestures (containing many of the representational gestures that have been correlated with language in earlier studies), and total number of gestures produced (see Table 9.2). TD children produced significantly more gestures of all types than did LPs and LCs, and LPs produced more than LCs at all

**Table 9.2.** Number of words understood and produced and number of gestures produced on the MacArthur-Bates Communicative Development Inventory: Words and Gestures (Fenson et al., 1993)

| | | Words Understood Age in months | | |
|---|---|---|---|---|
| Group | | 10 | 13 | 16 |
| Typically developing | | 52.51[a] | 141.01[a] | 230.67[a] |
| Late producers | | 42.53[b] | 117.46[b] | 208.23[b] |
| Late comprehenders | | 13.63 | 32.01 | 67.07 |
| | | Words Produced Age in months | | |
| Group | | 10[c] | 13[c] | 16[c] |
| Typically developing | | 3.99 | 19.24 | 63.81 |
| Late producers | | 1.32 | 3.97 | 7.59 |
| Late comprehenders | | .94 | 3.17 | 7.93 |
| | | Gestures Produced Age in months | | |
| Type of gesture | Group | 10 | 13 | 16 |
| | Typically developing | 9.10[a] | 13.19[a] | 15.31[a] |
| Early | Late producers | 7.91[b] | 11.80[b] | 14.23[b] |
| | Late comprehenders | .94 | 10.80 | 12.67 |
| | Typically developing | 8.07[a] | 20.39[a] | 30.22[a] |
| Later | Late producers | 6.20[b] | 16.98[b] | 26.66[b] |
| | Late comprehenders | 3.94 | 11.53 | 20.93 |
| | Typically developing | 17.18[a] | 33.58[a] | 45.53[a] |
| Total | Late producers | 14.12[b] | 28.78[b] | 40.89[b] |
| | Late comprehenders | 9.93 | 22.33 | 33.60 |

[a]Indicates that the scores were significantly higher than both other groups.
[b]Indicates that the scores were significantly higher than the late comprehenders only.
[c]Indicates that no analyses were done because of floor effects for late producers and late comprehenders.

three ages. TD children scored between the 50th and 60th percentiles, LPs scored between the 35th and 50th percentiles, and LCs scored between < 5th and the 25th percentiles. At 10 months the amount of variance accounted for was 10%, at 13 months it was 15%, and at 16 months it was 18%. As was seen with receptive vocabulary, the amount of variance accounted for increased at each age. However, gesture accounted for twice as much variance at 10 months and only about two thirds as much at 16 months compared with receptive vocabulary. Gender differences were variable and too small to be considered clinically significant. Girls in the TD and LC groups produced significantly more gestures of both kinds than did boys, but the reverse was true for the LP group.

In summary, looking across the three domains, it is clear that the differences among the groups established at 16 months were already evident in receptive vocabulary and use of gestures at 10 and 13 months of age. Moreover, LCs demonstrated representational skills that were much weaker than those of the LPs. Expressive vocabulary is not a useful measure at the younger ages because it has not yet developed sufficiently in any of the groups to provide a comparative measure.

**Table 9.3.** Expressive vocabulary and grammar on the MacArthur-Bates Communicative Development Inventory: Words and Sentences at 28 months of age (Fenson et al., 1993)

| Group | Vocabulary | Sentence Complexity | Mean of the 3 longest utterances |
|---|---|---|---|
| Typically developing | 539.23[a] | 24.45[a] | 7.96[a] |
| Late producers | 420.36[b] | 13.58[b] | 5.80[b] |
| Late comprehenders | 300.29 | 9.56 | 4.89 |

[a]Indicates that the scores were significantly higher than both other groups.
[b]Indicates that the scores were significantly higher than the late comprehenders only.

## Study 2: Group Differences in Vocabulary and Grammar at 28 Months

The goal of Study 2 was to determine if the pattern of development seen for receptive vocabulary and use of gestures in Study 1 was present in expressive vocabulary and grammar when the children were 28 months of age. That is, do LCs lag behind LPs, and do LPs continue to lag behind the TD children? The CDI: Words and Sentences was used to measure expressive vocabulary size (number of different words produced) and grammar (sentence complexity and the M3L) reported.

On these measures, TD children produced a significantly greater number of words than did LPs and LCs, and LPs produced a greater number than LCs, consistent with the results from younger ages (see Table 9.3). The same pattern was seen for both measures of grammar. We can also note that girls scored significantly higher than boys on all of the measures. The mean percentiles ranged from 55 to 70 for TD children, from 35 to 55 for LPs, and from 20 to 35 for LCs, demonstrating that all of the children scored within the normal range, although the substantial differences between the groups remained. The amount of variance accounted for was 23% for vocabulary size, 20% for grammatical complexity, and 10% for M3L.

## Study 3: Grammatical Development from 20 to 36 Months

In this study, the goal was to determine if the patterns identified in the previous two studies would be present in grammar across the age range from 20 to 36 months, and if they would be found across measures of the first signs of grammar (combining words) to levels of highest performance (M3L). Participants included 391 children (262 TD children, 86 LPs, and 43 LCs) from the longitudinal cohort whose parents completed the CDI: Words and Sentences at 20, 24, 28, and 36 months of age. The data for this study came from Part II, Section D of the CDI: Words and Sentences in which parents are asked whether their child was combining words yet and, if so, to give three examples of the longest utterances produced by their child. Sentences were considered to be complex if they contained object complementation, wh-embedded clauses, and coordinating or subordinating conjunctions; simple sentences contained only one clause. As shown in Table 9.4, all of the children in all three groups produced word combinations by 28 months of age. Prior to that time, more children in the TD group produced word combinations than children in either the LP or LC groups, but the two delayed groups did not differ from each other.

At 20 months of age, all three groups used primarily simple sentences. By 24 months, however, differences between groups emerged. At both 24 and 28 months

**Table 9.4.** Percentage of children combining words and using complex sentences reported and the mean of the 3 longest utterances produced on the CDI: Words and Sentences (Fenson et al., 1993)

| | Percent combining | | | |
|---|---|---|---|---|
| Group | 20 months | 24 months | 28 months | 36 months |
| Typically developing | 77%[a] | 91%[a] | 100% | 100% |
| Late producers | 24% | 59% | 100% | 100% |
| Late comprehenders | 25% | 51% | 100% | 100% |
| | Percent using complex sentences | | | |
| Group | 20 months | 24 months | 28 months | 36 months |
| Typically developing | 5% | 25%[a] | 50%[a] | 71%[b] |
| Late producers | 3% | 12%[b] | 35%[b] | 65%[b] |
| Late comprehenders | 0% | 4% | 15% | 46% |
| | Mean of the 3 longest utterances | | | |
| Group | 20 months | 24 months | 28 months | 36 months |
| Typically developing | 3.5[a] | 5.2[a] | 7.9[a] | 11.1[b] |
| Late producers | 2.8 | 3.7 | 6.4[b] | 10.9[b] |
| Late comprehenders | 2.5 | 3.4 | 4.7 | 8.8 |
| Males versus females | ns | Males < females | TDM = TDF<br>LPM < LPF<br>LCM < LCF | ns |

[a]Indicates that the scores were significantly higher than both other groups.
[b]Indicates that the scores were significantly higher than the late comprehenders only.
*Key:* F, female; LC, late comprehender; LP, late producer; M, male; TD, typically developing.

of age, TD children used significantly more complex sentences than children in the LP group, and LPs used significantly more than children in the LC group. By 36 months of age, however, LPs did not differ from children in the TD group, and both produced significantly more complex sentences than children in the LC group. Nonetheless, the percentage of complex sentences used increased consistently for all groups at all ages. Thus, although we observed considerable advances in grammatical development for all children across this important developmental period, children's profiles of later grammatical accomplishments were continuous with early lexical skills (e.g., Bates & Goodman, 1997). Most notably, those late-talking children with delays in early vocabulary comprehension were at the highest risk for later grammatical delays.

Looking at the second measure of grammatical skill, a similar pattern of developmental change, along with group differences, emerged. As shown in Table 9.4, at each age the M3L increased for all three groups, but the difference in M3L among groups changed with increasing age. At 20, 24, and 28 months, the mean M3L was significantly higher for TD children than for the LT group. At 20 and 24 months, the two LT groups did not differ from each other, but at 28 months LPs had a higher M3L than LCs. At 36 months there was no significant difference between TD children and LPs, and both were significantly higher than LCs. That is, the LPs had moved into the normal range but the LCs remained delayed. As with grammatical complexity, gender differences were also found for the M3L measure. At 24 months, males had a lower M3L than females. At 28 months TD males and females did not differ, whereas males from both LT groups had significantly lower M3L than females from those groups. No gender effects were found at 20 or 36 months of age.

In sum, the studies in Phase II demonstrated the close ties between language comprehension and gesture use between 10 and 16 months of age when expressive vocabulary size is too small to be useful for measuring level of language development. They also showed that the group differences seen in comprehension and use of gestures at those ages were still present in both expressive vocabulary and grammar at 28 months: TD children had the highest scores, LCs had the lowest scores, and LPs fell between them. By 36 months, however, LPs did not differ from TD children, but LCs continued to have significantly poorer language skills. Taken together, these results are consistent with the local homology model that predicts strong cross-domain continuities between early gesture and vocabulary, as well as early vocabulary and later grammar. Most notably, the results suggested that early language comprehension and/or gesture production may be reliable early predictors of long-term clinical outcomes for LTs.

## PHASE III

The studies in Phase III used standardized tests to measure the language and cognitive abilities of this prospective longitudinal cohort. When the children were 3 years of age, the families were invited to continue participating yearly until the children were 7 years old. At that time, 900 families agreed to continue through parent report measures and 90 agreed to continue to come into the lab.

At 4 and 5 years of age, a number of standardized tests were administered to the participants who came to the lab for testing, and standard scores were used to compare the LT groups. Language tests included the Peabody Picture Vocabulary Test, Revised (PPVT-R; Dunn & Dunn, 1981), The Expressive Vocabulary Test (EVT; Williams, 1997), and the preschool version of the Clinical Evaluation of Language Fundamentals (CELF-P; Wiig, Secord, & Semel, 1992). The Kaufman Assessment Battery for Children (K-ABC; Kauffman & Kauffman, 1983) was used to measure intelligence because it provided separate assessments of sequential versus simultaneous processing (thought to represent left versus right hemisphere brain capacities, respectively). The Nonword Repetiton Test (NRT; Dollaghan & Campbell, 1998) was also administered to examine phonological working memory.

At 5 years of age, parents ranked their children on the nine scales of the Minnesota Child Development Inventory (Minnesota CDI; Ireton, Thwing, & Currier, 1977). All parents were also asked if their children had received a diagnosis of speech disorder, language disorder, or learning or reading disability when they were between 4 and 7 years of age, and, if the answer was yes, they were asked to provide a copy of the clinical evaluation.

MANOVA, ANOVA, and Scheffé tests with the significance level set at $p < .05$ were used to compare the groups. Results from these studies showed patterns of development that are consistent with LT outcome reported by other researchers (Ellis Weimer, 2007; Paul, 1996; Rescorla, 2002; Rescorla, Dahlsgaard, & Roberts, 2000; Whitehurst & Fischel, 1994).

**Table 9.5.** Standardized test scores at 4 and 5 years of age

| | Age | | | | | |
| --- | --- | --- | --- | --- | --- | --- |
| | 4 years | | | 5 years | | |
| | Standard Scores | | | | | |
| | Typically developing | Late producers | Late comprehenders | Typically developing | Late producers | Late comprehenders |
| Vocabulary PPVT-R | 114.0 | 107.3 | 103.7 | 117.8[a] | 109.1 | 112.8 |
| EVT | 113.0[a] | 106.7 | NA | 114.4 | 111.9 | 113.0 |
| Language | | | | | | |
| CELF-P | | | | | | |
| Receptive | 114.7[a] | 105.3 | 105.2 | 114.7 | 111.4 | 105.0 |
| Expressive | 112.8[a] | 103.8 | 108.5 | 112.7 | 107.4 | 106.8 |
| Processing | | | | | | |
| K-ABC | | | | | | |
| Sequential | 111.9[a] | 106.1 | 98.5 | 108.7 | 108.7 | 106.4 |
| Simultaneous | 110.7 | 105.8 | 105.5 | 116.5 | 106.4 | 116.0 |

[a]Indicates that the scores were significantly higher than both other groups.

*Key:* PPVT-R, Peabody Picture Vocabulary Test–Revised (Dunn & Dunn, 1997); EVT, Expressive Vocabulary Test (Williams, 1997); CELF-P, Clinical Evaluation of Language Fundamentals–Preschool (Wiig, Secord, & Semel, 1992); K-ABC, Kaufman Assessment Battery for Children (Kaufman & Kaufman, 1983).

## Study 1: Links to Language and Cognitive Outcomes at 4 and 5 Years

Table 9.5 presents the results for the standardized language tests and the K-ABC. At both ages, all three groups had scores well within the normal range on these standardized tests. However, at 4 years of age, TD children achieved higher scores than both of the LT groups on the EVT, CELF-P Receptive and Expressive, and K-ABC Sequential Processing (composed of scores on word order, number recall, and sequential hand movements). No differences were found for these measures at 5 years of age. TD children scored significantly higher than both LT groups on the PPVT-R at 5 years (but not at 4 years) of age. There were no significant differences between any of the groups on the K-ABC simultaneous processing measures at either age.

## Study 2: Links to Phonological Working Memory

The NRT (Dollaghan & Campbell, 1998) was administered so that the outcomes from the LTs could be compared with results reported for children with SLI (Dollaghan & Campbell, 1998; Ellis Weismer et. al., 2000). Because all of the LTs who participated in these studies scored within the normal range on tests of language development, and because the number of LCs who participated was very small, the two LT groups were combined into a single group (combined late talkers [CLTs]). There were 64 children at 4 years of age: 44 TD children and 20 CLTs (Thal, Miller, Carlson, & Vega, 2005). At 5 years there were 65 children: 44 TD children and 21 CLTs (Thal, Miller, & Vega, 2006). The results are presented in Table 9.6.

**Table 9.6.** Scores on the Nonword Repetition Test (Dollaghan & Campbell, 1989)

| | Group | | | |
| --- | --- | --- | --- | --- |
| | 4 years | | 5 years | |
| | Typically developing | Combined late talkers | Typically developing | Combined late talkers |
| Test item | | | | |
| PPC 1 syllable | 82.4 | 76.2 | 86.5 | 85.3 |
| PPC 2 syllables | 89.3 | 83.7 | 91.9 | 89.3 |
| PPC 3 syllables | 83.2[a] | 71.2 | 83.4 | 78.9 |
| PPC 4 syllables | 72.8[a] | 55.1 | 74.4[a] | 62.8 |
| TPPC | 80.5[a] | 68.4 | 82.2[a] | 75.8 |

[a]Indicates the scores were significantly different.
*Key:* PPC, percent phonemes correct; TPPC, total percent of phonemes correct.

At 4 years of age the TD group scored significantly higher than the CLTs on the total percent of phonemes correct (TPPC) and also at the 3- and 4-syllable level. At 5 years, they scored significantly higher on TPPC and at the 4-syllable level. The scores for CLTs in these two studies are remarkably close to those reported for children with SLI by Dollaghan and Campbell (1998) and by Ellis Weismer et al. (2000), and by those for 5½-year-old LTs reported by Ellis Weismer (2007), supporting the hypothesis that late talking and SLI are not distinct phenomena.

## Study 3: Parent Report of Social, Motor, and Language Development

At 5 years of age, parents ranked their children on the nine scales of the Minnesota CDI (Ireton et al., 1977): General Development, Expressive Language, Receptive Language, Letters, Numbers, Social, Self Help, Gross Motor, and Fine Motor Development. No differences were found for the Social, Self Help, Gross Motor, or Fine Motor scales. On both the Letters and Numbers scales, all three groups scored within the normal range, but LPs and LCs scored significantly lower than TD children and did not differ from each other, a pattern that was also seen on the standardized tests of language. On the General Development, Expressive Language, and Receptive Language scales, TD children and LPs had scores in the average range and did not differ significantly from each other. LCs, however, scored below average and significantly lower than TD children or LPs. This pattern of greater delay in the LC group was also seen in parent report of language (the CDIs) multiple times at younger ages, depending on the ages of the children and the particular language skill examined.

## Study 4: Group Differences in Incidence of Clinical Diagnoses

In this study the goal was to determine whether different proportions of children in each of the groups identified at 16 months of age received a diagnosis of language impairment by a certified speech-language pathologist when they were between the ages of 4 and 7 years. All parents were asked if their children had received a diagnosis of language disorder at those ages, and, if the answer was yes, a copy

**Table 9.7.** Percent of children with a diagnosis of language impairment at any time between 4 and 7 years of age

| 16-month status | N | Percent with language impairment |
|---|---|---|
| Groups combined | 463 | 6.7% |
| Typically developing | 365 | 4.9% |
| Late producers | 70 | 11.4% |
| Late comprehenders | 28 | 17.8% |

of the official diagnostic report was obtained. Table 9.7 shows the percentage of children in each of the three groups identified at 16 months of age who received a diagnosis of language impairment at that time.

When the entire sample was considered as a single group, 6.7% of the children received a diagnosis of language impairment anytime between 4 and 7 years of age, a number that is comparable to that described for children diagnosed in the early school years (Tomblin et al., 1997). When the three groups identified at 16 months of age were examined separately, the TD group had the fewest diagnoses, LCs had the greatest percentage, and LPs fell in the middle. There was, however, no significant difference between the percentage of LPs and LCs who received a diagnosis of language impairment between 4 and 7 years of age. Significantly fewer of the TD children than children in either of the LT groups received a diagnosis of language impairment during this period.

Taken together the results of the studies in Phase III demonstrated the continuity of the individual differences identified in these children when they were 16 months of age through 7 years of age. Although significant differences varied depending on the measures used, when looked at across many measures of language, phonological working memory and cognitive processing, LCs had the weakest language skills. LPs had stronger language skills than LCs, but weaker than TD children. In addition, the significantly weaker sequential processing score of LTs at 4 years of age on the K-ABC (a composite score of the left hemisphere functions that test recall of word order, numbers, and sequential hand movements) provides further support for claims that LTs have a weakness in one or more language-related left hemisphere processing mechanisms. More generally, such findings add to the growing evidence for a dimensional view of language disorders (e.g., Rescorla, 2009).

## PHASE IV

Having established clear continuity in the individual differences in language skills from 10 months to preschool age for the groups identified as having delays or typical development at 16 months of age, the next goal was to determine whether language outcome could be *predicted* from earlier ages using the vocabulary and gesture measures from the CDIs in combination with medical and family history variables. We explored short-term prediction from 10 through 16 months to 28 months as well as longer-term prediction (to school age). This is an important question for those who wish to make a clinical diagnosis of language impairment as early as possible. Chi square, multiple and logistic regression, and hierarchical liner model-ing analyses were used (as specified in the following sections) to explore the abil-ity to predict categorical (delayed/language impaired or typical development) and continuous (staying in the same relative position within the sample) outcomes.

## Study 1: Predicting 28-Month Language
## Status from Language and Background Variables at 16 Months

The first goal of this study was to determine if the categorical language status of typical development versus language delay at 28 months could be predicted using the categorical language, gesture, medical, and family background characteristics at 16 months. To that end, two 28-month outcome measures of language from the CDI: Words and Sentences were used: the number of words produced (vocabulary size) and the grammatical complexity score. Children who scored at or below the 10th percentile on either of these were classified as having language delays (LDs). All others were classified as TD children.

The 16-month variables shown in Table 9.8 were examined as candidate pre-dictors. Family background and child health variables were first examined indi-vidually as categorical variables in association with the child's language status at 28 months using bivariate chi-square analysis. These were then combined within a stepwise logistic regression to determine the best background predictors of

**Table 9.8.**  16-month predictors of 28-month language status

| Communication | Language status at 28 months | | |
| | Delayed | Typically developing | Effect size |
| --- | --- | --- | --- |
| CDI Words Understood | 194.98 (85.33) | 219.87 (53.11) | Somer's D = .16 |
| CDI Words Produced | 39.32 (46.28) | 55.05. (55.58) | Somer's D = .22 |
| CDI Total Gestures | 42.30 (9.50) | 44.38 (7.81) | Somer's D = .12 |
| Medical | | | |
| Child history of ear infections by 16 months | 26.86% | 25.99% | $\varphi = -0.008$ |
| Family background | | | |
| Family history of speech and language disorders | 18.33% | 16.82.% | $\varphi = 0.02$ |
| Family history of learning disabilities | 18.73% | 20.09% | $\varphi = -0.01$ |
| Mother's education | 6 (4–7)[a] | 4 (4–7) | $\varphi = 0.15$ |
| Father's education | 6 (3–7)[a] | 6 (3–7) | $\varphi = 0.11$ |
| Family income | 3 (1–4)[a] | 4 (1–4) | $\varphi = 0.13$ |

[a]Median and range (in parentheses) where education levels were as follows:  3, partial high school; 4, high school graduate; 5, partial college; 6, college graduate; 7, graduate or professional school; and income was 1, less than $10,000; 2, $10,000–24,000; 3, $26,000–50,000; 4, $51,000 and higher.

*Key:* CDI, MacArthur-Bates Communicative Development Inventories (Fenson et al., 1993).

28-month outcomes. Likewise, the 16-month communication variables were first examined separately as continuous variables using logistic regression and then together using stepwise logistic regression. Finally, the background variables and the communication variables were combined in a stepwise logistic regression to determine which of the communication variables contributed uniquely to LD or TD classification at 28 months of age and which of the family/medical background variables added to the prediction.

The results of the bivariate analyses are shown in Table 9.8 in the form of effect sizes. Parent's education (both mother's and father's) and family income were associated with 28-month language status; however, as seen by the phi coefficients (that are similar to Pearson $r$ values), the effect sizes were small. Family history of speech language impairment and learning disabilities and the child's history of otitis media at 16 months were not significantly associated with 28-month language outcome. In contrast, all three of the 16-month communication variables were significantly related to language classification at 28 months of age. The effect sizes in each case were in the small to moderate range. When analyzed together in a stepwise logistic regression the relation between two combinations of communication variables (words produced and words understood or words produced and language status at 28 months) were similar to the single variable of words produced (Somer's D = .22). Words produced and understood accounted for 9% of the variance ($R^2$ = .09), whereas words and gestures produced accounted for 10% of the variance ($R^2$ = .10). Combining all three of the communication variables, and adding the family/medical history variables did not add any more predictive information. *These findings suggest that predicting a binary category of language delay outcome over 1 year from 16 months to 28 months of age can be done; however, the level of accuracy is not sufficient for clinical purposes.*

The rather low levels of association between the communication measures at 16 months and 28-month language status is likely due in part to the conversion of quantitative variables into categorical variables. Examination of the correlations between the 16-month and 28-month measures (in which the variables are continuous rather than categorical) demonstrated that they *are* significantly related with correlations in the moderate range (see Table 9.9). When all three 16-month

**Table 9.9.** Correlations between number of words produced, words understood, and gestures produced on the CDI: Words and Gestures at 16 months and words produced and grammatical complexity at 28 months on the CDI: Words and Sentences (Fenson et al., 1993)

|  | Words Produced | Sentence Complexity |
|---|---|---|
| Words Produced | .45<br>$n$ = 931<br>$p$ < .0001 | .50<br>$n$ = 921<br>$p$ < .0001 |
| Words Understood | .49<br>$n$ = 931<br>$p$ < .0001 | .41<br>$n$ = 921<br>$p$ < .0001 |
| Total Gestures | .40<br>$n$ = 931<br>$p$ < .0001 | .35<br>$n$ = 921<br>$p$ < .0001 |

communication variables were used to predict 28-month measures using a step-wise regression method, all three predictors were retained, resulting in medium to large effect sizes for both words produced ($r^2 = .30$) and sentence complexity ($r^2 = .29$). Thus, we can see that considerable information regarding 28-month language status is available from parent report when children are 16 months old.

## Study 2: Relationship Between Rate of Growth in Language from 10 Months to 16 Months and 28-Month Language Status

Given that impressive continuity in language status from 10 to 36 months of age was demonstrated in Phase II, the next question was whether *rate of growth* in language from 10 to 16 months of age would predict language level at 28 months of age. Hierarchical linear modeling (SAS Proc Mixed) was used to examine this question. Three specific questions were of interest: 1) Was rate of growth in either words produced or words understood from 10 to 16 months related to vocabulary size and grammatical knowledge as a continuous variable? 2) Was that relation (if found) the same for production and comprehension? 3) Was the ability to predict language delay at 28 months better using rate of growth than it was using just the 16-month data (described previously)? Scores from the CDI: Words and Gestures were used at 10, 13, and 16 months of age. The outcome measures, as for Study 1, were the number of words produced (vocabulary) and the sentence complexity score (grammar) on the CDI: Words and Sentences.

First, the relation between 28-month vocabulary scores and expressive vocabulary growth from 10 to 16 months for 900 children who had been given the CDI: Words and Sentences at 28 months was examined. When growth in words produced was tested as a predictor of 28-month vocabulary, the analyses indicated that both the association between 28-month vocabulary and the intercept at 10 months (Beta = 0.008, $t = 3.66$, $df = 911$, $p < .0003$) and the interaction of the rate of increase in expressive vocabulary size from 10 to 16 months with-28 month vocabulary (Beta = 0.004, $t = 15.30$, $df = 899$, $p < .0001$) were significant. A somewhat stronger relationship was found using growth in words understood. The intercept at 10 months (Beta = 0.06, $t = 6.24$, $df = 911$, $p < .0001$) and the interaction of the rate of increase in receptive vocabulary size with vocabulary status at 28 months (Beta = 0.03, $t = 16.07$, $df = 911$, $p < .0001$) were significantly associated.

The prediction of grammatical complexity showed that both the association of 28-month complexity with intercept levels at 10 months (Beta = 0.008, $t = 3.66$, $df = 911$, $p < .0003$) and the interaction of rate of increase in expressive vocabulary size with 28-month complexity (Beta = 0.004, $t = 15.56$, $df = 899$, $p < .0001$) were significant. When growth was measured by words understood, an even stronger pattern of association of the intercept (Beta = 0.07, $t = 6.24$, $df = 911$, $p < .0001$) and the interaction of growth with 28-month sentence complexity was found.

These results show that the levels of both word production and comprehension (that provided the intercept at 10 months of age) are associated, albeit weakly, with language status a year and a half later. Furthermore, differential slopes reflect differences in the rates of growth in both measures of vocabulary between 10 and 16 months. Such differences are also associated with individual differences in vocabulary and sentence complexity 1 year later. Although both vocabulary production and comprehension showed these patterns of association, the measures of word comprehension consistently showed a slightly stronger association.

## Study 3: Does Growth from 10 to 16 Months Improve Prediction of 28-Month Language Status?

The previous analyses demonstrated that 16-month scores on the CDIs (words understood, words produced, and gestures produced) as well as the measures of growth in words understood and words produced between 10 and 16 months all independently predicted 28-month language status. The next question examined was whether information about growth would improve the prediction of 28-month language status over just the 16-month CDI scores alone. Thus, a difference score for the increase in words produced and words understood from 10 to 16 months of age was calculated.

Initially each potential predictor variable (change in words understood, change in words produced, words understood at 16 months, words produced at 16 months and gestures produced at 16 months) was correlated with 28-month words produced on the CDI: Words and Sentences. The correlations for each of the five predictors were similar ($r = .47$ for change in words understood, $r = .45$ for change in words produced, $r = .49$ for words understood at 16 months, $r = .45$ for words produced at 16 months, and $r = .40$ for gestures produced). These variables were entered in a stepwise multiple regression to determine the degree to which they contained unique predictive information. Four of the predictor variables were retained as significantly adding predictive information regarding words produced at 28 months. Word comprehension at 16 months accounted for 24% of the variance, whereas the words produced at 16 months added another 5.4%, growth in words understood contributed 1%, and the 16-month score for total gestures added another 1%. This analysis shows that most of the predictive information for 28-month status could be obtained from a single observation point at 16 months that uses words understood, words produced, and gesture use. However, the growth trajectory of word understanding prior to that also provides some additional information.

## Study 4: Prediction of Diagnosis of Language Impairment Between 4 and 7 Years of Age

A subset of children ($n = 470$) who participated in the prior studies were followed, and parents provided information on the child's history of speech and language diagnosis. Of the total, 6.81% ($n = 32$) were reported by their parents to have received a diagnosis of language impairment between the ages of 4 and 7 years. Stepwise logistic regression was used to determine the strength of prediction of this outcome that could be made using 1) the CDI: Words and Gestures communication variables of number of words produced (expressive vocabulary), number of words understood (receptive vocabulary), and total number of gestures used at 16 months, and 2) the CDI: Words and Sentences measures of words produced and grammatical complexity at 28 months of age. This analysis resulted in a three-variable model that included number of words understood at 16 months, number of words produced at 28 months, and sentence complexity at 28 months. The predictive strength of this model was moderately strong, as indicated by a Somers' D score of 0.49.

**Table 9.10.** Classification accuracy (%) for the prediction of diagnosis of language impairment between 4 and 7 years of age based on a logistic model using number of words produced at 28 months and number of words understood at 16 months

| Prior probability of language impairment diagnosis | Sensitivity (number of true cases = 32) | Specificity (number of true noncases = 438) | Predictive value positive | Predictive value negative |
|---|---|---|---|---|
| 0.05 | 69 | 69 | 14 | 97 |
| 0.10 | 56 | 86 | 23 | 96 |
| 0.15 | 50 | 91 | 31 | 95 |
| 0.20 | 41 | 95 | 37 | 95 |

This logistic model can be evaluated with regard to its ability to predict the diagnostic outcome of children between 4 and 7 years of age. These predictions are in the form of classifications with respect to the rate of correctly identifying: true cases (sensitivity), true noncases (specificity), rates of predicted cases that are true cases (predictive values positive), and rates of predicted noncases that are true noncases (predictive values negative). Because the predictor variables are continuous, it is possible to vary the cutoff so that these different rates can be optimized; however, increasing one (e.g., sensitivity) will always come at the cost of decreasing the other (e.g., specificity). Table 9.10 presents the classification accuracy of two language measures taken when the children were very young (16-month words understood and 28-month words produced) for prediction of diagnosis of language impairment when the children were between 4 and 7 years old. As the cutoff point in terms of prior probability of language impairment is increased, the sensitivity declines, and the specificity increases. Thus, if one wants to identify most of the children who will go on to have language impairment, one should establish a low prior probability (e.g., 0.05). However, this will also result in misclassifying a large number of children who are not at risk, as can be seen in the very high false positive value (93%). If the cutoff point is raised to 0.20, 13 of the 32 children (41%) who will go on to have language impairment were identified along with 22 children who did not go on to have language impairment. Although this level of predictive value positive (37%) is still low, the absolute level of overidentification could be argued to be acceptable, particularly given that the children who are false positives in this case are likely to have low language skills and could very likely profit from early intervention.

## SUMMARY AND DISCUSSION

To our knowledge, this is the only research program in which children with early delays in language development were followed prospectively, as part of a larger unselected sample, from infancy to school age. Taken together, the studies provide strong evidence for the continuity of individual differences in language and language-related skills from 10 months of age to school age and for a dimensional perspective regarding language delay and disorders (Bishop, 2006; Dollaghan, 2004, 2011; Karmiloff-Smith, 2007; Leonard, 1987, 2009; Rescorla, 2009).

## Phases I and II: Late Talker
## Characterization and Outcome from 10 to 36 Months

Studies from the first phase of this project established that late-talking toddlers around 2 years of age used representational communicative gestures such as TD children in the single-word stage of language development. The use of gestural symbols was in advance of spoken verbal symbols, "traveling" instead with vocabulary comprehension. Moreover, this relationship predicted outcomes 1 year later: LTs who showed the normal range of comprehension and sufficient use of representational communicative gestures were more likely to move into the normal range, whereas those with delayed comprehension and infrequent communicative gesture use remained significantly delayed as a group. These results are consistent with Bates' model in which comprehension and *analyzed* production (i.e., language production based on comprehension rather than imitation or ritualized routines) at 13 months of age leads to growth in vocabulary and grammar at 20 and 28 months of age (Bates et al., 1979, 1988). In this case, the gestures used by the LPs indicated a level of representational ability that was less likely to be observed in the children with delayed comprehension. Because these predictive behaviors (i.e., vocabulary comprehension and use of gestures) appeared at a later age than in TD children, these results suggest that risks for poor outcomes are associated with delayed, underdeveloped, or weaker capacity for representing information mentally during the first years of life.

In the second phase, the same issues were explored with a sample of more than 1,100 children that was unselected and followed prospectively from 10 months to 3 years. At 16 months, the children were classified as TD (i.e., children who scored in the normal range on vocabulary comprehension and production), LPs who were in the normal range for comprehension but delayed in production, and LCs who were delayed in both comprehension and production. In the first study, results showed that the patterns found between language and gesture in Phase 1 were robust, and they were identifiable as early as 10 months of age. Children in both the LP and LC groups were at floor on the CDI: Words and Gestures for words produced at all ages between 10 and 16 months; however, the LPs understood more words and used more gestures than children in the LC group. The TD children understood more words and used more gestures than either of the LT groups. Again, the results showed that early comprehension and gesture use traveled together and distinguished those LTs at greater risk for later delays from those who showed some recovery.

Continuity between the lexicon and grammar were demonstrated in the next two studies. The results first showed the same pattern for expressive vocabulary, and the sentence complexity score at 28 months as was found for receptive vocabulary and gesture use at earlier ages. TD children had the largest expressive vocabulary and used the most complex sentences, followed by LPs, who were, in turn, higher than LCs. In Study 3, grammatical development was examined in more detail at 4-month intervals from 20 to 36 months. In these more fine-tuned observations, more TD children than either LPs or LCs produced word combinations at 20 and 24 months. By 28 months all of the children combined words. No differences were found on the sentence complexity score at 20 months, and the same pattern seen in Study 2 was found at 24 and 28 months (TD children > LPs > LCs). At 36 months, however, the pattern changed: TD children and LPs had equivalent sentence complexity scores, and they both produced more complex utterances than LCs. The pattern for the M3L reflected both the combining and the sentence complexity score results. TD children were higher than the other two groups at 20 and 24 months (as would be expected from the percent combining scores), and at 28 months TD children had longer M3L than LPs who, in turn, had longer M3L than LCs (e.g., the grammatical complexity score at 24 and 28 months). Finally, at 36 months, LPs did not differ from TD children, and both had more complex longest utterances than LCs.

At a number of levels and across a number of measures, then, we see greater weakness in the linguistic abilities examined in LCs, who were delayed in vocabulary comprehension and gesture use at 16 months of age. These children also appear to remain well behind through 36 months of age. The LPs (i.e., LTs who were not delayed in vocabulary comprehension or gesture use at 16 months) slowly moved into the normal range, such that by 36 months of age they no longer scored significantly lower than TD children in all areas at 16 months. Given that this "catch up" of the LP group was on measures of the earliest aspects of vocabulary and grammar, it may well reflect the notion of "illusory recovery" proposed by Scarborough and Dobrich (1990). If tested on language measures that provided newer challenges for them, they may still have achieved scores in the delayed range.

The results summarized so far provide strong support for the relation between gesture and vocabulary comprehension in LTs and for the continuity of the lexicon and grammar, as originally demonstrated in TD children by Bates and colleagues (Bates et al., 1979, 1988). In addition, the patterns of relations and continuities found in these studies of LTs are the same as those reported in other studies of TD monolingual children (Marchman & Bates, 1994); bilingual children (Conboy & Thal, 2006; Marchman, Martinez-Sussman, & Dale, 2004); and children at both extremes of the normal range, including linguistically precocious children, (Thal, Bates, Goodman, & Jahn-Samilo, 1997; Thal, Bates, Zappia, & Oroz, 1996), other LTs (Ellis Weismer, 2007; Moyle, Ellis Weismer, Evans, & Lindstrom, 2007), and children with language delays due to other etiologies as diverse as focal brain injury (Bates et al., 1997; Marchman, Saccuman, & Wulfeck, 2004) and Williams syndrome (Singer-Harris, Bellugi, Bates, Jones, & Rossen, 1997). Although the emergence of the various language abilities may be earlier or later in the exceptional children, the *pattern* of emergence is typically the same as that for TD children, indicating a difference in timing rather than kind. In addition, these late-talking children, who had patterns no different from TD children in early childhood, had patterns similar to later-identified LTs and children with SLI on a test of phonological working memory (Dollaghan & Campbell, 1998; Ellis Weismer, 2007; Ellis Weismer et al., 2000).

## Phase III: Language and Clinical Status at 4–7 Years of Age

Phase III was designed to explore the language levels and clinical status of the groups who were identified at 16 months of age when they were between 4 and 7 years of age to see how they compared with children from other studies of LTs and to children with SLI. On clinical tests of language and cognitive development at 4 and 5 years, children in all three groups scored within the normal range, on average. Nevertheless, children from both groups of LTs achieved scores that were significantly lower than the TD children on some tests at some ages, but they were not significantly different on others. These results are consistent with a large body of earlier research on LTs (Armstrong, 2006; Girolametto, Wiigs, Smyth, Weitzman, & Pearce, 2001; Moyle et al., 2007; Paul, 1996; Rescorla 2002; Rescorla et al., 2000; Rescorla & Lee, 2000; Whitehurst & Fischel, 1994), suggesting that although earlier delayed children may appear to catch up, they nevertheless may not achieve levels of skills that are characteristic of children who were never delayed. In addition, LTs had significantly poorer phonological working memory than TD children, and they had scores that were comparable to those reported in other studies of LTs (Ellis Weismer, 2007) and children with SLI (Dollaghan & Campbell, 1998; Ellis Weismer, 2007). The measures that used parent and clinician report reflected continued delay for more LTs than for TD children, and more significant delay for those LTs who had been delayed in comprehension at 16 months of age. More LTs than TD children received a clinical diagnosis of language impairment by a certified speech-language pathologist between the ages of 4 and 7 years. In addition, the mean scores for LCs on the expressive and receptive language subscales of the Minnesota CDI were below average in range and significantly lower than those of LPs and TD children. These findings are consistent with reports that LTs continue to have weakness in language and language-related skills into adolescence (Paul, Murray, Clancy, & Andrews, 1997; Rescorla, 2002, 2005, 2009; Stothard, Snowling, Bishop, Chipchase, & Kaplan, 1998; Tomblin, Zhang, Buckwalter, & O'Brien, 2003) and lead us to speculate that the weaknesses are likely to be more substantial for late-talking children who were delayed in comprehension as well as production at 16 months than for those who were delayed only in production.

## Phase IV: Prediction of Language Outcome

Finally, in Phase IV, the question of early prediction of later outcome was explored. Results of the studies in this phase showed that 16-month status was not a good predictor of a *categorical* classification of language delayed or typically developing at 28 months of age, but it was a moderately strong predictor of continuous measures of development (vocabulary size and grammatical complexity score). In other words, children stayed within the same range of strengths and weaknesses in the language skills examined over the year between 16 and 28 months of age. Vocabulary comprehension was the strongest predictor, but it was only slightly stronger than vocabulary production and use of gestures. Rate of growth in any of the 10–16-month measures did not improve prediction. Finally, prediction of a diagnosis of language impairment at 4 to 7 years of age from five early language measures (words understood, words produced, and gestures used at 16 months plus words produced and grammatical complexity score at 28 months) had good sensitivity, excellent specificity, and an excellent false negative rate. However, as found in other studies, the false positive rate was high. Many TD children would have been diagnosed as language impaired using the 16- and 28-month scores. Given the descriptive outcomes reported for all of the other studies, the poor categorical prediction over even 1 year, and the results of previous studies in which categorical prediction has been tested (see, e.g., Law, Boyle, Harris, Harkness, & Nye, 2000), this is perhaps not surprising.

## CONCLUSIONS

The results of the research reported here add to the large body of evidence supporting a dimensional definition of language development that has accumulated since the 1980s. Continuity has been demonstrated in children with SLI (Tomblin et al., 2003) and LTs (e.g., Paul, 1996; Rescorla, 2009), and early vocabulary comprehension has been identified as an important predictor of whether late-talking toddlers move into the normal range or remain delayed. In her early studies of individual differences in language development, Bates hypothesized about the cognitive mechanisms necessary to get language learning off the ground in somewhat general terms: comprehension, rote production, and analyzed production. Rote production was observed during the acquisition of a new label in the earliest stages of measurable expressive vocabulary (between 13 and 20 months) when a word was first encountered and used without comprehension, imitatively, or in a social ritual. Comprehension and analyzed production occurred between 13 and 28 months and were observed as words produced with comprehension for conveying information. A critical mass of analyzed expressive vocabulary was needed for use of grammatical forms to get off the ground, demonstrating a developmental link between the lexicon and grammar.

In a longitudinal study in which LTs were followed until 17 years of age, Rescorla (2009) suggested that fundamental skills supporting the acquisition of language may include auditory perception, word retrieval, verbal working memory, motor planning, phonological discrimination, and grammatical rule learning. In newer research with infants and toddlers, new methodologies and ideas have begun to refine our ideas about the cognitive mechanisms that may be essential for language learning and/or may be implicated in language impairment. These include processing speed, working memory, and implicit learning (see Evans, Saffran, & Robe Torres, 2009; Leonard et al., 2007). For example, experimental studies with very young children have shown that children's early skill at efficiently integrating linguistic and nonlinguistic information during real-time language comprehension is robustly correlated to vocabulary outcomes over the 2nd and 3rd years (Fernald, Perfors, & Marchman, 2006). In a study focusing on LTs, speed of spoken word recognition at 18 months differentiated those delayed toddlers who moved into the normal range from those who remained at risk for more persistent delays (Fernald & Marchman, 2012). Such language processing skills have also been shown to predict children's later language and cognitive outcomes at 8 years of age, suggesting that a broad range of cognitive and linguistic skills that are necessary for successful real-time comprehension are fundamental to language development (Marchman & Fernald, 2008). In another line of research using eye tracking, a methodology that provides fine-grained analysis of real-time language processing, Yu and Smith (2011) demonstrated different patterns of attention across slower and faster word learners to the linguistic stimuli presented. They concluded that a combination of selective attention and a learning mechanism that employs associative learning can provide a plausible implicit learning model of how very young children acquire vocabulary.

The studies reported in this chapter also represent considerable advances in our ability to identify language delays much earlier in development than had previously been considered. Given the continuities between language outcomes and early skills in the period prior to the onset of vocabulary production, the current studies reinforce the conclusion that research should continue to explore fundamental aspects of very early development that support language learning, notably those that are related to early comprehension. The current project relied on parent report methodologies to a large degree, and the results support the conclusion that this technique remains a useful tool in such early assessments. Nevertheless, some researchers and clinicians have voiced concerns that parents may be prone to bias, and clearly, caution is recommended when assessing early comprehension skills, especially in lower–socioeconomic status populations (Arriaga, Fenson, Cronan, & Pethick, 1998). It is our recommendation that research should continue to explore the validity of early parent report measures using large-scale studies that include children from broad and diverse populations of learners. Another critical direction is further evaluation of the promise of experimental techniques that assess early comprehension, such as real-time measures of spoken language understanding (e.g., Fernald & Marchman, 2012; see also Chapter 8). Such studies contribute to the mounting evidence that a variety of early speech processing skills are fundamental to children's developing linguistic knowledge (e.g., Kuhl, Conboy, Padden, Nelson, & Pruitt, 2005).

To our knowledge, the research described in this chapter is the largest study to have identified LTs younger than 2 years, and the only one that has examined the earlier-emerging cognitive linguistic abilities of vocabulary comprehension and symbolic gesture use as it relates to long-term development and/or continued delay. The studies described in this chapter showed continuity of the group status established at 16 months of age from 10 to 36 months of age and consistent relations between gesture, vocabulary, and grammar. Clearly, many questions remain regarding how these linguistic and nonlinguistic skills converge over the course of the first few years of life, as well as the additional endogenous and environmental factors that may further shape children's outcomes. Nevertheless, these results are consistent with the emergentist models proposed by Bates and provide further support for the continuity of individual differences in children (see Bates et al., 1995, and Marchman & Thal, 2005, for more discussion). Taken together, these results provide strong support for dimensional models of language development and SLI (Dollaghan, 2011; Leonard, 1987, 1991; Rescorla, 2009) and point to the need for research focused on the varying effects of multiple underlying factors that differ across individual children and that can shed further light on the nature and course of early language development and delay.

## REFERENCES

Acredolo, L.P., & Goodwyn, S.W. (1988). Symbolic gesturing in normal infants. *Child Development, 59,* 450–466.

Acredolo, L.P., & Goodwyn, S.W. (1990). Sign language in babies: The significance of symbolic gesturing for understanding language development. In R. Vasta (Ed.), *Annals of Child Development, Vol. 7* (pp. 1–42). London, United Kingdom: Jessica Kingsley Publishers.

Armstrong, E.S. (2006). School-age cognitive and achievement outcomes for LT and late bloomers: Do late bloomers really bloom? (Doctoral dissertation). Available from ProQuest Dissertations and Theses database. (UMI No. 3238575)

Arriaga, R.I., Fenson, L., Cronan, T., & Pethick, S.J. (1998). Scores on the MacArthur Communicative Development Inventory of children from low- and middle-income families. *Applied Psycholinguistics, 19*(2), 209–223.

Bates, E., Benigni, L., Bretherton, I., Camaioni, L., & Volterra, V. (1977). From gesture to the first word. In M. Lewis & L. Rosenblum (Eds.), *Interaction, conversation, and the development of language* (pp. 247–307). New York, NY: Wiley.

Bates, E., Benigni, L., Bretherton, I., Camaioni, L., & Volterra, V. (1979). *The emergence of symbols: Cognition and communication in infancy.* New York, NY: Academic Press.

Bates, E., Bretherton, I., Shore, C., & McNew, S. (1983). Names, gestures and objects: Symbolization in infancy and aphasia. In K. Nelson (Ed.), *Children's language: Vol. IV.* (pp. 59–123). Mahwah, NJ: Lawrence Erlbaum Associates.

Bates, E., Bretherton, I., & Snyder, L. (1988). *From first words to grammar: Individual differences and dissociable mechanisms.* Cambridge, MA: Cambridge University Press.

Bates, E., Bretherton, I., Snyder, L., Shore, L., & Volterra, V. (1980). Gestural and vocal symbols at 13 months. *Merrill-Palmer Quarterly, 26,* 407–423.

Bates, E., Dale, P.S., & Thal, D. (1995). Individual differences and their implications for theories of language development. In P. Fletcher & B. MacWhinney (Eds.), *Handbook of child language* (pp. 96–151). Cambridge, MA: Blackwell.

Bates, E., & Goodman, J. (1997). On the inseparability of grammar and the lexicon: Evidence from acquisition, aphasia and real-time processing. In G. Altmann (Ed.), Special issue on the lexicon. *Language and Cognitive Processes, 12*(5/6), 507–586.

Bates, E., Marchman, V., Thal, D., Fenson, L., Dale, P., Reznick, J.S., . . . Hartung, J. (1994). Developmental and stylistic variation in the composition of early vocabulary. *Journal of Child Language, 21*(1), 85–124.

Bates, E., & Thal, D. (1991). Associations and dissociations in language development. In J. Miller (Ed.), *Research on child language disorders: A decade of progress* (pp. 145–168). Austin, TX: PRO-ED.

Bates, E., Thal, D., Trauner, D., Fenson, L., Aram, D., Eisele, J., & Nass, R. (1997). From first words to grammar in children with focal brain injury. In D. Thal & J. Reilly (Eds.), Special Issue on the Origins of Communication Disorders. *Developmental Neuropsychology, 13*(3), 275–343.

Bates, E., Thal, D., Whitesell, K., Fenson, L., & Oakes, L. (1989). Integrating language and gesture in infancy. *Developmental Psychology, 25,* 1004–1019.

Bayley, N. (1993). *Bayley Scales of Infant Development–Second Edition.* San Antonio, TX: Harcourt Assessment.

Bishop, D. (2006). What causes specific language impairment? *Current Directions in Psychological Science, 15,* 217–221.

Bretherton, I., Bates, E., McNew, S., Shore, C., Williamson, C., & Beeghly-Smith, M. (1981). Comprehension and production of symbols in infancy. *Developmental Psychology, 17,* 728–736.

Brownell, C. (1988). Combinatorial skills: Converging developments over the second year. *Child Development, 59,* 675–685.

Chomsky, N. (1980). *Rules and representations.* New York NY: Columbia University Press.

Conboy, B., & Thal, D. (2006). Ties between the lexicon and grammar: Cross-sectional and longitudinal studies of bilingual toddlers. *Child Development, 77,* 712–735.

Dollaghan, C. (2004). Taxometric analysis of specific language impairment in 3- and 4-year-old children. *Journal of Speech, Language, and Hearing Research, 47,* 464–475.

Dollaghan, C. (2011). Taxometric analysis of specific language impairment in 6-year-old children. *Journal of Speech, Language, and Hearing Research, 54,* 1361–1371.

Dollaghan, C., & Campbell, T.F. (1998). Nonword repetition and child language impairment. *Journal of Speech, Language, and Hearing Research, 41,* 1136–1146.

Dunn, L., & Dunn, L. (1981). *Peabody Picture Vocabulary Test–R.* Circle Pines, MN: American Guidance Service.

Education of the Handicapped Act Amendments of 1986, PL 99–457, 20 U.S.C. §§ 1400 *et seq.*

Ellis Weismer, S. (2007). Typical talkers, LT, and children with specific language impairment: A language endowment spectrum? In R. Paul (Ed.), *Language disorders from a developmental perspective: Essays in honor of Robin S. Chapman* (pp. 83–102). Mahwah, NJ: Lawrence Erlbaum Associates.

Ellis Weismer, S., Tomblin, J.B., Zhang, X., Buckwalter, P., Chynoweth, J., & Jones, M. (2000). Nonword repetition performance in school-age children with and without language impairment. *Journal of Speech, Language, and Hearing Research, 43,* 865–878.

Escalona, S. (1973). Basic modes of social interaction: Their emergence during the first two years of life. *Merrill-Palmer Quarterly, 19,* 205–232.

Evans, J.L., Saffran, J.R., & Robe-Torres, K. (2009). Statistical learning in children with specific language impairment. *Journal of Speech, Language, and Hearing Research, 52,* 321–335.

Fenson, L., Dale, P., Reznick, J.S., Thal, D., Bates, E., Hartung, J., . . . Reilly, J. (1993). *MacArthur Communicative Development Inventories: User's guide and technical manual.* Baltimore, MD: Paul H. Brookes Publishing Co.

Fenson, L., Dale, P., Reznick, J.S., Thal, D., Bates, E., Hartung, J., & Pethick, S. (1994). Variability in early communicative development. *Monographs of the Society for Research in Child Development, Serial No. 242, 59*(5).

Fenson L., Flynn, D., Omens, J., Burgess, L., & Hartung, J. (1989, April). *Tools for the assessment of language in infants and toddlers using parental report.* Poster session presented at the biennial meeting of the Society for Research in Child Development, Kansas City, MO.

Fenson, L., Marchman, V.A., Thal, D.J., Dale, P.S., Reznick, J.S., & Bates, E. (2007). *MacArthur-Bates Communicative Development Inventories (CDIs)* (2nd ed.). Baltimore, MD: Paul H. Brookes Publishing Co.

Fenson, L., & Ramsay, D. (1981). Effects of modelling action sequences on the play of twelve-, fifteen-, and nineteen-month-old children. *Child Development, 32,* 1028–1036.

Fenson, L., Vella, D., Flynn, D., & Thal, D. (1988). *Developmental norms for 4 parental inventory reports of language and communication between 9 and 28 months.* Unpublished manuscript, San Diego State University and University of California, San Diego.

Fernald, A., & Marchman, V. (2012). Individual differences in lexical processing at 18 months predict vocabulary growth in typically developing and late-talking toddlers. *Child Development, 83,* 203–222.

Fernald, A., Perfors, A., & Marchman, V.A. (2006). Picking up speed in understanding: Speech processing efficiency and vocabulary growth across the second year. *Developmental Psychology, 42,* 98–116.

Fodor, J. (1983). *The modularity of mind.* Cambridge, MA: The MIT Press.

Girolametto, L., Wiigs, M., Smyth, R., Weitzman, E., & Pearce, P.S. (2001). Children with a history of expressive language delay: Outcomes at 5 years of age. *American Journal of Speech Language Pathology, 10,* 358–369.

Ireton, H.R., Thwing, E.F., & Currier, S. (1977). Minnesota Child Development Inventory: Identification of children with developmental disorders. *Journal of Pediatric Psychology, 2,* 18–22.

Iverson, J., & Goldin-Meadow, S. (Eds.). (1998). *The nature and functions of gesture in children's communication.* San Francisco, CA: Jossey-Bass.

Karmiloff-Smith, A. (2007). Atypical epigenesis. *Developmental Science, 10,* 84–88.

Kaufman, A., & Kaufman, N. (1983). *Kaufman Assessment Battery for Children.* Circle Pines, MN: American Guidance Service.

Kuhl, P.K., Conboy, B.T., Padden, D., Nelson, T., & Pruitt, J. (2005). Early speech perception and later language development: Implications for the 'critical period.' *Language Learning and Development, 1,* 237–264.

Law, J., Boyle, J., Harris, F., Harkness, A., & Nye, C. (2000). Prevalence and natural history of primary speech and language delay: Findings from a systematic review of the literature. *International Journal of Language and Communication Disorders, 35,* 165–188.

Leonard, L. (1987). Is specific language impairment a useful construct? In S. Rosenberg (Ed.), *Advances in applied psycholinguistics* (Vol.1): *Disorders of language development* (pp. 1–39). New York, NY: Cambridge University Press.

Leonard, L. (1991). Specific language impairment as a clinical category. *Language, Speech, and Hearing Services in Schools, 22,* 66–68.

Leonard, L. (2009). Is expressive language disorder an accurate diagnostic category? *American Journal of Speech-Language Pathology, 18,* 115–123.

Leonard, L., Ellis Weismer, S., Miller, C., Francis, D., Tomblin, J.B., & Kail, R. (2007). Speed of processing, working memory, and language impairment in children. *Journal of Speech, Language, and Hearing Research, 50,* 408–428.

Marchman, V.A., & Bates, E. (1994). Continuity in lexical and morphological development: A test of the critical mass hypothesis. *Journal of Child Language, 21*(2), 339–366.

Marchman, V.A., & Fernald, A. (2008). Speed of word recognition and vocabulary knowledge in infancy predict cognitive and language outcomes in later childhood. *Developmental Science, 11,* F9–F16.

Marchman, V.A., Martínez-Sussmann, C., & Dale, P.S. (2004). The language-specific nature of grammatical development: Evidence from bilingual language learners. *Developmental Science, 7*(2), 212–224.

Marchman, V.A., Saccuman, C., & Wulfeck, B. (2004). Productive language use in children with early focal brain injury and specific language impairment. *Brain & Language, 88,* 202–214.

Marchman, V.A., & Thal, D. (2005). Words and grammar. In M. Tomasello & D Slobin (Eds.), *Beyond nature and nurture: Essays in honor of Elizabeth Bates* (pp. 141–164). Mahwah, NJ: Lawrence Erlbaum Associates.

McCune-Nicolich, L. (1981). Toward symbolic functioning: Structure of early pretend games and potential parallels with language. *Child Development, 52,* 785–797.

McCune-Nicolich, L., & Bruskin, C. (1982). Combinatorial competency in play and language. In K. Rubin & D. Pepler (Eds.), *The play of children: Current theory and research* (pp. 30–40). New York, NY: Karger.

Miller, J., & Chapman, R., (1981). Procedures for analyzing free speech samples: Syntax and semantics. In J. Miller (Ed.), *Assessing language production in children* (pp. 21–72). Baltimore, MD: University Park Press.

Moyle, M., Ellis Weismer, S., Evans, J., & Lindstrom, M. (2007). Longitudinal relationships between lexical and grammatical development in typical and late-talking children. *Journal of Speech, Hearing, and Language Research, 50,* 508–528.

Nicolich, L. (1977). Beyond sensorimotor intelligence: Assessment of symbolic maturity through analysis of pretend play. *Merrill-Palmer Quarterly, 23,* 89–99.

O'Connell, B., & Gerard, A. (1985). Scripts and scraps: The development of sequential understanding. *Child Development, 56,* 671–681.

Paul, R. (1993). Patterns of development in LT: Preschool years. *Journal of Communication Disorders, 15,* 17–14.

Paul, R. (1996). Clinical implications of a natural history of slow expressive language development. *American Journal of Speech-Language Pathology, 5,* 5–21.

Paul, R., Murray, C., Clancy, K., & Andrews, D. (1997). Reading and metaphonological outcomes in LT. *Journal of Speech, Language, and Hearing Research, 40,* 1037–1047.

Piaget, J. (1952). *The origins of intelligence in children.* New York, NY: International Universities Press.

Piaget, J. (1962). *Play, dreams and imitation in childhood.* New York, NY: W.W. Norton.

Pinker, S. (1981). On the acquisition of grammatical morphemes. *Journal of Child Language, 8,* 477–484.

Pinker, S. (1982). A theory of the acquisition of lexical-interpretive grammars. In J. Bresnan (Ed.), *The mental representation of grammatical relations* (pp. 655–726). Cambridge, MA: The MIT Press.

Pinker, S. (1987). Constraint satisfaction networks as implementations of nativist theories of language acquisition. In B. MacWhinney (Ed.), *Mechanisms of language learning* (pp. 51–67. Mahwah, NJ: Lawrence Erlbaum Associates.

Rescorla, L. (1989). The Language Development Survey: A screening tool for delayed language in toddlers. *Journal of Speech and Hearing Disorders, 54,* 589–599.

Rescorla, L. (2002). Language and reading outcomes to age 9 in late-talking toddlers. *Journal of Speech, Language, and Hearing Research, 48,* 459–472.

Rescorla, L. (2005). Age 13 language and reading outcomes in late-talking toddlers. *Journal of Speech, Language, and Hearing Research, 48,* 459–472.

Rescorla, L. (2009). Age 17 language and reading outcomes in late-talking toddlers: Support for a dimensional perspective on language delay. *Journal of Speech, Language, and Hearing Research, 52,* 16–30.

Rescorla, L., Dahlsgaard, K., & Roberts, J. (2000). Late talking toddlers: MLU and IPSyn outcomes at 3;0 and 4;0. *Journal of Child Language, 27,* 643–664.

Rescorla, L., & Lee, E. (2000). Language impairments in young children. In T. Layton & L. Watson (Eds.), *Handbook of early language impairment in children: Volume 1: Nature* (pp. 1–38). New York, NY: Delmar.

Rescorla, L., & Schwartz, E. (1990). Outcome of toddlers with specific expressive language delay. *Applied Psycholinguistics, 11,* 393–408.

Reynell, J. (1977). *Reynell Developmental Language Scales–Revised.* Los Angeles, CA: Western Psychological Corporation.

Scarborough, H., & Dobrich, W. (1990). Development of children with early language delays. *Journal of Speech and Hearing Research, 33,* 70–83.

Shore, C. (1981). *Getting it together: An exploration in cognitive capacities related to multisymbol combinations.* Unpublished Doctoral Dissertation, University of Colorado, Boulder.

Shore, C. (1986). Combinatorial play, conceptual development and early multiword speech. *Developmental Psychology, 22,* 184–190.

Shore, C., Bates, E., Bretherton, I., Beeghly, M., & O'Connell, B. (1990). Vocal and gestural symbols: Similarities and differences from 13 to 28 months. In V. Volterra & C.J. Erting (Eds.), *From gesture to language in hearing and deaf children* (pp. 79–92). New York, NY: Springer-Verlag.

Shore, C., & Bauer, P. (1983). *Individual styles in language and symbolic play.* Paper presented at the American Psychological Association, Anaheim, California.

Shore, C., O'Connell, B., &Bates, E. (1984). First sentences in language and symbolic play. *Developmental Psychology, 20,* 872–880.

Siegel, S. (1956). *Nonparametric statistics.* New York, NY: McGraw Hill.

Singer-Harris, N., Bellugi, U., Bates, E., Jones, W., & Rossen, M. (1997). Contrasting profiles of language development in children with Williams and Down syndromes. In D. Thal & J. Reilly (Eds.), Special Issue on the Origins of Communication Disorders. *Developmental Neuropsychology, 13*(3), 275–343.

Snyder, L., Bates, E., & Bretherton, I. (1981). Content and context in early lexical development. *Journal of Child Language, 8,* 565–582.

Stothard, S., Snowling, M., Bishop, D., Chipchase, B., & Kaplan, C. (1998). Language-impaired preschoolers: A follow-up into adolescence. *Journal of Speech, Language, and Hearing Research, 41,* 407–418.

Thal, D., & Bates, E. (1988). Language and gesture in LT. *Journal of Speech and Hearing Research, 31,* 115–123.

Thal, D., & Bates, E. (1990). Continuity and variation in early language development. In J. Columbo & J. Fagan (Eds.), *Individual differences in infancy* (pp. 359–383). Mahwah, NJ: Lawrence Erlbaum Associates.

Thal, D., Bates, E., Goodman, J., & Jahn-Samilo, J. (1997). Continuity of language abilities: An exploratory study of late- and early-talking toddlers. *Developmental Neuropsychology, 13*(3), 239–274.

Thal, D., Bates, E., Zappia, M., & Oroz, M. (1996). Ties between lexical and grammatical development: Evidence from early talkers. *Journal of Child Language, 23*(2), 349–368.

Thal, D., Miller, S., Carlson, J., & Vega, M. (2005). Nonword repetition and language development in 4-year-old children with and without a history of early language delay. *Journal of Speech, Language, and Hearing Research, 48,* 1481–1495.

Thal, D., Miller, S., & Vega, M. (2006). *Nonword repetition and language development in 5-year-old children with and without a history of early language delay.* Unpublished manuscript.

Thal, D., & Tobias, S. (1992). Communicative gestures in children with delayed onset of oral expressive vocabulary. *Journal of Speech and Hearing Research, 35,* 1281–1289.

Thal, D., & Tobias, S. (1994). Relationships between language and gesture in normally developing and late-talking toddlers. *Journal of Speech and Hearing Research, 37,* 157–170.

Thal, D., Tobias, S., & Morrison, S. (1991). Language and gesture in LT: A one-year follow-up. *Journal of Speech and Hearing Research, 34,* 604–612.

Tomblin, J.B., Records, N.L., Buckwalter, P., Zhang, X., Smith, E., & O'Brien, M. (1997). Prevalence of specific language impairment in kindergarten. *Journal of Speech, Language, and Hearing Research, 40,* 1245–1260.

Tomblin, J.B., Zhang, X., Buckwalter, P., & O'Brien, M. (2003). The stability of primary language disorder: Four years after kindergarten diagnosis. *Journal of Speech, Language, and Hearing Research, 46,* 1283–1296.

Werner, H., & Kaplan, B. (1963). *Symbol formation: An organismic-developmental approach to language and the expression of thought.* New York, NY: Wiley.

Whitehurst, G.J., & Fischel, J.E. (1994). Early developmental language delay: What, if anything, should the clinician do about it? *Journal of Child Psychology and Psychiatry, 35,* 613–648.

Wiig, S.E., Secord, W., & Semel, E. (1992). *Clinical Evaluation of Language Fundamentals–Preschool.* San Antonio, TX: Psychological Corporation.

Williams, K. (1997). *Expressive Vocabulary Test.* Circle Pines, MN: American Guidance Service.

Yu, C., & Smith, L. (2011). What you learn is what you see: Using eye movements to study infant cross-situational word learning. *Developmental Science, 14,* 165–180.

Zimmerman, I.L., Steiner, V.G., & Pond, R.E. (1992). *Preschool Language Scale, Third Edition (PLS-3).* San Antonio, TX: Harcourt Assessment.

# 10

# Late Talking in Context

*The Clinical Implications
of Delayed Language Development*

Rhea Paul and Susan Ellis Weismer

Late talkers (LTs)—children who appear to be developing typically but do not begin speaking at the usual time, acquire words very slowly, and do not begin combining words at the typical ages—are usually identified in their second year or early in the third year of life. In fact, failure to acquire words and word combinations is the most common presenting problem in young children (Toppleberg & Shapiro, 2000). Research suggests that clinical diagnosis of autism spectrum disorders (ASDs) can also be assigned in the second or third year, and shows at least short-term stability (Matson, Wilkins, & Gonzales, 2008) when conferred by a team of experienced clinicians (Charman et al., 2005; Chawarska, Klin, Paul, & Volkmar, 2007; Cox et al., 1999; Eaves & Ho, 2004; Lord, 1995; Lord, Risi, & DiLavore, 2006; Stone et al., 1999; Turner, Stone, Pozdol, & Coonrod, 2006; Wetherby et al., 2004). Because both LTs and young children with ASDs evidence very limited communication skills, differentiating these two conditions during the second year can be difficult. In this chapter, we review evidence from studies of toddlers who present with poor communication and social skills drawn from independent investigations in our laboratories. These investigations examine profiles of communication in toddlers with delayed language development for information that can be used for differential diagnoses of these two conditions in a very young child. We then explore

Preparation of this chapter and results reported in this chapter were supported by Research Grant P01–03008 funded by the National Institute of Mental Health (NIMH); the National Institute of Deafness and Communication Disorders (NIDCD) R01 DC07129, R01 DC007223, and R01 DC00371; MidCareer Development Award K24 HD045576 funded by NIDCD; T32 DC005359 funded by NIDCD; NIMH Autism Center of Excellence grant P50 MH81756; and P30 HD03352 core grant to the Waisman Center funded by the National Institute of Child Health and Human Development; as well as by the National Alliance for Autism Research, and the Autism Speaks Foundation.

the degree to which late talking in toddlers is associated with serious risk not only for ASDs but also for other long-term disruptions in development. Our aim is to integrate findings from two independent sets of data on this population to look for convergent patterns that can inform our understanding of the implications of language delay in toddlers.

## DIFFERENTIATING AUTISIM SPECTRUM DISORDERS AND LATE TALKING

Research dating back to the 1970s has attempted to delineate the differences between the language of children with ASDs and those with more circumscribed language impairments. Bartak, Rutter, and Cox (1975) investigated these differences in school-age children. Their research suggested that boys with ASDs and developmental language disorders (DLDs) showed similar levels of nonverbal cognitive skills, as well as comparable levels of syntactic development. Strikingly, though, boys with ASDs had more severe receptive language impairments than peers with DLDs; more deviant language behaviors, such as echolalia; more difficulties in nonverbal communication, such as gestures; and more impaired pragmatic skills. These differences continue to be recognized as the primary criteria for differentiating ASDs from DLDs. However, until the early 21st century there have been few empirical data to support the use of these distinctions at the *early* stages of language development.

We are uniquely positioned to contribute to the discussion of similarities and differences between LTs and young children with ASDs because we have each conducted research focused on early language development in LTs (e.g., Ellis Weismer, 2007; Paul, 1991) and toddlers with ASDs (e.g., Ellis Weismer, 2012; Paul, Chawarska, Cicchetti, & Volkmar, 2008), as well as direct comparisons of these groups with each other or other children with delayed language development (e.g., Ellis Weismer et al., 2011; Paul, Chawarska, & Volkmar, 2008). In this chapter we summarize the complementary findings of both our laboratories that compare children who received clinical diagnoses of ASD and those who were identified as LTs in order to examine the patterns of behavior in the second and third years of life in these two groups.

### Findings from the Yale Laboratory of Developmental Communication Disorders

Paul, Chawarska, and Volkmar (2008) studied toddlers referred for suspicion of ASDs ($n = 174$) or classified as LTs ($n = 27$) who had nonverbal developmental levels within the normal range but had scores on the Mullen Scales of Early Learning (Mullen, 1995) Expressive Language domain more than one standard deviation (*SD*) below the mean for their age. A contrast group of 171 typically developing (TD) children matched to the other groups on age was also included. All participants were between 16 and 34 months of age, with no differences among groups in terms of their birth or medical histories. Families reported no known genetic syndromes or visual or hearing disorders. Extensive assessments (summarized in Table 10.1) were conducted in order to assign participants to diagnostic groups. These assessments included standardized testing, structured behavioral observation, and

**Table 10.1.**   Assessment procedures

|  | Area assessed |
|---|---|
| Communication and Symbolic Behavior Scales Developmental Profile™ (CSBS DP™; Wetherby & Prizant, 2002) | Social abilities Speech Symbolic behavior |
| Mullen Scales of Early Learning (Mullen, 1995) | Visual reception Fine and gross motor Expressive language Receptive language |
| The Autism Diagnostic Observation Schedule– Module 1 (Lord et al., 2000) | Social abilities Communication Imagination Repetitive behaviors |
| The Vineland Adaptive Behavior Scales (Sparrow, Balla, & Cicchetti, 1984) | Communication Socialization Daily living skills Motor skills |
| Autism Diagnostic Interview–Revised (Lord, Rutter, & Conture, 1994) | Social abilities Communication Repetitive behaviors |

extensive parent reports gathered through semistructured interviews and questionnaires. Diagnoses based on the *Diagnostic and Statistical Manual of Mental Disorders, Fourth Edition (DSM-IV)* guidelines (American Psychiatric Association, 1994) were conferred by consensus between two experienced clinicians based on informed clinical judgment following interaction with the child, formal testing, and review of parent reports and records. The Autism Diagnostic Observation Schedule–Module 1 (ADOS; Lord et al., 2000) and the Autism Diagnostic Interview–Revised (ADI-R; Lord, Rutter, & Conture, 1994) were also administered to children in the ASD and LT groups. Clinicians involved in conferring diagnoses had access to these results, but numerical scores from these measures were not used exclusively for making diagnostic decisions. That is, clinical judgment took these results into account, along with other tests and clinical observation, as stated previously.

As Table 10.2 shows, participants in all groups were predominantly male. Average age was approximately 2 years at intake. Nonverbal cognitive levels were significantly different among the groups at this time, as measured by the Visual Reception and Fine Motor Scales of the Mullen Scales of Early Learning (Mullen, 1995). The group with an ASD diagnosis scored below the average range and significantly lower than those assigned to the other two groups, which both scored within the normal range, on average, on these measures. Expressive language skills were measured both by parent report of expressive vocabulary size on the MacArthur-Bates Communicative Development Inventories (Fenson et al., 2007) and by parent interviews on adaptive communication on the Vineland Adaptive Behavior Scales (Sparrow, Balla, & Cicchetti, 1984). Expressive language levels were not significantly different between the ASD and LT groups; the TD group scored significantly higher than both the ASD and LT groups on this measure.

Standardized testing profiles of the groups on the Mullen Scales of Early Learning (Mullen, 1995) revealed that children with ASDs differed from same-age LT and

**Table 10.2.**   Group characteristics

|  | ASDs | LTs | TD |
|---|---|---|---|
| Age (years) | 2.3 (.61)[a] | 1.9 (.74)[b] | 1.9 (.78)[b] |
| % Male | 80[a] | 67[b] | 60[b] |
| Mullen Scales of Early Learning (Mullen, 1995) Visual Reception T-score | 34.8 (13.5)[a] | 49.6 (12.2)[b] | 53.2 (11.9)[b] |
| Mullen Scales of Early Learning (Mullen, 1995) Fine Motor T-score | 31.3 (12.6)[a] | 43.96 (9.9)[b] | 50.1 (9.5)[b] |
| MacArthur-Bates Communicative Development Inventories (CDIs; Fenson et al., 2007) Expressive Vocabulary | 66 (98)[a] | 76 (104)[a] | 175 (145)[b] |
| Vineland Adaptive Behavior Scales (Sparrow, Balla, & Cichetti, 1984) Communication Scale Age-Equivalent Score | 1.3 (.64)[a] | 1.4 (.58)[a] | 2.1 (.87)[b] |

From Paul, R., Chawarska, K., & Volkmar, F. (2008). Differentiating ASD from DLD in toddlers. *Perspectives on Language Learning and Education, 15*(3), 101–111; adapted by permission. © 2008 American-Speech-Language-Hearing Association

[a, b]Values with differing superscripts are significantly different (*p* < .05).

*Key:* ASDs, autism spectrum disorders; LTs, late talkers; TD, typically developing.

TD peers not only on nonverbal skills and expressive language scores but also on receptive language scores (see Figure 10.1). Notably, toddlers with ASDs scored *lower* on the Mullen Receptive Language scale than they did on the Expressive Language scale, a finding replicated by Ellis Weismer, Lord, and Esler, 2010, as discussed later in the chapter. Children with ASDs were significantly lower than LTs on both expressive and receptive scores; LTs were significantly lower on both of these measures than TD toddlers.

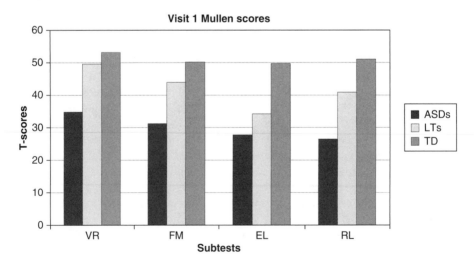

**Figure 10.1.**   Scores for three groups on the Mullen Scales of Early Learning (Mullen, 1995). (*Key:* ASDs, autism spectrum disorders; EL, expressive language; FM, fine motor; LTs, late talkers; RL, receptive language; TD, typically developing; VR, visual reception.) (From Paul, R., Chawarska, K., & Volkmar, F. [2008]. Differentiating ASD from DLD in toddlers. *Perspectives on Language Learning and Education, 15*[3], 101–111; adapted by permission. © 2008 American-Speech-Language-Hearing Association)

In addition, examination of communication behaviors measured on the Behavioral Sample of the Communication and Symbolic Behavior Scales (Wetherby & Prizant, 2002) showed that children with ASDs and LTs earned similar scores on measures of the use of gaze, sharing of emotion and reciprocity, production of sounds and words, and the expression of communicative acts (see Figure 10.2). Both groups performed significantly below TD toddlers on all of these measures, with the exception of number of communicative acts expressed. On this metric, the LT group was significantly different from neither the ASD or TD groups. The LT group scored significantly higher than the ASD group on understanding of language, use of objects in pretend play schemes, and use of gestures. On all of these measures, the LT and TD groups were on par.

These findings suggest that, when matched on expressive language level, toddlers with ASDs and LTs are similar, and less skilled than TD toddlers, on a range of communicative behaviors beyond the traditional measures of expressive language. These similarities include their rate of communication, their use of gaze to regulate interactions, their ability to share emotions with others and to engage in back-and-forth interactions, as well as the range of sounds and words produced. Areas in which LTs were significantly different from toddlers with ASDs, and similar to those with TD, included their nonverbal cognitive skills, use of gestures to communicate, use of pretend play, and ability to respond to language. These findings indicate that, perhaps contrary to expectations, LTs show some weaknesses in interpersonal skills—such as sharing affect, using gaze, and initiating communication—that go beyond the production of sounds and words. These impairments may initially raise questions about their risk for ASDs. However, superior skills in pretend play, gesture use, and responsiveness to language do differentiate them from same-age peers with ASDs. Interestingly, two of these factors—use of gestures and receptive language—are the same areas reported by Bartak et al. (1975) to

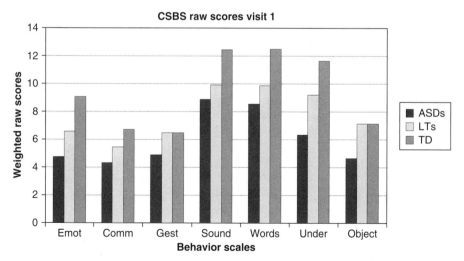

**Figure 10.2.** Scores for three groups on Communication and Symbolic Behavior Scales Developmental Profile™ (CSBS™; Wetherby & Prizant, 2002). (*Key:* ASDs, autism spectrum disorders; Comm, communication; Emot, emotion, gaze, and reciprocity; Gest, gesture use; LTs: late talkers; Object, use of objects in play schemes; Sound, sounds produced; TD: typically developing; Under, understanding of single words; Word: words used.) (From Paul, R., Chawarska, K., & Volkmar, F. [2008]. Differentiating ASD from DLD in toddlers. *Perspectives on Language Learning and Education, 15*[3], 101–111; adapted by permission. © 2008 American-Speech-Language-Hearing Association)

**Table 10.3.**   Similarities and differences: Children with ASDs versus LTs

| Skill | ASDs/LT Comparison |
|---|---|
| Nonverbal cognition (Paul, Chawarska, & Volkmar, 2008) | ASDs < LTs |
| Use of gaze, reciprocity (Paul, Chawarska, & Volkmar, 2008) | ASDs = LTs |
| Frequency of spontaneous communication (Paul, Chawarska, & Volkmar, 2008) | ASDs = LTs |
| Expression of joint attentional intentions (Wetherby et al., 2004) | ASDs < LTs |
| Expressive language (Paul, Chawarska, & Volkmar, 2008) | ASDs = LTs |
| Receptive language (Paul, Chawarska, & Volkmar, 2008) | ASDs < LTs |
| Use of conventional gestures (Paul, Chawarska, & Volkmar, 2008) | ASDs < LTs |
| Spontaneous pretend play (Paul, Chawarska, & Volkmar, 2008) | ASDs < LTs |
| Repetitive movements (Wetherby et al., 2004) | ASDs > LTs |
| Unusual vocalizations (Wetherby et al., 2004) | ASDs > LTs |

From Paul, R., Chawarska, K., & Volkmar, F. (2008). Differentiating ASD from DLD in toddlers. *Perspectives on Language Learning and Education, 15*(3), 101–111; adapted by permission. © 2008 American-Speech-Language-Hearing Association

*Key:* ASDs, autism spectrum disorders; LTs, late talkers.

distinguish school-age children with ASDs from those with language impairments. And although some symbolic play impairments have been reported in LTs (e.g., Rescorla & Goosens, 1992), this research suggests they are more similar to TD toddlers in this respect than they are to children with ASDs. Table 10.3 provides a summary of similarities and differences between LTs and toddlers with ASDs based on these findings (Paul Chawarska, & Volkmar, 2008) combined with results from an investigation by Wetherby and colleagues (2004) that included assessment of joint attention, repetitive movements, and unusual vocalizations.

## Findings from the University of Wisconsin–Madison Language Processes Laboratory

As the findings of the Yale laboratory highlight, LTs are typically identified on the basis of their limited productive vocabulary and/or lack of word combinations, with the vast majority of LTs displaying normal range language comprehension skills, or at least levels of comprehension higher than their productive skills. Ellis Weismer and colleagues have recently investigated the comprehension-production profile observed in toddlers with ASDs in two samples of children. Ellis Weismer, Lord, and Esler (2010) investigated language abilities in a sample of 2- to 3-year-old children, including 179 with autism, 78 with pervasive developmental disorder–not otherwise specified, and 69 with developmental delay (DD) without autism. The goal of this study was to characterize early language abilities of toddlers on the autism spectrum, using multiple measures of language development, and to compare their pattern of language acquisition with that of toddlers with nonspectrum DD. Language abilities were measured in this study using the Vineland Adaptive Behavior Scales (Sparrow et al., 1984) or Vineland–II Adaptive Behavior Scales (Sparrow, Cicchetti, & Balla, 2005), the Sequenced Inventory of Communication Development (SICD; Hendrick, Prather, & Tobin, 1984), and the Mullen Scales of Early Learning (Mullen, 1995).

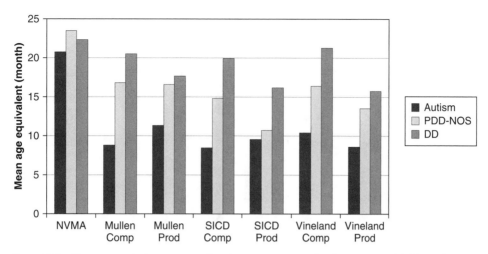

**Figure 10.3.** Mean age equivalent scores on three language measures for three groups of children relative to their nonverbal mental age (NVMA) scores. (*Key:* Autism, autism spectrum disorder group; PDD-NOS, pervasive developmental disorder–not otherwise specified group; DD, developmental delay without autism group; Mullen Comp, comprehension scale on Mullen Scales of Early Learning; Mullen Prod, production scale on Mullen Scales of Early Learning; SICD Comp, comprehension scale on Sequenced Inventory of Communication Development; SICD Prod, production scale on Sequenced Inventory of Communication Development; Vineland Comp, comprehension scale of the Vineland Adaptive Behavior Scales; Vineland Prod, production scale of the Vineland Adaptive Behavior Scales.) (*Source:* Ellis Weismer, Lord, & Esler, 2010.)

Toddlers with autism performed significantly worse than toddlers with DD and also exhibited a different comprehension-production profile than the DD group. As shown in Figure 10.3, toddlers who had DD without autism scored significantly higher on comprehension than production ($p < .05$) for each of the three language assessments. However, the autism group displayed the reverse pattern on two of three measures—that is, children in this group scored significantly lower on comprehension than production on the SICD and Mullen Scales ($p < .05$). These findings replicate not only the Yale laboratory results, but also those of other investigators examining language development in young children with ASDs (Charman, Drew, Baird, & Baird, 2003; Hudry et al., 2010; Thurm, Lord, Lee, & Newschaffer, 2007; Toth, Muson, Meltzoff, & Dawson, 2006). Although one can certainly question how useful the available standardized measures are for assessing comprehension abilities in toddlers with ASDs, their special difficulties with comprehension do not appear to be simply a matter of lack of compliance with clinician assessments in that similar results have been noted for both parent-report measures and direct clinician-administered measures. In the case of findings from the CDI (Charman et al., 2003), children comprehend more vocabulary words than they produce in absolute terms, but the *relative* degree of delay is more pronounced for comprehension than production. When comprehension of single-word vocabulary as well as sentence-level constructions (e.g., understanding questions) are assessed using standardized tests such as the Mullen Scales, young children with ASDs typically obtain age-equivalent scores that are lower for receptive than expressive language (Ellis Weismer et al., 2010; Paul, Chawarska, & Volkmar, 2008).

In another study, the relationship between language comprehension and production abilities was investigated longitudinally in 53 TD controls, 53 LTs, and 129 children with ASDs (Ellis Weismer, 2012). All groups had a mean age of 2½ years

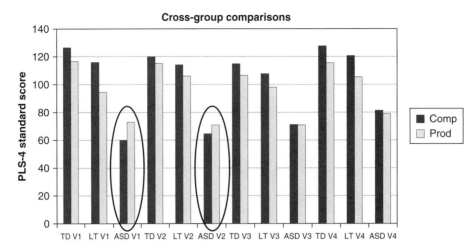

**Figure 10.4.** Longitudinal comparison of comprehension and production scores on the Preschool Language Scale, Fourth Edition (PLS-4; Zimmerman, Steiner, & Pond, 2002) for typical talkers, late talkers, and children with autism spectrum disorders. (*Key:* ASD, autism spectrum disorder group; Comp, comprehension [Auditory Comprehension Scale of PLS-4]; LT, late talker group; Prod, production [Expressive Communication Scale of PLS-4]; TD, typically developing group; V1, visit 1 at mean age of 2½ years; V2, visit 2 at mean age of 3½ years; V3, visit 3 at mean age of 4½ years; V4, visit 4 at mean age of 5½ years.)

at their initial assessment (Visit 1). As was the case for the studies conducted by Paul and colleagues that were described previously in this chapter, a diagnosis of ASD was made by an experienced interdisciplinary team and included use of the ADOS and ADI-R as well as clinical judgment. The Preschool Language Scales, Fourth Edition (PLS-4; Zimmerman, Steiner, & Pond, 2002) was used to evaluate language comprehension and production. As illustrated in Figure 10.4, the TD and LT groups scored significantly higher ($p < .05$) on the Auditory Comprehension subscale of the PLS-4 than on the Expressive Communication subscale across all four time points. At early points in development—ages 2½ (Visit 1) and 3½ years (Visit 2)—the ASD group displayed the opposite pattern in which comprehension was significantly worse than production ($p < .01$); however, by 5–6 years of age this profile appears to normalize relative to the patterns observed in TD and late talking children. Thus, if a child displays substantially more difficulty with language comprehension than production during these early periods of development, this may be reason for clinical concern.

Ellis Weismer et al. (2011) also investigated the extent to which LTs and toddlers with ASDs could be distinguished with respect to semantic and grammatical features of early language development. This study examined whether verbal toddlers with ASDs and LTs matched on overall productive vocabulary displayed similar use of semantic categories, psychological state terms, word combinations, and grammatical complexity. Two groups of toddlers (22–37 months) participated in this study—40 LTs and 40 toddlers with ASDs. Groups were matched on parent report of words produced (± 9 words) on the CDI: Words and Sentences (Fenson et al., 2007). The mean number of words produced was 108 ($SD = 76$) and 106 ($SD = 75$) for the ASD group and LT group, respectively. Matching on overall vocabulary resulted in a significant age difference ($p < .01$) between the groups such that the average age for the LT group was 25 months compared with 30 months for the ASD group. Findings revealed no significant differences between groups on the 18 CDI semantic categories that were analyzed (measured as number of words per category or as a percent of total vocabulary).

Next, analysis was conducted of psychological state terms from the CDI based on a combination of categories employed in prior research (Johnston, Miller, & Tallal, 2001; Lee & Rescorla, 2002), based on the hypothesis that the groups may differ with respect to specific vocabulary associated with expression of theory of mind. The psychological state categories consisted of emotion (e.g., "mad"), desire (e.g., "like"), cognitive (e.g., "think"), physiological (e.g., "hot"), and evaluation (e.g., "good") terms. Surprisingly, the two groups were equivalent with respect to the overall number of psychological state terms that parents reported that they had in their productive repertoire as well as the breakdown of the various categories. It is important to note that at this early point in development neither group was reported to use any cognitive state terms. Prior research with older children has shown that it is the cognitive terms (rather than other types of psychological state terms) that appear to be particularly problematic for children with autism compared with matched controls with developmental disabilities or specific language impairment (SLI; Tager-Flusberg, 1992; Ziatas, Durkin, & Pratt, 1998).

Bates and colleagues proposed that advances in grammar occur only after vocabulary reaches a critical mass (Bates & Goodman, 2001), and prior research has documented strong links between lexical and grammatical skills in typical development across various languages (e.g., Elin Thordardottir, Ellis Weismer, & Evans, 2002). When the association between vocabulary and early grammatical abilities for the LTs and toddlers with ASDs was examined, results indicated that the number of toddlers combining words was identical in the two groups and there was no significant group difference in CDI complexity scores. Even though the LTs and toddlers with ASDs were matched on total words produced and displayed very similar profiles of semantic category use, it was not a foregone conclusion that the groups would display the same level of early grammatical abilities. Because the data revealed close similarities across groups, we interpreted these findings to indicate that both groups showed equivalent patterns of lexical-grammatical associations.

To summarize, the study by Ellis Weismer et al. (2011) found that verbal toddlers with ASDs displayed a more severe delay in productive vocabulary development than LTs; that is, toddlers with ASDs were on average 30 months compared with the LTs who were 25 months of age when the groups were matched on number of words produced. However, the two groups were very similar in the semantic categories of words that they used, including the use of psychological state terms. Furthermore, qualitatively similar patterns of association between lexical and grammatical development were observed across these groups. One criticism that might be leveled against this study is that the standardized set of vocabulary contained on the CDI could not reveal actual differences in words used by the two groups. However, the CDI contains 680 words, and our sample of children produced an average of approximately 100 words, which seems to provide a reasonable opportunity to observe differences in semantic category use. Furthermore, both sets of parents were instructed to write in additional words, particularly any unusual or idiosyncratic words, which their child used that were not on the form. Using this approach, no notable group differences were observed. Given that children with ASDs often have a restricted range of interests, they may later develop a highly specialized vocabulary set related to these interests; however, our data suggest that at 2–3 years of age LTs and toddlers with ASDs (matched on overall vocabulary) cannot be distinguished on the basis of the words they use or their early grammatical abilities.

## UNDERSTANDING THE CLINICAL IMPACT OF LATE TALKING

How might these data inform clinical practice for LTs? Data reviewed in other chapters in this book demonstrate that 50%–75% of children identified as LTs move into the normal range for vocabulary by the end of the preschool period and perform within normal limits on standardized tests of language skills by kindergarten (Paul, 1996; Rescorla, Dahlsgaard, & Roberts, 2000; Rescorla & Lee, 2000; Rice, Taylor, & Zubrick, 2008; Roos & Ellis Weismer, 2008; Whitehurst & Fischel, 1994). Still, although most LTs would not be identified as having language disorders by early school age, they continue to score significantly lower, as a group, than TD peers from similar socioeconomic backgrounds (Paul, 1996; Rescorla, 2002, 2005; Rice et al., 2008; Thal, 2005).

In addition, Rescorla reported that her cohort of LTs showed significantly weaker reading decoding scores at age 9 and significantly weaker reading comprehension scores at age 13 than TD peers. However, none of the children who had been LTs were formally diagnosed with a reading disorder. These data suggest that students with a history of late talking continue to score within the typical range on tests of language and reading, perform similarly to same-age peers on reading mechanics and writing at many ages, and do not qualify for special educational services or a diagnostic label such as SLI for the most part. However, their scores are significantly lower than those of peers with similar socioeconomic status, and they demonstrate persistent weaknesses in basic and higher-order language skills, including vocabulary, grammar, verbal memory, figurative language, and reading comprehension. When Rescorla (2009) followed these individuals to age 17, they continued to obtain significantly lower scores on measures of vocabulary, grammar, and verbal memory than peers matched by socioeconomic status, although, again, none were identified as having special educational needs.

Rice and colleagues (2008) used growth curve modeling to investigate the language outcomes at age 7 for 128 children with a history of late talking and 109 peers with typical language histories. They found that although the LTs demonstrated skills within the average range on a global measure of language functioning, a significantly greater percentage of children in the late talking group demonstrated skills that were more than one *SD* below the mean in spoken language, syntax, and morphosyntax. Moreover, several other groups studying LTs have reported that although, on average, scores moved within the normal range by kindergarten age, some proportion of the LT sample, ranging from 15% to 30% depending upon the study (Paul & Fountain, 1999; Roos & Ellis Weismer, 2008), continued to perform significantly below average on measures of language at school age.

These data suggest that LTs can continue to show weaknesses in language and literacy, relative to socioeconomic peers, throughout the school years. Although in the populations studied so far, these weaknesses are not severe enough to qualify many children with a history of late talking for identification as having significant learning disabilities or to make them eligible for special educational services in school, persistent vulnerabilities have been identified in a range of studies, across a wide span of ages.

Given these findings, it might be tempting to conclude that LTs evidence little risk for long-range language and academic impairments. However, it must be remembered that the children in most cohorts followed in LT studies (e.g., Rescorla, 2009; Paul, 1996; Ellis & Thal, 2008) come from families that were exclusively middle class and relatively well-educated. It is likely that many children who evidence language-based learning difficulties sufficiently severe to qualify them for special education come from less advantageous circumstances. It is well documented, for example, that children who are raised in poverty are at considerable risk for delays in oral language and literacy development (Barnett, 2001; Hart & Risley, 1995; Roth & Troia, 2006; Tabors, Snow, & Dickinson, 2001). When a child with the relatively weak endowment in language that appears to characterize LTs (Ellis Weismer, 2007; Rescorla, 2009) experiences a limited set of language experiences, the result is likely to be a significant difficulty in acquiring the more literate aspects of oral language needed to support success in learning to read and its attendant academic skills.

## CONCLUSIONS: WHEN IS LATE TALKING A SIGNIFICANT RISK?

The preceding discussion provides some background for evaluating the degree to which late talking should be considered a serious risk for developmental or academic disability. Although several studies have attempted to identify predictors of long-term outcomes in LTs, the level of prediction has not proved to be very robust (Ellis & Thal, 2008). Nonetheless, several factors seen in children with slow expressive language development tend to be more strongly associated with long-term difficulties. These factors include the following:

- The presence of an atypical comprehension-production profile, with weakness in comprehension relative to production

- Limited response to language

- Infrequent vocalizations

- Limited number of consonants in babble

- Reduced spontaneous imitations

- Lack of symbolic play

- Reduced frequency of communicative gestures or vocalizations

- Low rate of nonverbal communication

- Communicative intents limited to requesting, with few comments expressed

- Family history of language delays or reading problems

Children who show several of these signs should, first, undergo in-depth evaluation in order to provide differential diagnosis from ASDs because data from our studies contrasting toddlers with ASDs and those with late talking suggest that several of the features on this list are shared by LTs and toddlers with ASDs. Like children with ASDs, LTs can appear less interested in interaction, less likely to use gaze to regulate communication, less able to engage in back-and-forth turn taking, and less apt to initiate communication than TD same-age peers. However, our data suggest that although they may show these weaknesses, as well as standard test scores in both expressive and receptive modes that are below the normal range, LTs are more likely to respond to language in natural settings. In addition, LTs, even when they have delays in receptive language, typically show comprehension that is at least on par with expressive language level. Toddlers with ASDs, however, are likely to show receptive language levels in both standard tests and structured play that are worse than their expressive abilities would suggest. LTs are also more able than same-age peers with ASDs to spontaneously demonstrate some pretend play skills and to use some conventional gestures to communicate, even if these skills are not as advanced as their chronological age would predict.

For LTs for whom ASDs can be ruled out by using these guidelines as well as clinical assessment, the issue of environmental input should also be considered. Research on LTs from advantaged families suggests that these children will be likely to perform within, though perhaps at the low end of, the expected range of academic achievement. This suggests that advice to middle-class families to do all they can to bolster language and preliteracy development in the context of everyday preschool experiences—including encouraging dialogic reading activities within the family (Whitehurst et al., 1988), as well as talking about "there and then" topics such as past experiences, projections about future events, and elaboration of pretend (Dickinson, Golinkoff, & Hirsh-Pasek, 2010)—may be sufficient. For children from less-privileged backgrounds, particularly those learning English as a second language (Keiffer, 2008), late talking may represent a more significant risk factor for long-term effects on language, literacy, and academic achievement. In these children, whose inherent vulnerabilities in language endowment are likely to be exacerbated by limitations in input and facilitative experience, a more aggressive approach, including early intervention and attempts to ameliorate the language environment through parent training and preschool education, are warranted.

Provision of these services may require more than clinical diagnoses, however; they may demand the commitment of resources to schools and agencies that address the needs of young children in poverty to provide intensified preschool education aimed at boosting lagging language skills to a level that can enable basic literacy acquisition. Emphasis on response-to-intervention approaches to early reading instruction, and the expansion of these approaches to preschool emergent literacy development, may help in accommodating the needs of these vulnerable children.

## REFERENCES

American Psychiatric Association. (1994). *Diagnostic and statistical manual of mental disorders* (4th ed.). Washington, DC: Author.

Barnett, W.S. (2001). Preschool education for economically disadvantaged children: Effects on reading achievement and related outcomes. In S.B. Neuman & D.K. Dickinson (Eds.), *Handbook of early literacy research* (pp. 421–443). New York, NY: Guilford.

Bartak, L., Rutter, M., & Cox, A. (1975). A comparative study of infantile autism and specific developmental receptive language disorder. *British Journal of Psychiatry, 126,* 127–145.

Bates, E., & Goodman, J. (2001). On the inseparability of grammar and the lexicon: Evidence from acquisition. In M. Tomasello & E. Bates (Eds.), *Language development: The essential readings* (pp. 134–162). Malden, MA: Blackwell.

Charman, T., Drew, A., Baird, C., & Baird, G. (2003). Measuring early language development in preschool children with autism spectrum disorder using the MacArthur Communicative Development Inventory (Infant Form). *Journal of Child Language, 30,* 213–236.

Charman, T., Taylor, E., Drew, A., Cockerill, H., Brown, J.A., & Baird, G. (2005). Outcome at 7 years of children diagnosed with autism at age 2: Predictive validity of assessments conducted at 2 and 3 years of age and pattern of symptom change over time. *Journal of Child Psychology & Psychiatry, 46,* 500–513.

Chawarska, K., Klin, A., Paul, R., & Volkmar, F. (2007). Autism spectrum disorder in the second year: Stability and change in syndrome expression. *Journal of Child Psychology & Psychiatry, 48,* 128–138.

Cox, A., Klein, K., Charman, T., Baird, G., Baron-Cohen, S., Swettenham, J., ... Wheelwright, S. (1999). Autism spectrum disorders at 20 and 42 months of age: Stability of clinical and ADI-R diagnosis. *Journal of Child Psychology & Psychiatry & Allied Disciplines, 40,* 719–732.

Dickinson, D., Golinkoff, R., & Hirsh-Pasek, K. (2010). Speaking out for language: Why language is central to reading development. *Educational Researcher, 39,* 305–310.

Eaves, L., & Ho, H. (2004). The very early identification of autism: Outcome to 4½–5. *Journal of Autism and Developmental Disorders, 34,* 367–378.

Elin Thordardottir, E., Ellis Weismer, S., & Evans, J.L. (2002).Continuity in lexical and morphological development in Icelandic and English-speaking 2-year-olds. *First Language, 22,* 3–28.

Ellis, E., & Thal, D. (2008). Early language delay and risk for language impairment. *Perspectives on Language Learning and Education, 15,* 93–100.

Ellis Weismer, S. (2007). Typical talkers, late talkers, and children with specific language impairment: A language endowment spectrum? In R. Paul (Ed.), *The influence of developmental perspectives on research and practice in communication disorders: A Festschrift for Robin S. Chapman* (pp. 83–102). Mahwah, NJ: Lawrence Erlbaum Associates.

Ellis Weismer, S. (2012, May). *Characterizing early language development and predicting outcomes for toddlers with autism.* Keynote address at the Zeigler Research Forum, Nursing and Health Sciences, University of Vermont, Burlington, VT.

Ellis Weismer, S., Gernsbacher, M.A., Stronach, S., Karasinski, C., Eernisse, E., Erickson, C., & Sindberg, H. (2011). Lexical and grammatical skills in toddlers on the autism spectrum compared to late talking toddlers. *Journal of Autism and Developmental Disorders, 41,* 1065–1075.

Ellis Weismer, S., Lord, C., & Esler, A. (2010). Early language patterns of toddlers on the autism spectrum compared to toddlers with developmental delay. *Journal of Autism and Developmental Disorders, 40,* 1259–1273.

Fenson, L., Marchman, V.A., Thal, D.J., Dale, P.S., Reznick, J.S., & Bates, E. (2007). *MacArthur-Bates Communicative Development Inventories (CDIs)* (2nd ed.). Baltimore, MD: Paul H. Brookes Publishing Co.

Hart, B., & Risley, T.R. (1995). *Meaningful differences in everyday experience of young American children.* Baltimore, MD: Paul H. Brookes Publishing Co.

Hendrick, D., Prather, E., & Tobin, A. (1984). *Sequenced inventory of communication development* (Rev. ed.). Seattle: University of Washington Press.

Hudry, K., Leadbitter, K., Temple, K., Slonims, V., McConache, H., Aldred, C., ... Charman, T. (2010). Preschoolers with autism show greater impairment in receptive compared with expressive language abilities. *International Journal of Language & Communication Disorders, 45,* 681–690.

Johnston, J.R., Miller, J.F., & Tallal, P. (2001). Use of cognitive state predicates by language-impaired children. *International Journal of Language & Communication Disorders, 36,* 349–370.

Keiffer, M. (2008). Catching up or falling behind? Initial English proficiency, concentrated poverty, and the reading growth of language minority learners in the U.S. *Journal of Educational Psychology, 100,* 851–868.

Lee, E.C., & Rescorla, L. (2002). The use of psychological state terms by late talkers at ages 3, 4, and 5 years. *Applied Psycholinguistics, 29,* 21–39.

Lord, C. (1995). Follow-up of two-year-olds referred for possible autism. *Journal of Child Psychology & Psychiatry & Allied Disciplines, 36,* 1365–1382.

Lord, C., Risi, S., & DiLavore, P. (2006). Autism from 2 to 9 years of age. *Archives of General Psychiatry, 63,* 694–701.

Lord, C., Risi, S., Lambrecht, L., Cook, E.H., Leventhal, B.L., DiLavore, P.C., . . . Rutter, M. (2000). The Autism Diagnostic Observation Schedule–Generic: A standard measure of social and communication deficits associated with the spectrum of autism. *Journal of Autism and Developmental Disorders, 30,* 205–223.

Lord, C., Rutter, M., & Conture, A. (1994). Autism Diagnostic Interview-Revised: A revised version of a diagnostic interview for caregivers of individuals with possible pervasive developmental disorders. *Journal of Autism and Developmental Disorders, 24,* 659–685.

Matson, J., Wilkins, J., & Gonzalez, M. (2008). Early identification and diagnosis in autism spectrum disorders in young children and infants: How early is too early? *Research in Autism Spectrum Disorders, 2,* 75–84.

Mullen, E. (1995). *Mullen Scales of Early Learning: AGS edition.* Circle Pines, MN: American Guidance Service.

Paul, R. (1991). Profiles of toddlers with slow expressive language development. *Topics in Language Disorders, 11,* 1–13.

Paul, R. (1996). Clinical implications of the natural history of slow expressive language development. *American Journal of Speech-Language Pathology, 5,* 5–30.

Paul, R., Chawarska, K., Cicchetti, D., & Volkmar, F. (2008). Language outcomes in toddlers with ASD: A 2 year follow-up. *Autism Research, 1,* 97–107.

Paul, R., Chawarska, K., & Volkmar, F. (2008). Differentiating ASD from DLD in toddlers. *Perspectives on Language Learning Disorders, 15*(3), 101–111.

Paul, R., & Fountain, R. (1999). Predicting outcomes of early expressive language delay. *Infant-Toddler Intervention: The Transdisciplinary Journal, 9,* 123–136.

Rescorla, L. (2002). Language and reading outcomes to age 9 in late-talking toddlers. *Journal of Speech, Language, and Hearing Research, 45,* 360–371.

Rescorla, L. (2005). Age 13 language and reading outcomes in late-talking toddlers. *Journal of Speech, Language, and Hearing Research, 48,* 459–472.

Rescorla, L. (2009). Age 17 language and reading outcomes in late-talking toddlers: Support for a dimensional perspective on language delay. *Journal of Speech, Language, and Hearing Research, 52,* 16–30.

Rescorla, L., Dahlsgaard, K., & Roberts, J. (2000). Late-talking toddlers: MLU and IPSyn Outcomes at 3;0 and 4;0. *Journal of Child Language, 27,* 643–664.

Rescorla, L., & Goossens, M. (1992). Symbolic play development in toddlers with expressive specific language impairment. *Journal of Speech and Hearing Research, 35,* 1290–1302.

Rescorla, L., & Lee, E.C. (2000). Language impairments in young children. In T. Layton & L. Watson (Eds.), *Handbook of early language impairment in children: Vol. I: Nature* (pp.1–38). New York, NY: Delmar.

Rice, M., Taylor, C., & Zubrick, S. (2008). Language outcomes of 7-year-old children with or without a history of late language emergence at 24 months. *Journal of Speech, Language, and Hearing Research, 51,* 394–407.

Roos, E., & Ellis Weismer, S. (2008). Language outcomes of late talking toddlers at preschool and beyond. *Perspectives on Language Learning Disorders, 15,* 119–126.

Roth, F., & Troia, B. (2006). Collaborative efforts to promote emergent literacy and efficient word recognition skills. *Topics in Language Disorders, 26*(1), 24–41.

Sparrow, S., Balla, D., & Cicchetti, D.V. (1984). *The Vineland Adaptive Behavior Scales (Survey Form).* Circle Pines, MN: American Guidance Service.

Sparrow, S., Cicchetti, D.V., & Balla, D. (2005). Vineland-II adaptive behavior scales. Circle Pines, MN: American Guidance Service.

Stone, W., Lee, E., Ashford, L., Brissie, J., Hepburn, S., Coonrod, E., & Weiss, B. (1999). Can autism be diagnosed accurately in children under 3 years? *Journal of Child Psychology and Psychiatry, 40,* 219–226.

Tabors, P.O., Snow, C., & Dickinson, D. (2001). Homes and schools together: Supporting language and literacy development. In D. Dickinson& P.O. Tabors (Eds.). *Beginning literacy with language: Young children learning at home and school* (pp. 313–334). Baltimore, MD: Paul H Brookes Publishing Co.

Tager-Flusberg, H. (1992). Autistic children's talk about psychological states: Deficits in the early acquisition of a theory of mind. *Child Development, 63,* 161–172.

Thal, D. (2005, April). *Early detection of risk for language impairment: What are the best strategies?* Paper presented at the Congress on Language and Speech Disorders, Urbino, Italy.

Thurm, A., Lord, C., Lee, L., & Newschaffer, C. (2007). Predictors of language acquisition in preschool children with autism spectrum disorders. *Journal of Autism and Developmental Disorders, 37,* 1721–1734.

Toppelberg, C.O., & Shapiro, T. (2000). Language disorders: A 10-year research update review. *Journal of the American Academy of Child and Adolescent Psychiatry, 39,* 143–152.

Toth, K., Munson, J., Meltzoff, A., & Dawson, G. (2006). Early predictors of communication development in young children with autism spectrum disorders: Joint attention, imitation, and toy play. *Journal of Autism & Developmental Disorders, 36,* 933–1005.

Turner, L., Stone, W., Pozdol, S., & Coonrod, E. (2006). Follow-up of children with autism spectrum disorders from age 2 to age 9. *Autism, 10,* 243–265.

Wetherby, A., & Prizant, B. (2002). *Communication and Symbolic Behavior Scales Developmental Profile™ (CSBS DP™).* Baltimore, MD: Paul H. Brookes Publishing Co.

Wetherby, A., Woods, J., Allen, L., Cleary, J., Dickinson, H., & Lord, C. (2004). Early indicators of autism spectrum disorders in the second year of life. *Journal of Autism and Developmental Disorders, 34,* 473–493.

Whitehurst, G., Falco, F., Lonigan, C., Fischel, J., DeBaryshe, B., Valdez-Menchaea, M., & Caulfield, M. (1988). Accelerating language development through picture-book reading. *Developmental Psychology, 24,* 552–558.

Whitehurst, G.J., & Fischel, J.E. (1994). Early developmental language delay: What, if anything, should a clinician do about it? *Journal of Child Psychology and Psychiatry, 35,* 613–648.

Ziatas, K., Durkin, K., & Pratt, C. (1998). Belief term development in children with autism, Asperger syndrome, specific language impairment, and normal development: Links to theory of mind development. *Journal of Child Psychology and Psychiatry, 39,* 755–763.

Zimmerman, I., Steiner, V., & Pond, R. (2002). *Preschool Language Scale* (4th ed.). San Antonio, TX: PsychCorp.

# Late-Talking Toddlers

*A 15-Year Follow-Up*

Leslie A. Rescorla

A delay in starting to talk is one of the most common reasons that young children are referred for evaluation (Rescorla & Lee, 2000; Whitehurst & Fischel, 1994). Early expressive language delay is often secondary to a more global primary disorder (Rescorla & Lee, 2000; Whitehurst & Fischel, 1994), such as intellectual disability (ID) or autism spectrum disorder (ASD). Children may also be slow to talk because of a hearing loss, a neurological disorder, or severe neglect. When none of these primary conditions is present, children ages 18–36 months who are slow to talk are often called late talkers (LTs). Some LTs have an expressive delay only, whereas others are also delayed in receptive language.

In this chapter, we summarize the outcomes of a group of LTs identified between 24 and 31 months of age and followed longitudinally for 15 years. When this study began in the mid-1980s, it was widely assumed that late-talking toddlers with normal receptive language, normal IQs, adequate hearing, typical social/emotional development, and middle to high socioeconomic status (SES) backgrounds would be talking normally by about age 3 and were hence at minimal risk for later language problems. To test this assumption, we recruited a cohort of 40 such "advantaged" LTs with the intention of following them until age 5. We also recruited a sample of typically developing (TD) children from the same demographic backgrounds so that we could compare development in the two groups. As it turned out, we continued the study until the children in both groups were 17 years old.

Previous reports of this research program have presented outcomes at different time points, such as at age 3 (Rescorla, Roberts, & Dahlsgaard, 1997), age 4 (Rescorla, Dahlsgaard, & Roberts, 2000; Rescorla & Roberts, 2002), age 9 (Rescorla, 2002), age 13 (Rescorla, 2005), and age 17 (Rescorla, 2009). However, this is the first report to summarize outcomes over the full 15 years of the study.

As will emerge in this chapter, most of our LTs did catch up in expressive language by age 5, but as a group, the LTs continued to have weaker language skills than the comparison children through age 17. However, there was substantial variability, both across LTs and across language domains. After highlighting the outcomes from the study, the chapter closes with a discussion of the theoretical and practical implications of our research findings.

## THE STUDY SAMPLE

The original LT cohort in this longitudinal study consisted of 40 LTs ages 24–31 months (36 boys and 4 girls), whereas the comparison group consisted of 39 toddlers with typical language histories (38 boys and 1 girl). LTs were recruited through newspaper advertisements, notices to pediatricians, and a local infant lab. All but one of the children in the original cohorts came from two-parent, middle to upper class Caucasian families (the parents of one LT were divorced). The LTs and the comparison children did not differ in age or in Hollingshead (1975) SES score.

The first inclusionary criterion for recruiting LTs was a score higher than 85 on the Bayley Mental Development Scale (Bayley, 1969). Because the LTs failed almost all expressive language items, they had to pass most of the other Bayley items to attain a score of 85 or higher. Importantly for our follow-up results, the LT and comparison groups were matched at intake on a nonverbal IQ score derived from summing all 19 nonverbal items on the Bayley above the basal level for all children (e.g., towering blocks, doing puzzles, drawing, inserting pegs).

To ensure that all LTs had normal receptive language skills, the children were required to score within 3 months of chronological age (CA) on the Reynell Receptive Language Scale (Reynell, 1977). Only one LT failed to meet this criterion, scoring 4 months below CA. All comparison children scored within 3 months of CA on the Reynell Receptive Language scale. When raw scores were converted to age-based $z$-scores using the Reynell manual, the LTs had a mean score close to zero, indicating normal receptive skills. However, it is important to note that the comparison children had above average receptive language skills. Thus, even though the LTs had fully normal receptive skills for their age, the groups differed significantly in receptive language as measured by the Reynell Receptive Language Scale $z$-score, with a Cohen's (1988) $d$ score of .78, or more than three quarters of a standard deviation (SD).

To ensure that the LTs had a significant expressive language delay, they were required to score at least 6 months below CA on the Reynell Expressive Language Scale. Comparison children had to have a Reynell Expressive Language Scale score within 3 months of CA; 38 comparison children met this criterion and one scored within 4 months of CA. The effect size for the group difference in the Reynell Expressive Language Scale $z$-score approached 2 SDs (–1.70 vs. 0.25). All LTs scored at least 1.2 SDs below age expectations (< 10th percentile), and many scored 1.5 SDs or more below age expectations (< 7th percentile). In addition, LTs had to have fewer than 50 words or no word combinations on the Language Development Survey (LDS; Rescorla, 1989). The LTs had a mean vocabulary of 20.75 words on the LDS, in contrast to a mean vocabulary of 226.79 words for the comparison group ($d > 2.0$).

No children with atypical behavioral/emotional development or ASDs were included in the LT cohort. On the contrary, the LTs were well-adjusted, engaging, and delightful toddlers, as were the comparison children. When Rescorla and Merrin (1998) compared communicative intent in the LTs and comparison children at intake, the late-talking toddlers produced fewer initiations and responses during free play with their mothers or with the examiner than age-matched TD peers, even when gestures and nonverbal vocalizations were included as communications. However, when total communicativeness was controlled for, LTs were just as likely to initiate, respond, and maintain joint attention as were their TD peers. In fact, children in both groups responded about 90% of the time when their partner (whether mother or examiner) initiated.

Rescorla and Fechnay (1996) studied a subset of the same late-talking and TD samples. They reported that mothers of LTs did not differ from comparison group mothers in degree of synchrony with their children or in their use of social cues. Rescorla and Fechnay also reported that LTs and comparison children did not differ significantly in play synchrony, compliance, or overall communicativeness. As would be expected, however, LTs produced more unintelligible utterances and relied more heavily on gestural and nonverbal communicative cues than their TD peers.

Although a delay in phonetic skills was not among the criteria for identification as an LT, studies by Mirak and Rescorla (1998) and Rescorla and Ratner (1996) indicated that the LT cohort had reduced phonetic repertoires, although they appeared to be acquiring consonants in approximately the same sequence as the TD comparison group. The LTs vocalized less, had much smaller consonant inventories, were much less likely to use consonants at the ends of words, and had a preponderance of simpler syllable shapes rather than more complex ones. This suggests that the late talkers were not only delayed in vocabulary but that they were also delayed in phonological development.

About one third of the LTs received some speech-language therapy during the preschool period, and a few participated in preschool programs for children with language impairments; two LTs were in special education classes in the early elementary school years. A few comparison children also received speech and language therapy or reading remediation. Because degree of remediation was so varied and because information about interventions was incomplete, the effects of intervention could not be analyzed.

As occurs in all longitudinal studies, there was some attrition over time. One parent of an LT and two parents of comparison children declined to participate in follow-up visits after the preschool period. Otherwise, children were missed at follow-up because they moved out of the area, could not be reached at their original numbers/addresses, or had scheduling conflicts. For LTs, we were able to see 34–37 children at age 9, 28 at age 13, and 26 at age 17. Retention was more difficult for the comparison group—about half of them had been in a pilot group that we initially did not intend to track longitudinally but then tried to contact again at age 6 when it was clear the study would continue past age 5. We were able to see 21 comparison children at age 3, 16 at age 4, 24 at age 5, 25–32 for ages 6–9, 25 at age 13, and 23 at age 17.

At every follow-up point, we tested for the possibility of selective attrition by running $t$-tests on major intake variables for the original cohorts and the children seen for follow-up. We found no differences even approaching significance, indicating that attrition was not selective in either group. That is, the LT and comparison follow-up samples at every age were comparable to the original cohorts on all intake variables. For every follow-up sample, LTs were similar to comparison group children in age, SES, and Bayley nonverbal scores, and they were significantly different in Reynell Receptive and Expressive $z$-scores and LDS vocabulary scores.

## LATE TALKER OUTCOMES TO AGE 3

Because the LTs were seen roughly bimonthly from intake to age 3, we were able to collect vocabulary data using the LDS across multiple time points. These data allowed us to use growth curve modeling to analyze individual vocabulary trajectories over time in LTs. Results of these analyses were reported by Rescorla, Mirak, and Singh (2000).

The LDS (Rescorla, 1989), the instrument used to collect vocabulary data for this study, is a one-page checklist containing 310 of the most frequently used words in children's early vocabularies. Parents are asked to check off words that their child uses spontaneously, to report use of two-word combinations, and to cite three of the child's longest sentences or phrases. The LDS consists of words belonging to 14 semantic categories (e.g., animals, body parts, clothes, foods, actions). The LDS was administered bimonthly from age of intake (at 24–31 months) until 36 months, unless an LT had already approached the ceiling of 310 words. Bimonthly visits were not part of the protocol for the earliest LTs recruited, and visits were occasionally missed for scheduling reasons, so we were only able to include 28 of the 40 LTs in the growth curve analyses. To be included, a child needed to have at least two LDS data points, with one being at 30 months (which might be the intake data point) and the other being between 30 and 36 months.

On average, vocabulary growth from 24 to 36 months for these 28 LTs resembled that from 12 to 24 months for TD children (e.g., the LT group had 18 words at 24 months, 89 words by 20 months, and 195 words by 36 months, with the 50-word vocabulary mark attained from 26 to 28 months). However, this aggregate pattern of vocabulary growth over time does not capture the wide individual differences among the LTs in their rates of vocabulary acquisition.

Growth curve analysis revealed that the LTs could be classified into two distinct groups based on whether or not they had attained 100 words by age 30 months. One group of 11 LTs showed a rapid vocabulary spurt between 26 and 32 months, reached 150–180 words by 30 months, and attained the LDS asymptote of about 300 words by 24 months. In contrast, a second group of 17 LTs still had a mean vocabulary of fewer than 30 words at 30 months, had less of a vocabulary spurt when they did start acquiring words, and attained 150–180 words by 36 months. Thus, the first group showed about a 6-month lag in LDS vocabulary relative to TD children, whereas the second group showed about a 12-month lag. Both groups showed something of a vocabulary spurt close to the 50-word mark, but the first group added words more rapidly during this spurt (70–80 words vs. 58 words per 2-month period).

As reported by Rescorla, Mirak, and Singh (2000), the vocabulary spurt appeared to be associated with a higher percentage of nouns in their LDS lexicons for both groups of LTs in this study. The 11 children who began their vocabulary spurt at about 26 months and attained 100 words by 30 months started out with an LDS noun percentage of 58%, below the 62% base rate of nouns on the LDS; they also showed considerable within-group variability in noun percentage. However, by 28 months, they manifested ≥ 60% noun percentage with minimal variability, which persisted to 36 months. By contrast, the 17 LTs who only attained 150–180 words by 36 months did not manifest a ≥ 60% noun percentage with minimal variability until 32 months of age. Therefore, the period in which LTs increased in noun percentage was the same period in which they began to add words to their lexicon more rapidly. This association was reflected in significant correlations between noun percentage and vocabulary size at all time points except 24 and 36 months. Furthermore, from 28 months on, correlations were significant between noun percentage and vocabulary size at the subsequent time point (.48, .68, .90, and .91).

## LATE TALKER OUTCOMES IN THE PRESCHOOL PERIOD

At the age 3 follow-up, 34 LTs and 21 comparison children were seen (Rescorla et al., 1997). Six LTs were not included in the speech sample analyses described here. These children were among the first participants recruited into the sample, and they had either played with different toys ($n = 5$) or had defective tapes ($n = 1$). The comparison children did not include the pilot group participants.

At age 3, naturalistic speech samples were collected during mother–child play with the Fisher Price Village, which contains a wide variety of elements conducive to make-believe (e.g., a fire engine; a garage; a barber shop; a post office; and many toy figures, vehicles, and other assorted props). After 100-utterance transcripts had been prepared, mean length of utterance (MLU; Brown, 1973) and the Index of Productive Syntax (IPSyn; Scarborough, 1990), an emergent syntax measure, were scored for each child. The children were also tested with the Reynell Expressive Language Scale (Reynell, 1977); the Test of Auditory Comprehension of Language–Revised (TACL-R; Carrow-Woolfolk, 1985); the Expressive One-Word Picture Vocabulary Test (EOPVT; Gardner, 1981); and the Leiter International Performance Scale (Leiter, 1948), a nonverbal IQ measure. In describing follow-up results at age 3 and all subsequent ages, we use the term *average range* to refer to scores within 1 *SD* of the mean (i.e., ≥ 16th percentile).

The LTs and comparison children did not differ in Leiter scores, consistent with their similar Bayley nonverbal scores at intake. Although the LTs scored in the average range in receptive language skills on the TACL-R, they differed significantly from the comparison children in receptive language (98.63 vs. 105.71; $d = .80$), as had been the case at intake.

For the expressive language measures at age 3, the percentage of LTs scoring in the average range (≥ 16th percentile) was 79% on the EOPVT, 58% on the Reynell Expressive Language Scale, 35% on MLU, and 24% on the IPSyn. More than three quarters of the LTs had caught up to age expectations in single-word expressive vocabulary by age 3 (group mean = 99.50), but they still scored significantly below the comparison group (group mean = 119.19), with a Cohen's *d* score of 1.22. About half the LTs scored in the average range on the Reynell at age 3, which assesses the ability to label pictured objects, define words, and describe pictorial scenes, as well as syntactic maturity as rated by the examiner. However, their mean *z*-score of –.65 was more than 2 *SD*s lower than the mean score of 1.48 obtained by the comparison group. The LTs showed the most substantial impairment in grammatical skills, with only one third scoring at age level on MLU and only one quarter scoring at age level on the IPSyn. Cohen's $d$ scores for age-based MLU and IPSyn $z$-scores were 2.64 and 2.61, respectively, indicating a major delay in syntactic development.

When Rescorla et al. (1997) used regression analyses to predict age 3 language outcomes on the EOPVT, Reynell, MLU, and IPSyn, intake Reynell Receptive $z$-scores and nonverbal ability scores were not significant predictors. However, intake Reynell Expressive $z$-scores accounted for 21%–34% of the variance in the age 3 outcome measures. Intake age, which was correlated –.76 with Reynell Expressive $z$-score, was also a significant correlate of age 3 outcomes (e.g., $r = -.60$ with IPSyn score), but it was not significant when entered last. Even though intake ranged from only 24 to 31 months, expressive language skills in TD children improve so rapidly in this period that the older a LT is within this time period, the lower his or her age-based $z$-score based on the normative sample. As Rescorla et al. (1997) noted, LTs who have < 50 words in the 24–30-month period are falling behind on a steeply accelerating vocabulary development curve.

Roberts, Rescorla, Giroux, and Stevens (1998) used the age 3 speech samples for 29 LTs and 19 comparison children to examine improvements in phonological skills since intake. By age 3, there was no longer a significant group difference in amount of vocalization, but group differences were significant in phonetic inventories, productive control of consonants, percent consonants correct, and overall intelligibility. Additional analyses indicated that about half of the LTs had caught up to the comparison peers in articulation, whereas the rest were still significantly delayed. When Pharr, Ratner, and Rescorla (2000) compared syllable shape use for 20 of the LTs and 15 of the comparison children at age 3, they found that LTs produced fewer syllable shapes with final consonants, > 1 consonant type, and consonant clusters than their comparison peers. In fact, 3-year-old LTs produced approximately the same proportion of syllable types as 2-year-old comparison children, except that the 2-year-old comparison children produced more consonant clusters than the 3-year-old LTs.

Rescorla, Bascome, Lampard, and Feeny (2001) compared 32 of the LTs and 21 of the comparison children at age 3 with respect to conversational patterns. The two groups did not differ in number of utterances, topic initiation, topic synchrony, use of commands, responses to commands, or conversational fillers during mother–child play. However, LTs asked fewer questions, provided fewer answers to maternal questions, made fewer declarative statements, and were less likely to elaborate on their own topics than comparison children. In both groups, mothers and children were highly synchronous. Rescorla et al. (2001) also noted that there were no differences in any of these conversational parameters between LTs with continuing delay at 3 and "late bloomers."

Rescorla, Dahlsgaard, and Roberts (2000) reported age 4 outcomes for 34 LTs and 16 of the comparison children seen at age 3. Whereas 41% of the LTs scored above the 10th percentile on MLU at age 3, 71% did so at age 4. Less progress was made on the IPSyn (34% and 29%), which provides a more in-depth measure of syntactic development than MLU. Although the LTs showed a greater increase in MLU and IPSyn score from age 3 to age 4 than did the comparison children, $z$-score differences between the groups still exceeded 2.5 $SD$s at age 4. These findings indicate that although the LTs were catching up to normative expectations, they were not closing the gap with their peers from the same SES backgrounds.

At age 5, 33 LTs and 24 comparison children were administered the Stanford-Binet Intelligence Scale: Fourth Edition (SB-IV; Thorndike, Hagen, & Sattler, 1986) and the Patterned Elicitation Syntax Test (PEST; Young & Perachio, 1983), as well as some phonological awareness measures and a letter and word identification test. On the SB-IV, there was a significant and large difference in Verbal IQ between the LT and comparison groups (106.09 vs. 129.62, $d$ = 1.58), even though the LTs scored in the average range. The LTs also had a lower mean score on Binet Nonverbal IQ at age 5 (95.76 vs. 105.17, $d$ = .88), the only time a nonverbal ability difference was found between the LT and comparison groups. On the PEST, the LTs obtained a score in the average range (52nd percentile), but the comparison children had a significantly higher mean score (82nd percentile), a difference of about 1 *SD*. Neither the LTs nor the comparison children were very proficient in the emerging skills of rhyming, initial consonant matching, phoneme deletion, letter identification, or word reading, and no significant group differences were found on these measures.

Lee and Rescorla (2008) examined use of four types of psychological state words (physiological, emotional, desire, and cognitive) during the mother–child play sessions at ages 3, 4, and 5 years for 30 of the LTs and 15 of the comparison children. By age 5, the LTs no longer differed from the comparison children in total number of words used or in *voc*D (MacWhinney, 2000), a measure of lexical diversity considered less sensitive to sample size than the type-token ratio. However, the LTs still differed significantly in MLU from the comparison children by age 5, with only 53% of LTs scoring within 1 *SD* of the comparison children's mean. The LTs used significantly more physiological state words (e.g., "hungry") at ages 3 and 4, but the two groups did not differ in their use of physiological state terms at age 5. The LTs and the comparison children did not differ in their use of emotional terms (e.g., "mad" or "sad") or desire terms (e.g., "want" or "need") at any age, and desire terms were the most frequently used psychological state terms for both groups at every age. In both groups, use of cognitive state terms increased significantly between the ages of 3 and 5 years, more so for the LTs than for the comparison children. However, the LTs used significantly fewer cognitive terms such as "think" and "know" than the comparison children at every age. In fact, the LTs' use of cognitive state terms at age 5 was comparable to use of these terms by MLU-matched comparison children at age 3.

The most striking syntactic difference that Lee and Rescorla (2008) found between the LT and comparison groups was in use of propositional complements, such as "I thought that the policeman was riding a motorcycle." The percentage of children using propositional complements increased significantly between the ages of 3 and 5 years for both groups, but the groups were significantly different at every age (7% vs. 40% at age 3, 33% vs. 93% at age 4, and 55% vs. 100% at age 5). In addition, the LTs rarely used propositional complements with contrastives to express false belief, as in "The baby thinks this is a park, but it is a jail." It should also be noted that the mothers of the LTs used fewer cognitive state words in conversations with their children than the mothers of the TD children, perhaps reflecting a perception of their children's limitations in the ability to talk about thoughts and beliefs.

## LATE TALKER OUTCOMES IN MIDDLE CHILDHOOD

The general pattern of LT group scores in the average range but significantly lower than comparison group scores persisted when the children entered elementary school. Rescorla (2002) reported age 6 outcomes for 34 LTs and 26 comparison children on the Test of Language Development–Primary 2 (TOLD-P:2; Newcomer & Hammill, 1988). Ten LTs (29%) had at least one TOLD-P:2 subtest score < 10th percentile, compared with 9% of the comparison group (whose low scores were on the TOLD-P:2 Word Discrimination subtest only). However, only two LTs (6%) had two TOLD-P:2 subtest scores below this 10th percentile benchmark. Based on clinical impression of conversational speech, six LTs manifested specific language impairment (SLI) at age 6 (17%). These youngsters, all of whom had normal receptive language, demonstrated many grammatical morpheme errors, limited intelligibility, word retrieval problems, poor formulation skills, and weak narratives; five of the six were receiving school-based speech-language services.

At each follow-up, we typically administered two or three measures to assess a particular skill (e.g., vocabulary, grammar, verbal memory, phonological awareness, reading decoding). To reduce the risk of finding significant differences because of multiple statistical tests (i.e., a Type I error) and to increase the reliability of measures by reducing the influence of chance fluctuations in any single measure, we aggregated similar measures to produce a smaller number of dependent variables for statistical analysis. The aggregation was based on a theoretical conceptualization of the skills the subtests measured, the known properties of the subtests as presented in their respective test manuals, and observed correlations among the subtests in our sample. When all measures to be aggregated had the same metric (e.g., standard scores with a mean of 10 and $SD$ of 3), we aggregated by averaging the component subtest scores (e.g., Vocabulary at ages 6 and 8; Grammar at ages 6, 7, and 8; Listening Comprehension at age 8; and Reading at ages 8 and 9). When measures to be aggregated had different metrics or lacked normed scores, we used the pooled samples to convert each score into a standard score and then averaged these standard scores. The mean scores for LT and comparison groups on the various language outcomes at ages 6, 7, and 8 are presented in Figure 11.1. All measures in the figure have a population mean of 10 and an $SD$ of 3.

At age 6, the Cohen's $d$ scores for group differences were 0.85 for the Vocabulary aggregate (TOLD-P:2 Oral Vocabulary and Picture Vocabulary), 0.64 for the Grammar aggregate (TOLD-P:2 Grammatic Completion and Grammatic Understanding), 0.91 for the Phonology aggregate (TOLD-P:2 Word Discrimination, plus phoneme deletion and matching initial consonants tasks), and 1.26 for TOLD-P:2 Sentence Imitation. The groups did not differ on rapid naming, verbal fluency, or reading tasks.

At age 7, the LT and comparison groups differed significantly on the Vocabulary aggregate composed of the Vocabulary subtest from the Wechsler Intelligence Scale for Children–Revised (WISC-R; Wechsler, 1974) and the Boston Naming Test (Kaplan, Goodglass, & Weintraub, 1983), with a Cohen's $d$ score of 1.53. They did not differ on the Grammar aggregate composed of the Formulated Sentences, Word Structure, and Sentence Structure subtests on the Clinical Evaluation of Language Fundamentals–Revised (CELF-R; Semel, Wiig, Secord, & Sabers, 1987) or on Phonological or Reading aggregates. The groups also did not differ at age 7 on WISC-R

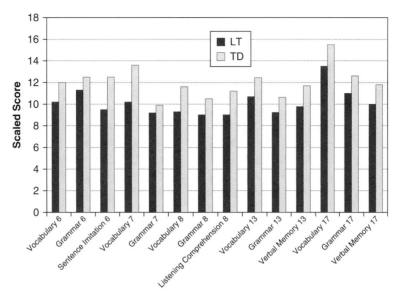

**Figure 11.1.** Language outcomes for late talker and comparison groups at ages 6, 7, 8, 13, and 17. (*Key:* LT, late talker; TD, typically developing.)

Block Design, Picture Arrangement, or Arithmetic subtests, indicating comparable nonverbal and math skills.

At age 8, the LTs had significantly lower scores on all four aggregates: Vocabulary (CELF-R Word Associations and Word Classes), with a Cohen's *d* score of 1.05; Grammar (CELF-R Linguistic Concepts, Formulated Sentences, Sentence Assembly), with a Cohen's *d* score of .94; Listening Comprehension (CELF-R Semantic Relationships and Listening to Paragraphs), with a Cohen's *d* score of 1.24; and Reading (Letter Word Identification and Passage Comprehension subtests on the Woodcock-Johnson Psychoeducational Battery–Revised [WJ-R; Woodcock & Johnson, 1989]), with a Cohen's *d* score of .84. At age 9, the groups differed significantly on an aggregate Reading measure composed of the Basic Reading and Reading Comprehension from the Wechsler Individual Achievement Test (WIAT; Wechsler, 1992) and the Dictation and Writing Samples subtests from the WJ-R, with a Cohen's *d* score of .72.

At ages 8 and 9, the children also participated in a narrative task involving the *Frog, Where Are You* wordless picture book (Manhardt & Rescorla, 2002). At age 9, the children narrated the story first independently and then when various elements were modeled and elicited (i.e., in the "supported" condition). Narratives were scored on four factors: advanced syntactic structures (e.g., propositional complements and relative clauses), story grammar components (e.g., initiating event, goal-directed action, consequence, resolution, and formal ending), cohesive ties (e.g., reference and conjunction), and evaluative information (e.g., causal connectors, references to emotions or cognitions, and direct or indirect speech). Significant group differences were found on three of the four narrative factors (not the cohesion factor). Cohen's *d* scores were obtained for group comparisons at age 8 and for both the standard and "supported" conditions at age 9. The Cohen's *d* score for syntax was smaller at age 8 than age 9 (.16 at age 8 vs. .47 and .51 at age 9). Effect sizes for the story grammar factors were substantial at both ages (.58 at age 8 and .70 and .56 at age 9), as were effect sizes for the evaluative information factor (.58 at age 8 and .61 and .63 at age 9). It is noteworthy that the "supported" condition benefited the comparison group as much as or more than the LT group, which is why the Cohen's $d$ score in the supported condition was generally not larger and sometimes smaller than that for the standard condition at age 9.

Although Manhardt and Rescorla (2002) noted that the story grammar differences were still present when the LTs' lower scores on the CELF-R were taken into account statistically, the LTs' story grammar weaknesses appeared to derive to some extent from the lack of complexity in their syntax that was not reflected in their CELF-R scores. Specifically, the LTs used fewer elements of complex syntax, such as expanded noun phrases (e.g., "He was a little green frog"), propositional complements (e.g., "He thought the frogs were sitting on the log"), relative clauses (e.g., "The frog who climbed out of the jar was green"), noun phrase complements (e.g., "There were ripples spreading through the pond"), adjectival complements (e.g., "They were happy that they had found it"), adverbial complements (e.g., "After the boy fell asleep, the frog escaped"), and Wh-clauses (e.g., "He saw the frog was missing when he woke up").

The kinds of complex syntactic structures largely absent from the LTs' narratives provide richness, elaboration, perspective, and depth to narrative exposition. They are also the kinds of devices used in written language, as well as in the more formal, elaborated speech used by better educated speakers and in school textbooks. However, these syntactic structures are not typically assessed in a basic clinical language evaluation or represented in any depth on tests such as the CELF. By the time they enter school, LTs have generally caught up to age expectations in vocabulary, basic syntax/morphology, and articulation. This allows them to perform in the average range on standardized tests and to appear to the casual listener not to have language impairments. However, the demands of a narrative task made it evident that the LTs manifested language weaknesses relative to peers from the same SES backgrounds when assessed with measures more sensitive to the advanced language elements necessary for conveying complex ideas.

For the aggregate measures for ages 6–9, Rescorla (2002) reported many significant concurrent cross-domain correlations (e.g., $r = .50$ between Vocabulary and Grammar at age 8), as well as many significant within-domain longitudinal correlations (e.g., $r = .70$ between Vocabulary at age 6 and age 7). The correlations that were significant at $p < .01$ (66 of 78) ranged from .33 to .99, with 32 being large effects ($\geq .50$) according to Cohen (1988). Rescorla (2002) also presented regression results, with predictors entered in chronological order. Vocabulary score on the LDS (Rescorla, 1989) at age 2, grammar skills at age 3 as measured by MLU and IPSyn scores (Scarborough, 1990), and grammar skills at 5 as measured by the PEST (Young & Perachio, 1983) collectively explained 35% of the variance in age 8 scores on the CELF-R (Semel et al., 1987). Age 2 LDS scores significantly predicted age 9 reading outcomes on the WIAT/WJ-R, but its beta weight declined once age 5 reading and phonology scores were entered as predictors. These three predictors (LDS, age 3 grammar, age 5 grammar) explained 54% of the variance in age 9 reading.

## LATE TALKER OUTCOMES IN ADOLESCENCE

Rescorla (2005) reported language and reading outcomes at age 13 for 28 of the LTs and 25 of the TD children. As in previous follow-ups, the two outcome groups were matched at intake on age, SES status, and nonverbal ability. LTs and comparison children did not differ significantly on the Wechsler Intelligence Scale for Children–Third Edition (WISC-III; Wechsler, 1991) Block Design. Thus, as was true at intake, these SES-matched groups were comparable in their nonverbal cognitive abilities. They were also similar in their performance on WISC-III Digit Span, indicating that their working memory skills were comparable for numbers. As a group, LTs performed in the average range on all standardized language and reading tasks at age 13. However, consistent with earlier follow-ups, they scored significantly lower than SES-matched peers on most measures.

On the Vocabulary aggregate, which was composed of the Vocabulary subtest from the WISC-III and the Listening Vocabulary and Reading Vocabulary subtests from the Test of Adolescent and Adult Language–Third Edition (TOAL-3; Hammill, Brown, Larsen, & Wiederholt, 1994), the LTs scored in the average range but significantly lower than the comparison children ($d = .67$). Similarly, on the Grammar aggregate, which was composed of the TOAL-3 Listening Grammar and Reading Grammar subtests, as well as the Formulated Sentences subtest on the CELF-R and the Ambiguous Sentences subtest from the Test of Language Competence–Expanded Edition (TLC; Wiig & Secord 1989), the LTs scored in the average range but significantly lower than the comparison children ($d = .64$). The same pattern emerged on the Verbal Memory aggregate, which was composed of the WISC-III Digit Span subtest, the CELF-R Recalling Sentences subtest, and a pseudoword repetition task ($d = .83$). Group means on these age 13 language scores are presented in Figure 11.1.

The LT and comparison groups did not differ significantly on the age 13 Reading Mechanics aggregate (which was composed of reading decoding, word and nonsense word timed reading, spelling, and reading rate and error scores) or on a Writing aggregate (composed of three subtests from the Test of Written Language–Third Edition (TOWL-3; Hammill & Larsen, 1996). However, there was a significant and large difference ($d = .84$) on Reading Comprehension at age 13, as measured by the comprehension questions on an expository passage from the Qualitative Reading Inventory–II (QRI-II; Leslie & Caldwell, 1995). This result is consistent with the well-established finding that reading comprehension is more closely associated with language skills than is reading decoding (Catts & Kamhi, 2005).

Correlations among age 13 outcome measures were moderately high. For example, Vocabulary was significantly correlated at the $p < .001$ level with Grammar (.59), Reading Mechanics (.59), and Reading Comprehension (.64)—all large effect sizes based on Cohen (1988). The Grammar aggregate had comparable correlations with Verbal Memory (.58) and Reading Mechanics (.60; $p < .001$). The Verbal Memory aggregate had a similar correlation with the Reading Mechanics aggregate (.50; $p < .001$). The Writing aggregate was correlated with Grammar (.35; $p < .01$) and Reading Mechanics (.51; $p < .001$). These correlations suggest considerable shared variance among the various language and reading/writing measures.

Regression analyses indicated that age 2 LDS vocabulary score was a significant predictor of age 13 Vocabulary, Grammar, Verbal Memory, and Reading

Comprehension (with $R^2$ values of 14%, 13%, 21%, and 14%, respectively). No other age 2 predictors were significant, including SES, Bayley nonverbal score, or Reynell Receptive Language score. As would be expected, age 6 Vocabulary score was a stronger predictor than age 2 LDS for age 13 outcomes (40% for Vocabulary, 15% for Grammar, 15% for Reading Mechanics, and 35% for Reading Comprehension). When age 2, age 6, and age 8 predictors were entered chronologically to predict age 13 aggregates, the total variance accounted for was 55% for Vocabulary, 53% for Grammar, 38% for Verbal Memory, 57% for Reading Mechanics, and 35% for Reading Comprehension, with age 2 LDS scores still a strong predictor of all four outcomes (14%–20% of the variance). These findings further confirm that slow language development at age 2–2½ was associated with a weakness in language-related skills into adolescence relative to TD peers.

Rescorla (2009) reported language and reading outcomes at age 17 for 26 LTs and 23 comparison children. LTs and comparison children did not differ significantly on either the Wechsler Adult Intelligence Scale–Third Edition (WAIS-III; Wechsler, 1997a) Block Design or the Woodcock-Johnson Psychoeducational Battery–III: Tests of Achievement (WJ-III, REF), Math Fluency, with both groups scoring somewhat above average on Block Design and in the average range on Math Fluency. Thus, as had been the case 15 years earlier, these two demographically matched groups of children were comparable in their nonverbal cognitive abilities.

As in previous follow-ups, LTs performed in the average range on all language and reading tasks at age 17, but they obtained significantly lower vocabulary, grammar, and verbal memory scores than peers with typical language histories. The largest Cohen's $d$ scores were found for the Vocabulary subtest on the WAIS-III ($d = .80$), the Grammatical Judgment subtest on the Comprehensive Assessment of Spoken Language (CASL; Carrow-Woolfolk, 1999; $d = .80$), and the Logical Memory subtest (narrative recall) on the Wechsler Memory Scale–Third Edition (WMS-III; Wechsler, 1997b; $d = 1.08$). Very few LTs scored below the 10th percentile on any of the language and reading outcome measures at age 17. The most challenging tasks for the LTs appeared to be WM-III Logical Memory and WM-III Verbal Paired Associates, but even on these difficult verbal memory tasks most LTs scored in the average range or above.

Figure 11.1 presents mean scores by group for the age 17 Vocabulary measure (WAIS-III Vocabulary), for the age 17 Grammar aggregate (mean of CASL Syntax Construction, Sentence Comprehension, Grammatical Judgment, and Ambiguous Sentences subtest scores, converted to standard scores with mean of 10, $SD$ of 3), and for the age 17 Verbal Memory aggregate (mean of WMS-III Logical Memory and Verbal Paired Associates scores). As was true at earlier ages, mean scores for the LT group were in the average range but lower than mean scores for the comparison children.

For statistical comparisons at age 17, the various subtests were grouped into aggregates, as was done at younger ages, but principal components analyses were then used to derive factor scores, thereby weighting the components of each factor according to their degree of association with the factor. For these analyses, Vocabulary and Grammar scores were combined into a single factor. LTs obtained significantly lower scores than comparison children on the age 17 Vocabulary/Grammar factors ($d = .92$) and Verbal Memory factor ($d = .93$), but the group difference on the Reading/Writing factor (mean of WJ-III Letter Word Identification, Reading Fluency, and Writing Fluency subtests) was not significant.

The age 17 Vocabulary/Grammar factor was correlated at .65 ($p < .001$) with the age 17 Verbal Memory factor and at .64 ($p < .001$) with the age 17 Reading/Writing factor. However, the Verbal Memory factor was correlated at only .37 with the Reading/Writing factor ($p < .05$). Thus, the age 17 Vocabulary/Grammar factor had a large $r$ with the two other age 17 outcome factors, but the $r$ between the other two factors was only medium in size.

Regression analysis indicated that age 2 LDS vocabulary score, entered first, explained 17% of the variance in the age 17 Vocabulary/Grammar factor. Reynell Expressive and Reynell Receptive scores, entered second, were not significant predictors. However, for the first time, Bayley nonverbal score, added last, explained an additional 13% of the variance. Results were similar for the Verbal Memory factor, with the LDS accounting for 17% and the Bayley nonverbal score accounting for an additional 11% of the variance. Thus, 28%–30% of the variance in age 17 language scores was explained by two age 2 measures.

## CONTEXTUALIZING OUR OUTCOME FINDINGS IN THE LATE TALKER LITERATURE

Our LT study is notable because it followed the children until age 17. However, our findings are quite consistent with results of other LT studies with shorter follow-up periods, many of which are summarized in other chapters in this book (e.g., Chapters 1, 2, 9, 10, and 12). For example, Fischel, Whitehurst, Caulfield, and DeBaryshe (1989) studied 22 LTs identified at 24–38 months who had mean vocabularies of < 20 words. The percentage of children scoring in the average range on the EOPVT (Gardner, 1981) was 35% by 5 months after intake and increased to 88% by age 3½ and to 95% by age 5½ (Whitehurst, Fischel, Arnold, & Lonigan, 1992). These findings indicating that most of the children had normal expressive vocabulary skills by age 3½ are very consistent with our results.

Thal, Tobias, and Morrison (1991) reported age 3 outcomes for 10 LTs identified at age 2. The four LTs who were still delayed 1 year later had also been delayed in receptive language and gestures at age 2, whereas the six LTs who had normal expressive language by age 3 had been developing typically in receptive and gesture skills at age 2. These findings indicated that many but not all late-talking toddlers perform in the average range by age 3, and that those with receptive language and gestural impairments were at higher risk for persistent delay than those with typical development in these areas.

Paul and colleagues studied 32 LTs identified between 20 and 34 months (Paul, 1993, 1996; Paul, Murray, Clancy, & Andrews, 1997). At ages 3 and 4, all of Paul's (1993) LTs scored in the average range for receptive and expressive vocabulary and for receptive grammar. By the criterion of > 10th percentile in Developmental Sentence Score (DSS; Lee, 1974), recovery was achieved by 41% of the sample by age 3, 57% by age 4, 74% by kindergarten and first grade, and 84% by second grade (Paul, 1996; Paul et al., 1997). However, consistent with our results, the LTs did more poorly than a group of TD comparison children at age 7 on the TOLD-P:2 (Newcomer & Hammill, 1988) Expressive language scale, even if they were classified as recovered.

Subsequent LT studies confirmed the results of the earlier outcome studies. For example, Girolametto, Wiigs, Smyth, Weitzman, and Pearce (2001) reported outcomes for 21 LTs identified at 24–33 months who had participated in an 11-week parent-based intervention program. At age 5 follow-up, most of the LTs scored in the average range on various language measures, but they scored significantly lower than children with typical language histories on most language measures at age 5, particularly on measures tapping more complex skills, such as narrating a story.

Thal, Miller, Carlson, and Vega (2005) reported age 4 outcomes for 20 LTs who scored < 10th percentile in expressive vocabulary on the MacArthur Communicative Development Inventories (CDIs; Fenson et al., 1993) at 16 months. Although the LT group scored in the average range on language and cognitive tests at age 4, they scored significantly lower than a group of 44 comparison children with typical language histories, consistent with our results. The LTs also scored lower than the comparison children on a nonword repetition task, consistent with our finding of weak verbal memory performance at many follow-up points.

Moyle, Ellis Weismer, Evans, and Lindstrom (2007) reported age 5 outcomes for 30 LTs first identified at age 2 by scores ≤ 10th percentile on the CDIs. Consistent with our findings, LTs at age 5 had significantly lower scores than comparison children matched on age, SES, gender, and nonverbal cognitive ability on three Test of Language Development–3 (TOLD-P:3) subtests (Newcomer & Hammill, 1997): Oral vocabulary, Grammatic Completion, and Sentence Imitation (Cohen's $d$ scores of .97, 1.46, and 1.52, respectively). Ellis Weismer (2007) reported age 5½ outcomes for another cohort of LTs—40 children identified at age 2. Only three of the LTs scored at least 1 $SD$ below the mean on TOLD-P:3 Speaking Quotient at age 5½. However, even with these three children excluded, the LTs obtained significantly lower scores than comparison children on both the Listening and Speaking Quotients of the TOLD-P:3. Group differences were particularly marked in sentence imitation, as found in our study.

Ellis and Thal (2008) summarized age 6 outcomes for 156 LTs identified using the CDIs in a sample of 577 children 16 months of age; 35 of the LTs were also delayed in receptive language. At age 6, 3.7% of the LTs with expressive language delay only and 8.5% of the LTs with concomitant receptive language delays were diagnosed with SLI. These findings underscore that early receptive/expressive delay confers greater risk for later SLI than does expressive delay only, but that most of the higher risk group still performed on the average range by age 6.

Our LT study is also consistent with studies that have identified LTs in large-scale epidemiological cohorts of young children. For example, Armstrong, Marchman, and Owen (2007) reported findings through fifth grade for 131 LTs identified in a sample of 689 children from the National Institute of Child Health and Human Development's Early Child Care Research Network data set. The LTs scored ≤ 10th percentile on the CDIs and < 85 on the Reynell at both 36 and 54 months. Differences between the LTs and both a TD group and a "late bloomer" group (delayed at 36 but not 54 months) persisted through fifth grade on the Picture Vocabulary, Letter Word Identification, and Memory for Sentences subtests of the WJ-R (Woodcock & Johnson, 1989), although the LT group scored in the average range on the first two subtests at all time points. For all measures, the LT group performed worst, the TD group performed best, and the late bloomer group performed in between the other two groups, with little change in the gaps between groups over time.

Dale, Price, Bishop, and Plomin (2003) identified LTs in a sample of twins in the United Kingdom at age 2 based on expressive vocabulary scores < 10th percentile (≤ 15 words) on the 100-word MacArthur Communicative Development Inventory UK Short Form (MCDI: UKSF; Dionne, Dale, Boivin, & Plomin, 2003). When a score ≤ 15th percentile on two of three language measures (vocabulary, grammar, and abstract language) was used to identify language delay, 44% and 40% of the 2-year-old LTs were still delayed at age 3 and age 4, respectively.

Finally, Rice, Taylor, and Zubrick (2008) reported age 7 outcomes for LTs identified in an Australian study by Zubrick, Taylor, Rice, and Slegers (2007) at 24 months. Using receptive and expressive language items of the Communication scale of the Ages & Stages Questionnaires® (ASQ; Bricker & Squires, 1999), 128 LTs (19% of the sample) were identified at age 2, 88 of whom also had receptive language delays. At age 7, the LTs did not differ from the TD group on SES/demographic variables or on nonverbal intelligence, and they scored in the average range on all language measures, consistent with our study. However, they had significantly lower scores on receptive vocabulary, articulation, and numerous grammatical scales, with the largest Cohen's $d$ scores on the morphosyntax measures. The percentages of LTs who were impaired (> 1 $SD$ below the mean) ranged from 4% to 23% across the 17 outcome measures, with significant group differences for seven of the measures.

In summary, a large body of research on LTs has yielded findings that are very consistent with the earliest studies in the field, even though the earliest studies (ours included) had relatively small and select samples. The definitive findings from this body of research include the following:

1. Most LTs attain language scores in the average range by age 5, 6, or 7.

2. LT groups consistently obtain significantly lower scores than groups with typical language histories on most language measures, even when the LTs perform in the average range.

3. LTs with receptive as well as expressive language delays have higher rates of persistent delay, but even most of these children end up scoring in the average range on expressive language measures by elementary school.

4. Vocabulary delays resolve more quickly and completely than morphosyntax delays, with the latter being persistent in some children.

5. A persistent impairment in verbal working memory is characteristic of many LTs.

## CONCLUSIONS

A first important finding from our research is that the LTs and TD comparison children differed significantly and substantially ($d$ = .78) in their receptive language skills at intake (24–31 months), even though all the LTs were required to have age-appropriate receptive language scores. This suggests that the LTs were not only delayed in their expressive language development at intake but that they also had weaker language skills in general. This substantial difference in receptive language skill persisted until age 17, suggesting an individual difference that was stable, rather than a temporary delay.

A second important finding from our research is that the LT and comparison groups showed very large differences in expressive language at intake when they were first identified (e.g., intake Reynell Expressive language $d = 1.95$; intake LDS $d > 2.0$), but that Cohen's $d$ scores for expressive language tasks stabilized at about .80 to 1 $SD$s once the LTs caught up to normative expectations in vocabulary. Thus, although the vocabulary delay by which LTs were identified was severe at intake, this severe delay did not persist. Rather, this early and severe delay presaged a mild but enduring expressive language weakness up to age 17.

A third important finding from our research is that the nature of the LTs' most substantial impairment changed over time, paralleling the language acquisition process. Thus, the LTs were first delayed in vocabulary and phonology. By age 3, 79% had caught up in expressive vocabulary on the EOPVT, and about half had caught up in phonology. However, only 24% were at age level in grammatical skills according to the IPSyn. A $> 2.5$ $SD$ difference in grammatical skills relative to the comparison children as measured by MLU and the IPSyn persisted through age 4. By age 5, most of the LTs appeared to have caught up in grammatical skills, as reflected in a score at the 52nd percentile on the PEST, although they still scored about 1 $SD$ lower than the comparison group. However, at age 5 they used only as many cognitive state terms as MLU-matched comparison children had done at age 3. Furthermore, only 55% of the LTs used propositional complement syntax, compared with 100% of their peers. When they had to define words, explain concepts and conventions, and describe pictorial absurdities on the Stanford-Binet IV Vocabulary scale, the LTs scored 1.58 $SD$s below the comparison children. Manhardt and Rescorla (2002), who compared LTs and comparison children in a narrative task at ages 8 and 9, reported substantial differences in use of complex syntax, including expanded noun phrases, relative clauses, Wh-clauses, and complementation (propositional, noun phrase, adjectival, and adverbial complements). These findings suggest that most of the LTs were able to catch up to normative expectations in vocabulary and grammar by the time they entered kindergarten, but that they continued to show weaknesses relative to TD peers in the ability to use complex, higher-order language for narration, definition, explanation, description, and exposition.

A fourth important finding from our research was that group differences in some domains were most likely to emerge in the middle of the learning curve for a skill, rather than early in the acquisition process, when neither group had much mastery of the skill, or late in the acquisition process, when both groups had mastered it. This was evident both in our phonological awareness tasks and in our reading decoding tasks. LTs did not differ from comparison children at age 5 on phonological skills such as matching consonants and phoneme deletion, when children in both groups were just beginning to master these skills. However, they differed significantly on the same skills at age 6 ($d = .91$), the point at which the comparison children had largely mastered them but LTs were still inconsistent. By age 7, however, the groups did not differ on our phonological tasks, as most children in both groups had mastered them. The same pattern emerged with reading decoding, with no significant differences at ages 6 and 7 (when children in both groups were emerging readers), substantial differences (Cohen's $d$ scores of .84 and .72) at ages 8 and 9 (when the comparison children were fluent readers but the LTs were more mixed in their reading skills), and no significant differences at age

13 (when both groups were skilled decoders). However, the large reading comprehension differences at age 13 indicated that the LTs were not as proficient readers as the comparison children. This might have been the case at age 17 as well, had we used a more challenging reading comprehension task. In summary, this pattern is reminiscent of Scarborough and Dobrich's (1990) *illusory recovery* notion, whereby children show initial delays in language and then appear to catch up, but in fact they have an enduring impairment that may emerge later in a somewhat different form.

A fifth important finding from our research is that vocabulary, grammar, verbal memory, phonological, and reading measures were consistently correlated with each other. For example, at age 17, the Vocabulary/Grammar factor was correlated at .65 ($p < .001$) with the Verbal Memory factor and at .64 ($p < .001$) with the Reading/Writing factor. The 10 correlations among the five age 17 vocabulary and grammar subtests ranged from .32 to .69, with nine of the correlations > .45. This pattern is reminiscent of the "positive manifold" or pattern of positive correlations consistently found among most mental tests, which is captured by the notion of "*g*." Our study suggests a common core of language-related abilities that is shared by most of the vocabulary, grammar, verbal memory, and reading measures we used over 15 years, with somewhat tighter links among the three explicitly language skills than with reading skills. We would argue that it is this common core of language abilities that explains the enduring correlation between LDS scores at age 2 and language outcomes 15 years later. Because acquiring an expressive vocabulary is a key developmental task from 12 to 24 months, we would argue that those children who do it much more slowly are likely to have some underlying impairment, albeit mild, that first manifests as being an LT but that persists in lower language scores than those obtained by TD peers, even though their delay is resolved.

Findings from our LT studies as well as from those reported in other chapters in this book provide support for a dimensional account of language delay, according to which LTs are positioned somewhat to the left of the distribution relative to children with typical language development on a hypothetical language ability spectrum (Rescorla, 2009). According to this view, the difference between LTs and TD children is therefore more quantitative than qualitative. This notion of a spectrum of language ability is consistent with formulations provided by Leonard (1991), Bishop and Edmundson (1987), Ellis Weismer (2007), and Dollaghan (2004).

As articulated by Rescorla (2002, 2005, 2009), the language ability spectrum, like intelligence, can be conceptualized as deriving from variation in many discrete skills. The distinct yet interrelated abilities hypothesized to subserve language include auditory perception/processing, word retrieval, verbal working memory, motor planning, phonological discrimination, and grammatical rule learning.

Research by Fernald and Marchman (2012) and Marchman and Fernald (2008) and summarized in this book suggests that weaker language processing skills may be one of the most critical impairments leading to late talking. Their research has shown that reaction time and accuracy in a lexical processing task at 18 months significantly predicted later vocabulary growth in both TD children and LTs, as well as predicting age 8 working memory. These findings are noteworthy because verbal memory impairments are among the most robust and enduring weaknesses manifested by LTs, even when they perform in the average range at follow-up.

It is likely that children vary in their inborn language processing ability, but it is also likely that this ability is shaped by subsequent language environments. This suggests that children with richer language environments develop more fully and rapidly in their ability to efficiently process lexical information than children with less rich language environments. Fernald and Marchman's (2012) finding that variation in maternal speech to children predicted later lexical processing skill at 24 months provides support for the notion that environmental factors may have an impact on processing skills.

In summary, language is a complex set of skills. Many biopsychosocial factors contribute to individual differences in the skills that subserve language ability. We would suggest that "advantaged" LTs with good receptive language, normal nonverbal skills, typical personality development, and middle to high SES families—such as those who participated in our 15-year longitudinal study—most likely were slow to talk because of constitutional differences in language endowment. Family history information supported this speculation. Having been an LT was reported for ≥ 1 parent and/or ≥ 1 siblings for 12 of the 40 LTs but for only 3 of the 39 comparison children. The fact that mothers of LTs did not differ from mothers of comparison children in synchrony, reciprocity, or other social characteristics generally associated with promoting good language acquisition further suggests that the LTs we studied were not slow to talk due to deficient environments. However, we know that inborn characteristics can be influenced by environmental factors. Therefore, as children enter the preschool period, psychosocial factors such as how much (and how well) parents talk to them become increasingly important (Hart & Risley, 1995). We expect that a small percentage of children who manifest SLI at age 5 have poor language endowment and have manifested delayed language since they were toddlers. However, most school-age children with SLI are probably at more psychosocial risk than the children we studied, few of whom were diagnosable with SLI by the time they were 6 or 7. Children at psychosocial risk have poorly developed listening skills, limited vocabularies, weak grammatical skills, and poorly developed higher level language abilities such as defining, describing, and narrating. In each of these domains of language, our LTs generally scored within 1 *SD* of their peers, and hence in the average range, broadly defined. However, they had weaker skills in these domains than TD peers with the same advantaged backgrounds and comparable nonverbal abilities, consistent with the notion of enduring differences in language endowment.

## REFERENCES

Armstrong, E.S., Marchman, V.A., & Owen, M.T. (2007). School age cognitive and achievement outcomes for late talkers and late bloomers: Do late bloomers really bloom? Poster presented at American Speech-Hearing Association Annual Conference, Boston, MA.

Bayley, N. (1969). *The Bayley Scales of Infant Development.* San Antonio, TX: The Psychological Corporation.

Bishop, D.V.M., & Edmundson, A. (1987). Language impaired 4-year-olds: Distinguishing transient from persistent impairment. *Journal of Speech and Hearing Disorders, 52,* 156–173.

Bricker, D., & Squires, J. (1999). *Ages & Stages Questionnaires®: A parent-completed, child-monitoring system* (2nd ed.). Baltimore, MD: Paul H. Brookes Publishing Co.

Brown, R. (1973). *A first language: The early stages.* Cambridge, MA: Harvard University Press.

Carrow-Woolfolk, E. (1985). *Test for Auditory Comprehension of Language, Revised.* Austin, TX: PRO-ED.

Carrow-Woolfolk, E. (1999). *Comprehensive Assessment of Spoken Language.* Circle Pines, MN: American Guidance Service.

Catts, H.W., & Kamhi, A.G. (Eds.). (2005). *The connections between language and reading disabilities.* Mahwah, NJ: Lawrence Erlbaum Associates.

Cohen, J. (1988). *Statistical power analysis for the behavioral sciences* (2nd ed.) New York, NY: Academic Press.

Dale, P.S., Price, T.S., Bishop, D.V., & Plomin, R. (2003). Outcomes of early language delay: I. Predicting persistent and transient language difficulties at 3 and 4 years. *Journal of Speech, Language, and Hearing Research, 46*(3), 544–560.

Dionne, G., Dale, P.S., Boivin, M., & Plomin, R. (2003). Genetic evidence for bidirectional effects of early lexical and grammatical development. *Child Development, 74,* 391–412.

Dollaghan, C.A. (2004). Taxometric analysis of specific language impairment in 3- and 4-year-old children. *Journal of Speech, Language, and Hearing Research, 47,* 464–475.

Ellis, E.M., & Thal, D.J. (2008). Early language delay and risk for language impairment. *Perspectives, 15,* 93–100.

Ellis Weismer, S. (2007). Typical talkers, late talkers, and children with specific language impairment: A language endowment spectrum? In R. Paul (Ed.), *The influence of developmental perspectives on research and practice in communication disorders: A festschrift for Robin S. Chapman* (pp. 83–101). Mahwah, NJ: Lawrence Erlbaum Associates.

Fenson, L., Dale, P.S., Reznick, J.S., Thal, D., Bates, E., Hartung, J.P., . . . Reilly, J.S. (1993). *The MacArthur Communicative Development Inventories: User's Guide and Technical Manual.* Baltimore, MD: Paul H. Brookes Publishing Co.

Fernald, A., & Marchman, V.A. (2012). Individual differences in lexical processing at 18 months predict vocabulary growth in typically developing and late-talking toddlers. *Child Development, 83,* 203–222.

Fischel, J., Whitehurst, G., Caulfield, M., & DeBaryshe, B. (1989). Language growth in children with expressive language delay. *Pediatrics, 82,* 218–227.

Gardner, M.F. (1981). *Expressive One-Word Picture Vocabulary Test.* Novato, CA: Academic Therapy Publications.

Girolametto L., Wiigs, M., Smyth R., Weitzman E., & Pearce, P.S. (2001). Children with a history of expressive language delay: Outcomes at 5 years of age. *American Journal of Speech-Language Pathology, 10,* 358–369.

Hammill, D.D., Brown, V.L., Larsen, S.C., & Wiederholt, J.L. (1994). *Test of Adolescent and Adult Language–Third Edition.* Austin, TX: PRO-ED.

Hammill, D.D., & Larsen, S.C. (1996). *Test of Written Language–Third edition.* Austin, TX: PRO-ED.

Hart, N., & Risley, T. (1995). *Meaningful differences in everyday experiences of young American children.* Baltimore, MD: Paul H. Brookes Publishing Co.

Hollingshead, A. (1975). *Four-factor index of social status.* Unpublished manuscript.

Kaplan, E., Goodglass, H., & Weintraub, S. (1983). *Boston Naming Test.* Philadelphia, PA: Lea & Febiger.

Lee, E.C., & Rescorla, L. (2008). The use of psychological state terms by late talkers at ages 3, 4, and 5. *Applied Psycholinguistics, 29,* 21–39.

Lee, L. (1974). *Developmental sentence analysis: A grammatical assessment procedure for speech and language clinicians.* Evanston, IL: Northwestern University Press.

Leiter, R.G. (1948). *Leiter International Performance Scale.* Chicago, IL: Stoelting Co.

Leonard, LB. (1991). Specific language impairment as a clinical category. *Language, Speech, and Hearing Services in Schools, 22,* 66–68.

Leslie, L., & Caldwell, J. (1995). *Qualitative Reading Inventory–II.* New York, NY: Harper Collins.

MacWhinney, B. (2000). *The CHILDES project: Tools for analyzing talk.* Mahwah, NJ: Lawrence Erlbaum Associates.

Manhardt, J., & Rescorla, L. (2002). Oral narrative Skills of late talkers at ages eight and nine. *Applied Psycholinguistics, 23,* 1–21.

Marchman, V.A., & Fernald, A., (2008). Speed of word recognition and vocabulary knowledge in infancy predict cognitive and language outcomes in later childhood. *Developmental Science, 11,* F9–F16.

Mirak, J., & Rescorla, L. (1998). Phonetic skills and vocabulary size in late talkers: Concurrent and predictive relationships. *Applied Psycholinguistics, 19,* 1–17.

Moyle, M.J., Ellis Weismer, S., Lindstrom, M., & Evans, J. (2007). Longitudinal relationships between lexical and grammatical development in typical and late talking children. *Journal of Speech, Language, and Hearing Research, 50,* 508–528.

Newcomer, P.L, & Hammill, D.D (1988). *Test of Language Development–Primary, Second Edition* Austin, TX: PRO-ED.

Newcomer, P., & Hammill, D. (1997). *Test of Language Development–Primary, Third edition.* Austin, TX: PRO-ED.

Paul, R. (1993). Outcomes of early expressive language delay. *Journal of Childhood Communication Disorders, 15,* 7–14.

Paul, R. (1996). Clinical implications of the natural history of slow expressive language development. *American Journal of Speech-Language Pathology, 5*(2), 5–21.

Paul, R., Murray, C., Clancy, K., & Andrews, D. (1997). Reading and metaphonological outcomes in late talkers. *Journal of Speech, Language, and Hearing Research, 40,* 1037–1047.

Pharr, A.B., Ratner, N.B., & Rescorla, L. (2000). Syllable structure development of toddlers with expressive specific language impairment. *Applied Psycholinguistics, 21,* 429–449.

Rescorla, L. (1989). The Language Development Survey: A screening tool for delayed language in toddlers. *Journal of Speech and Hearing Disorders, 54*(4), 587–599.

Rescorla, L. (2002). Language and reading outcomes to age 9 in late-talking toddlers. *Journal of Speech, Language, and Hearing Research, 45*(2), 360–371.

Rescorla, L. (2005). Age 13 language and reading outcomes of late-talking toddlers. *Journal of Speech, Language, and Hearing Research, 48,* 459–472.

Rescorla, L. (2009). Age 17 language and reading outcomes in late-talking toddlers: Support for a dimensional perspective on language delay. *Journal of Speech, Language, and Hearing Research, 52*(1), 16–30.

Rescorla, L., Bascome, A., & Lampard, J., & Feeny, N. (2001) Conversational patterns in late talkers at age 3. *Applied Psycholinguistics, 22,* 235–251.

Rescorla, L., Dahlsgaard, K., & Roberts, J. (2000). Late-talking toddlers: MLU and IPSyn outcomes at 3;0 and 4;0. *Journal of Child Language, 27,* 643–664.

Rescorla, L., & Fechnay, T. (1996). Mother-child synchrony and communicative reciprocity in late-talking toddlers. *Journal of Speech and Hearing Research, 39,* 200–208.

Rescorla, L., & Lee, E.C. (2000). Language impairments in young children. In T. Layton & L. Watson (Eds.), *Handbook of early language impairment in children: Vol. I: Nature.* New York, NY: Delmar Publishing Company.

Rescorla, L., & Merrin, L., (1998). Communicative intent in late-talking toddlers. *Applied Psycholinguistics, 1,* 393–414.

Rescorla, L., Mirak, J., & Singh, L. (2000). Vocabulary acquisition in late talkers: Lexical development from 2;0 to 3;0. *Journal of Child Language, 27,* 293–311.

Rescorla, L., & Ratner, T. (1996). Phonetic profiles of toddlers with specific expressive language impairment (SLI-E). *Journal of Speech and Hearing Research, 39,* 153–165.

Rescorla, L., & Roberts, J. (2002). Nominal vs. verbal morpheme use in late talkers at ages 3 and 4. *Journal of Speech, Language, and Hearing Research, 45,* 1219–1231.

Rescorla, L., Roberts, J., & Dahlsgaard, K. (1997). Late talkers at 2: Outcome at age 3. *Journal of Speech and Hearing Research, 40,* 556–566.

Reynell, J.K. (1977). *Reynell Developmental Language Scales.* Windsor, United Kingdom: NFER.

Rice, M.L., Taylor, C.L., & Zubrick, S.R. (2008). Language outcomes of 7-year-old children with or without a history of late language emergence at 24 months. *Journal of Speech, Language, and Hearing Research, 51,* 394–407.

Roberts, J., Rescorla, L., Giroux, J., & Stevens, L. (1998). Phonological skills of children with specific expressive language impairment (SLI-E): Outcome at age 3. *Journal of Speech, Language, and Hearing Research, 41,* 374–384.

Scarborough, H.S. (1990). Index of Productive Syntax. *Applied Psycholinguistics, 11,* 1–12.

Scarborough, H.S., & Dobrich, W. (1990). Development of children with early language delays. *Journal of Speech and Hearing Research, 33,* 70–83.

Semel, E., Wiig, E., Secord, W., & Sabers, D. (1987). *Clinical Evaluation of Language Fundamentals–Revised.* San Antonio, TX: The Psychological Corporation

Thal, D.J., Miller, S., Carlson, J., & Vega, M.M. (2005). Nonword repetition and language development in 4-year-old children with and without a history of early language delay. *Journal of Speech, Language, and Hearing Research, 48,* 1481–1495.

Thal, D.J., Tobias, S., & Morrison, D. (1991). Language and gesture in late talkers: A 1-year follow-up. *Journal of Speech and Hearing Research, 34*(3), 604–612.

Thorndike, R.L., Hagen, E.P., & Sattler, J.M. *(1986). The Stanford-Binet Intelligence Scale: Fourth edition.* Chicago, IL: Riverside.

Wechsler, D. (1974). *The Wechsler Intelligence Scale for Children–Revised.* San Antonio, TX: Psychological Corporation Wechsler.

Wechsler, D. (1991). *The Wechsler Intelligence Scale for Children–Third Edition.* San Antonio, TX: Psychological Corporation.

Wechsler, D. (1992). *The Wechsler Individual Achievement Test.* San Antonio, TX: Psychological Corporation.

Wechsler, D. (1997a). *The Wechsler Adult Intelligence Scale–Third Edition.* San Antonio, TX: Psychological Corporation.

Wechsler, D. (1997b). *The Wechsler Memory Scale–Third Edition.* San Antonio, TX: Psychological Corporation.

Whitehurst, G., & Fischel, J. (1994). Early developmental language delay: What, if anything, should the clinician do about it? *Journal of Child Psychology and Psychiatry, 35,* 613–648.

Whitehurst, G.J., Fischel, J.E., Arnold, D.S., & Lonigan, C.J. (1992). Evaluating outcomes with children with expressive language delay. In S.F. Warren & J. Reichle (Eds.), *Causes and effects in communication and language intervention, Vol. 1* (pp. 277–313). Baltimore, MD: Paul H. Brookes Publishing Co.

Wiig, W.H., & Secord, W. (1989). *Test of Language Competence–Expanded Edition.* San Antonio, TX: Psychological Corporation.

Woodcock, R.W., & Johnson, M.B. (1989). *Woodcock-Johnson Psychoeducational Battery-Revised.* Chicago, IL: Riverside Publishing.

Woodcock, R.W., McGrew, K.S., & Mather, N. (2001).*Woodcock-Johnson Psychoeducational Battery–Third Edition.* Chicago, IL: Riverside Publishing.

Young, E.C., & Perachio, J.J. (1983). *Patterned Elicitation Syntax Test, Revised.* Tucson, AZ: Communication Skill Builders.

Zubrick, S.R., Taylor, C.L., Rice, M.L., & Slegers, D.W. (2007). Late language emergence at 24 months: An epidemiological study of prevalence, predictors, and covariates. *Journal of Speech, Language, and Hearing Research, 50*(6), 1562–1592.

# 12

# Outcomes for Late Talkers

*A Twin Study*

Philip S. Dale and Marianna E. Hayiou-Thomas

C hildren whose early language development is delayed, known as late talkers (LTs), present a dilemma for both developmental theorists and speech-language interventionists alike. On the one hand, late talking is demonstrably a risk condition for below average language development throughout childhood and into adolescence (Chapter 11). Although typically the mean of a late-talking group on later measures is within the normal range, it is below the level of matched controls, and given the substantial variance with such groups, some proportion would be classified as falling in the clinical range. On the other hand, it is also well established by now that many children with language delays at age 2 or 3 will score in the normal range 2 or 3 years later. Discriminating persistent from transient early delay would have both theoretical and applied significance: theoretical significance for the light it would shed on the changing nature of the task of learning language over time and possible variations in learning strategies, and applied significance for the ability to target intervention services to the children who most need them. Although previous research (see Chapters 1, 2, 9, and 11) has implicated a number of factors that may influence outcome—particularly severity of early delay, receptive language abilities, gestural communication, and family history of speech-language or literacy delay—the degree of prediction is still too weak to be of practical use.

Thus we have made only modest progress at present in addressing three of the core questions about the phenomenon of late talking:

We gratefully acknowledge the ongoing contribution of the parents and children in the Twins Early Development Study (TEDS). This research is supported by grants from the United Kingdom Medical Research Council (G0500079) and the United States National Institute of Child Health and Human Development (HD044454, HD046167, HD059215).

1.  Why are some children notably slow in beginning language development?

2.  Why do many of these children appear to catch up by the beginning of school?

3.  Even if we cannot *explain* catching up, can we *predict* which children will catch up so that intervention can be focused on those children who most need it? And does our ability to predict improve substantially if we wait until age 3?

In this chapter, we bring a new source of evidence, behavior genetic analysis, to bear on these questions, drawn from a longitudinal twin study of language and literacy development. Twin studies (along with other genetically sensitive designs, such as adoption and pedigree studies, which have been less often used for language development) are uniquely capable of distinguishing genetic and environmental influences on development. They offer a "wide-angle-lens" view of development, in at least two senses. First, they are analyses of the variance within large samples of children rather than measures of individual children, and second, in their most common forms they do not by themselves identify specific genes or specific environmental features. In both respects, twin studies serve to complement other research designs that are more "close-up" in nature, in that they examine in more detail the abilities of smaller numbers of children. In addition, the very large sample in the present study, although not an epidemiological study, is nonetheless highly representative of the relevant population. These features afford considerable power to detect even small effects and correlations, which is of value when examining questions of outcome.

## THE LOGIC AND ASSUMPTIONS OF THE TWIN METHOD

Twinning provides a naturally occurring quasi-experimental situation that can illuminate the relative influence of nature and nurture (Plomin, DeFries, McClearn, & McGuffin, 2008). Identical, or monozygotic (MZ), twins derive from one zygote (fertilized egg) and are genetically identical. Fraternal, or dizygotic (DZ), twins develop from separately fertilized eggs, and, on average, share only 50% of varying human DNA. Half of all DZ twin pairs are same-sex and half are opposite-sex, whereas all MZ twin pairs are same-sex. If genetic factors are important for a trait, MZ pairs should be more similar than DZ pairs. And to the extent that family level environmental variables influence the measure, the correlation should be high for both MZ and DZ pairs. Thus, comparisons of correlations between MZ twins and those for DZ twins make it possible to analyze (divide) the total variance on a measure into three components:

1.  Variance due to genetic variance among individuals, known as *heritability,* symbolized $a^2$ or $h^2$

2.  Variance due to shared environmental factors, that is, environmental factors such as neighborhood and socioeconomic status that are common to family members and that tend to make siblings similar to each other, symbolized $c^2$

3.  Variance due to nonshared environmental factors, that is, those that affect individual children, such as illness and child-specific school experiences, and thus tend to make siblings less similar to each other, symbolized $e^2$

This broad framework somewhat oversimplifies the complexity of ways in which genes and environment can interact to affect development. There are also gene–gene interactions, in which the effect of a gene is influenced by the presence or absence of other genes (nonadditive effects); gene–environment interactions, in which the effect of a gene is influenced by the environment (often the effect of genes for cognitive and language processes is higher in more advantaged, low-risk environments); and gene–environment correlation, in which an individual's exposure to, or susceptibility to, specific environments is partly influenced by, or correlated with, that individual's genes (e.g., a child whose time with puzzles, blocks, and geometric designs is partly governed by genetically driven interests).

The following three examples from the Twins Early Development Study, which will be discussed in the next section, demonstrate how behavior genetic analysis can be applied to measures of language and literature. Spinath, Price, Dale, and Plomin (2004) estimated heritability to be .29 and .18 for age 2 vocabulary for boys and girls, respectively, based on a 100-item vocabulary checklist for parents. Kovas et al. (2005) estimated heritability to be .38 for a measure of phonological awareness at 4.5 years. And Harlaar, Spinath, Dale, and Plomin (2005) estimated heritability to be about .66 for a measure of word decoding at 7 years (.65 for boys, .67 for girls). These results also illustrate two frequently observed trends: First, heritability tends to rise with age, and second, it is generally higher for speech and speech-related skills such as printed word decoding than it is for language skills.

This fundamental analysis, often called univariate individual differences analysis, has been extended in several ways, two of which are especially relevant for the questions posed in this chapter. In the first extension, called DF analysis after its developers John DeFries and David Fulker (1988), the focus is on the extremes of the distribution, usually the lower extreme, in contrast to variability across the entire distribution. (The same logic can be used for the high extreme in studies of giftedness.) The question becomes the extent to which genetic and environmental factors are responsible for placement of some children at the extremes. The logic of the analysis is straightforward. We can expect that the children who score at the low extreme (probands) will have, on average, co-twins who also score lower than average, as the co-twins share both genetic and environmental factors with the probands. But to the extent that genetic factors have influence, the co-twins in MZ pairs will score even lower than the co-twins in DZ pairs. Thus, the difference between the mean scores for MZ co-twins and DZ co-twins is an index of genetic influence. In practice, a regression analysis is used here, and it generates group heritability ($h^2_g$), group shared environment ($c^2_g$), and group nonshared environment ($e^2_g$) influences. These statistics are analogous to the three measures for individual differences analyses introduced previously but are specifically addressed to the issue of extreme performance. Group heritability is often of the same general magnitude as individual differences heritability, but it is sometimes larger, suggesting a greater influence at the extremes. Spinath et al. (2004), for example, analyzed parent-reported language at 2, 3, and 4 years, as well as a composite measure. Group heritabilities for scores in the lowest 5% or 10% were almost always larger than individual differences heritability, and in some cases significantly so. For example, the individual differences heritability for the composite measure was .27 for boys and .18 for girls, whereas the group heritability was significantly larger, at .49 for both boys and girls. In contrast, Harlaar et al. (2005) obtained group heritabilities for word decoding of .67 for boys and .50 for girls, which were comparable to the individual differences heritabilities described earlier in this section (.65, .67), suggesting no greater influence at the extreme than across the distribution as a whole.

Another very useful extension of twin analysis has been the development of multivariate analyses (Plomin et al., 2008), which permit the investigation of the etiology of the *relationships* among two or more measures. Here we ask if an observed correlation between two measures is due to the influence of common genetic factors on both measures, due to common environmental influences on both measures, or due to some combination of the two kinds of influence. Like univariate analyses, multivariate analyses contrast correlations for MZ and DZ twins, in which the magnitude of the discrepancy between them indexes a genetic effect, and the overall magnitude of the correlations regardless of zygosity (MZ or DZ) indexes a shared environmental effect. But in multivariate analyses, the relevant correlation is across measures, as well as across twins. For example, the correlation is calculated between measure A for twin 1 and measure B for twin 2 in each twin pair. A special case of multivariate analysis of particular interest to developmental science is longitudinal analysis, in which measure A and measure B (possibly the same measure, possibly different ones) are obtained at different points in time. These longitudinal genetic analyses estimate genetic and environmental contributions to continuity and change.

Multivariate analysis can provide either or both of two sets of statistical results. The first set includes an estimate of the genetic correlation, $r_A$, which measures the overlap of genetic influences on the two measures. Roughly speaking, this is the probability that a gene that influences one measure will also influence the other. The shared environment correlation, $r_C$, and the nonshared environment correlation, $r_E$, provide analogous estimates of the overlap of shared environmental influences and of nonshared environmental influences, respectively. The second set of statistics includes bivariate heritability, which is the proportion of the observed phenotypic correlation that is due to common genetic effects; there are comparable statistics for bivariate shared environment and bivariate nonshared environment. Thus, these multivariate techniques allow us to understand more deeply the relationship among different skills (e.g., vocabulary and grammar, oral language and literacy) as well as longitudinal relationships (e.g., language at age 2 and 4). As an example, Hayiou-Thomas, Harlaar, Dale, Bishop, and Plomin (2010) examined the relationship between language and speech measures at 4.5 years and reading measures in the early school years. They observed a phenotypic correlation of .43 between a language composite at 4.5 and a measure of word decoding at 7. The bivariate statistics revealed that most of the correlation (.34, which is 80% of .43) was due to common environmental influences, although some was due to common genetic influences (.08, which is 19% of .43). The genetic and environmental correlations revealed that the environmental influences were essentially identical for both the language composite and word decoding measures (shared environmental correlation of 1.0), but there were substantially different genetic influences (genetic correlation of only .22).

Finally, it is possible to combine the DF and multivariate methods to understand the relationship between extreme performance on two measures. Examples of that approach are presented later in this chapter in the section What Are the Genetic and Environmental Contributions to the Relation Between Early Language and the Outcomes Measures?

Like every research method, the twin design rests on some crucial assumptions, two of which are noted here. The equal environment assumption assumes that environmentally caused similarity is roughly the same for both types of twins. If the assumption were violated because identical twins experience more similar environments and consequently develop more similarly than nonidentical twins, this violation would inflate estimates of genetic influence. There is, in fact, evidence that MZ twins are treated more similarly than their DZ counterparts. For example, as children, MZ twins are more likely than DZ twins to have the same playmates, share the same room, and dress alike. As adults, MZ twins are more likely than same-sex DZ twins to keep in contact (Evans & Martins, 2000). However, the equal environment assumption would only be violated if this greater similarity for MZ twins led to a greater similarity for phenotypes of interest—that is, the feature that shows greater similarity in the environment would need to be one that actually affects the trait of interest. The equal environments assumption has been tested in several ways and appears reasonable for most traits. For example, environmental similarity during childhood does not predict twin similarity in personality, attitudes, intelligence, or a range of psychiatric disorders (Evans & Martin, 2000). Moreover, both greater similarity of parental treatment of MZ twins and greater physical similarity between MZ twins are uncorrelated with twin similarity for personality, vocational interests, and cognitive abilities.

The second assumption is that the results of studies with twins can be safely generalized to singletons. On the whole, this assumption also appears to be valid. Results with twins are generally confirmed by adoption studies when available. In the case of language, although twins are initially a few months behind (Dale et al., 1998), the delay generally disappears prior to school entry, their pattern of language development is the same as that of singletons, and there is agreement between twin and adoption studies with respect to the relative magnitude of genetic and environmental influences.

## THE TWINS EARLY DEVELOPMENT STUDY AND RESULTS CONCERNING LATE TALKERS FROM THE PRESCHOOL YEARS

### Participants

The Twins Early Development Study (TEDS) is a longitudinal study of twins ascertained from population records of live twin births in England and Wales (Kovas, Haworth, Dale, & Plomin, 2007; Oliver & Plomin, 2007). After checking for infant mortality, all families identified by the United Kingdom Office for National Statistics as having twins born in these years were invited to participate in TEDS when the twins were about 18 months old. The twins were assessed on measures of language, cognitive, and behavioral development at 2, 3, 4, 7, 9, 10, 12, and 16 years of age, using a variety of methods, including parent questionnaires, telephone testing, and web-based assessment. Informed consent was obtained by post or online consent forms, and a test administrator was assigned to call the families and provide assistance and encouragement.

Over time, the sample has remained reasonably representative of the U.K. population, as determined by comparison with Office of National Statistics census data (Dale, Harlaar, Hayiou-Thomas, & Plomin, 2010; Oliver & Plomin, 2007).

We excluded from the present analyses data twin pairs with any of the standard set of genetic, medical, and data quality exclusion criteria in TEDS (see Kovas et al., 2007, for details) or severe medical problems. Zygosity was determined by a combination of parent questionnaires at 18 months, 3 years, and 4 years, and by DNA tests for a subsample when the twins' zygosity was doubtful or the parents requested it (Kovas et al., 2007). We included only twins whose first language was English to eliminate variability due to differences in exposure to English. We also included only twins whose parents reported their ethnicity as "white," which was 93% of this U.K. sample. This exclusion was selected to maximize genetic similarity in preparation for later molecular genetic analysis of the sample. Finally, the vocabulary and grammar measures used for defining LTs had to be complete at ages 2, 3, and 4. The final sample for the present analyses thus included 2,794 pairs: 958 MZ pairs, 913 same-sex DZ pairs, and 923 opposite-sex DZ pairs.

## Early Language Measures

*Vocabulary*  At 2 and 3 years of age, children's expressive vocabulary was assessed by parent report, using adaptations of the McArthur-Bates Communicative Development Inventories (CDIs; Fenson et al., 2007). Parents were asked to complete a checklist, indicating which words their children could say (disregarding pronunciation errors). At age 2, 100 words from the full CDIs (Fenson et al., 2000) were selected and anglicized where necessary. At 3 years, 45 words were retained from the 2-year measure, and 55 new words chosen on the basis of literature review and pilot testing to be age-appropriate. This version, which was developed for TEDS, was later distributed more widely as the CDI-III (Fenson et al., 2007). Reliability, internal consistency, and validity information for these two measures is presented in Fenson et al. (2007). For the age 4 measure, 48 new words were chosen on the basis of literature review and pilot testing. Little direct evidence on validity for this measure is available, but several papers have selected children at age 4 on the basis of low parent report and confirmed that assessment with direct testing (Bishop & Hayiou-Thomas, 2008; Hayiou-Thomas, Oliver, & Plomin, 2005; Viding et al., 2003).

*Syntax*  The adapted versions of the CDI used in TEDS also include a measure of children's sentence complexity. At ages 2 and 3, the first question asks whether children are able to combine words, and 12 subsequent items present two sentences with similar meanings, one of which is in a developmentally simpler form (e.g. at 2, "I no do it" vs. "I can't do it"; at 3, "Why he run away" vs. "Why did he run away?"; Fenson et al., 2007). Parents indicate which of the two more closely resembles what their child is able to say. The vocabulary and syntax measures were combined to form a composite language measure at each age. The evidence for validity of the syntax measures is similar to that for vocabulary, discussed previously (Fenson et al., 2007); very high validity for the 2-year measures (concurrent correlations with criterion measures .70–.88), and somewhat lower for the 3-year measure (.60–.75). At age 4, parents were asked to indicate on a scale of 1–6 a global rating of the complexity of their child's language, with 1 being "not yet talking" and 6 being "talking in long and complicated sentences." Although there is little direct evidence for the 4-year measure, etiological analysis of the three syntax measures has produced very similar results (Dionne, Dale, Boivin, & Plomin, 2003; Spinath et al., 2004).

At each age, the standardized vocabulary and grammar scores were averaged, and a $-1.25$ standard deviation ($SD$) criterion was used for defining late talking.

## Nonverbal Ability

The Parent Report of Children's Abilities (PARCA; Oliver et al., 2002; Saudino et al., 1998) consists of both parent-report questions and parent-administered items (e.g., copying shapes, imitating actions). The original 2-year version was extended to include content suitable for 3- and 4-year-old children. Total scores were converted to z-scores relative to the whole sample.

## Additional Family and Early Development Measures

When the twins entered the study, parents provided comprehensive information on prenatal and perinatal events. As noted previously, children with severe medical problems have been excluded from most analyses. However, a binary measure of preterm birth was developed. Because twins are typically born early, the usual criterion of 35 weeks' gestation was too liberal, as it would have included nearly half the sample. Instead, a criterion of less than 33 weeks was used, as it identified approximately 7% of the sample. When the twins were about 9 years old, their parents were asked if either of them had experienced difficulties in learning to talk or to read. This information was used to construct a binary measure of parent history.

## Persistent and Transient Delay During Early Childhood

Two previous papers have investigated the outcomes of early delay within the genetically sensitive design of the TEDS project. Both are focussed on the persistence and transience of delay between age 2 and age 4. In the first paper, Dale, Price, Bishop, and Plomin (2003) defined early language delay (ELD) as vocabulary in the lowest 10% at 24 months on the 100-item vocabulary parent-report checklist. Outcome at age 4 was used to define persistent versus transient early difficulty in two ways. The first approach used parent-report measures of vocabulary, grammar, and abstract language use; specifically, children's outcome was classified as persistent difficulty if their scores on at least two of these three language measures were at or below the 15th percentile. The second approach used parental expression of concern about the child's speech and language or professional involvement for the child as indices of persistent difficulty. Consistent with previous research, only about 40% of the children in the ELD group were classified as showing persistent language difficulties at age 4 on these measures. The odds ratio for ELD as a predictor of persisting difficulty at age 4 was 7.2. A number of phenotypic and environmental measures were weakly, though significantly, related to outcome within the ELD group, including degree of early delay, grammar, displaced reference in language, nonverbal cognition, gender, mother's educational qualifications, and a cumulative ear infection score. But even taken together, the prediction was far too poor to be of clinical use, as at best only 68.5 % of the ELD cases could be correctly classified.

In the second paper, Bishop, Price, Dale, and Plomin (2003) then examined the etiology of these categories, using the twin design. A concordance analysis that was focussed on pairs in which both twins were classified as ELD at age 2 revealed significantly higher concordance for outcome at age 4 for MZ pairs than for DZ pairs, implicating a genetic distinction *within* the ELD group at age 2 related to outcome. This was followed by DF extremes analysis (DeFries & Fulker, 1988) conducted separately for two subsamples of the ELD group at age 2: those whose delay would persist and those whose delay was transient. When the division was done by language measures at age 4, there were no differences in the results. However, DF extremes analysis revealed that heritability of 2-year vocabulary was significantly higher ($h^2_g = .41$) for children who would have professional involvement by age 4 than for children who would not have professional involvement ($h^2_g = .08$). (Further discussion of the difference in results depending on the criteria chosen is provided in Bishop et al., 2003.)

## QUESTIONS FOR THE PRESENT STUDY

In this chapter, we extend the scope of questions beyond those of Dale et al. (2003) and Bishop et al. (2003) in several respects, most notably looking at three outcome measures at later points in development: oral language at 7 and 12 years, and reading at 12 years.

1. What is the etiology of the age 2 and age 3 language measures and the three outcome measures?

2. How much does prediction to these outcome measures improve if we identify LTs at age 3 rather than at age 2?

3. *Within* the set of children identified as LTs at either age, we can use severity of delay as a baseline predictor of outcome. How much can we improve prediction if we add gender, preterm birth, family history of language/reading difficulties, and nonverbal ability as predictors?

4. Based on multivariate analyses, what is the contribution of genetic and environmental factors to change and continuity between each of the two early measures and each of the three outcome measures?

## NEW MEASURES

### Middle Childhood Language Measure: Teacher Assessment

All state schools in England and Wales are required to provide teacher assessments of students' abilities in core academic areas in the latter part of each school year, using the National Curriculum level descriptions provided by the Qualifications and Curriculum Authority (2003). The level descriptions apply from Year 1 through Year 9 of school (ages 6–14). These school years are divided into Key Stage 1 (Years 1 and 2; ages 5–7), Key Stage 2 (Years 3–6; ages 8–11), and Key Stage 3 (Years 7–9; ages 12–14). In the present analyses, we focus on the English: Speaking and Listening scale at Level 1, as detailed in Figure 12.1. On average, a 7-year-old would be expected to perform at Level 2. A score of W or 1 was used to define language impairment; this criterion identified 9.9% of the sample as having impairments.

**W. Not yet functioning at Level 1.**

1  Pupils talk about matters of immediate interest. They listen to others and usually respond appropriately. They convey simple meanings to a range of listeners, speaking audibly, and begin to extend their ideas or accounts by providing some detail.

2  Pupils begin to show confidence in talking and listening, particularly where the topics interest them. On occasions, they show awareness of the needs of the listener by including relevant details. In developing and explaining their ideas they speak clearly and use a growing vocabulary. They usually listen carefully and respond with increasing appropriateness to what others say. They are beginning to be aware that in some situations a more formal vocabulary and tone of voice are used.

3  Pupils talk and listen confidently in different contexts, exploring and communicating ideas. In discussion, they show understanding of the main points. Through relevant comments and questions, they show they have listened carefully. They begin to adapt what they say to the needs of the listener, varying the use of vocabulary and the level of details. They are beginning to be aware of Standard English and when it is used.

4  4+. Speaking and listening are substantially more advanced than most pupils at Level 3.

**Figure 12.1.**  National Curriculum Key Stage 1 (5–7 years) Teacher Assessment Scale for English: Speaking and Listening. Teachers selected one of five boxes to indicate the twins' level of attainment; the criteria are listed above. (From Qualifications and Curriculum Authority, Department of Education. [2003]. *QCA key stage 1. Assessment and reporting arrangements*. Great Britain: Qualifications and Curriculum Authority. © Crown copyright 2013.)

## Adolescent Language Measures

At age 12, participants were assessed on a web-based set of four receptive language measures, all of which are subtests of well-established published test batteries whose manuals report details of test validation and reliability. The development of the web-based battery and details of the testing procedures are reported in Haworth et al. (2007).

*Vocabulary*  The Wechsler Intelligence Scale for Children, Third Edition, UK. Vocabulary Multiple Choice subtest (Wechsler, 1992) was the core semantic measure.

*Nonliteral Semantics*  In addition to vocabulary, semantics was assessed using the Figurative Language subtest of the Test of Language Competence–Expanded Edition, Level 2 (Wiig, Secord, & Sabers, 1989). This subtest assesses the interpretation of idioms and metaphors; correct understanding of such nonliteral language requires rich semantic representation as well as an awareness of the ambiguity of many expressions between their literal and figurative meaning. The child heard a sentence auditorally and chose one of four answers, presented in both written and auditory forms.

*Syntax*  Syntax was assessed using the Listening Grammar subtest of the Test of Adolescent and Adult Language, Third Edition (TOAL-3; Hammill, Brown, Larsen, & Wiederholt, 1994). Children were required to select two sentences that have nearly the same meaning from a set of three options. The sentences were presented auditorily only.

*Pragmatics*  The Making Inferences subtest of the Test of Language Competence–Expanded Edition, Level 2 (Wiig et al., 1989) requires participants to make permissible inferences on the basis of existing, but incomplete, causal relationships in the context of short paragraphs presented orally. The child chose two of four responses, presented in both written and auditory form, that best explained what could have happened.

A latent factor score based on these four receptive language measures was computed, as described in Dale et al. (2010), and a −1.25 *SD* criterion was used to identify language impairment.

## Adolescent Reading Measures

Four reading measures were administered, including two decoding measures and two comprehension measures. Three were administered by web as part of the battery including the language measures just discussed, and one (the Test of Word Reading Efficiency, described in the next section) was administered by telephone (see Harlaar, Kovas, Dale, Petrill, & Plomin, 2012, for further details).

***Word Decoding***   Word decoding was assessed using the Woodcock-Johnson III (WJ-III) Reading Fluency Test (Woodcock, McGrew, & Mather, 2001) and the Test of Word Reading Efficiency (TOWRE; Torgesen, Wagner, & Rashotte, 1999). The WJ-III Reading Fluency Test (98 items) requires participants to read and comprehend simple sentences quickly. The TOWRE (167 items) assesses fluency and accuracy in word reading and phonemic decoding. The WJ-III Reading Fluency Test has a 3-minute time limit, and the TOWRE has a 2-minute time limit.

***Reading Comprehension***   Reading comprehension was assessed using the reading comprehension subtest of the Peabody Individual Achievement Test (PIAT$_{rc}$; Markwardt, 1997) and the GOAL Formative Assessment in Literacy for Key Stage 3 (Global Online Assessment for Learning, 2002). The PIATrc uses a multiple-choice picture format to test literal comprehension of sentences (82 items). The GOAL assessment uses questions about words, sentences, and short paragraphs to assess both literal and inferential reading comprehension (40 items in each category).

The four reading measures were standardized and averaged, and a criterion of −1.25 *SD* was applied to define reading impairment.

## RESULTS

### Who Is a Late Talker?

Do LTs differ from typically developing (TD) children in sufficiently consistent ways that we can predict or explain their LT status? Table 12.1 summarizes the comparison of LTs and TD children on several dimensions that are known to have some association with individual differences in early language development. (As is customary, all nongenetic analyses are based on one randomly selected twin from each pair, to preserve independence of data.) All differences were in the expected direction. At both age 2 and age 3, there were more boys than girls who were LTs, but the difference was relatively small (approximately 1.3:1), as is typical for population-based samples in contrast to clinic-based samples. Mother's educational qualifications (essentially a measure of years of education) were also significantly higher for TD children than LTs, though the difference was small at both ages. For LTs at age 2, there was a somewhat higher incidence of preterm

**Table 12.1.** Comparison of late talkers and typically developing children at 2 and 3 years on selected measures (significance and effect size); based on one randomly selected twin from each pair

| Age | Group (N) | % boys: % girls | Mother's educational qualifications M (SD) | Nonverbal z-score (PARCA) M (SD) | Preterm birth (< 33 weeks) % | Family history of language or reading difficulty |
|---|---|---|---|---|---|---|
| 2 years | LTs 383 | 60.6:39.4[a] | 3.64 (1.86)[a] | −.54 (.98)[a] | 9.7%[a] | 17.3[b] |
| | TD 2,411 | 45.6:54.4 | 3.96 (2.01) | .14 (.93) | 6.7% | 12.7 |
| 3 years | LTs 286 | 59.4:40.6[a] | 3.42 (1.85)[a] | −.78 (.95)[a] | 4.9% | 16.1 |
| | TD 2,508 | 46.3:53.7 | 3.97 (2.00) | .14 (.92) | 7.4% | 13.0 |

[a] $p < .05$.
[b] $p < .10$; all tests two-tailed.
*Key:* LTs, late talkers; TD, typically developing.

birth, and a marginally significant trend for there to be a parent history of early learning difficulty, though neither held for LTs identified at age 3. Finally, nonverbal scores were significantly higher for TD children than for LTs; the difference was moderate at age 2 and large at age 3. This difference is difficult to interpret, however; even though the concepts being tested on the PARCA are considered nonverbal (e.g., counting, shapes), language is often used to communicate the tasks to them, and so some association is to be expected.

Based on these modest relationships, a logistic regression was conducted at both age 2 and age 3. The regression attempted to predict LT status on the basis of gender, parent history, preterm birth, and mother's education. Nonverbal performance was not included, due to its ambiguity. At both ages, parent history and mother's education remained as significant contributors in the final equation, but the prediction was even worse than the default of predicting every child would be TD, which would have 88.7% accuracy despite being completely uninformative. Thus it is not possible with the available measures to predict, much less explain, why some children are slow to develop language.

Although univariate genetic analyses do not identify specific genetic or environmental measures that would explain LT status, they can provide an overall estimate of the role of factors of these two types. The first two rows of Table 12.2 provide this information for LT status at age 2 and age 3. Probandwise concordance is the probability that a twin who is an LT will have an LT co-twin. The concordances are high for both MZ and DZ twins. For example, 89% of the MZ co-twins and 80% of the DZ co-twins of late talking probands were also LTs. This high level in both types of twins suggests a strong family (shared environment) influence. The concordances are somewhat higher for MZ than DZ twins, which suggests a genetic influence as well. The results of the full analysis are shown in the last three columns. The heritability of late talking at 2 is .28, whereas the influence of shared environmental factors is substantially higher, at .66. At age 3, the heritability has increased, and is approximately equal to shared environmental influence.

**Table 12.2.** The etiology of late talking at 2 and 3 years, and impaired performance on outcome measures at 7 and 12 years

| Measure | Probandwise concordance (MZ;DZ) | $h^2_g$ | $c^2_g$ | $e^2_g$ |
|---|---|---|---|---|
| Late talking at 2 | .89;.80 | .28 | .66 | .06 |
| Late talking at 3 | .89;.67 | .49 | .43 | .08 |
| Oral language impairment at 7 | .87;.66 | .51 | .29 | .20 |
| Receptive language impairment at 12 | .66;.51 | .53 | .14 | .33 |
| Reading impairment at 12 | .71;.36 | .75 | .00 | .25 |

*Key:* $h^2_g$, group heritability; $c^2_g$, group shared environment; $e^2_g$, group nonshared environment; MZ, monozygotic; DZ, dizygotic.

Nonshared environmental influence is low at both ages. These analyses confirm that there are important environmental influences, even if they have not yet been identified, as well as genetic influences. At age 2, the environmental influence is stronger than genetic influences.

### What Are the Interrelationships Among and Etiology of the Three Outcome Measures?

Before turning to the central issue of prediction from LT status to later outcomes, it is useful to examine the outcome measures themselves. They are diverse, in that they represent two ages (7 and 12), developmental change, and modality (receptive and expressive oral language vs. reading). The three measures are only modestly related; the contingency coefficient for language impairment at age 7 with language impairment at age 12 was .213; for language impairment at age 12 with reading impairment at age 12 was .299; and for language impairment at age 7 with reading impairment at age 12 was .301. Expressed differently, although there were 110 twins with language impairment at age 7 (a), 153 with language impairment at age 12 (b), and 143 with reading impairment at age 12 (c), only 27 had both a and b, 52 had both b and c, and 47 had both a and c. (Recall that these analyses, like all the phenotypic analyses, are based on one randomly selected twin from each pair.) Thus it is likely that the patterns of prediction from LTs will differ among these outcomes.

Table 12.2 also includes the etiological analysis of these measures. All of them have substantial genetic influence, and it is highest for the reading measure, consistent with previous research. In addition, at this age there is a substantial nonshared environmental influence. As children become older, their experiences are less fully determined by family and more likely to be individual. This is especially likely for children who are having language or academic difficulties (Hayiou-Thomas, Dale, & Plomin, 2013).

### Is Prediction to the Outcome Measures Substantially Better from Age 3 than from Age 2?

We now turn to the core issue of prediction of outcome measures. Table 12.3 summarizes analyses of prediction from LT status at ages 2 and 3 to the three outcome measures. As the fourth and fifth columns illustrate, LT status is clearly a risk factor for later impairment, more so for language than for reading, but the effect is relatively modest, and the great majority of LTs are not in the impaired range later.

The same moderate level of effect is seen for the question of whether prediction is better from age 3 than from age 2. The percentage rates and odds ratios confirm that there is improvement in the prediction, but again it is not large.

## How Much Better Is the Prediction if We Take into Account Severity, Gender, Preterm Birth, Parental History, and Maternal Education?

In practice, LT status alone would not be used to make a significant decision about a child; all available information should be used, based on research on predictive validity of specific measures. LTs vary in the severity of their delay as reflected in their language scores, and several other kinds of information are also likely to be available. In the present study, information on gender, preterm birth, parental history, and maternal education appeared to be the most likely to be useful available measures as predictors *within* the late talking group. For this reason, six logistic regression analyses were performed. In each case, the sample was restricted to children who met the late talking criterion at age 2 or age 3, and the goal was prediction of impairment versus nonimpairment on one of the three outcome measures. With respect to prediction within the late talking group at age 2, the results were almost entirely negative. In no case could the equation predict an impaired outcome, and

**Table 12.3.** Prediction from late talking at 2 and 3 years to outcomes at 7 and 12 years; based on one randomly selected twin from each pair

| Predictor | Outcome measure | Mean outcome score (SD) for LTs and TD twins[a,b] | % LTs impaired at outcome/ % TD impaired at outcome | Odds ratio for delay at outcome relative to baseline |
|---|---|---|---|---|
| Late talking at 2 | Speaking and listening at 7 | LTs: 1.91 (.69) TD: 2.20 (.61) | 21.2/8.3 | 2.97 |
| | Receptive language at 12 | LTs: −.31 (1.04) TD: .08 (.99) | 20.9/10.6 | 2.23 |
| | Reading composite at 12 | LTs: −.19 (1.0) TD: .14 (.98) | 13.7/9.1 | 1.59 |
| Late talking at 3 | Speaking and listening at 7 | LTs: 1.80 (.73) TD: 2.20 (.60) | 26.6/8.3 | 4.00 |
| | Receptive language at 12 | LTs: −.67 (1.04) TD: .11 (.97) | 30.9/9.9 | 4.07 |
| | Reading composite at 12 | LTs: −.42 (1.06) TD: .15 (.96) | 18.4/8.5 | 2.43 |

[a]Standardized z-scores.

[b]All differences between LTs and TD are significant at p < .01.

*Key:* LTs, late talkers; *SD*, standard deviation; TD, typically developing.

thus the best prediction was the default (i.e., that all twins would be nonimpaired), as this gives better than 80% accuracy. With respect to prediction within the late talking group at age 3, the results were very slightly improved, in that a small number of children were predicted to be impaired later, but the prediction had very low sensitivity with respect to later difficulties (in every case, less than .1). Thus, overall it was not possible to predict long-term outcomes for individual children within the late talking group with any degree of accuracy or clinical utility.

## What Are the Genetic and Environmental Contributions to the Relation Between Early Language and the Outcome Measures?

Although the analyses just reported demonstrate only a modest relationship between early LT status and later outcomes, it is of interest to ask about the underlying basis for that relationship. That is, to the extent that low performance on an early language measure is related to low performance on a later measure such as reading, we can ask if it is due to genetic influences acting on both measures, or shared environmental influences, or nonshared environmental influences. This is an example of a multivariate (bivariate when we are comparing just two measures at a time, as is the case here) DF analysis. The fundamental idea is to consider each twin who is low on, say, age 2 language, and ask if his or her co-twin is low on an outcome measure, such as reading—and then compare the results for MZ and DZ twin pairs. Table 12.4 summarizes the results of these analyses.

Before turning to the genetic analysis, it is useful to clarify a measure of the predictive relationship between delay on one measure and delay on another. The third column of the table is one useful way to quantify the relationship, especially as a prelude to genetic analysis. It has sometimes been labeled "phenotypic group correlation" (Oliver, Dale, & Plomin, 2004). It is based on examining, for each twin who is low on one of the measures, how far below the mean *that same twin* is on the other measure, even if he or she does not qualify as impaired on that second measure. As we noted previously, the relationships are small to moderate. The genetic analysis then divides the association listed in the third column into three components, which represent the extent to which the prediction reflects the three broad factors of genetics, shared environment, and nonshared environment. Note

**Table 12.4.**  Genetic and environmental contributions to the relation between late talking and later impairments

| Predictor | Outcome measure and age | Phenotypic association | $h^2_g$ | $c^2_g$ | $e^2_g$ |
|---|---|---|---|---|---|
| Late talking at 2 | Speaking and listening at 7 | .23 | .13 | .08 | .02 |
| | Receptive language at 12 | .27 | .00 | .20 | .07 |
| | Reading composite at 12 | .11 | .00 | .08 | .03 |
| Late talking at 3 | Speaking and listening at 7 | .32 | .14 | .18 | .00 |
| | Receptive language at 12 | .39 | .14 | .24 | .01 |
| | Reading composite at 12 | .26[a] | .13 | .14 | .00 |

[a]The three parameter estimates do not appear to sum to this value due to rounding.

*Key:* $h^2_g$, group heritability; $c^2_g$, group shared environment; $e^2_g$, group nonshared environment.

that the values in the fourth, fifth, and sixth columns of the table add up to the value in the third column.

Consistent with the analyses presented earlier, the third column confirms that prediction is better from age 3 than from age 2. In five of the six cases, the largest contribution to the longitudinal association is shared environment, which includes family and, in most cases, school features. However, in the majority of cases, and especially from age 3, there is a genetic contribution to the association. This finding is consistent with the result in Table 12.2 that late talking has higher heritability at 3 than at 2. One interpretation of this is that late talking at 3 is a more accurate reflection of the child's genetic endowment.

## CONCLUSIONS

The results of this large, population-representative study are generally quite consistent with other smaller studies in that they fit the "half-full/half-empty" metaphor. On the one hand, it is clear that late talking at age 2 or age 3 is a substantial risk factor for later language and reading problems, at least to age 12. On the other hand, our ability to make predictions at an individual level is far from being clinically useful, even when we add in some of the factors known to be related to variability in development, such as gender, parent history of difficulty, preterm birth, and maternal education. Although the prediction is somewhat better from age 3 than from age 2, the improvement is not enough to give confidence to predictions.

To some extent, the failure to predict individual outcomes may reflect some limitations in the present dataset. For example, no early measure of comprehension was included, although the work of Marchman and Fernald (Chapter 8), Paul and Weismer (Chapter 10), Rescorla (Chapter 11), and Thal and colleagues (Chapter 9), among others, suggests that it plays a positive predictive role, as does early gestural ability. Furthermore, the requirement of a very large sample size for behavior genetic analyses meant that no direct measure of either the child or the home environment was available. Information on social/pragmatic development at 24 months may also have a substantial predictive role, as discussed by Paul and Ellis Weismer (Chapter 10). And information about parent–child interaction might, in principle, distinguish late talking that reflects an impoverished environment for language learning from late talking with a purely internal cause. Nevertheless, the relatively negative findings from so many studies suggest that these kinds of measures will have limited success. Process measures, such as those described in Marchman and Fernald (Chapter 8) may be more successful.

The etiological analyses, taking advantage of the twin design, do add a new perspective. Although all of the measures have substantial genetic influence, they also show substantial environmental influence. The pattern is especially strong for the outcomes of late talking, as shown in Table 12.4. This implies that there are environmental—and hopefully malleable—features that can improve the chances of a positive outcome. It is our task to identify them.

## REFERENCES

Bishop, D.V.M., & Hayiou-Thomas, M.E. (2008). Heritability of specific language impairment depends on diagnostic criteria. *Genes, Brain and Behavior, 7,* 365–372.

Bishop, D.V.M., Price, T., Dale, P.S., & Plomin, R. (2003). Outcomes of early language delay: II. Etiology of transient and persistent language difficulties. *Journal of Speech, Language, and Hearing Research, 46,* 561–575.

Dale, P.S., Harlaar, N., Hayiou-Thomas, M.E., & Plomin, R. (2010). The etiology of diverse receptive language skills at 12. *Journal of Speech, Language, & Hearing Research, 53,* 982–992.

Dale, P.S., Price, T.S., Bishop, D.V.M., & Plomin, R. (2003). Outcomes of early language delay: I. Predicting persistent and transient language difficulties at 3 and 4 years. *Journal of Speech, Language, and Hearing Research, 46,* 544–560.

Dale, P.S., Simonoff, E., Bishop, D.M., Eley, T.C., Oliver, B., Price, T.S., . . . Plomin, R. (1998). Genetic influence on language delay in two-year-old children. *Nature Neuroscience, 1*(4), 324–328. doi:10.1038/1142

DeFries, J.C., & Fulker, D.W. (1988). Multiple regression analysis of twin data: Etiology of deviant scores versus individual differences. *Acta Geneticae Medicae et Gemellologiae, 37,* 205–216.

Dionne, G., Dale, P.S., Boivin, M., & Plomin, R. (2003). Genetic evidence for bidirectional effects of early lexical and grammatical development. *Child Development, 74,* 394–412.

Evans, D.M., & Martin, M.G. (2000). The validity of twin studies. *GeneScreen, 1,* 77–79.

Fenson, L., Marchman, V.A., Thal, D.J., Dale, P.S., Reznick, J.S., & Bates, E. (2007). *MacArthur-Bates Communicative Development Inventories (CDIs)* (2nd ed.). Baltimore, MD: Paul H. Brookes Publishing Co.

Fenson, L., Pethick, S., Renda, C., Cox, J.L., Dale, P.S., & Reznick, J.S. (2000). Short-form versions of the MacArthur Communicative Development Inventories. *Applied Psycholinguistics, 21,* 95–116.

Global Online Assessment for Learning. (2002). *GOAL formative assessment: Key Stage 3.* London, United Kingdom: Hodder & Stoughton.

Hammill, D.D., Brown, V.L., Larsen, S.C., & Wiederholt, J.L. (1994). *Test of Adolescent and Adult Language, Third Edition (TOAL-3).* Austin, TX: PRO-ED.

Harlaar, N., Kovas, Y., Dale, P.S., Petrill, S.A., & Plomin, R. (2012). Mathematics is differentially related to reading comprehension and word decoding: Evidence from a genetically sensitive design. *Journal of Educational Psychology, 104,* 622–635.

Harlaar, N., Spinath, F.M., Dale, P.S., & Plomin, R. (2005). Genetic influences on early word recognition abilities and disabilities: A study of 7-year-old twins. *Journal of Child Psychology and Psychiatry, 46*(4), 373–384. doi:10.1111/j.1469–7610.2004.00358.x

Haworth, C.M.A., Harlaar, N., Kovas, Y., Davis, O.S., Oliver, B.R., Hayiou-Thomas, M.E., . . . Plomin, R. (2007). Internet cognitive testing of large samples needed in genetic research. *Twin Research and Human Genetics, 10,* 554–563.

Hayiou-Thomas, M.E., Dale, P.S., & Plomin, R. (2013). *Language impairment from 4 to 12 years: Prediction and etiology.* Manuscript under review.

Hayiou-Thomas, M.E., Harlaar, N., Dale, P.S., Bishop, D.V.M., & Plomin, R. (2010). Preschool language skills and reading at 7, 9 and 10 years: Etiology of the relationship. *Journal of Speech, Language, and Hearing Research, 53,* 311–332.

Hayiou-Thomas, M.E., Oliver, B., & Plomin, R. (2005). Genetic influences on specific versus non-specific language impairment in 4-year-old twins. *Journal of Learning Disabilities, 38,* 222–232.

Kovas, Y., Haworth, C.M.A., Dale, P.S., & Plomin, R. (2007). The genetic and environmental origins of learning abilities and disabilities in the early school years. *Monographs of the Society for Research in Child Development, 72*(3), 1–144.

Kovas, Y., Hayiou-Thomas, M.E., Oliver, B., Dale, P.S., Bishop, D.M., & Plomin, R. (2005). Genetic influences in different aspects of language development: The etiology of language skills in 4.5-year-old twins. *Child Development, 76*(3), 632–651. doi:10.111 1/j.1467–8624.2005.00868

Markwardt, F.C., Jr. (1997). *Peabody Individual Achievement Test–Revised–Normative Update.* Bloomington, MN: Pearson Assessments.

Oliver, B., Dale, P.S., & Plomin, R. (2004). Verbal and nonverbal predictors of early language problems: An analysis of twins in early childhood back to infancy. *Journal of Child Language, 31,* 609–631.

Oliver, B., Dale, P.S., Saudino, K.J., Petrill, S.A., Pike, A., & Plomin, R. (2002). The validity of a parent-based assessment of the nonverbal cognitive abilities of three-year-olds. *Early Child Development and Care, 17,* 337–348.

Oliver, B.R., & Plomin, R. (2007). Twins Early Development Study (TEDS): A multivariate, longitudinal genetic investigation of language, cognition and behavior problems from childhood through adolescence. *Twin Research and Human Genetics, 10,* 96–105.

Plomin, R., DeFries, J.C., McClearn, G.E., & McGuffin, P. (2008). *Behavioral genetics* (5th ed.). New York, NY: Worth.

Qualifications and Curriculum Authority. (2003). *QCA key stage 1. Assessment and reporting arrangements.* Great Britain: Author.

Saudino, K.J., Dale, P.S., Oliver, B., Petrill, S.A., Richardson, V., Rutter, M., . . . Plomin, R. (1998). The validity of parent-based assessment of the cognitive abilities of two-year-olds. *British Journal of Developmental Psychology, 16,* 349–363.

Spinath, F.M., Price, T.S., Dale, P.S., & Plomin, R. (2004). The genetic and environmental origins of language disability and ability. *Child Development, 75,* 445–454.

Torgesen, J.K., Wagner, R.K., & Rashotte, C.A. (1999). *Test of Word Reading Efficiency.* Austin, TX: PRO-ED.

Viding, E., Price, T.S., Spinath, F.M., Bishop, D.V., Dale, P.S., & Plomin, R. (2003). Genetic and environmental mediation of the relationship between language and nonverbal impairment in 4-year-old twins. *Journal of Speech, Language, and Hearing Research, 46,* 1271–1282.

Wechsler, D. (1992). *Wechsler Intelligence Scale for Children manual* (3rd ed., UK; WISC-III-UK). London, United Kingdom: Psychological Corporation.

Wiig, E.H., Secord, W., & Sabers, D. (1989). *Test of Language Competence* (Expanded ed.). San Antonio, TX: Psychological Corporation.

Woodcock, R.W., McGrew, K.S., & Mather, N. (2001). *Woodcock-Johnson III Tests of Achievement.* Itasca, IL: Riverside Publishing.

# Interventions

# 13

# From Words to Early Sentences

*Parent-Implemented*
*Intervention for Late-Talking Toddlers*

Luigi Girolametto, Elaine Weitzman, and Cindy Earle

There are three alternative recommendations for the clinical management of late-talking toddlers: "wait and see," "watch and see" (Paul, 1996), and early intervention (Girolametto, Pearce, & Weitzman, 1996; Robertson & Ellis Weismer, 1999). A wait and see approach implies no action, whereas Paul (1996) describes a watch and see approach as careful and consistent monitoring with reevaluations every 3–6 months during the preschool period. The intervention model presented in this chapter advocates a proactive stance to the management of late-talking toddlers and recommends a short-term, parent-implemented early intervention. Parent-implemented interventions, in which parents learn to integrate language intervention strategies into their daily routines, are minimally intrusive for the child, cost effective, and time efficient. Recommended practices dictate that early intervention services provided to children and their families should be family centered, with the ultimate goal of empowering families and enhancing their sense of competence and self-worth (Prelock & Hutchins, 2008). Empowering parents of late-talking toddlers involves supporting and strengthening their capacity to access knowledge and gain practical skills that, in turn, bolsters their sense of self-efficacy in relation to fostering their child's development (Dempsey & Dunst, 2004). Teaching parents to facilitate their child's language skills enables them to play a major role in their child's development and is a critical component of any early language intervention program (Roberts & Kaiser, 2011).

Parent-implemented language intervention programs have been shown to have positive, significant effects on children's receptive and expressive language skills (Roberts & Kaiser, 2011). The parent-implemented model shifts the role of the speech-language pathologist (SLP) from direct interventionist to one of facilitator or mediator who forms a therapeutic alliance with parents to help them acquire the skills that are known to improve children's language outcomes (American Speech-Language-Hearing Association [ASHA], 2008b).

Considering that children who are late talkers (LTs) are frequently referred for intervention at a very young age, training their parents to be their child's language facilitator is an ideal avenue for supporting the child's development. Target Word–The Hanen Program for Parents of Children who are Late Talkers (Earle & Lowry, 2011a) allows parents to gain the interactive skills to make language intervention an ongoing process in their child's natural environment. This program was developed to meet the needs of toddlers ages 16–30 months, focusing on building expressive vocabulary through responsive, child-centered interactions with their parents. Target Word is one of four Hanen programs for parents. The other three programs include 1) It Takes Two to Talk–The Hanen Program for Parents of Children with Language Delays (Pepper & Weitzman, 2004), 2) More Than Words–The Hanen Program for Parents of Children on the Autism Spectrum (Sussman, 1999), and 3) TalkAbility–The Hanen Program for Parents of Verbal Children on the Autism Spectrum (Sussman, 2006). More Than Words is designed to improve the social interactions (e.g., joint attention, initiations) and early communicative abilities (e.g., pragmatic intentions, vocabulary) of children with autism spectrum disorders. Talkability differs from More Than Words in that it is for children with autism spectrum disorders who speak in sentences and focuses on improving their theory of mind in order to build their conversational and peer interaction skills.

The Hanen parent-implemented programs are offered to small groups of parents and are led by SLPs who have received specialized training in the delivery of a specific program. Each program has its own supportive resource materials for both parents and the SLP. Although formats vary somewhat from program to program, all Hanen programs combine a series of group training sessions for caregivers with individual consultations that include video recording the parent–child interaction and providing feedback to the parents.

The first section of this chapter describes the various roles of the speech-language pathologist in the Target Word program. The second section summarizes the research completed using parent-implemented intervention with toddlers who were LTs and the evidence base that was used to create the Target Word program. The third section describes the Target Word program's content and format in more detail. Finally, the last section concludes with an informal evaluation of the Target Word program's effect using consumer satisfaction data and one case study.

## WORKING WITH PARENTS IN THE TARGET WORD PROGRAM

In leading a parent-implemented intervention program, the SLP's focus is on helping the parent learn specific responsive language strategies that are known to facilitate children's expressive language development. This parent-implemented approach requires the SLP to expand the role of service provider to include three distinct roles: early language interventionist, adult educator, and coach (Girolametto & Weitzman, 2006).

## SPEECH-LANGUAGE PATHOLOGIST AS EARLY LANGUAGE INTERVENTIONIST

The role of early language interventionist is fundamental to the successful outcome of the Target Word program. In this role, the SLP draws on his or her therapeutic expertise in order to help parents learn the program's responsive language strategies. In order to facilitate parents' learning, the SLP must him- or herself be able to apply these language strategies effectively in interactions with children and to demonstrate this to parents (Wlodkowski, 1993). This includes being able to adapt or modify the application of the strategy to ensure maximum effectiveness for individual children. Being an effective interventionist also allows the SLP to observe the parents' interactions with the child and to identify whether the program strategy is being effectively implemented and, if not, how to modify it (ASHA, 2008a; Girolametto & Weitzman, 2006; Kaiser & Hancock, 2003).

## SPEECH-LANGUAGE PATHOLOGIST AS ADULT EDUCATOR

The second role of the SLP is that of adult educator. The SLP's ability to support the child in a parent-implemented intervention program is dependent on his or her skill as an educator in facilitating the parents' acquisition and generalization of the program's strategies. This requires recognition of parents as adult learners who have diverse learning styles, abilities, and levels of motivation. It also requires these factors to be accommodated within the format of the program. One important aspect of accommodating the needs of a diverse group of adult learners involves using teaching methods that match their various learning preferences at least some of the time.

Like all Hanen programs, the Target Word program uses a four-part teaching-learning cycle that facilitates skill acquisition while addressing four different learning styles that reflect varying preferences for perceiving and processing information (Kolb, 1984). Each of the program's responsive strategies is taught by guiding learners sequentially through this four-part cycle, with each learning style being addressed within one part of the cycle. This approach to facilitating behavior change in parents who participate in a parent program is motivated by the assumption that, although learners feel most comfortable in the part of the cycle that matches their learning style, they must participate fully in each part of the cycle in order to learn to apply the responsive strategy effectively.

The first part of the teaching-learning cycle introduces the topic and provides the rationale for what is being learned. This addresses the needs of learners who require a "big picture" view of what is to be learned and why it is important (MacKeracher, 1996). To this end, teaching a strategy begins with parents participating in a concrete, experiential activity that is used to illustrate the rationale for use of the strategy, while drawing on their background knowledge and life experiences. An example of this might involve a simulated interaction between two parents who have been given specific instructions in terms of use of a communicative strategy in an adult–adult conversation. Then, in a small or large group, parents analyze the effect of the strategy on the interaction between the two adults. The SLP relates these conclusions to interactions with children, providing the context and rationale for use of that specific communicative strategy within the family's daily interactions. For example, having parents analyze the variety of ways adults send important nonverbal messages to each other in a noisy environment enables the SLP to facilitate parents' recognition of the many ways children communicate nonverbally. It also highlights the fact that because LTs use few or no words, they use a wide variety of nonverbal means to communicate.

The second part of the teaching-learning cycle involves presenting specific information about each strategy. This part of the cycle accommodates the preferences of learners who enjoy obtaining new information from reading books or from listening to experts who provide information that expands their understanding of the topic (MacKeracher, 1996). Presentations in a program session involve the SLP providing information that facilitates parents' understanding of why a strategy is important and how it is applied for children at different developmental stages. Using varied media such as flip charts, PowerPoint slides, and relevant props, new information is presented in an interesting and engaging manner, along with video examples of a specific strategy to demonstrate its real-life application (Girolametto & Weitzman, 2006). Group discussion and individualization of program content are an integral part of presenting new material because this facilitates learning (MacKeracher, 1996). This includes asking parents focused questions, such as why they think a strategy (e.g., waiting for an initiation) might be effective in facilitating a particular communication skill, when the strategy would best be applied during their everyday interactions with their child (e.g., bath time, putting the child in the car seat), and how they expect their child to respond to it (e.g., gestures, vocalizations, word attempts). The presentation always includes discussion in relation to the strategy's application to each individual child in the group, ensuring that the information remains practical and individualized.

The third stage of the teaching-learning cycle involves application and practice of newly learned skills in simulated contexts and engagement of the learner in evaluating the effect of the applied skill (Trivette, Dunst, Hamby, & O'Herin, 2009). This part of the cycle appeals to parents who learn best through experiential activities once they have a basic understanding of the task and goals (MacKeracher, 1996). Opportunities for simulated practice frequently involve role plays (e.g., enacting how parents might join their child's play with toys by imitating the child's play). Prior to the role play, parents are given specific instructions regarding the context for application of the strategy with a partner who role-plays the child. Because learners need feedback about how close their performance is to the specific strategy being taught, there is always a debriefing after the role play (MacKeracher, 1996). This involves the SLP asking parents to reflect on how well they think they applied the strategy, what was difficult, and how the parent role-playing the child felt about the parent's use of the strategy. It may also include a discussion on how parents can use metacognitive techniques to remind themselves to use the responsive strategy or to modify their behavior if they realize they are not using the strategy correctly (Clarke, 1984; Paris & Winograd, 1990). An example of a metacognitive strategy used by parents involves having them put a list of their child's target words on the refrigerator to remind the parents to think about and apply a *focused stimulation* strategy aimed at these target words. Another context for application of newly learned skills involves setting a problem-solving task for parents, such as watching a video of a parent–child interaction and analyzing whether or not the strategy was applied effectively. If the parents conclude that the strategy was not applied effectively, they are asked to suggest how the parent could have modified his or her behavior. In addition, brainstorming activities are used to facilitate application of new learning. For example, parents may be asked to suggest solutions for expanding their child's play when he or she is engaged in restricted pretend play sequences.

The fourth and final component of the teaching-learning cycle involves individualized planning for implementation of the strategy in the home (Clarke, 1984;

Girolametto & Weitzman, 2006). This is accomplished by the parent developing a written plan with respect to how he or she will apply the strategy to facilitate the child's achievement of his or her communication goals. Although this stage of the teaching-learning cycle appeals to learners who prefer to jump in and try it, it is an important step for all parents because the more specific the plan, the more likely it is to be implemented. The outcome of the plan is shared with the large group at the next session.

In the role of adult educator, the SLP is an expert facilitator, helping parents adjust to the new environment, guiding them in their learning and helping them apply new knowledge and skills to interactions with their own child. As the group forms and establishes its own identity, the SLP's role changes. Initially, he or she bears much of the responsibility for leading the group and setting up learning activities that encourage interaction among its members. Once the group is comfortable in the learning environment and parents come to rely on one another as sources of support and information, the SLP further adjusts his or her role. The SLP facilitates more autonomy on the part of the parent group by setting up activities in which parents can take more responsibility for their own learning. The role of adult educator in a parent-implemented intervention program is dynamic, requiring a skillful shifting of roles as the SLP supports the parents to become more autonomous, independent learners who acquire skills they can generalize to a variety of interactions with their child (Clarke, 1984; Girolametto & Weitzman, 2006).

## SPEECH-LANGUAGE PATHOLOGIST AS COACH

The final role of the SLP is that of coach. Coaching is an adult learning strategy that supports the parent in improving existing skills, gaining new skills, or gaining a greater understanding of current skills. Coaching involves collaboration with parents in which the parents and SLP share their skills, knowledge, and expertise with the ultimate goal of increasing the parents' capacity to support their child's development (Rush & Sheldon, 2008). For example, the role of coach is assumed when the SLP works with the family to choose their child's vocabulary goals and select program strategies to achieve these goals (e.g., label, expand). When working with parents, this aspect of the SLP's role is critical to empowering the parent to implement strategies independently and flexibly across contexts.

Although the SLP assumes the role of coach intermittently throughout the program, a more specific context for coaching occurs during the two individual consultations, when parents are video recorded while interacting with their child. In this context, the parent draws on what has been learned to demonstrate the use of program strategies while the SLP observes. From time to time, the SLP may provide a brief but specific suggestion that allows the parent to modify his or her behavior (Kaiser & Hancock, 2003). For example, the SLP might say, "Remember to *wait* to give her a chance to imitate." The result of this coaching during a parent–child interaction is usually a change in the parent's interactive behavior, an enhanced response from the child, and a more successful interaction that the SLP and parent then review while watching the video recorded interaction together (Girolametto & Weitzman, 2006; Hanft, Rush, & Shelden, 2004). Thus, the purpose of coaching during individual consultations is to offer specific feedback to help a parent apply a strategy appropriately.

Another context for coaching occurs when the parent and SLP review the video recorded parent–child interaction together right after it has been filmed. In this situation, the SLP's role of coach becomes one of supporting the parent's continual improvement, and the optimal approach uses a reflective discussion, which is a core component of coaching and should take place immediately after the video recording (Hanft et al., 2004). Reflective discussion includes the coach's targeted questions, active listening, informational feedback, and provision of relevant information to promote the parent's learning through a process of self-discovery. Rather than telling parents where they need to improve and exactly what they need to change, the coach uses the video recording to help parents discover what they are already doing well, what requires further modification, and how to make the necessary changes. The ultimate goal of the coaching process during the postvideo discussion is to blend the learner's new and existing skills and to promote self-observation, self-evaluation, and self-reflection (Girolametto & Weitzman, 2006; Hanft et al., 2004; Rush & Shelden, 2011).

As a coach, the SLP's ability to listen to what the parent says in response to questions about the video recorded interaction is critical in terms of providing opportunities for the sharing of ideas, feelings, and concerns. Attentive listening also provides valuable insights into the parent's level of self-awareness and awareness of the child's needs and abilities. Appreciation of the parent's stage in the learning process determines how the SLP facilitates the reflective discussion. For example, if the parent demonstrates little awareness of the fact that he or she was not following the child's lead until he or she was coached, the SLP needs to highlight the before-coaching and after-coaching sections of the video recording to show the difference in the parent's behavior and its impact on the child's response. However, if the parent demonstrates intermittent use of a strategy and is aware of this, the SLP can work toward helping the parent use the strategy more consistently.

Coaching during a video recording and feedback session also involves providing some specific feedback on parents' use of strategies. Feedback can be helpful in terms of offering new insights or perspectives on the parent's skills and should be precise and informative, as opposed to evaluative (Hanft et al., 2004). In effect, this means that feedback should provide knowledge of results so parents can use it to modify their behavior or cement emerging skills (Bruner, 1968). By linking the child's positive response to the parent's behavior (e.g., "When you repeated the word *jump* and waited while he was jumping up and down, he said 'jump'"), the parent views him- or herself as the locus of causality for the child's improvement, which increases the parent's intrinsic motivation to continue to learn and apply his or her learning. This kind of feedback is more effective than extrinsic rewards such as praise, which does not support a parent's sense of autonomy or self-efficacy and does not facilitate generalization of new behaviors (Wlodkowski, 1993).

## RESEARCH ON PARENT-IMPLEMENTED
## INTERVENTION WITH LATE-TALKING TODDLERS

The Target Word program is an outgrowth of an efficacy study using The Hanen Centre's It Takes Two to Talk program with a group of toddlers with expressive vocabulary delays. The efficacy study results demonstrated that the parent-implemented program, modified to include focused stimulation, accelerated the expressive language development of late-talking toddlers compared with a no-treatment control group (Girolametto et al., 1996; Girolametto, Pearce, & Weitzman, 1997). In focused stimulation, the parent repeats a specific goal (e.g., a target word) three to five times within a brief and meaningful interaction. The outcomes of this study were used to inform clinical practice with respect to children with delayed expressive vocabulary development and led to the creation of a program specifically designed for late-talking toddlers. The results of this research are discussed in more detail in this section.

The It Takes Two to Talk program was the intervention model used in this research. This parent-implemented intervention program was considered to be suitable for young toddlers because it focused on language stimulation in natural settings using naturalistic strategies. This intervention was considered to be a cost- and time-effective service delivery model, given the young age of the children and the involvement of parents as primary change agents.

A community sample of 25 toddlers with expressive vocabulary delays were recruited from waiting lists for assessment in a large metropolitan city. The children were between 23 and 33 months of age and were at the single-word stage of language development. None of the children had sensory impairments (e.g., hearing loss) or oral motor problems, nor did they have frank neurological problems, pervasive developmental disorders, or autism, as determined informally by an SLP at the intake assessment. English was the only language spoken in the homes for all 25 children. A full description of the children's characteristics and study results can be found in Girolametto et al. (1996, 1997).

Based on an assessment performed at intake into the study, the children had vocabulary sizes that ranged from 8 to 18 words, placing all of them in the lower 5th percentile on the MacArthur Communicative Development Inventories (CDIs; Fenson et al., 1993). A 30-minute language sample was transcribed to yield further information on the children's language development. The language sample consisted of two 15-minute video recordings of parent–child interactions (filmed 1 week apart). Based on the language sample, 5 of the 25 children produced a few two-word utterances. The five children who combined words used between one and six two-word combinations in total, and according to parent report, these phrases had been learned as single units (e.g., "want tea"). In addition, four children had receptive language delays that were greater than 6 months as measured by the Sequenced Inventory of Communication Development (SICD; Hedrick, Prather, & Tobin, 1984).

All 25 children and their mothers participated in an 11-week parent-implemented intervention program that included eight evening sessions for parents and three home visits to individualize the information for families. The strategies taught to parents included focused stimulation of target words coupled with responsive language strategies that are consistent with social-interactionist perspectives of language acquisition (e.g., expand children's utterances, use self-talk, follow the child's lead). Theoretically, this interactive model of language intervention assumes that teaching parents to increase their responsiveness and decrease directiveness will provide increased opportunities for their children to participate in interaction. In turn, these increased opportunities to participate in reciprocal interactions provide children with simplified and responsive language input from which children can learn advanced sociocommunicative skills and language.

Half of the children and their mothers (i.e., 12) were randomly assigned to the first treatment group, whereas the remainder (i.e., 13) was assigned to a waiting list control group. This permitted a comparison of treatment effects to a control group that did not receive treatment. The mothers and children in the control group received the same intervention program immediately after the program post-test. Based on the children's vocabularies at intake (i.e., their pretest assessment results), 10 target words were individually selected for each of the 25 children. The target words were given to the mothers in the experimental group but were not shared with mothers in the control group. All target words started with a consonant that was within the child's phonetic repertoire, was a word that the child comprehended, and was a word that the child did not use expressively as determined by parent report and direct probe using toys and objects. The mothers were coached to select target words that were meaningful and motivating for their children and that had the potential to occur frequently in their daily routines. Finally, target words were selected to represent both action words (i.e., verbs) and nouns.

The effect of the 11-week program was measured on the mothers as well as on the children. Greater detail can be found in Girolametto et al. (1996, 1997). Following the intervention, the mothers in the experimental group used fewer words per minute and a shorter mean length of utterance (morphemes) than mothers in the control group. In addition, mothers in the experimental group used target words and focused stimulation (three repetitions of the target words) more often than the mothers in the control group. Thus, mothers in the experimental group learned to speak more slowly and simplify their utterances. They also learned to use the focused stimulation strategy and applied it appropriately to the target words assigned to their children.

The results for the children were highly positive (see Table 13.1 for a summary). Following intervention, the children in the experimental group had a significantly larger vocabulary as measured by the CDIs. In addition, these children used a significantly greater number of different words in free-play interaction with their parents and a significantly greater number of target words relative to the control group.

**Table 13.1.** Mean (*SD*) values for children's outcomes at posttest

| Measure | Experimental group (*n* = 12) | Control group (*n* = 13) | *p* |
|---|---|---|---|
| Vocabulary size (CDIs) | 187.7 (181) | 65.4 (66) | ≤ .05 |
| Number of different words (free play) | 64.5 (46) | 25.2 (22) | ≤ .01 |
| Number of target words (probes) | 5.9 (3.3) | 3.3 (2.5) | ≤ .05 |
| Number of word combinations (free play) | 43.4 (61) | 11.5 (23) | ≤ .05 |
| Number of CVC and CVCV syllable structures (free play) | 17.6 (11) | 7.5 (9) | ≤ .01 |
| Number of early consonants | 8.0 (4) | 4.5 (3) | ≤ .05 |
| Number of middle consonants | 4.2 (2) | 1.8 (2) | ≤ .05 |
| Number of late consonants | 1.4 (1) | 0.7 (1) | ≤ .05 |

From Girolametto, L., Pearce, P., & Weitzman, E. (1996). Interactive focused stimulation for toddlers with expressive vocabulary delays. *Journal of Speech and Hearing Research, 39*(6), 1274–1283 and Girolametto, L., Pearce, P., & Weitzman, E. (1997). Effects of lexical intervention on the phonology of late talkers. *Journal of Speech, Language, and Hearing Research, 40*(1), 338–348; adapted by permission. © 1996 and 1997 American Speech-Language-Hearing Association

*Key:* CDIs, MacArthur Communicative Development Inventories (Fenson et al., 1993); CVC, consonant-vowel-consonant; CVCV, consonant-vowel-consonant-vowel. *Note:* Early consonants include /h, w j, m, n, d, p, b, f/; middle consonants include /k, g, t, s, dʒ, ŋ/; and late consonants include /v, l, r, θ, ð, tʃ, ʒ, ʃ/ (Irwin & Wong, 1983).

The children in the experimental group also used significantly more multi-word combinations during free play language samples relative to the control group, showing program effects on word combining. In their word structure, children in the experimental group used significantly more consonant-vowel-consonant (CVC) and consonant-vowel-consonant-vowel (CVCV) syllable types and a greater number of different consonants. Thus, the effects of the parent-implemented intervention were observed not only on vocabulary but also on the children's production of word combinations and phonology.

After the intervention was completed, we examined the relation of maternal strategies to language outcomes to determine which of the parental strategies was most highly correlated with children's treatment gains (Girolametto, Weitzman, Wiigs, & Pearce, 2000). The results revealed robust correlations between maternal imitations and expansions and children's language progress as measured by the number of different words, the number of word combinations, and the expressive language score on the SICD. For this group of children, maternal strategies that repeated or built on the children's utterances appeared to be most highly related to advances in language development.

Approximately 3 years later, when the children were between 5 and 6 years of age, 21 of the 25 families agreed to a follow-up assessment. The 21 children were between 64 and 70 months of age. Because all of the families had now participated in the program, a comparison group of typically developing (TD) children, matched for age and sex, were also recruited to permit comparison to same-age peers (Girolametto, Wiigs, Smyth, Weitzman, & Pearce, 2001). Following their involvement in the parent-implemented intervention, 13 of the 21 families of late-talking toddlers had participated in subsequent speech and language therapy: Five received direct intervention for articulation disorders, six received direct intervention for both articulation and language disorders, and the families of the two remaining children received home programs and follow-up assessments every 6 months. Relative to the comparison group of TD children, the 21 late-talking children received lower scores on the Test of Language Development–Primary, Second Edition (TOLD-P:2; Newcomer & Hammill, 1988), the Preschool Language Assessment Instrument (PLAI; Blank, Rose, & Berlin, 1978), and narrative competence as determined by narrative stage and cohesion scores from a story generation task using a book titled *A Boy, A Dog, and a Frog* (Mayer, 1967). Effect sizes (measured as Cohen's *d* score) were large for the significant differences obtained on the TOLD-P:2, PLAI, and the cohesion score on the narrative generation task. The effect size for narrative stage was medium. Thus, the children in the LT group were significantly different from their age-matched peers on a range of language measures, including semantic, syntactic, and narrative skills.

In summary, the majority of the late-talking children performed within normal limits on norm-referenced tests of language development by 5 years of age. However, group comparisons with TD peers indicated that the late-talking children continued to exhibit multiple language weaknesses relative to peers in skills tapping classroom discourse, grammatical perspective taking, and narrative ability. Thus, on tasks designed to "stress the language system" (e.g., perspective taking, abstract language, narratives), the late-talking children continued to demonstrate significant difficulties. The large effect sizes obtained in this study indicated that the group comparisons yielded important findings.

The conclusion we derived from following a group of 21 late-talking toddlers to age 6 years is that an early parent-implemented intervention is effective relative to a wait and see approach (i.e., the waiting list control group). We estimated conservatively that parents who adopted the program strategies for a total of 84 hours during the 11-week intervention—that is, for 2 hours a day for the final 6 weeks (this assumed that parents first learning the strategies would take up to 5 weeks to begin applying them consistently and across the day). Thus, parents delivered an intensive intervention that boosted children's language development from the single-word stage to word combining. However, more than half of the children (i.e., 62%) required additional intervention during the preschool years, and at 5 years, these children still scored significantly lower than a comparison group on all language measures. Consequently, monitoring LTs as they enter the school system and providing successive interventions may be necessary to ensure their developmental progress across the preschool and school-age years.

## DESCRIPTION OF THE TARGET WORD PROGRAM

The results of this research with late-talking children led to the development of a parent-implemented program that would deliver a similar intensity of intervention as It Takes Two to Talk, but with fewer contacts with the SLP. Consistent with the aim of providing a less costly and less intrusive intervention for late-talking children (who are not identified as having a language disorder), the number of parent sessions in the Target Word program was reduced from eight to five, and the number of individual consultations from three to two. Content from the three evening sessions that were omitted from the original program were integrated by 1) combining the information from the first two sessions (Let Your Child Initiate and Follow Your Child's Lead) and 2) amalgamating information from two sessions on book reading and music into one session on play.

The Target Word program consists of a preprogram assessment, five group sessions, and two individual consultation sessions with video recording and feedback (see Table 13.2 for a week-by-week schedule). Group sessions are offered once every 2 weeks over a 10- to 12-week period to groups of six to eight families. This

**Table 13.2.** Schedule for the Target Word program (Earle & Lowry, 2011a)

| Time frame | Session and content |
| --- | --- |
| Prior to program | Preprogram assessment |
| Week 1 | Introductory Session: Getting Started |
| Week 2 | Session 1: Let Your Child Lead |
| Week 3 | No session |
| Weeks 4 and 5 | Individual Consultation 1 |
| Week 6 | Session 2: Continue the Conversation |
| Week 7 | No session |
| Week 8 | Session 3: Expand Your Child's Message |
| Week 9 | No session |
| Weeks 10 and 11 | Individual Consultation 2 |
| Week 12 | Session 4: Expand Your Child's Play |

*Note:* There are no sessions during Weeks 3, 7, and 9 to allow parents time to consolidate their learning.

spaced training gives parents sufficient time to practice the program's strategies and observe their effect on the child's communication skills. These parent programs are offered by a Hanen-certified SLP who leads the program as specified in the *Target Word Making Hanen Happen Leader's Guide* (Earle & Lowry, 2011a), which is a manual outlining the content and format for each session. The *Leader's Guide* is supported by a DVD that contains PowerPoint slides with embedded video examples.

Children are referred to this program if they are

- 16–20 months of age and using fewer than 24 words

- 21–24 months of age and using fewer than 40 words

- 24–30 months of age and using fewer than 100 words and/or using limited word combinations

- Positive for the presence of at least two risk factors (see Table 13.3) and have no other developmental concerns

These criteria for late-talking children are derived from the work of Rescorla (1991) and Paul (1993) and are designed to capture young children who fall below the 15th percentile on the MacArthur-Bates Communicative Development Inventories (CDIs; Fenson et al., 2007). Essential to the definition is that the child must be positive for the presence of additional risk factors but have no other developmental concerns. Risk factors can be found in Table 13.3 and are derived from the work of Olswang, Rodriguez, and Timler (1998).

## Preprogram Assessment

Prior to the program, children and their parents participate in a preprogram assessment. Parents bring with them a completed CDI form, which is mailed to them several weeks before the appointment. During the assessment, the SLP observes a 15- to 20-minute free play interaction between the parent and child and notes

**Table 13.3.**   Risk factors that may indicate language delays

Quiet as an infant/limited babbling

Delayed comprehension skills

Family history of language delay

Low socioeconomic status or limiting parent interaction style

Limited consonant repertoire

Limited gesture use

Presence of social/behavior problems

Continuous history of otitis media

No spontaneous verbal imitation

Limited change over time

Lack of sequenced pretend play

Limited vocabulary consisting mainly of nouns

*Source:* Olswang, Rodriguez, and Timler (1998).

information about the child's play skills, repertoire of speech sounds, nonverbal communication, gesture use, and pragmatics. After the observation, the SLP may interact with the child for a few minutes to determine the child's stimulability for pretend play and word imitation. Next, the SLP administers a receptive test of language development to rule out a significant receptive language delay. The SLP and parents then complete a survey of risk factors (see Table 13.3) and review the child's list of speech sounds together. Finally, the parents and SLP agree on the child's communication goal. Each child in the program will have one of four communication goals: 1) increase the frequency of vocalizations and/or word approximations, 2) increase the frequency of spontaneous imitation of words, 3) increase the frequency of spontaneous word use, or 4) increase the frequency of word combinations. At the end of the assessment parents are asked to confirm their commitment to participating in the program and to consider attending with another caregiver, if possible.

## Introductory Session: Getting Started

The introductory session is 2 hours long and has several key components, including a description of communication development, an overview of the program and its purpose, and an introduction to several responsive strategies (e.g., face-to-face interaction, focused stimulation). For the purposes of the program, focused stimulation is defined as the repetition of a target word at least five times within a joint activity without pressure for the child to imitate or say the word (e.g., Ellis Weismer & Robertson, 2006). A variety of examples of parents using focused stimulation are presented, illustrating how program strategies can fit into the family's existing routines with their child. At the end of the session parents receive the *Target Word Parent Handbook* (Earle & Lowry, 2011b), which includes specific information about the program strategies, pages to take notes, home activity sheets, and charts/diaries for tracking their child's progress.

## Session 1: Let Your Child Lead

Session 1 is 2.5 hours long and occurs 1 week after the introductory session. The session starts with a debriefing of the parents' home activities and an opportunity for parents to ask questions and comment on the assigned readings. The new information focuses on establishing joint interactions and creating opportunities for the child to communicate. Specifically, parents are taught the importance of being face to face with their child and observing, waiting, and listening for their child's message. Once their child communicates, parents are taught to follow their child's lead by interpreting the child's message and/or joining in the child's play.

*Interpreting* is described as modeling the word(s) the parent thinks the child would say in the context, if he or she could say a single word. For example, when a child points to her doll's mouth, vocalizes, and looks at the parent, the parent may interpret this message by saying, "mouth" or "eat." Parents then are encouraged to put the word in a short sentence or phrase, pause, and then repeat the word, thereby providing a model that the child may imitate (e.g., if the child is feeding a doll, the parent might interpret by saying, "Your dolly wants to eat").

During an interactive presentation with video recorded examples, the SLP illustrates how parents can join in the child's play by imitating what their child is doing with toys and at the same time modeling the word(s) appropriate to the context. For example, if a child is brushing a doll's hair, the parent can get his or her own doll and say, "Brushing. I'm brushing the doll's hair . . . brushing," as he or she imitates the child's actions. At the end of Session 1, the SLP assigns home practice and confirms the appointments for the first individual consultation. Parents are also asked to provide a list of their child's favorite things before the individual consultation to provide information that will be used to select the child's target words.

## Individual Consultation 1

The first individual consultation appointment occurs in the clinic and is scheduled 2–3 weeks after Session 1 in order to give parents sufficient time to practice using the program strategies. This 90-minute consultation includes video recording with feedback and the selection of target words. Prior to recording, the program strategies are reviewed and parents are given an opportunity to ask questions. The SLP then video records 5–10 minutes of parent–child interaction using a standard set of toys (e.g., tea set, frying pans, dolls, bathtub, comb, brush, shape sorter, nesting cups, pretend food). During the filming, the SLP may decide to coach by providing the parent with a verbal reminder to use a specific program strategy. For example, if a parent is not waiting long enough for the child to respond, the SLP may say, "Wait longer so he can initiate" and continue recording. After the video recording, the SLP and the parent view and discuss the interaction, with much of the discussion and feedback focusing on the parents' use of the program strategies and their impact on the child's communication. Parents then complete a summary page in their handbook that lists the program strategies and activities they will continue to use and how they will remember to include the strategies in their interactions at home. At the end of the first individual consultation, the SLP and parents select 10 target words for the child, which include nouns and at least four action words/verbs, using the following guidelines (adapted from Paul, 2007):

- The word must be motivating for the child to say

- The word must be understood by the child (parents review their copy of the completed CDI)

- The word must start with a sound already in the child's speech sound repertoire (parents review the child's speech sound checklist)

- The child must not already have a verbal representation for the word

- The word should occur throughout the day and be present in play and book reading

Verbs are carefully chosen to facilitate early word combinations (e.g., "kick ball," "daddy jump") because the ultimate goal for these children is the development of early sentence use. Parents are asked not to focus on their target words until Session 2.

## Session 2: Continue the Conversation

Session 2 is 2.5 hours long. At the beginning of the session, the SLP shows a short video clip from each family's individual consultation as a means of reviewing the previous session's information. The new information focuses on specific strategies to help children learn their target words. The acronym "TARGET" is used to remind parents of these new strategies.

T = take your time (slow down)

A = adjust the length (to a single word or short sentence)

R = repeat (try for at least five times in an activity)

G = add a gesture or show the object

E = emphasize (e.g., pause before saying the word, increase or decrease the volume, elongate the word)

T = try other situations (remember to think of all the contexts in which a word can be used)

The second half of Session 2 focuses on using comments and questions to continue the conversation (e.g., Yoder, Davies, Bishop, & Munson, 1994). Parents are encouraged to examine the types of questions they ask their child and why they ask them. If the question is genuine and at an appropriate developmental level, the SLP recommends that parents continue to ask it. But when questions are not genuine, parents are advised to replace them with comments. For example, instead of asking, "Do you want to put your coat on?" parents can use a comment such as, "It's time to put your coat on." Choice questions are very important for this group of children, as the response is part of the choice (e.g., "Do you want a cookie or a cracker?"). When a child responds nonverbally, the parent may interpret the child's message and pause, thereby creating an opportunity for the child to imitate the word. Home activities designed to have parents practice the new strategies and use questions and comments to continue the conversation are planned and shared before the end of the session.

## Session 3: Expand Your Child's Message

Session 3 is held 2 weeks after Session 2 and lasts 2.5 hours. Session 3 is usually 8 weeks after the preprogram assessment, and some of the children may now be spontaneously imitating or using single words. The session focuses on teaching parents how to expand or recast the child's verbal turn by adding one or two words to the child's message (e.g., Nelson, Camarata, Welsh, Butkovsky, & Camarata, 1996). For example, when a child shows his parent an apple and says, "apple," the parent can now expand the child's verbal turn and say, "We're eating apples" or "Apples taste good." Parents are reminded to take their best guess at using an expansion that is appropriate for the context.

Session 3 includes using songs and games to model target words. Parents learn how to pause before the target word in a song or game, thereby creating an opportunity for the child to take a turn. Parents view video examples of songs and games and then adapt a song or game in which to include one or two of their child's target words.

## Individual Consultation 2

The next session is the second individual consultation, which is typically 45 minutes long. Prior to recording, the SLP and parent review the child's progress and select a new communication goal, if appropriate. The SLP then video records 5–10 minutes of parent–child interaction, including the song or game parents prepared in the previous evening session. Once again, the SLP may coach the parent to use a recently taught program strategy (e.g., expand or recast) and then facilitates a discussion with the parent during a review of the video recording. At the end of the video feedback discussion, parents identify which strategies they will continue to work on and how they will include them in a variety of activities in the home.

### Session 4: Expand Your Child's Play

This final session of the Target Word program is 2.5 hours long and occurs approximately 11 or 12 weeks after the preprogram assessment. The SLP teaches parents strategies to expand their child's pretend play sequences (e.g., Vandermaas-Peeler, Nelson, Bumpass, & Sassine, 2009). Parents identify pretend play activities in which their child uses repetitive actions with little elaboration (e.g., pouring tea and handing the cup to the parent to drink), then they learn to add one new step to the pretend play sequence (e.g., adding milk or sugar, dunking a cookie, blowing on the tea before drinking). As this is the final group session, the SLP reviews typical expectations for speech sound acquisition so that parents understand the next steps in their child's articulation development. Parents are encouraged to monitor their child's progress and contact the SLP in the absence of weekly changes. Parents update their child's CDI form and speech sound checklist, and they complete a final program evaluation. Finally, the SLP makes an appointment with the family for a follow-up assessment when the child turns 30 months.

## RESEARCH USING THE TARGET WORD PROGRAM

Preliminary research using the Target Word program with parents of late-talking toddlers includes 1) consumer satisfaction data on program effects and 2) a descriptive case study.

### Consumer Satisfaction

Parental evaluations of the program's impact and format were obtained by collecting evaluations from six consecutive parent groups, totaling 37 parents in all. All parent programs were taught by the third author of this chapter. Evaluations were completed at the end of the last session. The first five items on the evaluation form examined the impact of the program on the parent/child and the extent to which five statements were true using a 5-point Likert scale from 1 (*not at all*) to 5 (*a lot*). For the remaining 8 items, parents rated the usefulness of the program activities using a frequency scale from 1 (*not at all*) to 5 (*a lot*). Table 13.4 displays the mean, minimum, and maximum ratings.

Parents consistently assigned positive ratings to the first five items evaluating the program's impact. In particular, the ratings for parental awareness of their own communication (Item 1) and knowledge of the child's communication (Item 2) had the highest ratings overall, with all parents rating these items as a 4 or 5 on the 5-point scale. The ratings for items regarding parents' use of language facilitation strategies (Item 4) and observed changes in the children (Item 5) were more variable, ranging from 3 to 5.

**Table 13.4.** Parents' evaluations of the Target Word program (Earle & Lowry, 2011a)

| Rating scale items | Mean | Minimum–Maximum |
|---|---|---|
| **Impact of program** | | |
| 1. Increased your awareness of your communication and interactions with your child | 4.89 | 4–5 |
| 2. Increased your knowledge of your child's communication and interaction with you | 4.92 | 4–5 |
| 3. Increased your knowledge of language facilitation strategies | 4.82 | 3–5 |
| 4. Increased your use of language facilitation strategies with your child | 4.76 | 3–5 |
| 5. Observed changes in how your child communicates with you | 4.76 | 3–5 |
| **Usefulness of group activities** | | |
| 6. Information presented by the speech-language pathologist | 4.79 | 4–5 |
| 7. Large-group discussions, brainstorming, and problem solving | 4.55 | 3–5 |
| 8. Viewing video recordings of parent–child interactions | 4.74 | 3–5 |
| 9. Small-group activities to practice and apply new information (e.g., role playing) | 4.00 | 1–5 |
| **Usefulness of Individual Activities** | | |
| 10. Reading the *It Takes Two to Talk* guidebook (Pepper & Weitzman, 2004) | 4.26 | 3–5 |
| 11. Practicing in class | 4.58 | 2–5 |
| 12. Practicing at home | 4.79 | 4–5 |
| 13. Practicing in video recording and feedback sessions | 4.79 | 4–5 |

Group learning activities also received consistently high ratings, with the exception of small-group activities. Parents rated the presentations by the SLP (Item 6) and viewing video recordings (Item 8) as the most useful learning activities. However, there was considerable variability in the ratings for small-group activities, such as role playing (Item 9), with nine parents assigning ratings of 3 or lower for these activities. The data indicate that the small-group activities may not have been useful for promoting parents' learning. Future evaluations may need to tease out which small-group activities are beneficial and for what purpose.

Finally, there was also variation in how parents rated individual activities. The highest ratings were assigned to practicing strategies with their children at home (Item 12) and practicing strategies during the clinic visits (Item 13). Lower ratings were assigned to practicing strategies in class (13 parents rated this item 3 or lower) and reading printed material (5 parents rated this item as 3). Thus, parents appeared to value activities that were directly relevant to their children.

## Case Study

Our experiences with late-talking toddlers have yielded four profiles of outcomes following intervention. The first group includes children who achieve vocabulary scores on the CDIs that are within in the normal range (i.e., greater than the 20th percentile) and whose expressive language is age appropriate. A second group includes children who make significant gains in vocabulary acquisition and expressive language but remain below the 20th percentile on the CDIs. A third group includes children who make important gains in vocabulary but whose vocabulary and expressive language score on the CDIs remain below the 15th percentile. And a fourth group includes children who make minimal progress and remain significantly delayed in vocabulary development and expressive language development. The child profiled in this case study is representative of children in the second group.

# ( ( ( ( ( Sam ) ) ) ) )

Sam was seen by an SLP at 22 months of age because his parents were concerned that he used few words. He typically communicated by pointing, screaming, or gesturing for the objects he wanted. His parents had no concerns about his hearing, comprehension, play, or social skills. On a standardized test of communication development, he scored below the 10th percentile on the expressive scale. However, his receptive language score was within normal limits, confirming the parents' impressions of his comprehension. On the CDI, his vocabulary size was estimated to be 11 words, which was below the 5th percentile. Participation in a parent-implemented program was recommended.

Sam and his parents participated in a Target Word preprogram assessment when he was 24 months of age. Both parents felt there had been little change in Sam's expressive language development and that he was notably more frustrated. The parents updated his CDI form, and Sam was now using 17 words (a gain of only 6 words over a 2-month time span), which continued to be below the 5th percentile for his age group. During the assessment, the SLP observed that he had good pretend play skills, social interaction abilities, and comprehension. He used the words *mommy* or *daddy* consistently to initiate an interaction or to take his turn. Discussion with Sam's parents indicated that he was positive for four risk factors for ongoing speech and language delays: He was quiet as an infant and vocalized little, he did not imitate sounds or words, his vocabulary consisted mostly of nouns with few verbs, and he had made few gains in expressive vocabulary over time.

During the first individual consultation, Sam's parents and the SLP selected a total of 11 target words composed of 7 verbs (i.e., *dump, come, pour, toss, push, cut, open*), 3 nouns (i.e., *car, poo, vacuum*), and 1 proper name (i.e., *grandma*). These target words reflected objects, activities, and people that Sam's parents believed were highly interesting and motivating for him. During the program sessions, his parents identified four strategies that they needed to emphasize, including 1) joining in Sam's play by imitating his actions, 2) using focused stimulation consistently to model the preselected target words, 3) interpreting Sam's vocalizations and gestures using short sentences, and 4) expanding Sam's word approximations by adding one or two words. The SLP supported the parents in developing these skills during the individual consultations and discussions following video recordings. By the end of the program, Sam's parents achieved a high level of consistency in the use of these program strategies, and Sam had acquired 10 of his 11 target words. His parents updated the CDI form prior to the final session of the program, approximately 11 weeks after the preprogram evaluation. Sam's parents reported that he was now saying 110 words (below the 10th percentile for his age group) and was often using two- and three-word combinations (e.g., "baby eat," "baby sleep," "me can't daddy," "cat go away").

Sam and his parents were seen for follow-up evaluation when he was 30 months of age, approximately 3 months after the final session of the program. Sam was now using 324 words on the CDI, placing him at the 20th percentile for his age group. He communicated using short utterances of three to five words in length. His parents felt that they understood Sam most of the time; however, they felt that he was still lagging behind other children of the same age in terms of the completeness of his sentences. The SLP recommended that Sam and his parents receive home programming suggestions on a monthly basis to ensure his continued speech and language development. She recommended integrating some new goals concerning morphosyntax and embedding these goals within joint story book reading to increase Sam's exposure to literacy. She suggested that parents help Sam reenact familiar stories with props to improve his use of oral language to recount narratives. Finally, his parents were counseled to continue to expand his utterances and extend his pretend play.

## Outcome Profiles

This case study illustrates one of the four types of profiles observed following intervention, namely children who make significant gains in vocabulary acquisition and expressive language development but remain below the 20th percentile on the CDIs. For many of the children with this profile, the focus of therapy continues to be the development of additional vocabulary, morphosyntax, and sentence complexity. Outcome profiles for each of the four general profiles that are based on the gains children experience during the course of the program are detailed in this section. All children in these profiles make important gains in communication development from preprogram to postprogram and achieve their initial communication goals. These profiles may be helpful for guiding clinicians to make subsequent treatment recommendations concerning next steps, including the goals of therapy and type of service delivery model best suited for the child.

*Excellent Progress*    The first profile includes children who make "excellent" progress. Generally, across 67 families who participated in Target Word programs taught by the third author of this chapter between 2006 and 2009, 12% of the children fit this profile and were discharged from further treatment. Following intervention, the children's scores on the CDI (i.e., vocabulary, utterance length, and sentence complexity) were within expectations (i.e., above the 20th percentile). Although many of these children had developmental articulation errors (e.g., cluster reduction, stopping for some fricatives), these were age appropriate. These children used a variety of verb phrases and sentence types in their language samples, and most of their utterances were multiword utterances that were grammatically correct. Their parents were no longer concerned about expressive language development but were encouraged to monitor their child's emergent literacy development and contact the clinician if they had any concerns.

*Good Progress*    A second profile consists of children who make "good" progress during the program, comprising 11% of the 67 children who completed the Target Word programs between 2006 and 2009. During intervention, these children made important gains in vocabulary, but their vocabulary size on the CDI at the end of the 12-week intervention remained below the 20th percentile for their age group. In addition, they continued to lag behind in terms of expressive language development—their verb phrases and sentence forms were incomplete and/or agrammatical. In language samples, these children used single-word phrases, two-word utterances, and some early sentences. Their articulation included developmental error patterns, such as final consonant deletion and fronting of velars. All of these children were placed on a watch and see monitoring schedule. In other words, their families received reevaluation sessions when their child reached 30 months of age and two to three times per year, during which the children's progress was assessed. At each appointment, the parent–child interaction was observed, and the parents were given specific suggestions for facilitating their children's vocabulary and language development based on the child's communication skills and the parents' interactive behavior.

***Fair Progress***   A third profile includes children who make "fair" progress in phonology, vocabulary, and language development, comprising 63% of the children seen between 2006 and 2009. These children typically achieved their initial communication goals that were set at the preprogram consultation. Generally, the vocabulary size of these children remained below the 15th percentile for their age group. These children acquired a number of word types, new consonant sounds, and used a variety of syllable shapes. Their expressive language consisted of single-word and two-word utterances. However, they required therapy focusing on either articulation or morphosyntax or both. Given the risk factors that many of these children present with at intake, many of these children go on to develop specific language impairment. This is the group of children that continues to need ongoing support to develop their language and academic abilities across the preschool and school-age periods.

***Poor Progress***   A fourth profile includes children who make "poor" progress during the intervention. This profile comprised 14% of the children seen between 2006 and 2009. Following intervention, they became more communicative using vocalizations and gestures and, as a consequence, the parents' and children's frustration levels decreased. However, these children made very limited gains in expressive vocabulary development, possibly due to motor speech delays. In terms of expressive vocabulary, their vocabulary size remains well below the 10th percentile on the CDI. Their language samples consisted primarily of one-word phrases, many of which were unintelligible. They used few two-word utterances. All of these children were referred for direct, ongoing speech and language services. These children who demonstrated this fourth profile typically required more intensive, direct intervention for motor speech issues immediately after the Target Word program was completed.

***Families in Which English Is Not The First Language***   Programs often have families for whom English is not their first language. These families are referred to the program because the parents are concerned about their children's vocabulary development in their home language. Guided by recommended practices (e.g., Kohnert, 2010; van Kleeck, 1994), the SLP leading a Target Word program works with the family to choose target words in their first language. If the family is bilingual (e.g., Spanish-speaking mother and English-speaking father), the SLP may work with the parents to select target words in both languages, but never the same word in the two languages. Parents are asked to complete a speech sound checklist to reflect the speech sounds the child has acquired in the home language, and the SLP will engage the family in a discussion about sounds in the first language that do not appear in English. Time is spent at the preprogram assessment determining how the family views the child's functioning and current communication skills. Other family members who are involved in the child's upbringing (e.g., grandparents, older siblings) are encouraged to attend the program. However, future research is required to determine the efficacy of this program for English language learners and their families. Moreover, long-term follow-up is a critical component of future research to delineate whether late-talking children catch up with their peers or if their late vocabulary onset has a longer lasting impact on their expressive language development and academic/literacy abilities.

## CONCLUSIONS

The development of a parent-implemented program for late-talking toddlers was informed by research on the effects of parent training for young children with expressive vocabulary delays (Girolametto et al., 1996). The effectiveness of the focused stimulation strategy, as well as other responsive interaction strategies (e.g., imitating, interpreting, expanding) in facilitating the language development of the children in that study led to these strategies being incorporated into a parent training program specifically for late-talking toddlers. Although further research is needed to demonstrate the efficacy of the Target Word program, its implementation to date shows that it is feasible and well-received by parents, and that children's vocabularies increase from preprogram to postprogram. In addition, it provides clinicians with a short-term intervention that can guide subsequent intervention recommendations. Finally, parents need information that is useful and applicable. As one parent wrote in her evaluation form,

> Sharing experiences with others has reduced my frustration. The most important thing I learned was to allow my child to initiate play and to wait for him to engage. . . . [I learned] that there are things we can do to give [L.] the confidence to talk.

## REFERENCES

American Speech-Language-Hearing Association. (2008a). *Core knowledge and skills in early intervention speech-language pathology practice.* Rockville, MD: Author.
American Speech-Language-Hearing Association. (2008b). *Roles and responsibilities of speech-language pathologists in early intervention: Guidelines.* Rockville, MD: Author.
Blank, M., Rose, S., & Berlin, L. (1978). *The Preschool Language Assessment Instrument.* New York, NY: Grune & Stratton.
Bruner, J. (1968). *Toward a theory of instruction.* New York, NY: W.W. Norton.
Clarke, J.I. (1984). *Who, me lead a group?* San Francisco, CA: Harper and Row.
Dempsey, I., & Dunst, C. (2004). Help giving styles and parent empowerment in families with a young child with a disability. *Journal of Intellectual and Developmental Disability, 29*(1), 40–51.
Earle, C., & Lowry, L. (2011a). *Target Word making Hanen happen leaders guide* (3rd ed.). Toronto, ON, Canada: The Hanen Centre.
Earle, C., & Lowry, L. (2011b). *Target Word parent handbook* (3rd ed.). Toronto, ON, Canada: The Hanen Centre.

Ellis Weismer, S., & Robertson, S. (2006). Focused stimulation approach to language intervention. In R.J. McCauley & M.E. Fey (Eds.), *Treatment of language disorders in children* (pp. 175–202). Baltimore, MD: Paul H. Brookes Publishing Co.

Fenson, L., Dale, P.S., Reznick, J.S., Thal, D., Bates, E., Hartung, J.P., . . . Reilly, J.S. (1993). *MacArthur Communicative Development Inventories: User's guide and technical manual.* Baltimore, MD: Paul H. Brookes Publishing Co.

Fenson, L., Marchman, V.A., Thal, D.J., Dale, P.S., Reznick, J.S., & Bates, E. (2007). *MacArthur-Bates Communicative Development Inventories (CDIs)* (2nd ed.). Baltimore, MD: Paul H. Brookes Publishing Co.

Girolametto, L., Pearce, P., & Weitzman, E. (1996). Interactive focused stimulation for toddlers with expressive vocabulary delays. *Journal of Speech and Hearing Research, 39*(6), 1274–1283.

Girolametto, L., Pearce, P., & Weitzman, E. (1997). Effects of lexical intervention on the phonology of late talkers. *Journal of Speech, Language, and Hearing Research, 40*(1), 338–348.

Girolametto, L., & Weitzman, E. (2006). It Takes Two To Talk–The Hanen Program For Parents: Early language intervention through caregiver training. In R. McCauley & M. Fey (Eds.), *Treatment of language disorders in children* (pp. 77–103). Baltimore, MD: Paul H. Brookes Publishing Co.

Girolametto, L., Weitzman, E., Wiigs, M., & Pearce, P. (2000). The relationship between maternal language measures and language development. *American Journal of Speech-Language Pathology, 8*(4), 364–374.

Girolametto, L., Wiigs, M., Smyth, R., Weitzman, E., & Pearce, P. (2001). Children with a history of expressive language delay: Outcomes at 5 years of age. *American Journal of Speech-Language Pathology, 10,* 358–369.

Hanft, B.E., Rush, D.D., & Shelden, M.L. (2004). *Coaching families and colleagues in early childhood.* Baltimore, MD: Paul H. Brookes Publishing Co.

Hedrick, D., Prather, E., & Tobin, A. (1984). *The Sequenced Inventory of Communication Development* (Rev. ed.). Seattle: University of Washington Press.

Irwin, J.V., & Wong, S.P. (Eds.). (1983). *Phonological development in children 18 to 72 months.* Carbondale: Southern Illinois University Press.

Kaiser, A., & Hancock, T. (2003). Teaching parents new skills to support their young children's development. *Infants and Young Children, 16,* 9–21.

Kohnert, K. (2010). Bilingual children with primary language impairment: Issues, evidence, and implications for clinical actions. *Journal of Communication Disorders, 43*(6), 456–473.

Kolb, D.A. (1984). *Experiential learning: Experience as the source of learning and development.* Englewood Cliffs, NJ: Prentice Hall.

MacKeracher, D. (1996). *Making sense of adult learning.* Toronto, ON, Canada: Culture Concepts.

Mayer, M. (1967). *A boy, a dog, and a frog.* New York, NY: Dial Books for Young Readers.

Nelson, K., Camarata, S., Welsh, J., Butkovsky, L., & Camarata, M. (1996). Effects of conversational recasting treatment on the acquisition of grammar in children with specific language impairment and younger language-normal children. *Journal of Speech and Hearing Research, 39*(4), 850–859.

Newcomer, P., & Hammill, D. (1988). *Test of Language Development–Primary, Second Edition.* Austin, TX: PRO-ED.

Olswang, L., Rodriguez, B., & Timler, G. (1998). Recommending intervention for toddlers with specific language learning difficulties: We may not have all the answers, but we know a lot. *American Journal of Speech-Language Pathology, 7*(1), 23–32.

Paris, S., & Winograd, P. (1990). How metacognition can promote academic learning and instruction. In B. Fly Jones & L. Idol (Eds.), *Dimensions of thinking and cognitive instruction* (pp. 15–51). Mahwah, NJ: Lawrence Erlbaum Associates.

Paul, R. (1993). Patterns of development in late talkers: Preschool years. *Journal of Childhood Communication Disorders, 15*(1), 7–14.

Paul, R. (1996). Clinical implications of the natural history of slow expressive language development. *American Journal of Speech Language Pathology, 5*(2), 5–20.

Paul, R. (2007). *Language disorders from infancy through adolescence* (3rd ed.). St. Louis, MO: Mosby Elsevier.

Pepper, J., & Weitzman, E. (2004). *It Takes Two To Talk: A practical guide For parents of children with language delays* (2nd ed.). Toronto, ON, Canada: The Hanen Centre.

Prelock, P., & Hutchins, T. (2008). The role of family-centred care in research: Supporting the social communication of children with autism spectrum disorder. *Topics in Language Disorders, 28*(4), 323–339.

Rescorla, L. (1991). Identifying expressive language delay at age two. *Topics in Language Disorders, 11*(4), 14–20.

Roberts, M., & Kaiser, A. (2011). The effectiveness of parent-implemented language intervention: A meta-analysis. *American Journal of Speech-Language Pathology, 20,* 180–199.

Robertson, S., & Ellis Weismer, S. (1999). Effects of treatment on linguistic and social skills in toddlers with delayed language development. *Journal of Speech, Language, and Hearing Research, 42*(5), 1234–1248.

Rush, D., & Shelden, M.L. (2008). Tips and techniques for effective coaching interactions. *Brief Case, 1*(2), 1–4.

Rush, D.D., & Shelden, M.L. (2011). *The early childhood coaching handbook.* Baltimore, MD: Paul H. Brookes Publishing Co.

Sussman, F. (1999). *More than words: Helping parents promote communication and social skills in children with autism spectrum disorder.* Toronto, ON, Canada: The Hanen Centre.

Sussman, F. (2006). *TalkAbility.* Toronto, ON, Canada: The Hanen Centre.

Trivette, C.M., Dunst, C., Hamby, D., & O'Herin, C.E. (2009). Characteristics and consequences of adult learning methods and strategies. *Practical Evaluation Reports, 2*(1), 1–32.

Vandermaas-Peeler, M., Nelson, J., Bumpass, C., & Sassine, B. (2009). Social contexts of development: Parent-child interactions during reading and play. *Journal of Early Childhood Literacy, 9*(3), 295–317.

van Kleeck, A. (1994). Potential cultural bias in training parents as conversational partners with their children who have delays in language development. *American Journal of Speech-Language Pathology, 3*(1), 67–78.

Wlodkowski, R.J. (1993). *Enhancing adult motivation to learn.* San Francisco, CA: Jossey-Bass.

Yoder, P., Davies, B., Bishop, K., & Munson, L. (1994). Effect of adult continuing wh-questions on conversational participation in children with developmental disabilities. *Journal of Speech and Hearing Research, 37*(1), 193–204.

# 14

# Evidence-Based Language Intervention Approaches for Young Late Talkers

Lizbeth H. Finestack and Marc E. Fey

Speech-language pathologists working with 2-year-olds identified as late talkers (LTs) have several options when planning and implementing speech-language services. For example, there is a broad range of language intervention approaches that have been developed and evaluated for young children from other clinical populations—such as children with autism, Down syndrome, specific language impairment (SLI), and specific speech sound disorder—that clinicians may consider using with LTs. In addition, there are a few studies that have evaluated language intervention efficacy specifically with LTs as participants and even a very few comparative intervention studies that have examined the benefits of one intervention approach over another. However, based on the external evidence of published research, there is no single intervention approach that is best for all LTs.

Although the intervention approach implemented by a clinician should be supported by external evidence, every evidence-based management decision also requires consideration of internal evidence (i.e., an individual child's profile, familial preferences, and clinician expertise and experience; Fey & Justice, 2007). When limited external evidence is available or when each intervention approach is equally supported, the service plan the clinician adopts must hinge on these internal factors.

We begin this chapter by discussing approaches to language intervention that are suitable for children who are considered LTs, highlighting investigations that have focused on late-talking children. We then introduce four children who may be considered LTs and their families. Based on the external and internal evidence presented with each child, we discuss an intervention approach that appears most suitable for that child and family.

## LANGUAGE INTERVENTION OPTIONS

When working with a child considered to be an LT, a clinician may choose not to deliver intervention services but instead to monitor the child's progress aggressively. Alternative approaches, all of which entail the delivery of direct intervention services, include general language stimulation, focused stimulation, milieu teaching, or the use of augmentative and alternative communication.

### A Nonintervention Option: Watch and See

The only intervention approach designed specifically to accommodate LTs is the "watch and see" approach (Paul, 1996). Based on her longitudinal study of 2-year-old children who had an expressive vocabulary of fewer than 50 words or were not yet combining words, Paul found that 23 of the 31 children in her study had grown out of their initial language delay by the time they reached first grade. That is, in first grade, 74% of children previously meeting criteria for being an LT performed no differently than children with typical language development on measures of grammatical complexity, reading recognition, and reading comprehension. These children with a history of expressive language delay performed in the average range on standardized language assessments, even though their scores were still significantly lower than those of the control children with typical language development histories. These findings align closely with other studies that have found that, based on norm-referenced instruments, the majority of late-talking children catch up with their peers by 5 years of age, though they may still lag behind control children who have been followed longitudinally (e.g., Girolametto, Wiigs, Smyth, Weitzman, & Pearce, 2001; Rescorla, 2002; Whitehurst et al., 1991). It is important to note that although the majority of children appeared to catch up on several measures, on more complex language tasks, including classroom discourse, grammatical perspective taking, narrative ability, and reading, clinically significant language delays persisted or reappeared throughout the elementary years (Manhardt & Rescorla, 2002; Paul, Hernandez, Taylor, & Johnson, 1996; Rescorla, 2002). Based on her early findings, Paul recommended that late-talking children of middle-class families should *not* be eligible for intervention that is provided at public expense. Instead, she argued that they should be aggressively monitored during the early years. This watch and see approach entailed systematically reexamining the late-talking child for evidence of clinically significant slow language growth every 3–6 months between the ages of 2 and 3 years and every 6–12 months between the ages of 3 and 5 years.

Paul (1996) included several caveats to this recommendation, however. First, it would be appropriate only for children identified as LTs for whom the only concern is expressive language; receptive language is not significantly delayed; and there are no concerns with cognitive, behavioral, hearing, medical, emotional, or neurological development. Second, direct services should be provided if the child's speech is significantly impaired such that family, friends, and peers cannot readily understand the child. Third, Paul insists that the watch and see approach is only appropriate for children from well-educated, middle-class families who are not otherwise at risk for language impairment. Finally, the watch and see recommendation is appropriate only as long as the child's language skills continue to develop in terms of lexical and grammatical complexity, conversational participation, and speech intelligibility. When implementing a watch and see program, Paul proposed that at the time of assessment and decision to watch and see, the clinician identify a set of speech and language goals that would be appropriate for the child if intervention were to be recommended. At the subsequent reevaluation, the clinician's objective would be to determine whether these goals had been met without therapy. If they had been, there would be no call for initiating intervention; instead, new goals would be selected for later evaluation. If the reevaluation provided evidence that goals were not being met without treatment, the clinician would have strong evidence in support of starting treatment and an effective baseline, which would be helpful in measuring the effects of that treatment.

Paul's watch and see policy position was challenged by several child language development and intervention researchers, as well as practicing speech-language pathologists (e.g., Nippold, 1996; Nippold & Schwarz, 1996; van Kleeck, Gillam, & Davis, 1997). Experts argued that the available outcome data revealing that most LTs grow out of their delays are short-term, and they cannot be depended on for decisions that have such long-term consequences. In response, Paul maintained that early language delays that qualify children as LTs should be viewed as risk factors for language disorders but should not be considered disorders or impairments in and of themselves (Paul, 1997). Children who have no significant delays in development other than in communication and who are not at risk for language learning difficulties due to environmental or known neurodevelopmental factors are likely to be well-suited for the watch and see approach, never requiring direct intervention services.

As a service delivery option, adoption of the watch and see approach is supported primarily by the weak evidence provided by the results of studies with longitudinal observational designs. These study results broadly indicate that LTs who do not receive language intervention tend to catch up with their peers. However, the watch and see approach has never been tested experimentally as an alternative either to intervention or to a less aggressive wait and see option. Still, the available evidence is consistent; each prospective study that has been designed to study the natural history of early language delay (Girolametto et al., 2001; Paul, 1996; Rescorla, 2002; Thal, Bates, Goodman, & Jahn Samilo, 1997; Whitehurst et al., 1991) has found that the majority of children identified at 20–34 months of age as late talking no longer demonstrated delays in language performance by the time they reached school age. Thus, a watch and see approach should be considered a viable alternative for some children who have been identified as LTs yet have few or no additional concerns.

## General Language Stimulation

At their core, all general language stimulation approaches involve modifications of the physical and linguistic environments that aim to increase opportunities for children to hear frequent adult models of developmentally appropriate language and to use language at the edge of their abilities. Thus, intervention agents (e.g., parents, clinicians) performing general language stimulation limit their use of controlling behaviors, such as commands and questions, and increase their levels of responsiveness to the child and the child's communicative acts. General language stimulation does not target specific language forms or communication acts, and the intervention agent never tells the child directly to produce any specific words, word combinations, or grammatical constructions. Instead, the intervention focuses on creating a rich language environment that is tailored to the child's interests and abilities. Children may then focus on those aspects of language that they are most prepared to learn.

General stimulation activities may include reading a book, playing house, baking a cake, or making lemonade, depending on how well each activity provides opportunities and creates the need for the child to talk and for the intervention agent, such as the parent or clinician, to employ the intervention procedures. Typical procedures include 1) following the child's lead, 2) talking about the object to which the child is attending (i.e., parallel talk), and 3) responding to the child's verbalizations with semantically and grammatically contingent responses. Perhaps most significantly, the intervention agent produces recasts, namely responses to the child's utterances that repeat parts or all of the child's utterance while adding semantic and grammatical detail to the child's verbal contributions (Fey, Krulik, Loeb, & Proctor-Williams, 1999).

There are a few studies that have examined general stimulation approaches for young children with the clinician or teacher as the intervention agent (e.g., Boyd, 1980; Robertson & Ellis Weismer, 1999; Weiss, 1981). Robertson and Ellis Weismer (1999) conducted the most rigorous of these investigations. Their randomized controlled trial compared the outcomes of a 12-week clinician-delivered intervention with those of a no-treatment condition. The 21 children in the study, all identified as late-talking toddlers, ranged from 21 to 30 months in age and averaged 15 spoken words. Each participant in the treatment group received two 75-min group treatment sessions per week. The children in the treatment group made both statistically and clinically significant gains on a diverse set of measures of child behavior, including words produced, speech intelligibility, and socialization. Effect sizes ($d$) ranged from 0.63 to 1.67. Perhaps even more important was the significant reduction in parent stress ($d = .41$), presumably stemming from the children's improved communication skills. Robertson and Ellis Weismer suggested that the children's positive response to treatment led parents to view their child as more similar to peers with typical development. This, in turn, helped parents to accept their child despite his or her language limitations. In addition, the authors argued that the children's increases in verbal communication resulted in more parent–child communicative exchanges, which reinforced parents' efforts to communicate with their children and yielded even more linguistic input directed toward the children. Thus, there was a bidirectional, or transactional, effect of this general stimulation approach in which the gains made by the children led to changes in the parents' communication and interaction patterns, which presumably fostered continued growth in child and parent communication.

General language stimulation approaches have been studied most frequently in parent-implemented treatments with children with varying diagnoses, including autism and Down syndrome (e.g., Aldred, Green, & Adams, 2004; Buschmann et al., 2009; Carter et al., 2011; Girolametto, 1988; Tannock, Girolametto, & Siegel, 1992). Although general stimulation approaches have largely been successful in leading to more balanced parent–child verbal interactions, limiting parents' controlling behaviors, and increasing parents' responsiveness to their child (see Carter et al., 2011), the effects on children with autism and intellectual disabilities have been mixed, and this has led some researchers to consider focused stimulation or milieu teaching for these children (Girolametto, Pearce, & Weitzman, 1996), as discussed in the next section.

Two studies have evaluated the efficacy of a parent-delivered general stimulation with LTs (Baxendale & Hesketh, 2003; Buschmann et al., 2009). The most rigorous of these studies, and thus, the one that yields the strongest evidence in support of general stimulation with LTs, is a study by Buschmann et al. (2009). In this study, 58 children between the ages of 24 and 27 months were randomly assigned to either a parent-implemented treatment group or a no-treatment group. All of the child participants had receptive language abilities and nonverbal cognitive abilities in the average range and had expressive vocabularies of less than 50 words. Parents in the treatment group completed seven 2-hour group sessions that taught them to use language facilitation techniques, especially during activities involving picture books. Twelve months after treatment onset, the children of parents in the intervention group outperformed the children assigned to the no-treatment group on both parental report measures of vocabulary, morphology, and syntax and norm-referenced clinician-administered tests of vocabulary and syntax. The effect sizes for all measures were medium to large ($d = 0.72–1.16$), indicating clinical significance. The strongest claim of clinical significance, however, was that 75% of the children in the treatment group no longer met criteria for late talking postintervention, compared with 44% of children in the no-treatment group.

In sum, although some studies have reported small or no effects of general stimulation on children with autism or other developmental disabilities (Carter et al., 2011; Tannock et al., 1992), studies with LTs have generally been successful, whether the intervention agent is a clinician or the child's parent. Thus, LTs who exhibit clinically significant limitations in the number of communication acts produced, responsiveness to the adult partner, and the use of words and early grammatical constructions may be viable candidates for some variation of this approach. However, when there is a need to target specific vocabulary items or grammatical forms, a more specified intervention approach may be necessary, such as focused language stimulation or milieu teaching.

## Focused Language Stimulation

Focused stimulation is very similar to general stimulation but differs in one fundamental respect, which leads to many other smaller differences between these approaches. Unlike general stimulation, in which the clinician does not target specific words, grammatical constructions, or communication skills, focused stimulation involves the identification of one or, more typically, several specific language targets on which the clinician's teaching efforts and the child's language learning resources are to be focused. Consider a child who produces minimal action words and a handful of object words. An appropriate specific goal for this child might be for the child to use specified action (e.g., "go," "stop") and object (e.g., "car," "boat," "bus," "grapes," "cookie," "juice," "milk") words that are relevant to the child's particular needs and play interests when requesting or commenting on events. In focused stimulation, appropriate activities are not just interesting and fun for the child (e.g., play with a city set), and they are not designed to facilitate child talking in a general way; instead, they must provide many opportunities for adult models of child targets (e.g., "Watch the car go," "The bus will stop") and encourage child attempts at the use of child targets (e.g. "Should the car stop or go?" "Do you want to play with the boat or the bus?"). In general, then, the child's target forms are presented at a high density in meaningful and functional contexts (Fey, 1986). Importantly, when using focused stimulation techniques, the child is never required to imitate the target form.

Girolametto and his colleagues (1996) experimentally evaluated the parent-implemented Hanen Program for Parents, which comprises eight weekly group sessions and three home visits across 11 weeks. The sessions are focused on teaching parents to use general language stimulation techniques, such as to follow the child's lead, model language that is contingent on the child's attentional focus, and promote turn taking. In addition, the study intervention included a focused stimulation component such that parents were given a list of 10 target words to incorporate into their daily activities. They also were taught how to replace these target words once their child produced the target at least three times in three different contexts in a 1-week time frame.

The participants in Girolametto et al.'s (1996) study included 15 children between the ages of 23 and 33 months with standardized IQ scores ranging from low to high average (79–116). All of the children had expressive vocabularies in the lower 5th percentile and were in the single-word stage of language development, not producing any two-word phrases. Aside from language, the children had no other evidence of developmental delay. Children were randomly assigned to receive the intervention immediately ($n = 8$) or after a waiting period ($n = 7$).

Following treatment, the mothers who received the Hanen parent education used significantly fewer words per minute, shorter utterances, and more target words than mothers in the control group. Moreover, the children of mothers who received Hanen education had significantly larger vocabularies; used a significantly greater number of different words, including target and control words; and produced significantly more multiword combinations than the children in the control group. These statistically significant findings were supported by large effect sizes ($d$), ranging from 0.70 to more than 1.0. In addition, the focused stimulation treatment indirectly resulted in significant gains in phonology. The children who received the intervention produced more complex syllable shapes and expanded their phonetic inventories to include more consonant sounds (Girolametto, Pearce, & Weitzman, 1997). Thus, there is strong evidence that parent-implemented focused stimulation can be used to expand the vocabularies, early grammatical constructions, and phonetic inventories of LTs. In fact, at a 3-year follow-up, when the children were 5 years of age, the majority of the LTs studied by Girolametto et al. (1996, 1997) performed in the average range on norm-referenced language assessment instruments. Despite these encouraging findings, it is important to note that on tests of higher level language abilities, such as narration and interpretation of ambiguous sentences, these same 5-year-olds exhibited significant weaknesses that could require additional language services (Girolametto et al., 2001).

## Milieu Teaching

In most respects, milieu teaching closely resembles the other language intervention approaches that have been proposed for LTs. Like both general and focused language stimulation, milieu teaching takes place during meaningful, naturalistic activities. As in focused language stimulation, the clinician identifies one or more specific goals on which the intervention is to focus. Then, the clinician modifies the physical and linguistic contexts to increase the opportunities for the child to talk and, more specifically, to attempt to use the target language behaviors. The intervention agent must be highly responsive to the communication efforts of the child, making special efforts to recast child attempts at the targets into appropriate lexical and grammatical forms.

Despite these similarities between milieu teaching and, especially, focused stimulation approaches, there is one key feature that always distinguishes these models. In focused stimulation, the child may be queried in a manner designed to yield an attempt at production of some targeted language form or communication act (e.g., "Tell me about the car. What is the car going to do?"), but the child is *never* given an imitative prompt to produce any language forms (e.g., "Say, 'stop'"). The child is not required to attempt the form or produce the target correctly. Incorrect attempts at the target are likely to be followed by recasts. In contrast, when using milieu teaching, the intervention agent expects the child to use the target language forms correctly during each teaching episode. If the child does not respond correctly to nonimitative prompts for production of a target, the form is modeled and the child is required to imitate. A recast is then used to expand the child's utterance semantically and/or grammatically (Hancock & Kaiser, 2006). For example, when targeting the noun *milk,* the interventionist may begin by asking the child, "What do you want to drink?" If the child points to the milk, but does not respond verbally, the intervention would explicitly prompt the child to produce the form by providing an imitative model such as, "Say, 'milk.'" If the child appropriately responds with the target "milk," the interventionist would provide a recast such as, "You want milk."

There are two studies that have compared the effects of clinician-implemented milieu teaching, which for every teaching episode included imitative prompts in the prompt hierarchy, with the effects of focused stimulation on LTs (Ellis Weismer, Murray Branch, & Miller, 1993; Kouri, 2005). The Ellis Weismer et al. study used a single-subject experimental design to compare treatment approaches, whereas the Kouri study used a more rigorous randomized experimental design to teach expressive vocabulary.

Findings from the Kouri (2005) study provided some limited evidence that imitative prompts may significantly enhance classic focused stimulation. The 29 participants in the Kouri study ranged in age from 19 to 36 months and evidenced expressive language delays at least 1.5 *SD*s below the mean. All participants exhibited reduced expressive vocabularies relative to chronological age. Fifteen participants were randomly assigned to a milieu teaching treatment group, and 14 participants to a modeling only, focused stimulation group. Regardless of group assignment, each child participated in ten 50-minute individual treatment sessions. Based on data collected during the treatment sessions, results indicated that participants who received prompts for imitation acquired more target words than did the participants in the focused stimulation group ($d = 0.73$). However, there were no differences between groups based on measures derived from children's interactions with their mothers at home.

It is essential to keep in mind that there will be individual variation in treatment outcomes, as the results of Ellis Weismer and colleagues (1993) demonstrate. This study included three children between 27 and 28 months of age with oral vocabularies ranging from 25 to 87 words. All children performed within 6 months of age expectations on receptive language and cognitive measures. Using a single-subject alternating treatments design, each participant received a milieu teaching intervention targeting a predetermined set of words as well as a focused stimulation intervention targeting a different set of words. Participants received twenty-four 1-hour sessions that incorporated both group and individual instruction. Based on visual inspection of individual data, participant performance across the treatment approaches varied greatly: One participant demonstrated greater gains in the milieu teaching condition, another participant demonstrated greater gains in the focused stimulation condition, and the third participant had limited gains in both treatments.

Although it appears that providing LTs prompts to imitate target words is generally effective, as is highlighted by the Ellis Weismer et al. (1993) study, there is considerable individual outcome variability, and imitative prompts may not always be maximally beneficial for all LTs. During the assessment phase or during the first few treatment sessions while the clinician is monitoring a child's progress, it is important for clinicians to use dynamic assessment to determine which approach is likely to be best suited for a child. For example, assume that a clinician is examining a child's use of nominative case pronouns in subject position, and the child says, "Him work every day." The clinician could systematically observe the child's responses to requests for clarification (e.g., "What?") versus recasts (e.g., "He works every day") versus prompts for imitation (e.g., "Say, 'he works'"). The child's response may provide the clinician with information about whether the target should be treated and, if so, what types of language intervention procedures may be especially effective (Olswang, Bain, & Johnson, 1992).

## Changing Modalities: Augmentative and Alternative Communication

When designing an intervention program for an individual child, there are several intervention decisions (e.g., specific treatment procedures, treatment intensity, intervention context) that must be made; however, typically the first intervention planning decisions involve the treatment goals. Thus far, in our overview of treatment options for LTs, we have assumed that the treatment goals focus on spoken language. However, there is a growing body of empirical evidence suggesting that if the initial target and focus of intervention is an increase in the child's range and amount of spoken language, augmentative and alternative communication (AAC), including the use of manual signs and graphic symbols, may help the child transition to spoken communication.

For example, Baumann Leech, and Cress (2011) examined the use of milieu teaching to target communicative use of picture symbols and signs with a 40-month-old child identified as an LT. This study used a single-subject, alternative treatment, baseline research design. The child completed fifteen 1.5-hour treatment sessions over the course of 10 weeks. The treatment used the milieu teaching least-to-most hierarchy of cuing, ending with prompts modeling the target sign or giving the target picture symbol, and, if necessary, hand-over-hand modeling to produce the target sign or provide the symbol. The child was never prompted to produce the target form orally. The child failed to meet criterion (i.e., 75% accurate use when the clinician presented an expectant pause or verbal prompt) for all targets in both the sign and symbol modes. However, he reached criteria for all targets in the verbal mode. Thus, although the clinician never prompted the participant to produce the spoken targets (but did prompt for AAC productions), the child made significant gains in spoken productions.

Dunst, Meter, and Hamby (2011) conducted a meta-analysis examining the influences of combined sign and oral language interventions on vocal and verbal outcomes. The meta-analysis included studies with participants with varying diagnoses (e.g., Down syndrome, autism, intellectual and developmental disabilities). Across studies, the child participants ranged in age from 7 months to 12 years. Results indicated that interventions targeting sign production yielded clinically significant gains in oral language. The average effect size ($d$) for studies implementing a group design ($n = 33$) was 0.72, and the average effect size for studies implementing a single-subject design ($n = 60$) was 1.48. Additional analyses indicated that the specific diagnoses or severity of impairment level did not differentially affect outcomes. Thus, targeting sign language had a positive impact on the oral language of a wide range of child participants.

The results from both Dunst et al. (2011) and Baumann Leech and Cress (2011) suggest that for a child who does not positively respond to prompts to orally imitate models of language targets, presenting targets using AAC, whether sign or symbol, may be a reasonable option. In such cases, the basic intervention goal is for the child to communicate verbally, but the more specific goals may be adjusted to incorporate the targeted mode of communication. There is no clear evidence explaining why targeting AAC use may lead to gains in verbal communication. We can speculate that targeting AAC helps to strengthen prelinguistic foundations necessary for language development or that it frees cognitive resources to allow the child to more efficiently process and learn the targeted forms. Importantly, the evidence suggests that targeting AAC is not detrimental to and may well facilitate the development of verbal communication.

Although there are only a few intervention studies specifically focused on children who may be described as LTs, the preceding review highlights several empirically supported intervention approaches that may be viable options for increasing the expressive vocabularies of late-talking children. These approaches include parent- and clinician-implemented treatments, varying levels of models and prompts, and multiple modes of communication. There is not a single language intervention program that has proven to be more effective than other intervention approaches for all children identified as LTs. Similarly, we cannot select with absolute certainty the approach that will be best for any particular child.

## MAKING DECISIONS FOR INDIVIDUAL CHILDREN

When initially developing an intervention program, it is imperative for the clinician to consider and be sensitive to the characteristics of the child, including cognitive and language abilities, and to the child's family situation and concern, as well as the clinician's own skills and preferences based on objective evaluation of his or her own experience. To illustrate how different treatment approaches may each be appropriate in a given clinical case, the remaining sections of this chapter present the profiles of four hypothetical children who may be considered LTs. Based on each child's profile, we then suggest an initial intervention approach for each child. To help put our clinician decisions in a broader context, we begin with an overview of federal laws pertinent to intervention services for LTs.

## State Criteria for Part C Eligibility

Under federal law—specifically Part C of the Individuals with Disabilities Education Improvement Act (IDEA) of 2004 (PL 108–446)—children younger than 3 years of age with disabilities are entitled to early intervention services. In September 2011, Part C of IDEA was updated to include children with developmental delays as well as children who have conditions that may lead to future developmental delays (U.S. Department of Education, n.d.). IDEA Part C services are established for children and their families by multidisciplinary teams, which include the child's parent(s), using individualized family service plans. It is important to note that IDEA funding is administered at the state level and that states are allowed flexibility in establishing eligibility criteria for the provision of IDEA Part C services (Danaher, Goode, & Lazara, 2011). Table 14.1 lists the requirements for infant and toddler

**Table 14.1.**   Examples of state criteria for early intervention eligibility

|  | Minnesota | Kansas |
|---|---|---|
| Criteria for eligibility for services | 1. Have a disability, or<br>2. Have a developmental delay, or<br>3. Have a diagnosed physical or mental condition or disorder that has a high probability of resulting in developmental delay regardless of whether the child has a demonstrated need or delay | 1. Have a developmental delay,<br>2. Have a known condition leading to a developmental delay, or<br>3. Have an established risk (physical or mental) for developmental delay in which the common history of the disorder indicates the need for early intervention services |
| Criteria for developmental delay | A score of 1.5 standard deviations or more below the mean, as measured by the appropriate diagnostic measures and procedures, in one or more of the following areas:<br>a. Cognitive development<br>b. Physical development, including vision and hearing<br>c. Communication development<br>d. Social or emotional development<br>e. Adaptive development. | 1. There is a discrepancy of 25% or more between chronological age, after correction for prematurity and developmental age in any one of the following areas:<br>a. Cognitive development<br>b. Physical development, including vision and hearing<br>c. Communication development<br>d. Social or emotional development<br>e. Adaptive development<br>2. The child is functioning at 1.5 standard deviations below the mean in any one area listed in #1.<br>3. There are delays of at least 20% or at least one standard deviation below the mean in two or more areas listed in #1.<br>4. The clinical judgment of the multidisciplinary team concludes that a developmental delay exists when specific tests are not available or when testing does not reflect the child's actual performance. |

*Sources:* Kansas Department of Health and Environment (n.d.); Minnesota Department of Health (n.d.).

intervention services for Minnesota (The Office of the Revisor of Statutes, 2007) and Kansas (Kansas Department of Health and Environment, n.d.) as examples.

Even if it is determined that an LT is not eligible for government-funded intervention services, parents have the right to seek privately funded services. These services may be financially supported through individual health insurance or private funds. Thus, failing to meet the criteria presented in Table 14.1 does not preclude a child from receiving treatment. Moreover, for a child who does meet state-eligibility criteria, parents may want their child to receive alternatively funded services, either to supplement state-funded services or instead of state-funded services.

## Late Talker Cases

Although they have relatively specific delays in speech, language, and communication in common, children diagnosed as LTs can have dramatically different communication profiles. These profile differences, which make up part of the internal evidence needed for evidence-based intervention decisions, are highly relevant in determining the most appropriate service delivery option for any given child.

Table 14.2 details the child and family characteristics of four hypothetical children, ages 22–25 months old, who meet the standard criteria for LTs. For each case, we can assume that based on assessment by multiple professionals, the child does

**Table 14.2.**   Illustrative profiles of four children identified as late talkers

|  | Leo | Neva | Caleb | Ilsa |
|---|---|---|---|---|
| Child |  |  |  |  |
| Chronological age | 22 months | 22 months | 24 months | 25 months |
| Cognitive development standard score[a] | 95 | 85 | 105 | 85 |
| Receptive language standard score[a] | 115 | 83 | 110 | 80 |
| Expressive language standard score[a] | 78 | 76 | 71 | 68 |
| CDI: Words and Sentences total spoken words | 20 | 42 | 21 | 30 |
| Word-initial/final consonants | 8/3 | 5/0 | 6/0 | 4/0 |
| Family |  |  |  |  |
| Parental status | Two-parent household | Two-parent household | Single-parent household | Two-parent household |
| Parental education |  |  |  |  |
| Mother | College degree | College degree | 11th grade | College degree |
| Father | College degree | College degree |  | College degree |
| Birth order | 2/2 | 2/2 | 4/5 | 3/4 |
| Family history of language delay/reading difficulties | Yes | No | Yes | Yes |

[a]Assume mean = 100 and standard deviation = 15.
*Note:* Sensory and motor functioning are within the normal range for all four children.
*Key:* CDI, MacArthur-Bates Communicative Development Inventories (Fenson et al., 2007).

not have a hearing, intellectual, or motor impairment; a syndrome known to affect communication development (e.g., Down syndrome, Williams syndrome); or known neurological pathology (e.g., seizure disorder, stroke). We can also assume that based on screenings and careful consideration of the possibility, there are limited or no concerns about autism (see Chapter 15).

# ( ( ( ( ( Leo ) ) ) ) )

Leo, 22 months old, is the younger of two children in a well-educated, middle-class family. He does not communicate frequently, but he does produce requests as well as comments using his small set of spoken words plus a range of gestures, including a distal point, several conventional gestures (e.g., hand wave, head nod to indicate "yes," index finger to mouth to indicate quiet), and hand and body actions to refer to objects for which he has no words. According to the MacArthur-Bates Communication Development Inventory: Words and Sentences (CDI: Words and Sentences; Fenson et al., 2007), a parent report checklist, Leo has 20 spoken words. This places him below the 5th percentile for boys his age. Leo's words are consistently articulated and generally intelligible. He has 8 initial consonants and 3 final consonants in his phonetic inventory, and many of his words and babbled utterances contain two different consonants.

Leo has begun to produce some two-word utterances to express functional and semantic relations (e.g., "more juice," "my car"). His mother reported on the CDI: Words and Sentences that his three longest recent utterances contained one, two, and two words, respectively, which is below the 10th percentile compared with other 22-month-olds. Leo's play skills are well developed for his age. He has begun to sequence play events meaningfully (e.g., stirring in a bowl with a toy spoon and then feeding a doll with the spoon). Leo's grandmother reports that his father was also an LT, but his father has no residual indicators of this early developmental delay. Leo's parents are not overly concerned about his language development, although they recognize that he is not nearly as far along in his language development as his older brother was by the same age, which is why they sought a speech-language evaluation. However, they believe that even if Leo's assessment demonstrates that he is clinically significantly behind, he will progress more quickly at home with his mother or the family's child care provider than at the available state-supported infant-toddler program.

Based on both the Minnesota and Kansas criteria for early intervention eligibility, Leo qualifies for speech-language services due to his expressive language standard score of 78, which is right at the cutoff of 1.5 SDs below the mean. In addition, his performance on the CDI: Words and Sentences places him at or below the −1.5 cutoff level. It is important to note the findings of Heilmann and his colleagues (2005), which support using the 11th percentile as a cutoff for impairment: According to this diagnostic accuracy study, children falling below the 11th percentile on the CDI: Words and Sentences had language delays that were likely to persist through 30 months of age. Despite his borderline scores, therefore, Leo qualifies for government-funded speech-language services. Even if Leo did not have standardized test scores in one area at least 1.5 SDs below the mean, in Kansas, the multidisciplinary evaluation team could argue that Leo's substantial delay in expressive language constitutes such a significant threat to the child's developmental progress that services should be provided immediately. Minnesota and many other states do not explicitly have this option.

Each of the intervention options reviewed previously in this chapter may be appropriate for Leo, and each should be discussed with his parents as defensible options. Leo's profile, however, is one that might be appropriately suited for the watch and see approach. Specific strengths in Leo's profile that may lead a clinician to feel comfortable with a watch and see approach include his young age (i.e., 22 months), his strong receptive language and cognitive skills, and his well-developed phonetic inventory. In addition, Leo has relatively strong prelinguistic communication skills (see Chapter 9), and his use of some functional and semantic relations in two-word constructions is another indication that his development could normalize over the next 6–12 months without intervention (Kelly, 1998; Olswang, Rodriguez, & Timler, 1998). However, these strengths must be cautiously considered given the findings of Dale et al. (2003), which indicated that LTs with less severe language delays at age 2 were not necessarily the children who grew out of their delay by age 3 or 4. Thus, it cannot be assumed that children with profiles similar to Leo's will consistently be among those children who grow out of the delay.

Additional internal evidence that must be weighed as part of the clinical decision process is familial preference. It is crucial for parents to be committed and supportive of the intervention plan designed for their child. In Leo's case, his parents were comfortable when the watch and see was presented as a management option. With Leo's father's normalization after a history of language delay, Leo's young age, and the high-quality care Leo gets in the home, Leo's parents are not convinced that intervention services are required at this point. However, they would like for Leo to be reevaluated every 3 months to monitor his progress. Evidence-based practice *always* requires speech-language pathologists to look to family circumstances and parent preferences as a viable form of evidence regarding service decisions. This is especially true for those LTs who have few concerns indicating additional risk for persistent delay and many positive prognosticators. This is true of the case with Leo for whom we believe watch and see is defensible and appropriate, despite the fact that he qualifies for intervention services through the state IDEA program.

# ( ( ( ( ( Neva ) ) ) ) )

Like Leo, Neva is 22 months old; comes from a well-educated, middle-class family; and is the younger of two children. She communicates using some gestures combined with canonical vocalizations, but she does not seem to connect with adults during play. She often plays by herself and does not attend closely to her partner or her partner's objects of attention, even when she is clearly trying to communicate something with or without words. Most of her communicative acts are requests, but she does produce some comments. Neva also enjoys playing ritual games with adults, such as Peekaboo and itsy-bitsy spider. She makes good eye contact during these playful interactions. Neva's performance on standardized, norm-referenced assessments indicates that her expressive language is below average. Furthermore, her cognitive and receptive language abilities are in the low average range. Neva's parents reported that her productive vocabulary includes 42 words, which places her below the 10th percentile relative to other girls her age. Neva has only five initial consonants (and no final consonants) in her phonetic inventory and uses consonant-vowel syllable shapes for most all of her words. Unlike Leo, Neva is not combining words. Although she plays appropriately with most toys, she does not combine play schemes in a complex manner, as Leo does. Neva's parents are anxious about her slow language development and express an interest in doing whatever is necessary to get Neva the help she needs.

As was the case with Leo, Neva's standardized language assessment scores place her just below -1.5 *SD* and thus eligible for speech-language services in both Minnesota and Kansas and many other states. Specifically, her expressive language score falls more than 1.5 *SD*s below the mean for her age, and her CDI: Words and Sentences productive language performance is well below the 11th percentile cutoff recommended by Heilmann et al. (2005). However, similar to Leo, neither her cognitive nor her receptive language scores are more than 1.5 *SD*s below the mean.

Neva's limited prelinguistic communication, lack of initiations to communicate, reduced phonetic inventory, and underdeveloped play skills should be considered potential concerns associated with significant persistent delays in future language development (Fasolo, Majorano, & D'Odorico, 2008; Paul & Shiffer, 1991; Rescorla & Goossens, 1992; Thal, Tobias, & Morrison, 1991). We are confident in our position that watch and see is a viable option for many children such as Leo. We are equally confident, however, in our stance that watch and see is not a responsible choice for many LTs, such as Neva. The case for intervention for Neva is made even stronger by Neva's parents' concern about her development and their desire for Neva to receive an active treatment targeting her language delay as well as their interest in participating in such a program.

Having ruled out watch and see, the question becomes, which is the most appropriate intervention option for Neva and her family? There are many considerations involving factors that have not been presented, but based on available internal evidence, a program with parents as intervention agents would be a desirable option. General and focused stimulation approaches have generally required far fewer parent sessions than milieu approaches (Hancock & Kaiser, 2006) to yield the expected changes in parental behaviors, and effects on parental behaviors have generally been strong. Thus, one or the other of these approaches would seem to be the best fit for Neva and her family. There is no compelling evidence to indicate that one form of parent-based intervention is better than another for LTs. Either approach would take advantage of the parents' eagerness to be involved by teaching Neva's parents specific strategies to support her language development, which may or may not include specified treatment targets. With either program, it will be important for the speech-language pathologist to frequently monitor both the parents' and Neva's progress to determine if modifications to the selected treatment approach are necessary or if an entirely new approach is needed.

# ( ( ( ( ( Caleb ) ) ) ) )

Caleb, 24 months old, was born 6 weeks premature to a low-income single mother. He has three older brothers (8 years, 6 years, 5 years), all of whom were slow to talk, like Caleb, and a younger sister (11 months). Caleb's oldest brother currently receives special services for reading and math. Caleb uses gestures combined with a range of canonical vocalizations and consistent coordinated joint attention to indicate his intentions.

He readily communicates requests and occasionally comments on objects and events of interest. He is a good imitator of gross and fine motor actions. According to his performance on the CDI: Words and Sentences, Caleb's expressive vocabulary includes 21 spoken words, placing him well below the 5th percentile for boys his age. He also uses three signs (*eat*, *sleep*, and *dog*) that he learned when his mother started playing an infant sign video for him. Standardized testing confirms Caleb's expressive language impairment, but his receptive language abilities and cognitive skills are in the upper average range. Caleb uses only six consonants, one of which is a retroflex [s], and he imitates these sounds on command. However, he does not attempt to produce consonants that are not in his phonetic inventory following imitative prompts to do so.

Caleb is not yet combining words, but he readily sequences pretend play schemes throughout his play with real or toy objects. Despite her limited resources, Caleb's mother is actively seeking services to support his language development. As Caleb's oldest brother advances grades in elementary school, Caleb's mother is well aware of the brother's struggles. She would like to prevent such learning difficulties for Caleb, if possible.

Caleb's performance on the norm-referenced, standardized expressive language test unequivocally makes him eligible to receive early intervention services in Minnesota or Kansas and other states. His low performance (approximately 2 *SD*s below the mean) is further supported by his reduced expressive vocabulary reported on the CDI: Words and Sentences.

As was the case for Neva, a watch and see approach may be dismissed as a service option for Caleb because he has a number of negative prognostic indicators in his profile that suggest the need for a more aggressive intervention. In addition to significant delays in expressive language, there is a history of language delay and reading impairment in Caleb's immediate family, he comes from a low socioeconomic household, and he has an extremely limited phonetic inventory. Caleb's mother has indicated that she wants an intervention program for Caleb.

Regarding the specific type of treatment best-suited for Caleb, there are several factors that Caleb's speech-language pathologist should consider. First, Caleb's mother is supportive of services and could make herself available to participate in Caleb's intervention in some capacity. But she does not believe she is in a position to serve as his primary intervention agent. In most cases such as Caleb's, the intervention agent is likely to be the speech-language pathologist, at least at first. Second, it is diagnostically significant that Caleb has strong imitation skills of gross and fine motor movement as well as of consonants that are within his phonetic repertoire. This evidence suggests that, although Caleb may not require an intervention that includes prompts for imitation, if the clinician believes there are advantages to such approaches, he is well suited for one of them (Ellis Weismer & Murray Branch, 1989; Kouri, 2005). In addition, given Caleb's high-level use of gesture and the ease with which he learned and began to use manual signs, targeting AAC might prove to be an effective approach for Caleb. Targeting AAC in the sign modality may be a short-term way to alleviate both parent and child frustration levels due to communication breakdowns, while indirectly leading to long-term gains in oral vocabulary. As noted previously, there is strong evidence that adoption of an alternative communication method does not limit acquisition of oral language and some evidence that it can speed that development, regardless of whether the children clearly have the capacity to speak (Romski et al., 2010). Initially focusing on AAC would also give Caleb time to further develop his phonetic inventory, which his speech-language pathologist may simultaneously target in his intervention program.

# ( ( ( ( ( Ilsa ) ) ) ) )

Ilsa is 25 months old and the third of four children in a well-educated, middle-class family. There is no family history of speech or language delay, although Ilsa's older brother gets extra help with reading at school. Ilsa communicates a broad range of communication acts using a small set of words and a range of pointing, conventional, and iconic gestures combined with coordinated eye gaze. According to the CDI: Words and Sentences, Ilsa's expressive vocabulary includes 30 spoken words, which places her well below the 5th percentile compared with other girls her age. Her consonant inventory is limited to /b/, /d/, /m/, and /w/ in initial or intervocalic position.

Ilsa is not yet combining words, but she makes use of meaningful sequences of play schemes (e.g., pretending to eat with a toy spoon and then wash the dishes). Standardized testing confirms Ilsa's expressive language impairment, but her receptive language abilities are only slightly below average, and her cognitive skills are right at the low average cutoff. She has been receiving speech-language services for 3 months. Ilsa's parents, both of whom work in high-pressure professional positions, at first were unwilling to admit that Ilsa was having communication difficulties. Over the past 2 months, though, they have become frustrated by Ilsa's limited language ability and occasional tantrum behaviors that she has begun to display when her communication efforts are not understood. They have tried to get Ilsa to imitate words to get objects and services she requests using gestures or other means to indicate her needs, but she firmly rejects efforts to get her to imitate. Now, her parents are certain that intervention is needed, and they are highly motivated to find more appropriate services for Ilsa.

As was the case for Caleb, Ilsa's weak performance on the norm-referenced, standardized expressive language test makes her automatically eligible to receive early intervention services in either Minnesota or Kansas as well as many other states. Her performance on the CDI: Words and Sentences further supports her eligibility.

Given that Ilsa had already been receiving intervention services with minimal gains, a watch and see approach is not an option for her. Additional indicators in Ilsa's profile that suggest that an active intervention approach is necessary include a family history of reading difficulties, an extremely restricted phonetic inventory, and low to average receptive language and cognitive abilities. Perhaps most importantly, Ilsa's behavioral issues due to a lack of communication abilities and her parents' related frustrations also clearly support an active intervention program for Ilsa. Similar to the other cases, each of the previously described intervention approaches remains a potential option for Ilsa. However, close examination of the internal evidence in regard to Ilsa's treatment history helps to inform the development of an initial treatment plan.

The fact that Ilsa did not respond positively to a previous intervention plan or to her parents' requests for imitation is strong internal evidence indicating that Ilsa requires an intensive intervention program. Her previous intervention included a

clinician-implemented general stimulation approach aimed to create more opportunities for Ilsa to communicate during playtime and meals. Thus, it appears that
Ilsa may benefit from a more focused intervention approach, which identifies specific vocabulary items to target in treatment, or a milieu approach implemented by
a clinician rather than the parents. If Ilsa responds well to the speech-language
pathologist's prompts for imitation such that she attempts to imitate the target word
and does not appear stressed or anxious with the prompting, the use of a milieu
teaching approach would be a practical option. In comparison to a focused stimulation approach, prompts for imitation, although less naturalistic, are part of a more
direct approach that may lead to gains more quickly. In addition, an approach that
uses both Ilsa's parents and the speech-language pathologist as intervention agents
may be most appropriate for Ilsa at this point. The speech-language pathologist
should have identified targets, which would make this intervention more aggressive than her previous intervention. The parents, however, may benefit more from
participation in a parent-implemented general stimulation approach. This type of
program could target changes in parent–child interaction and increase Ilsa's production of spontaneous communication acts while helping her parents learn to
limit their attempts to elicit specific behaviors from Ilsa when she is not inclined to
produce responses to such imitative stimuli.

The results of the Ellis Weismer et al. (1993) study, which highlighted that
children even with similar behavioral profiles respond to treatment differently,
illustrate how important it is to closely monitor Ilsa's progress to ensure that she is
making gains. If Ilsa does not respond positively to the milieu teaching approach,
the speech-language pathologist would need to explore the other treatment options,
including AAC approaches.

## CONCLUSIONS

In this chapter, we have illustrated numerous clinical options that may be appropriate for children identified as LTs. However, we discussed only the most fundamental features that distinguish the approaches. There are many other treatment
details (e.g., higher or lower dosage, lexical or semantic-syntactic specific goals,
more structured or more naturalistic activities) that complicate the decision processes on which we have focused and generate confounding problems in their own
right.

We also have demonstrated some ways in which external and internal evidence can be weighed to select a management approach that is best for the child
and family and is viewed as appropriate by the speech-language pathologist. For
the most part, we have shown that studies of efficacy with LTs support the claim
that spoken language development can be sped up significantly with intervention,
which may take varying shapes and be employed on varying schedules.

The clinical category of LTs is integrally associated with the clinical research
objective of determining which children who get slow starts in language development will have persistent language disorders and which children will recover and
suffer no other associated negative consequences over their lifetime. It is important to note, then, that the efficacy evidence, to date, reflects relatively short-term
effects of relatively short-term interventions. We simply do not know whether
2-year-old LTs who respond well to treatment and appear to have normalized by

age 4 or 5 will remain free of clinically significant spoken and written language problems during school or as adults. From this perspective, we have made impressive progress, but we still have a long way to go.

## REFERENCES

Aldred, C., Green, J., & Adams, C. (2004). A new social communication intervention for children with autism: Pilot randomized controlled treatment study suggesting effectiveness. *Journal of Child Psychology and Psychiatry, 45*(8), 1420–1430.

Baumann Leech, E.R., & Cress, C.J. (2011). Indirect facilitation of speech in a late talking child by prompted production of picture symbols or signs. *AAC: Augmentative and Alternative Communication, 27*(1), 40–52. doi:

Baxendale, J., & Hesketh, A. (2003). Comparison of the effectiveness of the Hanen Parent Programme and traditional clinic therapy. *International Journal of Language and Communication Disorders, 38*(4), 397–415.

Boyd, R.M. (1980). Language intervention for grade one children. *Language, Speech, and Hearing Services in Schools, 11*(1), 30–40.

Buschmann, A., Jooss, B., Rupp, A., Feldhusen, F., Pietz, J., & Philippi, H. (2009). Parent based language intervention for 2-year-old children with specific expressive language delay: A randomised controlled trial. *Archives of Disease in Childhood, 94,* 110–116. doi:10.1136/adc.2008.141572

Carter, A.S., Messinger, D.S., Stone, W.L., Celimli, S., Nahmias, A.S., & Yoder, P. (2011). A randomized controlled trial of Hanen's 'More Than Words' in toddlers with early autism symptoms. *Journal of Child Psychology and Psychiatry, 52*(7), 741–752. doi:10.1111/j.1469–7610.2011.02395.x

Dale, P.S., Price, T.S., Bishop, D.V.M., & Plomin, R. (2003). Outcomes of early language delay: I. Predicting persistent and transient language difficulties at 3 and 4 years. *Journal of Speech, Language, and Hearing Research, 46*(3), 544–560. doi:10.1044/1092–4388(2003/044)

Danaher, J., Goode, S., & Lazara, A. (2011). *Part C updates* (12th ed.). Chapel Hill, NC: NECTAC.

Dunst, C.J., Meter, D., & Hamby, D. (2011). Influences of sign and oral language interventions on the speech and oral language production of young children with disabilities. *CELLreviews, 4*(4), 1–20.

Ellis Weismer, S., & Murray Branch, J. (1989). Modeling versus modeling plus evoked production training: A comparison of two language intervention methods. *Journal of Speech and Hearing Disorders, 54*(2), 269–281.

Ellis Weismer, S., Murray Branch, J., & Miller, J.F. (1993). Comparison of two methods for promoting productive vocabulary in late talkers. *Journal of Speech and Hearing Research, 36*(5), 1037–1050.

Fasolo, M., Majorano, M., & D'Odorico, L. (2008). Babbling and first words in children with slow expressive development. *Clinical Linguistics & Phonetics, 22*(2), 83–94. doi:10.1080/02699200701600015

Fenson, L., Marchman, V.A., Thal, D.J., Dale, P.S., Reznick, J.S., & Bates, E. (2007). *MacArthur-Bates Communicative Development Inventories (CDIs).* (2nd ed.). Baltimore, MD: Paul H. Brookes Publishing Co.

Fey, M.E. (1986). *Language intervention with young children.* San Diego, CA: College-Hill Press.

Fey, M.E., & Justice, L.M. (2007). Evidence-based decision making in communication intervention. In R. Paul & P.W. Cascella (Eds.), *Introduction to clinical methods in communication disorders* (2nd ed.; pp. 179–202). Baltimore, MD: Paul H. Brookes Publishing Co.

Fey, M.E., Krulik, T.E., Loeb, D.F., & Proctor-Williams, K. (1999). Sentence recast use by parents of children with typical language and children with specific language impairment. *American Journal of Speech-Language Pathology, 8,* 273–286.

Girolametto, L. (1988). Improving the social-conversational skills of developmentally delayed children: An intervention study. *Journal of Speech and Hearing Research, 53*(2), 156–167.

Girolametto, L., Pearce, P.S., & Weitzman, E. (1996). Interactive focused stimulation for toddlers with expressive vocabulary delays. *Journal of Speech and Hearing Research, 39*(6), 1274–1283.

Girolametto, L., Pearce, P.S., & Weitzman, E. (1997). Effects of lexical intervention on the phonology of late talkers. *Journal of Speech, Language, and Hearing Research, 40*(2), 338–348.

Girolametto, L., Wiigs, M., Smyth, R., Weitzman, E., & Pearce, P.S. (2001). Children with a history of expressive vocabulary delay: Outcomes at 5 years of age. *American Journal of Speech-Language Pathology, 10*(4), 358–369.

Hancock, T.B., & Kaiser, A.P. (2006). Enhanced milieu teaching. In R.J. McCauley & M.E. Fey (Eds.), *Treatment of language disorders in children* (pp. 203–236). Baltimore, MD: Paul H. Brookes Publishing Co.

Heilmann, J., Ellis Weismer, S., Evans, J., & Hollar, C. (2005). Utility of the MacArthur-Bates Communicative Development Inventory in identifying language abilities of late-talking and typically developing toddlers. *American Journal of Speech-Language Pathology, 14*(1), 40–51. doi:10.1044/1058–0360%282005/006%29

Individuals with Disabilities Education Improvement Act (IDEA) of 2004, PL 108–446, 20 U.S.C. §§ 1400 *et seq.*

Kansas Department of Health and Environment. (n.d.). Permanent Administrative Regulations, Infant and Toddler Program, *KAR 28-4, 28-4-550 to 572.* Retrieved from http://www.kdheks.gov/its/kar28-4-550to572.html

Kelly, D.J. (1998). A clinical synthesis of the "late talker" literature: Implications for service delivery. *Language, Speech & Hearing Services in Schools, 29*(2), 76–84.

Kouri, T.A. (2005). Lexical training through modeling and elicitation procedures with late talkers who have specific language impairment and developmental delays. *Journal of Speech, Language, and Hearing Research, 48*(1), 157–171. doi:10.1044/1092–4388 (2005/012)

Manhardt, J., & Rescorla, L. (2002). Oral narrative skills of late talkers at ages 8 and 9. *Applied Psycholinguistics, 23*(1), 1–21.

Minnesota Department of Health, Infant and Toddler Intervention Services. (n.d.) *Guidelines for making eligibility decisions.* Retrieved from http://www.health.state.mn.us/divs/fh/mcshn/ecipelig/

Nippold, M.A. (1996). Slow expressive language development: A call for more data. *American Journal of Speech-Language Pathology, 5*(2), 29–30.

Nippold, M.A., & Schwarz, I.E. (1996). Children with slow expressive language development: What is the forecast for school achievement? *American Journal of Speech-Language Pathology, 5*(2), 22–25.

The Office of the Revisor of Statutes. (2007). *Minnesota administrative rules.* Retrieved from https://www.revisor.mn.gov/rules/?id = 3525.1350

Olswang, L.B., Bain, B.A., & Johnson, G.A. (1992). Using dynamic assessment with children with language disorders. In S.F. Warren & J.E. Reichle (Series Eds. & Vol. Eds.), *Communication and Language Intervention Series: Vol. 1. Causes and effects in communication and language intervention* (pp. 187–216). Baltimore, MD: Paul H. Brookes Publishing Co.

Olswang, L.B., Rodriguez, B., & Timler, G. (1998). Recommending intervention for toddlers with specific language learning difficulties: We may not have all the answers, but we know a lot. *American Journal of Speech-Language Pathology, 7*(1), 23–32.

Paul, R. (1996). Clinical implications of the natural history of slow expressive language development. *American Journal of Speech-Language Pathology, 5*(2), 5–21.

Paul, R. (1997). Understanding language delay: A response to van Kleeck, Gillam, and Davis. *American Journal of Speech-Language Pathology, 6*(2), 40–49.

Paul, R., Hernandez, R., Taylor, L., & Johnson, K. (1996). Narrative development in late talkers: Early school age. *Journal of Speech and Hearing Research, 39*(6), 1295–1303.

Paul, R., & Shiffer, M.E. (1991). Communicative initiations in normal and late-talking toddlers. *Applied Psycholinguistics, 12*(4), 419–431.

Rescorla, L. (2002). Language and reading outcomes to age 9 in late-talking toddlers. *Journal of Speech, Language, and Hearing Research, 45*(2), 360–371.

Rescorla, L., & Goossens, M. (1992). Symbolic play development in toddlers with expressive specific language impairment (SLI-E). *Journal of Speech and Hearing Research, 35*(6), 1290–1302.

Robertson, S.B., & Ellis Weismer, S. (1999). Effects of treatment on linguistic and social skills in toddlers with delayed language development. *Journal of Speech, Language, and Hearing Research, 42*(5), 1234–1248.

Romski, M., Sevcik, R.A., Adamson, L.B., Cheslock, M., Smith, A., Barker, R., & Bakeman, R. (2010). Randomized comparison of augmented and non-augmented language interventions for toddlers with developmental delays and their parents. *Journal of Speech, Language, and Hearing Research, 53*(2), 350–364. doi: 10.1044/1092–4388(2009/08–0156)

Tannock, R., Girolametto, L., & Siegel, L.S. (1992). Language intervention with children who have developmental delays: Effects of an interactive approach. *American Journal on Mental Retardation, 97*(2), 145–160.

Thal, D.J., Bates, E., Goodman, J., & Jahn Samilo, J. (1997). Continuity of language abilities: An exploratory study of late- and early-talking toddlers. *Developmental Neuropsychology, 13*(3), 239–273.

Thal, D.J., Tobias, S., & Morrison, D. (1991). Language and gesture in late talkers: A 1-year follow-up. *Journal of Speech and Hearing Research, 34*(3), 604–612.

U.S. Department of Education. (n.d.). *IDEA 2004: Building the legacy: Part C (bith–2 years old).* Retreived from http://idea.ed.gov/part-c/search/new

van Kleeck, A., Gillam, R.B., & Davis, B. (1997). When is "watch and see" warranted? A response to Paul's 1996 article, "Clinical Implications of the Natural History of Slow Expressive Language Development." *American Journal of Speech-Language Pathology, 6*(2), 34–39.

Weiss, R.S. (1981). INREAL intervention for language handicapped and bilingual children. *Journal of Early Intervention, 4*(1), 40–51. doi:10.1177/105381518100400106

Whitehurst, G.J., Fischel, J.E., Lonigan, C.J., Valdez Menchaca, M.C., Arnold, D.S., & Smith, M. (1991). Treatment of early expressive language delay: If, when, and how. *Topics in Language Disorders, 11*(4), 55–68.

# 15

# Which Late Talkers Require Intervention?

*Matching Child Characteristics
and Risk Factors to Treatment*

Stephen Camarata

For the purposes of this chapter, the term *late talker* (LT) refers to ALL children with a late onset of word production, regardless of whether this is a temporary developmental phase that will eventually normalize (often also referred to as a "late bloomer") or the late talking is an indication of a broader and more pervasive condition such as receptive language disorder, autism, or global intellectual disability. As this perspective implies, "late talking" applies to a diverse population with many potential factors contributing directly or indirectly to the late onset of words and to its consequences. Not surprisingly, the developmental and treatment course of these various conditions is quite diverse, even though the core explicit feature—talking late—is shared.

The goal of this chapter is to describe some of the potential conditions that lead to late talking, including late blooming, and, if intervention is warranted, matching the intervention to a given child's characteristics. Intervention approaches can be strikingly different depending on these child characteristics, ranging from a "wait and see" approach (Paul, 1996; see also Chapter 14 in this book) to intensive daily treatment (Lovaas, 1987), even though the primary feature that triggered the original referral is the late onset of talking. In addition, the chapter focuses on developmental approaches that are appropriate for children at or near the age when late talking is usually first evident: toddlers younger than 36 months old. This is an important consideration because some intervention approaches that may be appropriately applied to preschoolers or early school-age children may not be suitable for toddlers.

## BACKGROUND

Talking is one of the most salient developmental milestones in early childhood. To a parent's delight, most children start talking around the time they celebrate their first birthday. More than 90% of children begin using words by 18 months of age. But the remaining 10% are late to begin talking, at least to some extent. (Fenson et al., 2007). A key question for clinicians and for parents is whether the late onset of words is simply typical developmental variation without any long-term effects or whether it is an indication of broader developmental disabilities.

## What Is Late Talking?

A parent once contacted me and was concerned that her child was not using words at 13 months of age. She had read that first words come in by 12 months and was rather distraught that her son had not met this milestone. Like many developmental milestones, talking has a rather variable onset, with a typical distribution from approximately 9 to 16 months. That is, according to Fenson et al. (2007), a majority of typically developing children will begin using first words somewhere within this age range. In terms of age-equivalency and "percent delay," a metric often used for early intervention (EI) eligibility, this is a broad span. Consider that an age deviation (age of onset minus median age of onset divided by median age of onset) would yield a 33% delay for a 16-month-old child (16–12)/12 = 4/12 x 100) who in actuality is within the typical developmental onset of first words. In the absence of a more general developmental condition (e.g., Down syndrome), such a "delay" would simply be normal variation around the median age toddlers typically start using words. For the purposes of this chapter, if a child is not using true words by 17 months of age, this would be considered late talking.

## Assessment Considerations

The first thing to be said about all late talking cases is that a medical evaluation should be completed to rule out any medical factors such as seizures or known genetic conditions that may be contributing to the late onset of speech and/or language. In addition, an audiological examination should be performed to ensure that hearing loss, which is a major risk factor for late talking, can be ruled out. Also, it is important to bear in mind that many children who talk late are "nonclinical" in that they may display significantly delayed language abilities at 2 or even 3 years of age but subsequently catch up and do not have a clinical conditions such as autism or apraxia.

Although some clinicians appear to approach late talking from a particular developmental orientation—such as Agin, Geng, and Nicholl (2004) applying apraxia as a framework to account for late talking—there are actually a number of clinical conditions that include late talking as a symptom. Assessment should focus on differential diagnosis of the conditions associated with the late onset of words *rather than confirming a particular diagnosis such as apraxia*. The text revision of the American Psychiatric Association's (APA's) *Diagnostic and Statistical Manual of Mental Disorders, Fourth Edition (DSM-IV-TR;* APA, 2000)—the most current *DSM* at the time of this writing—lists various conditions that first appear in childhood that include late talking as a symptom or diagnostic marker. The most prevalent of these include Expressive Language Disorder; Mixed Expressive-Receptive Language Disorder; Phonological Disorder; Mental Retardation; and some of the pervasive developmental disorders, including Autistic Disorder, Rett's Disorder, and Pervasive Developmental Disorder Not Otherwise Specified (PDD-NOS). Note that Asperger's Disorder is characterized in the

*DSM-IV-TR* with typical onset of language, *indicating that late talking is not a symptom of this condition.* Children who talk late should not be labeled as having Asperger syndrome (see also Camarata, in press).

Note that a common classification for one form of late talking, specific language impairment (SLI), combines the *DSM* categories of expressive language disorder and mixed expressive-receptive language disorders. Also note that apraxia, or childhood apraxia of speech (CAS), would be considered a subtype of phonological disorder (articulation disorder) in the *DSM* classification scheme and that a child can have multiple diagnoses (e.g., autism and articulation disorder). But, it is clear that very few children are LTs because of apraxia (Delaney & Kent, 2004; Shriberg, Aram, & Kwiatkowski, 1997). Finally, there are diagnoses commonly used for LTs such as sensory integration deficit (Ayres, 1970; Miller, Anzalone, Lane, Cermak, & Osten, 2007) that may be employed by some clinicians, but these have not been sufficiently developed and/or validated to be included in the *DSM* or other standard diagnostic classifications. (See also the policy statement on sensory integration from the American Academy of Pediatrics [Zimmer & Desch, 2012].)

## Differential Diagnosis of Late Talking

The broad question of how one can tell if a child will grow out of late talking or has a clinical condition likely to persist, such as phonological disorders, intellectual disabilities, autism spectrum disorders (ASDs), PDD-NOS, language disorder, or some combination of these (e.g., phonological disorder and an ASD) is a primary focus of the initial (and ongoing) assessments. The process of differential diagnosis requires careful observation of the child in a variety of contexts. More importantly, the evaluation process should include a detailed examination of potential risk factors rather than attempting to confirm a particular preconceived diagnosis such as an ASD. In general, the fewer risk factors evident and the lower the severity level of these risk factors, the more likely the late talking is a developmental variation rather than a clinical condition such that the child may ultimately normalize. For example, several studies since the early 1990s have indicated that if the only trait evident in the child is late onset of words at age 2, then there is a relatively high probability that the vocabulary size will be within the normal range at the age of 4 (Paul, 1993, 2000; Whitehurst, Fischel, Arnold, & Lonigan, 1992). In contrast, Paul (1996) reported that late-talking children who also had phonological (speech sound) disorders were more likely to continue to have language difficulty beyond age 4. This suggests that a diagnostic model should provide a systematic analysis of risk factors when recommending treatment for LTs.

If a child is not talking, what skills *other than the late talking (word production)* are important? As mentioned previously, the quality of the child's vocalizations (e.g., Does the child use a variety of sounds in babbling? Is the child producing protowords?) is predictive of later growth and whether immediate treatment or wait and see should be implemented. In addition, the child's receptive language skills are important. The children who subsequently normalized in Whitehurst et al.'s (1992) and Thal et al.'s (1991) studies had normal (age-appropriate) comprehension, and subsequent studies (e.g., Botting et al., 2001; Law, Tomblin & Zhang, 2008) have indicated that receptive ability is among the strongest predictors of subsequent language ability. Stated simply, poor receptive language level is an important risk factor for late talking (see Chapter 9).

Another important domain is the nature and quality of the child's nonverbal social interactions. Children with serious problems such as autism are less likely to initiate nonverbal social interactions than children who are likely to normalize. Indeed, reduced social interaction that cannot be accounted for by late talking itself is a hallmark characteristic of autism or other forms of PDD (APA, 2000). The original description of autism by Leo Kanner in 1943, which was based on observations of children with intellectual disabilities, was focused on the striking reduction in motivation for social interaction, even relative to others with intellectual disabilities and, presumably, with reduced expressive and receptive language ability.

Although the precise genetics are not currently known, it does appear that familial occurrence also constitutes risk for late talking. But, it is important to bear in mind that first- or second-order relatives may have talked late and normalized without direct intervention. Familial late talking, however, can be considered a risk factor in the broad autism phenotype (Tager-Flusberg & Cooper, 1999).

Finally, a child's nonlinguistic cognitive abilities are an important factor. It is not surprising that LTs often fall below expected levels on verbally based intelligence assessments. After all, how many of us could do well on a test given in a language we don't understand? But, LTs who are otherwise unimpaired should fall within the normal range on tests that examine nonverbal cognitive abilities (e.g., the Leiter International Performance Scale–Revised [Leiter-R]; Roid & Miller, 1997). If the LT is below expected levels on nonverbal tests (in addition to verbal tests), this suggests a more comprehensive intellectual disability. In simple terms, these kinds of tests predict a child's rate of learning, and if cognitive abilities are below expected levels, it is likely that the child will learn more slowly and require more attention than peers not only in the area of speech and language development but in other learning as well.

## AN OVERVIEW: A DEVELOPMENTAL PERSPECTIVE ON RISK FACTORS AND INTERVENTION STRATEGIES

There are at least two divergent perspectives on risk factors for late talking and how these lead to intervention. In order to interpret the diverse intervention perspectives and approaches applied to children who talk late, it is helpful to first understand these different clinical orientations. The first is broadly based on a speech and auditory processing perspective and employs speech motor and cognitive processing factors as the basis for remediating speech and language disorders. Within this framework, any delay in talking arises from one or more impairments in the special skills or "processing" abilities hypothesized to underlie speech and language. For example, late talking could be viewed as a disruption in the motor planning and peripheral execution of the articulation gestures required to produce intelligible speech (Agin et al., 2004). This then would lead to interventions based on improving volitional execution of tongue movements thought to underlie phoneme production in order to treat late talking. Under this rubric, intervention targets may include oral motor exercises, blowing, activities designed to increase awareness of tongue position and oral sensation, and even facial massage in the hopes of increasing mastery of these subcomponents hypothesized to be required for speaking. A processing perspective also may hold that the ability to discriminate individual speech sounds is a prerequisite skill for auditory comprehension and, in some models, for accurate speech production. In these approaches, the starting point for intervention is the simple fact that a child is late in beginning to talk so that the "processing infrastructure" must be supplemented using intervention. In the absence of direct evidence and studies testing causal linkage between the special skills and the late talking, it is mere speculation as to which special skills are necessary precursors to speaking.

An alternative competing view of assessment and intervention arises from the extensive literature on typical developmental processes. In this view, deviations from typical development are analyzed in order to determine how to augment the child's existing speech and language systems and bring them through the next steps in language development. In this developmental perspective, intervention goals would include speech sounds (phonemes), words (vocabulary), morphemes, and syntax within an appropriate social (pragmatic) context. For example, Keith Nelson's (1989) foundational work on recast intervention wherein words, grammatical morphemes, and syntactic structures are targeted by clinician (or parent) modeling of these forms following a child initiation would be considered a developmental intervention approach.

Not surprisingly, these two approaches have very different diagnostic processes. Broadly, and at the risk of oversimplification, processing models simply require demonstration that there is an impairment in order to initiate intervention on the special skills thought to be necessary for speech and language production. Again broadly, and again at the risk of oversimplification, a standard approach to late talking could be to initiate intervention using nonspeech oral motor exercises believed to be the foundation of learning to talk. There no doubt is an appealing face validity to the notion that talking requires a tongue that is strong enough and sufficiently agile to fluidly move through the rapid and complex gestures required to generate intelligible speech. Also, because speech is a product of effectively valving the airflow through the oral cavity, there is an intuitive appeal to remedial activities such as blowing bubbles and whistles in order facilitate speech development. Despite the face validity and intuitive appeal to a special skills/processing approach to late talking, there is a surprisingly weak evidence base to support intervention for LTs arising from this perspective. For example, Lof and Watson (2008) provided a convincing critique of nonspeech oral motor exercises. Perhaps the most challenging counter evidence for employing these special skills interventions with late-talking toddlers is that many typically developing toddlers are unable to complete the special skills hypothesized to underlie typical development. For example, if the ability to blow bubbles is a necessary prerequisite skill for talking, why is it that so many 2-year-olds who speak perfectly fine for their age level are unable to blow bubbles?

In contrast, a developmental perspective seeks to examine the child's current developmental level, and to some degree, the ambient environment including parent input in order to individualize intervention. The purpose of this chapter is not to provide a critique of the special skills or processing diagnostic and intervention approach, although there is a reasonably extensive literature addressing this issue. Rather, the risk factors and intervention framework presented herein will follow a developmental perspective. Finestak and Fey (Chapter 14) provide an excellent orientation to a number of approaches within a developmental framework and theoretical case presentations designed to illustrate intervention arising from these perspectives. This chapter augments the information in Chapter 14 by providing a general developmental problem-solving approach to late talking.

## Transactions: The Foundations of Development

Sameroff (1975) presented a general model of child development rooted in the notion that interactions and transactions between the child and the environment are a core foundation of development. Nelson (1989) adapted this model specifically for language development, and a number of researchers—including Snyder-McLean and McLean (1987); MacDonald and Gillette (1988); Kaiser, Hancock, and Trent (2007); Yoder and Warren (1993); Fey et al. (2006); Camarata, Nelson, and Camarata (1994); and Koegel and Koegel (2006)—have adopted this general theoretical orientation to the problem of diagnosing and treating speech and language disorders in children with disabilities. For late-talking toddlers, the work of Kaiser et al., Yoder and Warren, and Camarata et al. are especially relevant, and the Hanen program (see Chapter 13) is an example of a parent training intervention approach based on transactional theory.

Broadly, the transactional approach to development views talking as a long-term product of parent–child interaction (Moerk, 1992), with incremental advancements induced by a series of learning episodes. The parent (or clinician) reacts to a child's communicative initiations with a linguistic model of a more advanced language target. For example, in a toddler an initiation "ba" when the child is looking at a ball will trigger a parent (or clinician) response with the lexical and phonologically more advanced form "Ball; yes, a ball" (Camarata, 2010). For morphological and syntactic growth, a child's initiation "ball roll" would elicit a parent (or clinician) response of "The ball is rolling." When the child's initiations begin to incorporate even more advanced forms (e.g., "The ball is rolling"), the parent (or clinician) provides additional syntactic, morphological, and semantic information, such as "Yes, the ball is rolling down the hill" (See Figure 15.1; see also Moerk, 1992; Nelson, 1989).

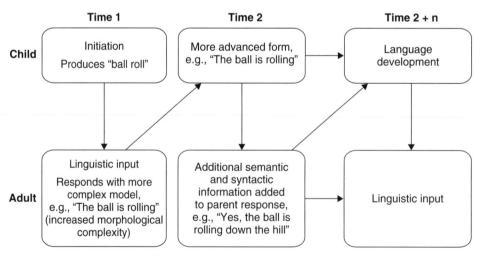

**Figure 15.1.**  Transactional approach to language development.

## Differential Diagnosis and Risk Factors

Studies of the transactional model as the basis of development have demonstrated that there are literally hundreds of thousands or even millions of transactions delivered to children before they enter school (Hart & Risley, 1995). Indeed, Hart and Risley characterized transactions in the hundreds of thousands as being relatively impoverished compared with the millions of opportunities delivered by many parents. By adapting the transactional model to the problem of differential diagnosis and risk factors in late-talking toddlers, the goal becomes identifying the barriers to accessing typical developmental opportunities. For example, because children with autism have a reduced or absent motivation for social interaction, the rate of initiations that trigger a parent model becomes severely limited (Koegel, Koegel, & McNerney, 2001). Also, Koegel et al. reported that baseline levels of initiations by children with autism is one of the strongest predictors of later growth in terms of communication development. In contrast, children with phonological disorders only do initiate and are motivated socially, but their initiations may not be sufficiently intelligible for parents to deliver lexical, morphological, and/or syntactic models that accurately map the child's intended message. Finally, children with global intellectual impairments learn in a manner that parallels typical development but at a much lower rate. In these children, for example, the typical lexical fast mapping becomes "slow mapping" wherein the two or three presentations needed for an initial word acquisition in typical development becomes presentations in the hundreds.

The notion of risk factors then is viewed within the context of whether and to what extent elements of the transactions that are readily available in the child's every day environment can be 1) triggered, 2) delivered by a parent (or clinician), and 3) processed and stored by the child. So, a wait and see approach may be acceptable for a child who readily initiates, is intelligible when he or she does initiate, is in a home or child care situation in which parent/teacher/peer models are delivered in response to initiation, and whose comprehension skills are sufficient to process and store the additional linguistic elements provided by the model. From a theoretical perspective, intervention would be indicated when the child has limitations in any of these aspects of development. And, at least theoretically, the more severe and more pervasive the risk factors, the more intense the intervention should be (Wetherby et al., 2004).

This directly parallels the differential diagnosis process. That is, after directly determining that the child is indeed late in talking, the next step is to determine whether he or she meets the diagnostic criteria for global intellectual impairments, autism, SLI, phonological disorder, or some other form of pervasive developmental disorder. At a minimum, this will require assessing the child's social engagement, receptive language ability, and cognitive abilities independently of the late talking symptomology, and conducting a speech/articulation/phonological assessment. These data then can be applied to the problem of whether a wait and see minimal parent training approach or more intensive intervention is indicated.

Note that the differential diagnosis process is NOT identical to the eligibility process. Eligibility criteria are laid out in part C of the Individuals with Disabilities Education Improvement Act (IDEA) of 2004 (PL 108–446) and are designed to identify which toddlers will gain access to special education services under assessment procedures and cutoff scores/levels determined by each state under federal guidelines (Ringwalt, 2012). For example, the results of the developmental checklist may be sufficient to gain child eligibility for EI access under the broad rubric of developmental delays but will not provide a differential diagnosis of whether the developmental delay is a specific language impairment, global intellectual impairment, or autism. I have seen all of these, and also some late-talking toddlers who normalized while waiting for service, labeled as developmentally delayed for access to EI services.

## INTERVENTION FOR LATE TALKING: MATCHING CHILD CHARACTERISTICS TO INTERVENTION APPROACHES

Although some clinicians may employ a monolithic "one size fits all" approach to intervention, medical and behavioral treatments are moving increasingly to an individualized approach. Such a perspective is adopted herein, with different intervention approaches being applicable to children with different developmental profiles. As an example, consider what is commonly referred to as an applied behavior analysis (ABA) approach to autism treatment. This approach, popularized by Ivar Lovaas (e.g., Lovaas, 1987), uses imitative prompts and food rewards to elicit words and is based on B.F. Skinner's (1957) description of operant language learning. This approach is widely used on LTs, but many late-talking children may resist responding to imitative prompts and thus not be good candidates for this approach. For example, Gillum, Camarata, Nelson, and Camarata (2003) reported that children with low scores on the sentence imitation subtest of the Test of Language Development, Third Edition (Newcomer & Hamill, 1988) performed poorly in the kind of discrete ABA trials Lovaas (1987) described. Similarly, Nelson et al. (1995) reported that typical development was slowed when imitation and prompts were used to elicit grammatical forms. The point here is that no one approach will be applicable to all cases, even with a shared diagnosis such as ASDs. This point is examined in detail in Yoder, Kaiser, and Alpert (1991). In the case of LTs with heterogeneous diagnoses and risk factors, matching child characteristics to intervention approaches is even more important.

### Controlling for Spontaneous Growth and Superstitious Treatment Effects

The language skills of any LT, regardless of diagnosis, and many typically developing children as well, can be accelerated by applying focused stimulation on words, word endings, sentences, and speech sounds. If the only factor in the late talking is the late onset of words, there is a very high likelihood that the child will normalize within a relatively short time. All children with disabilities can learn, so more serious problems can be improved with appropriate treatment. It is comforting to know that the overwhelming majority of individuals with disabilities learn to talk. But, this also increases the need for studies that test treatments against spontaneous growth. That is, if treatment is applied to an LT who would have otherwise normalized even without treatment, the family and the clinician may mistakenly attribute the growth to the intervention.

Also, an important challenge in more serious conditions such as autism is making sure that the focus of language is on truly functional skills (e.g., useful words) and making sure that the goals are coordinated among the special educators, preschool teachers, speech-language pathologists, and parents, as these children will likely benefit from learning the same words in each context. Unfortunately, there are many unproven (and often expensive) treatments being offered to families that do not directly improve talking and whose supporting evidence appears to be testimonials from parents and clinicians without adequate control for spontaneous growth in LTs who may have initially been misidentified as having an ASD. At this time, unlike the research to support directly teaching a child to talk, there is not scientific evidence to support the use of special diets, massage, muscle exercises, nonlanguage auditory training, or chelation therapy to treat late talking. Moreover as Paul (2000) noted, late talking may simply be a developmental stage or it may be a symptom of a more severe condition. Many LTs will normalize without treatment, many others will normalize with an appropriate treatment program, and some may never speak, but regardless of whether the late talking is a stage or a symptom, all can learn. It is important to have an accurate diagnosis, and if needed, appropriate treatment.

Because the general condition of late talking is a behavioral trait for many different clinical conditions, as well as a variation on nonclinical development, clinicians hypothesize that late-talking toddlers are a very interesting group for developing neural, genetic, and auditory perceptual signatures that will yield useful diagnostic information and perhaps provide important prognostic indictors for treatment. And, there is an ongoing need to critically evaluate treatment to improve on what Paul (2000) has characterized as a relatively low accuracy rate in predicting later development in late-talking 2-year-olds.

## Matching Risk Factors and Intervention Approaches

Some children who talk late have difficulty learning speech and language skills and many require learning support to maximize their potential, whereas many others normalize after adopting a wait and see approach. This later approach is in direct contrast to applying EI to all LTs. It is perhaps unsurprising that there have been many different types of intervention developed that have very different methods of teaching speech and language skills. The array of intervention choices and orientations can make it difficult for parents and clinicians to determine which services are most likely to be effective with their child.

## Divergent Intervention Perspectives

When parents discover that their child has a disabling condition with associated speech and language ramifications, it may be difficult for them to find accurate information on the ways to enhance learning. There have been widely different causes and intervention approaches proposed, and parents are often confronted with conflicting and perhaps even contradictory proposals on what services are needed to help their child learn to talk.

Accounts provided in the media or in product information brochures appear to promise the potential for seemingly miraculous results; one intervention plan touts "dramatic results in only six weeks" from a program that acts like "glasses for the ears" (Blakeslee, 1995; see also Merzenich et al., 1996). A book by Thomas Sowell (1998) described late-talking children who evidently get a late start in language and/or speech acquisition but manage to learn to talk with little or no intervention support. Opinions on speech and language intervention approaches at a national conference of the American Speech-Language-Hearing Association (ASHA, n.d.) ranged from the aforementioned "glasses for the ears" that employ computer games designed to enhance speech sound discrimination, to strictly controlled imitation practice completed in pull-out clinical settings, to naturalistic intervention completed in inclusive settings in the classrooms.

As one might guess, the goals and the proposed outcomes of these approaches are directly predicated on the assumptions about causation of late talking underlying the intervention approach. Some approaches include training in special skills thought to underlie speech and language acquisition, with an emphasis on the proposed components of talking. For example, the FastForWord intervention focuses directly on formant transitions, the zones of acoustic information within speech sounds that play a major role in speech discrimination. In this approach, speech and language disabilities (and more general learning disabilities) are believed to result from a reduced ability to use this acoustic information, so the intervention includes drills on this special skill in the hopes that improvement in speech sound discrimination will lead to broader gains in speech and language performance. But, at this time, it is unclear whether this kind of instruction will actually result in improved speaking and listening skills in everyday contexts such as at home and school. Also, it is unclear whether all children with speech and language disabilities actually have difficulties with speech discrimination. Moreover, the results of a randomized control trial conducted in Great Britain (Cohen et al., 2005) testing an intervention approach designed to improve speech discrimination did not support this approach (see also, Camarata, 2008). In addition, it has become increasingly clear that speech discrimination impairments cannot account for speech and language disorders. For example, one of the children in the Scottish Rite Child Language Disorders Center at Vanderbilt University had speech discrimination skills that exceeded the abilities of most adults, but his speech was largely unintelligible, and a recent review by Fey et al. (2011) indicated a lack of evidence for auditory processing approaches to treating delayed language.

Whole language programs (Norris & Hoffman, 1994) are perhaps at the opposing end of the spectrum; intervention includes nonspecific enrichment activities and teaching episodes that directly parallel what happens during communication exchanges at home and in school within typical language and includes no specific skills training whatsoever. But, if the child is having problems learning to talk, it is unclear whether simply adding more of these activities without a developmentally appropriate focus will be sufficient to enhance speech and language acquisition. Given these options and a range of gradations incorporating elements of special skills, imitation and drill, and naturalistic intervention components, how can one determine which approach is most likely to be effective?

## Validation of Intervention Effectiveness

Ultimately, the resolution of these debates can only come from clinical researchers conducting fair and objective comparisons of the various intervention approaches. There is actually a relatively large database on treating the various disabilities for which late talking is a symptom. For example, there are direct comparisons of imitation and drill types of instruction versus intervention patterned after how children without disabilities learn to talk. The first thing to be said is that literally hundreds of articles demonstrate that direct and indirect methods of teaching vocabulary, morphology, syntax, and phonology within a developmentally appropriate framework can dramatically increase a child's rate of progress. Although persistent and at times heated arguments regarding whether targets should be taught under tightly controlled conditions or more naturalistic contexts have been going on for more than 3 decades, (e.g., see Muma, 1977) a broader look at the data shows that if, for example, words are taught, then words will be learned. This is not meant to trivialize the real differences in, for example, the ABA discrete trials approach (Lovaas, 1987) to teaching vocabulary as opposed to, say, enhanced milieu teaching (Kasier et al., 2007) or conversational recast (Camarata, 2010), but rather to highlight the fundamental notion that children will learn what they are taught.

In contrast, nonlinguistic specific skills approaches may not lead to gains in generalized speech and language skills. For example, teaching children to discriminate speech sounds will often improve performance on tests of speech discrimination but may not translate into improvements in talking ability at home or in the classroom (Camarata, 2008; Fey et al., 2011). Moreover, it is clear that significant gains in speech and language skills do not require direct training in speech sound discrimination or in any other underlying special skill (e.g., auditory sequencing).

Finally, and perhaps most importantly, this research has indicated that individual children require different levels of intervention support to learn speech and language. Most children in this research learned when provided with repeated models of developmentally appropriate language goals. A typically developing child can often learn a new word in one or two presentations. A child with language learning disabilities can learn in exactly the same setting, but may require 50 or even 100 presentations (Nelson et al., 1995). But, some children require even more support to learn, such as strict stimulus control within imitation and drill activities (Camarata et al., 1994). For example, one child needed more than 1,500 presentations to learn the auxiliary form (see also Leonard, Camarata, Brown, & Camarata, 2008). A few children learn very slowly no matter which intervention approach is applied, but most make rapid progress with intervention. Contributing factors can include receptive language levels, presence or absence of behavior challenges such as attention-deficit/hyperactivity disorder or disruptive behavior, lacks motivation to communicate, or displays other challenges in addition to the language impairments (e.g., anxiety disorder).

These findings suggest that miracle cures are not likely to produce real, long-term improvements in speech and language skills, and that effective intervention is a systematic, focused process that directly targets the skills that are developmentally appropriate for each child. A tentative starting point for intervention should be presentations that parallel and enhance the learning process in the home and/or school setting. If little progress is observed with this approach, additional support should be provided in terms of frequency of intervention and in terms of traditional imitation and drill activities (see the model in Camarata, 1996). Perhaps most importantly, these studies suggest that the overwhelming majority of children with speech and language disabilities make significant progress during intervention, which should provide hope and encouragement for families of toddlers who talk late.

## TYING IT ALL TOGETHER: CASE EXAMPLES

Chapter 14 provides four excellent case presentations for differing intervention approaches. A case-study approach is also adopted here by presenting composite, prototypical case presentations based on multiple exemplars seen in the Vanderbilt University research clinic in the Department of Hearing and Speech Sciences at the Wilkerson Center. Each prototypical case includes multiple features adapted from a specific child and represents real-life examples.

These case presentations will include late-talking children who initially met eligibility criteria or were diagnosed with relatively severe conditions and then subsequently normalized while waiting for intervention; children with severe conditions, including one case with intellectual impairments and another with autism whose parents disagreed with the initial diagnoses and only subsequently realized that their child's late talking was actually a symptom of a more severe condition; children diagnosed with apraxia, including one who continues to have severe speech disability and another who normalized without traditional speech intervention; and a child with receptive language disorder who initially was diagnosed with more global intellectual impairments but whose subsequent developmental course indicated that the global intellectual impairments perspective was inaccurate, although extensive intervention support was required in order for the child to learn language.

### Wait and See

The first case, which illustrates a child with an initial severe eligibility who normalized within an inadvertent wait and see approach, is a Caucasian girl who was 18 months at the time she was referred for eligibility testing for EI. The initial EI evaluation resulted in an eligibility determination of an ASD, and this diagnosis was provided to the family. It is perhaps noteworthy that this assessment included a parent interview and a developmental checklist based on, according to the parents, relatively brief direct observation of the child. Bear in mind that the goal of this initial assessment was to determine whether she met the state mandated criteria for EI and was not designed to provide a differential diagnosis. The child's father was a physician and her mother was a developmental psychologist, and they both disagreed with the eligibility determination of an ASD.

A subsequent speech and language and general developmental evaluation was completed 1 month later at the age of 19 months with a different focus. Rather than screening for an ASD in order to establish eligibility for EI by matching symptoms to an ASD checklist, an evaluation designed to provide a differential diagnosis was completed. The parents reported that the child was relatively unchanged in terms of her development, but she was less reticent to respond to the examiner in the second evaluation. This second evaluation indicated that receptive language abilities were above average, nonverbal social engagement was high, performance on the Merrill-Palmer-Revised Scales of Development (Roid & Sampers, 2004) was advanced, and the child vocalized extensively while using a variety of age-appropriate phonological forms. The conclusion of this latter evaluation suggested that this child was "expressive" in that she paralleled the descriptions in Katherine Nelson's (1973) landmark monograph describing early lexical development: The child spoke in relatively long syllabic strings with appropriate intonation but used few identifiable words. Although the parents disagreed with the autism eligibility, they were sufficiently concerned that they accepted enrollment in EI services. However, as is often the case, there was a significant wait between eligibility testing and initiation of these services so that more than 6 months elapsed before they were able to start EI services. Because their child had made so much progress in the interim, the parents returned her for an evaluation prior to initiating services. This subsequent evaluation indicated that her mean length of utterance (MLU) had reached 3.6, and that expressive skills as measured on the third edition of the Preschool Language Scale (PLS-3; Zimmerman, Steiner, & Pond, 1992) were within the normal range. She also maintained her advanced status in receptive language ability and in nonverbal cognitive levels. The only relative weakness seen was in phonological abilities, but these also were within the broad range of typical. The parents declined enrollment in EI and subsequently did not enroll in treatment of any kind. Long-term follow-up was completed when the child was in the second grade using the Woodcock-Johnson III Tests of Cognitive Ability and Tests of Achievement (Woodcock, McGrew, & Mather, 2000a, 2000b). This testing indicated advanced performance across cognitive and achievement domains: The overwhelming majority of the child's scores, including those that were language related, such as reading/passage comprehension, were within the 90th percentile or above. Extensive speech and language testing indicated that the only residual from the early late onset of talking was a mildly distorted /r/.

This child provides an example of the effectiveness of a wait and see approach in the absence of risk factors other than the late onset of words: Her nonverbal social engagement, play, receptive skills, cognitive development, and phonetic inventory were within typical ranges, and there were no medical factors to account for the expressive delay. Admittedly, the initial impression of autism proved to be inaccurate, and the wait and see approach was simply a byproduct of a relatively inefficient initiation of prescribed EI services. One can imagine, however, that if EI had been delivered and these services did not derail the otherwise typical development this child displayed, that the parents and the clinicians may have superstitiously believed that the EI was a causal factor in the positive outcome.

### Severe Cases in Which Parents Hoped the Wait and See Approach Would Be Effective    The first of these cases was a 30-month-old boy from a Latino background who was using 15 words at the time of his initial evaluation. His parents reported that they spoke only English at home, but his maternal grandmother, who was living with the family, only spoke Spanish. The child's words included only English forms, but it was clear that he was also exposed to Spanish forms as well. A phonetic inventory indicated age-appropriate syllable structure, vowel production, and consonant inventory, so it appeared that phonological skills were not inhibiting development. Cognitive testing controlling for language levels (appropriate both because of the late talking and because of the multilingual home environment) indicated that fluid reasoning was significantly below expected levels (a quotient of 63 was observed). The expressive portion of the fourth edition of the Preschool Language Scale (PLS-4; Zimmerman, Steiner, & Pond, 2002) was in accord with the cognitive quotient, with a score of 58. Interestingly, the child's parents reported that he understood everything they said, but the receptive quotient (60) on the

PLS-4 was also in the low range. Naturally, the PLS-4 quotients are based on English competency and did not take into account his potential competency in Spanish. The child's nonverbal and verbal social engagement was strong, he used his single-word productions socially, and he readily responded to nonverbal social overtures from his parents. The results for this toddler appeared to indicate global intellectual impairments, with cognitive levels, expressive language, and receptive language converging on quotients in the low 60s/high 50s. When this information was presented to the child's parents—who had previously expressed a hope that he would grow out of the late talking—they disagreed with the assessment, pointing out that he could point to letters they named and also complete simple puzzles. Although an intervention placement was offered, they refused and insisted on continuing a wait and see approach. The clinician indicated that they could return for follow-up testing and, if they changed their mind, enroll in intervention.

Approximately 20 months later, the child's parents became concerned about whether he would be ready for kindergarten and brought him in for follow-up testing. The follow-up testing indicated that he had made progress, but that developmental quotients across domains were relatively stable at the low 60/high 50 level: The brief IQ on the Leiter-R was a 59, and both the expressive and receptive quotients on the PLS-4 were in the low 60s. His phonological development, as measured on the Goldman-Fristoe Test of Articulation 2 (GFTA-2; Goldman & Fristoe, 2000) was within the normal range (quotient of 97). By now, at the age of 50 months, it was abundantly clear that this child was progressing more slowly than his peers and that the late talking was in fact a symptom of general developmental delay. Moreover, the wait and see approach revealed that he was not catching up to his peers either in talking or in intellectual maturity. The parents accepted eligibility and placement in a special education preschool for developmental delays.

The second of these severe cases was a 26-month-old African American boy who was previously enrolled in EI services and given an ASD eligibility and also a diagnosis of autism. His parents came to our clinic because they disagreed with the first diagnosis and wanted a second opinion. As described in Chapter 10, the goal of the evaluation was to provide an additional insight into the original assessment. The second evaluation appeared to confirm the first. The child played with toys in a restricted manner, picking up trains and rolling their wheels in front of his eyes while refusing to put them on a track or roll them back and forth with the clinician. He did not use words, and vocalizations primarily consisted of squealing. Attempts to engage in interactive play were met with withdrawal, as he turned his back and moved away from the clinician. Social overtures, including joint attention, reciprocal gaze, and pointing, were not observed. The results of the Modified Checklist for Autism in Toddlers (M-CHAT; Robins, Fein, & Barton, 1999), which includes asking the parents questions such as "Does your child enjoy playing Peekaboo?" and "Does your child ever use his finger to point at something?" suggested autism. In addition, he was not using canonical syllables and used few consonants so that phonological skills were also likely restricted, but it was also clear that this finding did not account for the reduced social engagement. Receptive and expressive skills could not be assessed interactively, as the child would not cooperate with the PLS-3 or other standardized test, but the MacArthur-Bates Communicative Development Inventories (CDIs; Fenson et al., 2007), completed by his parents, revealed performance below the 10th percentile in both domains. The Vineland Adaptive Behavior

Scales-II (Sparrow, Chicchetti, & Balla, 2006) confirmed broad delays in development as well. The results of the assessment indicated that the child displayed features of classic autism as well as more global developmental delays. The parents did not agree with this diagnosis and refused EI services, preferring to wait and see in the hopes that their child would normalize without additional intervention. Indeed, they told the clinician that their child would prove him wrong with regard to autism, to which the clinician said, "I don't think he will, but I hope he does!"

Unfortunately, more than 2 years elapsed while the parents continued to wait and see. The clinician contacted the family at 6-month intervals to check whether they had an interest in EI and then as the child grew older, preschool services, but they did not take advantage of these opportunities to initiate treatment. Finally, as the child neared 5 years of age, they returned for a follow-up assessment. At this point, it was abundantly clear that this child did indeed have autism, as he produced fewer than 50 words, and these were all nouns used to access preferred foods and objects. Auditory comprehension was measured as a quotient of 43 on the Test of Auditory Comprehension of Language (Third Edition, Carrow-Woolfolk, 1998) and cognitive abilities on the Primary Test of Nonverbal Intelligence (P-TONI; Ehler & McGee, 2008) were in the low 50s. The family then accepted the autism eligibility and enrolled him in an intensive home-based behavioral intervention program for autism (i.e., Pivotal Response Treatment; Koegel & Koegel, 2006).

In both of these cases, the late talking was a symptom of severe developmental disabilities (intellectual disabilities and autism, respectively) so that wait and see was an inadvisable intervention approach.

## CASES INITIALLY IDENTIFIED AS APRAXIA

ASHA defines CAS as a *motor speech disorder.*

> Children with CAS have problems saying sounds, syllables, and words. This is not because of muscle weakness or paralysis. The brain has problems planning to move the body parts (e.g., lips, jaw, tongue) needed for speech. The child knows what he or she wants to say, but his/her brain has difficulty coordinating the muscle movements necessary to say those words. (ASHA, n.d.)

Although mapping what a toddler wants to say may not be straightforward or completely accurate, it is not unusual for LTs to be identified as having apraxia. Also, although ASHA's definition specifically excludes muscle weakness as a causal element in apraxia, the diagnosis all too often is used as an entrée into nonspeech oral motor activities. Furthermore, a book on late-talking children by Agin et al. (2004) appears to indicate that apraxia is an important underlying factor for late talking.

The first case of apraxia is a 26-month-old boy who produced no identifiable words but whose comprehension was above average so that his score from the Peabody Picture Vocabulary Test–Third Edition (PPVT-III; Dunn & Dunn, 1997) yielded a quotient greater than 130. His social engagement was high, he had no problems with object play, and he readily responded to a whole series of verbal instructions. A medical evaluation turned up no significant illnesses or ancillary features to account for the late talking. The apraxia diagnosis resulted in a thorough Internet search by his mother, who became quite anxious about her child's future abilities. The child's father reported that his mother with so concerned about her child facing a future without speech that she was unable to sleep and considered a pantheon of unproven alternative diets and treatments in the hopes of helping her child. His evaluation indicated that although canonical syllables were being produced, his vowel (vocant) and consonant (closant) inventories were limited, being restricted to primarily central vowels and bilabial oral and nasal stops. Interestingly, he would often produce a range of articulatory gestures when imitating animal sounds—for example, using a sustained *s* when asked what sound a snake makes and a using high back round when asked what sound and owl makes ("who"). Our working hypothesis was that the late talking was exacerbated by a restricted phonemic inventory, although this was not completely explanatory because simple words such as "ba" for "ball" were within his phonemic capabilities. Because of this, he was enrolled in a parent training program focusing on phonological recasts (Camarata, 2010) and seen twice weekly for speech and language intervention using a phonological recast and responsive interaction approach. No nonspeech oral motor exercises, massage, or articulation drill were provided within this intervention context, and the child's mother reported that he was not enrolled in any outside intervention, including any that would be delivering these latter exercises. In short, no apraxia types of intervention procedures were employed with this child.

Yearly follow-up testing was completed for the child through the age of 7. By the age of 54 months, expressive vocabulary testing yielded quotients above 130, and his receptive vocabulary continued at this similar high-performance range. Achievement testing completed when he was 7 indicated that reading decoding and reading comprehension were both in the 120–130 range, and that mathematical abilities were similarly advanced. Not surprisingly, cognitive abilities including fluid reasoning were also in the 120–130 range at that time. More extensive testing for morphology and syntax at the age of 7 indicated no residual weaknesses in these domains either, although the quotients for these areas were within the broad range of typical (in the 110–115 range). Thankfully, despite the initial dire predictions of reduced long-term speech abilities arising from apraxia, this child appeared to have completely normalized by the age of 7. The intervention was not wait and see; rather, parent training and direct instruction were employed. However, it is important to note that the original intervention path of nonspeech oral motor exercises and articulation drill were not delivered and, therefore, cannot account for this positive outcome.

The second case of apraxia, initially seen at 28 months, was a Caucasian girl who also had previously received an apraxia diagnosis. In contrast with the first apraxia case, she displayed a marked difference in her ability to complete voluntary as compared with involuntary movements not only with regard to oral motor gestures but also with regard to pointing and imitating hand gestures. Her phonemic inventory was similarly impoverished. Our evaluation suggested not only CAS but also motor apraxia of her hands. Intensive speech therapy was recommended, and, in the meantime, introduction of an augmentative device as a means of communication. The child's mother was concerned that the use of AAC would inadvertently delay speech development and refused this recommendation. However, the child's parents did enroll her in extensive EI and then preschool services through the public school system where she lived. In addition, in a desire to leave no stone unturned, her family also enrolled her in nonspeech oral motor programs and sensory integration therapy, placed her on a gluten-free diet, and administered essential fatty acid vitamins, all at high financial expense. Although the clinician informed the family that none of these approaches had any evidence base for inducing talking generally or improving speech apraxia specifically, it is perhaps understandable that the family chose to disregard such advice and plow ahead with the alternative treatments in the face of their daughter's severe disability. The clinician maintained contact with the child's mother, who indicated that at age 6 the child still did not produce any intelligible words and continued to display a restricted phoneme inventory. At this point, the family agreed to an augmentative evaluation in their school district, perhaps in part because the child had herself begun using an iPad to communicate. For this late-talking child, the original diagnosis of apraxia appears to have been accurate.

## SOCIAL IMPACT OF HIGHLY STRUCTURED BEHAVIORAL INTERVENTIONS

The next case is an African American boy who was 38 months when he came into the clinic. He had been identified as having an ASD at approximately 22 months of age and was immediately enrolled in a 40-hour per week discrete trials intervention. When seen at 38 months, he imitated nearly every verbal production by the clinician conducting the evaluation. Also, he watched the clinician's hands rather than looking at her face. The results of testing indicated that his receptive language ability was within the broad range of typical and that his nonverbal cognitive skills, as measured by the Leiter International Performance Scale–Revised (Roid & Miller, 1997) was also within the broad range of typical. The child's phonological production was highly accurate, and his nonimitative MLU was approximately 2.5. The child's mother, who accompanied him to the assessment session, noted that the discrete trials approach appeared to have been highly successful in teaching him to imitate whatever an adult said and that she was now hoping to increase his spontaneous productions and decrease his echoed productions.

This child was rotated out of discrete trials and enrolled in a Hanen-style parent training program so that the mother was taught to respond and expand his initiations. At that time, he was not enrolled in preschool, so his mother provided the treatment. A 1-year follow-up indicated that the child's expressive language was now trending into the typical range and he maintained strengths in receptive language and cognitive abilities. The most striking advance, though, was in the area of social language. He no longer imitated (echoed) adult verbalizations and displayed typical levels of eye contact, readily looking his mother and clinicians in the eye. Interestingly, the prior discrete trials treatment had included prompting for him to look at the clinician (or his mother) prior to delivering a prompt. However, he appeared to resist this demand and primarily looked at the clinician's hands. After the Hanen treatment implemented by his mother, he readily looked adults and peers in the eye without prompting. To be sure, in a case of this kind, it is impossible to know what the outcome would have been if the original discrete trials intervention had not been provided. Perhaps this was the platform on which subsequent growth was based. However, it is likely that the discrete trials taught him to echo what the adult said, as this imitation behavior was directly rewarded during therapy. Also, it is likely that he learned to look at the clinician's hands because they were the source of the food rewards he received. (For a more detailed discussion of the social implications of discrete trials intervention, see Camarata, 2000.)

This case illustrates that approaches that differ sharply from transactions that parallel typical development potentially have a cost in the social domain. It seems that higher levels of support that move farther and farther from the child's natural, functional communication context require much more extensive fading and generalization training to transfer the targets to naturalistic communicative contexts (Camarata, 1996). To be sure, some LTs with severe disabilities require discrete trials support to learn words. Most, however, do not, so this approach should not be viewed as an appropriate treatment for all LTs. Indeed, it should be used judiciously because extensive efforts will be needed to transfer the learned skills to new contexts and because typical social development may be derailed (Spradlin & Siegel, 1982).

## CONCLUSIONS

Because late talking can simply be a developmental stage some children pass through or a symptom of broader linguistic and perhaps social impairments, treatment, if needed, should address individual child characteristics. A number of intervention approaches are employed with toddlers to accelerate language growth, and these are often based on the eligibility criteria a child was enrolled under (e.g., ASDs), rather than individual risk factors or profiles. Because children who talk late include late bloomers as well as children with autism, intellectual disabilities, language disorders, and phonological disorders, a clinician should complete assessment with an eye toward matching child characteristics to levels of support needed to accelerate language growth and should not apply a one size fits all approach to diagnosis or treatment.

## REFERENCES

Agin, M.C., Geng, L.F., & Nicholl, M.J. (2004). *The late talker: What to do if your child isn't talking yet.* New York, NY: St. Martin's Griffin.

American Psychiatric Association. (2000). *Diagnostic and statistical manual of mental disorders* (4th ed., text rev.). Washington, DC: Author.

American Speech-Language-Hearing Association. (n.d.). *Childhood apraxia of speech.* Retrieved from http://www.asha.org/public/speech/disorders/childhoodapraxia.htm

Ayres, A.J. (1970). *Sensory integration and the child.* Los Angeles, CA: Western Psychological Services.

Blakeslee, S. (1995, November 14). *Glasses for the ears' easing children's language woes.* Retrieved from http://www.nytimes.com/1995/11/14/science/glasses-for-the-ears-easing-children-s-language-woes.html?pagewanted=all&src=pm

Botting, N., Faragher, B., Simkin, Z., Knox, E., & Conti-Ramsden, G. (2001). Predicting pathways of specific language impairment: What differentiates good and poor outcomes. *Journal of Child Psychology and Psychiatry, 42,* 1013–1020.

Camarata, S.M. (1996). On the importance of integrating naturalistic language, social intervention, and speech-intelligibility training. In L.K. Koegel, R.L. Koegel, & G. Dunlap (Eds.), *Positive behavioral support* (pp. 333–351). Baltimore, MD: Paul H. Brookes Publishing Co.

Camarata, S.M. (2000). The pragmatics of paediatric language intervention: Issues and analysis. In N. Müller (Ed.), *Pragmatics in speech and language pathology: Studies in clinical applications* (pp. 139–163) Amsterdam, Netherlands: John Benjamins Publishing.

Camarata, S. (2008). Fast ForWord® does not significantly improve language skills in children with language disorders. *Evidence-Based Communication Assessment and Intervention, 2,* 96–98.

Camarata, S.M. (2010). Naturalistic intervention for speech intelligibility and speech accuracy. In L.A. Williams, S. McLeod, & R.J. McCauley (Eds.), *Interventions for speech sound disorders in children* (pp. 381–406). Baltimore, MD: Paul H. Brookes Publishing Co.

Camarata, S. (2011). *Auditory comprehension in autism and autism spectrum disorders.* Paper presented at the Annual Symposium for Research in Child Language Disorders, Madison, WI.

Camarata, S. (in press). Early identification and early intervention in autism spectrum disorders: Accurate and effective? *International Journal of Speech-Language Pathology.*

Camarata, S., Nelson, K.E., & Camarata, M. (1994). A comparison of conversation based imitation based procedures for training grammatical structures in specifically language impaired children. *Journal of Speech and Hearing Research, 37,* 1414–1423.

Carrow-Woolfolk, E (1998). *Test of Auditory Comprehension of Language–Third Edition.* Austin, TX: PRO-ED.

Cohen, W., Hodson, A., O'Hare, A., Boyle, J., Durrani, T., McCartney, E., . . . Watson, J. (2005). Effects of computer-based intervention through acoustically modified speech (Fast ForWord) in severe mixed receptive-expressive language impairment: Outcomes from a randomized controlled trial. *Journal of Speech, Language, and Hearing Research, 48*(3), 715–729.

Delaney, A.L., & Kent, R.D. (2004, November). *Developmental profiles of children diagnosed with apraxia of speech.* Poster session presented at the annual convention of the American-Speech-Language-Hearing Association, Philadelphia, PA.

Dunn, L.M., & Dunn, L.M. (1997). *Peabody Picture Vocabulary Test–Third Edition (PPVT-III).* Circle Pines, MN: American Guidance Service.

Ehler, D., & McGee, R. (2008). *Primary Test of Nonverbal Intelligence (P-TONI).* Austin, TX: PRO-ED.

Fenson, L., Marchman, V.A., Thal, D.J., Dale, P.S., Reznick, J.S., & Bates, E. (2007). *MacArthur-Bates Communicative Development Inventories (CDIs)* (2nd ed.). Baltimore, MD: Paul H. Brookes Publishing Co.

Fey, M.E., Richard, G.J., Geffner, D., Kamhi, A.G., Medwetsky, L., Paul, D., . . . Schooling, T. (2011). Auditory processing disorder and auditory/language interventions: An evidence-based systematic review. *Language, Speech, and Hearing Services in Schools, 42*(3), 246–264.

Fey, M.E., Warren, S.F., Brady, N., Finestack, L.H., Bredin-Oja, S., Fairchild, M., . . . Yoder, P.J. (2006). Early effects of responsivity education/prelinguistic milieu teaching for children with developmental delays and their parents. *Journal of Speech, Language, and Hearing Research, 49*(3), 526–547.

Gillum, H., Camarata, S., Nelson, K.E., & Camarata, M. (2003). Pre-intervention imitation skills as a predictor of treatment effects in children with specific language impairment. *Journal of Positive Behavior Intervention, 5*(3), 171–178.

Goldman, R., & Fristoe, M. (2000). *Goldman-Fristoe Test of Articulation 2 (GFTA-2).* San Antonio, TX: Pearson.

Hart, B., & Risley, T.R. (1995). *Meaningful differences in the everyday experience of young American children.* Baltimore, MD: Paul H. Brookes Publishing Co.

Individuals with Disabilities Education Improvement Act (IDEA) of 2004, PL 108–446, 20 U.S.C. §§ 1400 *et seq.*

Kaiser, A.P., Hancock, T.B., & Trent, J.A. (2007). Teaching parents communication strategies. *Early Childhood Services: An Interdisciplinary Journal of Effectiveness, 1*(2), 107–136.

Kanner L. (1943) Autistic disturbances of affective contact. *Nervous Child, 2,* 217–250.

Koegel, R., & Koegel, L.K. (2006). *Pivotal Response Treatments for autism: Communication, social, and academic development.* Baltimore, MD: Paul H. Brookes Publishing Co.

Koegel, R., Koegel, L., & McNerney, E. (2001). Pivotal areas of intervention in autism. *Journal of Clinical Child Psychology,30,* 19–32.

Law, J., Tomblin, J.B., & Zhang, X (2008). Characterizing the growth trajectories of language impaired children between 7 and 11 years of age. *Journal of Speech, Language, and Hearing Research, 51,* 739–749.

Leonard, L., Camarata, S., Brown, B., & Camarata, M. (2008). The acquisition of tense and agreement in the speech of children with specific language impairment: Patterns of generalization through intervention. *Journal of Speech, Language, and Hearing Research, 51,* 120–125.

Lof, G., & Watson, M. (2008). A nationwide survey of nonspeech oral motor exercise use: Implications for evidence-based practice. *Language, Speech, and Hearing Services in Schools, 39,* 392–407.

Lovaas, O.I. (1987). Behavioral treatment and normal educational and intellectual functioning in young autistic children. *Journal of Consulting and Clinical Psychology, 55,* 3–9.

MacDonald, J.D., & Gillette, Y. (1988). Communicating partners: A conversational model for building parent-child relationships with handicapped children. In K. Marfo (Ed.), *Parent-child interaction and developmental disabilities: Theory, research, and intervention.* (pp. 220–241). New York, NY: Praeger.

Merzenich, M.M., Jenkins, W.M., Johnston, P., Schreiner, C., Miller, S.L., & Tallal, P. (1996). Temporal processing deficits of language-learning impaired children ameliorated by training. *Science, 271*(5245), 77–81.

Miller, L.J., Anzalone, M.E., Lane, S.J., Cermak, S.A. & Osten, E.T. (2007). Concept evolution in sensory integration: A proposed nosology for diagnosis. *American Journal of Occupational Therapy, 61,* 135–140.

Moerk, E.L. (1992). *A first language taught and learned.* Baltimore, MD: Paul H. Brookes Publishing Co.

Muma, J. (1977). Language intervention strategies. *Language Speech and Hearing Services in Schools, 8,* 107–125.

Nelson, K. (1973). Structure and strategy in learning to talk. *Monographs of the Society for Research in Child Development, 38*(1–2), 136–136.

Nelson, K.E. (1989). Strategies for first language teaching. In M.L. Rice & R.L. Schiefelbusch (Eds.), *The teachability of language* (pp. 263–310). Baltimore, MD, Paul H. Brookes Publishing Co.

Nelson, K.E., Welsh, J., Camarata, S., Butkowsky, L., & Camarata, M. (1995). Available input and available language learning mechanisms for specifically language-delayed and language-normal children. *First Language, 15,* 1–17.

Newcomer, P., & Hammill, D. (1988). *Test of Language Development–Primary, Third Edition.* Austin, TX: PRO-ED.

Norris, J.A., & Hoffman, P.R. (1994). Whole language and representational theories: Helping children to build a network of associations. *Journal of Childhood Communication Disorders, 16*(1), 5–12.

Paul, R. (1993). Patterns of development in late talkers: Preschool years. *Journal of Childhood Communication Disorders, 15,* 7–14.

Paul, R. (1996). Clinical Implications of the natural history of slow expressive language development. *American Journal of Speech-Language Pathology, 5*(2), 5–21.

Paul, R. (2000). Predicting outcomes of early expressive language delay: Ethical implications. In D. Bishop & L. Laurence (Eds), *Speech and language impairments in children: Causes, characteristics, intervention and outcome* (pp. 195–209). East Sussex, United Kingdom: Psychology Press.

Ringwalt, S. (2012, June). Summary table of states' and territories' definitions of/criteria for IDEA Part C eligibility. Retrieved from http://www.nectac.org/~pdfs/topics/earlyid/partc_elig_table.pdf

Robins, D., Fein, D., & Barton, M. (1999). *Modified Checklist for Autism in Toddlers (M-CHAT).* Retrieved from https://m-chat.org

Roid, G., & Miller, L. (1997). *Leiter International Performance Scale–Revised (Leiter-R).* Wood Dale, IL: Stoelting Co.

Roid, G., & Sampers J. (2004). *Merrill-Palmer-Revised Scales of Development (M-P-R)*. Wood Dale, IL: Stoelting Press.

Roesler, C.P., Friedman, J.T., Realpe-Bonilla, T., Flax, J., Choudhury, N., & Benasich A.A. (2008). *Computer-based intervention hones skills in language content and structure*. Paper presented at the annual conference of the American Speech-Language-Hearing Association, Chicago, IL

Sameroff, A.J. (1975). Early influences on development: Fact or fancy? *Merrill-Palmer Quarterly, 21*(4), 267–294.

Shriberg, L.D., Aram, D.M., & Kwiatkowski, J. (1997). Developmental apraxia of speech: I. Descriptive and theoretical perspectives. *Journal of Speech, Language, and Hearing Research, 40*, 273–285.

Skinner, B. (1957). *Verbal behavior*. Acton, MA: Copley Publishing Group.

Snyder-McLean, L., & McLean, J.E. (1987). Effectiveness of early intervention for children with language and communication disorders. In M.J. Guralnick & F.C. Bennett (Eds.), *The effectiveness of early intervention for at-risk and handicapped children* (pp. 213–274). San Diego, CA: Academic Press.

Sowell, T. (1998). *Late-talking children*. New York, NY: Basic Books.

Sparrow, S., Chicchetti, D., & Balla, D. (2006). *Vineland II: The Vineland Adaptive Behavior Scales, Second Edition*. Minneapolis, MN: Pearson Assessments.

Spradlin, J.E., & Siegel, G.M. (1982). Language training in natural and clinical environments. *Journal of Speech & Hearing Disorders, 47*(1), 2–6.

Tager-Flusberg, H., & Cooper, J. (1999). Present and future possibilities for defining a phenotype for specific language impairment. *Journal of Speech, Language, and Hearing Research, 42*, 1275–1278.

Thal, D., Tobias, S., & Morrison, D. (1991). Language and gesture in late talkers: A 1-year follow-up. *Journal of Speech and Hearing Research, 34*, 604–612.

Wetherby, A.M., Woods, J., Allen, L., Cleary, J., Dickinson, H., & Lord, C. (2004). Early indicators of autism spectrum disorders in the second year of life. *Journal of Autism and Developmental Disorders, 34*(5), 473–493.

Whitehurst,G.J., Fischel, J.E., Arnold, D.S., & Lonigan, C.J. (1992). Evaluating outcomes with children with expressive language delay. In S.F. Warren & J.E. Reichle (Series Eds. & Vol. Eds.), *Communication and Language Intervention Series: Vol. 1. Causes and effects in communication and language intervention* (pp. 277–314). Baltimore, MD: Paul H. Brookes Publishing Co.

Woodcock, R.W., McGrew, K.S., & Mather, N. (2000a). *Woodcock-Johnson III Tests of Achievement*. Itasca, IL: Riverside.

Woodcock, R.W., McGrew, K.S., & Mather, N. (2000b). *Woodcock-Johnson III Tests of Cognitive Ability*. Itasca, IL: Riverside.

Yoder, P.J., Kaiser, A.P., & Alpert, C.L. (1991). An exploratory study of the interaction between language teaching methods and child characteristics. *Journal of Speech and Hearing Research, 34*(1), 155–167.

Yoder, P.J., & Warren, S.F. (1993). Can developmentally delayed children's language development be enhanced through prelinguistic intervention? In S.F. Warren & J. Reichle (Series Eds.) & A.P. Kaiser & D.B. Gray (Vol. Eds.), *Communication and Language Intervention Series: Vol. 2. Enhancing children's communication: Research foundations for intervention* (pp. 35–62). Baltimore, MD: Paul H. Brookes Publishing Co.

Zimmer, M., & Desch, L. (2012). Policy statement: Sensory integration therapies for children with developmental and behavioral disorders. *Pediatrics, 129*, 1186–1189.

Zimmerman, I., Steiner, V., & Pond, R. (1992). *Preschool Language Scale–3 (PLS-3)*. San Antonio, TX: Harcourt Assessment.

Zimmerman, I., Steiner, V., & Pond, R. (2002). *Preschool Language Scale–Fourth Edition (PLS-4)*. San Antonio, TX: Harcourt Assessment.

# 16

# Environmental Modification, Intervention, and the Late-Talking Child from a Public Health Perspective

James Law

This chapter explores what clinicians can do about late emerging language given what is known about the consequences. Can interventions be used, and what effects can be predicted from them? To answer this question, this chapter begins with a discussion of the interpretation of the term *late talker (LT)* and then examines it in relation to what clinicians understand by the term *public health*—a phrase that has, up until now, been rarely used in the context of early language development. The chapter then outlines and elaborates on the different levels of intervention (i.e., universal, targeted, and specialist). This chapter adopts a broadly epidemiological or population-based perspective and explores its relationship to public health interventions before going on to review more targeted interventions: those that are offered to groups of children who have been identified as being at risk by virtue of the fact that they are slow to start speaking. The chapter ends with a discussion about universal intervention for late-talking children.

## THE TARGET GROUP

Before looking at intervention and the extent to which it can change outcomes for children, a definition of LTs needs to be addressed. A number of authors have tried to define LTs (Desmarais, Sylvestre, Meyer, Bairati, & Rouleau, 2008; Roos & Language, 2008). However, as with many efforts to divide children into diagnostic or other groups, it rapidly becomes clear that such distinctions are essentially arbitrary and there will always be children just the other side of any given boundary who are in similar need. So, for example, taking a group of children ages 24–36 months with expressive vocabulary delay and with sociodemographic risk, as Cable and Domsch (2011) did in their review of the relevant intervention literature, leaves one asking whether children older or younger than those ages are having similar problems. This is one aspect of a growing consensus that most variation in language skills is dimensional (i.e., continuous), in contrast to a strongly categorical view (see Chapters 5 and 11).

There is a related issue of whether it is really relevant to separate out a group of children whose difficulties are confined exclusively to expressive language, given what clinicians are now coming to understand about the multidimensional nature of language. Language impairment among LTs, as among older children, is highly heterogenous (see Chapter 9). For example, in their study of somewhat older children, Tomblin and colleagues (Tomblin & Zhang, 2006; Tomblin, Zhang, Weiss, Catts, & Ellis-Weismer, 2004) obtained a comprehensive evaluation of a representative sample of 604 kindergarten children in Iowa. Based on the profiles of individual children, Tomblin et al. concluded that there were some children whose social communication skills were stronger than their language structure skills (phonology, syntax, semantics), and others whose pragmatic skills were weaker than their language structure skills. In their words, "There appeared to be two constellations in our universe formed principally by their relative strength and weaknesses in semantics and syntax versus social communication" (Tomblin & Zhang, 2006, p. 68). However, no distinct group of children solely with expressive language learning difficulties emerged in their results. Given that "expressive only" versus "expressive plus receptive" groups have been repeatedly identified in LTs in the age range of 24 to 36 months, it may be that the subgroups of children with delayed language skills change from ages 2–3 to ages 5–6. This is a topic that deserves further research.

Because these issues are discussed at length elsewhere in this book, this chapter will not elaborate on them further except to say that, aside from research purposes, there seems to be little reason to draw such strict demarcation lines. Accordingly, for the purpose of this chapter, LTs are defined as all children who are late to start speaking, even those who potentially start speaking at the appropriate time but whose performance appears to fall behind after 3 years of age (Law, Rush, Anandan, Cox, & Wood, 2012; Ukoumunne et al., 2012), a phenomenon that may appear counterintuitive to many clinicians with a strongly developmental perspective. Nevertheless, one of the key factors on which most practitioners, service managers, and researchers would agree is that the number of children having late emerging language is likely to be high. How high depends on the extent to which children from socially disadvantaged backgrounds are included in any given analysis. The prevalence figure most often cited for specific speech and language difficulties is Tomblin's 7.4% at school entry (Tomblin et al., 1997). However, if a "delay" represents more than one standard deviation (*SD*) below the mean on a standardized language test, the percentage may go up as high as 40% or 50% of some populations of preschoolers (Locke, Ginsborg, & Peers, 2002). By any definition, the percentage of the population with delayed speech and language development is high, and it may be exceptionally high in some circumstances. The point here is not to get into the debate about the percentage but to highlight the fact that conventional services, such as those provided by speech-language pathologists, are not developed to deal with these sorts of numbers. There are simply too few people to go around in services that were conventionally set up within a rehabilitation model, in which numbers are relatively low but needs are high. To address the needs of children with speech and language difficulties, it is necessary to investigate service delivery from a public health perspective.

## PUBLIC HEALTH AND LATE TALKERS

The relevance of public health to LTs is especially relevant in the United Kingdom, with its prioritization of public health services (HM Government, 2010), but it is also pertinent in other countries where services are publicly funded, such as within the U.S. public school system (Logemann & Baum, 1998). Of course, this issue of providing services to the whole population is not new, in the United Kingdom at least. As early as 1972, Randolph Quirk, in his report *Committee of Enquiry into Speech Therapy,* recommended that speech therapy, unlike many other clinical services, should be seen as a universal service, accessible to all. With the exception of a few attempts to capture and describe the populations that it serves (e.g., Enderby & Philipp, 1989), speech therapy has tended to emphasize the individual with a disorder at the expense of understanding the broader population perspective and social factors that drive communication competence—an issue that we (the author of this chapter and colleagues) feel needs to be addressed (Law & Elliott, 2009; Law, Reilly, & Snow, 2012).

Underpinning public health or epidemiological approaches is the assumption that, although the causes of ill-health/disability may be within the individual (e.g., inherited predispositions, physical or sensory disabilities), the *solutions* to many problems are socially, rather than individually, determined. The Faculty of Public Health in the United Kingdom defines public health as

> The science and art of promoting and protecting health and wellbeing, preventing ill health and prolonging life through the organised efforts of society. There are three domains of public health: health improvement (including people's lifestyles as well as inequalities in health and the wider social influences of health), health protection (including infectious diseases, environmental hazards and emergency preparedness) and health services (including service planning, efficiency, audit and evaluation. (HM Government, 2010, p. 11)

Central to public health thinking is an understanding of the social and environmental determinants of the processes underpinning health and the need for equity in opportunities for health and access to services. This begins at the policy level and includes a range of strategies, from the simple dissemination of positive health messages in the community via health *education* to whole-of-government (e.g., health, education, transport, employment, housing) policy and practice approaches to health *promotion* targeting drivers of health inequity. Public health approaches also encompass systematic data gathering about populations through surveillance and screening for conditions that can be effectively treated if detected early. In developed nations, they also increasingly include chronic disease management in the community to improve the interface between primary, secondary, and tertiary services.

Two types of public health approaches are commonly identified in the literature: "Old" public health was concerned with air and water quality; adequate nutrition; and ensuring people do not live in squalor, where they are at a high risk of contracting diseases that are now largely preventable, in developed countries at least, through immunization programs. By contrast, "new" public health concentrates on preventable conditions associated with interactions between economic well-being; lifestyle; and environmental exposure, such as stress and inadequate economic and psychosocial resources and access to services in different populations, as a function of geographic location, ethnicity, and socioeconomic status. Many conditions, such as poor mental health, childhood accidents, smoking, or alcohol abuse, are both outcomes of disadvantage and determinants of further adversity across the lifespan (Baum, 2002).

Key to the use of the term *public health* are social determinants of health, or "factors characterizing the environments that individuals are 'exposed' to and that can influence lifelong developmental and health outcomes" (Maggi, Irwin, Siddiqi, & Hertzman, 2010, p. 627). Social determinants create a "health gradient" that results in poorer health for those with the poorest economic circumstances. It is important to note, however, that this gradient is also relevant to the more advantaged, such that those who have the highest incomes have better health than those in the second highest income- group, and so forth (Fosse, 2011).

This concept of a social gradient with respect to language development has been well captured in what has become a seminal work in the discussion of the relationship between language development and social disadvantage (Hart & Risley 1995), but the authors of this study specifically selected a relatively small number of families from more extreme subgroups within their population. To give some idea as to whether this gradient holds across whole population, it is necessary to study large scale population cohorts. Figure 16.1 provides data from such a cohort of children born in the United Kingdom beginning in 2000. The Millenium Cohort Study recruited upwards of 18,000 children, all born during 2000–2001, and has been following them since that time using parent reports, teacher reports, and direct assessment. This chapter looks at the 3-year-olds ($N = 15,029$) and specifically their performance (T scores) on the naming vocabulary scale of the British Ability Scales (Elliott, Smith, & McCulloch, 1997). This equates to the type of skills commonly associated with late talking. The T scores on the British Ability Scales provides a scaled score between 1 and 100 accounting for the child's age at testing, with an average range between 40 and 60. To establish the extent to which the children's performance is socially determined, it has been examined against quintiles of the Index of Multiple Deprivation (IMD; Department for Communities and Local Government, 2011), a scale made up of a variety of different aspects of the context in which the child is developing (e.g., parental income, employment, health, education, training, access/barriers to services, living environment/housing, physical environment, and crime). Each child can be assigned a score according to his or her postcode. This approach is rather different from the poverty threshold commonly employed in the United States (Silver & Miller, 2003).

If there is no health gradient, the same median score would be expected for the children in each of the quintiles. However, Figure 16.1 shows that this is not the case. That is, children in the lowest IMD quintile have a median score that sits just over the threshold for delay. In fact, as the figure suggests, there is a difference between each IMD quintile, and these differences are statistically significant. The means and SDs for the five quintiles are as follows: first quintile, 45.3 (11.6); second quintile, 48.8 (11.00); third quintile, 50.4 (10.7); fourth quintile, 52.2 (10.4); fifth quintile, 53.0 (10.1). The proportion of children with scores outside the normal range (–1 SD below the mean) was 27.7% for the first quintile, dropping to 16.2%,

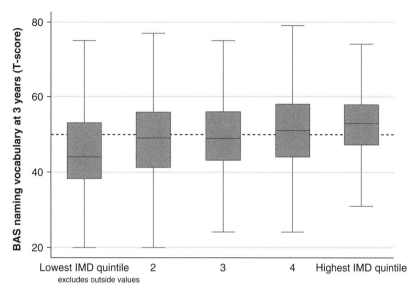

**Figure 16.1.**  T scores for naming vocabulary on the British Ability Scales (BAS; Elliott, Smith, & McCulloch, 1997) for 3-year-old children in the UK Millenium Cohort Study (*N* = 15,029). The dashed line represents the mean for the test. (*Key:* IMD, Index of Multiple Deprivation [Department for Communities and Local Government, 2001].)

12.7%, 8.6%, and 6.7% in the following four quintiles, respectively, demonstrating that the prevalence of late talking is very sensitive to social disadvantage. It is important to add, however, that with this type of sample size, statistical differences are relatively commonplace. The most marked drop is between the first two quintiles.

## Conceptualizing Provision for Late Talkers within a Public Health Model

It is critically important to conceptualize the model of service delivery that would be needed to adopt a public health perspective for LTs. One approach to gaining popularity in the United Kingdom is to consider need in terms of a pyramid, with the services offered described as *universal, targeted,* or *specialist* (Gascoigne, 2006). Universal services are available for all children. They are usually provided by health care workers, early education workers, and the like, and they provide messages and procedures for drawing the issue in question to the attention of parents or by providing services to the children themselves. In contrast, targeted services only are provided to a group of children who are deemed to be in need of such services and not to the rest of the population. Finally, specialist services are provided to those children who have the most severe difficulties and correspondingly the highest level of need. These children will all have received the universal services but may not have gone through targeted services.

This distinction between different service levels is sometimes captured in epidemiological terms as primary, secondary, and tertiary prevention, as shown in Figure 16.2. Universal services would be seen as primary prevention, the aim being to prevent the child's difficulties from emerging altogether. Targeted interventions would be seen as secondary prevention, the aim being to identify and effectively treat the condition at the most appropriate time so that it does not become persistent.

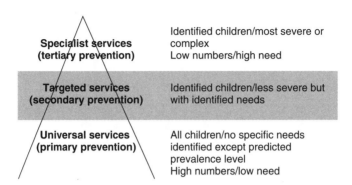

**Figure 16.2.**  Universal, targeted, and specialist interventions. (*Source:* Gascoigne 2006.)

Specialist intervention would be seen as tertiary prevention, in which the condition is assumed to be persistent and the intervention is aimed at preventing secondary difficulties. So, in the case of children with severe speech and language impairment, a decision may be made that the child's communication difficulty is likely to be persistent and that the intervention should be aimed at, for example, improving curriculum access or reducing potential mental health difficulties.

In some respects, this model is congruent with the response to intervention model used in the United States, whereby children move from one level or tier to another because of their response to a given intervention. The difference between the response to intervention system in the United States and that employed in the U.K. system may be that in the latter the level of need can be identified prior to intervention. Of course, although this is presented here as a way of conceptualizing services for late-talking children, this model is equally appropriate to any number of high-prevalence conditions, many of which have a social dimension, such as obesity or type 2 diabetes. Specialist interventions are reserved for those with the most intransigent difficulties. This tends not to be the LT group, although it conceivably could be if they remain LTs after intervention or as they move into school. For this reason the chapter now turns to targeted and then universal interventions for LTs.

## TARGETED INTERVENTIONS FOR LATE TALKERS

The evidence presented in this section draws on a systematic review of the literature (Law, Garrett, Nye, & Dennis, 2013) that was first published in 2003 but has since been updated on two occasions, the most recent being in 2011/2012. A systematic review is designed to be an explicit piece of replicable research, unlike narrative reviews that are considered to be partial and selective in their reporting. The review is published in Cochrane Library (http://www.thecochranelibrary.com), one of the most highly cited of all health journals. The review is housed specifically within the Cochrane Development, Psychosocial and Learning Problems Group (http://dplpg.cochrane.org), one of a range of review groups covering all aspects of health care. Distinctive criteria of such reviews are that they should have explicit inclusion and exclusion criteria, not only for the outcomes and the interventions but also for the study designs. Cochrane reviews commonly focus on the highest level of evidence if it is available, namely the randomized controlled trial. The review process makes an explicit statement about the "risk of bias" in each study according to how participants are allocated to groups and whether assessors are blinded to the assessment/intervention status.

To give some indication of the changing shape of intervention in the area of late talking, searches conducted for the original (2003) version of this review identified 634 records (studies); this figure rose to 986 by 2011. In the 2003 version of the review, 33 studies were included, of which 25 had sufficient data to be included in the review meta-analyses. By 2011 there were 65 studies, of which 54, involving 3,872 children, were included in the meta-analyses. It is important to acknowledge that since the initial review was completed, there have been other systematic reviews that are relevant as far as the subject of LTs is concerned. For example, there has been a review of interventions for school-age children (Cirrin & Gillam, 2008) and of parent-implemented interventions, the majority of which are delivered in the preschool period (Roberts & Kaiser, 2011). The results, on the whole, are positive, but with reservations commonly expressed about size and heterogeneity of samples together with the length of follow-up. The latter is of critical importance given the level of spontaneous catch up among LTs.

For the purposes of this chapter on LTs, children who are identified as having delayed expressive and/or receptive language development up to the age of 6 years are included. This study, therefore, includes both LTs, as defined in this other chapters in this book (i.e., children identified as slow to talk before age 4) and children with primary language delay/disorder (i.e., children identified as slow to talk after age 4). Both receptive and expressive language outcomes are included because it is not always easy to be clear about the nature of the children's difficulties. Using below-average expressive language skills before 6 years of age as the criteria for slow talking, 25 studies met the criteria for inclusion, and these are summarized in Table 16.1 (arranged in the order in which they were published).

It is important to acknowledge that some authors of the studies listed in Table 16.1 do use the term *late talkers,* whereas others talk about children with specific language problems or delayed language development. In other cases, children being referred to speech and language therapy services is the criteria, with an emphasis on language in the outcomes used. Our relatively liberal criteria do not draw a distinction between these groups at this early stage in development. All would have been late to speak, with the difficulties of some resolving earlier than others. Few children, if any, have receptive difficulties in the absence of expressive difficulties, although the literature indicates that some children with autism have more advanced expressive language than they do receptive language skills, especially in the early years. But it is quite common for children with expressive language difficulties to have receptive language difficulties as well—the level of overlap between the two at least in part a function of the measures used to ascertain levels and thresholds. Two studies are included in which the age range spanned 6 years, one only marginally (Courtright & Courtright, 1979) and one in which the ages of the included children covered the whole of childhood but in which the majority of the children fell below 6 years (Broomfield & Dodd, 2011). Studies of children who received interventions for phonological or articulation delays are not included, although these groups are analyzed separately in the original review. In all, the 25 studies included 1,982 children.

The first thing to note about these studies is that they have been published over nearly a 40-year period. Although 11 of the studies were published since 2000, it is clear that intervention to enhance late language emergence has been of interest

**Table 16.1.** Intervention studies to enhance the language development of children with late emerging language (*N* = 25)

| Date | First author | *n* | Age | Criteria for inclusion | Intervention | Results |
|---|---|---|---|---|---|---|
| 2011 | Yoder | 62 | Mean = 42 months in both groups | SLI with MLU in morphemes 1.29 *SD*s below that expected for their age or a score below the 11th percentile on the Expressive Communication subscale of the Preschool Language Scale, Third Edition (Zimmerman, Steiner, & Pond, 1992) | BTR versus MLT | Children with initially low MLU, but not children with initially high MLU, responded to MLT. |
| 2011 | Washington | 22 | Mean = 52 months | SLI and expressive difficulties but normal receptive abilities | CAT program using color-coded screens to develop 'children's sentence structure versus standard SLT (n-CAT) with tabletop procedures versus wait list controls | Both interventions showed significant gains relative to controls, but no differences were reported between the two interventions. |
| 2011 | Wake | 301 | Mean = 13.3 months | Children assessed as slow to talk as toddlers via the Communication and Symbolic Behavior Scales Developmental Profile™ (CSBS DP™; Wetherby & Prizant, 2002) | "You Make the Difference" Hanen program directed at parents versus "usual care"/no treatment control | The Hanen program was feasible and acceptable, but there was little evidence that it improved language or behavior either immediately or at age 3 years. |
| 2011 | Broomfield | 730 | Range = 0–16 years | Referral | Community SLT versus no treatment | Intervention showed significant results relative to no intervention over a 6-month period. |
| 2009 | Buschmann | 58 | Range = 23–24.5 months | Less than 50 words on a vocabulary checklist | Parent language training versus wait list control | Seventy-five percent of children in the intervention group caught up (within normal limits) compared with 44% in the control group. |
| 2009 | Gallagher | 24 | Range = 42–51 months | – 2 *SD*s below E/C | Clinician-administered "intensive intervention" versus joint intervention with nursery staff and an SLT versus no treatment | Clinician-administered intensive intervention was more effective than the joint intervention, and both were more effective than no intervention. |

| Year | Author | | N | | Comparison | Results |
|------|--------|------|-----|------|------------|---------|
| 2008 | Bowyer-Crane | Group means = 57.53 and 56.83 months | 152 | The eight children with the lowest scores on the Wechsler Preschool and Primary Scale of Intelligence Vocabulary and Word Reasoning scales (Wechsler, 2002) in target schools; cutoff points varied by school and ranged from a mean scaled score between 5.56 and 8.75. | Phonological versus oral language | Intervention effects were demonstrated for respective interventions but not generalized to other skills. Results were sustained over a 5-month period. |
| 2006 | van Kleeck | Mean = 52 months | 30 | Below 1.4 E,70 nonverbal IQ | Narrative intervention versus no treatment | Significant group differences favoring intervention with medium to large effect sizes were found between pre- and posttest scores. |
| 2003 | Evans | Mean = 8 months | 60 | −1 SD for E/C | Parent-administered language intervention versus no treatment control | Substantial within group change was noted for both groups, but no between-group differences were found. |
| 2002 | Fey and Loeb | Mean = 38 months | 16 | MLU −1 SD and DSS Developmental Sentence Scores < 10th percentile (Lee, 1974) | Clinician-administered intervention versus general play | No significant differences were found between conditions, and the authors concluded that "Inverted questions may be too complex to foster the initial acquisition of auxiliaries in children not already using them productively" (p. 160). |
| 2000 | Glogowska | Range = 18–42 months | 159 | < 1.25 SD | Clinician intervention versus delayed intervention | Positive results favoring intervention were found for comprehension but not for other measures. Seventy percent of all children continued to have difficulties postintervention. |

*(continued)*

**Table 16.1.** (continued)

| Date | First author | Age | n | Criteria for inclusion | Intervention | Results |
|---|---|---|---|---|---|---|
| 1999 | Law | Range 33–39 months | 43 | More than 1.5 $SD$s below the mean E/C | Clinician- or parent-administered expressive and receptive language intervention versus delayed treatment; clinician therapy focused on auditory processing and word mapping; parent therapy used Hanen principles. | Significant within-group effect for the main language measures were found, but there were no between-group differences. |
| 1999 | Sutton | Mean = 7 months | 22 | $< -1\ SD$ E/C | Ward Infant Language Screening Test, Assessment, Acceleration and Remediation (Ward, 1999) parent-administered general language intervention designed to facilitate language development in first year of life versus no treatment control | Significant within group changes were found, but these were not reflected in the between-group comparison. |
| 1999 | Robertson | Mean = 19 months | 24 | < 10th percentile on the CDIs vocabulary measure | Clinician-administered intervention for expressive vocabulary and syntax and child-centred approach to provide general stimulation versus delayed intervention | Significant group differences were found for MLU, total number of words, number of different words, lexical repertoire, percentage of intelligible utterances, socialization, and parental stress. |
| 1997 | Fey | Range = 55–58 months | 28 | Original inclusion below the 10th percentile in expressive language for the lower of chronological age OR mental age | Five months extension to original study with rerandomization to the clinician- or parent-administered intervention | High variability was found, but both intervention groups increased significantly, with clinician group increases significantly higher than the parent group. |

| 1997 | Robertson | Range = 42–61 months | 20 | SLI < 2 *SDs* E/C | Play intervention for expressive language delivered in pairs versus with a typically developing peer | The intervention group produced significantly more words in their script reports than the comparison group both immediately after treatment and at follow-up. |
| 1996a | Girolametto | Range = 22–38 months | 16 | < 5th percentile on CDIs | Parent-administered expressive vocabulary intervention based on Hanen principles and adapted for focused stimulation versus delayed treatment | The experimental group used significantly more multiword combinations and early morphemes than children in the control group. |
| 1996a | Girolametto | Range = 23–35 months | 25 | < 5th percentile on CDIs | Parent-administered expressive vocabulary intervention based on Hanen principles versus delayed intervention | Language input was slower, less complex, and more focused for the mothers in the experimental group than mothers in the control group. Concomitantly, children in the experimental group used more target words in naturalistic probes, used more words in free-play interaction, and were reported to have larger vocabularies overall as measured by parent report. In addition, the treatment had an effect on language development such that children in the experimental group used more multiword combinations and early morphemes than children in the control group. |

*(continued)*

**Table 16.1.**  *(continued)*

| Date | First author | Age | n | Criteria for inclusion | Intervention | Results |
|------|--------------|-----|---|------------------------|--------------|---------|
| 1994 | Gibbard | Range = 27–39 | 36 | Fewer than 30 words and at a one-word stage of development based on mother report | Two experiments: 1) Parent-administered expressive syntax intervention versus no intervention 2) Clinician-delivered expressive syntax intervention therapy versus parent-delivered therapy of the same type versus parent control "Portage" therapy focusing on general learning skills | The two intervention groups performed significantly better than the parent control group; no differences were found between the parent versus clinician intervention. |
| 1993 | Fey | Range = 44–70 months | 30 | < 10th percentile in expressive language for the lower of chronological age OR mental age | Parent- or clinician-administered expressive syntax intervention based on focused stimulation versus wait list control | Large treatment effects were observed for both treatment groups on three of four measures of grammatical expression. Clinician treatment effects were more consistent than those for the parent treatment. |
| 1991 | Wilcox | Range = 20–47 months | 20 | < 1.5 SDs E/C | Clinician-administered expressive vocabulary intervention versus classroom-based group intervention | In terms of initial lexical training, both approaches were effective. Children in the classroom intervention condition demonstrated a greater degree of productive use of target words in the home generalization measures than did children in the individual intervention condition. The children also demonstrated differences in use of target words in treatment versus home settings. |

| Year | Author | Age range | N | Inclusion criteria | Comparison | Findings |
|---|---|---|---|---|---|---|
| 1991 | Barratt | Range = 37–43 months | 42 | −1 SD for E or C | Weekly versus intensive intervention | Both methods of delivery showed comparable significant improvements. |
| 1986 | Cole | Range = 38–69 months | 44 | −1.5 SDs for E or C | Directive versus interactive intervention | Direct and interactive language instruction both significantly improved children's semantic and syntactic skills, but there was no difference between the two approaches. |
| 1985 | Schwartz | Range = 32–40 months | 10 | Nonverbal skills within normal range; 6m–9m below maturation age for C; 12m–16m below for E | Clinician-administered intervention with experimental and nonexperimental stimuli presented as an object-play activity versus control group receiving play sessions with unfamiliar objects | There was a substantial increase in the number of multiword productions for most of the children in the experimental group but not for controls. |
| 1979 | Courtright | Range = 45–73 months | 36 | < 10th percentile for E | Mimicry versus modelling | Modeling techniques were superior to mimicry in their ability to teach abstract grammatical rules, but retention and generalization of such learning also are enhanced by such training methods. |

*Key:* BTR, broad target recasts; CAT, computer assisted treatment; CDIs, MacArthur-Bates Communicative Development Inventories (Fenson et al., 1993); MLT, milieu language teaching; MLU, mean length of utterance; SD, standard deviation; SLI, specific language impairment; SLT, speech-language therapy; E, expression; C, comprehension.

to practitioners and researchers for many years. Only four of the studies have had more than 100 participants, and these have all been published since 2000. Thus, the majority have relatively small samples, and few have follow-up periods of more than 6 months. Although many provide evidence of positive short-term outcomes, there is little conclusive evidence that intervention makes early delays resolve, simply because the question has only rarely been expressed in that way. It is interesting to note that one study that did not meet the criteria for inclusion suggested that very early parent–child interaction intervention had long-term consequences in terms of preventing children entering special educational provision (Ward, 1999). This study has not been replicated, despite the fact that two studies deliberately set out to do so (Evans, 2003; Sutton & Tapper, 1999). This is especially significant because replication remains relatively rare in this literature.

In the studies reviewed, a variety of thresholds were adopted, ranging from –1 *SD* to –2 *SD*s below the mean on a given standardized language measure and various descriptive criteria in between. Nine studies included children younger than 24 months (Broomfield & Dodd, 2011; Buschmann et al., 2009; Evans, 2003; Girolametto, Pearce, & Weitzman, 1996a, 1996b; Glogowska, Roulstone, Enderby, & Peters, 2000; Sutton & Tapper, 1999; Wake et al., 2011; Wilcox, Kouri, & Caswell, 1991). In terms of the interventions offered, these fall into broadly four types: 1) those that focus on parent–child interaction in some form, 2) those that examine the effectiveness of speech and language therapy (however delivered), 3) those that compare particular methods of delivering intervention in terms of specific techniques (e.g., imitation, directive, recasting, narrative intervention, play focused intervention), and 4) those that focus on broader service delivery issues (e.g., indirect vs. direct intervention, weekly/intensive, computer assisted therapy).

Predictably, quite a variety of results are reported. Perhaps surprisingly given the interest in very early intervention, the results for the interventions delivered prior to 24 months do not look especially promising, not because they do not lead to change in the children identified but because the comparison groups also appear to change to such an extent that no between-group differences are identified. Indeed, this pattern is found in a number of the studies, irrespective of the included children's ages. Probably the most successful study in this early group comes from Germany (Buschmann et al., 2009) and reported that 75% of children in the intervention group had caught up compared with 44% in the control group.

Outcome data for the largest study included within this review (Broomfield & Dodd, 2011) have so far been published only in the form of *z* scores summarizing improvement in speech and language outcomes from a large number of scales/assessments (eight of which are listed in the review as "main assessments"). The variety of instruments used reflect the range necessary to deal appropriately with the very different speech and language problems of a sample of 730 children from 1 to 16 years. This study summarized outcomes for children of any age who were referred to the department for difficulties in one or more areas of phonology, expressive language, or receptive language. The comparisons involved standard speech-language therapy (SLT) intervention delivered after intake for 6 months and standard SLT delivered as a wait list control. Intervention for the wait list control group began after intervention had ceased for those randomized to the immediate treatment group. Outcomes were measured according to the child's primary area of difficulty (e.g., phonology, expressive and/or receptive language). The study reported that speech and language therapy, as it was delivered within the clinic setting, was effective when compared with a delayed therapy control group. The analysis using $z$ scores showed the mean change in $z$-score at each assessment point. The children receiving treatment ($n$ = 479) had a mean change in z-score of 0.67 compared with those receiving no treatment ($n$ = 231) who had a change in z-score of 0.12. The means reflect a statistically significant difference as shown by an adjusted $t$-test using $z$-score change over time between the treatment and no treatment groups ($t$ = 11.58; $df$ = 660.67, $p < 0.001$). This significant finding shows that intervention promoted a much greater improvement in speech and language functioning than would have occurred through maturation alone.

In the review, we examined the differences between new interventions and common practice, or what is known as "treatment as usual." This is quite a difficult criterion to impose, given the years covered by the review, because it is likely that this year's new intervention becomes next year's treatment as usual. One feature that is rarely extracted from these papers is the relationship between the severity of the children's initial difficulties and the apparent effect of the intervention. It would appear that those studies that include children with more severe difficulties, identified either by the inclusion criteria or because they were referred to clinics because they had some sort of identified need, made the most progress. Note that these studies were included because the children had primary language delay. That is, they were not included in the studies if they had general developmental delays.

Exclusion criteria were operationalized in different ways in these studies, but essentially these children had pronounced language learning difficulties in the absence of other developmental difficulties. The clearest examples of these are Gallagher (2009) and Robertson (1997), both of which only included children with language delays > 2 $SD$s below the mean. As Cable and Domsch (2011) suggested in their review, there does appear to be a good case for recommending parent–child intervention with "focused stimulation" for children with identifiable albeit less pronounced difficulties (Gibbard, 1994; Girolametto, Pearce & Weitzman, 1996a). On the other hand, care has to be taken not to assume that such an approach is a panacea that will work equally well whatever the dosage and whatever the population. As Wake and colleagues (2011) have well demonstrated, if the dosage is very low and the parental population relatively well educated, it may well be that it is impossible to detect differences because parents in the control group are already doing what is being suggested for those in the intervention group. Of course, the reverse may also be true, as illustrated by Law's study of specifically impaired children from low socioeconomic backgrounds, in which the authors reached the conclusion that the amount of intervention (25–30 hours) was simply too short to affect the way that the parents adapted to their children's communication needs (Law, Kot, Barnett, 1999).

In summary, the emphasis of the intervention studies tends to change over time, with operant models giving way to more context-sensitive models of intervention. But the study designs differ quite considerably. Even though the study designs to be included in the review were all randomized controlled trials, they vary considerably in terms of their details. Into the foreseeable future, vocabulary interventions will continue to be the key to LT populations, perhaps applied in a public health setting and with longer follow-ups than have been adopted hitherto. More parent–child interaction studies can also be expected, although the Wake et al. (2011) study provides a caveat about assuming that parent–child interaction problems necessarily underpin early language delays. The data tend to suggest that computer-delivered intervention may not be very useful for promoting oral language skills, but it is likely that other innovative uses of technology (e.g., intervention delivered by phone "app") will start to play a part. In general, study quality has improved, although the heterogeneity of findings remains a distinct issue. It seems likely that the number of such studies will continue to increase, and LTs will continue to be a key target. However, it seems probable, given what the field is coming to understand about the spontaneous recovery rates of LTs and covered extensively elsewhere in this volume, that this will need to be built into the sample selection. This will help avoid providing intervention to those who may not need it and target those who are least likely to improve without assistance.

## How the Intervention Might Work

The majority of interventions are *behavioral* in origin. This is likely to involve the training of specific behaviors (e.g., vocabulary, sentence structures) accompanied by reinforcement of some type. Most commonly, the intervention involves rewards of some form (e.g., stickers, tokens, praise). The assumption behind overt behavioral techniques is that language or speech can be explicitly taught and, furthermore, that gaps in the child's skills can be filled by instruction. Since the 1990s, most therapy has shifted from explicit training paradigms to one based on social learning theory, which assumes that children learn most effectively if they are trained within a social context. Although children are often seen individually, especially when they are being assessed, it is common for them to be treated in groups in which they can interact with and learn from one another. There has also been an increasing emphasis on working through parent–child or professional–child interaction and using play to model specific behaviors. This is based on a belief that if a behavior is modeled in the right context the child will come to adopt that behavior within that context and then start to generalize that behavior to other contexts.

In addition, the majority of interventions used with children adopt a *developmental* approach. That is, they follow a developmental sequence, whereby it is assumed that earlier skills will be targeted first. Recently, that emphasis has shifted somewhat, especially as the child gets older, toward a more functional approach whereby children are taught skills that are most useful for them at that moment. As the child gets older, the emphasis often shifts from instruction to a more cognitive, or as it is sometimes known a "meta-cognitive" approach, whereby the therapist or teacher will encourage children to reflect on what they hear and then adopt it into their own repertoire. Often the therapist will present children with alternatives and encourage them to make judgments based on their intrinsic grammatical or phonological knowledge. It is assumed that the process of making a judgment increases children's chances of modifying their language or speech performance. In the case of typical LTs, the level adopted is developmentally simpler, often focusing on the acquisition of vocabulary, as demonstrated in the focused stimulation approach, in which the child's attention is explicitly drawn to a specific set of words rather than grammatical structures. Thus, psycholinguistic approaches are adopted to establish where the nature of the child's difficulties lie and to ensure that the tasks are closely tied into the area of greatest difficulty. Although this is rarely considered in intervention studies in this area, motivation is a critical issue in therapy. Speech and language therapists pay considerable attention to the best means of fostering the child's interest in the tasks.

In terms of specific mechanisms, speech and language therapies rely heavily on the auditory channel and the assumption that improving the child's listening is likely to enhance performance. There has been an ongoing discussion as to whether the child's auditory skills are the key underlying problem or whether the breakdown is primarily linguistic in nature. The data remain inconclusive, and the reality is that there are probably a number of different routes into speech and language impairment. There is also an awareness among practitioners that although visual perception is not likely to be an integral part of the child's difficulties, it is often seen as a part of the solution. Widespread use is made of pictorial support materials, visual timetables, and the like to help children make better use of auditory material. It is assumed that practice is one of the cornerstones to the process of reinforcement and that repetition makes it easy for children to learn what they have not otherwise acquired. For many therapists, children's social skills and their ability to integrate with peers and negotiate the curriculum are key outcomes, although the evidence supporting the explicit teaching of social skills especially for those with more pronounced developmental difficulties is not strong (Gresham, Sugai, & Horner, 2001).

## UNIVERSAL INTERVENTIONS FOR LATE TALKERS

It is not uncommon in countries where there is a relatively high level of socialized health and social care for politicians to try to influence the messages given to the parents of young children. The message is that the state has a role to play in supporting parents. Of course, this can manifest in a number of ways and, although there is agreement that it is a good idea to support parents, how best to do it remains an issue. By way of example, parenting programs have been introduced to teach young parents how to look after their children, the assumption being that the breakdown of the nuclear family in many areas has led to a corresponding breakdown in the intergenerational transmission of parenting skills. Intended for those from vulnerable families, these parenting classes have come to be seen as stigmatizing, and uptake has been low. In response, the U.K. government launched a new approach to parenting classes supported by a voucher system allocated to all parents. This explicitly removes that sense of stigma and tries to normalize the support offered, effectively shifting parenting classes from being a targeted to a universal provision, at the same time raising concerns about the relationship between the state and the family (see "David Cameron Says," 2012). Other proposals include parents being contacted by text or e-mail and reminded about specific aspects of their child's health or development. It is important to note that such schemes are not explicitly designed to target early language skills, but early child development is likely to be recognized as a key component and is indeed now commonly referred to by politicians as one of the reasons for supporting families and enhancing the child's chance of being ready for school (Allen & Duncan Smith, 2008; Field, 2010; Marmot, 2010).

Turning more explicitly to universal interventions for children with slow developing language, three areas can be identified in which services have been developed or are developing to enhance early language development. The first is developmental screening and health promotion; the second is community intervention to promote, among other things, child development; and the third is early education and the role that plays in fostering early interaction and communication skills.

## Developmental Screening and Health Promotion

Screening children with early language delays is both important and problematic. It is important both because of parental concerns about their children's early development and because of the political impetus (Field, 2010; Marmot, 2010; Tickell, 2011), which reflects both improving understanding about the potential negative sequelae of early language delays (Law et al., 2009) on the one hand and the evidence for widening health and social inequalities associated with early cognitive development on the other. Despite the impetus from such diffferent quarters, screening per se remains problematic because although a great many screening tests are available—whether parental report of concerns (Laing et al., 2002), measurement of specific communication behaviors, or speech and language milestones (Coplan & Gleason, 1990)—no one assessment has been demonstrated to be sufficiently accurate to warrant introduction at a population level. Specifically, there is a tendency for such measures to have low sensitivity relative to specificity (i.e., they tend to underreport difficulties). There is also concern that developmental screening may be especially prone to bias (Camp, 2007). This finding was first reported in the United Kingdom in a review of the 70 or so published screening tests identified in the late 1990s (Law, Boyle, Harris, Harkness, & Nye, 1998) and then reported by the U.S. Preventive Services Task Force (Nelson, Nygren, Walker, & Panoscha, 2006). Of course, it is possible to adjust thresholds to address the issue of underreporting (Klee, Pearce, & Carson, 2000), but this issue has rarely been addressed.

One measure that has attracted considerable attention in the research community since the 1990s is the MacArthur-Bates Communicative Development Inventories (CDIs; Fenson et al., 2007), a parental report of the words that their child is using (Law & Roy, 2008). Originally developed as a tool for obtaining comprehensive language samples in children up to 30 months old using a 680-item word list, the inventories were reduced to a 100-item list and subsequently a 50-item list for more general use. In these reduced formats, it has been adapted and standardized for use in Sure Start programs across England (Roy, Kersley, & Law, 2005) and then used to survey the language performance of more than 6,000 children in three national audits (Harris, Law, & Roy, 2004, 2005). This latter version of the CDIs was combined with elements of the Parental Evaluation of Developmental Status (PEDS; Glascoe, 1997) into what has become known as the Sure Start Language Measure (SSLM). The PEDS is a simple set of questions to parents about their concerns about their child's development, behavior, language development, and so forth. The CDIs focus exclusively on parent report of vocabulary and specific aspects of early grammar. The SSLM does not include the full range of questions about the development of early grammatical forms because parents found these questions difficult to answer and those carrying out the scale difficult to score. The SSLM in this format was standardized for ages 16–30 months (Roy et al., 2005). Two versions of the word list within the SSLM are employed in this study, one of 100 words and one of 50 words, both derived directly from the original U.S. versions of the CDIs (Dale, Dione, Eley, & Plomin, 2000). As such, the measure has been shown to have good face validity and to be feasible for health visitors or community child health nurses to use. The issue with this measure, however, is the extent to which it accurately identifies the right children.

We examined this issue in a small study of 129 children across a reasonably representative sample in England (Brown, Roy, & Law, 2012) using the Reynell Developmental Language Scales (Edwards et al., 1997) as the gold standard. We set the threshold at the 10th percentile, which would predict the identification of 10% of a normal sample of children as language delayed (LD), a rate within the estimated prevalence range (Tomblin et al., 1997). Of course, if the pretest probability of having language delay was higher, as it would be in more socially disadvantaged populations, we anticipate this figure also being higher given the same threshold—an assumption born out in the data from the Millenium Cohort Study described previously in this chapter. It is conceivable that the thresholds might be adjusted for different populations, but this was not considered in the present analysis. Initially, receiver operator characteristic (ROC) curves were constructed for both versions of the vocabulary measure. The curves were used to identify the optimum threshold for each version as well as the overall accuracy represented by the area under the curve (Zweig & Campbell, 1993). The optimum threshold is that which maximizes specificity and sensitivity and is thus the most functionally useful in identifying the target group, that is the group falling below the 10th percentile. Sensitivity, specificity, and both positive and negative likelihood ratios (Sackett, Haynes, Guyatt, & Tugwell, 1991) were calculated for the screen using the optimal thresholds identified using the ROC analysis. Sensitivity measures whether children who are slow talkers are being correctly identified, specificity measures whether those who do not have difficulties are not being identified. Low sensitivity means that children are being missed, whereas low specificity means that they are being overidentified. Likelihood ratios are employed to estimate the relationship between sensitivity and specificity. A positive likelihood ratio is a measure of how confident we are that those with problems are being identified; a negative likelihood ratio measures how confident we are that we are not missing children. Comparable figures were calculated for parental concern.

The test-retest reliability of the SSLM was excellent for the two versions of the measure: 98.5% for the 50-word measure and 98.4% for the 100-word measure. Likewise, there were highly significant associations between screen result and diagnosis of LD for both versions (Fisher's exact $p < .001$) and between parental concern and identification of LD (Fisher's exact $p < .001$). Table 16.2 provides the productivity figures for both versions of the SSLM alone, as well as when they were combined disjunctively with parental concern (e.g., < 30 words OR parental concern). Productivity figures were calculated using the best thresholds identified by the ROC curves. Likelihood ratios are expressed as pre- and posttest probabilities calculated according to Bayesian theory from pretest and posttest odds and positive and negative likelihood ratios.

As the table shows, the performance of the two scales are rather different. Taken on its own, the 100-word version of the SSLM looks to be more consistent with acceptable levels of both sensitivity and specificity, whereas the sensitivity of the 50-word list falls well below expectations, but the specificity is higher. The 50-word list is thus better at saying who does not have a difficulty than who does. However, when we set the criterion to below threshold vocabulary OR parental concern, the pattern changes. The sensitivity in the case of the 100-word list improves and the specificity drops somewhat, whereas the reverse happens in the case of the 50-word list.

It is important to add at this point that what is and what is not an acceptable level of specificity or sensitivity is essentially arbitrary, although commentators often indicate that a threshold needs to reach 0.8 to be acceptable. What these thresholds mean depends on what weight should be attached to them. Thus, if it is as important to identify all the right children as it is not to overidentify children, then specificity and sensitivity should be equally weighted. If children are missed, they will not receive services. If those services have been shown to be effective, the children will almost certainly be losing out, and their parents could reasonably have a grievance about their child being missed. By contrast, the costs associated with overidentification are the unwarranted demands on the services concerned and also perhaps in the raised levels of anxiety for the parents who have been told that they should be concerned. In the end, it is a societal decision in the context of the information available at any one point, and the balance may shift as the evidence changes. As clinicians get better at predicting which children will be in need of services, specificity can be increased by separating out LTs who are likely to catch up from those who are likely not to do so, and the specificity will improve. As interventions improve, the pressure goes the other way, and the salience of sensitivity increases. At the moment, it probably could be said that sensitivity is more important. It is better not to miss children, but this, of course, is a matter for discussion, and the balance may change in different societies in which the health and education systems are funded differently.

The discussion now returns to Table 16.2 and the likelihood ratio, a decision statistic that allows making a judgment about the relative relationship between specificity and sensitivity. Likelihood ratios are used to calculate probability shifts from pre- to posttest (Deeks, 2004) and are related to benchmark levels at which a screen may be deemed to conclusively rule in or rule out the condition in question. These benchmark levels are a positive likelihood ratio higher than 10 for ruling in

**Table 16.2.** Combined thresholds for 50- and 100-word vocabulary screens together with parental concern

| Criterion | 100 words < 30 | 50 words < 9 | 100 words < 30 OR parental concern | 50 words < 9 OR parental concern |
|---|---|---|---|---|
| Sensitivity | 0.80 | 0.64 | 0.91 | 0.73 |
| Specificity | 0.85 | 0.93 | 0.78 | 0.85 |
| Positive likelihood ratio | 5.33 | 9.14 | 4.14 | 4.87 |
| Negative likelihood ratio | 0.24 | 0.39 | 0.12 | 0.32 |

and a negative likelihood ratio less than 0.2 for ruling out (Arkkila, Rasanen, & Vilkman, 2008; Jaeschke, Guyatt, & Lijmer, 1994), although again overreliance on rules of thumb, which are likely to be sensitive to context and interpretation, should be avoided. All but one of the likelihood ratio figures in Table 16.2 fall between 0.2 and 10, except the negative likelihood ratio for the combination of the 100 word list OR parental concern, which would appear to accurately rule children out, reflecting the relatively high sensitivity (0.91) of this particular combination.

Our results from the Sure Start program suggest that use of the SSLM is both feasible and acceptable, although care has to be taken not to assume that face validity alone is sufficient in introducing such measures. With the appropriate thresholds, it is likely we can identify children with a higher level of accuracy than has been reported for many such measures, and the SSLM would thus appear to be a good method of identifying a group of children who are in need of further investigation, and accurately ruling out those for whom referral is not necessary. Yet whether this is the measure of choice for identifying early language delays depends on the weights attributed to the different options. Are we content that the 10th percentile is the optimum threshold in the sense that those with scores falling below this level are the children most likely to develop persistent difficulties unless they receive intervention? To what extent is this decision sensitive to the population concerned? Would we find the same relationship across different sociodemographic quintiles? And, finally, if we are able to rule out the children who do not have delays, can we be confident that they will not have delays in the future? There has been an assumption in the literature that children need to be identified early and that they are unlikely to develop difficulties later on if they don't have early difficulties—an assumption that has been questioned by the data from large-scale longitudinal studies (Dale, Price, Bishop, & Plomin, 2003; Henrichs et al., 2011; Law, Rush, et al., 2012; Reilly et al., 2007, 2010).

So, despite the persistent optimism associated with screening, it is probably wise to not put too much faith in specific measures. The primary purpose of such measures is not to sort children out into sheep and goats at a single time point but to allow a space for the parent and professional to engage in the discussion of the child's well-being and development. This is termed the "health promotion" approach, in the sense that it does promote well-being for all, but, of course, it does mean that the professionals concerned must have access to their populations at regular intervals and that the majority of parents must use the services. The reality is that in some countries, such services do not exist, while in others, such as those in Scandanavia, such services exist and are well used by parents. In other countries, such as in the United Kingdom, such services exist but are not universally used by all parents, especially as the children get older. In short, the identification process needs to be seen as the starting point rather than an end in itself, a direction of travel that has been well captured in the recent U.K. Sure Start initiative.

## Sure Start and the Population Approach to Early Intervention

The single most significant endeavor in the population approach to early intervention has been the Head Start program in the United States, which began in the 1960s to promote readiness for school in children from very socially disadvantaged backgrounds. Encouraging the development of children's language was only ever one element of this approach. This section turns to a particular initiative in the United Kingdom known as Sure Start, which had a similar purpose to Head Start but which was always intended to be more community focused. Originally set up by the U.K. government in 1999, it ran through the subsequent decade. It remains in place in some areas in the United Kingdom, although it has changed somewhat since its first inception. One of the features of Sure Start was that it had a series of targets against which it was monitored, and one of these targets was specific to language. This was modified as Sure Start progressed, but latterly it was to achieve by 2005/6 "an increase in the proportion of children aged five with normal levels of communication, language and literacy for their age and an increase in the proportion of young children with satisfactory speech and language development at age 2 years" (Department for Education and Skills, 2006, p. 68).

As far as we are aware, it is the first time that intervention to promote early language development has ever been mandated for such a program. The emphasis was on providing a genuinely universal service to those within Sure Start areas— those with high levels of social disadvantage—focusing on developing community involvement and promoting child development and school readiness. Speech/language constituted a key component of this initiative. However, it needs to be stressed that the program was not regulated, and it is difficult to know exactly what was being done from one program to another. The programs had five core services:

1.   Outreach and home visiting

2.   Support for families and parents

3.   Good quality play, learning, and child care

4.   Primary and community health care, including advice about child and family health

5.   Support for children and parents with specialized needs

Although there was no manual, there was a specific set of guidance developed for the so-called Sure Start areas (Law & Harris, 2001). There were a formal evaluation of the program, but more relevant to the specific issue of LTs were three audits of 2-year-old children's language skills across the whole of England (Harris, Law, & Roy, 2005) using the SSLM. An audit in this case refers to data collected routinely on children receiving services within Sure Start. The SSLM data were collected on a proportion of children from each of the 250 or so Sure Start programs across England. We used the number of words reported by parents, their reporting of two-word combinations, and their level of concern as the criteria for whether Sure Start appeared to be making a difference in the populations concerned.

Tables 16.3–16.5 tell an interesting story. Table 16.3 shows the average word count on the 50-word checklist rose consistently over the three time points, although this was not statistically significant. We looked at whether the number of children with relatively high word scores (more than 13 in the case of the 50-word list) had risen over the same period, and indeed this is the case (Chi-square, $p < .05$) Over the same period, the percentage of parents with language concerns went down significantly ($p < .05$). The number of word combinations reported fluctuated but

**Table 16.3.** Word scores on the three audits of children's language within Sure Start (English speakers only)

| Implementation year | Time 1 | Time 2 | Time 3 |
|---|---|---|---|
| Number of children | 800 | 1,046 | 1,094 |
| Average word count score on the 50-word list (*SD*) | 25.4 (12.9) | 26 (12.7) | 26.3 (12.5) |
| Children combining words (sometimes or often) (%) | 85.7 | 87.1 | 85 |
| Parents with language concerns (%) | 21.9 | 19.3 | 17.9 |

From Harris, F., Law, J., & Roy, P. (2005). *The third implementation of the Sure Start language measure.* Nottingham, United Kingdom: Sure Start. © Crown copyright 2013; adapted by permission.

essentially remained static. Given the potential noise in the system attributable to the variability in the programs and the sample, one would not assume that such a process would be able to detect change of this sort, suggesting that indeed vocabulary may be a sensitive indicator for these programs.

Table 16.4 suggests that the changes appear to be coming from boys rather than the girls, whose scores are predictably higher than those of the boys to start with but remain static. This difference was statistically significant (ANOVA, $p < .05$). Finally, Table 16.5 turns to another issue that is of considerable interest in the study of LTs, and that is the children who come from bilingual backgrounds or from backgrounds in which no English is spoken in the home. These children tend to be studied by those who focus on bilingualism and are often excluded from studies of early language development. By contrast, these children are a key element of any such intervention study because they are commonly the children of families of economic migrants in socially disadvantaged areas and thus may be particularly vulnerable. Indeed, the group of children who were bilingual but did not have English as one of their languages had significantly lower levels of reported vocabulary (ANOVA, $p < .05$), lower levels of word combinations (ANOVA, $p < .05$), and higher levels of parental concern (ANOVA, $p < .05$) than their English-speaking peers, whereas the bilingual children who did have English as one of their languages had similar scores to their English-speaking peers.

It is important to stress at this stage that these data are not from an experimental study. There is no control group with which to compare outcomes, and there are no data about the longer term outcomes. Thus, care needs to be taken not to extrapolate too readily from one to another. The fact that these are different children at each time point also begs the question of the comparability across the three different time points.

**Table 16.4.** Word scores on the three audits of boys' and girls' language within Sure Start

| Implementation year | Time 1 | Time 2 | Time 3 |
|---|---|---|---|
| Number of boys | 489 | 657 | 716 |
| Scores | 22.2 (12.4) | 23.4 (12.7) | 24.3 (12.9) |
| Number of girls | 433 | 644 | 687 |
| Scores | 28.8 (12.8) | 28.1 (12.3) | 28.2 (11.7) |

From Harris, F., Law, J., & Roy, P. (2005). *The third implementation of the Sure Start language measure.* Nottingham, United Kingdom: Sure Start. © Crown copyright 2013; adapted by permission.

**Table 16.5.** Performance of English- and non–English-speaking group at Time 3

| Language background | English only | Bilingual with English | Non-English speaking |
|---|---|---|---|
| Number of children | 2,943 | 565 | 125 |
| Average word count score on the 50-word list (*SD*) | 26.3 (12.5) | 26.4 (12.7) | 24.8 (13.9) |
| Combining words (%) | 85 | 84.3 | 76.5 |
| Parents with language concerns (%) | 17.9 | 16.9 | 23.5 |

From Harris, F., Law, J., & Roy, P. (2005). *The third implementation of the Sure Start language measure.* Nottingham, United Kingdom: Sure Start. © Crown copyright 2013; adapted by permission.

In summary, these data derived from use of the SSLM at a population level yield several important policy implications. First, its use appears to be feasible. Second, the SSLM appears to have the potential to provide baseline information against which future service outcomes could be compared. It is interesting that there is a statistically significant difference in the level of parental concern over time, and that the boys' scores change more from a lower base than do the girls' scores. How important this is depends on the needs of those interpreting the data. Although the changes are relatively modest in real terms, those responsible for monitoring the performance of children in Sure Start responded positively to these data. It is also of interest that the average is well above the threshold identified on the SSLM from the ROC curves previously noted (i.e., a score of 9), suggesting that although these scores may be relatively low, they do not indicate that the majority of children were experiencing problems in starting to speak. We obviously do not have comparison data for this study because, by definition, the children came from Sure Start areas and were relatively socially disadvantaged. In the end, although it is possible to increase awareness of these issues and we can encourage parents to make use of services, the only way that we can ensure that all children receive appropriate support to help them develop their early language skills is by focusing on their communication experiences in preschool classrooms, and this is what the chapter turns to next. It is, of course, important to point out that although two thirds of children go to preschool in the United Kingdom, the health services are the only services that are technically universal.

## The "Communication Friendly" Classroom

An alternative population approach to intervention with children who are slow to start to speak is to address the issue in early years schooling provision (3–6 years in England). To what extent the state pays for such provision obviously varies from country to country, but it is increasingly recognized in developed countries that such early provision can be key to encouraging mothers to return to work while facilitating the development of the core academic and social skills in the young children. The problem is that beyond the initial training provided to teachers, we have relatively little control of their practice. Despite years of research into what helps promote the communication skills of young children, such practices do not necessarily filter through to practice in the classroom. This is especially true at the nursery level (3–4 years), in which it is often assumed that leaving the children to experience resources for themselves is sufficient for the children to experience the full benefits of the nursery school environment. Evidence-based measures are needed that allow assessment of the quality of the input given to the children. These should not just be process measures such as class size or more academic measures such as school readiness but should focus on what is being done in the classroom with individuals and with groups of children. For this reason we have developed the Communication Supporting Classrooms (CsC) Observation Tool (Dockrell, Bakopoulou, Law, Spencer, & Lindsay, 2012).

The main focus of the CsC Observation Tool is to capture what is happening in the classroom in real time. To this end, observations of the classroom are made and are then used to profile the language learning classroom environment. The CsC Observation Tool does not focus on the whole-school environment, liaison with other professionals, or staff training. Similarly, it does not focus on the speech and language therapist or specialist who visits the school on an intermittent basis. In contrast, the CsC Observation Tool was designed to be sensitive to the key elements in the activities within classrooms that support oral language growth. Our aim has been to create a tool that identifies key classroom features related to oral language development and that supports school staff to monitor the opportunities children have for language learning as well as the adult–child interactions that take place in their own classrooms. By doing so, the CsC Observation Tool provides a flexible measure to support school staff in developing their practices, targeting areas for specific action in relation to the school population, and identifying needs for further training.

We started the process of developing the CsC Observation Tool by turning to the relevant literature. This helped us identify the features in the classroom environment and the techniques used by adults talking with children that have been demonstrated to support the development of oral language skills. A three-stage review model was used in order to identify the relevant literature. The first stage consisted of identifying studies that met the review inclusion criteria. The second stage consisted of in-depth review of the selected studies in order to identify key elements and processes involved in classroom environments that enhance language development. These features were then used to develop the CsC Observation Tool. To contextualize the tool within standard practice, we also identified elements of supportive oral language practice highlighted in government educational reports; government documentation; and policy documents related to "speech language and communication needs," the term used in the United Kingdom to denote children with any type of communication need. At the final stage, the studies used to develop the CsC Observation Tool were rated on a three-point scale to indicate the strength of the evidence of the included studies.

**Identifying and Rating Studies**   The search strategy identified abstracts, which were then subjected to a screening process of exclusion and inclusion criteria. This narrowed the focus of the studies and ensured that only papers relevant to the aims of the project and the target population were reviewed. Studies were included on the following criteria:

1.  The study specifically examined elements that support oral language development, including both receptive and expressive language.

2.  The mean age group of the participants in the study was between 2 and 12 years, or the documentation referred to early years and primary school settings.

3.  The paper was an empirical study, a review of empirical studies, government documentation, policy, or documentation related to speech, language, and communication needs (SLCN).

4.  The paper was published in English.

5.  The paper was published and within the public domain after 1984.

The evidence derived from 62 papers was rated based on the studies' research questions and design. Studies were included if they had sufficient power (sample size) to draw reliable conclusions, appropriate designs to identify change or causality, and were peer reviewed. The criteria used for the three scale-rating were

Strong:  Randomized intervention studies, quasi-experimental intervention studies measuring targeted and nontargeted variables, population studies monitoring progress and identifying factors that predicted progress

Moderate:  Quasi-experimental intervention studies in which only targeted language variables were measured; reviews of empirical studies, typically book chapters that reviewed a minimum of 10 studies and provided details of the studies reviewed

Indicative:  Single studies without matched comparisons or nontargeted measures

Other:  Government documentation or policies, SLCN frameworks, SLCN documentation, elements/items contained in a standardized rating scale derived from empirical sources and influencing current practice

Twenty-two papers met the rating criteria for a strong research design, 27 papers for moderate, and 5 for indicative. Eight papers were included as important SLCN documentation or government policy related to SLCN. The review of the literature and rating of the evidence identified three main factors that support communication in the classroom: 1) the classroom environment, 2) the learning opportunities, and 3) the adult–child interactions that occurred in the classroom settings.

Key features within the classroom's physical environment and learning context provide an important infrastructure to enable the quality and quantity of children's oral language experiences (Roskos & Neuman, 2002). In communication supporting environments, the physical environment provides support for facilitating children's exposure to diverse aspects of language. Consideration of the organization of space and provision of materials was highlighted in the literature as important for maximizing language richness. We termed these aspects the *language learning environment*. In the final scale it included such items as "Learning areas are clearly defined throughout the classroom"; "Book specific areas are available"; and "Background noise levels are managed consistently throughout the observation, and children and adults are able to hear one another with ease."[1] The elements of the language learning environment were coded as being either present or absent (i.e., a binary scale).

---

[1]Communication Supporting Classrooms (CsC) Observation Tool items on pages 350–351 from Dockrell et al. (2012). London, United Kingdom: Department for Education. © Crown copyright 2013.

The research evidence also pointed to the importance of particular opportunities children have throughout the day to learn and practice their language skills. These opportunities characterize a communication-supporting environment and include small-group work, interactive book reading, and structured opportunities for high-quality verbal input among peers and adults. We termed these aspects *language learning opportunities.* Specific examples include "Children have opportunities to engage in interactive book reading facilitated by an adult (for example: asking predictive questions, joining in with repetitions, story packs etc.)" and "Children have opportunities to engage in structured conversations with peers (Talking partners)." The scale was scored out of a maximum of five observations of the specific behavior.

The language learning environment and language learning opportunities may be necessary aspects of the communication-supporting classroom, but they are unlikely to be sufficient to promote good oral language. Exposure to particular types of oral language exchanges and opportunities to practice and use oral language in interaction with others are both associated with robust language gains by children. Specifically, the quality of child–adult interactions was identified as a significant factor in the development of children's oral language skills. Adult–child verbal interactions that are characterized by high levels of adult responsiveness have been shown to be specific supports of children's oral language development. The adults' role (both class teachers and support staff) is thus central within the classroom environment and involves frequently and consistently responding to a child's communicative acts in a way that is sensitive to the child's developing oral language skills. These dimensions were captured in the third category in the scale, which we termed *language learning interactions,* such as "Adults use symbols, pictures and props (real objects) to reinforce language." Some components of this category included "Pacing: Adult uses a slow pace during conversation; give children plenty of time to respond and take turns in interacting with them" and "Scripting: Adult provides a routine to the child for representing an activity (e.g. First, you go up to the counter. Then you say 'I want milk.') and engages the child in known routines (e.g. 'Now it is time for circle time. What do we do first?')." Again these were scored as seen or not seen and then counted up to a maximum of five instances identified during the hour of observation.

The target group for the CsC Observation Tool was the initial stage of primary school (Reception [the year that the children reach the age of 5 ] and the two subsequent years in primary school, Year 1 and Year 2); however, given the breadth of the review and the nature of the items, it was envisaged that the tool could also be used in early years settings. As an observation tool, it was designed to be used during a regular classroom teaching session, usually during the literacy or numeracy lesson. The average length of time necessary to collect a representative sample of behavior was established at 1 hour in the classroom, with an additional 20 minutes prior to the observation period to become familiar with the classroom setting and available resources.

The three dimensions of the CsC Observation Tool can be thought of as fulfilling different functions and need to be considered as capturing different dimensions and, perhaps, highlighting the need for collecting additional information.

These functions will vary as a result of the nature of the items in the three dimensions and the representativeness of the observations.

**_Interpreting the Communication Supporting Classrooms Observation Tool Profile_** Classrooms are not expected to demonstrate all items in the dimensions all the time, but the overall patterns offer opportunities for the development of practice. Where gaps are identified, it is important to consider whether there are any reasons why these features might not occur during the observation period or whether the gaps are typical of a more general approach to teaching and learning within that class or across the school. Patterns across classrooms and schools provide the basis for identifying features that are strengths and activities or techniques that require future training and development.

We selected what are termed in the United Kingdom "mainstream school" classrooms. This meant that we specifically excluded classrooms with specialist resources such as "language units" or "language resource bases" or "dyslexia friendly schools," which one might expect would perform particularly well on our criteria. We also excluded any schools that were "under special measures," a term used to refer to schools that on audit were seen to be underperforming. Finally, we excluded any schools that had higher than national average educational attainments and no children on the special needs register. It is not that these schools would not have been interesting to examine, but rather that their inclusion might be expected to distort the results in one way or another.

We first examined interrater reliability for each dimension of the CsC Observation Tool in nine schools. Based on 13 classroom observations conducted in these 9 schools by the research team, interrater reliability for the CsC Observation Tool was consistently high, with greater than 83% agreement between raters for the dimension of the language learning environment being achieved for 12 of the 13 observations. This was also the case for the presence of language learning opportunities, in which agreement between raters was higher than 71% for 11 of the 13 observations, and language learning interactions, in which agreement between raters was higher than 84% for 12 of the 13 observations. Reliability for the frequency of language learning interactions was lower than for the other two dimensions but achieved acceptable levels for the majority of the observations. Following the second phase of the pilot, and prior to the main feasibility study, final amendments of the CsC Observation Tool were made to enhance reliability of the language learning interactions scale and modify items that were unclear.

To trial the use of the CsC Observation Tool, 101 different classrooms in 39 different schools across the North and Southeast of England were then observed. The schools were drawn from 10 different local authorities, and we sampled Reception classes ($N = 38$), Year 1 classes ($N = 35$), and Year 2 classes ($N = 28$). This discussion reports on patterns across the three dimensions—environment, opportunities, and interactions—and then focuses more closely on the differences between opportunities and interactions.

Each dimension of the CsC Observation Tool resulted in different total numbers of scores (language learning environment = 19, language learning opportunities = 25, language learning interactions = 100). To account for the different numbers of items across the three dimensions, proportion scores were created. Proportion scores were derived by dividing the actual number of observations by

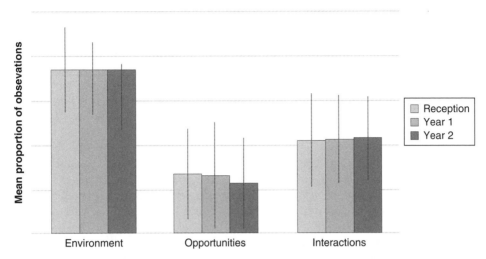

**Figure 16.3.** Mean (+/– *SD*) proportion score for the Communication Supporting Classrooms Observation Tool (Dockrell, Bakopoulou, Law, Spencer, & Lindsay, 2012) dimensions for the 3-year groups. (From Dockrell, J., Bakopoulou, I., Law, J., Spencer, S., & Lindsay, G. [2012]. *Developing a Communication Supporting Classrooms Observation Tool* [Department for Education research report DEF-RR247-BCRP8]. London, United Kingdom: Department for Education. © Crown copyright 2013.)

the total number of possible observations. These proportion scores range from 0 (not recorded) to 1 (maximum possible numbers of occurrences), in which items were rated on the basis of a maximum of five occurrences.

Figure 16.3 presents the mean proportion scores and their *SD*s for the three dimensions. As Figure 16.3 shows, there were significant differences across the three dimensions. Overall, a large number of the classrooms observed scored high on the language learning environment dimension, but scores for language learning opportunities and language learning interactions were lower. For all year groups, scores for the language learning environment dimension were significantly higher than scores for language learning interactions, and scores for language learning interactions were significantly higher than those for language learning opportunities This is an interesting observation given the level of material investment in schools in the United Kingdom since the late 1990s. But having the relevant materials is not necesarily the same as using them appropriately, and this is why we put such store by the other elements of the scale.

Figure 16.3 shows that there were differences in the relevant aspects of the communication environment across the 3-year group. The proportions decline significantly as the children get older and the curriculum takes over from materials designed to promote communication for its own sake. By contrast, although the opportunities were lower than the interactions, in all cases the differences between the year groups did not differ. These differences may, of course, reflect the classrooms sampled, aspects of teaching and learning in Year 2, or different assessment targets, but they provide interesting insights against which future observations can be compared.

## CONCLUSIONS

As seen in a number of the chapters in this book, late emergence of language, or late talking, is certainly a risk factor for a range of negative outcomes. Equally, children who do not progress well in school or who are identified with difficulties often have records of late language development and would probably have been construed as LTs had they interacted with services that were in a position to make such a judgment. Care must be taken not to be deterministic when considering this issue. Differences or difficulties identified at a later stage in the child's development are not necessarily a marker of unmet need or of children not meeting their potential. It may just be that these children are at risk for a variety of reasons, and language is taken to be key because it is relatively easy to assess. But, of course, the difficulties of these children are rarely confined to language, at least not by the time they are well into their school years. The number of children with truly specific language difficulties that remain specific across childhood is probably very low indeed. So identifying them on the basis of their slow language development alone is probably not a very sensible way of developing services. Probably more important are the patterns of change in children's language learning more generally, whether it be the substantial proportion of LTs who go on to develop typically, or those who are not LTs in the sense of the term used in this volume but whose development seems to falter despite having typically developing language in the first 3 years of life.

We have seen that targeted interventions have the potential to change children's profiles relative to controls, although care must be taken to ensure that the right children are included in such programs and enough intervention is provided. There would seem to be reasonable evidence that this sort of approach operates in a rather similar fashion to an injection given to a risk group (in this case those with low language scores), which bolsters the child's resilience by heightening parental awareness and thus increasing the early vocabulary. The challenge is that it can be very common for children to be slow to talk and although some children from middle-class backgrounds do experience late talking, it is much more common and probably has a far greater impact on socially disadvantaged populations. This means that clinicians either have to sit back and wait for concerned parents to come to them, in which case there is likely to be an accentuation of the inverse care law, whereby those who are better educated make more use of services, or clinicians have to examine what can be offered in terms of universal services. This remains a major challenge to all those providing services across developing countries. The population or public health approach allows us to examine the potential impact of developmental screening relative to health promotion or population monitoring. The former has proved problematic for the reasons discussed, but it is not known whether the latter is more effective, in part because there are very few examples of population monitoring measured in terms of intervention outcomes, especially in the medium to long term. Sure Start has offered an interesting angle on this, as services target whole populations of children from disadvantaged socioeconomic backgrounds with language recognized as one of the key outcomes. The SSLM, the tool developed for measuring language in these populations, has been shown to be clinically adequate at least for ruling out children who do not have a problem. This measure has been used with some success in Australia, Scotland, and England, but it needs more widespread application with closely monitored outcomes. Finally, we turned to the school environment, describing a measure we developed to be used by schools themselves to see how "communication friendly" they really are. We anticipate that this will generate considerable interest among a wider range of different early years' professionals in the future and may allow the measure to be included as a part of an intervention package that has yet to be developed.

In fact, the foregoing discussion highlights the difference between targeted and universal interventions. Although the former can be relatively circumscribed and specific, inputs and outputs closely tied together and outcomes readily measurable, the latter, of necessity, functions in a more generic way, perhaps focusing on family well-being or cognitive skills in general rather than language per se. The key issue at this stage is to articulate these different elements as done in this chapter and see how they interact across and within generations, as well as between home, school and, where appropriate, social services. There is almost certainly no one solution, but different combinations of these key universal elements that can be made to work together in different contexts. Whatever the combination, the key issue is to monitor the child's performance on a range of measures of which language is an integral element.

One recommendation for taking the ideas in this chapter forward is to apply a public health approach to raising the language levels of LTs, making sure that those most likely to have persistent difficulties are included. But it is not enough to design such a service. It must be evaluated, applying carefully designed services in one population and comparing outcomes with those in a demographically comparable community where children receive whatever help is available—a treatment as usual model. Interventions could be designed using the three-tier (universal, targeted, and specialist) model described previously in this chapter. Indeed there are already plenty of targeted interventions that show promise. Less is known about public health interventions. A stepped-care model, familiar in the provision of mental health services, could be introduced, with children moving back and forth across the steps according to need. Of course, such evaluations are complex to design, but they will be needed for the adoption of a public health approach to the late-talking child.

## REFERENCES

Allen, G., & Duncan Smith, I. (2008). *Early intervention: Good parents, great kids, better citizens.* London, United Kingdom: The Centre for Social Justice and the Smith Institute.

Arkkila, E., Rasanen, P., Roine, R.P., & Vilkman, E. (2008). Specific language impairment in childhood is associated with impaired mental and social well-being in adulthood. *Logopedics Phoniatrics Vocology, 33,* 179–189.

Barratt, J., Littlejohns, P., & Thompson, J. (1991). Trial of intensive compared to weekly speech therapy in preschool children. *Archives of Disease in Childhood, 671,* 106–108.

Baum, F. (2002). *The new public health: An Australian perspective* (2nd ed.). Melbourne, Australia: Oxford University Press.

Bowyer-Crane, C., Snowling, M.J., Duff, F.J., Fieldsend, E., Carroll, J.M., Miles, J.M.V., & Hulme, C. (2008). Improving early language and literacy skills: Differential effects of an oral language versus a phonology with reading intervention. *The Journal of Child Psychology and Psychiatry, 49,* 422–432.

Broomfield, J., & Dodd, B. (2011). Is speech and language therapy effective for children with primary speech and language impairment? Report of a randomized control trial. *International Journal of Language & Communication Disorders, 46*(6), 628–640. doi:10.1111/j.1460–6984.2011.00039.x

Brown, H., Roy, P., & Law, J. (2012). *Screening for early language delay using the Sure Start language measure: Thresholds, productivity and power.* Manuscript submitted for publication.

Buschmann, A., Jooss, B., Rupp, A., Feldhusen, F., Pietz, J., & Philippi, H. (2009). Parent based language intervention for 2-year-old children with specific expressive language delay: a randomised controlled trial. *Archives of Disease in Childhood, 94,* 110–116.

Cable, A.L., & Domsch, C. (2011). Systematic review of the literature on the treatment of children with late language emergence. *International Journal of Language & Communication Disorders, 46*(2), 138–154.

Camp, B.W.C. (2007). Evaluating bias in validity studies of developmental/behavioural screening tests. *Journal of Developmental and Behavioural Pediatrics, 28,* 234–240.

Cirrin, F.M., & Gillam, R.B. (2008). Language intervention practices for school-age children with spoken language disorders: A systematic review. *Language, Speech, and Hearing Services in Schools, 39,* S110–S137. doi:10.1044/0161–1461(2008/012

Cole, K.N., & Dale P.S. (1986). Direct language instruction and interactive language instruction with language delayed preschool children: A comparison study. *Journal of Speech and Hearing Research, 29,* 206–217.

Coplan, J., & Gleason, J.R. (1990). Quantifying language development from birth to 3 years using the Early Language Milestone Scale. *Pediatrics, 86,* 963–971.

Courtright, J.A., & Courtright, I.C. (1979). Imitative modeling as a language intervention strategy: The effects of two mediating variables. *Journal of Speech and Hearing Research, 22,* 366–388.

Dale, P.S., Dionne, G., Eley, T.C., & Plomin, R. (2000). Lexical and grammatical development: A behavioural genetic perspective. *Journal of Child Language, 27,* 619–642.

Dale, P.S., Price, T.S., Bishop, D.V.M., & Plomin, R. (2003). Outcomes of early language delay I. Predicting persistent and transient language difficulties at 3 and 4 years. *Journal of Speech, Language, and Hearing Research, 46,* 544–560. doi:10.1044/1092–4388(2003/044)

David Cameron says parenting classes are not "nanny state." (2012, May 18). *The Independent.* Retrieved from http://www.independent.co.uk/news/uk/politics/david-cameron-says-parenting-classes-are-not-nanny-state-7765666.html

Deeks, J.A.D. (2004). Diagnostic Tests 4: Likelihood ratios. *British Medical Journal, 329,* 168–169.

Department for Communities and Local Government. (2011). *The index of multiple deprivation (IMD).* London, United Kingdom: Author.

Department for Education and Skills. (2006). *Autumn Performance Report 2006: Achievement against public service agreement targets.* Runcorn, United Kingdom: Author.

Desmarais, C., Sylvestre, A., Meyer, F., Bairati, I., & Rouleau, N. (2008). Systematic review of the literature of characteristics of late-talking toddlers. *International Journal of Language and Communication Disorders, 43,* 544–560.

Dockrell, J., Bakopoulou, I., Law, J., Spencer, S., & Lindsay, G. (2012). *Developing a Communication Supporting Classrooms Observation Tool* (Department for Education research report DEF-RR247-BCRP8). London, United Kingdom: Department for Education. Retrieved from http://www.education.gov.uk/publications/standard/publicationDetail/page1/DFE-RR247-BCRP8

Edwards, S., Fletcher, P., Garman, M., Hughes, A., Letts, C., & Sinker, I. (1997). *The Reynell Developmental Language Scales III.* University of Reading edition. Windsor, United Kingdom: Nelson.

Elliott, C., Smith, P., & McCulloch, K. (1997). *British Ability Scales* (2nd ed.). London, United Kingdom: NFER Nelson.

Enderby, P., & Davies, P. (1989). Communication disorders: Planning a service to meet the needs. *International Journal of Language & Communication Disorders, 24,* 301–331 doi: 10.3109/13682828909019893

Evans, C. (2003). *The Kenilworth project: A randomised control trial of WILSTAAR.* Unpublished manuscript.

Fenson, L., Dale, P.S., Reznick, J.S., Thal, D., Bates, E., Hartung, J.P., . . . Reilly, J.S. (1993). *MacArthur Communicative Development Inventories: User's guide and technical manual.* Baltimore, MD: Paul H. Brookes Publishing Co.

Fenson, L., Marchman, V.A., Thal, D.J., Dale, P.S., Reznick, J.S., & Bates, E. (2007). *MacArthur-Bates Communicative Development Inventories (CDIs)* (2nd ed.). Baltimore, MD: Paul H. Brookes Publishing Co.

Fey, M.E., Cleave, P.L., & Long, S.H. (1997). Two models of grammar facilitation in children with language impairments: Phase 2. *Journal of Speech and Hearing Research, 40,* 5–19.

Fey, M.E., Cleave, P.L., Long, S.H., & Hughes, D.L. (1993). Two approaches to the facilitation of grammar in children with language impairment: An experimental evaluation. *Journal of Speech and Hearing Research, 36,* 141–157.

Fey, M., & Loeb, D.F. (2002). An evaluation of the facilitative effects of inverted yes-no questions on the acquisition of auxiliary verbs. *Journal of Speech, Language, Hearing Research, 45,*160–174.

Field, F. (2010). *The foundation years: Preventing poor children becoming poor adults: The report of the independent review on poverty and life chances.* London, United Kingdom: HM Government.

Fosse, E. (2011). *Policies to reduce health inequalities in families with children. Document analysis in four European countries.* [Working document from GRADIENT project, Work Package 5 (Tackling the Gradient: Applying Public Health Policies to Effectively Reduce Health Inequalities amongst Families and Children)]. Retrieved December 23, 2011, from thttp://members.kwitelle.be/GRADIENT/_images/policyhealthinequalities.pdf

Gallagher, A., & Chiat, S. (2009). Evaluation of speech and language therapy interventions for preschool children with specific language impairment a comparison of outcomes following specialist intensive, nursery-based and no intervention. *International Journal of Language and Communication Disorders, 44,* 616–638.

Gascoigne, M. (2006). *Supporting children with speech, language and communication needs within integrated children's services RCSLT position paper.* London, United Kingdom: Royal College of Speech and Language Therapists.

Gibbard, D. (1994). Parental-based intervention with pre-school language-delayed children. *European Journal of Disorders of Communication, 29,* 131–150.

Girolametto, L., Pearce, P.S., & Weitzman, E. (1996a).The effects of focused stimulation for promoting vocabulary in young children with delays: A pilot study. *Journal of Children's Communication Development, 17,* 39–49.

Girolametto, L., Pearce, P.S., & Weitzman, E. (1996b). Interactive focused stimulation for toddlers with expressive vocabulary delays. *Journal of Speech and Hearing Research, 39,* 1274–1283.

Glascoe, F.P. (1997). *PEDS: Parental Evaluation of Developmental Status.* Nashville, TN: Ellsworth & Vandermeer Press.

Glogowska, M., Roulstone, S., Enderby, P., & Peters, T.J. (2000). Randomised controlled trial of community based speech and language therapy in preschool children. *British Medical Journal, 321,* 923–926.

Gresham, F.M., Sugai, G., & Horner, R.H. (2001). Interpreting outcomes of social skills training for students with high-incidence disabilities. *Exceptional Children, 67,* 331–344.

Harris, F., Law, J., & Roy, P. (2004). *The development of a 50 word adaptation of the UK short form of the MCDI for use with two years olds in Sure Start Programmes in England* [Paper prepared by the team responsible for this further development of the CDI in the United Kingdom for Professor Larry Fenson and the MCDI team in San Diego, California]. Available from the second author c/o School of Education, Communication and Language Sciences, University of Newcastle, Newcastle-upon-Tyne, United Kingdom, NE1 7RU.

Harris, F., Law, J., & Roy, P. (2005). *The third implementation of the Sure Start language measure.* Nottingham, United Kingdom: Sure Start.

Hart, B.R., & Risley, T.R. (1995). *Meaningful differences in the everyday experiences of young American children.* Baltimore, MD: Paul H. Brookes Publishing Co.

Henrichs, J., Rescorla, L., Schenk, J., Schmidt, H.G., Jaddoe, V.W.V., Raat, H., . . . Tiemeier, H. (2011). Examining continuity of early expressive vocabulary development: The Generation R Study. *Journal of Speech, Language, and Hearing Research, 54,* 854–869. doi:10.1044/1092–4388(2010/09–0255

HM Government. (2010). *Healthy lives, healthy people: Our strategy for public health in England.* London, United Kingdom: HMSO.

Jaeschke, R., Guyatt S., & Lijmer J. (1994). Diagnostic tests. In G. Guyatt & D. Rennie (Eds.), *Users' Guides to the Medical Literature: A Manual for Evidence-Based Clinical Practice* (pp. 121–139). Chicago, IL: AMA Press.

Klee, T., Pearce, K., & Carson, D.K. (2000). Improving the positive predictive value of screening for developmental language disorder. *Journal of Speech, Language, and Hearing Research, 43,* 821–833.

Laing, G., Logan, S., Law, J., & Levin, A. (2002). Evaluation of a structured test and a parent led method for screening for speech and language problems: Prospective population based study. *British Medical Journal, 325,* 1–5.

Law, J., Boyle, J., Harris, F., Harkness, A., & Nye, C. (1998). Screening for speech and language delay: A systematic review of the literature. *Health Technology Assessment, 2,* 1–184.

Law, J., Boyle, J., Harris, F., Harkness, A., & Nye, C. (2000). The feasibility of universal screening for primary speech and language delay: A systematic review of the literature. *Developmental Medicine and Child Neurology, 42,* 190–200.

Law, J., & Elliott, L. (2009). The relationship between communication and behaviour in children: A case for public mental health. *The Journal of Public Mental Health, 8*(1), 4–11.

Law, J., Garrett, Z., Nye, C., & Dennis, J. (2013). Speech and language therapy interventions for children with primary speech and language delay or disorder. *Cochrane Database of Reviews, 2003,* 3. Art. No.: CD004110. doi:10.1002/14651858.CD004110

Law, J., & Harris, F. (2001). *Promoting language development in Sure Start areas.* Nottingham, United Kingdom: Sure Start.

Law, J., Kot, A., & Barnett, G. (1999). *The efficacy of intervention for young children with severe language impairment: report to North Thames Regional Health Authority.* Available from the first author c/o School of Education, Communication and Language Sciences, University of Newcastle, Newcastle-upon-Tyne, United Kingdom, NE1 7RU.

Law, J., Reilly, S., & Snow, P. (2012). *Speech, language and communication need in the context of public health: A new direction for the speech and language therapy profession.* Manuscript submitted for publication.

Law, J., & Roy, P. (2008). Parental report of infant language skills: A review of the development and application of the Communicative Development Inventories. *Child and Adolescent Mental Health, 13,* 198–206.

Law, J., Rush, R., Anandan, C., Cox, M., & Wood, R. (2012). Predicting language change between three and five years and its implications for early identification: Findings from the Millennium Cohort Study. *Pediatrics, 130*(1). doi:10.1542/peds.2011–1673

Law, J., Tomblin, J.B., & Zhang, X. (2009). Modeling developmental language difficulties from school entry into adulthood: Literacy, mental health, and employment outcomes. *Journal of Speech, Language, and Hearing Research, 52,* 1401–1416.

Lee, L. (1974). *Developmental sentence analysis.* Evanston, IL: Northwestern University Press.

Locke, A., Ginsborg, J., & Peers, I. (2002). Development and disadvantage: Implications for the early years and beyond. *International Journal of Language and Communication Disorders, 37*(1), 3–15.

Logemann, J.A., & Baum, H.M. (1998). Speech-language hearing interventions in the schools: A public health perspective on measuring their short-term and long-term impact. *Language, Speech and Hearing Services in Schools, 29,* 270–273.

Maggi, S., Irwin, L.J., Siddiqi, A., & Hertzman, C. (2010). The social determinants of early child development: An overview. *Journal of Paediatrics and Child Health, 46,* 627–635.

Marmot, D. (2010). *Fair society, healthier lives: Strategic review of health inequalities in England Post-2010.* London, United Kingdom: The Marmot Review.

Nelson, H.D., Nygren, P., Walker, M., & Panoscha, R. (2006). Screening for speech and language delay in preschool children: Systematic evidence review for the US preventive services task force. *Pediatrics, 117.*

Quirk, R. (1972). *Committee of enquiry into speech therapy.* London, United Kingdom: HMSO.

Reilly, S., Wake, M., Bavin, E.L., Prior, M., Williams, J., Bretherton, L., . . . Ukoumunne, O.C. (2007). Predicting language at 2 years of age: A prospective community study. *Pediatrics, 120,* 1441–1449.

Reilly, S., Wake, M., Ukoumunne, O.C., Bavin, E., Prior, M., Cini, E., . . . Bretherton, L. (2010). Predicting language outcomes at 4 years of age: Findings from Early Language in Victoria Study. *Pediatrics, 126,* e1530–e1537. doi:10.1542/peds.2010–0254

Roberts, M., & Kaiser, A. (2011). The effectiveness of parent-implemented language intervention: A meta-analysis. *American Journal of Speech-Language Pathology, 20,* 180–189.

Robertson, S.B. (1997). The influence of peer models on the play scripts of children with specific language impairment. *Journal of Speech, Language, and Hearing Research, 40,* 49–61.

Robertson, S.B., & Weismer, S. (1999). Effects of treatment on linguistic and social skills in toddlers with delayed language development. *Journal of Speech, Language and Hearing Research, 42,* 1234–1248.

Roos, E.M., & Language, S. (2008). Outcomes of late talking toddlers at preschool and beyond. *Perspectives on Language Learning and Education, 15*(3): 119–126. doi: 10.1044/lle15.3.119

Roskos, K., & Neuman, S. (2002). Environment and its influences for early literacy teaching and learning. In S.B. Neuman & D.K. Dickinson (Eds.), *Handbook of early literacy research* (pp. 281–294). New York, NY: Guilford.

Roy, P., Kersley, H., & Law, J. (2005). *The Sure Start Language Measure Standardisation Study: Report to the Sure Start Unit London.* Nottingham, United Kingsom: Sure Start. Available from the first author c/o Department of Language and Communication Science, City University, London, United Kingdom.

Sackett, D.L., Haynes, R.B., Guyatt, G.H., & Tugwell, P. (Eds.). (1991). *Epidemiology: A basic science for clinical medicine.* Boston, MA: Little, Brown and Company.

Schwartz, R.G., Chapman, K., Terrell, B.Y., Prelock, P., & Rowan, L. (1985) Facilitating word combination in language impaired children through discourse structure. *Journal of Speech and Hearing Disorders, 50,* 31–39.

Silver, H., & Miller, S.M. (2003). The European approach to social disadvantage. *Indicators, 2,* 5–21.

Sutton, L., & Tapper, L. (1999). Investigating WILSTAAR. *Bulletin of the Royal College of Speech and Language Therapists,* 8–9.

Tickell, C. (2011). *The early years: Foundations for life, health and learning.* London, United Kingdom: DFE.

Tomblin, J.B., Records, N., Buckwalter, P., Zhang, X., Smith, E., & O'Brien, M. (1997). Prevalence of specific language impairment in kindergarten children. *Journal of Speech, Language, and Hearing Research, 4,* 1245–1269.

Tomblin, J.B., & Zhang, X. (2006). The dimensionality of language ability in school-age children. *Journal of Speech, Language, and Hearing Research, 49,* 1193–1208.

Tomblin, J.B., Zhang, X., Weiss, A., Catts, H., & Ellis Weismer, S.E. (2004). Dimensions of individual differences in communication skills among primary grade children. In M. Rice, & S. Warren (Eds.). (2004). *Developmental disorders: From phenotypes to aetiologies.* Mahwah, NJ: Lawrence Erlbaum Associations.

Ukoumunne, O.C., Wake, M., Carlin, J., Bavin, E.L., Lum, J., Skeat, J., . . . Reilly, S. (2012). Profiles of language development in preschool children: A longitudinal latent class analysis of data from the Early Language in Victoria Study. *Child Care Health and Development, 38,* 341–349.

van Kleeck, A., Van der Woude, J., & Hammett, L. (2006). Fostering literal and inferential language skills in Head Start preschoolers with language impairment using scripted book-sharing discussions. *American Journal of Speech-Language Pathology, 15*(1), 85–95.

Wake, M., Tobin, S., Girolametto, L., Ukoumunne, O.C., Gold, L., Levickis, P., J., . . . Reilly, S. (2011). Outcomes of population based language promotion for slow to talk toddlers at ages 2 and 3 years: Let's Learn Language cluster randomised controlled trial. *BMJ, 343,* d741.

Ward, S. (1999). An investigation into the effectiveness of an early intervention method for delayed language development in young children. *International Journal of Language & Communication Disorders, 34,* 243–264.

Washington, K.N., Warr-Leeper, G., & Thomas-Stonell, N. (2011). Exploring the outcomes of a novel computer-assisted treatment program targeting expressive-grammar deficits in preschoolers with SLI. *Journal of Communication Disorders, 44,* 315–330.

Wechsler, D. (2002). *Wechsler Preschool and Primary Scale of Intelligence–Third Edition (WPPSI-III)*. San Antonio, TX: Harcourt Assessment.

Wetherby, A., Prizant, B. (2002). *Communication and Symbolic Behavior Scales Developmental Profile™ (CSBS DP™)*. Baltimore, MD: Paul H. Brookes Publishing Co.

Wilcox, M.J., Kouri, T.A., & Caswell, S.B. (1991). Early language intervention: A comparison of classroom and individual treatment. *American Journal of Speech-Language Pathology, 1,* 49–61.

Yoder, P.J., Molfese, D., & Gardner, E. (2011). Initial mean length of utterance predicts the relative efficacy of two grammatical treatments in preschoolers with specific language impairment. *Journal of Speech, Language, and Hearing Research, 54,* 1170–1181.

Zimmerman, I., Steiner, V., & Pond, R. (1992). *Preschool Language Scale, Third Edition.* San Antonio, TX: Psychological Corporation.

Zweig, M.H., & Campbell, G. (1993). Receiver-operating characteristic (ROC) plots: A fundamental evaluation tool in clinical medicine. *Clinical Chemistry, 39,* 561–577.

# Conclusion

# 17

# Alternative Routes
# to Language Impairment

Laurence B. Leonard

The proportion of late talkers (LTs) who later meet the criteria for specific language impairment (SLI) vastly underestimates the documented prevalence of SLI (e.g., Ellis Weismer, 2007; Paul, 2000; Rescorla, 2002; Thal, 2005; Whitehurst & Fischel, 1994). This finding holds across major laboratories and different outcome measures of spoken language ability. For example, Ellis Weismer (2007) found that at age 5.5 years, only 7.5% of LTs scored at least 1 standard deviation (*SD*) below the mean on an expressive measure of language development, and none scored this low on a receptive measure of language development. Such a finding is noteworthy considering that the prevalence of SLI at 5 years of age is taken to be 7% (Tomblin, Records, et al., 1997). Paul (2000) found a somewhat higher percentage at 7 years for the LTs in her study: On one expressive syntax measure, 16% of LTs scored below the 10th percentile. However, these children were within normal limits on a formal test of expressive and receptive language. Rescorla (2002) reported that 15% of LTs scored below average levels on a test of expressive grammar at 5 years of age. At age 6 years, 6% of these children scored below the 10th percentile on at least two of six subtests of a comprehensive test of spoken language. Performance on those subtests that involved language comprehension was considerably higher than performance on subtests assessing language production. Thal (2005) found that only 8.8% of the LTs in her study met the criteria for SLI at 5 years of age. If all children exhibiting SLI at age 5 years come from the LT population, these percentages should be much higher, as LTs constitute only a small proportion of 2-year-olds.

The gross underestimation of SLI based on LT outcomes is all the more noteworthy considering that these studies have been of high quality. Most studies in this area have been prospective, longitudinal studies, with careful matching between children in the LT and typically developing (TD) language groups. This chapter discusses some possible reasons for this underestimation. These reasons are divided into three broad categories. Some of the reasons have been discussed by the authors of these studies themselves; they usually concern methodological details. Other reasons are more conceptual and, possibly, more responsible than any other reason for the small proportion of children with SLI who are identified through the LT method.

## MATCHING ON CHARACTERISTICS THAT ARE UNEQUAL IN CHILDREN WITH LANGUAGE IMPAIRMENTS AND TYPICALLY DEVELOPING CHILDREN

To determine the unique contribution of LT status to language outcomes, it makes sense to match LTs and TD children on factors such as nonverbal IQ and maternal education level (or some other measure related to socioeconomic status). The disadvantage of this approach is that, on average, children with SLI score lower than their same-age TD peers on measures of nonverbal IQ and are more likely to come from families in which parents have completed fewer years of formal education. For example, in group comparison studies, when children are not specifically matched on nonverbal IQ, differences favoring the TD group are customary (e.g., Krantz & Leonard, 2007; Spaulding, Plante, & Vance, 2008). Regarding maternal education level, Tomblin, Smith, and Zhang (1997) found that mothers of children with SLI completed fewer years of education than mothers of TD children. Of particular importance here is the fact that this investigation was an epidemiological study and hence less vulnerable to biases that can often accompany a clinically referred sample.

The potentially misleading consequences of matching according to characteristics such as nonverbal IQ and maternal education level are clear. The outcomes of LTs may appear especially favorable because other LTs with characteristics more representative of children with SLI did not provide a close match with their non–late-talking peers and were therefore excluded.

There are other characteristics that seem to be associated with a higher likelihood of a diagnosis of SLI. Although they are not often used as a basis for exclusion, their correlation with socioeconomic status makes it less likely that they will be represented among LT groups if socioeconomic status matching is employed. These include the following risk factors that have proved significant in predicting an outcome of SLI: maternal age at child's birth, late or no prenatal care, high birth order, limited or no breast feeding, and paternal smoking (e.g., Delgado, Vagi, & Scott, 2005; Reilly et al., 2010; Stanton-Chapman, Chapman, Bainbridge, & Scott, 2002; Tomblin, Smith, & Zhang, 1997).

It would seem advisable to allow more factors to vary in comparisons between LTs and their peers. Not only do investigators reduce the likelihood of finding major differences in outcome when they match children on macrovariables (e.g., socioeconomic status) that may subsume multiple microvariables, but if they do find outcome differences, the explanatory value of the outcome findings may be compromised. For example, some factors may be correlated with, but not entirely explained by, socioeconomic status. These factors, if free to vary and to be monitored, might help to explain some significant portion of the variance in the children's outcomes. Without information of this type, if LTs are found to be at greater risk for SLI than their peers, the reasons for their LT status in the first place will be unknown. Efforts may be made to accelerate these children's rate of language development, but prevention efforts will be hampered by not knowing which factors increase the likelihood that a child will be late in talking.

The one factor that is carefully monitored while being left free to vary is a positive history of language-related problems. Many of the earliest prospective studies of LTs have reported that they are more likely than their peers to have family members with a history of spoken language and/or reading difficulties (e.g., Ellis Weismer, Murray-Branch, & Miller, 1994; Paul, 1991; Rescorla & Schwartz, 1990). The potential importance of this fact is discussed later, in the Next Steps section of this chapter.

## RISK CONSTITUTES A CONTINUUM

LT status does seem to have predictive value inasmuch as LTs, as a group, score below the level of matched peers on a variety of language measures from preschool into the adolescent years. The problem is that the lower-scoring children with an LT history typically score above the threshold needed for a diagnosis of SLI. However, such results should not be viewed as disappointing if one views SLI as falling on a continuum with below-average, average, above-average, and superior language ability (Dollaghan, 2004, 2011; Leonard, 1987, 1991). That is, because the LTs did not have some of the accompanying risk factors (as a result of exclusion or group matching decisions), they were probably not among the most seriously at risk in the first place. Their outcomes placing them below the level of their peers but within normal limits should therefore not be surprising.

Recall that LTs are more likely to come from families with a positive history of language-related problems. It is also well known that there is a genetic component in many cases of SLI (Bishop, Adams, & Norbury, 2006; Stromswold, 2008). However, the molecular genetic evidence paints a picture of SLI as a multifactorial condition in which combinations of genetic variants, or genetic variants coupled with environmental factors, lead to SLI. Such a picture is quite compatible with the view that SLI is a point on a continuum. The same factors in different combinations (or fewer variants operating in combination) might lead to an ability level best described as below-average rather than impaired. Thus, many LTs who do not quite reach the threshold of SLI might differ from children with SLI in just this way. These may not be qualitative differences. After all, what makes the lowest end of the continuum (SLI) classified as an impairment is the fact that poor language has an adverse effect on a child's communicative (Fujiki, Spackman, Brinton, & Hall, 2004; Jerome, Fujiki, Brinton, & James, 2002), academic (Catts, Fey, Tomblin, & Zhang, 2002), and emotional (Conti-Ramsden & Botting, 2008; Fujiki, Brinton, & Clarke, 2002) functioning. These negative consequences distinguish language abilities at the low end of the continuum from comparably low abilities in areas such as music proficiency and physical agility. Quality of life might well be affected if a child is not musical or graceful, but the consequences will be much broader and deeper if language is the area that is extremely weak.

## THE SPECIFIC LANGUAGE IMPAIRMENT PROFILE IS A PRESCHOOL AND SCHOOL-AGE CHARACTERISTIC THAT EMERGES

A very understandable assumption of the prospective studies on LT outcomes is that children with SLI had an SLI-like profile from the beginning. That is, if language was the primary weakness by preschool, language was likewise the primary weakness at age 2. The alternative possibilities are twofold.

## Many Children Destined for a Diagnosis of Specific Language Impairment Fail to Meet Late Talker Selection Criteria

By now, the unstable nature of the SLI category is well known (Botting, 2005; Conti-Ramsden & Botting, 1999). Some of this instability has taken the form of children shifting from nonspecific language impairment (NLI) to SLI. This change has also been captured in prospective studies that retained children even when they did not initially meet the customary criteria for SLI (e.g., Miller et al., 2006). Such observations suggest that some children meeting the criteria for SLI at preschool age or beyond did not show the SLI-like profile at the outset. Such children might well have been excluded from studies of LTs.

An illustration of this issue is provided in Figure 17.1. Assume that the top panel of the figure reflects typical development, with children showing developmentally comparable abilities in motor, nonverbal cognitive, and language abilities. Absolute ability, of course, increases with age. The scenario in the middle panel of Figure 17.1 reflects the LT situation, in which the children are clearly delayed in language, but seem (based on the top panel) to be reaching milestones appropriately in motor and nonverbal cognitive abilities. This middle panel illustrates that the children's language development continues to trail their development in these other areas. Whether the children's language ability will catch up to these other abilities in subsequent years is, of course, one of the most central questions that is asked in LT studies.

The bottom panel of Figure 17.1 represents a case in which children might have been excluded as participants in LT studies because their motor and nonverbal cognitive development were still below age level at 24 months, a common age for participant recruitment. If it turns out that, for some children, motor and nonverbal cognitive development begin to outpace language development, we could have the children meeting the criteria for SLI at a later age after being excluded for appearing to have broader disabilities at an earlier age.

This change from a broader impairment to SLI is not the remarkable transformation in children that it may seem. For example, there is growing evidence that the nonverbal IQ cutoff of 85, though statistically sensible given that it represents $-1SD$, does not serve as a valid means of distinguishing diagnostically separable groups. For example, Tomblin and Zhang (1999) found very similar linguistic profiles when comparing children with language impairments whose nonverbal IQs were above or below the 85 cutoff. In addition, results from treatment studies indicate that children below the 85 cutoff benefit from language treatment to the same degree as those above the cutoff (Cole, Dale, & Mills, 1990; Fey, Long, & Cleave, 1994). After considering the evidence that children with nonverbal IQs in the 75–84 range cannot be easily distinguished from children with language impairments with nonverbal IQs of 85 and above, Tager-Flusberg and Cooper (1999) recommended that children in the lower IQ range be included in group studies of SLI until or unless future evidence reveals a distinction between the two IQ levels. This relaxing of the nonverbal IQ standard emerged only after the initial publication of many of the prospective studies of LTs that employed an IQ level of 85 or higher as one of the

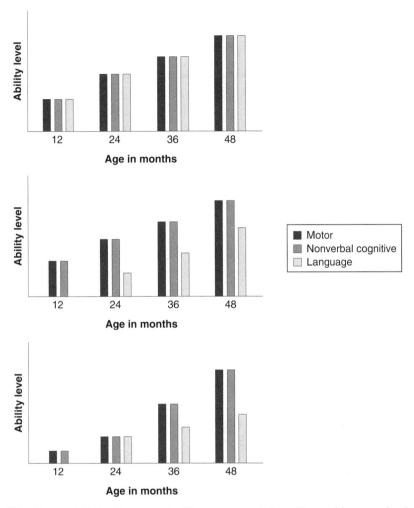

**Figure 17.1.** Top panel: Typical development with motor, nonverbal cognitive, and language development proceeding as expected. Middle panel: Late talkers who show slow lexical development relative to their age-appropriate development in the motor and nonverbal cognitive domains. Bottom panel: Children who are initially slow in all three areas but begin to catch up to peers in all but language development.

selection criteria. The major point here is that NLI-to-SLI shifts over time should not be unexpected given that the boundary between them was not established on the basis of empirical evidence.

Additional risk factors for SLI—those that can and often have served as a basis for excluding children from studies of LTs—include the presence of a congenital condition, a multiple birth, a low 5-minute Apgar score, and very low birth weight (Delgado et al., 2005; Reilly et al., 2010; Stanton-Chapman et al., 2002). Not all studies have identified the same risk factors. For example, in a study by Tomblin, Smith, and Zhang (1997), the 95% confidence interval surrounding the odds ratio for low birth weight rendered this factor nonsignificant. However, meta-analysis does suggest that very low birth weight serves as a significant risk factor for poor language ability (Barre, Morgan, Doyle, & Anderson, 2011).

Some of the genetic evidence related to SLI suggests how some of these other factors can become associated with the language disorder. For example, variants of the gene CNTNAP2 in chromosome region 7q36 seem to be correlated with weaknesses on a range of language measures (Vernes et al., 2008). However, disruptions in this gene have also been associated with neurodevelopmental weaknesses in addition to language. The developmental course and rate of some of these functions could well differ, producing initial profiles that include weaknesses in areas beyond language, with the language impairment persisting as other weak areas gain strength.

Locke (1994) advanced a proposal that is founded on the idea that children with SLI initially show a more general neuromaturational delay that includes not only the late emergence of words but also a delay in achieving motor and other developmental milestones. These children gradually overcome these delays, but the language problem persists. According to Locke, a sufficient number of words must be acquired before a biologically based grammatical analysis mechanism is set in motion. This analysis mechanism has an optimal period of functioning; if words are accumulated quite slowly, the mechanism will not yet be operational for a portion of the optimal period. The result will be compromised learning of grammar—a hallmark of SLI.

It is ironic that factors that have been used as a basis for exclusion because they constitute nonlinguistic developmental complications can actually be useful predictors of the SLI profile in which language is the primary impairment. This type of evidence serves as yet another reason to employ a more liberal set of selection criteria in our studies of LTs.

## Small and Delayed Vocabularies May Not Characterize Many Instances of Specific Language Impairment

The fact that common symptoms of SLI take the form of weaker morphosyntactic abilities rather than lexical abilities, coupled with the fact that some children with SLI show age-appropriate vocabularies, raises the possibility that, in principle, children with SLI do not have to start out with small and late-developing vocabularies.

This state of affairs is depicted in Figure 17.2. Assume the top panel reflects typical development. At 12 months of age, TD children may be expressing words, but grammar has probably not yet emerged. By 24 months, the children's lexicons will have expanded, and grammatical ability will now be detectable. By around 48 months, TD children will provide ample evidence of grammatical sentences and a rich vocabulary. (Of course, development will continue in both domains; for the purposes of this chapter, 48 months seems an appropriate end point.)

The middle panel of Figure 17.2 resembles portions of the top panel, with ages shifted to the right. This seems to be the common situation in which children with a limited lexicon at 24 months might be selected in an LT study. If these children were to progress in a manner similar to that of the children in the top panel, grammar would soon emerge, so that at 36 and 48 months, these LTs might look much like the TD children at 24 and 36 months, respectively. By following the LTs further across time, it could be determined if these children eventually catch up to their peers.

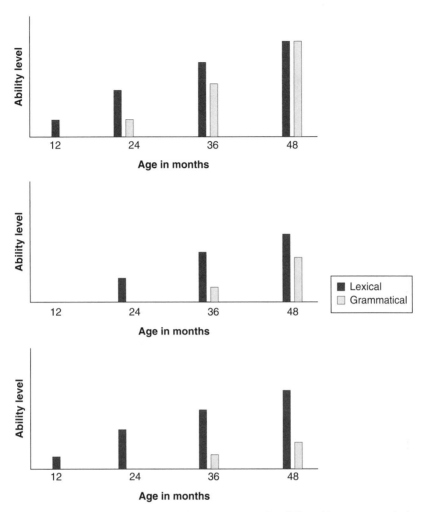

**Figure 17.2.**   Top panel: Typical development with words emerging first, followed by grammar, and subsequent development in both domains. Middle panel: Late talkers who show the expected profile but at a later age. Bottom panel: Children who do not appear to be slow in lexical development but show a significant lag in their development of grammar.

However, another possibility exists, shown in the bottom panel of Figure 17.2. Any children showing this profile would probably not be considered an LT because the size of their vocabularies approximates that seen in typical language development. Yet their grammar does not keep pace with their lexical development. Such children would probably meet the criteria for SLI, either because their weak grammatical skills would pull down their composite language score, or because of the weak grammatical skills in their own right.

Certainly it is true that correlations hold between scores on lexical and morphosyntactic measures. However, all tests and measures that exhibit good sensitivity and specificity for language impairment seem to deal with morphosyntax (use of tense/agreement, comprehension of syntax) or phonological memory (nonword repetition). Vocabulary comprehension or production measures have not yet shown acceptable diagnostic accuracy. This has very little to do with the quality of the standardization of these tests; some of these tests are of high quality. The problem rests with the fact that the area of vocabulary does not provide a very sharp distinction between SLI and typical language development. It stands to reason, then, that vocabulary status may not be a universal characteristic of children who will be diagnosed with SLI a few years down the line.

Of course, it is natural for studies of LT outcomes to choose vocabulary as the central focal point; most TD children are only just beginning to produce multiword utterances at 24 months of age, so their most conspicuous language achievement is a relatively rich vocabulary. In addition, the ultimate goal in some of this LT research is to devise measures that have clinical utility. Parents can judge, with some accuracy, the approximate number of words their children produce. For this reason, they can be in a position to alert professionals if their children are accumulating too few words for their age. Such a decision can be very helpful to the extent that a small vocabulary proves to have important prognostic value in predicting future language impairment.

Yet, consider how it might be possible for some children to acquire an adequate lexical inventory yet stumble when words must be integrated with morphosyntax. For example, Kelly and Rice (1994) presented to children a set of novel verbs whose meanings could be interpreted in terms of either a change of state (e.g., action completion) or type of motion. Young TD children showed a preference for the change of state interpretation; children with SLI, however, showed no such tendency. This relative insensitivity to temporal information at the lexical level could put children with SLI at a disadvantage when acquiring tense and aspect, even though the verbs themselves might be learned. Leonard, Miller, and Gerber (1999) found that children with SLI made significantly less use of tense and agreement morphemes than younger TD children who were matched on the number of different verbs they produced. Thus, relative to their younger peers, the children with SLI seemed less equipped to put their available verb inventory to work in expressing morphosyntactic notions. Grela and Leonard (1997) found that children with SLI had greater difficulty than younger peers matched for verb diversity in using subjects with unaccusative verbs—that is, verbs whose subjects are themes rather than agents (e.g., "fall"). The problem did not seem to rest in the core verb meaning but in using a theme in subject position when, with most verbs of this type, themes are used in postverb position.

Unfortunately, identifying children at risk for language impairment on the basis of late grammatical development means that professionals must wait beyond the age (24–30 months) that is characteristically used in LT studies. It appears, however, that once identified as at-risk at this older age, children are more likely to have been identified correctly. A study by Leonard, Camarata, Brown, and Camarata (2004) provides an example. These investigators identified 31 children with a mean age of 3;6 as being at risk on the basis of low scores on measures of morphosyntactic development. The children then participated in a 12-week intervention program that produced statistically reliable, though somewhat modest, gains in language development. Nevertheless, following the 12-week intervention period, all 31 children continued to show significant impairments in morphosyntactic ability. Twenty-five of the children received an additional 12 weeks of intervention. Although significant gains were made in the second 12-week period of intervention,

20 of the 25 children continued to exhibit significant impairment in morphosyntax after this period (Leonard, Camarata, Pawłowska, Brown, & Camarata, 2006).

## NEXT STEPS

Much work remains to be done before children at risk for language impairment can be accurately identified at a young age. As this work is pursued, questions about the role of late talker status and the relative importance to be placed on particular risk factors will have to be addressed. Some of the issues are discussed here.

### Using Late Talker Status as an Additional, Rather than Primary, Predictor

There is little doubt that LT status can play an important role in solving the puzzle of SLI. However, because the many high-quality prospective studies of LTs have not led to outcomes that reflect the prevalence of SLI, it might be time to rethink how LT status might be put to use in predictor studies. The LT–non-LT distinction might be better implemented if investigators determine if LT status explains additional unique variance in children's outcomes—that is, variance over and beyond the variance explained by other factors suspected to have a detrimental effect on language development. The Reilly et al. (2010) study cited earlier is an example of an investigation that employed this type of strategy. These researchers found that LT status improved predictability over and beyond factors such as socioeconomic status and positive family history. Of course, this is only a first step. As reported by Reilly et al., even after adding LT status to the regression model, success in predicting children's language outcomes was modest at best.

### Policy Issues

Assuming that with time researchers become more accurate in predicting children's language outcomes, the distinction between successful prediction at the group level and accurate prediction at the individual child level will become paramount. However, as predictions at the individual child level become more feasible, important policy issues will arise as practitioners contemplate how best to put these successful predictors into general practice. The most important issue might be how to deal with predictors that apply to only a small segment of the at-risk population. Some risk factors—although very real—occur with low enough frequency in the SLI population that they may not rise to the level of characterizing the group as a whole. Thus, although a factor may prove important in contributing to the likelihood that an individual child will be diagnosed with SLI, the low frequency of occurrence of this factor may not warrant incorporating this factor into a screening protocol for the general population (Mason, Scott, Chapman, & Tu, 2000). It may be possible in the future to incorporate items about rare but highly prognostic conditions in less time-consuming questionnaires while devoting more testing time to more common risk factors.

### Developing and Refining New Measures for Identifying Risk

As knowledge of genetic and environmental risk factors continues to expand, the ability to predict language outcomes of young children will likely increase. It will also be necessary to develop and refine measures obtained from the children themselves. These include measures that can be obtained at or before the typical age of LT identification (around 24 months) as well as those measures more suitable for a slightly later age (between 24 and 36 months) that is still somewhat younger than the age at which SLI can be diagnosed with confidence.

Measures of the first type include speech processing measures. Such measures might be used on their own, in combination with a LT–non-LT distinction, and/or with other risk factors such as positive family history for language impairment. The method of employing response time as a measure of efficiency in word recognition, as developed by Fernald and her colleagues (e.g., Fernald & Marchman, 2012; see also Chapter 8), serves as an excellent example of such a measure that shows great promise. Of course, at this point, this measure seems to predict children's future rate of lexical development. As noted earlier, small vocabularies at, say, 3 years of age, may not necessarily be predictive of later language impairment. However, Fernald and her colleagues have also shown that the same looking-while-listening paradigm can also detect young children's sensitivity to grammatical cues, such as a Spanish-speaking child's use of the article "la" to anticipate an object whose name (e.g., "pelota" for "ball") has feminine gender (Lew-Williams & Fernald, 2007). Because grammar seems to be an especially weak area in children with SLI, such methods may prove to have predictive value.

With further development, instruments such as LENA (Language ENvironment Analysis, LENA Research Foundation, Boulder, CO) may contribute to researchers' ability to identify children at risk for language impairment. For example, Zimmerman et al. (2009) found that the number of conversational turns (as estimated by the LENA algorithm) between adults and children (mean age = 14 months) in 12-hour samples could predict the children's scores on the Preschool Language Scale–4 (PLS-4; Zimmerman, Steiner, & Pond, 2002) 18 months later. The number of conversational turns accounted for unique variance in the later PLS-4 scores even after PLS-4 scores obtained at the earlier age were entered in the model as an additional predictor. Obviously, the term *conversational turn* must be defined quite broadly given the children's young ages at the outset of the study. However, the massive language samples that are available through LENA might allow researchers to probe deeper into these interactions to determine whether particular types of conversational turns are the operative ones. Of course, it must also be determined whether measures such as the number of conversational turns prove to be significant predictors of language impairment. At this point, predictions have been limited to the range of language test scores seen in children who were well within the normal range of language development.

Measures more suitable for a slightly later age range could be based on closely monitoring children from about 2–3 years of age to determine whether their emerging grammar matches that of TD children. This type of measure, too, might stand alone or be used in tandem with other risk factors, including LT status. Hadley and Short (2005) have developed a set of measures that seem to hold considerable promise. These investigators found that the productivity that young children showed in using tense/agreement morphemes (e.g., third-person singular –s, copula *is*) during very early grammatical development was related to their future language status. The measures used by Hadley and Short were quite conservative in that the number of different verbs used with a particular verb inflection was taken into consideration, and copula and auxiliary forms that were contracted with pronominal subjects (as in "that's," "he's") were excluded on the grounds that they may have been learned as unanalyzed wholes. Positive instances were the focus; the many omissions of tense/agreement forms were not a factor in their tallies.

Assuming researchers are at least a decade away from having an accurate set of measures for predicting future language impairment, practitioners are faced with a dilemma. Even if measures such as those of Hadley and Short (2005) live up to expectations, they are useful only to the extent that young children are seen for repeated sessions over 1–2 years. It might be difficult to justify multiple trips to the laboratory/clinic (or to the child's home) if the process is strictly for diagnostic or prognostic purposes. Alternatively, practitioners might invite families to have their children regularly participate in language stimulation groups—so called because the children's unclear diagnostic status probably does not warrant a more formal language treatment regimen. Indeed, given the continuum of language abilities likely to be represented in such groups, activities of this type could prove beneficial to all children—those who might have achieved typical (albeit below average) language abilities even without these experiences, as well as those whose avoidance of a future language impairment may depend on it.

## CONCLUSIONS

This chapter has considered some of the reasons why the proportion of LTs who later meet the criteria for language impairment is so much lower than expected given the prevalence of such impairments in the preschool population. One likely factor is that careful matching of LT and TD groups on particular characteristics has probably led to the selection of those LTs with the fewest risk factors and hence the best prognosis. Certainly even these most advantaged of LTs are later found to be weaker in language than their matched peers, but in most instances their language skills nevertheless fall within normal limits. This finding is quite consistent with the view that there is a continuum of language ability and a corresponding continuum of factors that influence this ability.

Another factor that might lead to underestimations of the prevalence of language impairment is that the SLI profile seen in the preschool years is not the profile that characterizes toddlers who will meet the criteria for SLI later on. Broader neuromaturational delays may be seen in many of these children, with the weaknesses narrowing and residing primarily in language by 4 or 5 years of age. Perhaps the most neglected possibility is that some children with language impairment do not exhibit a significant delay in their lexical development. For these children, lexical inventories—even if slightly below average in size—may exceed the number of words required to qualify as an LT. Across time, grammar may prove to be these children's Achilles' heel, a weakness that could not be observed at the age when LTs are first identified.

LT status remains an important prognostic factor. However, this factor may prove most useful if it is used as an additional predictor rather than as a primary predictor in longitudinal studies. Finally, along with continued development of other measures that can be used during early development, we should probably consider applying measures of the early stages of grammar in our search for predictors of subsequent language impairment. Use of such measures must be postponed until children approach 3 years of age or later, but until alternative infant and toddler measures are ready for diagnostic use, these grammatically based metrics might serve to increase practitioners' current accuracy in identifying those children who will exhibit an impairment in language ability by preschool age.

## REFERENCES

Barre, N., Morgan, A., Doyle, L., & Anderson, P. (2011). Language abilities in children who were very preterm and/or very low birth weight: A meta-analysis. *The Journal of Pediatrics, 158,* 766–774.

Bishop, D.V.M., Adams, C., & Norbury, C.F. (2006). Distinct genetic influences on grammar and phonological short-term memory deficits: Evidence from 6-year-old twins. *Genes, Brain and Behavior, 5,* 158–169.

Botting, N. (2005). Non-verbal cognitive development and language impairment. *Journal of Child Psychology and Psychiatry, 46,* 317–326.

Catts, H., Fey, M., Tomblin, J.B., & Zhang, X. (2002). A longitudinal investigation of reading outcomes in children with language impairments. *Journal of Speech, Language, and Hearing Research, 45,* 1142–1157.

Cole, K., Dale, P., & Mills, P. (1990). Defining language delay in young children by cognitive referencing: Are we saying more than we know? *Applied Psycholinguistics, 11,* 291–302.

Conti-Ramsden, G., & Botting, N. (1999). Classification of children with specific language impairment. *Journal of Speech, Language, and Hearing Research, 42,* 1195–1205.

Conti-Ramsden, G., & Botting, N. (2008). Emotional health in adolescents with and without a history of specific language impairment. *Journal of Child Psychology and Psychiatry, 49,* 516–525.

Delgado, C., Vagi, S., & Scott, K. (2005). Early risk factors for speech and language impairments. *Exceptionality, 13,* 173–191.

Dollaghan, C. (2004). Taxometric analyses of specific language impairment in 3- and 4-year-old children. *Journal of Speech, Language, and Hearing Research, 47,* 464–475.

Dollaghan, C. (2011). Taxometric analyses of specific language impairment in 6-year-old children. *Journal of Speech, Language, and Hearing Research, 54,* 1361–1371.

Ellis Weismer, S. (2007). Typical talkers, late talkers, and children with specific language impairment: A language endowment spectrum? In R. Paul (Ed.), *Language disorders from a developmental perspective* (pp. 83–101). Mahwah, NJ: Lawrence Erlbaum Associates.

Ellis Weismer, S., Murray-Branch, J., & Miller, J. (1994). A prospective longitudinal study of language development in late talkers. *Journal of Speech and Hearing Research, 37,* 852–867.

Fernald, A., & Marchman, V. (2012). Individual differences in lexical processing at 18 months predict vocabulary growth in typically developing and late-talking toddlers. *Child Development, 83,* 203–222.

Fey, M.E., Long, S.H., & Cleave, P.L. (1994). Reconsideration of IQ criteria in the definition of specific language impairment. In R.V. Watkins & M.L. Rice (Eds.), *Specific language impairments in children* (pp. 161–178). Baltimore, MD: Paul H. Brookes Publishing Co.

Fujiki, M., Brinton, B., & Clarke, D. (2002). Emotion regulation in children with specific language impairment. *Language, Speech, and Hearing Services in Schools, 33,* 102–111.

Fujiki, M., Spackman, M., Brinton, B., & Hall, A. (2004). The relationship of language and emotion regulation skills to reticence in children with specific language impairment. *Journal of Speech, Language, and Hearing Research, 47,* 637–646.

Grela, B., & Leonard, L. (1997). The use of subject arguments by children with specific language impairment. *Journal of Clinical Linguistics and Phonetics, 11,* 443–453.

Hadley, P., & Short, H. (2005). The onset of tense marking in children at risk for specific language impairment. *Journal of Speech, Language, and Hearing Research, 48,* 1344–1362.

Jerome, A., Fujiki, M., Brinton, B., & James, S. (2002). Self-esteem in children with specific language impairment. *Journal of Speech, Language, and Hearing Research, 45,* 700–714.

Kelly, D., & Rice, M. (1994). Preferences for verb interpretation in children with specific language impairment. *Journal of Speech and Hearing Research, 37,* 182–192.

Krantz, L., & Leonard, L. (2007). The effect of temporal adverbials on past tense production by children with specific language impairment. *Journal of Speech, Language, and Hearing Research, 50,* 137–148.

Leonard, L. (1987). Is specific language impairment a useful construct? In S. Rosenberg (Eds.), *Advances in applied psycholinguistics: Volume 1. Disorders of first-language development* (pp. 1–39). New York, NY: Cambridge University Press.

Leonard, L. (1991). Specific language impairment as a clinical category. *Language, Speech, and Hearing Services in Schools, 22,* 66–68.

Leonard, L., Camarata, S., Brown, B., & Camarata, M. (2004). Tense and agreement in the speech of children with specific language impairment: Patterns of generalization through intervention. *Journal of Speech, Language, and Hearing Research, 47,* 1363–1379.

Leonard, L., Camarata, S., Pawłowska, M., Brown, B., & Camarata, M. (2006). Tense and agreement morphemes in the speech of children with specific language impairment during intervention: Phase 2. *Journal of Speech, Language, and Hearing Research, 49,* 749–770.

Leonard, L., Miller, C., & Gerber, E. (1999). Grammatical morphology and the lexicon in children with specific language impairment. *Journal of Speech, Language, and Hearing Research, 42,* 678–689.

Lew-Williams, C., & Fernald, A. (2007). Young children learning Spanish make rapid use of grammatical gender in spoken word recognition. *Psychological Science, 18,* 193–198.

Locke, J. (1994). Gradual emergence of developmental language disorders. *Journal of Speech and Hearing Research, 37,* 608–616.

Mason, C., Scott, K., Chapman, D., & Tu, S. (2000). A review of some individual- and community-level effect size indices for the study of risk factors for child and adolescent development. *Educational and Psychological Measurement, 56,* 45–62.

Miller, C., Leonard, L., Kail, R., Zhang, X., Tomblin, J.B., & Francis, D. (2006). Response time in 14-year-olds with language impairment. *Journal of Speech, Language, and Hearing Research, 49,* 712–728.

Paul, R. (1991). Profiles of toddlers with slow expressive language development. *Topics in Language Disorders, 11,* 1–13.

Paul, R. (2000). Predicting outcomes of early expressive language delay: Ethical implications. In D.V.M. Bishop & L.B. Leonard (Eds.), *Speech and language impairments in children: Causes, characteristics, intervention and outcome* (pp. 195–209). Hove, United Kingdom: Psychology Press.

Reilly, S., Wake, M., Ukoumunne, O., Bavin, E., Prior, M., Cini, E., . . . Bretherton, L. (2010). Predicting language outcomes at 4 years of age: Findings from Early Language in Victoria Study. *Pediatrics, 126,* 1530–1537.

Rescorla, L. (2002). Language and reading outcomes to age 9 in late-talking toddlers. *Journal of Speech, Language, and Hearing Research, 45,* 360–371.

Rescorla, L., & Schwartz, E. (1990). Outcomes of toddlers with specific expressive language delay. *Applied Psycholinguistics, 11,* 393–407.

Spaulding, T., Plante, E., & Vance, R. (2008). Sustained selective attention skills of preschool children with specific language impairment: Evidence for separate attentional capacities. *Journal of Speech, Language, and Hearing Research, 51,* 16–34.

Stanton-Chapman, T., Chapman, D., Bainbridge, N., & Scott, K. (2002). Identification of early risk factors for language impairment. *Research in Developmental Disabilities, 23,* 390–405.

Stromswold, K. (2008). The genetics of speech and language impairments. *New England Journal of Medicine, 359,* 2381–2383.

Tager-Flusberg, H., & Cooper, J. (1999). Present and future possibilities for defining a phenotype for specific language impairment. *Journal of Speech, Language, and Hearing Research, 42,* 1275–1278.

Thal, D. (2005). *Early detection of risk for language impairment.* Presentation at the Annual Convention of the American Speech-Language-Hearing Association, San Diego, CA.

Tomblin, J.B., Records, N., Buckwalter, P., Zhang, X., Smith, E., & O'Brien, M. (1997). The prevalence of specific language impairment in kindergarten children. *Journal of Speech, Language, and Hearing Research, 40,* 1245–1260.

Tomblin, J.B., Smith, E., & Zhang, X. (1997). Epidemiology of specific language impairment: Prenatal and perinatal risk factors. *Journal of Communication Disorders, 30,* 325–344.

Tomblin, J.B., & Zhang, X. (1999). Language patterns and etiology in children with specific language impairment. In H. Tager-Flusberg (Ed.), *Neurodevelopmental disorders* (pp. 361–382). Cambridge, MA: The MIT Press.

Vernes, S., Newbury, D., Abrahams, B., Winchester, L., Nicod, J., Groszer, M., . . . Geschwind, D. (2008). A functional genetic link between distinct developmental language disorders. *New England Journal of Medicine, 359,* 2337–2345.

Whitehurst, G., & Fischel, J. (1994). Early developmental language delay: What, if anything, should the clinician do about it? *Journal of Child Psychology and Psychiatry, 35,* 613–648.

Zimmerman, F., Gilkerson, J., Richards, J., Christakis, D., Xu, D., Gray, S., & Yapanel, U. (2009). Teaching by listening: The importance of adult-child conversations to language development. *Pediatrics, 124,* 342–349.

Zimmerman, I., Steiner, V., & Pond, R. (2002). *Preschool Language Scale–4.* San Antonio, TX: Psychological Corporation.

# 18

# Where Do We Stand Now?

*Conclusions and Future Directions*

Leslie A. Rescorla and Philip S. Dale

The chapters in this book have provided a wealth of information about late talkers (LTs)—too much to be fully summarized in this concluding chapter. Instead, this chapter outlines some of the major conclusions that can be drawn from the research presented in this book, organized around its four major themes. In many respects, these conclusions are so well supported by research conducted by numerous investigators that they can be taken as definitive both by researchers and practitioners. In others, we suggest additional research that would strengthen the conclusions and their relevance for clinical work. Finally, in each section we outline some of the major issues we think should be explored in future research on LTs.

## IDENTIFICATION AND CLASSIFICATION OF LATE TALKERS

Reliable and valid screening tools are available for identifying children who are slow to talk in general population samples. In additional, clinical instruments are available for differential diagnosis of children who are slow to talk. However, more research is needed with large epidemiological samples to determine the optimal cutpoints for identifying LTs and other children who are slow to talk, as well as for ascertaining the prevalence of the different conditions associated with slow language development.

### Conclusion 1

There are now practical methods by which it is possible to identify LTs in the general population in the age range of 18–36 months. The instruments that have been most widely validated for this purpose—the Language Development Survey (LDS; Rescorla, 1989) and the MacArthur-Bates Communicative Development Inventories

(CDIs; Fenson et al., 2007)—are easy to administer, do not require professional time to complete, and are well-received by parents (Chapters 9, 11, and 12). Both instruments have excellent psychometric properties, such as strong test-retest and internal consistency reliability, as well as strong concurrent validity with direct assessments of expressive language. Because both instruments are continuous measures, users can set a delay criterion that best suits their needs, whether it be a percentile cutoff (e.g., the 10th or the 15th percentile) or a specific language mile-stone (e.g., < 50 words or no word combinations). Finally, these checklists provide efficient screening tools whereby practitioners can identify virtually all children in this age range likely to have an expressive language delay. Once these children are identified, they can be further evaluated to determine the degree and breadth of their developmental delay (Chapter 15).

Despite these achievements, there is still little scientific basis for selecting the precise criterion, especially one that can be used across a range of ages. Should it be the 10th or the 15th percentile? Should it be 1, 1.25, or 1.5 standard deviations (*SDs*) below the mean? The most appropriate criterion may vary with the language, as there are differences in rate of early language development (Chapter 3). An even more complex issue is the selection of appropriate criteria for bilingual children (Chapter 4). An important related issue that has yet to be addressed is whether the same criterion should be used for boys and girls, or whether gender-specific criteria should be employed, given the known, albeit modest, gender differences. Specifically, there is a category of girls who would not be identified as LTs by a common, unisex criterion, but would be picked up by girl-specific norms. Are those girls indeed at higher risk than girls not selected as having delays? These and other questions about selection of criteria can only be addressed by longitudinal studies of population-representative samples.

## Conclusion 2

Children in the age range of 18–36 months who are slow to talk are a heterogeneous group (Chapters 10 and 15). Within this broad group are children with intellec-tual disability, autism spectrum disorders, hearing impairment, and environmental neglect, as well as children with language delay only, whom we refer to as LTs. Differential diagnosis is essential because some of those other conditions, such as autism, have even higher risk for continuing delay than late talking by itself. Even within the group of LTs, there are at least two subgroups, namely children with expressive delay only and children with mixed expressive/receptive delays, and they are likely to benefit from different forms of intervention.

## Conclusion 3

Individual differences in early vocabulary development are dramatic, as indicated by very large *SDs* on the LDS and the CDIs. Thus, "typical development" at age 2 encompasses a very wide range of vocabulary sizes. LTs, by definition, occupy a posi-tion at about the 10th or 15th percentile on the left-hand side of a distribution that is broadly normal, rather than containing a distinct "hump" at the lower end. This observation about distribution, along with outcome and genetic studies (Chapters 11 and 12), suggests strongly that LTs are *quantitatively* different from typically developing (TD) peers in their vocabulary size, rather than forming a qualitatively distinct, taxometrically identifiable category or class (Chapter 5). Research does not support the idea that LTs form a categorical disease entity (Chapter 5).

## Conclusion 4

Although LTs are typically identified because they have small vocabularies, failure to produce word combinations at age 2 is also widely used as an alternative, or supplementary, criterion for late talking (Chapters 2 and 11). Some children appear to be more delayed in their emerging syntax than they are in their vocabulary development, although it is not yet known how common this is. The fact that vocabulary delays often resolve by age 3 but syntactic delays are more enduring further highlights the importance of syntax delay in LTs and the need for further research on individual differences in emerging syntax (Chapter 17).

## Conclusion 5

Although initial LT studies focused on small, advantaged, and "pure" samples (Chapter 17), later studies that have identified LTs in general population samples have revealed the multifactorial nature of language delay. Most importantly, these studies have brought an important public health perspective to the study of language delay (Chapters 1, 2, 12, and 16).

## Future Directions: Identification and Classification of Late Talkers

It is well accepted that children who are slow to talk from 18 to 36 months of age comprise various subgroups (e.g., autism spectrum disorders, intellectual disabilities, hearing impairment, environmental neglect, LTs with receptive delays, LTs with expressive delay only). However, very limited information is available from large population-based studies regarding the percentages of children with delayed expressive categories who fall in to these major subgroups. Therefore, an important future direction is to identify all children with an expressive language delay in large epidemiological cohorts and to have sufficient diagnostic assessment data to determine differential diagnoses. Prevalence information for disorders is an essential public health tool for the design of screening programs, as well as for planning and delivering intervention programs. In addition, it provides a framework for evaluation of treatment effectiveness and cost-benefit ratios at a population level.

## CHARACTERISTICS AND CAUSE

Three decades of research have yielded a rich and quite consistent portrait of the characteristics of LTs. On the other hand, the etiological factors that cause late talking are still largely unknown. Most factors that have been identified as significant do not explain much of the variance, indicating a strong need for further research.

## Conclusion 6

The factors most predictive of being an LT at around age 2 appear to be neurobiological rather than socioeconomic (Chapters 1 and 2). That is, family factors such as maternal education, family socioeconomic status, and ethnicity explain very small amounts of the variance in predicting late talking at age 2, if they are statistically significant at all. In contrast, being a boy, having positive family history, and having perinatal risk (e.g., low birth weight) are generally better predictors, but even these predictors explain small amounts of variance. Twin studies provide an important caution here, however. They suggest that environmental factors taken as a whole, even if we do not know what they are, have a very substantial influence (Chapter 12). Thus socioeconomic status can only be a first attempt at specifying the features of the environment that matter. The best predictors of late talking at age 2 are "nearby" measures: weak language/communication skills at earlier ages. Taken as a whole, the lesson of current research is that much of the variance in being a late talker at age 2 is still unexplained.

## Conclusion 7

Even when LTs and comparison groups at age 2 are matched on socioeconomic status and nonverbal ability at intake and a requirement is imposed that the LTs have typical receptive language, the LTs generally differ significantly and substantially in their receptive language skills from age-matched peers. This suggests that LTs are not only delayed in their expressive language development at intake but that they have weaker language skills on average (Chapter 11). This finding has implications for theories of the emergence of late talking, as well as prediction of outcomes (Chapter 9). Further exploration is needed to determine the prevalence, severity, and predictors of receptive delay.

## Conclusion 8

A promising predictor of being an LT at age 2 is efficiency of real-time language processing, such as measured in the looking-while-listening (LWL) laboratory task (Chapter 8). The fact that speed of spoken word recognition at 12–18 months is a measurable individual difference predictive of slower expressive language development suggests that this task may reflect one of the core skills underlying the development of expressive language, and thus predict the occurrence of late talking. Furthermore, young children's early skill at efficiently integrating linguistic and nonlinguistic information during real-time language processing is significantly correlated with vocabulary growth to age 3, and proves a useful predictor of outcomes for LTs. As noted later in this chapter, additional research along these lines is needed to identify other skills underlying language development that can be measured before LTs can be identified. The causal direction also needs further examination: Does having a larger vocabulary aid in recognizing individual words, or does skill in recognizing words facilitate developing a larger vocabulary? These are not mutually exclusive possibilities, of course.

## Conclusion 9

LTs show delays not only in their expressive vocabulary (and therefore in their emerging syntax) but also in their phonological skills (Chapters 6, 7, and 11). When identified at age 2, LTs differ from their TD peers by vocalizing less, having smaller consonant inventories, and producing simpler syllable shapes. Furthermore, LTs generally have a history of delayed or reduced babbling relative to TD peers.

In addition, some research suggests that differences in receptive phonology or speech perception during infancy may be predictive of late talking (Chapter 6). Although further work is needed in this area, it appears that infant speech perception may be an even earlier emerging skill than real-time lexical processing that is predictive of late talking. Another potentially illuminating line of research is work by Stokes and others (discussed in Chapter 6) that shows that children differ in their sensitivity to phonological neighborhood density in learning words (i.e., whether there are many or few words that are phonologically similar), and that this may contribute to differences in vocabulary growth rate.

### Future Directions: Characteristics and Causes

As noted previously, online lexical processing and receptive and expressive phonology appear to be two promising early markers for underlying language endowment. These skills, which can be measured at about 12 months of age, are both associated with rate of language progress in the first 3 years of life. However, as suggested by Rescorla (2005, 2009), many skills probably subserve the acquisition of language and hence contribute to language endowment. Although some of these skills are obviously language-related, such as lexical processing and phonological perception/categorization, others may be more general cognitive mechanisms that are used by the language learning system and hence contribute to language endowment. For example, vocabulary acquisition involves an associative learning process. That is, the child must learn that the sounds comprising the word *dog,* for example, refer to a furry, four-legged barking creature. Similarly, development of grammar involves extracting regularities and inferring rules from the language of others (e.g., that most plurals involve adding an /s/ or /z/, that most past tenses are formed by adding /d/ or /t/). Variation in associative learning skills might help account for individual differences in rate of lexical acquisition, whereas variations in inferential rule learning might help explain individual differences in grammar. Both types of skills were well studied in young children decades ago and therefore established methodologies exist for assessing them. However, to our knowledge, they have not been assessed in conjunction with individual differences in language acquisition. Therefore, a promising avenue for future research would be to explore whether individual differences in some of these less specifically linguistic skills are significant predictors of late talking.

## LONGITUDINAL COURSE/OUTCOMES

Most LTs do not turn out to be school-age children with SLI. Correspondingly, most school-age children with SLI were not LTs. These two findings indicate a pressing need for longitudinal studies conducted with large general population samples to further illuminate outcomes of LTs and to identify precursors of SLI.

### Conclusion 10

Many young children change language delay status in the period from 18 to 36 months (Chapters 1 and 12). Specifically, many children delayed in expressive language at 18 months are no longer delayed at age 2. Similarly, many children delayed at age 2 are no longer delayed at age 3. Furthermore, many children delayed at age

3 were not delayed at 18 months or at 2 years. This means that although it is possible to reliably identify children in this age period who are LTs, the consistency in LT status across the age period is quite low. Findings from the Twins Early Development Study (TEDS; see Chapter 12) suggest that both genetic and environmental factors have a substantial influence on the outcome of late talking, with the latter probably the more important. However, as we noted in Conclusion 5, the field is far from understanding which environmental factors are the most predictive of outcome (Chapter 12).

## Conclusion 11

Research evidence to date suggests that socioeconomic status factors become increasingly important predictors of language skills as children move through the preschool period and into the school-age period. Significant socioeconomic status differences in vocabulary size are present by age 2, but prevalence of late talking is not markedly elevated in children from lower socioeconomic status families relative to children from middle or upper socioeconomic status families. A parallel pattern appears to be seen in children from bilingual home environments, inasmuch as onset of first words is not delayed but growth in the lexicon may be slower than in children from monolingual home environments (Chapter 4). However, socioeconomic status differences in language skills become more marked by age 3 and appear to continue to do so as children approach kindergarten. As noted later in this chapter, further research is needed to elucidate this hypothesized increasing role of socioeconomic status in predicting language skills with age. The methodological challenge is that the environmental factors that mediate socioeconomic status effects at a proximal level—such as amount of talking, responsivity, sentence recasting, and the like—are very labor intensive to study and hence are typically used only in relatively small samples, but it is necessary to know more about them on a larger, public health scale (Chapter 16). Furthermore, parents who provide an impoverished language environment may also have weaker genetic endowment for language (i.e., "passive" genetic-environment correlation), underscoring the need for twin studies to disentangle this confound.

## Conclusion 12

Most LTs at age 2 perform in the normal range on a variety of expressive language measures by age 5 (Chapters 9–11). Thus, by the time LTs enter kindergarten, only a small fraction of them meet the criteria for specific language impairment (SLI). In Conclusion 11 we considered the role of environment in this variability of outcome. Within the domain of language and communication itself, the area that takes the longest to resolve is morphosyntax (Chapters 2 and 11). However, by age 6 or 7, most LTs score in the average range even on morphosyntax measures. Some LTs, however, are diagnosed with SLI as they get older. Among the risk factors predicting persistent language problems are comprehension delays, delayed phonology/babbling, limited communicative intent/responsivity to language, weak imitative skills, delayed symbolic play, limited nonverbal communication, and family history of language of reading problems (Chapter 10).

## Conclusion 13

Despite achieving age-level expectations in language skills by the time they enter school, LTs continue to have significantly lower language scores than comparison children from the same backgrounds into adolescence. Thus, late talking is not a strong predictor of later impairment, but it is a predictor of relative language weakness relative to peers through childhood and adolescence. It is likely that this pattern occurs in reverse as well: Children who have weak skills but do not qualify as LTs as toddlers probably make up the majority of children who will eventually be classified with SLI (Chapter 17).

## Conclusion 14

The largest differences between LTs and TD comparison children as they age appear to be on tasks measuring verbal memory (e.g., nonword, word, and sentence imitation tasks; Chapters 1, 9, 10, and 11). Weakness in verbal memory skills, therefore, appears to be among the most enduring and significant difference between LTs and their peers. As we noted for Conclusion 8, more research is needed to clarify the causal direction. Does verbal memory help acquire new words, or does having a large language repertoire facilitate verbal memory? In this area, training studies could play a useful role.

## Conclusion 15

Differences between LTs and TD peers show a developmental progression over time, tracking the development of language itself. A general pattern noted in several studies is that as large delays in one area resolve into age-appropriate but still weaker performance, delays become evident in a newly emerging domain of language functioning (Chapters 10 and 11). Thus, early differences in phonology and vocabulary are followed by later differences in syntax, which are followed in turn by differences in higher-order discourse skills such as narration, exposition, and reading comprehension. This pattern, as well as the finding of strong correlations among many different language tasks, suggests a common core of language-related abilities that is shared by phonology, vocabulary, grammar, verbal memory, and discourse skills. This in turn supports the notion of a spectrum of language ability (Chapters 5, 10, 11, and 17), on which LTs have somewhat weaker endowment than TD peers.

## Future Directions: Longitudinal Course/Outcomes

It is well-established from small-scale longitudinal studies that LTs from middle-class families generally outgrow their language delay by the time the enter school, with only a minority being diagnosed with SLI. It is equally clear that some proportion of LTs will later manifest communication disorders broader than SLI. At the level of public health planning, as discussed in the Future Direction: Identification and Classification of Late Talkers section, we have a strong need to determine on a population basis which LTs will persist in language delay (whether with SLI or another condition), as well as which children who were not LTs will develop SLI (or a broader language delay). This question will require large-scale longitudinal studies of diverse epidemiological samples. The Early Language in Victoria Study (ELVS; see Chapter 1), the TEDS, and the Dutch Generation R study (Henrichs et al., 2010), as well as work by Law (Chapter 16), suggest the increasing importance of socioeconomic status in explaining the etiology of language impairment as children advance in age. Future research needs to be designed to focus more systematically on socioeconomic status and other more proximal environmental features. Specifically, how do language endowment and environmental risk contribute to language delay, and how do their relative importance as etiological factors change with the child's age?

Even within SLI as a potential outcome of late talking, there is much heterogeneity. The epidemiological study by Tomblin and colleagues (Tomblin, Records, Buckwalter, et al., 1997; Tomblin, Records, & Zhang, 1996) made a very important contribution to understanding SLI in the school years at a population level. However, that study did not have a major focus on subgroups within the SLI population, beyond differentiating between SLI and nonspecific language impairment (children without an IQ/language discrepancy). To increase understanding of SLI and how it relates to late talking in early childhood, future research with large and diverse general population samples should identify subgroups within the broad class of children with language impairments. This subgrouping analysis should take into account numerous factors, including family history of language/reading problems, prenatal/perinatal history and gender, early history of language development, socioeconomic status/bilingual demographic factors, nonverbal cognitive abilities and language, and language profile (receptive vs. expressive, phonological, lexical, grammatical, and pragmatic/discourse). The goal of this analysis would be to identify and characterize the major subgroups of school-age children with language problems on the basis of these factors. For example, one subgroup might be boys from middle socioeconomic status families with a family history of language and reading problems who were LTs; have weak verbal memory and weak phonological processing skills; typical nonverbal skills; good lexical skills; and weaknesses in higher-level receptive and expressive grammatical skills, language processing, and reading comprehension when task demands are great (i.e., "recovered late talkers" such as those described in Chapters 9–11). Another subgroup might be children from lower socioeconomic status or minority families (with no family history of late talking but generally low educational attainment of parents) who were not LTs and have average phonological skills, but who have low average nonverbal abilities and who increasingly fall behind age expectations in lexical, grammatical, and discourse abilities as they get older.

Another future direction concerns the changing developmental nature of language development in middle childhood and adolescence. As noted in Chapter 11, higher-level language skills in LTs appear to be compromised relative to those of peers, despite scores in the average range on comprehensive, broad-scale language tests such as the Test of Language Development (TOLD; Newcomer & Hammill, 1988, 1997) and the Clinical Evaluation of Language Fundamentals (CELF; Semel, Wiig, & Secord, 1995; Semel, Wiig, Secord, & Sabers, 1987). This suggests that an important future direction is the development of more sophisticated and sensitive tools for assessing advanced syntax and complex discourse skills. Language problems in middle childhood and adolescence tend not to be associated with basic grammatical impairments such as the use of past tense markers, but rather by language that is too simple to express and understand complex ideas. Examples include such syntactic features as compound and complex sentences, relative clauses, Wh-clauses, and complementation, as well as mastery of lexical elements shaping sentence meaning such as "nevertheless," "although," "however," and "despite."

## INTERVENTIONS

Much is known about interventions that are effective with LTs. However, research regarding which types and amounts of intervention are best for different subgroups of LTs is sorely needed. Furthermore, progress is needed in applying public health approaches to late talking, given the heterogeneity among children who manifest this condition.

### Conclusion 16

A variety of intervention approaches have been found to be effective for LTs, suggesting that expressive language in LTs can be sped up significantly with intervention. Interventions differ on many parameters (e.g., more structured vs. more naturalistic, lexical vs. syntactic vs. pragmatic focus, parent delivered vs. practitioner delivered, higher vs. lower dosage). Which approach to intervention is likely to work best with an individual LT appears to depend on a variety of child and family characteristics (Chapters 13–16). Because children who talk late include children with autism spectrum disorders and intellectual disabilities, and because LTs with no other primary condition vary in receptive language skills and phonological skills, an in-depth clinical assessment is recommended so that the appropriate type and level of treatment can be provided (Chapter 15). At present, these decisions must be based on clinical experience and theoretical models; there is a strong need for empirically based evidence as well. Response to intervention should be studied at an individual level, whether in single-subject designs or aptitude-by-treatment group designs, to determine if measureable aspects of children can be used to predict the optimal intervention.

### Conclusion 17

Most efficacy studies to date have been relatively short-term, both in length of the intervention and length of the follow-up. Research is lacking with regard to how LTs who respond well to treatment at age 2 or 3 and appear to have caught up by age 4 or 5 will look by the time they reach middle childhood or adolescence (Chapter 14). Whether early intervention can bring some or all of them to the level of functioning of demographically matched peers, and whether they can maintain that growth, is currently unknown. Of particular relevance here is Scarborough's notion of "illusory recovery" (Scarborough & Dobrich, 1990), discussed in Chapter 11, which suggests that LTs may catch up in the area of intervention, but their underlying language impairment will result in weakness in other aspects of language learning and functioning later on in their development.

## Conclusion 18

Socioeconomic status factors appear to be important in determining which LTs need intervention and what form that intervention should take (Chapter 10). Because most LTs from advantaged families are likely to perform in the average range by school age without intensive intervention, advice to parents about how to foster language in the context of everyday preschool experiences may suffice. For socially disadvantaged populations, late talking is likely to have a much greater impact on subsequent development. Therefore, LTs from low socioeconomic status backgrounds may need a more comprehensive and aggressive approach to intervention, given the risks for language and literacy impairments even typically endowed children from such families manifest. Often targeted individual intervention services plus more generic intervention in the form of enhanced preschool services are needed to make a difference on outcomes for these at-risk children (Chapter 16).

### Future Directions: Interventions

In Conclusion 16 we suggested that intervention research should focus downward on the response of individual children to treatment, not just the group as a whole. Here we suggest an upward shift as well. Research in communication disorders has almost always addressed assessment and intervention as separate components of clinical work. In contrast, public health research in the medical domain has understood the need to examine them together in making policy decisions. For example, the most appropriate evaluation for breast cancer or prostate cancer is to establish a screening program, provide treatment for diagnosed individuals, and then compare outcomes for the screened and treated population with those for people who did not participate in the screening and treatment program. Perhaps surprisingly, the case for prostate cancer screening is very weak, and even for breast cancer screening the case is stronger at some ages than others. Base rates of the disorder, the accuracy of screening, normal developmental change, and the effectiveness of intervention all have a substantial effect on the overall outcome. Rigorous examination of the benefits of screening and intervention for late talking at a population level is equally needed (Chapter 16).

Another broad intervention question concerns the potential contributions of parents, preschool educators, and speech-language pathologists as agents of intervention. Research has demonstrated that each of these groups can have a significant effect on young children's language. They do bring different sets of strengths and weaknesses, including background and training, motivation, other demands, and time. Which kinds of intervention are appropriate for which group, and how can they work together in a mutually supportive way?

## CONCLUDING THOUGHTS

The findings summarized in this book represent the fruits of research by a relatively small group of scholars, many of whom began studying LTs more than three decades ago. Although there has been some collaboration and certainly much communication among the various research groups who have studied LTs, the field has benefited by the fact that several rather parallel but nonetheless independent studies have come to the same basic conclusions about LTs. However, as summarized in this chapter, there is still much to learn about how to identify and classify LTs, what etiological factors are most important at various ages, the factors influencing longitudinal course, the subtypes of school-age SLI, the effectiveness of different kinds of intervention, and the most effective public health approaches to language problems across the early years. We hope that the next generation of researchers in the field, many of whom contributed to this book, will explore these important research and practice questions.

## REFERENCES

Fenson, L., Marchman, V.A., Thal, D.J., Dale, P.S., Reznick, J.S., & Bates, E. (2007). *MacArthur-Bates Communicative Development Inventories (CDIs)* (2nd ed.). Baltimore, MD: Paul H. Brookes Publishing Co.

Henrichs, J., Rescorla, L., Schenk, J.J., Schmidt, H.G., Jaddoe, V.W.V., Hofman, A., . . . Tiemeier, H. (2011). Examining continuity of early expressive vocabulary development: The Generation R Study. *Journal of Speech, Language, and Hearing Research, 54*(3), 854–869.

Newcomer, P., & Hammill, D. (1988). *Test of Language Development-2 (Primary).* Austin, TX: PRO-ED.

Newcomer, P., & Hammill, D. (1997). *Test of Language Development-3 (Primary).* Austin, TX: PRO-ED.

Oliver, B.R., & Plomin, R. (2007). Twins Early Development Study (TEDS): A multivariate, longitudinal genetic investigation of language, cognition and behavior problems from childhood through adolescence. *Twin Research and Human Genetics, 10,* 96–105.

Rescorla, L. (1989). The Language Development Survey: A screening tool for delayed language in toddlers. *Journal of Speech and Hearing Disorders, 54,* 587–599.

Rescorla, L. (2005). Age 13 language and reading outcomes of late-talking toddlers. *Journal of Speech, Language, and Hearing Research, 48,* 459–472.

Rescorla, L. (2009). Age 17 language and reading outcomes in late-talking toddlers: Support for a dimensional perspective on language delay. *Journal of Speech, Language, and Hearing Research, 52*(1), 16–30.

Scarborough, H.S., & Dobrich, W. (1990). Development of children with early language delays. *Journal of Speech and Hearing Research, 33,* 70–83.

Semel, E., Wiig, E., & Secord, W. (1995). *Clinical Evaluation of Language Fundamentals– Third Edition.* San Antonio, TX: Psychological Corporation.

Semel, E., Wiig, E., Secord, W., & Sabers, D. (1987). *Clinical Evaluation of Language Fundamentals–Revised.* San Antonio, TX: Psychological Corporation.

Tomblin, J.B., Records, N.L., Buckwalter, P., Zhang, X., Smith, E., & O'Brien, M. (1997). Prevalence of specific language impairment in kindergarten children. *Journal of Speech, Language, and Hearing Research, 40,* 1245–1260.

Tomblin, J.B., Records, N.L., & Zang, Z. (1996). A system of diagnosis of specific language impairment in kindergarten children. *Journal of Speech and Hearing Research, 39,* 1284–1294.

# Index

References to tables and figures are indicated with *t* and *f*, respectively.